Puerto Rico

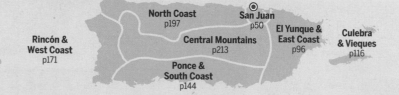

North Coast
p197

San Juan
p50

**Rincón &
West Coast**
p171

Central Mountains
p213

**El Yunque &
East Coast**
p96

**Culebra
& Vieques**
p116

**Ponce &
South Coast**
p144

Liza Prado, Luke Waterson

Contents

PLAN YOUR TRIP

Welcome to Puerto Rico . . 4

Puerto Rico Map 6

Puerto Rico's Top 17 8

Need to Know 18

First Time Puerto Rico . . 20

If You Like... 22

Month by Month 25

Itineraries 28

Eat & Drink
Like a Local 34

Puerto Rico Outdoors . . 39

Travel with Children 45

Regions at a Glance 47

ON THE ROAD

SAN JUAN 50

Sights 54

Beaches 69

Activities 70

Courses 72

Tours 73

Festivals & Events 74

Sleeping 74

Eating 78

Drinking & Nightlife 83

Entertainment 85

Shopping 88

Around San Juan 92

Cataño & Bayamón 92

Piñones 93

Loíza 94

EL YUNQUE &
EAST COAST 96

El Yunque 98

Luquillo & Around 105

Fajardo & Around 107

Naguabo & Around 111

Yabucoa & Around 114

CULEBRA &
VIEQUES 116

Culebra 118

Vieques 128

SURFING IN RINCÓN, P176

MANGROVES, P257

JAMES MCGRAGHAN/500PX ©

AMONTES/SHUTTERSTOCK ©

WALTER BIBIKOW/GETTY IMAGES ©

Contents

PONCE & SOUTH COAST 144

Ponce 146
Guayama & Pozuelo. 155
Bahía de Jobos 157
Playa Salinas. 158
Coamo 159
Yauco & Around 162
Guánica & Around 163
La Parguera. 166

RINCÓN & WEST COAST. 171

Rincón 173
Mayagüez. 182

Cabo Rojo Area. 186
Playa de Joyuda 186
Boquerón. 188
El Combate 190
Refugio Nacional
Cabo Rojo 191
San Germán 192
Isla Mona. 195

NORTH COAST 197

Dorado 199
Arecibo. 201
Around Arecibo. 203
Isabela & Around 207
Aguadilla 210

CENTRAL MOUNTAINS 213

Caguas. 215
Bosque Estatal
de Carite 216
Aibonito & Around 217
Barranquitas & Around. . 218
Guavate 219
Reserva Forestal
Toro Negro. 220
Jayuya 222
Adjuntas & Around. 223
Maricao 224
San Sebastián
& Around 225

UNDERSTAND

Puerto Rico Today 228
History 230
Life in Puerto Rico. . . . 240
Sounds of
Puerto Rico 245
Arts. 250
Puerto Rico
Landscapes 254
Wildlife of
Puerto Rico 258

SURVIVAL GUIDE

Directory A–Z 262
Transportation 268
Language. 272
Index. 281
Map Legend. 287

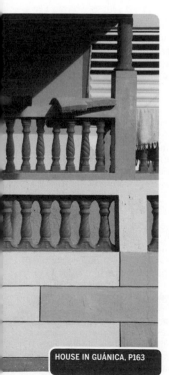

HOUSE IN GUÁNICA, P163

SPECIAL FEATURES

Eat & Drink
Like a Local. 34
Puerto Rico Outdoors . . 39
Travel with Children. . . . 45
Sounds of
Puerto Rico 245
Wildlife of
Puerto Rico 258

Welcome to Puerto Rico

Scented by slow-roasted pork and sea breezes, and colored by swashbuckling history, this sun-washed medley of Spanish and American influences is a paradise-seeker's pleasure dome.

Caribbean Beaches

Puerto Rico inspires Caribbean daydreams for good reason: it can satisfy both the lethargic beach bum and the budding big-wave surfer – all in a long weekend. Its coral reefs host a riot of fantastical fish and the shores shimmer like crushed pearls. On some beaches you'll have plenty of company. In other places like Vieques or Cabo Rojo you might have some of the world's best stretches of sand entirely to yourself. If the island tempts you to stay, you can opt for sizeable resorts or independent guesthouses for watching those seaside sunsets from your room.

Cultural Vibrancy

The island's culture is of the visceral kind. Search for it beyond the condo towers and congested roads. Sometimes it seems Puerto Rico doesn't wish to show outsiders its cultural magnitude. Then, suddenly, you'll smell it in the smoke arising from *lechoneras* (eateries specializing in suckling pig), or hear it in the intoxicating patters of salsa beats. You'll glimpse it as sunlight sparkles across coffee plantations, or in museums celebrating everything from failed revolution to classical European painting. Puerto Rican traditions have been shaped by generations of cultural synthesis, celebration and setback, and it emerges today as vivid and indomitable.

Happening History

Puerto Rico's past brims with cannon fire and colonization, repression and revolt. Legend abounds: from San Juan's fortresses, scoured by siege, to the crumbling South Coast sugar refineries once powering the island's economy. European settlers built pretty plazas in harbor cities while political revolutionaries schemed rebellion in mountain villages. History buffs can wander precolonial Taíno ruins or coffee haciendas. Even if your interest is scant, it's hard not to get immersed in Puerto Rico's tempestuous story in Old San Juan, where echoes of bygone times – of colonists and swashbucklers and smugglers – reverberate still.

Forest Thrills

Even those who stick to the coast cannot escape the alluring shadow of Puerto Rico's thick forests, as knotted labyrinths of mangroves create crucial shoreside wildlife reserves and the green glint of the inland forested hills is rarely out of sight.

The island's dense foliage invites a perpetual mystery to blanket it, as coqui frogs chant and roots reduce so-called roads to rubble. The forests here are internationally important, such as El Yunque, the only tropical rainforest in the US. A journey into them guarantees to awaken the adventurer within.

Why I Love Puerto Rico

By Luke Waterson, Writer

The island seems to specialise in making seemingly run-of-the-mill experiences rapidly erupt into life-long memories. The first time I traveled along the ramshackle south coast, I remember expressing interest to some passersby in an off-shore cay and no sooner had the words left my mouth than the impromptu offers to take me out there flooded in. This epitomizes Puerto Rico for me: one moment a stroll along a crumbling sea wall and the next, a float in azure, mangrove-backed waters with a cold beer in hand.

For more about our writers, see p288

Above: Paseo de la Princesa (p58), San Juan

Puerto Rico

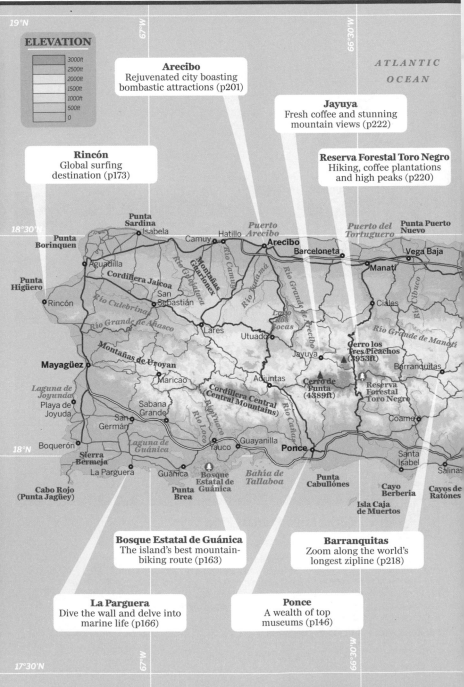

ELEVATION

3000ft
2500ft
2000ft
1500ft
1000ft
500ft
0

Arecibo
Rejuvenated city boasting
bombastic attractions (p201)

Jayuya
Fresh coffee and stunning
mountain views (p222)

Rincón
Global surfing
destination (p173)

Reserva Forestal Toro Negro
Hiking, coffee plantations
and high peaks (p220)

*ATLANTIC
OCEAN*

Bosque Estatal de Guánica
The island's best mountain-
biking route (p163)

Barranquitas
Zoom along the world's
longest zipline (p218)

La Parguera
Dive the wall and delve into
marine life (p166)

Ponce
A wealth of top
museums (p146)

19°N
67°W
66°30'W
18°30'N
18°N
17°30'N
67°W
66°30'W

Punta
Sardina
Isabela
Camuy
Hatillo
*Puerto
Arecibo*
Arecibo
*Puerto del
Tortuguero*
Punta Puerto
Nuevo
Punta
Borinquen
Barceloneta
Vega Baja
Aguadilla
Cordillera Jaicoa
*Montañas
Guamomex*
Manatí
Punta
Higüero
Río Culebrinas
San
Sebastián
Río Grande de Arecibo
Cíales
Rincón
Río Grande de Añasco
Lares
*Lago
Dos
Bocas*
Río Grande de Manatí
Utuado
Río Tibuco
Mayagüez
Montañas de Uroyan
Jayuya
Cerro los
Tres Picachos
(3953ft)
Barranquitas
Maricao
Adjuntas
*Cordillera Central
(Central Mountains)*
Cerro de
Punta
(4389ft)
Reserva
Forestal
Toro Negro
*Laguna de
Joyunda*
Playa de
Joyuda
Sabana
Grande
Río Loco
Río Yauco
Río Cañas
Coamo
San
Germán
Boquerón
*Laguna de
Guánica*
Yauco
Guayanilla
Ponce
Santa
Isabel
Salinas
**Sierra
Bermeja**
La Parguera
Guánica
Bosque
Estatal de
Guánica
*Bahía de
Tallaboa*
Punta
Cabullónes
Cayo
Berbería
Cayos de
Ratónes
Cabo Rojo
(Punta Jagüey)
Punta
Brea
Isla Caja
de Muertos
Punta
Borinquen
Río Guayo
Río Camuy

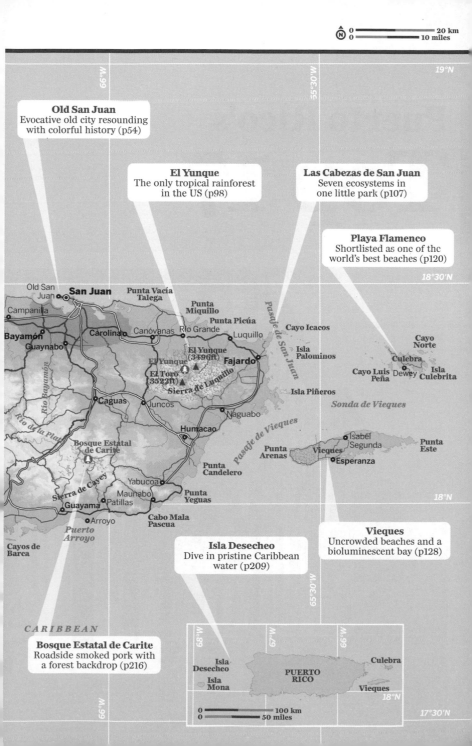

Old San Juan
Evocative old city resounding with colorful history (p54)

El Yunque
The only tropical rainforest in the US (p98)

Las Cabezas de San Juan
Seven ecosystems in one little park (p107)

Playa Flamenco
Shortlisted as one of the world's best beaches (p120)

Isla Desecheo
Dive in pristine Caribbean water (p209)

Vieques
Uncrowded beaches and a bioluminescent bay (p128)

Bosque Estatal de Carite
Roadside smoked pork with a forest backdrop (p216)

0 ——— 20 km
0 ——— 10 miles

19°N
18°30'N
18°N
17°30'N

Old San Juan
San Juan
Campanilla
Bayamón
Guaynabo
Río Bayamón
Río de la Plata
Punta Vacía Talega
Punta Miquillo
Punta Picúa
Carolina
Canóvanas
Río Grande
Luquillo
Cayo Icacos
Isla Palominos
El Yunque (3496ft)
El Yunque
El Toro (3522ft)
Sierra de Luquillo
Fajardo
Pasaje de San Juan
Cayo Norte
Cayo Luis Peña
Culebra
Dewey
Isla Culebrita
Isla Piñeros
Caguas
Juncos
Naguabo
Sonda de Vieques
Pasaje de Vieques
Humacao
Bosque Estatal de Carite
Punta Candelero
Punta Arenas
Isabel Segunda
Vieques
Esperanza
Punta Este
Sierra de Cayey
Yabucoa
Maunabo
Patillas
Punta Yeguas
Cabo Mala Pascua
Guayama
Arroyo
Puerto Arroyo
Cayos de Barca
CARIBBEAN

Isla Desecheo
Isla Mona
PUERTO RICO
Culebra
Vieques
18°N

0 ——— 100 km
0 ——— 50 miles

65°30'W
65°W

Puerto Rico's
Top 17

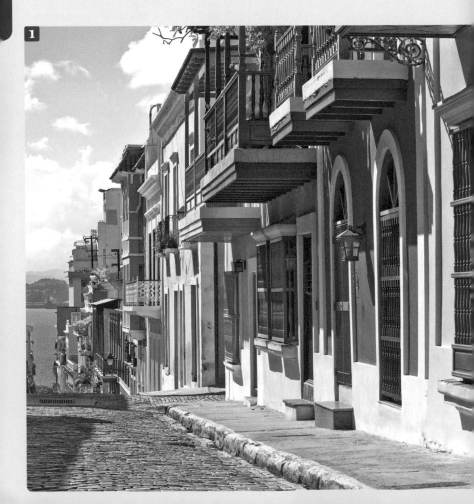

1

Evocative Old San Juan

1 Even those limited to a quick visit find it easy to fall under the beguiling spell of the cobblestone streets, pastel-painted colonial buildings and grand fortresses of Old San Juan (p54). From the ramparts of El Morro, the allure of this place is evident in every direction: in the maze of crooked lanes and in the endless sparkle of the Atlantic. By day, lose yourself in historical stories of blood and drama; by night, tap in (and tap along) to the condensed cluster of bars and clubs constituting the neighborhood's nightlife. Calle San Justo

Glorious Beaches

2 The rub of sand between your toes, the dazzling shimmer of turquoise water and the rhythmic shush of cresting waves – Puerto Rico's beaches possess all the qualities of a daydream. Take your pick from the golden, crescent-shaped heaven of Culebra's Playa Flamenco (p120; considered among the world's best beaches); the embarrassment of riches on Vieques; the coconut-oil-scented crowds of Playa Isla Verde, San Juan's own little slice of Brazil; the secluded, mangrove-shaded hideaways in the south; or the roaring surf of the west, culminating in isolated bays like Playa Santa. Beach at Palmas del Mar (p112)

DAVIE MADISON/GETTY IMAGES ©

FRANZ MARC FREI/GETTY IMAGES ©

El Yunque Tropical Rainforest

3 Lush forests, verdant hills and crashing waterfalls attract visitors to El Yunque (p98), the only true rainforest in the US National Forest System. It's a place to embark on hikes (short and sweet, with information boards, or long and lonely, with coqui frogs for company) through the mist and gawk at Jurassic-sized ferns. Bring a raincoat and binoculars, too; of the 26 species found only here, you'll want to keep an eye out for the Puerto Rican parrot, one of the world's 10 most endangered birds.

Ponce

4 Ponce (p147), the so-called 'Pearl of the South,' boasts a wealth of museums with enough diversity to satisfy the most intellectually rapacious museum hunter. The city is proud of its action-packed past: sample its glory days at ornate Casa Wiechers Villaronga, its grimmer days at Casa de la Masacre de Ponce, and beeline to the Caribbean's best art museum, Museo de Arte de Ponce. Then absorb the island's premier indigenous site, Centro Ceremonial Indigena de Tibes, and round off your historical romp in the beautiful Plaza Las Delicias. Fire truck on display at Parque de Bombas (p149)

DENNIS VAN DE WATER/SHUTTERSTOCK ©

FRANZ MARC FREI/GETTY IMAGES ©

WALTER BIBIKOW/GETTY IMAGES ©

Architectural Gems

5 If you tried to savor every single example of colonial grandeur – all the fountains and historic squares, every dignified plantation house and buttressed 19th-century municipal hall – Puerto Rico's architectural gems would demand a stay of months. But if just one location outside of Old San Juan earns time on your agenda, take a stroll around Ponce and its historic main square (p147). In the west, Puerto Rico's second oldest city, San Germán (p192), dates to 1511, an age that blows away anything in the continental US. Architectural detail, San Germán

6

7

GARY BOGDON/GETTY IMAGES ©

PIANOMANIA/GETTY IMAGES ©

Catching Some Baseball

6 The bleachers at island *béisbol* (baseball) stadiums reveal a lot more than nine innings of play – they offer a glimpse at the Caribbean love affair with this sport. Even if their numbers are sometimes small, Puerto Ricans love the low-key games and dirt-cheap tickets that get fans right up to the Winter League Baseball action. Witness upstart farm leaguers looking for their big shot: they'll be facing off against fading stars of the Major League, who, in turn, will be looking to go out in a blaze of glory in San Juan's Hiram Bithorn Stadium (p88).

San Juan's Great Food

7 San Juan's restaurants (p78) impress with the Caribbean's most inventive fine dining. Recent years have seen a revolving door of hot restaurants in Old San Juan, while in the Santurce district you'll find creative, high-profile eateries and a burgeoning food-truck culture. The foodie scene on Calle Loíza will also keep your taste buds tingling. Expect the traditional, elemental essence of Puerto Rican flavors fused with preparations from across the globe. A glut of great cafes await across the capital.

Swimming, Snorkeling & Diving

8 Many of the island's best places for snorkeling and swimming lie on satellite islands off the main island's east or south coast and at coral reefs in the southwest. Waters in these areas are crystal clear and usually calm enough to enjoy visibility up to 75ft. Expect brightly colored fish, coral formations and even a lazy ray or two. The legendary reefs at La Parguera (p168) on the South Coast and the consistently clear waters of Isla Desecheo, off the West Coast, attract divers and snorkelers. Diving at La Parguera

Salsa

9 Let the scholars debate over whether the origins of salsa are rooted in the clubs of New York or the islands of the Caribbean and just feel the beat. There's no doubt that it lives on as the essential heartbeat of Puerto Rico (especially at venues in San Juan; p85). You'll hear the basic rhythm of the *clavé* (percussion instrument; literally 'keystone') driving Puerto Rican pop music and traditional songs. The secret to grooving to its rhythms on the dance floor is handed down from one generation to the next.

Salsa band at Nuyorican Café (p85), San Juan

MICHAEL DWYER/ALAMY STOCK PHOTO ©

Coffee in the Central Mountains

10 Puerto Rico's legendary coffee plantations offer caffeine junkies a rare opportunity. In the remote Central Mountains, you can sip fresh coffee while looking over the rolling hills and quiet valleys where the beans are grown, roasted and brewed. The winding Ruta Panorámica, a scenic route through the peaks, takes travelers past one picturesque plantation after the next; go through the village of Jayuya, in the heart of coffee country, where haciendas such as Pomarrosa (p220) or San Pedro (p223) offer tasty and hugely informative coffee breaks. Hacienda San Pedro

Mountain Biking

11 Spend half a day rumbling down the rocky, cactus-lined paths of Bosque Estatal de Guánica (p163) and you will traverse some of the most interesting mountain-biking terrain in the Caribbean. They're not well groomed or technical, but trails in this Unesco–protected site, or those in less-traveled karst country forests like Bosque Estatal de Susúa, bring the DIY thrills of the sport to Puerto Rico's unique subtropical wilds. For calmer rides, consider the rough yet quiet nature-reserve roads on Vieques or the cycle trails and lanes behind the beaches in Isabela.

Bioluminescent Bays

12 Few experiences can inspire the awe of floating on inky waves under a canopy of stars and witnessing one of nature's most tactile magic tricks: the otherworldly sparkle of bioluminescent waters. Kayaking into Puerto Rico's bioluminescent bays and seeing the jeweled flicker of water drip from your hands or illuminate a paddle stroke promises an experience of profound wonder. Or you can just glide along on an electric boat. Best bet: the bioluminescent bay at Vieques (p131).

11

12

Big Wave Surfing at Rincón

13 In winter, the cold weather brings righteous swells to the island's west-coast surfing capital of Rincón (p176), where some of the most consistent and exciting surf locations in the Caribbean can be found. And while the double overheads and excellent tubes attract an international set of would-be pros, beginners can paddle out to tamer breaks nearby. At sunset, crowds of locals and visitors replenish themselves with inexpensive eats and ice-cold beer in suave restaurants, laid-back beach bars and around bonfires on the sand.

Las Cabezas de San Juan Reserva Natural

14 The diverse ecosystem of the Las Cabezas de San Juan nature reserve (p107) is only a day trip from San Juan; it highlights the island's ecological eclecticism at every turn. After a trip through the visitors center, travelers begin touring the flora and fauna. The sea grass waves along mangrove forest and coral-protected lagoons, while crabs and giant iguanas scuttle around. A historic lighthouse boasts sweeping views of the coastline. At night, there's bioluminescent action.

DANITA DELIMONT/GETTY IMAGES ©

EFRAIN PADRO/ALAMY STOCK PHOTO ©

Adventure Parks

15 Puerto Rico's interior might, in its wild forests, rushing white water and limestone karst systems, already be screaming 'adventure' at you, but the island has made things easier by turning some of its wildernesses into high-adrenaline destinations. Toro Verde Nature Adventure Park (p219) near Barranquitas now has the world's longest zipline, where you whoosh a number of kilometers over a valley. Puerto Rico's only professionally designed mountain-bike circuit is here too. Other great parks also dot the Central Mountains, like the family-friendly Batey Zipline Adventures. Ziplining in El Yunque

Island Wildlife

16 Maybe the syncopated sounds of salsa rule the island's nightlife, but the croak of the coqui frogs rules the night. These creatures are the unofficial mascot of the island and its most constant soundtrack. Puerto Rico's wild population also includes rare birds in Bosque Estatal de Guánica (p163) and lazy reptiles on the remote Isla Mona, sometimes dubbed the Galápagos of the Caribbean. While not native to Puerto Rico, monkeys can be spied at locales like Cayo Santiago off Playa Humaco. In the waters offshore, the sea life adds to a naturalist's agenda, with tropical fish, coral, turtles and even manatee. Coqui frog

Feasting on Roast Pork

17 If you were to draw the Puerto Rican food pyramid, it might only have four elements – rice, beans, plantains and pork. Of these, pork rules the roost; you'll find it fried, grilled, stewed and skewered. But it's the mighty *lechón* (savory, smoky, suckling pig, spit-roasted for up to eight hours) that remains the island's favorite lunch. On the weekends, the roadsides near Guavate abutting the Bosque Estatal de Carite (p216) are a virtual parking lot for *lechoneras* (eateries specializing in suckling pig), with locals and visitors feasting alike.

Need to Know

For more information, see Survival Guide (p261)

Currency
US dollars ($)

Language
Spanish, some English

Visas
Visa formalities are exactly the same as for the mainland US.

Money
ATMs dispensing US currency are easily found. Credit and debit cards are widely accepted. Watch for mandatory fees at upscale hotels and resorts.

Cell Phones
All major US cell-phone carriers provide service in Puerto Rico, so US travelers do not have to suffer high international calling rates. Foreign travelers who are going to be in Puerto Rico for an extended period should look into getting a prepaid cellular phone.

Time
Atlantic Standard/Daylight Time (GMT/UTC minus four hours)

When to Go

San Juan
GO Dec–Apr

Rincón
GO Nov–Apr

Vieques
GO Dec–Apr

Ponce
GO Dec–Jan,
Jun–Aug

 Tropical climate, rain year-round
Warm to hot summers, cold winters

High Season
(mid-Dec–mid-Apr & Jul)

➡ Crowds escaping the frosty US mainland in winter see hotels rates go up and seasonal attractions come to life.

➡ In July, local families create a second high season, filling beach towns.

Shoulder
(Sep–Nov & mid-Apr–May)

➡ Puerto Rico's tourist infrastructure takes a breather to regroup during shoulder season, though there isn't a significant fluctuation in prices or services.

Low Season
(Jun–Nov)

➡ Apart from July, things get pretty lethargic during hurricane season; some resorts offer discounted packages, but prices at small hotels don't drop precipitously.

Useful Websites

See Puerto Rico (www.see puertorico.com) Official tourist site.

Eye Tour Puerto Rico (http://places.eyetour.com) Excellent short videos.

Welcome to Puerto Rico (http://welcome.topuertorico.org) Part encyclopedia, part travel guide.

Puerto Rico Day Trips (www.puertoricodaytrips.com) Fun days out from cities across the Commonwealth.

Lonely Planet (www.lonelyplanet.com/puerto-rico) Destination information, hotel bookings, traveler forum and more.

El Nuevo Dia (www.elnuevodia.com/english) The latest news online from Puerto Rico's main news publication.

Important Numbers

Puerto Rico's country code	☏1
International access code	☏011
Directory assistance	☏411
Emergency	☏911

Exchange Rates

Australia	A$1	$0.75
Canada	C$1	$0.75
Europe	€1	$1.07
Japan	¥100	$0.88
New Zealand	NZ$1	$0.72
UK	UK£1	$1.25

For current exchange rates see www.xe.com.

Daily Costs

Budget: Less than $120

➡ Public transportation/taxis: $25

➡ Double room in a budget guesthouse: $60–90

➡ Museum entry: Free–$10

Midrange: $120–250

➡ Rental car: $25–50

➡ Double room in a midrange hotel: $80–175

➡ *Lechonera* meal and drinks: $25

Top end: More than $250

➡ Double room in a boutique hotel or resort: from $200

➡ Dinner and drinks for two at a top restaurant: from $80

➡ Guided tours of bioluminescent bays or snorkeling excursions: from $50

Opening Hours

Hours can vary from those posted and they change sporadically, so check before setting off.

Bars 2pm–2am, often later in San Juan

Government offices 8:30am–4:30pm Monday to Friday

Museums 9:30am–5pm, often closed Monday and Tuesday

Restaurants 11am–10pm, later in San Juan

Shops 9am–6pm Monday to Saturday, 11am–5pm Sunday, later in malls

Banks 8am-4pm Monday to Friday, 9:30am-noon Saturday

Post offices 8am-4pm Monday to Friday, 8am-1pm Saturday

Arriving in Puerto Rico

San Juan's **Luis Muñoz Marín International Airport** (SJU) receives the vast majority of flights to Puerto Rico, especially international ones. It has all services (except wi-fi), including major car-rental companies and fairly cheap, flat-rate taxis to the nearby tourist centers.

Cruise ships dock at the busy **Old San Juan** and **Ponce Piers** ports at the base of Old San Juan and at Port of the Americas near Ponce's La Guancha Paseo Tablado. Nerarby you'll find excellent food and drink, although from Ponce's port you'll need a taxi to get to the center.

Getting Around

Most visitors drive themselves around Puerto Rico when they travel the island; this is far and away the advised means of getting about.

Bus Regular large urban buses run on routes convenient for visitors in San Juan.

Car Exploring Puerto Rico will be more rewarding with your own vehicle, although chaotic local driving habits and poor road conditions mean you won't want to plan any extended road trips. Note that a car is unnecessary while staying in San Juan: parking is scarce, traffic terrible.

Ferries & Planes Only used for trips to the major islands of Culebra and Vieques.

Taxi Within San Juan, taxis are reasonable. Travel between towns, though, and costs fly up.

For much more on **getting around**, see p268

First Time Puerto Rico

For more information, see Survival Guide (p261)

Checklist

➡ Reserve as far in advance as possible for flights and hotels in high season.

➡ Don't worry about a passport if you're a US citizen; a valid state ID or driver's license will do.

➡ Brush up on your high-school Spanish; a few simple phrases will be greatly appreciated.

➡ Stream some salsa to get a sense of local beats.

What to Pack

➡ Bathing suit

➡ Shorts

➡ Sandals

➡ Sun hat

➡ Sunglasses

➡ Flash duds for salsa dancing

➡ US cell phone: most plans include Puerto Rico

➡ Refillable water bottle: tap water is drinkable

➡ Books: you'll be relaxing lots

➡ A wad of US dollars: avoid international bank charges

➡ A driver's license: public transport here sucks

Top Tips for Your Trip

➡ Relax. Puerto Rico is easy, particularly for US travelers. US citizens don't need passports and the currency is the US dollar. If you forget something you can easily buy it at familiar stores like Walgreens.

➡ Save time to just chill and save plenty of time for the beaches. While there are countless reasons to go exploring, you'll find that road conditions can make endless days in a car stressful. Also, as you do move around, hit the pause button in places like Vieques, which are much more rewarding over several days as opposed to a super-quick day trip from San Juan.

➡ Eat like a local. You can get great international fare or even find familiar fast-food outlets, but why bother? Stands, food trucks and humble open-air cafes dish up the Commonwealth's delicious cuisine, which boasts an enticing medley of Caribbean and Spanish flavors.

What to Wear

Puerto Rico is mostly quite casual. Shorts and a T-shirt will suffice anytime you're near a beach, whether it's for a daytime frolic or a sunset cocktail at an open-air bar. Long pants, shirts that tuck in and skirts will suffice for nicer restaurants in San Juan, although there's no limit to how snazzy you can be if you're hitting the cutting-edge clubs.

Sleeping

Puerto Rico has a wide range of accommodations. We advise booking ahead in high season.

Hotels Available all over the island in price ranges from $60 to $400+ nightly, with a good selection under $200.

Bed-and-breakfasts This is a relatively new mid-range option; owners always live on or near the premises and breakfast is included.

Guesthouses These range from family-run places with a few rooms to larger motel-like stays; many are also apartments under another name.

Resorts World-class properties line San Juan's beachfront and other coastal areas, however, few are all-inclusive.

Camping Possible on Culebra and in a handful of nature parks.

Taxes

Sales tax stands at a whopping 11.5%: the highest of any US state or territory. Room tax is 7–11% of the bill depending on what type of lodging you are in.

Bargaining

Except for larger items like paintings in souvenir stalls, you'll find few places where it's appropriate to bargain. Prices in stores and most markets are firm and attempts at negotiation will not be welcome.

Tipping

Generally, you tip in Puerto Rico as you would on the US mainland.

➡ **Bars** $1 per drink.

➡ **Luggage attendants** $1 to $2 per bag for anyone who helps with your luggage.

➡ **Restaurants** 15% of the bill.

➡ **Taxis** 15% of the fare.

➡ Check for service charges included in your bill at touristy restaurants, even for groups smaller than six.

➡ If possible, tip servers with cash even when paying by credit card; this precludes management taking a cut.

Language

Spanish is the main language spoken, although most people speak at least some English and many are fluent. Travelers with no Spanish-language skills will still have no problems as even locals who don't speak English are used to visitors who don't speak Spanish and know how to get by.

El Morro (p54), San Juan

Etiquette

Puerto Rico is pretty laid back, but your welcome will be even warmer if you grasp a few principles of local etiquette.

Eating Meals, even a pause for a coffee, are meant to be unhurried affairs.

Greetings When entering a restaurant or cafe, offer a general greeting to those around you: 'Buen provecho' (enjoy your meal), coupled with a salutation appropriate to the time of day.

Politics Understand that Puerto Rico is part of the United States (residents pay taxes and serve in the military), but that it is not a state with voting rights in Congress, and know that questions about the Commonwealth's future political status are cause for intense local debate.

If You Like...

Perfect Beaches

If you've come to laze on the beach, there's only one decision to make: where to spread your towel.

Balneario Escambrón Nice sand, good snorkeling and a nearby fort make this San Juan's most evocative beach. (p69)

Playa Flamenco Often short-listed among the world's best beaches, this pristine strip on Culebra is largely undeveloped. (p120)

Playa Santa This southwest-coast cove stands in the shadow of a majestic 19th-century lighthouse and is perfect for swimming. (p192)

Playa Survival A solitary sea-bashed swathe of sand around Isabela devoid of any tourist manicuring. (p207)

Playa Caracas Just one of the amazing buffet of beaches on the south coast of Vieques. (p132)

Live Music

Catching live music is a surprisingly difficult task in Puerto Rico, where many of the clubs prefer raging reggaetón to live salsa. There are some options, though.

Nuyorican Café The best place for live music; the musicians carry the torch of Puerto Rican's musical legacy. (p249)

Carli's Café Fine Bistro & Piano For resonant live jazz in an atmospheric art-deco setting, this San Juan spot cannot be beaten. (p80)

El Centro de Bellas Artes Luis A Ferré Sparkling venue in San Juan where you can hear bombastic international acts, or the Puerto Rican Symphony Orchestra. (p85)

Romantic Escapes

With swaying palms, brilliant red sunsets and highland forest hideaways, Puerto Rico suffers no lack of romance.

Casa Flamboyant A sophisticated, adult-only retreat in El Yunque with its own private selection of trails for guest use. (p104)

Horned Dorset Primavera For very special occasions, this secluded west-coast boutique resort is as romantic as they get. (p178)

Mary Lee's by the Sea These exceedingly fashionable independently owned cliffside apartments are made for couples who want no interruptions. (p165)

Blue Horizon Boutique Resort On a quiet beach in Vieques, the bungalows here make for a delightful escape from the world. (p139)

Hacienda Pomarrosa Near remote Reserva Forestal Toro Negro, this tucked-away coffee hacienda has three secluded *casitas* at which you can stay. (p222)

Colonial Architecture

The grand edifices of Puerto Rico's past are strewn around the island and are still singing hymns of by-gone colonial dignity.

Old San Juan This historic port town has a wealth of lovingly restored buildings. (p54)

Plaza Las Delicias Ponce's historical core surrounds this grand public plaza, which boasts the magnificent Fuente de los Leones. (p147)

San Germán One of the oldest established cities, where beautifully restored historic homes stand beside the crumbling remains of the neglected ones. (p192)

Palacete Los Moreau Isabela offers visitors a refreshing break from its beach scene with this graceful former coffee hacienda with landscaped grounds. (p207)

Top: Plaza Las Delicias (p147), Ponce
Bottom: Parque Ceremonial Indígena Caguana (p204)

Wildlife-watching

Under sea and overhead, Puerto Rico's colorful wildlife is ever present.

El Yunque This rainforest is crawling with lizards and exotic birds; look for the exceptionally rare Puerto Rican parrot. (p98)

Bosque Estatal de Guánica This amazingly arid patch of dry forest is teeming with birds that nest in the cacti and scrub-covered hills. (p163)

Isla Mona The so-called Galápagos of the Caribbean; snorkel clear waters with colorful fish and sharks and hike past giant iguanas. (p195)

Bahía de Jobos2 Kayakers and hikers navigate the elaborate mangrove channels and coves to spot pelicans, herons and manatee here. (p157)

Diving & Snorkeling

Due to big swells on the north coast, most of the best diving and snorkeling lies away from San Juan.

La Parguera Just offshore here is 'The Wall,' which drops to over 1500ft and offers the chance to see rare black coral. (p168)

Fajardo Enormous coral heads and a great assortment of reef fish make this a great destination in the east. (p107)

Culebra & Vieques These two islands have charter trips to tiny, off-lying cays and snorkeling beaches within walking distance of each other. (p116)

Isla Desecheo This island hosts great dives when the sea is calm, with reliable visibility over 100ft. (p209)

Unique Cuisine

The dining is mighty fine across Puerto Rico, but there are a few one-of-a-kind eating experiences.

Mayagüez This often-overlooked west-coast city is the home of the island-wide delicacy brazo gitano. (p185)

Guavate Chow down at one of Guavate's legendary *lechoneras* (roadside pork-roast stands) alongside exuberant weekending Puerto Ricans. (p219)

Vieques Guzzle back a glass of *bilí*, a unique drink made with the island's *queñapa* fruit – and of course liberal amounts of rum. (p128)

Jayuya Coffee haciendas in Puerto Rico produce cracking coffee and Jayuya sits amidst a hotbed of pretty plantations. (p223)

Hiking

Don't expect much by way of well-marked trails, but Puerto Rico's hikes offer excellent DIY adventures.

El Yunque Short, easy hikes through this soaking rainforest should top every outdoors agenda, whilst more arduous traipses await for the intrepid. (p98)

Bosque Estatal de Guánica With amazing views and a bizarre landscape of cacti and scrub, the blazing hot hikes here are among Puerto Rico's weirdest. (p163)

Refugio Nacional Cabo Rojo Eerie salt flats, remote headlands, beautiful beaches and an absence of cars make for wanders where nature still rules. (p186)

Bosque Estatal de Guajataca Navigate deep limestone sink-holes, karst-country terrain and sudden cliffs in this untouched state forest. (p225)

Reserva Forestal Toro Negro The island's highest peak, Cerro la Punta, plus a network of virtually untrammeled forest trails. (p221)

Pre-Colombian Culture

Much of Puerto Rico's pre-colonial past is no longer in evidence, but these noteworthy exceptions are mesmerizing detours.

Cueva del Indio A curious cave near Arecibo with early Taíno inscriptions on the walls. (p202)

Museo de las Américas An evocative journey through time showing the influences on the development of Puerto Rico from Taíno to Spanish. (p55)

Centro Ceremonial Indígena de Tibes Extensive ruins near Ponce bring indigenous Puerto Rico to life. (p154)

Parque Ceremonial Indígena Caguana A small but poignant site preserving Taíno ball courts, evidence of the game of batey which held huge cultural significance. (p204)

Interesting Art

Puerto Rico boasts brilliant museum spaces dedicated to showing the island's propensity for highlighting plights, fights and fortunes in captivating art.

Santurce San Juan's new hub of counter-culture shot to hipster prominence mainly thanks to its riveting street-art murals. (p65)

Museo de Arte de Ponce For a small city, Ponce's art scene packs a punch. It's here that you'll find the finest collection of art in all the Caribbean. (p147)

Caguas The biggest town in the Central Mountains has become an artistic powerhouse, particularly well known for its exquisite *retablos* (three-dimensional miniature scenes). (p215)

Museo de Arte Contemporáneo de Puerto Rico A truly bombastic collection of art from the mid-20th century onwards at this San Juan museum. (p67)

Adventure Sports

Swooping forests and dramatic canyons with dangling wires enabling you to zipline over the lot: welcome to Puerto Rico's particular brand of adventure.

Kalichi Adventures Vertiginous leaps of waterfalls, rappelling and tough jungle hikes in El Yunque. (p103)

Toro Verde Nature Adventure Park The main allure is the planet's longest zipline, but the mountain-biking circuit is phenomenal too. (p219)

Cañon de San Cristóbal The place to try canyoning and climbing in the Central Mountains. (p217)

Tanamá River Adventures River tubing, kayaking and other blood-quickening escapades in the karst country south of Arecibo. (p206)

Month by Month

TOP EVENTS

Día de los Reyes, January

Carnaval, February

Feria Dulce Sueño, March

Fiesta de San Juan Bautista, June

Thanksgiving, November

January

Travelers looking to escape the cold find balmy solace in Puerto Rico, where temps hover between the high 70s and 80s and where the Christmas after-party rumbles on.

🎉 Día de los Reyes

This island-wide party on 6 January toasts the three kings (the Magi) and is the high of the Christmas cel-ebrations. Many towns have festivals in their plazas and families exchange gifts.

🎉 Fiestas de la Calle San Sebastián

This is a week-long shindig of parades, food, dancing and music in Old San Juan. One of the island's hippest street carnivals, it's usually held over January's third weekend. (p74)

🐋 Whale-watching

From late January to late March, migrating humpback whales can be seen off west-coast shores. Dive boats double as whale-watching operators, but you may also spot them from the light-houses at Cabo Rojo and Rincón. (p175)

February

Though the mountains are coolest during this time, temperatures stay fairly consistent along the coast. It's also one of the driest times of year, with only rare, brief, afternoon showers.

🎉 Carnaval

During the days preceding Lent, Ponce parties *hard* before giving up vices. While this event is not as wild as Rio de Janeiro's Carnival or New Orleans' Mardi Gras, it's fun to see parading *ve-jigantes* (traditional horned masks) and beauty pageants at Carnaval. (p151)

🎉 Maricao Coffee Festival

Held midmonth, the an-nual Maricao Coffee Festi-val has demonstrations of traditional coffee making and local crafting. The rugged mountain backdrop is sublime and the fresh air fills with the scent of roast-ing beans. (p224)

March

Snowbird tourists return north, but the weather remains remarkably beautiful, with warm temperatures and little rain. This may be the slowest month of tourism, leaving parks virtually empty.

🎉 Feria Dulce Sueño

The streets of Guayama fill with the elegant gait of Paso Fino horses during the two-day Feria Dulce Sueño (Fair of Sweet Dreams). Competi-tions take place in a digni-fied rodeo atmosphere and the city goes horse crazy. (p156)

☆ Puerto Rico JazzFest

Hosted at the Tito Puente Amphitheater in San Juan in mid-March, the festival draws international artists and jazz fans. (p74)

April

Trade winds bring a bit more precipitation to the north coast, though rainfall is mostly in the afternoon and temperatures continue to increase.

🍷 Ironwood Wine

People in little Juana Díaz near Ponce get tipsy with their Taíno heritage, celebrating Mavi Carnival and toasting a fermented drink made from the bark of an ironwood tree. Festivities include lots of costumes, food and fairly intense hangovers.

🎆 Semana Santa

The Catholic holiday of Easter gets celebrated for an entire week at Semana Santa festivals across the island. The most vivid festivals will have a procession through the streets to reenact the crucifixion – using a real person tied to a cross.

May

Many of the little agricultural towns of the south celebrate the arrival of spring with the fruit of their harvests – including an assortment of coconut, mango, shrimp and oysters.

☆ Semana de la Danza

Ponce's Semana de la Danza, held in mid-May, features a week of music and dance concerts that celebrate the stately music of string quartets and 19th-century ballroom dance. Many of the events are free. (p151)

June

Locals switch to summer mode, with shorter work days and time off school. The tourist season – when

road-tripping Puerto Ricans join foreigners – swings into high gear.

🍴 Festival del Juey

Guánica's mid-June Festival del Juey delights crab eaters and brings an open-air fair to the town's seaside. The crustaceans are consumed in every preparation imaginable and washed back with a whole lot of cold beer.

🎆 Fiesta de San Juan Bautista

On June 24 Old San Juan explodes with the island capital's *fiesta patronal* (patron saint's festival). Party animals eventually walk backwards into the sea (or sometimes fountains) to demonstrate loyalty to the saint of Christian baptism.

July

Blazing-hot temperatures drive Puerto Rican families to the beaches in droves. This is high season for sun-seeking locals, so expect company at the beach.

🎆 Fiesta de Santiago

This Loíza fiesta, held at the end of the month, brings Puerto Ricans of African descent to a festival worthy of Bahía in Brazil: parades, fabulous drum ensembles, masks and costumes revive saints and incarnations of West African gods. (p95)

August

Tropical rains start at the start of the peak of hurricane season, but parties continue.

☆ Bomba y Plena

The music of plantation workers fills the air at Bomba y Plena festivals. Explosive drumbeats and folk songs are the custom; reliably rowdy ones happen in Ponce and in the nearby mountain villages of Juana Díaz and Aguas Buenas.

October

Though this is the slow tourist season, the island's typical range of parties for patron saints are scattered throughout the month. A lack of crowds make this a great month for a visit.

🎆 Día del Descubrimiento de América

Though Christopher Columbus is loathed throughout most of Latin America, Puerto Rico celebrates his arrival – the so-called Discovery of America Day – with parades and street festivals on October 12.

November

American tourists begin descending on the island as the weather turns cold in the north.

🎆 Jayuya Indigenous Festival

Although all pure-blooded Taíno have been gone for about 400 years, this Jayuya festival, held midmonth, revives the games, costumes, food and music of the original islanders. As with almost all Puerto Rican fiestas, there's a beauty pageant, this time with women in Indian dress. (p223)

Top: Hatillo Mask Festival (p203)
Bottom: Puerto Rico JazzFest (p74)

☆ Play Ball!

Winter League Baseball is in full swing and stadiums throughout the island host teams of aspiring major leaguers, young players hoping to get a bit more experience over the winter and older players in the twilight of their careers.

✗ Thanksgiving

Puerto Ricans celebrate Thanksgiving similarly to folks in the continental US: as a largely family affair, on the fourth Thursday of November. Touristy restaurants put on special menus but otherwise places close down on this day, which marks the start of the island's lengthy Christmas season.

December

Twinkling lights make central plazas sparkle as Puerto Rico gets geared up for Christmas. Near the end of the month, every town celebrates the nativity.

🏃 Waves in the West

Cold fronts push huge waves to the island's west coast, making it the high season for surfing Rincón and beaches near Isabela and Aguadilla. With perfect tubes and tons of tourists, you'll need to reserve a board and lessons early.

🎭 Hatillo Mask Festival

Held on December 28, the festival features masked devils prowling the streets as incarnations of the agents of King Herod, who sent soldiers to find and kill the Christ Child. Kids run and hide from the maskers. (p203)

Itineraries

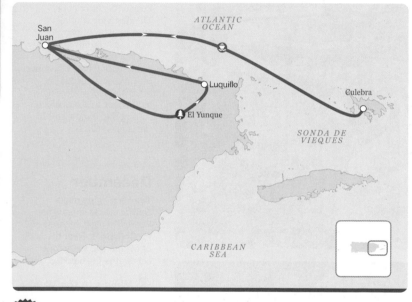

 **San Juan & Around**

This 3-day itinerary whisks you into the thick of the action of San Juan, the island's capital. Labyrinthine Old Town gives way to beachy outer neighborhoods and the city is well-located for exploring some of the island's other key draws.

It's easy to get caught up in **San Juan**, one of the Caribbean's most versatile cities. Spend a lazy first day exploring historic Old San Juan, rounding off the sightseeing with the edgy – and tasty – wonders of Santurce in the late afternoon and evening. On day two, make a beeline for one of the urban beaches, such as Playa Isla Grande, and wind up with live music back in Old San Juan at Nuyorican. But there is plenty to see and do just outside the capital that will give you a much broader picture of Puerto Rico's diverse pleasures.

Day three: choice time. Consider joining one of the sailing day trips out to either **Culebra** or **Vieques** where you'll enjoy some sensational snorkeling, or head on a day tour up to the lush rainforest wonders of **El Yunque**. As you drive Hwy 191, you'll climb ever higher into the misty peaks where you can take your pick of waterfalls and nature hikes. Spend the night at a mountain retreat before returning to San Juan via **Luquillo**, with its natural wonders, beaches and scrumptious food stands.

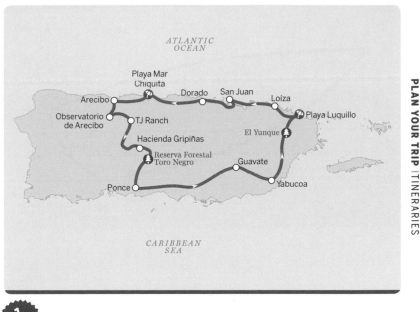

Essential Puerto Rico

1 WEEK

This week-long waltz around the island takes you from the capital out along the north coast, then down to the Central Mountains and Puerto Rico's culture-packed second city, Ponce, before spinning you back to San Juan via the tropical rainforest of El Yunque.

Arrive in **San Juan** and get to the beaches, exploring Isla Verde, Condado and Ocean Park. Spend day two weaving through the Unesco treasures of Old San Juan and posing by the ramparts of El Morro. Finish with an evening at Santurce's bars and restaurants.

Go west on day three, stopping first at **Dorado**, where you can play world-class golf or hide out at **Playa Mar Chiquita**, where you can watch waves explode over the coral reefs.

Keep along the coast road to **Arecibo,** a region becoming known for its bombastic monuments. First up, there's the tallest statue in North America, the Birth of the New World Statue. Turn south, winding into the mountains up to **Observatorio de Arecibo**. If you're extraordinarily lucky, this might be the day this mountain-sized icon, the world's largest radio telescope, detects life on another planet. Bunk nearby at the remote **TJ Ranch**.

Next morning, meander south into coffee country around Jayuya and take a tour of the bean-to-cup process at a hacienda here, such as **Hacienda Gripiñas.** Forge your way along the Ruta Panorámica, heading toward Puerto Rico's tallest peak, Cerro de Punta in **Reserva Forestal Toro Negro**. Head to historic **Ponce** to dine and sleep. The next day start slow and enjoy the city's excellent museums, then head east to sample smoky pork at one of the famed roadside *lechoneras* (eateries specializing in suckling pig) in **Guavate**. Continue east to sleep at a beach house in **Yabucoa**. The cool, green interior of **El Yunque** and its magical rainforest starts day six, which finishes on the white sands of **Playa Luquillo**. At night, glide across the glowing waters of the bioluminescent bay at Laguna Grande.

Before returning to San Juan, have a meal from one of the famous *friquitines* (beach kiosks) at Playa Luquillo. Drive back via **Loíza**, where you can buy a *vejigante* (traditional horned mask), then pass the evening wandering the back streets of Old San Juan. Stop for a drink and join locals and other visitors doing just the same.

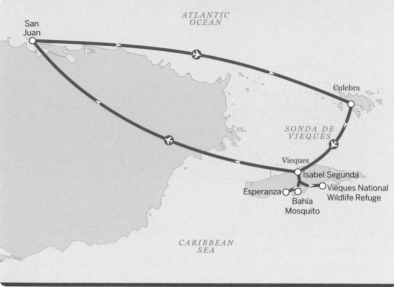

10 DAYS Escape to Culebra and Vieques

If you've come to Puerto Rico for dreamy tranquil islands – and everything that they might entail, from sun-worshipping to bioluminescent bay gazing – this itinerary is for you.

After time in the capital of **San Juan**, hightail it out of town for your island break. A trip to the islands of Culebra and Vieques displays Puerto Rico in its best light: perfect sand, laid-back atmosphere and ramshackle nightlife. Take a scenic flight to leave the capital: it's affordable and saves you the hassle and expense of getting to the ferries at Fajardo, plus the daredevil approach to Culebra rivals the best thrill ride.

Start in **Culebra**, which doesn't have much in the way of fancy resorts and clubs; the focus here is on the world-class beaches, reef snorkeling and wildlife refuges. With few cars on the island and long, deserted stretches of sand, Culebra offers the serenity that can be all too rare on the crowded Puerto Rican mainland. Visitors can soak in the expansive views of the ocean, breathe the fresh island air and explore beaches, from the renowned Playa Flamenco to the remote and enticing Playa Zoni. Save time for the beautiful snorkeling at Luis Peña Marine Reserve.

After dark, the little harbor at Dewey comes alive with affable expats whose love of karaoke crooning is only rivaled by their thirst for cold cans of Medalla.

Next up is surprising **Vieques**, the larger island just southwest of Culebra. You can take a ferry back to the mainland and another out to Vieques, but flying is vastly quicker and more fun. Once you touch down in **Isabel Segunda**, hang around this atmospheric town for a bit before heading south to **Esperanza**, the perfect place to enjoy the slow pace of the tropics while enjoying some fine places to stay, eat and drink. You may not want to leave. Spend the next few days exploring the wealth of south-coast beaches in the **Vieques National Wildlife Refuge**. You will be hard-pressed to choose your favorite as you marvel at crowd-free coves and bays.

Save one night for the magically glowing waters of the bioluminescent bay, **Bahía Mosquito**, where you can paddle out in a quiet kayak or glide silently in an electric boat.

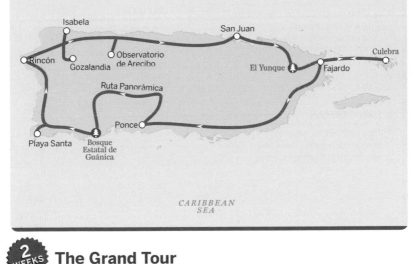

2 WEEKS The Grand Tour

You won't miss any highlights with this best-of-the-best clockwise circuit from San Juan.

Spend four days in **San Juan** and the surrounding areas, getting plenty of beach time and making sure to see Old San Juan. Spend at least one night listening to live salsa and taking in the dance-floor action at Nuyorican Café, the best live-music club on the island. Head to **El Yunque** for a day of hiking, then spend the night in **Fajardo** and experience the wonder of the bioluminescent bay at Laguna Grande.

The next morning head east aboard the ferry for **Culebra**. The next few days will go by too quickly, snorkeling and swimming at some of the best beaches in the world and taking a charter trip off to the abandoned white-sand paradise of Isla Culebrita.

Now that your batteries are fully recharged, get exploring. Make for the mainland and follow quiet roads past the sleepy sugar towns of the south coast toward **Ponce**. Spend a couple of days exploring the colonial buildings and excellent food in the so-called 'Pearl of the South.' Out of the center, you can also visit the impressive indigenous site of Centro Ceremonial Indígena de Tibes or detour up into the Central Mountains to hike and sip the island's famous coffee at dreamy stop-offs along the **Ruta Panorámica.**

Definitely allow one day (preferably with an early start so you can be done by midafternoon when the sun is at its hottest) for the rugged, bone-dry forest of **Bosque Estatal de Guánica**. After hiking, drive scenic Rte 333 along the south coast and stop to swim at tiny mangrove-enclosed beaches and spend the night in an isolated resort.

You can either spend the day swimming the turquoise water at **Playa Santa** in Refugio Nacional Cabo Rojo or head straight to the final destination, **Rincón**. The last few days of the trip will be spent surfing (or taking lessons) on perfect waves and soaking up the island's best sunsets with an icy rum drink in hand, perhaps with some time spent in nearby **Isabela**. Complete the circuit, breaking up the drive with a stop in the mountains at either the gorgeous waterfalls of **Gozalandia** near San Sebastián or grabbing insights into the stars at **Observatorio de Arecibo**, before arriving back in San Juan for your final evening.

Off the Beaten Track: Puerto Rico

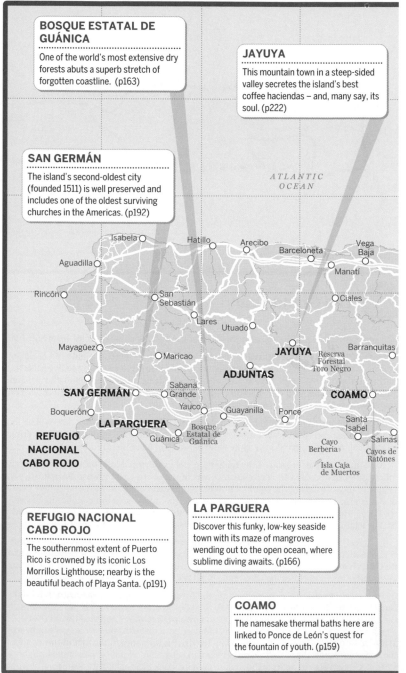

BOSQUE ESTATAL DE GUÁNICA

One of the world's most extensive dry forests abuts a superb stretch of forgotten coastline. (p163)

JAYUYA

This mountain town in a steep-sided valley secretes the island's best coffee haciendas – and, many say, its soul. (p222)

SAN GERMÁN

The island's second-oldest city (founded 1511) is well preserved and includes one of the oldest surviving churches in the Americas. (p192)

ATLANTIC
OCEAN

Isabela   Hatillo   Arecibo   Vega
                              Barceloneta   Baja
Aguadilla   Manatí
Rincón   San
         Sebastián   Ciales
         Lares   Utuado
Mayagüez   Barranquitas
         Maricao   JAYUYA   Reserva
                            Forestal
                   ADJUNTAS Toro Negro
         Sabana
SAN GERMÁN Grande   COAMO
Boquerón   Yauco   Guayanilla   Ponce
LA PARGUERA Bosque   Santa
             Estatal de   Isabel
REFUGIO   Guánica Guánica   Salinas
NACIONAL   Cayo   Cayos de
CABO ROJO   Berberia Ratónes
                            Isla Caja
                            de Muertos

REFUGIO NACIONAL CABO ROJO

The southernmost extent of Puerto Rico is crowned by its iconic Los Morrillos Lighthouse; nearby is the beautiful beach of Playa Santa. (p191)

LA PARGUERA

Discover this funky, low-key seaside town with its maze of mangroves wending out to the open ocean, where sublime diving awaits. (p166)

COAMO

The namesake thermal baths here are linked to Ponce de León's quest for the fountain of youth. (p159)

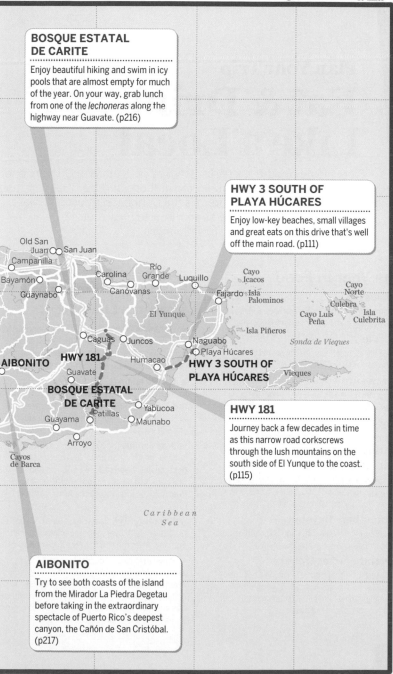

BOSQUE ESTATAL DE CARITE

Enjoy beautiful hiking and swim in icy pools that are almost empty for much of the year. On your way, grab lunch from one of the *lechoneras* along the highway near Guavate. (p216)

HWY 3 SOUTH OF PLAYA HÚCARES

Enjoy low-key beaches, small villages and great eats on this drive that's well off the main road. (p111)

HWY 181

Journey back a few decades in time as this narrow road corkscrews through the lush mountains on the south side of El Yunque to the coast. (p115)

AIBONITO

Try to see both coasts of the island from the Mirador La Piedra Degetau before taking in the extraordinary spectacle of Puerto Rico's deepest canyon, the Cañón de San Cristóbal. (p217)

Plan Your Trip

Eat & Drink Like a Local

From hipster food-truck parks, smoked pork stalls of Guavate and wacky beach bars to mountain-top grill-ups and gourmet San Juan restaurants, Puerto Rico's food is the Caribbean's best and most diverse. Comida criolla (traditional Puerto Rican cuisine) is an exciting blend of wide-ranging influences.

The Year in Food

January
Continued Christmas festivities keep treats like coquito (a rum-and-coconut drink) a-coming.

February
Coffee harvesting begins; Maricao and Jayuya celebrate coffee festivals.

March–April
The season hosts San Juan's rum festival, Barranquitas' celery festival and even a food-truck festival.

May
Sugarcane is celebrated in Hatillo, beer in San Juan and pineapples in Lajas.

June–August
Puerto Rico Restaurant Week and Lares' Banana Festival honor the start of summer. Avocado season begins; Old San Juan throws a culinary festival.

September–October
Mayagüez reveres sangria, Luquillo coconuts and Corozal plantains in the autumn festival line-up.

November–December
Thanksgiving kick-starts a two-month Christmas party. Watch for mofongo-stuffed turkey, tembleque (coconut pudding) and pernil (roast pork shoulder), other typical seasonal offerings.

Food Experiences

Meals of a Lifetime

➡ **El Rancho Original** (p219) Locals and visitors alike will always argue over which of Guavate's lechoneras is the best – but this place will almost certainly always be a contender.

➡ **El Gato Negro** (p187) Join local families – from tiny nippers to gossiping grandparents – at this authentic waterside diner at Playa Joyuda for some of the freshest and tastiest seafood you will ever eat.

➡ **José Enrique** (p82) For San Juan's best cuisine, head to Santurce, and for Santurce's best cuisine, head to José Enrique's eponymous restaurant to discover some of the best food Puerto Rico, and indeed, the Americas, has to offer.

➡ **Kasalta** (p81) A classic San Juan cafe and restaurant with every local specialty you can imagine, from the soups to the superb desserts.

➡ **Restaurante La Guardarraya** (p163) This esoteric old wooden house on stilts near Yauco invented one of the Commonwealth's best culinary dalliances: chuletas can can, or pork prepared with ribs and fat left on so that it blows up when cooked to resemble a cancan dancer's skirt.

Cheap Treats

Cheap, cheerful and indisputably Puerto Rican, *friquitines,* also known as *quioscos, kioskos,* food trucks or just plain food stalls, offer some of the island's best cheap snacks. Running the gamut from smoky holes-in-the-wall to mobile trucks parked up on the roadside, these cheap, informal eats offer fast food that is invariably home-made, locally sourced and tasty.

The island's most famous cluster of permanent *friquitines* (more than 60 in all) lines the beachfront at Luquillo (p106). Other more movable feasts operate at weekends in places such as Piñones near San Juan and Boquerón on the west coast, although you can come across them almost anywhere.

Among the favorites on offer:

➡ *Surullitos* (fried cornmeal and cheese sticks)

➡ *Empanadillas* (meat or fish turnovers)

➡ *Alcapurrias* (fritters made with mashed plantains and ground meat)

➡ *Bacalaítos* (salt-cod fritters seasoned with oregano, garlic and sweet chili peppers)

But don't think your choices are limited: everything from fabulous Mexican to smokey barbecue and much more is on offer.

When it's hot, keep an eye out for *piragüeros,* vendors who sell syrupy *piraguas* (cones of shaved ice covered in sweet fruity sauces such as raspberry, guava, tamarind or coconut). Another treat are fresh smoothies made from your choice of an abundance of fruit.

The food truck is the latest trendy reincarnation of the Puerto Rican move-able feast and, truth be told, it's a step up in class from the *friquitines.* Whilst a fairly familiar concept across the western world, Puerto Rico's food trucks are a reaction against the plethora of fast-food chains and mediocre supermarket fare in many parts of the island. Now they are generally parked in specific areas of towns with their own chairs, tables and awnings, and resound to the animated buzz of Puerto Rico's bright young hip-ster crowd, as well as a fair few families and in-the-know foreigners. Food trucks found their reputation on offering great, cheap meals (you'll fill your belly for under $5 sometimes and never more than $10). Alcohol is not permitted in food truck parks, so the fun all revolves around the taste buds.

Favorite food trucks:

Blue Fin Food Truck (p212), Aguadilla

Santurce Food Trucks (p82), San Juan

El Panino (p125), Culebra

Sol Food (p140), Vieques

El Chifrijo Food Truck (p81), San Juan

Antohaus Food Truck (Frente Universidad del Turabo, Gurabo; ☺6-11pm), Caguas

Local Specialties

Meat

First things first: Puerto Ricans adore meat. They smoke it, stew it, fry it and fillet it. They make bold claims about it (apparently modern barbecue descends from the roast pork that the Taíno called *barbicoa*), they mash it up with all kinds of starches (*mofongo,* anyone?) and they form it into outlandish designs (such as *chuletas can-can,* fringed like a showgirl's skirt).

But fancy or no-frills, the top of the Puerto Rican food chain is a smoky, savory *lechón asado,* which is cooked on a spit over a charcoal fire. When it's done right, the pig is liberally seasoned with a distinctive seasoning called *adobo* (garlic, oregano, paprika, peppercorns, salt, olive, lime juice and vinegar worked into a paste). *Adobo* comes from Spain and is often associated with Filipino food. The meat is then basted with *achiote* (annatio seeds) and juice from *naranjas* (the island's sour oranges). Finally, after it's cooked to crispness, the meat is served with *ajili-mójili* (tangy garlic sauce).

For less festive occasions, Puerto Rican dinners include roast *cabro* (kid goat), *ternera* (veal), *pollo* (chicken) or *carne mechada* (roast beef).

Seafood

Despite all that ocean, seafood takes a sec-ond place to pork on Puerto Rican menus. But that doesn't mean that it's not popular. A favored way to prepare seafood – from *pulpo* (octopus) to *mero* (sea bass) – is *en escabeche.* This technique yields a fried then chilled seafood, pickled in vinegar, oil, peppercorns, salt, onions, bay leaves and lime juice. Be warned this is not the same as ceviche, which uses a different preparation technique, but is often mistranslated as such on menus.

Fried fish is popular at beachside stalls and cafes. It's often topped with *mojo isleño* (a piquant sauce of vinegar, tomato sauce, capers and spices). If you're passing by Arecibo, be sure to try the local delicacy of *ceti* (small transparent fish often fried and piled into an empanada). Cheap and tasty, *bacalaitos* (fried codfish fritters) are ubiquitous. The fritters are often made with other seafood, like conch (sea snail).

Jueyes (land crabs) have long been a staple of islanders who can simply gather them from the beaches. An easy way to enjoy the taste is to eat *empanadillas de jueyes (*crab meat is picked from the shells, seasoned and baked in a wrap with *casabe* paste, which is made from yucca). Fish lovers should also try a bowl of *sopón de pescado* (fish soup), with its scent of onions, garlic and a subtle taste of sherry.

Shrimp and prawns are often marinated in garlic, grilled and served with *mofongo*, a heavenly pairing.

Soups & Stews

Soups and stews fill the humble cafeterias serving *comida criolla* and offer a genuine fusion of Taíno, European and African flavors. Many include island vegetables for texture: *yautia* (tanier; a starchy tuber that is very similar to taro), *batata* (sweet potato), yucca, chayote squash and *grelos*

COFFEE PLANTATIONS

Somewhat off the beaten path, Puerto Rico's historic coffee plantations let you enjoy a fresh brew amid trees laden with beans and with stunning scenery. The tortuous Ruta Panorámica takes travelers past one mountainside plantation after another. Among our favorites there and elsewhere:

Hacienda Tres Angeles (p224), Adjuntas

Hacienda San Pedro (p223), Jayuya

Hacienda Pomarrosa (p220), Reserva Forestal Toro Negro

Hacienda Buena Vista (p154), Ponce

(turnip greens). *Sancocho* (Caribbean soup) blends these vegetables with plantains – peeled and diced – and coarsely chopped tomatoes, green pepper, chilis, cilantro, onion and corn. Cooks then add water, tomato sauce, chopped beef and pork ribs for flavoring.

Another delicious, common dish is *asopao de pollo,* a rich and spicy chicken stew soaked in *adobo.*

Fruits

Puerto Rico grows and exports bananas, papayas, fresh and processed pineapples, as well as a bewildering variety of exotic tropical fruits. It's also one of the planet's largest producers of citron and you'll see a long swath of fields around Adjuntas dedicated to this fruit. Markets and stalls selling fruits (and fresh vegetables like perfect ripe tomatoes) are common.

Desserts

Puerto Ricans love their sweets and even the smallest town will usually have a bakery where you can get fresh cakes and other treats. In larger cities, stylish cafes will have their own bakery section where you can choose from an array of temptations.

Look for the flavors of passion fruit and other tropical treats in desserts like flan. In fact this version of custard is customized in myriad ways; versions with chocolate are highly prized. *Arroz con leche* (rice pudding) is best when topped with a dusting of freshly ground cinnamon. Some sweet treats only really come out at festival time, like *tembleque,* a coconut pudding with a consistency like pannacotta.

Coffee & Juice

Coffee, grown in Adjuntas, Jayuya and many other mountain regions, is a staple at all hours. In fact Puerto Rico is fast gaining a reputation for some of the best coffee in the hemisphere. Locally owned coffee houses are springing up, with an especially impressive collection in Old San Juan.

Cafe con leche (coffee with milk) is a Puerto Rican version of a cafe latte and is a staple at breakfast. Easily tossed back, it's the perfect start to a day.

Fruit juices, such as *guanábana* juice, are locally made in both carbonated and noncarbonated varieties. *Mavi* is something

PUERTO RICO'S FAVORITE FOOD & DRINK

Mofongo The Commonwealth's delicious staple, *mofongo* is made from plantains mashed and cooked with garlic, spices, broth and bits of pork for richness and flavor. No two versions are the same; it's so popular that plantains are imported from the Dominican Republic to meet demand.

Lechón Asado The heavenly smell of *lechón asado* (roast suckling pig) wafts from countless stalls and simple open-air restaurants. Succulent, juicy and lavishly seasoned, it's always popular. In fact, many make the pilgrimage to Guavate, where scores of outlets compete for business, just for a plate or two.

Rum As the home of Bacardi, the world's largest producer of rum, it's no surprise that Puerto Rico loves the spirit in its many forms, from crystal clear to amber, mild to complex. Look for sipping varieties in bars or just enjoy that perennial crowd pleaser, a fruity rum punch.

like root beer, made from the bark of the ironwood tree. As in much of the tropics, beach and street vendors sell *cocos fríos* (chilled green coconuts) with tops lopped off on the spot and straws inserted to reach the uber-refreshing juice inside.

Rum & Beer

Simply put, *ron* (rum) is the national drink. Puerto Rico is the largest producer of rum in the world and distilleries prop up the island's economy. The headquarters of the Bacardí Rum Factory is in Cataño, but most Puerto Ricans drink locally made Don Q or Castillo. Sipping a fine rum (flavors can include a rich medley of caramel and molasses) is a treat in many bars; Barrilito Three Star is aged in old sherry barrels for up to 10 years and is much lauded. Of course, many prefer their rum in one of the island's ubiquitous cocktails: piña colada and rum punch.

To really get into the spirit of things in San Juan, try a tour of the Casa Bacardí Rum Factory (p93), which even runs mixology classes, or a trip to the bar where the piña colada was purportedly first invented, the **Caribe Hilton** (Map p66; 787-721-0303; www.caribehilton.com; 1 San Geronimo, Puerta de Tierra; r $305-335, ste $365-435; P❀@☎☻).

But a beer revolution is sparking across the island. Medalla Light *might* be still the most popular beer locals knock back (it usually costs no more than $2 in bars and cafes) but a new breed of discerning small breweries are ratcheting up the quality and international perception of Puerto Rican beer. Breweries to look out for include the Boquerón Brewing Company in Cabo Rojo and the Old Harbor Brewery in San Juan.

Where to Eat

Book tables in advance in San Juan's posher joints; tip 15% island-wide for meals.

Friquitines Street vendors; ubiquitous.

Reposterías The place for a morning café con leche (coffee and steamed milk) and baked goodies is the local bakery: even small villages have them.

Food Trucks The island's latest culinary craze; generally serving more gourmet fast food than the *friquitines* – from trucks.

Cafes In myriad forms, from corner joints serving simple foods, to ornate eateries serving excellent Puerto Rico–grown coffees.

Restaurants Ranging from basic cafeterias rustling up cheap plates of local staples to grand seaside venues noted for fresh seafood.

Top: *Mofongo*

Bottom: Fried fish with plantains

Plan Your Trip
Puerto Rico Outdoors

Puerto Rico has it all: vistas of turquoise water, bushwhacking through dense jungle, kayaking over warm waves and heavenly surf breaks. The range of outdoor adventures in Puerto Rico is limited only by your ambition; the island's diverse forests, balmy beaches and crinkled karst formations are calling.

Surfing

Lapped on four sides by warm ocean, Puerto Rico has earned the right to consider itself the 'Hawaii of the Atlantic,' with the most consistent surf breaks in the world. Thanks to legendary waves at beaches such as Tres Palmas (p176), Crash Boat (p211) and Jobos (p207), Puerto Rico has a deeply ingrained surfing culture based around some of the best breaks in the Americas.

When to Go

October–April Winter is the time when cold fronts and low pressure systems from the north bring the biggest waves to Rincón and other surfing destinations on the west and north shores.

When Not to Go

December, June & July Even though you can surf in the west year-round, rates spike in December, when hordes of Americans on Christmas vacation invade, making for crowded waters and competitive accommodations. In June and July there are smaller, if surfable swells, but vacationing Puerto Ricans arrive in droves and many accommodations enforce a three-night minimum stay.

Puerto Rico's Most Memorable Trails

La Mina Trail
Navigate through an old mine tunnel in El Yunque rainforest, ending at a lovely waterfall. (p102)

El Yunque Trail
This moderately challenging hike summits the highest point in Puerto Rico's rainforest. (p102)

Cueva del Viento
Test your navigation skills on the poorly-marked plant-rich trails of the Guajataca forest and find this spooky cave. (p226)

Vereda Meseta
A coastal path in the Bosque Estatal after the terminus of Hwy 333, heading via a tempting scoop of sandy beach. (p164)

Vereda La Torre
Clamber up through the Reserva Forestal Toro Negro on a steep path to an observation tower overlooking all the island's highest peaks. (p221)

Los Morrillos Lighthouse
Scramble up to the windswept headlands and old lighthouse overlooking Puerto Rico's remote southwest corner, then swim on the beguiling beach of Playa Santa. (p192)

SURF ESCAPES FROM SAN JUAN

If the west coast's waves are too big, or if its dudes are too cool or the drive is too far, there are a number of lesser-known options for surfers who want to make a quick day trip from San Juan. Along the north coast there are a few decent breaks for expert surfers around Manatí and Arecibo and those with less experience can enjoy the shallow-water thrills of boogie boarding. There are even reasonable surfing lessons to be had in the capital, San Juan.

Die-hards will take what they can get at Balneario Escambrón in Puerta de Tierra, while the best stuff can be found over in Piñones at Los Aviónes. East of San Juan, the best place to surf barrels is at La Pared in Luquillo or the wildlife reserve at La Selva.

Where to Surf

Although there are opportunities to surf the north and east coasts (Luquillo has a popular break), the best of Puerto Rico's surfing is off the famous west coast.

Rincón In 1968 the World Surfing Championships were held at Rincón and the island hasn't looked back since. Surfers from around the world come here for a long annual season. The huge variety of breaks include plenty of stuff for beginners and experts. This is Puerto Rico's surfing capital.

Aguadilla (p211) Some locals actually favor the breaks near here, which are generally a bit more challenging than those at Rincón. Surfer's Beach is kind to beginners, while Gas Chambers is a superb right-hand break for experienced surfers.

Isabela (p207) To avoid the crowds, rent an apartment on the cliff-edge out-of-the-way beach communities around Isabela. Playa Jobos, a long beach good for all levels, is here and just east, enlightened surfers also dig the breaks of the aptly named Secret Spot.

Board Rentals & Lessons

Anywhere there is surfing on Puerto Rico you can expect to find board rentals, surf shops and usually places for lessons. The local scene is popular enough that there

is demand for good gear. In San Juan, especially, you'll find many highly promoted daytime surf camps for people of all ages. The northwest, around Rincón and Isabela, has a reputation for making some of the world's very best boards.

Underwater Adventure

Most Caribbean islands boast a formidable diving scene and Puerto Rico is no exception, with an exciting selection of walls, drop-offs, reefs and underwater caves.

Where to Dive

Parguera Wall The first of Puerto Rico's truly world-class dive areas is near La Parguera (p168) in the south. The underwater wall falls from 60ft to over 1500ft due to a huge drop in the continental shelf below the sea bed. With more than 25 named dive sites, the area is awash with trenches, valleys, coral gardens and colorful fish.

Isla Desecheo Thirteen miles northwest of Aguadilla, Desecheo has a number of spectacular dive sites and visibility that is often at least 100ft.

Isla Mona This is where real adventurers head for diving. It's expensive to charter a trip, but the unblemished waters are frequented by turtles and seals.

Culebra The protected waters of the Luis Peña Marine Preserve gain more followers every year.

San Juan If you can't stray far from the capital, there is good diving right off shore at Balneario Escambrón (p69) in the caves and overhangs at Horseshoe Reef, Figure Eight and the Molar. There's decent diving along the chain of islands called 'La Cordillera,' east of Las Cabezas de San Juan (p108; in the Fajardo area), with about 60ft to 70ft visibility.

Humacao There are some cracking dive sites off the coast around Humacao, near Naguabo, with an offshore wall secreting coral reefs, caves and trenches galore.

Where to Snorkel

Culebra & Vieques The best snorkeling in Puerto Rico can be found off the sheltered islands Culebra and Vieques, where you can snorkel directly from the beach. The former offers Punta Melones, the Luis Peña Marine Preserve and the wonderfully isolated Playa Carlos Rosario; the latter boasts an array of options on the west and south coasts.

Isla Caja de Muertos The south coast faces clear Caribbean waters that suffer low river runoff. Taking the day trip out to this island near Ponce can satisfy hikers as well.

La Parguera These warm waters have some decent snorkeling and DIY adventurers can access hidden mangrove beaches via kayak.

Dive Planning Basics

Generally speaking, the waters off the north and west coasts of Puerto Rico are rough and better suited to surfing. You may, however, get some luck on calm days snorkeling the fringe reefs off Condado and Playa Isla Verde in San Juan or at either Playa Shacks or Playa Steps in Rincón. Even though west-coast waters are calmer in summer, snorkeling still isn't great there.

Dive Operators

Dive operators run day trips out of the major ports and resort hotels around the island.

Many operators run highly promoted day trips on catamarans to Culebra and Vieques from San Juan. These are fun outings and include beach visits along with time underwater.

Across Puerto Rico, you'll find good operators on the islands and at Rincón, La Parguera and Fajardo among others, often with extras like a sunset cruise or whale-watching thrown in.

Hiking

Hiking in Puerto Rico has plenty of potential. But what you actually get out of it depends largely on your individual expectations and how willing you are to strike out on your own (often without a decent map). It would be wrong to paint a picture of the island as some kind of hiker's nirvana. Although the scenery is lush and the coastline wonderfully idyllic, a lack of well-kept paths and a dearth of accurate information are the main challenges.

Where to Hike

El Yunque National Forest (p98) The most popular hikes by far are in the emblematic El Yunque rainforest, where a 37km network of largely paved trails has opened up the area to mass tourism. Hikes here are usually short and easily accessible, and there are plenty of eco-minded tour operators happy to guide you through the main sights. The forest also contains Puerto Rico's only true backcountry adventure, the seven-hour trek to the top of El Toro (3522ft) and back.

SAFETY GUIDELINES FOR DIVING & SNORKELING

Before embarking on a scuba-diving, skin-diving or snorkeling trip, carefully consider the following points to ensure a safe and enjoyable experience:

➡ Possess a current diving certification card from a recognized scuba-diving instructional agency (if scuba diving).

➡ Be sure you are healthy and feel comfortable diving.

➡ Obtain reliable information about physical and environmental conditions at the dive site from a reputable local dive operation.

➡ Be aware of local laws, regulations and etiquette about marine life and the environment.

➡ Dive only at sites within your realm of experience; if available, engage the services of a competent, professionally trained dive instructor or dive master.

➡ Be aware that underwater conditions vary significantly from one region, or even one site, to another. Seasonal changes can significantly alter any site and dive conditions. These differences influence the way divers dress for a dive and what diving techniques they use.

➡ Ask about the environmental characteristics that can affect your diving and how trained local divers deal with these considerations.

Bosque Estatal de Guánica (p163) The foil for El Yunque in every way, this forest is on the opposite corner of the island, the climate is bone-dry and instead of palms the trails are lined with cacti. This remote place has fantastic trails, although many are often 'closed' for maintenance. For bird-watching or sublime simultaneous views of the Caribbean, it's a magical place.

Reserva Forestal Toro Negro (p220) For the island's most dramatic and isolated hikes, head toward the center of the island, on Puerto Rico's misty rooftop. Be prepared to get your shoes dirty here as clouds often shroud the peaks and the trails are invariably damp and muddy. Typical of the numerous forest reserves scattered along the Ruta Panorámica – others include Maricao, Carite and Guilarte – Toro Negro is rarely staffed in low season and you'll be lucky to spot more than a handful of fellow hikers enjoying the views.

Bosque Estatal de Guajataca (p225) The 43km maze of rough trails is more extensive than El Yunque's. It's good for a DIY hiker who doesn't mind a bit of bushwhacking, including a side trip to the spooky Cueva del Viento.

What to Expect

With its verdant mountains, numerous protected parks and highly developed infrastructure, Puerto Rico ought to be a country perfectly suited to hiking. Yet in reality, decent well-signposted trails are few and far between, and many of the Commonwealth's carefully protected forest reserves are rarely utilized.

This paucity of backcountry information can be something of a shock to aspiring wilderness hikers fresh from bushwhacking their way through the Sierra Nevada or dragging their crampons across the European Alps. But, contrary to what the gushing tourist brochures would have you believe, Puerto Rico is no Yosemite. Nor are the Puerto Ricans – with some obvious exceptions – a nation of hikers.

Outside El Yunque National Forest, the island's two dozen or so forest reserves are invariably poorly staffed and lacking in any accurate trail maps (although Bosque Estatal de Guajataca in the Central Mountains and Bosque Estatal de Guánica on the South Coast have equally extensive trail networks to El Yunque).

Yet, plan ahead and a little-used Eden is yours for the exploring. Persistence is important. Try the Departamento de Recursos Naturales y Ambientales (p262) in San Juan, ask around at the various adventure tour agencies and – best of all – question the more outdoor-minded locals. You'll be surprised by what you can find.

You can just chance it and turn up, too. Your wanderings will stand an increased chance of winding you up on some dead-end track with a need to backtrack, but who is to say that won't in itself be memorable?

Cycling

On an island often clogged with cars, cycling is not a contender. Still, you'll find that places to pedal and bicycle rentals – or leads to same – are becoming more common at guesthouses and hotels. San Juan has some good bike tours and rides along the beaches suitable for even the most casual cyclist.

Where to Cycle

Vieques (p136) The protected wildlife refuges on this beautiful island are great places to cycle with minimal auto intrusion – although be prepared for road conditions that favor the sturdiest of mountain bikes.

Isabela Coast (p208) The coastal bike path here is great for a casual afternoon ride. You'll pass the crashing surf and plenty of coastal beaches to take a dip. The hills back behind the main highway are great too, with plenty of rarely driven lanes. You can rent bikes in nearby Aguadilla.

Piñones (p93) The specially designed bike trails in Piñones make for an easy, enjoyable ride on this small island.

HIKING ACROSS THE ISLAND

Fondo de Mejoramiento (www. facebook.com/fondodemejoramiento) runs day hikes covering the entire length of the island from east to west along the Cordillera Central (Central Mountains). The idea is to cover the whole Ruta Panorámica in different weekend segments over a period of three months (February to April). The 'Ruta' was actually designed by Luis Muñoz Marín in the 1950s primarily as a hiking route.

ALTERNATIVE OUTDOOR ADVENTURES

➡ There's a lot of rewarding **kayaking** through the bays, mangroves and nature preserves of San Juan and the east. There are many tours to choose from, the most popular and memorable being the nighttime journeys over the glowing waters of the bioluminescent bays near Fajardo (p110) and Vieques (p131).

➡ Hit the Reserva Forestal Toro Negro with San Juan–based adventure company, Acampa Nature Adventure Tours (p221), and you could find yourself **rappelling** off 60ft cliffs and ziplining above the tree line.

➡ **Kitesurfing** has taken off big time, particularly in Playa Isla Verde (p69) in San Juan and in the Dorado (p199) area.

➡ **Rincón** is the best place to go for **whale-watching**; humpbacks appear in the Pasaje de la Mona around December. You can organize a boat trip with Taíno Divers (p177) or sometimes catch a glimpse from outside the Punta Higüero Lighthouse (p175).

➡ The adventure to dwarf all others is the choppy boat trip out to Isla Mona (p195), possible (with a deal of advance planning) through a handful of operators such as Adventures Tourmarine. (p187)

Central Mountains (p219) The Toro Verde Nature Adventure Park has a professionally groomed single-track trail that offers the island's best mountain biking.

Bosque Estatal de Guánica (p163) They're not dedicated mountain-bike trails, but the surreal scenery of this dry forest and the paucity of other people makes the pedaling here a pleasure.

Before You Go

If you want to do serious cycling in Puerto Rico, you'll find that it's more cost-effective to fly with your bike. The options for long-term rentals on the island are still quite scarce and expensive. Also, remember to bring plenty of extra tubes, a spare tire, basic tools and a couple of replacement spokes so the island's combination of rough roads and scant bike shops doesn't leave you out of commission.

Guided Tours

While nothing can compete with the adventure of planning and executing a wilderness trip on your own, these tour operators can take a lot of the worry out of the adventure and give you a chance to interact with fellow adventure travelers:

Acampa (p73) For Isla Mona, Reserva Forestal Toro Negro, El Yunque, Río Camuy or any other adventure spot on the island, Acampa has all the latest gadgets.

Aquatica Dive & Surf (p211) Dive & Bike Adventures Bicycle tours in Aguadilla, Cabo Rojo and Quebradillas, with the option of taking a swim en route.

Aventuras Tierra Adentro (p73) Camping, caving, rock climbing and river touring, with a specialty in canyon adventures.

Excursiones Eco (p70) For all the sides to San Juan and vicinity you wouldn't see on a standard tour, from unsung city lagoons to squatter communities, giving colourful history and background info; proceeds go back into the communities they tour through.

Kalichi Adventures (p103) Has hardcore adventure tours to the truly wild parts of El Yunque as its raison d'être.

Tanamá River Adventures (p206) Caving, kayaking, cave tubing, off-piste hiking in the forested karst country south of Arecibo.

Vieques Adventure Company (p137) For everything Vieques and adventure related; snorkeling, hiking, mountain biking, history tours, gear rental.

PHOTOGRAPHER LINDA WHITWAM/GETTY IMAGES ©

GREG JOHNSTON/GETTY IMAGES ©

Top: La Mina Trail
(p102)

Bottom: Diving in
Culebra (p122)

Plan Your Trip
Travel with Children

Combining comforts of home and lots of all-ages outdoor adventures, Puerto Rico is an excellent destination for travelers with children. The options for family activities on the island are extensive and happen mostly outdoors. Snorkeling, cave exploring, rainforest adventures and just plain beach fun are some of the highlights.

Puerto Rico for Kids

Puerto Rico is a safe and fun destination for kids, with perhaps the best services for families in the Caribbean. Facilities are comfortable and you'll receive fewer icy stares from curmudgeonly yachters than you might do elsewhere. Families will find it easy to fill their agendas.

Children's Highlights

Beaches

➡ **Condado** (p69) San Juan's most famous beach is also a family winner. Beautiful sand, gentle surf and lots of nearby places for treats.

➡ **Isla Verde** (p69) San Juan's other main beach can be a little quieter than Condado, which makes for more sandcastle-building solitude.

➡ **Sun Bay** (p135) The original public beach on Vieques has the facilities some of the wilder beaches around the island lack: changing rooms, bathrooms and picnic benches.

➡ **Playa Flamenco** (p120) Culebra's famous beach is also famously fun for families. The gentle surf offers a relaxing frolic, while there are many vendors selling beach toys, snacks and other treats.

Best Regions for Kids

San Juan
Young travelers will be thrilled by San Juan's vibrant culture, wide beaches and kid-friendly museums. San Juan's historic sights have a lot of diversions for kids and the tunnels and turrets of El Morro and Fuerte San Cristóbal capture young imaginations with stories of pirates and seafaring adventure. (p50)

Culebra & Vieques
Snorkeling and swimming in the clear, calm waters is excellent for kids and the islands boast holiday home and apartment rentals, which can be an affordable option for families. (p116)

El Yunque & East Coast
Rainforests and frogs, drippy palms and mountain lookouts – the easy hikes of El Yunque rainforest are thrilling. The bioluminescent waters of Fajardo are also magical. (p96)

West Coast
The west coast has excellent surfing and boogie boarding, with waves big enough or small enough to match all abilities. And it's fun to get off the beaten path. (p171)

MIND-BLOWING SIGHTS FOR CHILDREN

Bioluminescent Bays Near Fajardo in the east and on Vieques (p131), the waters glow on dark nights, which produces many a delighted shriek as you float along by kayak or small electric boat.

Observatorio de Arecibo (p203) This mountain-top radio telescope is like a giant ear listening to the heavens.

Marine life in Culebra Coral, tropical fish and clear waters make for excellent snorkeling and the island is fun and relaxed.

Rainforest flora in El Yunque The soggy trails of North America's only rainforest, El Yunque (p98), lead past fascinating flora and fauna, often with fun information posted en route.

➡ **Playa Luquillo** (p105) Visiting families can join scores of local families at this beach popular with young and old. There's plenty of shade and the famous stalls sell every treat imaginable.

➡ **Playa Jobos** (p207) Watch surfers offshore beyond the reef, while enjoying protected waters close to shore. There are some good cafes for lunch.

➡ **Playa Shacks** (p207) Older kids will enjoy the underwater caves here for snorkeling at this somewhat secluded beach.

Hikes

The best hikes for the whole family are in the rainforest of El Yunque (p98). Unlike virtually every other forest on the island, these trails are well marked, easy to follow and easy enough for shorter legs. A favorite is the popular Big Tree Trail (p102), which ends at a waterfall where kids who are brave enough can take an icy dip. The rainforest also has informative ranger-led walks.

Remember that the trails in El Yunque can get pretty crowded after 11am, so it's good to start early. Also, it's essential to bring water on your hike, as there are no facilities on the trails. The Las Cabezas de San Juan (p107) nature reserve is another great natural area for families, with minitours through a diverse coastal environment, a tram and lots of skeletons of marine animals.

Adventures

Families will also find a number of more adventurous activities in parts of the island further afield, though the winding hairpin turns of the central mountains are not recommended. Following the coast, there's lots to keep a family busy: you can ride a horse along the beach in Isabela (p208), explore the mysterious subterranean caves at the Río Camuy (p204) or hit the pirate-themed historical amusement park in Faro y Parque Histórico de Arecibo (p202).

Planning

Although fast-food chains and strip malls can be a bit off-putting for more adventure-some adults, the familiar sights make Puerto Rico more comfortable for kids. That said, there are several things parents can do to ensure a delightful visit.

➡ **Call ahead** Puerto Rican attractions can be notoriously unpredictable with their hours of operation – particularly in state-operated parks – so confirm opening hours before you go.

➡ **Know your accommodations** Look carefully at your hotel options to see what offerings they have for kids. Even though many of the hotels have swimming pools, some are tiny and not kid-friendly; others splash out with mini water parks. Check if resorts have evening programs designed to occupy younger travelers, which can give parents time for a moonlit stroll down the beach. Many major resorts offer 'kids clubs' during the day with myriad activities.

➡ **Consider an apartment** Holiday rental apartments are common and often quite affordable. Besides a lot more space than a hotel room, they offer cooking facilities for the vagaries of young appetites. Many have pools and are close to a beach.

➡ **Find a sitter** Getting someone to mind the kids is not always easy. Resorts and large hotels usually have agencies they recommend; elsewhere, finding a sitter you trust can be haphazard.

Regions at a Glance

San Juan

Nightlife
History
Food

All-night Parties

The rollicking drinking and sensational eating of the Santurce district is reason enough to head out for the night in San Juan. Old San Juan is another great option; join locals and tourists dancing to the libidinous late-night rhythms of a salsa band. Still not done? The casinos are open all night.

Colonial Grandeur

In Old San Juan history of the Americas comes alive in full color. From the ramparts of grand forts, visitors take in pastel-painted facades and tight cobblestone streets in one direction and the endless sparkle of the Atlantic in the other.

Caribbean's Classiest Cuisine

San Juan's cool cafes and exquisite, inventive restaurants combine to make the city the Caribbean's most varied and exciting destination for foodies.

p50

El Yunque & East Coast

Rainforest
Beaches
Nature

Tropical Trails

The trails in El Yunque's humid hills are loaded with surprises: misty waterfalls, the colorful shock of tropical birds or flowers and unexpected views of the canopy-covered hills. And this is only the beginning of the natural attractions.

Bioluminescent Bay

Though Puerto Rico is blessed with several bodies of bioluminescent waters, the one at Laguna Grande near Fajardo is a favorite: the route begins in a thick mangrove forest. Those who haven't experienced the phenomenon will be in awe.

Fantastic Fauna

It's not only El Yunque with ecological diversity: at Las Cabezas de San Juan you can experience seven different ecosystems within a single reserve!

p96

Culebra & Vieques

Beaches
Water Sports
Culture

World-beating Beach Basking

These are Puerto Rico's loveliest and most diverse beaches – some of which, such as Culebra's Playa Flamenco, are commonly listed among the best in the world. Visitors splash and soak up the essence of the Caribbean dream.

Snorkeling

The clear water, variety of fish and coral structures are mesmerizing, and this makes snorkeling particularly appealing. The best sights here are within a short swim of the sandy beach.

Relaxation

Both islands have a zany, sedate charm that is irresistible. A mix of characterful locals and long-term idiosyncratic expats create an utterly mellow and distinctive lifestyle that seems a world away from the 'mainland.'

p116

Ponce & South Coast

Architecture
Culture
Archaeology

Magnificent Mansions

A mix of elegantly restored colonial mansions, experimental turn-of-the-century edifices and tattered historic structures, Ponce has some of the island's most interesting architecture.

Museums

Ponce hosts museums of political revolution, musical heritage and history, but the one that's worth the trip is the renovated Museo de Arte de Ponce, the best art museum in Puerto Rico if not the Caribbean.

Indigenous Intrigue

Just outside the southern capital is the largest Taíno site in the Caribbean, where quiet ceremonial ball courts and comprehensive displays pay homage to the island's distant past and its pre-Columbian people.

p144

Rincón & West Coast

Water Sports
Adventure
Food and Drink

Surfing and Diving

The Beach Boys didn't sing about Rincón for nothing. The immaculate breaks near the point make for some of the best surfing on the planet. It's great for diving, too.

Capes and Isles

The lonely Cabo Rojo and its roads are amazing for cycling; a scramble around the lighthouse-crowned headland and its bays and salt flats is heart-racing. A trip to Isla Mona, 80km out in the ocean, is undoubtedly Puerto Rico's most memorable odyssey.

Ecclectic Dining

Rincón's fabulous restaurant scene seems to improve by the week and a culinary range of quality and variety you'd normally only find in a big city permeates this picturesque little town.

p171

North Coast

Golf
Surfing
Architecture

Caribbean's Top Swinging

Dorado's long fairways, challenging courses and jaw-dropping views attract golfers from around the globe. The best courses in the Caribbean within chipping distance of one another.

Surf and Turf

Rincón gets the glory, but many claim the serious surfing happens to the north, near the towns of Isabela and Aguadilla. Isabela's land-based action consists of superb golfing and horseback riding await.

Bizarre Buildings

The north coast boasts two of the strangest, most sizeable structures in the world. The planet's biggest radio-telescope crests a hill south of Arecibo while one of the world's tallest statues rears above the coastline.

p197

Central Mountains

Food and Drink
Outdoor Activities
Rural Culture

Coffee Haciendas

Many places cultivate coffee, but in Puerto Rico they strive to make this a riveting visitor experience. You can take a tour, kick back in an espresso bar and even stay within the fascinating, far-flung coffee haciendas here.

Hiking

Dramatic scenery and isolation make the untrammeled forests here appealing to gutsy outdoor adventurers. Sure, few of the trails are marked or maintained, but that's part of the fun.

Roadside Lechón

The little towns seem lonely until you stumble on the right *lechonera,* where a plate of smoky pork and a spontaneous dance party appear out of nowhere.

p213

On the
Road

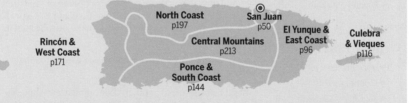

Rincón &
West Coast
p171

North Coast
p197

San Juan
p50

Central Mountains
p213

El Yunque &
East Coast
p96

Culebra
& Vieques
p116

Ponce &
South Coast
p144

San Juan

POP 368,000

Includes ➡

Sights	54
Beaches	69
Activities	70
Courses	72
Tours	73
Festivals & Events	74
Sleeping	74
Eating	78
Drinking & Nightlife	83
Entertainment	85
Shopping	88
Around San Juan	92

Best Places to Eat

➡ José Enrique (p82)

➡ Cocobana (p81)

➡ Acapulco Taqueria Mexicana (p81)

➡ Kasalta (p81)

➡ Marmalade (p80)

Best Places to Sleep

➡ Casa Sol (p75)

➡ Condado Vanderbilt Hotel (p76)

➡ Olive (p76)

➡ Dream Inn (p76)

Why Go?

Established in 1521, San Juan is the second-oldest European-founded settlement in the Americas and the oldest under US jurisdiction. Shoehorned onto a tiny islet that guards the entrance to San Juan harbor, the old town was inaugurated almost a century before the *Mayflower* laid anchor in what is now Massachusetts, and it is now a historic wonderland that juxtaposes historical authenticity with pulsating modern energy.

Beyond its timeworn 15ft-thick walls, San Juan is far more than a collection of well-polished colonial-era artifacts – it's also a mosaic of ever-evolving neighborhoods such as Santurce, which has a raw vitality fueled by street art, superb restaurants and a bar scene that takes over the streets at night.

And then there's the beaches. Silky ribbons of sand line San Juan's northern edge from swanky Condado to resort-filled Isla Verde. You can land at the airport and be splashing in the azure waters an hour later.

When to Go

Winter is the most popular time to visit San Juan as the frozen masses from colder climes come to thaw out. The weather also happens to be at its best – highs in the mid-80s, lows in the high 70s and little humidity.

During the high season (December to February), Old San Juan's streets fill with cruise-ship passengers and bookings are essential at the hottest hotels and restaurants. The boisterous street party of Festival de San Sebastián in mid-January is a high point, especially for locals.

At other times of the year, San Juan is much quieter, even though the beaches remain alluring year-round. From April to October you'll find fewer crowds and plenty of deals, especially in the bigger hotels.

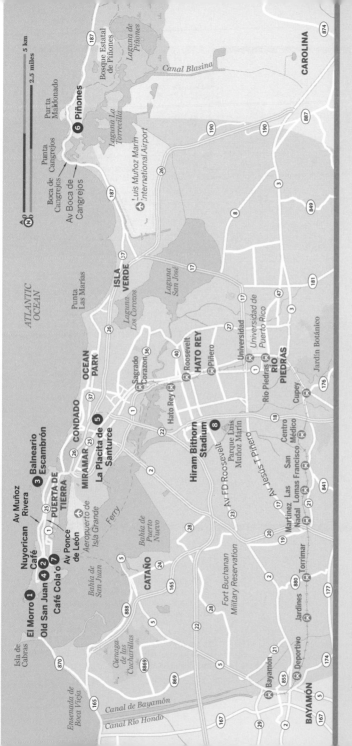

San Juan Highlights

1 El Morro (p54) Exploring 16th-century forts transports you back in time.

2 Nuyorican Café (p85) Feeling the rhythm during a late-night salsa session.

3 Balneario Escambrón (p69) Hitting some of the best urban beaches you'll find anywhere.

4 Old San Juan (p54) Being seduced by the charm of the old town while wandering the blue cobblestone streets.

5 La Placita de Santurce (p84) Losing yourself in the narrow streets around Santurce's market street party.

6 Piñones (p93) Exploring bike paths and beaches amid the wild beauty.

7 Café Cola'o (p83) Savoring locally grown coffee at an exquisite cafe.

8 Hiram Bithorn Stadium (p88) Cheering on the home baseball team as the Cangrejeros de Santurce knock it out of the park.

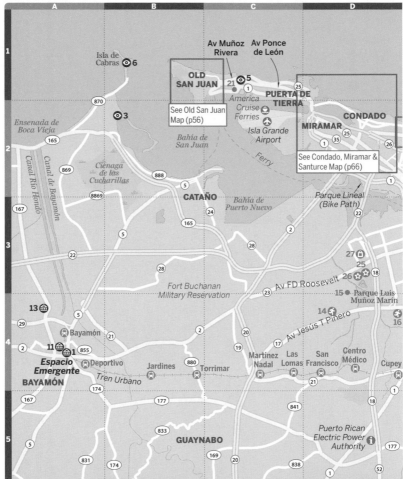

San Juan

◎ **Top Sights**
1 Espacio Emergente A4

◎ **Sights**
2 Balneario de Carolina G2
3 Casa Bacardí Rum Factory B2
4 Centro Cultural Ecoturístico de
   Piñones G2
5 El Capitolio C1
6 Isla de Cabras B1
7 Jardín Botánico de la
   Universidad de Puerto Rico E4

8 Mercado de Río Piedras E4
9 Museo de Entomología y
   Biodiversidad Tropical E4
10 Museo de Historia,
    Antropología y Arte de Río
    Piedras E4
11 Museo de Oller A4
12 Museo del Niño de Carolina H3
13 Parque de las Ciencias Luis A
    Ferré A4

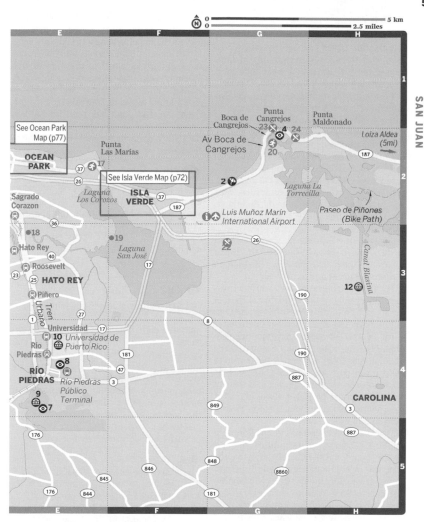

See Ocean Park Map (p77)

See Isla Verde Map (p72)

🟢 **Activities, Courses & Tours**
14	Acampa	D4
15	Acampa Nature Adventure Tours	D3
16	Aventuras Tierra Adentro	D4
17	Castillo Tours & Watersports	E2
	Corporación Piñones Se Integra	(see 4)
18	Excursiones Eco	E3
19	Expediciones Península	F3
20	Magic Tarpon	G2
21	Rent the Bicycle	C1

🔴 **Eating**
22	Bebo's BBQ	G3
23	El Nuevo Acuario	G2
24	Mi Casita Seafood	G2

🟢 **Entertainment**
| 25 | Hiram Bithorn Stadium | D3 |
| 26 | Roberto Clemente Coliseum | D3 |

🔵 **Shopping**
| 27 | Plaza Las Américas | D3 |

History

When the Spaniards arrived with their colonization plans in the early 1500s, San Juan was merely a deserted spit of land dominated by dramatic headlands and strong trade winds.

They settled just south of present-day San Juan in what was little more than a low-land outpost called Caparra. However, the settlement encountered constant Indian attacks and mosquito-borne malaria, so in 1521 the colonists retreated to the rocky outcrop and christened it Puerto Rico (Rich Port). A few years later a Spanish cartographer accidentally transposed Puerto Rico with San Juan Bautista – the name the Spaniards had given to the whole island – and the name change stuck.

The gigantic fortress, El Morro, with its 140ft ramparts, soon rose above the ocean cliffs, and the Catholic Church built a church, a convent and a cathedral.

For the next three centuries, San Juan was the primary military and legislative outpost of the Spanish empire in the Caribbean and Central America. But economically it stagnated.

All of that changed after the Spanish-American War of 1898. The US annexed the island as a territory and designated San Juan the primary port. Agricultural goods such as sugar, tobacco and coffee flowed into the city. *Jíbaros* (country people) flocked into port for work and old villages such as Río Piedras were swallowed up.

WWII brought capital and development as the US beefed up its military defense on the island and the Caribbean. After the war, the monumental economic initiative called Operation Bootstrap began changing Puerto Rico from an agricultural to a manufacturing-based economy and hundreds of US factories relocated to San Juan after the island gained commonwealth status in 1951, to take advantage of tax breaks. Foreign and US banks arrived en masse, the first high-rise buildings went up, and tourist zones took shape along the beachfront of the burgeoning city.

The unchecked growth was a nightmare for city planners, who struggled to provide services, roads and housing. By the 1980s, unemployment was rampant and crime high. Ironically, Old San Juan was considered the epicenter of all that was wrong with the city. Tourists kept to the beach resorts of Condado and Isla Verde.

In 1992, the 500-year anniversary of the arrival of Columbus to the Americas gave city leaders the impetus to restore Old San Juan.

The new millennium has brought several successful projects such as the efficient Tren Urbano (metro) that opened in 2005, a convention center in Miramar, and a series of redeveloped hotels in Condado.

Of late, San Juan has been hit hard by Puerto Rico's economic upheaval. Tourism is now more important than ever to the local economy.

◉ Sights

Most of San Juan's major attractions, including museums and art galleries, are in Old San Juan. Beaches dominate the appeal of Condado, Ocean Park and Isla Verde (as they should), while Santurce offers buzzy, gritty delights. Be aware that most museums are closed on Mondays.

◉ Old San Juan

Old San Juan is a colorful kaleidoscope of life, music, legend and history. It's an unmissable sight, the crown jewel of Puerto Rico. From the blue-toned, cobblestoned streets to 400-plus historically listed buildings to the stunning ocean views, the visual treats seem boundless. Add to this the quarter's sensuous yet subtle mood swings: tranquil at dawn, languid during the midday heat, romantic at dusk and positively ebullient after dark. Prepare to be surprised, entranced and delighted.

★ El Morro   FORT

(Fuerte San Felipe del Morro; Map p56; ☑ 787-729-7423; www.nps.gov/saju; 501 Norzagaray, Old San Juan; adult/child $5/free; ⊙ 9am-6pm; ☒ Fort) The star of Old San Juan, El Morro juts aggressively over bold headlands, glowering across the Atlantic at would-be conquerors. The 140ft walls (some up to 15ft thick) date back to 1539 and El Morro is said to be the oldest Spanish fort in the New World. Displays document the construction of the fort, which took almost 200 years, as well as El Morro's role in rebuffing attacks on the island by the British, the Dutch and, later, the US military. A short film providing a historical overview of the fort is screened every 15 minutes.

The gray, castellated **lighthouse** on the 6th floor has been in operation since 1846 (although the tower itself dates from 1906), making it the island's oldest light station still in use today. After suffering severe damage during a US navy bombardment during the 1898 Spanish-American War, the original lighthouse was rebuilt with unique Spanish-Moorish features, a style that blends in surprisingly well with the rest of the fort.

At a minimum, try to make the climb up the ramparts to the sentries' walks along the Santa Barbara Bastion and Austria Half-Bastion for the views of the sea, the bay, Old San Juan, modern San Juan, El Yunque and the island's mountainous spine. Steep walks and countless staircases can make wearing flip flops tough – consider wearing a more comfortable shoe instead.

The **National Park Service** (NPS; Map p56; ☑787-729-6777; www.nps.gov; Fuerte San Cristóbal, 501 Norzagaray, Old San Juan; ☺9am-6pm) maintains this fort and the small military museum on the premises. It was declared a Unesco World Heritage Site in 1983.

On weekends, the fields leading up to the fort are alive with picnickers, lovers and kite flyers. The scene becomes a kind of impromptu festival with food vendors' carts on the perimeter.

★**Fuerte San Cristóbal**   FORT
(San Cristóbal Fort; Map p56; ☑787-729-6777; www.nps.gov/saju; 501 Norzagaray, Old San Juan; adult/child $5/free; ☺9am-6pm; 🔒Fort) San Juan's second major fort is Fuerte San Cristóbal, one of the largest military installations the Spanish built in the Americas. In its prime,

San Cristóbal covered 27 acres with a maze of six interconnected forts protecting a central core with 150ft walls, moats, booby-trapped bridges and tunnels. The fort has a fascinating museum, a store, military archives, a reproduction of military barracks, and stunning Atlantic and city views.

The fort was constructed to defend Old San Juan against land attacks from the east via Puerta de Tierra. The imaginative design came from the famous Irish mercenary Alejandro O'Reilly and his compatriot Thomas O'Daly (hired by Spain). Construction began in 1634 in response to an attack by the Dutch a decade previously, though the main period of enlargement occurred between 1765 and 1783.

Seven acres were lopped off the fort in 1897 to ease congestion in the old town and the following year the Spanish marked Puerto Rico's entry into the Spanish-American War by firing at the battleship USS *Yale* from its cannon battery. The fort became a National Historic Site in 1949 and part of the Unesco World Heritage Site in 1983.

★**Museo de las Américas**   MUSEUM
(Museum of the Americas; Map p56; ☑787-724-5052; www.museolasamericas.org; cnr Cuartel de Ballajá, Norzagaray & Calle del Morro, Old San Juan; adult/child $6/4; ☺9am-noon & 1-4pm Tue-Fri, 10am-5pm Sat, noon-5pm Sun; 🔒Fort) This museum presents an impressive overview of cultural

---

ℹ VISITING OLD SAN JUAN'S FORTS

A visit to the two megastars of the San Juan National Historic Site, El Morro and Fuerte San Cristóbal, can be made even more rewarding with a just bit of planning.

Visitor centers Each fort has a small and useful visitor center where you can learn more about the structures and buy books that delve deeper into their history.

Joint admission Tickets are good for both forts and are valid for seven days. If you can, try to visit each on a different day so that all those walls don't start looking the same.

Orientation talks There are short, highly useful free introductory talks every hour at each fort, provided there are rangers available. Ask when you buy your ticket.

Tunnel tours Hour-long free guided tours roam the tunnels at Fuerte San Cristóbal every Saturday (English) and Sunday (Spanish) at 10:30am and 12:30pm. Come at least half an hour beforehand (or earlier) and add your name to the sign-up list. Guides walk you through three of the fort's tunnels, including one that's otherwise closed to the public.

Outworks walks Hour-long free guided tours of the fortifications show how Fuerte San Cristóbal remained impregnable. The walks are held every Saturday (Spanish) and Sunday (English) at 2:30pm. Sign up at least half an hour beforehand (or earlier).

El Morro life On the third Sunday each month, guides and recreators give an idea of what life was like for a soldier in El Morro during the 18th century when drills and duty dominated. While the recreations don't capture the smells of a time when bathing was a luxury, they do show what happens when you explode the black powder used in cannons.

Old San Juan

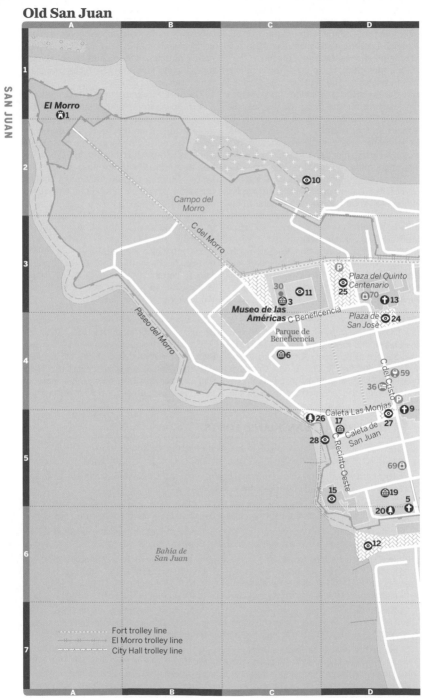

El Morro
1

10

Campo del
Morro

C del Morro

Paseo del Morro

Plaza del Quinto
Centenario

30
3
11
25
70
13

Museo de las
Américas C Beneficencia

Plaza de
San José
24

Parque de
Beneficencia

6

C del Cristo
59

36

Caleta Las Monjas
9

26
17
27

Caleta de
San Juan

28

C Recinto Oeste

69

15
19 5

20 1

12

Bahía de
San Juan

········· Fort trolley line
—II—II— El Morro trolley line
— — — — City Hall trolley line

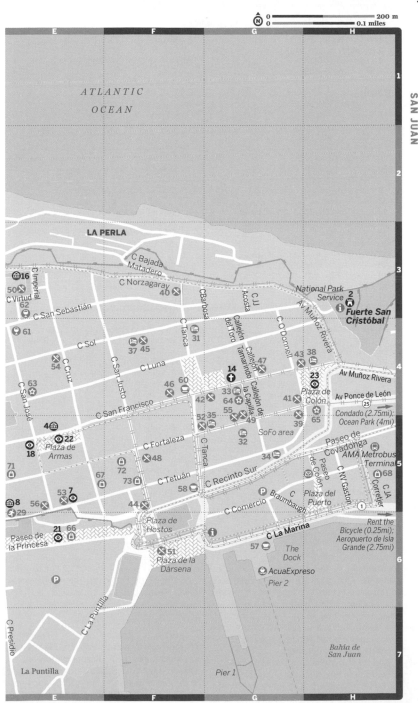

0   200 m
0   0.1 miles

ATLANTIC OCEAN

LA PERLA

C Bajada Matadero

C Norzagaray — 40

C Imperial — 16
50
C Virtud 62
61
C San Sebastián

National Park Service 2
Fuerte San Cristóbal

C Barbosa

C JI Acosta

C O'Donnell

Av Muñoz Rivera

C Sol

C Tanca

Callejón del Toro
Callejón Tamarindo

31

37 45

Av Muñoz Rivera

C Cruz
54
C San Justo

C Luna

46 60

14

47
43 38
23

Av Ponce de León
25

63
C San José

C San Francisco

42 33
64
55 49
52 35 45
32

41
Plaza de Colón

65
39

Condado (2.75mi);
Ocean Park (4mi)

4
22
Plaza de Armas
18

C Fortaleza

C Tanca

SoFo area

34

Paseo de Covadonga
AMA Metrobus Terminal

71

72
48

C Tetuán

C Recinto Sur

Paseo de Colón

C NV Gastón

68
C JA Corretjer

67
73
58

C Comercio

P

Plaza del Puerto

1

8
29
56
53 7

44

Plaza de Hostos

Braumbaugh

C La Marina

Rent the Bicycle (0.25mi);
Aeropuerto de Isla Grande (2.75mi)

21 66
Paseo de la Princesa

51
Plaza de la Dársena

57

The Dock

AcuaExpreso
Pier 2

P

C La Puntilla

C Presidio

La Puntilla

Bahía de San Juan

Pier 1

Old San Juan

◎ Top Sights
1 El Morro...A1
2 Fuerte San Cristóbal..........................H3
3 Museo de las Américas......................C3

◎ Sights
4 Alcaldía...E5
5 Capilla del Cristo...............................D6
6 Casa Blanca..C4
7 Casa de Ramón Power y Giralt.............E5
8 Casa del Libro....................................E5
9 Catedral de San Juan.........................D4
10 Cementerio Santa María
    Magdalena de Pazzis........................C2
11 Cuartel de Ballajá...............................C3
12 Fuente Raíces.....................................D6
13 Iglesia de San José.............................D3
14 Iglesia San Francisco de Asís.............G4
15 La Fortaleza.......................................D5
16 Museo de San Juan.............................E3
17 Museo Felisa Rincón de Gautier..........D5
18 Palacio de la Real Intendencia............E5
19 Palacio Rojo.......................................D5
20 Parque de las Palomas.......................D6
21 Paseo de la Princesa..........................E6
22 Plaza de Armas..................................E5
23 Plaza de Colón...................................H4
24 Plaza de San José..............................D4
25 Plaza del Quinto Centenario...............D3
26 Plazuela de la Rogativa......................C5
27 Plazuela Las Monjas...........................D5
28 Puerta de San Juan............................D5

⊕ Activities, Courses & Tours
29 Anam Spa & Cocktail Lounge..............E6
30 DanzActiva...C3
    Para la Naturaleza.....................(see 7)

⊜ Sleeping
31 Casa Sol...F4
32 Casablanca Hotel................................G5
33 Da House...G4
34 El Cervantes Hotel..............................G5
35 Fortaleza Guest House........................G5
36 Hotel El Convento...............................D4
37 La Terraza de San Juan.......................F4
38 Posada San Francisco.........................H4

◈ Eating
39 Aguaviva..G4
40 Antojitos del Callejón.........................F3
41 Café Puerto Rico................................G4
42 Cafeteria Mallorca..............................G4
43 Caficultura...G4
44 Carli's Café Fine Bistro &
    Piano...F5
45 El Jibarito...F4
46 La Bombonera.....................................F4
47 La Madre...G4
48 Manolín...F5
49 Marmalade..G4
50 Old San Juan Farmers Market.............E3
51 Old San Juan Food Trucks..................F6
52 Pirilo..F5
53 Señor Paleta.......................................E5
54 St Germain Bistro & Café....................E4
55 Trois Cent Onze..................................G5
56 Verde Mesa...E5

◉ Drinking & Nightlife
57 Café Cola'o...G6
58 Café Cuatro Sombras.........................F5
59 El Batey..D4
60 Finca Cialitos.....................................F4
61 La Factoría...E4
62 La Taberna Lúpulo.............................E3
    Mezzanine.................................(see 54)

◎ Entertainment
63 Amigos del Corralón...........................E4
64 Nuyorican Café...................................G4
65 Teatro Tapia.......................................H4

◎ Shopping
66 Artisans Fair......................................E6
67 Butterfly People.................................E5
68 Cigarros Antillas................................H5
69 Galería Botello...................................D5
70 Librería Instituto de Cultura
    Puertorriqueña................................D3
71 Olé..E5
72 Puerto Rican Art & Crafts...................F5
73 Pure Soul...F5

development in the Americas, including indigenous, African and European influences. Four permanent exhibits integrate art, history and sociology in thoughtful and provocative ways; the coverage of slavery is particularly moving, including a recreation of travel on a slave ship. Audiovisual highlights and knowledgeable guides enrich visits.

Every Saturday at 2pm, workshops ($1) are offered to introduce the public to various forms of folk art of the Americas. Though geared towards children, all are welcome;

reservations recommended. If you're interested in buying folk art, the museum also hosts Domingo de Artesanos the first Sunday of every month, where local artists showcase and sell their works.

Paseo de la Princesa   WATERFRONT
(Walkway of the Princess; Map p56; Old San Juan) Evoking a distinctly European feeling, the Paseo de la Princesa is a 19th-century esplanade just outside the city walls. Lined with antique streetlamps, trees, statues, benches,

food vendors' carts and street entertainers, this romantic walkway ends at the magnificent **Raíces Fountain** (Roots Fountain; Map p56), a stunning sculpture and water feature that depicts the island's eclectic Taíno, African and Spanish heritage. Festivals and fairs are often held here, including the weekend artisans fair (p89).

Puerta de San Juan GATE
(San Juan Gate; Map p56; Paseo de la Princesa, Old San Juan) Spanish ships once anchored in the cove just off these ramparts to unload colonists and supplies, all of which entered the city through a tall red portal known as Puerta de San Juan. This tunnel through the wall dates from the 1630s.

Catedral de San Juan CHURCH
(Map p56; ☑787-722-0861; 153 Calle del Cristo, Old San Juan; ⊙8am-4pm) FREE Although noticeably smaller and more austere than other Spanish churches, the Catedral de San Juan nonetheless retains a simple earthy elegance. Founded originally in 1521, the first church on this site was destroyed in a hurricane in 1529. A replacement was constructed in 1540 and, over a period of centuries, it slowly evolved into the neoclassical-inspired monument seen today.

Most people come to see the marble tomb of Ponce de León and the body of religious martyr St Pio displayed under glass.

Iglesia de San José CHURCH
(Map p56; ☑787-918-3800; www.iglesiasanjosepr.org; Plaza de San José, cnr Calle del Cristo & Beneficiencia, Old San Juan) What it lacks in grandiosity it makes up for in age: the Iglesia de San José is the second-oldest church in the Americas, after the cathedral in Santo Domingo in the Dominican Republic. Established in 1532 by Dominicans, this church, with its vaulted Gothic ceilings, still bears the coat of arms of Juan Ponce de León (whose family worshipped here), a striking carving of the Crucifixion and ornate processional floats.

The church has been under renovation since 2003, effectively making it a construction site that visitors are no longer able to enter. An extensive bilingual exhibit just outside its walls highlights some of the archaeological discoveries made during the restoration process.

Capilla del Cristo CHURCH
(Christ's Chapel; Map p56; cnr Calle del Cristo & Tetuán, Old San Juan; ⊙noon-6pm Tue & religious holidays) Over the centuries, tens of thousands of penitents have come to pray for miracles at the Capilla del Cristo, the tiny sanctuary at the end of a pedestrian street and adjacent to Parque de las Palomas. You can view the chapel and its ornate gold and silver altar at any time, but the iron fence across the front is only open on Tuesday afternoons and on religious holidays.

Casa del Libro MUSEUM
(House of Books; Map p56; ☑787-723-0354; www.lacasadellibro.org; 255 Calle del Cristo, Old San Juan; ⊙11am-5pm Mon-Sat or by appointment) FREE Bibliophiles will be in awe of this tiny but worthwhile collection of more than 5000 manuscripts and texts that date back 2000 years. The collection includes one of the most respected assemblages of incunabula (texts produced prior to 1501) in the Americas, including documents signed by King Ferdinand II and Queen Isabela.

Museo de San Juan MUSEUM
(Map p56; ☑787-480-3547; museodesanjuan@sanjuanciudadpatria.com; 150 Norzagaray, Old San Juan; by donation; ⊙9am-noon & 1-4pm Tue-Sat, 11am-5pm Sun; ☐Fort) Located in what was once the city marketplace, the Museo de San Juan offers the definitive take on the city's 500-year history. A permanent exhibit showcases well-laid-out pictorial and photographic testimonies from the Caparra ruins to modern-day neighborhoods. There's also a half-hour video about the history of San Juan and a temporary exhibition space that often features work from emerging artists. Every Saturday morning a small farmers market (p78) is held in the pretty inner courtyard.

Museo Felisa Rincón de Gautier MUSEUM
(Map p56; ☑787-724-7239; www.museofelisarincon.com; 51 Caleta de San Juan, Old San Juan; ⊙9am-4pm Mon-Fri, 10am-3pm Sat) FREE This museum, an attractive neoclassical townhouse, was the longtime home of San Juan's beloved mayor, Doña Felisa. She presided over the growth of the city with personal style and political acumen for more than 20 years during the Operation Bootstrap days of the 1940s, '50s and '60s. Awards, photos, paintings and several odd mannequins help tell the story of this remarkable leader.

Plaza de Colón SQUARE
(Columbus Plaza; Map p56; cnr San Francisco & Tetuán, Old San Juan) Tracing its roots back more than a century to the 400-year anniversary of Columbus' first expedition, the

Plaza de Colón is dominated by its towering statue of Columbus atop a pillar. Ringed with tall trees and outdoor cafes, the plaza sees a lot of action. At this end of Old San Juan, the city wall was torn down in 1897 and the plaza stands on the site of one of the city's original gated entries, Puerta Santiago.

Plaza de Armas   SQUARE
(Armaments Plaza; Map p56; cnr San Francisco & San José, Old San Juan; ☉ City Hall) Follow Calle San Francisco into the heart of the old city where it opens on to the Plaza de Armas. This is the city's nominal 'central' square, laid out in the 16th century with the classic look of plazas from Madrid and Mexico. A highlight of the plaza is the **Alcaldía** (City Hall; Map p56; ☑ 787-724-7171; www.sanjuanciudadpatria. com; ☉ 8am-4pm Mon-Fri), which dates from 1789 and has twin turrets resembling those of its counterpart in Madrid. This building houses the mayor's office and is the site of periodic exhibitions.

In its time, the plaza has served as a military parade ground (hence its name), a vegetable market and a social center. Shade trees, banks of seats, a fountain and a couple of old-fashioned coffee booths still make the plaza the destination of choice for couples taking their evening stroll. The beat of bomba drums often light up evenings, especially on weekends.

Plazuela Las Monjas   SQUARE
(Little Plaza of the Nuns; Map p56; cnr Calle del Cristo & Caleta Las Monjas, Old San Juan) This pleasant little park faces the Catedral de San Juan (p59). Its ironwork benches and shade trees make it a good place for people watching, especially on weekends when brides and *quinceañeras* parade through the church.

Plaza del Quinto Centenario   SQUARE
(Map p56; cnr Beneficiencia & Calle del Cristo, Old San Juan; ☉ Fort) This modern square is shoehorned in among several architectural landmarks and offers great views over El Morro and the ocean beyond. Built in 1992 for a rumored $10 million to honor the 500-year anniversary of Columbus' first voyage to the Americas, it is dominated by a stylized granite and clay totem pole – **El Tótem Telúrico** – by Puerto Rican artist Jaime Suárez. Using clay from across the Americas, it is meant to signify the origins of the people of the Americas.

SAN JUAN IN...

Two Days

Stay in Old San Juan. Start your first day with an exquisite cup of Puerto Rican coffee at **Finca Cialitos** (p83). Explore the historical sights of the **colonial quarter** and catch the sunset from an old wall. Wander till you find the perfect eatery before heading to **Nuyorican Café** (p85) for salsa music. Hit **Isla Verde** (p69) on day two for some beach time and then consider **Ocean Park** for dinner.

Four Days

Go on a museum crawl around Old San Juan, starting with the must-see **Museo de las Américas** (p55). Be sure to throw in a visit by ferry to the other side of the bay, either for more museum hopping in Bayamón (p92) or to explore **Isla de Cabras** (p92) in Cataño. Join an ecotour company for a daytime tour of **El Yunque** (p73). By night, prowl the nightclubs of the big hotels in **Condado** and **Isla Verde** and try not to lose your savings in a glitzy resort casino.

One Week

Explore Santurce's museums and galleries, starting with the world-class **Museo de Arte de Puerto Rico** (p66). Afterwards, wander the neighborhood, checking out the spectacular street art (p79). Join local hipsters for dinner from one of the **Santurce Food Trucks** (p82). Afterwards, head to **La Placita de Santurce** (p84) for drinks and dancing under the stars. Rent a bike and cycle to Piñones (p93), taking time to explore the wild beaches and stopping to enjoy a meal and a mojito at **El Nuevo Acuario** (p94). Round it up at **Balneario Escambrón** (p69) by frolicking in the surf or snorkeling to the **marine park** (p64) just in front.

SAN JUAN'S NEIGHBORHOODS

Metro San Juan, like many great cities, is an amalgamation of its neighborhoods, with each area exhibiting its own vicissitudes, atmosphere and charms. Here's a quick rundown of what to expect.

Old San Juan The soul of the city, Old San Juan's compact Unesco World Heritage Site is packed with historical relics and endless opportunities for strolling, plus eclectic and alluring nightlife.

Puerta de Tierra This thin slither of land that links Old San Juan with the rest of the city is an amalgam of tatty housing projects, an impressive capitol building, expansive city parks and one of the best beaches on the island.

Condado San Juan's original resort strip is a revitalized urban neighborhood replete with designer shops, pretty parks and massive beachfront resorts.

Miramar A leafy residential quarter of eclectic middle-class houses and plush lakeside condos.

Santurce The city's hottest neighborhood has bounced back from decay with galleries, museums, offbeat cafes and a revitalized market quarter with great bars and restaurants.

Ocean Park A beachside community with genteel guesthouses, high-rise condos and a quiet swath of beach juxtaposed with a burgeoning foodie scene on edgy Calle Loíza.

Isla Verde The city's premier hotel strip mixes condo towers and swanky resorts in an architectural mishmash. The beach is sublime.

Hato Rey San Juan's financial hub is a dense cluster of glass-tower blocks.

Río Piedras The low-rise academic quarter boasts a thriving market, a lovely botanical garden and an art museum with renowned works of Puerto Rican art.

Plaza de San José　　　　　　　　SQUARE
(Map p56; cnr Calle del Cristo & San Sebastián, Old San Juan) This small cobblestone plaza is dominated by a statue of Juan Ponce de León, cast from English cannons captured in the raid of 1797. It's a popular spot on weekend evenings.

Plazuela de la Rogativa　　　　　　PARK
(Map p56; Recinto Oeste, Old San Juan) This tiny gem of a plaza with lovely views of the bay is home to an interesting, stylized bronze sculpture of the bishop of San Juan and three women bearing torches.

According to legend, the women of San Juan held a religious procession one night in 1797 holding torches, ringing bells and singing hymns, which tricked British Lieutenant General Abercromby (who was preparing to lay siege to San Juan with 8000 troops and a flotilla of over 50 vessels) into believing that reinforcements were flooding the city. Fearful of being outnumbered, Abercromby and his fleet withdrew.

Parque de las Palomas　　　　　　PARK
(Pigeon Park; Map p56; cnr Calle del Cristo & Tetuán, Old San Juan) On the southern end of Calle del Cristo, Parque de las Palomas is in a tree-shaded cobblestone courtyard on the top of the city wall, with brilliant views of Bahía de San Juan and the crisscrossing water traffic that often includes Brobdingnagian cruise ships.

Paloma means 'dove' or 'pigeon' and it's the latter you'll encounter in the hundreds. With a lot more class than their often-scrabbling-about urban brethren, these pigeons fly in and out of dovecote-like holes in the wall and offer up a chorus of coos when at rest. Some folks come to the park just to feed them; small children come to chase them. Buy birdseed from a vendor by the gate.

La Fortaleza　　　　　　HISTORIC SITE
(El Palacio de Santa Catalina; Map p56; ☑ ext 2211 787-721-7000; www.fortaleza.gobierno.pr; Calle Recinto, Old San Juan; suggested donation $3; ☺ tours 9am-3:30pm Mon-Fri) Guarded iron gates mark La Fortaleza. This imposing building, dating from 1533, is the oldest executive mansion in continuous use in the western hemisphere. The original fortress for the young colony, La Fortaleza eventually yielded its military preeminence to the city's newer and larger forts and was remodeled and expanded to

domicile island governors for more than three centuries. You can take a 30-minute guided tour that includes the mansion's Moorish gardens, the dungeon and the chapel.

Casa Blanca
HISTORIC BUILDING

(White House; Map p56; ☑787-725-1454; Calle San Sebastián, Old San Juan; entrance $3; ⊙8am-noon & 1-4pm Wed-Sun) First constructed in 1521 as a residence for Puerto Rico's pioneering governor, Juan Ponce de León (who died before he could move in), Casa Blanca is the oldest continuously occupied house in the western hemisphere. Today it's a historic monument containing a museum and an Alhambra-style garden with a series of fountains. The interior rooms are furnished with antiques and paintings from the 16th and 17th centuries; the views of the bay from the 2nd floor are among the best in Old San Juan.

Cementerio Santa María Magdalena de Pazzis
CEMETERY

(Map p56; Calle Cementerio, Old San Juan) Sitting just outside the northern fortifications of the old city, the neoclassical chapel in the cemetery provides a focal point among the graves. The colony's earliest citizens are buried here, as well as the famous Puerto Rican freedom fighter Pedro Albizu Campos. This Harvard-educated chemical engineer, lawyer and politician led the agricultural workers' strikes in 1934 and was at the forefront of the movement for Puerto Rican independence until his arrest and imprisonment in 1936. Muggings have occurred here, so be careful if venturing in.

⊙ La Perla

Wedged tightly between the roaring Atlantic surf and Old San Juan's thick perimeter walls is the compact neighborhood of La Perla. Originally the site of a 19th-century slaughterhouse, today it's a ramshackle hodgepodge of pastel houses; it's considered one of San Juan's roughest neighborhoods, known mostly for drug-related violence.

La Perla was the subject of a controversial 1966 nonfiction book called *La Vida* by American anthropologist Oscar Lewis. Lewis won a National Book Award for detailing what he described as a tragic cycle of poverty and prostitution, but many Puerto Ricans decried it as stereotypical.

During the mid-2000s, the Puerto Rican government made regular (unsuccessful)

🏃 City Walk Old San Juan

START CAFÉ COLA'O
END LA TABERNA LÚPULO
LENGTH 2.75 MILES; THREE TO FOUR HOURS

Start with an early-morning caffeine hit at ❶ **Café Cola'o** (p83) next to Pier 2. Stroll west and take in the soaring 12-story elegance of the 1937 ❷ **Banco Popular building**, an art-deco gem at the corner of San Justo and Tetuán. Continue along ❸ **Paseo de la Princesa** (p58), a shaded 19th-century esplanade that tracks alongside the formidable old city walls to the brink of the Bahía de San Juan. If it's the weekend, peruse the outdoor artisans fair.

Turn north briefly on Calle del Cristo, then west on Fortaleza. Here you'll find buildings such as the ❹ **Palacio Rojo** that date back to the height of the colonial era. It's easy to see why this 1792 building is called the Red Palace. Its rouge walls once housed the Spanish commanding officers. Now, retrace your steps to the Paseo de la Princesa through ❺ **Parque de las Palomas** (p61) where you can buy some birdseed to feed the pigeons.

Head back down to the Paseo de la Princesa. As you feel the Atlantic breeze on your face, you'll spy the city's legendary perimeter wall as well as the imposing bronze ❻ **Fuente Raíces** (p59), which depicts Taíno, European and African gods and goddesses rising amid a shower of cascading water.

Behind the fountain, follow the Paseo de la Princesa as it cuts northwest along the waterfront. In the 17th and 18th centuries, Spanish ships once anchored in the cove just off these ramparts to unload colonists and supplies, all of which entered the city through a tall red portal known as ❼ **Puerta de San Juan** (p59).

Pass through the gate and turn right onto Recinto Oeste. This short cobblestoned street leads to the guarded iron gates of ❽ **La Fortaleza** (p61), the governor's mansion and executive office. Head back northwest, taking a moment to gaze over the water from the diminutive ❾ **Plazuela de la Rogativa** (p61) and admire its bronze sculpture of a religious procession.

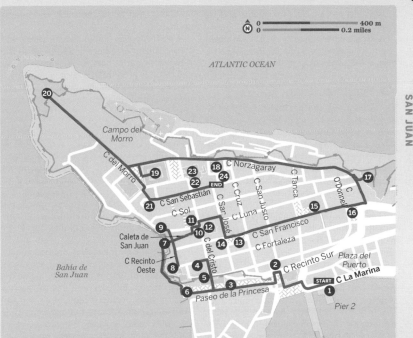

Follow the leafy Caleta de San Juan up the slope to the beautiful ⑩ **Plazuela Las Monjas** (p60), where stray cats stretch and romantic couples linger. On the north side of the plaza is ⑪ **Hotel El Convento** (p75), a historic building dating to 1651 and one of Puerto Rico's grandest hotels, well worth a casual inspection. To the east lies the ⑫ **Catedral de San Juan** (p59), a relatively austere religious building whose importance is enhanced by its age (dating from 1540) and the fact that the remains of Juan Ponce de León rest inside.

Cut along Luna for a block before taking a right down San José. Take a left onto San Francisco, which will bring you to the ⑬ **Plaza de Armas** (p60), an expansive square with government buildings like the imposing ⑭ **Palacio de la Real Intendencia**. Continue east on San Francisco, pausing to window-shop along the way and peek into the ⑮ **Iglesia San Francisco de Asís**; arrive at the ⑯ **Plaza de Colón** (p59), named for the great Genovese explorer. Cut north up Av Muñoz Rivera and you'll come to ⑰ **Fuerte San Cristóbal** (p55), the old city's other major fortification.

Walking west along Norzagaray, you can see the faded pastel houses of La Perla, a low-income neighborhood sitting along the

tempestuous Atlantic. Hidden in a former market building to your left is the ⑱ **Museo de San Juan** (p59). Just west, the intriguing ⑲ **Cuartel de Ballajá** houses the Museo de las Américas, which provides a fascinating overview of cultural development in the Americas. Across the grassy expanses of Campo del Morro, picnickers fly kites and the stately fort of ⑳ **El Morro** (p54) beckons. Stroll the former sentries' walks for panoramic views of San Juan and the sea.

Head down Calle del Morro to the ㉑ **Casa Blanca** (p62), the ancestral home for 250 years of the descendants of Juan Ponce de León and the oldest permanent residence in the Americas.

A stone's throw to the east lies the ㉒ **Plaza de San José** (p61), with its statue of Juan Ponce de León, cast from an English cannon captured in the raid of 1797. More antiquity overlooks the plaza from the north in the shape of the ㉓ **Iglesia de San José** (p59), the second-oldest church in the Americas, under renovation since 2003. From here, you'll probably be ready for a cold draft beer at ㉔ **La Taberna Lúpulo** (p83).

bids to buy out La Perla's residents and re-develop the area.

A steep, narrow access road leads down from Norzagaray to La Perla. Tourists, how-ever, should steer clear of it.

◉ Puerta de Tierra

The area along the peninsula east of Old San Juan is less than 2 miles long and only a quarter of a mile wide. This district, Puer-ta de Tierra, takes its name from its posi-tion as the 'gateway to land' leading up to the walls of Old San Juan. When attacking by land, the waves of English and Dutch invaders had to march through here. Cen-turies ago, it was the neighborhood where free blacks and multiracial people lived, outside of the protection of the city walls, which harbored the Spaniards and *criollos* (islanders of European descent).

Today the district is the conduit for cars entering Old San Juan, though its north coast is an awe-inspiring sight: a dramatic wave-pummeled shore with the palm tree-laden beach, Balneario Escambrón (p69), towards the eastern end. Just offshore is Es-cambrón Marine Park, a preserve featuring an array of corals and underwater life popu-lar with divers and snorkelers. Inland lies the sun-dappled Parque Luis Muñoz Rivera, the grand Capitolio and, further east, the **Fuerte San Gerónimo** (Saint Geronimo Fort; Map p66; Paseo Caribe, Puerta de Tierra).

Escambrón Marine Park   NATURE RESERVE
(Map p66; off Av Muñoz Rivera, Puerta de Tierra; 🚌 D53, T3, T5, T21) Adjacent to the gorgeous Balneario Escambrón, this marine park of the same name is a popular destination for snorkelers and divers. See schools of blue tangs, sergeant majors and damsel fish darting around huge brain coral and a col-lapsed bridge. For the best snorkeling from shore, head out towards the huge rock di-rectly across from the center of the beach; the western side is best. Visibility ranges from 5ft to 20ft, depending on conditions.

Parques Luis Muñoz Rivera &
Parque del Tercer Milenio   PARK
(Map p66; 🖉 787-721-6133; Av Muñoz Rivera, Puerta de Tierra) Spanning the broad swath between the Atlantic and Av Ponce de León, Parque Luis Muñoz Rivera dates back over 50 years and injects much-needed breathing space into the surrounding urban landscape. Trails wind under shade trees to a playground,

fountains and a pavilion for community events.

Across Avenida Muñoz Rivera, Parque del Tercer Milenio was the site of the eighth Pan American Games, held in 1979, and is now home to an array of activities, a good play-ground, the popular Balneario Escambrón (p69) beach and offshore diving at Escambrón Marine Park.

El Capitolio   NOTABLE BUILDING
(Palacio de Leyes; Map p52; 🖉 787-724-2030, ext 4609; www.senado.pr.gov/visitantes/pages/historiadelcapitolio.aspx; off Av Muñoz Rivera, Puerta de Tierra; ⊗8:30am-5pm Mon-Fri; 🚌 Ci-ty Hall) **FREE** The capitol of the Common-wealth is in an impressive columned and domed neoclassical building in a com-manding location overlooking Puerta de Tierra's wave-lashed coast. The much-revered constitution of the Commonwealth, which moved the island further away from colonialism in 1951, is on display inside the 80ft rotunda. Regular sessions of the leg-islature meet inside, while rallies for and against statehood occur outside every time the government debates the issue. Guided tours available by appointment only.

◉ Condado

In the 1960s, Condado is where Puerto Rico's tourist boom was first ignited, spearheaded by exiled Cuban businessmen and rum-drunk Americans. But, as fashions ebbed and flowed, Condado went the way of Miami Beach: a tawdry time in the 1970s and 1980s was followed by a rebirth.

Today Condado buzzes with top-end resorts, the odd celebrity and legions of beachgoers fleeing cold weather up north. Dotted in among the high-rises, you'll still find a few old eclectic 1920s villas, along with a handful of pretty parks that serve as spacious windows to the sea.

Besides having a wonderful water view, the Parque Nacional Laguna del Condado Jaime Benítez, a park on the southeastern shore of the lagoon, has displays about on-going mangrove habitat restoration. Most days, paddleboard and kayak enthusiasts can be seen on the water.

Parque la Ventana al Mar   PARK
(Window to the Sea Park; Map p66; Av Ashford, Condado) This small grassy park has public art, benches and shade trees. Best of all, it has great views of and easy access to Playa

SAN JUAN FOR CHILDREN

Puerto Rico is a family-friendly destination and children are very much a part of daily life across San Juan. You'll see children at all manner of restaurants and events and no doubt running around plazas late into the evening. Sidewalks are typically in decent condition and wide enough for strollers (though baby-changing facilities are few and far between).

Most resorts have children's clubs or programs; only a few boutique properties have age restrictions. Large swaths of the beaches are reef-protected so waves are gentle. **Playa Ocean Park** (p69) and **Playa Isla Verde** (p69) are particular favorites for local families.

In and around San Juan there are several attractions that children really enjoy. The **Museo del Niño de Carolina** (p94) is always a big hit, as is **Parque de las Ciencias** (p92) in Bayamón. If your kiddos like bugs (which ones don't?), hit up the **Museo de Entomología y Biodiversidad Tropical** (p69) to check out some doozies. Afterwards, let them run wild – the kids, not the bugs – in the **University Botanic Gardens** (p69) outside.

Two must-visit sights are **El Morro** (p54) and **San Cristóbal** (p55) in Old San Juan. What could be better than huge fortresses complete with tales of gold, plunder and pirates? Kids can explore the walls and tunnels for hours.

In season, a winter league baseball game at **Hiram Bithorn Stadium** (p88) is classic family fun.

Condado (p69). On the first Sunday of the month, a lively farmers market (p80) is held here.

Parque Nacional Laguna del Condado Jaime Benítez   PARK

(Parque Jaime Benítez; Map p66; ☏787-449-1483; www.estuario.org; 1110 Vieques, Condado; P; ☐ D53, T21) Sitting along the calm waters of Laguna del Condado, this park is a popular launching spot for kayakers and paddleboarders. There's a boardwalk and a ramp for easy access to the water. On the first Saturday of the month, at 7pm, free movies are shown on a huge inflatable screen on the great lawn. Locals come out in full force with picnic blankets, chairs and snacks – a full-on outdoor house party. There's a parking lot and well-maintained bathrooms too.

◉ Ocean Park

Just east of Condado lies Ocean Park, with its associated neighborhood of Punta Las Marías, a collection of private homes, beach retreats and a handful of seaside guesthouses. Calle Loíza, a bustling urban street, runs through the middle with a restaurant scene that features some of the most innovative menus in town.

◉ Santurce

Santurce is one of San Juan's most vibrant *barrios,* actually incorporating Condado and Miramar, but typically used to describe the area south of Expressway 26 and north of Hato Rey.

The '40s and '50s were a boom time here, when color and life seeped from Santurce's energetic streets, spurred on by the buoyancy of Operation Bootstrap. Back then, Santurce was a financial center and a residential quarter of some repute. The nosedive began in the 1970s when the business district headed south to Hato Rey and Santurce was left to fester.

Since then Santurce has worked hard to get back on its feet, its renaissance spearheaded by art museums, galleries, a performing arts center, trendy clubs and some of the city's best and most popular restaurants, cafes and bars. Much of the action in the neighborhood can be found in and around **La Placita de Santurce** (Map p66; Calle Dos Hermanos, Santurce; ☺6am-late; ☐T3, T5), the small square that's home to the Santurce Mercado, as well as along Avenida Ponce de León.

As evident from the stunning street art (p79) and murals, the local art scene is hot, with small galleries and cultural spaces organizing all manner of shows and events.

Condado, Miramar & Santurce

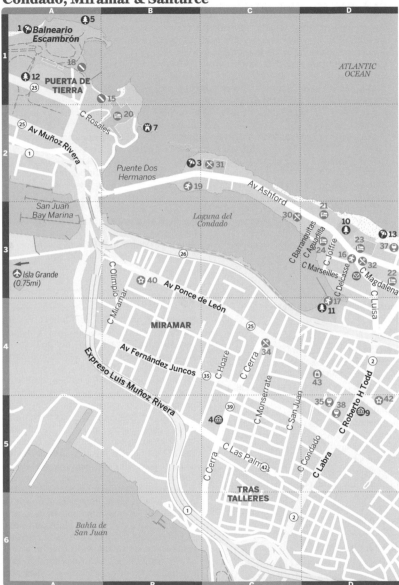

★ **Museo de Arte de Puerto Rico** MUSEUM
(MAPR; Map p66; ☑787-977-6277; www.mapr.org;
299 Av de Diego, Santurce; adult/concession $6/3,
Wed after 2pm free; ☺10am-8pm Wed, to 5pm Thu-
Sat, 11am-6pm Sun; ☐T5, T21) San Juan boasts
one of the largest and most celebrated
art museums in the Caribbean. Housed in
a splendid neoclassical building that was
at one time the city's Municipal Hospital,
MAPR boasts 18 exhibition halls spread
over an area of 130,000 sq feet. The artistic
collection includes paintings, sculptures,

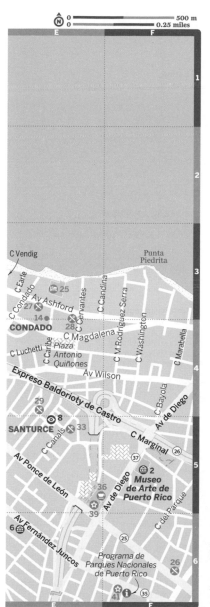

Adding distinction to diversity, the facility also boasts a hands-on exhibition space for kids, a 2.5-acre sculpture garden, a conservation laboratory, a theater and a good shop. Creative workshops are regularly offered for children too.

Don't miss the gardens, where winding paths invite visitors to stroll past 16 sculptures and more than 100,000 plants in a scene reminiscent of Monet's water lilies.

Museo de Arte Contemporáneo de Puerto Rico MUSEUM
(MAC; Map p66; ☑787-977-4030; www.mac-pr.org; cnr Av Ponce de León & Roberto H Todd, Santurce; admission $5; ☉10am-4pm Tue-Fri, 11am-5pm Sat; ☐T5) The Museo de Arte Contemporáneo de Puerto Rico sits just down the road from the Museo de Arte de Puerto Rico in an eye-catching neoclassical Georgian building – the former Rafael M de Labra school – dating from 1918. The museum showcases artists from the mid-20th century onwards, mostly from Puerto Rico, the Caribbean and Latin America. The permanent collection is a study in the challenges and struggles that are faced by modern-day society and the solutions offered by its creatives.

C787 Studios GALLERY
(Map p66; c787studios@gmail.com; 734 Cerra, Santurce; ☉hours vary; ☐T5) **FREE** This modern gallery in a bohemian section of Santurce often has thought-provoking work from emerging artists and musicians. Contemporary, conceptual, and experimental art and music are typically featured. Don't miss the murals lining the streets as you approach.

Espacio 1414 GALLERY
(Map p66; ☑787-725-3899; www.espacio1414.org; 1414 Av Fernández Juncos, Santurce; ☉by appointment only; ☐T9) **FREE** Housed in an austere yet modern building, this gallery celebrates contemporary Latin American art. There are regular special shows in addition to the permanent displays of the Berezdivin Collection, which has works from across the region.

◉ Hato Rey

South of Santurce, the urban grit of the former business district is replaced by the sleekness of its successor, Hato Rey. Sagrado Corazón station is the gleaming first stop on San Juan's Tren Urbano (p93). The mighty

posters and carvings from the 17th to the 21st century, chronicling such renowned Puerto Rican artists as José Campeche, Francisco Oller, Nick Quijano and Rafael Ferrer.

Condado, Miramar & Santurce

⊙ **Top Sights**
1 Balneario Escambrón.............................A1
2 Museo de Arte de Puerto Rico..............F5

⊙ **Sights**
3 Balneario Condado.............................. B2
4 C787 Studios.......................................C5
5 Escambrón Marine Park.......................A1
6 Espacio 1414.......................................E6
7 Fuerte San Gerónimo...........................B2
8 La Placita de Santurce.........................E5
9 Museo de Arte Contemporáneo
   de Puerto Rico.................................. D5
10 Parque la Ventana al Mar.....................D3
11 Parque Nacional Laguna del
   Condado Jaime Benítez.....................D4
12 Parques Luis Muñoz Rivera &
   Parque del Tercer Milenio...................A1
13 Playa Condado.....................................D3

⊙ **Activities, Courses & Tours**
14 Atelier at Cocina Abierta......................E3
15 Caribe Aquatic Adventures..................B1
16 Euforia...D3
17 Paddle Yoga Puerto Rico.....................D4
18 Scuba Dogs..A1
19 Velauno..B2

⊛ **Sleeping**
20 Caribe Hilton..B2
21 Condado Vanderbilt Hotel....................D3
22 Coral Princess Hotel.............................D3
23 La Concha...D3
24 Olive...D3

25 San Juan Marriott Resort &
   Stellaris Casino.................................E3

⊗ **Eating**
26 Abracadabra Counter Cafe...................F6
27 Alí Baba..E3
   El Mercado Urbano......................(see 10)
28 Freshmart...E3
29 José Enrique...E4
30 Kabanas Food Truck.............................C3
   Perla..(see 23)
31 Pikayo..C2
32 Pinky's West...D3
33 Santaella...E5
34 Santurce Food Trucks...........................C4

⊙ **Drinking & Nightlife**
35 Circo Bar...D5
36 Hacienda San Pedro Coffee
   Shop...E5
   La Concha Lobby Bar...................(see 23)
   La Placita de Santurce..................(see 8)
37 Oceano...D3
38 Scandalo The Club................................D5

⊙ **Entertainment**
39 El Centro de Bellas Artes Luis A
   Ferré..E5
40 Fine Arts Miramar.................................B3
41 La Respuesta...F6
42 Metro Cinemas......................................D5

⊙ **Shopping**
43 Santurce POP..D4

glass towers all around are the Caribbean's Wall Street. That moaning you hear might be the bankers contemplating the island's perilous financial state.

⊙ Río Piedras

The flatness of Hato Rey soon gives way to the leafy uplands of Río Piedras. Founded in 1714 and existing as a separate town until 1951, Río Piedras is the home of the University of Puerto Rico and harbors a thriving academic community. You'll find cheap cafes, a cut-price shopping street (José de Diego), and the island's largest farmers market.

The university is set in verdant, palm-filled grounds and is distinguished by its signature minaret-like clock tower. It's home to a small museum featuring some of the island's most important cultural pieces, including art by impressionist Francisco

Oller. Down the street sits the university's lush botanical garden.

The Río Piedras Tren Urbano station is right in the center.

Museo de Historia, Antropología y Arte de Río Piedras MUSEUM
(Museum of History, Anthropology & Art of Río Piedras; Map p52; ☎787-763-3939; www.upr.edu; University of Puerto Rico, cnr Av Ponce de León & Av Universidad, Río Piedras; ⊙8am-noon & 1-4:30pm Mon-Fri; ℗; Ⓜ Universidad) FREE Founded in 1951 as Puerto Rico's first national museum, this is home to some of the island's most important cultural pieces, including Francisco Oller's *El Velorio*, historical documents and archaeological artifacts dating back over a thousand years. The museum has three wings but structural damage resulting from the construction of a nearby metro line has forced it to close all but one room and a hallway. There, rotating exhibits of the permanent collection as well as temporary exhibits are displayed.

Jardín Botánico de la Universidad de Puerto Rico
GARDENS

(University of Puerto Rico Botanical Garden; Map p52; ✍ext 6578 787-250-0000; www.upr.edu/jardin-botanico; off Hwy 1, Río Piedras; ⊘6am-6pm; Ⓜ Río Piedras) FREE This 75-acre tract of greenery is a good urban respite. Hiking trails through cathedrals of bamboo lead to a lotus lagoon, an orchid garden with more than 30,000 flowers and a plantation of more than 120 species of palm. The air smells of heliconia blossoms, nutmeg and cinnamon trees. Pick up a free map at the small cafe and gift shop near the entrance.

Museo de Entomología y Biodiversidad Tropical
MUSEUM

(Museum of Entomology & Tropical Biodiversity; Map p52; ✍ ext 2174 787-767-9705; Jardín Botánico de UPR, off Hwy 1, Río Piedras; donations welcome; ⊘1-4pm Wed, 8:30-11am & 1-4pm Thu-Fri, tours by appointment only; Ⓜ Río Piedras) FREE This small but fascinating museum houses one of the largest collections of insects in the Caribbean. The three rooms contain case upon case of winged insects, jars of larvae big and small, even slides of microscopic creatures. The building also serves as a research center for entomologists at the University of Puerto Rico. Tours by resident experts are gladly given with advance notice. Located on the grounds of the university's Jardín Botánico, near the nursery.

Mercado de Río Piedras
MARKET

(Río Piedras Market; Map p52; ✍787-250-1818; Paseo de Diego, Río Piedras; ⊘9am-6pm Mon-Sat; Ⓜ Río Piedras) If you like the smell of fish and oranges, the bustle of people and trading jests in Spanish as you bargain for a bunch of bananas, this market is for you. As much a scene as a place to shop, the market continues the colonial-era tradition of an indoor market that spills into the streets. It's a short walk from the Río Piedras metro station.

🐚 Beaches

San Juan has some of the best municipal beaches this side of Rio de Janeiro. Starting a mile or so east of the old town, you can go from rustic to swanky and back to rustic all in the space of 7.5 miles.

★ Balneario Escambrón
BEACH

(Map p66; off Av Muñoz Rivera, Puerta de Tierra; parking $5; ⊘8:30am-6pm; 🚌D53, T3, T5, T21) A sheltered arc of raked sand, decent surf breaks, plenty of local action and a 17th-century Spanish fort shimmering in the distance are the hallmarks of this fine beach only a stone's throw from Old San Juan and the busy tourist strip of Condado. Best of all, it's often uncrowded.

★ Playa Ocean Park
BEACH

(Map p77; off McLeary, Ocean Park) Ocean Park's lesser fame is its hidden blessing. Fronted by leafy residential streets and embellished by B&Bs, its wide sweep of fine, diamond-dust sand is protected by offshore reefs and caressed by cooling seasonal trade winds. The neighborhood's namesake beach is perfectly tranquil, yet open to all: just pick a road through the low-rise gated community and follow it toward the water.

★ Playa Isla Verde
BEACH

(Map p72; off Av Isla Verde, Isla Verde) With its legions of tanned bodies and dexterous beach bums flexing their triceps around the volleyball net, Playa Isla Verde basks in its reputation as the Copacabana of Puerto Rico. Serenity seekers may prefer to head west to Ocean Park (p69) and dodge the extended families and colonizing spring-break hedonists that stake space here. Whatever your view, this broad, mile-long wedge of sand that lies between Punta Las Marías and Piñones is an undeniable beauty.

Playa Condado
BEACH

(Map p66; off Av Ashford, Condado) Hemmed in by hotel towers and punctuated by rocky outcrops, Condado's narrow beaches are busier than Ocean Park's, but less exclusive than Isla Verde's. Expect boisterous games of volleyball and plenty of crashing Atlantic surf. Families congregate around the big hotels, while gay men like the beach at the end of Calle Vendig. Parque de la Ventana al Mar (p64) has lovely waterfront views.

Balneario Condado
BEACH

(Map p66; cnr Av Ashford & Puente Dos Hermanos, Condado; 🚌D53, T21) Condado's official public beach is Balneario Condado, a small arc of sand, adjacent to the Dos Hermanos bridge, that faces west toward Fuerte San Gerónimo across the inlet. A line of rocks breaks the water here, making the sea calm and bathing relatively safe. Lifeguards police the area on weekdays and snack bars are open daily.

Balneario de Carolina
BEACH

(Map p52; Rte 187, Isla Verde; parking $5; ⊘8am-5pm Tue-Sun; 🚌D45) Wedged in between the high-rise hotel strip of Isla Verde and the

DON'T MISS

SAN JUAN'S URBAN LAGOONS

While it's easy to focus on the beautiful waters off San Juan's beaches, the city also has some remarkable waters just inland. Estuaries back up most of the coastal lands and surround the airport. The mangroves here are home to over 100 species of birds, 300 types of plants, dozens of different kinds of fish and even the odd manatee. Unfortunately, there's also a lot of trash that's typical of urban waterways. Recently, groups have begun cleaning up these sprawling lagoons and waterways, and while it's thought that a real clean-up would cost an unaffordable $600 million, locals realize that you have to start somewhere.

The following community groups offer ways to get out on these waters, which are truly the heart of the city. Away from the high rises and traffic, you discover the city's serene side.

Excursiones Eco (Map p52; ☑ 787-565-0089; www.excursioneseco.com; walking/boat tours from $15/45) Offers guided trips through the Caño de Martín Peña, a 3.5-mile tidal channel that connects the Bahía de San Juan with the Laguna San José. Passengers explore its mangrove forest and bird habitat while learning about its history and the current struggles of the low-income neighborhoods surrounding it. Walking tours that visit these underserved former squatter communities, which now house some 27,000 people, are also on offer.

Expediciones Península (Map p52; ☑ 787-753-3203; www.expedicionespeninsula.com; ⊘ tours Sat & Sun) Has well-organized weekend tours of the main lagoons, focusing on wildlife and the culture of the people living around the waters. Tours last up to three hours and combine a boat ride with walking. Call to reserve and confirm times and meeting point.

Corporación Piñones Se Integra (p93) A community-based nonprofit working to improve life in Puerto Rico's poorer *barrios*, as well as to protect the urban waterways. Headquartered in the **Centro Cultural Ecoturístico de Piñones** (p93), the group rents out kayaks for self-guided explorations of the adjacent Laguna Torrecilla, a beautiful mangrove-ringed body of water just east of the airport.

rustic delights of Piñones, Balneario de Carolina is a fine, clean beach that's positioned right in front of Luis Muñoz Marín International Airport (except for the periodic views of jumbo jets overhead you'd never know it). Equipped with plenty of lifeguards, bathrooms, showers and barbecue pits, the beach is a party zone on weekends but you're likely to have it to yourself the rest of the week.

🏃 Activities

The glittering azure waters are an obvious draw for outdoor fun in San Juan. Beaches that open to the Atlantic are great for kitesurfing and surfing, while the reefs draw snorkelers and divers. The city's glassy lagoons and waterways are perfect for kayaking and paddleboarding. On land you can get out and about in the nearby green hills and mangrove forests.

Water Sports

San Juan doesn't match Rincón in the surfing stakes, but no matter. You'll find the best waves and biggest *surfero* scene east of Isla Verde out toward Piñones and beyond, when the morning and evening breezes glass off a 4ft swell. Popular breaks include **Pine Grove** and **Los Aviónes** along Hwy 187.

At most of the city's beaches, you'll find vendors that will rent you pretty much anything that floats, or simply take you for a ride: banana boats, wave runners, paddleboards, kayaks and small catamarans. Or get airborne with some parasailing or kitesurfing.

15 Knots　　　　　　　　　　　KITESURFING
(Map p72; ☑ 787-215-5667; www.15knots.com; Beach House Hotel, 4851 Av Isla Verde, Isla Verde; rental per hour from $50, lessons from $295; ⊘ 10am-6pm) The often gusty conditions off San Juan's beaches make the waters prime kitesurfing territory. This recommended outfit offers rentals and lessons.

Velauno　　　　　　　　　　　WATER SPORTS
(Map p66; ☑ 787-470-9099; www.velauno.com; 860 Av Ashford, Condado; 1hr paddleboard & kayak rental from $25, tours from $55; ⊘ 9am-5pm)

Velauno offers stand-up paddleboarding classes and rentals. It also has single and double kayak rentals and tours.

Pine Grove Surf Club WATER SPORTS
(☑787-361-5531; www.pinegrovesurfclub.com; tours/lessons from $35/45, ☺7am-6pm) Owned and operated by the friendly Nogales brothers, Pine Grove Surf Club offers fun surf lessons on Pine Grove beach, paddleboarding tours in the lagoons of Piñones and snorkeling excursions off gorgeous Balneario Escambrón.

Tres Palmas SURFING
(Map p77; ☑787-728-3377; www.trespalmaspr.com; 1911 McLeary, Ocean Park; rentals per day from $35; ☺9am-7pm Mon-Sat, 10am-6pm Sun) Tres Palmas offers surfboard, paddleboard and boogie-board rentals. Lessons can be arranged, including ones geared towards children.

Watersports 4U WATER SPORTS
(Map p72; ☑939/969-4510; www.parasailpuertorico.com; Playa Isla Verde, 6063 Av Isla Verde, Isla Verde; banana boats/parasailing per person $20/75, small catamarans per hour US$95; ☺9am-5pm) This beachfront stand offers bananaboat rides and trips on small catamarans, including a captain. Or get airborne with some parasailing. Situated on Playa Isla Verde.

Diving & Snorkeling

While Puerto Rico is well known for its first-class diving, San Juan is not always the best place for it, with strong winds often churning up the water. On calm days, though, Escambrón Marine Park (p64) offers good snorkeling from the shore and near Condado there's an easy dive that takes you through a pass between the inner and outer reefs into coral caverns, overhangs, grottoes and tunnels.

Caribe Aquatic Adventures DIVING, SNORKELING
(Map p66; ☑787-281-8858; www.caribe-aquatic-adventures.com; snorkeling $55, 1-tank dive incl equipment from $65) This outfit does dives near San Juan and further afield around the islands off the coast of Fajardo (Icacos for snorkeling, and Palominos and Palominitos for diving). The dives from the shore at Balneario Escambrón are highly recommended. Divemaster Karen Vega has decades of local experience and is excellent with children.

Scuba Dogs DIVING, SNORKELING
(Map p66; ☑787-783-6377; www.scubadogs.net; Parque del Tercer Milenio, Puerta de Tierra; dives from $75; ☺9am-7pm Mon-Sat) This large, long-running outfit has been a tireless supporter of the offshore coral wonderland that is Escambrón Marine Park (p64). The Dogs offer gear rental, an array of shore and boat dive trips, plus training. Its shop is in Parque del Tercer Milenio.

Fishing

San Juan is an excellent base for serious deep-sea fishing for prized fish that include dolphin fish, tuna, wahoo, and white and blue marlin.

Castillo Tours & Watersports FISHING
(Map p52; ☑787-791-6195; www.castillotours.com; 101 Doncella, Ocean Park; boat charters from $700) The Castillo family offers deep-sea fishing for blue marlin, wahoo, tuna and mahimahi, as well as snorkeling and sailing excursions.

Magic Tarpon FISHING
(Map p52; ☑787-644-1444; www.magictarpon.com; Cangrejos Yacht Club Marina, Km 3.8, Hwy 187, Carolina; 4hr charters from $330) Huge tarpon up to 8ft long and weighing well over 200lb lurk in the mangroves of San Juan's lagoons. This outfit uses small boats and light tackle; it offers special instruction to kids, who may be dwarfed by the fish they catch.

Spas

Most of the major resorts have in-house spas, which are also open to nonguests. Many are affiliated with international spa chains.

Anam Spa & Cocktail Lounge SPA
(Map p56; ☑787-962-6479; www.anamspacocktaillounge.com; 259 Calle del Christo, Old San Juan; manicure/pedicure from $15/25, massage per min from $1; ☺11am-7pm) This spa with fine views of the water and far-off mountains has hit upon a genius gimmick: offer free drinks to customers. Most treatments and sessions include at least one free cocktail and the expert bartenders will sell you more. While you tipple, your aches and pains can be rubbed away and your nails are buffed to a shine.

Euforia SPA
(Map p66; ☑787-289-0808; www.euforiapr.com; 1102 Av Magdalena, Condado; manicure/pedicure/massage from $22/38/75; ☺10am-7pm Sun-Thu, 9am-7pm Fri & Sat) This small spa in the

Isla Verde

Isla Verde

◉ Top Sights
1 Playa Isla Verde C1

✦ Activities, Courses & Tours
2 15 Knots B1
3 Watersports 4U D1
4 WOW Surfing School D1

🛏 Sleeping
5 Boriquen Beach Inn C2
6 El Patio Guesthouse B2
7 El San Juan Hotel D1
8 InterContinental San Juan
  Resort & Casino C2

9 La Playita D1
10 Water Beach Club Hotel C1

✕ Eating
11 Ceviche House A1
12 Metropol D2
13 Playa Papaya C2
14 Yamiko Sushi C2

◉ Drinking & Nightlife
Club Brava .... (see 7)
El San Juan Hotel Lobby
  Bars .... (see 7)

heart of Condado offers everything from mani-pedis to deep-tissue massages. Cheese and hummus plates, desserts and all sorts of drinks are prepared for guests at the on-site cafe. Service is top notch.

🎓 Courses

Atelier at Cocina Abierta   COOKING
(Map p66; ☑ 787-946-3116; www.ateliercocina abierta.com; 58 Caribe, Condado; classes per person from $65) This cooking school offers one- to multiday classes in a wide variety of cuisines and methods. Learn the secrets of perfectly stuffed *mofongo*, prepare a classic French brunch or take a refresher on food-wine pairings. Classes are led by some of San Juan's best chefs, mixologists and sommeliers. Classes typically run two to three hours. Suitable for all levels.

Paddle Yoga Puerto Rico   YOGA
(Map p66; ☑ 787-698-1239; www.facebook.com/paddleyogapuertorico; Condado; classes from $43; ☺ hours vary) Take your yoga practice to another level, or at least to the water. Longtime yoga instructor Oscar Guerrero leads two-hour yoga classes on paddleboards, floating in the middle of Laguna del Condado. Classes are typically offered in the early morning or evening, when the water is calm and the kayak traffic minimal. Moonlight classes are particularly peaceful.Located off Parque Laguna del Condado Jaime Benítez.

Ashtanga Yoga Puerto Rico   YOGA
(Map p77; ☑ 787-677-7585; www.ashtangayoga pr.com; 1950 McLeary, Ocean Park; classes from $19; ☺ hours vary) Modified Ashtanga yoga classes are offered at this long-running school. The studio itself is bright and airy but also on the small side – arrive early

to get a good spot. Discounts for multiple visits and for signing up for drop-in classes online.

Dance

To learn a basic break step, the best venue in town is Nuyorican Café (p85) in Old San Juan, where free lessons are offered most Wednesdays from 9pm to 11pm. In Condado, Oceano (p84) also offers free salsa lessons every Tuesday night before the masses take the floor. Join the crowd and practice your moves.

DanzActiva   DANCING
(Map p56; ☑ 787-775-9438; www.danzactiva.com; Cuartel de Ballajá, cnr Norzagaray & Calle del Morro, Old San Juan; per month from $50; ⊙ hours vary) If you'll be in San Juan for an extended period, consider signing up for some classes to learn a few *bomba* moves, a traditional Afro-Puerto Rican dance involving live drumming and singing.

☞ Tours

Flavors of San Juan   FOOD & DRINK
(☑ 787-964-2447; www.sanjuanfoodtours.com; adult/child $80/70) If eating your way around the old town is your style, Flavors of San Juan conducts three-hour walking tours that give you a tasty dose of the local cuisine. Rum tastings and a primer on prepping *mofongo* folded in too.

Rent the Bicycle   CYCLING
(Map p52; ☑ 787-602-9696; www.rentthebicycle.net; 100 Del Muelle, Old San Juan; rentals per day from $27, tours from $52; ⊙ 9am-4:30pm Mon-Fri, to 4pm Sat & Sun) Offers tours of San Juan led by guides certified by the National Park Service (p55). It also rents sturdy banana-yellow cruiser bikes with lock and helmet. Rentals can be delivered to your hotel or you can arrange for pickup after a one-way ride. The shop is near Pier 6; the staff are brilliant with advice.

Legends of Puerto Rico   CULTURAL
(☑ 787-605-9060; www.legendsofpr.com; tours adult/child from $25/19; ⊙ daily tour schedule varies) Debbie Molina-Ramos is a well-respected guide for Legends of Puerto Rico, whose popular 'Night Tales in Old San Juan' tours book up early. She offers engaging discussions of history at places like old jails not usually seen by tourists, as well as movie locations. Other walking tours cover Old San Juan by day, food and cultural themes. Customized tours also offered, including for people with walking limitations. Tours meet and depart from various locations.

☞ Beyond San Juan

A number of tours outside of San Juan make for a great day trip and fun escape from the city.

★ Para la Naturaleza   ECOTOUR
(Para la Naturaleza; Map p56; ☑ 787-722-5834; www.paralanaturaleza.org; Casa de Ramón Power y Giralt, 155 Tetuán, Old San Juan; ⊙ 9am-5:30pm Mon-Fri, tour schedule varies) Para la Naturaleza manages 45 private nature reserves on the island – representing over 25,000 acres – including the very popular Cabezas de San Juan (p107) near Fajardo. Part of the **Conservation Trust of Puerto Rico** (Map p56; www.fideicomiso.org; ⊙ 9am-5pm Tue-Sat) **FREE**, it hopes to fully protect one-third of the island by 2033. Check for its many excellent tours, which include hiking, exploring caves, canyoneering and kayaking on Puerto Rico's bioluminescent waters.

Explora   OUTDOORS
(☑ 787-900-7755; www.explorapr.com; tours from $140; ⊙ 8am-7pm, tour schedule varies) Explora offers half- and full-day adventure tours in private nature preserves. Caving, rappelling, rock climbing and 'body rafting' through canyons are woven into different tours. Guides are knowledgeable naturalists as well as certified in various rescue techniques. Gear is high-end. Prepare to get wet and muddy.

Aventuras Tierra Adentro   OUTDOORS
(Map p52; ☑ 787-766-0470; www.aventuraspr.com; 268 Av Jesús T Piñero; day trip $170-195; ⊙ shop 10am-6pm Tue-Fri, to 4pm Sat, tour schedule varies) Aventuras Tierra Adentro is a favorite store for climbers and hikers in Puerto Rico. It's also a tour operator specializing in rock climbing and rappelling trips to the Río Camuy caves, and canyoning trips in El Yunque. Guides also lead zip-lining over the mouth of Camuy's Angeles sinkhole. It's 1 mile west of the university.

Acampa   OUTDOORS
(Map p52; ☑ 787-706-0695; www.acampapr.com; 1221 Av Jesús T Piñero, Los Caobos; tours from $80; ⊙ 10am-6pm Mon-Fri, 10:30am-5:30pm Sat, tour schedule varies) One of the best places in town to buy or rent outdoor gear, including camping equipment. It also runs a number of excellent tours all over the island, including hiking, mountaineering, kayaking and paddleboarding.

✨ Festivals & Events

★ Fiestas de la Calle San Sebastián
CULTURAL

(Calle San Sebastián, Old San Juan; ⊙ mid-Jan) For a full week around the third weekend of January, Old San Juan's Calle San Sebastián hums with processions, music, food stalls and larger-than-ever crowds. During the day, it's folk art and crafts; at night, it's raucous revelry.

★ Festival Casals
MUSIC

(☎ 787-723-5005; http://corporacionartesmusicales. pr; El Centro de Bellas Artes Luis A Ferré, 22 Av Ponce de León, Santurce; tickets $15-75; ⊙ late Feb-early Mar) Since 1956 renowned soloists and orchestras have come from all over the world to join the Puerto Rico Symphony Orchestra in performing virtuoso concerts night after night, primarily at El Centro de Bellas Artes Luis A Ferré (p85). The performances usually stretch over about three weeks from late February into March.

Puerto Rico JazzFest
MUSIC

(www.prheinekenjazz.com; passes from $35; ⊙ mid-Mar) Puerto Rico's largest jazz fest is held for four days around the third weekend in March. It attracts the best Latin jazz artists from all over the Caribbean. The late great Tito Puente sometimes played here and Eddie Palmieri often still does. Four-day passes, including early entry to concerts, are available. It's held at San Juan's Anfiteatro Tito Puente in Parque Luis Muñoz Marín.

Fiesta de San Juan Bautista
CULTURAL

(⊙ late Jun) Celebration of the island's patron saint and a summer solstice party, Latin style. Staged during the week preceding June 24, the heart of the action is in Old San Juan. But you can catch the festivities – including religious processions, wandering minstrels, fireworks, food stalls, drunken sailors and beauty queens (straight and otherwise) – in the rest of the city (and country).

Playa Isla Verde is a major focus on the last day of the festival, when at midnight thousands of people march into the water backwards and dunk themselves three times in order to cleanse themselves of evil spirits and attract good luck.

Culinary Festival
FOOD & DRINK

(www.facebook.com/sofoculinaryfest; ⊙ Aug & Dec) SoFo's alfresco culinary festival is a moveable feast that in recent years has tended to happen twice a year, in August and December. During the three-night event, a two-block wedge of Fortaleza is closed to traffic and commandeered by local restaurateurs who set up their tables in the street and rustle up their best dishes. Live bands drop by, belly dancers entertain diners and the food is sizzlingly good.

Festival de Cine Internacional de San Juan
FILM

(San Juan International Film Festival; ☎ 787-946-9730; www.festivalcinesanjuan.com; tickets from $7.75; ⊙ Oct) Screens new films over one week in October, with an emphasis on Caribbean cinema. Given the number of Puerto Ricans/Nuyoricans making good on the big screen – J Lo, Benicio del Toro, Jimmy Smits (and Raul Julia, who was given a state funeral when he died of cancer in 1994) – this event has been pulling in bigger luminaries each year.

Puerto Rico Queer Filmfest
FILM

(www.puertoricoqueerfilmfest.com; ⊙ mid-Nov) Established in 2009, the Puerto Rico Queer Filmfest is considered the first and largest LGBTQ film festival in the Caribbean. Critically acclaimed submissions include international and Puerto Rico films, both in long and short form.

🛏 Sleeping

San Juan has a huge variety of accommodations, many situated right on its stunning beaches. Upscale, midscale, boutique or B&B: take your pick. Only budget options are few and far between. Old San Juan offers historical havens and old-world charm. Condado has lots of big hotels and small inns. Ocean Park is home mostly to guesthouses and B&Bs. Isla Verde has a few boutique options flanked by mega resorts.

There are plenty of hotels in this town – both chain and indie options. Rates can vary significantly season by season. Note that the large hotels tack on substantial resort, service and parking fees.

🛏 Old San Juan

Posada San Francisco
HOSTEL, GUESTHOUSE $

(Map p56; ☎ 787-996-0324; www.posada-colonial-puertorico.com; Plaza de Colón, 405 San Francisco, Old San Juan; dm $22, d with shared bathroom $60, all incl breakfast; ✲ 🛜; 🚍 El Morro, Fort) This family-run posada makes up for lackluster service by being spacious and clean. Double- and twin-bedded rooms have high ceilings, fridges and classic tile floors. Exquisite 5th-floor-patio views, plenty of bathrooms (no waiting in line for the showers) and a guest kitchen top it off. Continental breakfast included. The elevator can be cranky – take the stairs if you don't want to chance it.

Fortaleza Guest House HOSTEL, GUESTHOUSE $
(Map p56; ☑ 787-721-7112; 303 Fortaleza, Old San Juan; dm with air-con $20, r with shared barthroom $40-50; ☀☎) Centrally located in Old San Juan, these budget rooms are a little worn around the edges but reasonably clean and comfortable, though not for the fussy. Tiny rooms have either air-con and no natural light or a fan and a somewhat loud street-side balcony. Perks include three spick-and-span kitchens, a washer/dryer for guest use and a breezy rooftop terrace. It's also a good place to meet other travelers.

Da House HOTEL $$
(Map p56; ☑ 787-977-1180; www.dahousehotel pr.com; 312 San Francisco, Old San Juan; r $110-140; ☀@☎) One of Old San Juan's boho hotels is also one of its best bargains, with boutique-style rooms kitted out with chic furnishings and eye-catching contemporary art. Each room in the creamy peach building is dedicated to a different local artist. For the musically inclined, one of San Juan's best salsa bars, the Nuyorican Café (p85), is downstairs; for the less enamored (or sleep-deprived), staff will ruefully give out ear plugs.

El Cervantes Hotel HOTEL $$
(Map p56; ☑ 787-724-7722; www.cervantespr.com; 329 Recinto Sur, Old San Juan; r $130-180, ste $250-450; ☀☎; ⊡City Hall, El Morro, Fort) Designed as a boutique hotel by local guru Nono Maldonado, the Cervantes is about as luxurious as Puerto Rico gets. Inside, this Parisian-influenced beauty has 12 rooms on six floors, intimate decor and a remarkable level of all-round opulence. Take in the eye-catching art and enjoy the gadgets deftly splashed around the angular rooms before you step outside into Old San Juan's action.

Casablanca Hotel HOTEL $$
(Map p56; ☑ 787-725-3436; www.hotelcasa blancapr.com; 316 Fortaleza, Old San Juan; r $150-200; ☀☎) This stylish SoFo hotel blends a luxurious mix of colonial-era and contemporary styles. Five floors of rooms are swathed in vibrant fabrics and decorated with original art. Many are smallish but all are decked out with high-end amenities; some bathrooms

even sparkle with gorgeous mother-of-pearl sinks. Greet the morning on the roof deck with inspirational views of El Morro and El Yunque, or swan around in one of the soaking tubs.

★**Casa Sol** B&B $$
(Map p56; ☑ 787-980-9700, 787-399-0105; www. casasolbnb.com; 316 Sol, Old San Juan; r $170-230; ☀☎) This charming B&B is located in a beautifully restored 18th-century building in the heart of the old town. Rooms are spacious and nicely decorated, each with unique furnishings, folk art and touches like fresh flowers. The cheery central courtyard doubles as a dining area where a homemade breakfast is served each morning; fittingly for its name and address, it's done up in a radiant yellow. The affable owners live on-site and are generous with their local knowledge.

★**Hotel El Convento** HISTORIC HOTEL $$$
(Map p56; ☑ 787-723-9020; www.elconvento.com; 100 Calle del Cristo, Old San Juan; r $270-400, ste $660-1440; P☀@☎☒) Historic monument, tapas restaurant, meeting place, coffee bar and evocative colonial-era building. El Convento is Puerto Rico's most complete atmospheric and multifaceted hotel. Built in 1651 as the New World's first Carmelite convent, the 67 rooms and five suites (2nd-floor rooms have the highest ceilings) are gorgeously decorated with Andalusian tiles, mahogany and thick rugs. Service is impeccable from reception to the bar.

La Terraza de San Juan BOUTIQUE HOTEL $$$
(Map p56; ☑ 787-722-2014; www.laterraza hotelsanjuan.com; 262 Sol, Old San Juan; r $220-310; ☀☎☒) The 24 rooms in this boutique hotel are set in two 18th-century buildings combined into one. Most have gorgeous *talavera* tile floors, impressive high ceilings and furnishings that combine old-world style with modern comfort. The rooftop *terraza* (hence the name) is spectacular, giving guests a 360-degree view of Old San Juan. A plunge pool and a restaurant make it easy to enjoy.

▨ Condado

★**Coral Princess Hotel** HOTEL $$
(Map p66; ☑ 787-977-7700; www.coralpr.com; 1159 Magdalena, Condado; r incl breakfast $100-175; ☀☎☒) The Coral Princess is a 25-room boutique hotel that punches way above

its weight. Sitting in Condado's midrange bracket, it offers all the luxuries of the fancy resorts – spacious rooms, flat-screen TVs, marble floors and original art – but with enough intimacy and Latin flavor to remind you that you're still in Puerto Rico. A rooftop Jacuzzi and well-maintained pool make it that much better.

★ **Olive**   BOUTIQUE HOTEL **$$$**
(Map p66; ☑787-705-9994; www.oliveboutique hotel.com; 55 Aguadilla, Condado; r incl breakfast $200-430; ✺🛜) If there's a place to get away from it all, Olive is it. A Mediterranean-inspired hotel, this boutique inn has details like *talavera* tile floors, fountains and tropical wood features. Rooms are small but luxurious with big windows, deep beds and glass-enclosed showers as centerpieces (toilets are separate). Some have outdoor patios with Jacuzzis and plush seating areas.

Breakfast is served on the gorgeous rooftop lounge with sweeping views of Laguna Condado, or instead have it delivered to your room so you can lounge in bed just a little bit longer.

La Concha   RESORT **$$$**
(Map p66; ☑787-721-7500; www.laconcharesort. com; 1077 Av Ashford, Condado; r $290-310, ste $330-430; 🅿✺@🛜🏊) Popular La Concha will wow you. Spacious and serene white rooms pop with flashes of color and blue-lit showers exude an otherworldly underwater glow. Add in its three pools (one adults-only), gorgeous indoor and outdoor seating areas, hallways in crayon colors, a 24-hour casino, a sushi bar and the drop-dead gorgeous **Perla restaurant** (Map p66; ☑787-977-7886; www.perlarestaurant.com; mains $25-55; ☺6-10pm Sun-Thu, to 11pm Fri & Sat) and you won't feel the need to venture far.

★ **Condado**
Vanderbilt Hotel   LUXURY HOTEL **$$$**
(Map p66; ☑787-721-5500; www.condadovan derbilt.com; 1055 Av Ashford, Condado; r/ste from $350/445; 🅿✺@🛜🏊) One of the most opulent hotels when it opened in 1919, the Condado Vanderbilt Hotel reopened in 2014 after a lavish restoration and expansion. Its 323 rooms, including 90 rooms in the original building, are spacious and exude modern elegance; many have breathtaking city or ocean views. Service is tops, with concierges stationed on every floor and doormen who greet you by name.

🛏 Ocean Park

★ **The Dream Catcher**   B&B **$$**
(Map p77; ☑787-455-8259; www.dreamcatcher pr.com; 2009 España, Ocean Park; r $125-190, ste $230-290; ✺🛜) The Dream Catcher wows with its whimsical elegance: fine art and knick-knacks, luxurious linens and quirky wallpaper, designer furnishings and lazy hammocks, plants and sunlight everywhere, the outdoors brought in. It's high-end boho living at its best. Guests enjoy outdoor showers, quiet nooks for relaxing, common kitchens for socializing and a vegetarian restaurant serving some of the best breakfasts in town. Service is impeccable. And the beach is just two blocks away.

★ **Dream Inn**   HOTEL **$$**
(Map p77; ☑787-200-6340; www.dreaminnpr. com; r incl breakfast $140-175; 🅿✺🛜🏊) A hipster with a big heart. That's how Dream Inn feels. An urban architectural beauty – cement rules – with ecofriendly features like cross-breeze walls, solar panels and rainwater collection bins. Units are bright and spotless with art by local artists; many enjoy private balconies. A rooftop terrace and a lap pool are perfect places to relax. Breakfast at nearby Kasalta (p81) is included.

Numero Uno   GUESTHOUSE **$$**
(Map p77; ☑787-726-5010; www.numero1guest house.com; 1 Santa Ana, Ocean Park; r $130-230, apt $190-290; ✺🛜🏊) Hidden behind the walls of a whitewashed 1940s beachfront house, surrounded by palms and topped by a luminous kidney-shaped swimming pool, the 12 rooms and four apartments here are run by a former New Yorker whose soaring vision has inspired an inn of spiffy rooms, intimate service and an exquisite on-site seafood restaurant.

Andalucía Guest House   GUESTHOUSE **$$**
(Map p77; ☑787-309-3373; www.andaluciapr.com; 2011 McLeary, Ocean Park; d $100-120, with kitchenette $120-140; 🅿✺@🛜) Within striking distance of Ocean Park's excellent restaurants and beaches, this comfortable guesthouse makes you feel like you're part of the neighborhood. Its 11 rooms sport pretty tiling and striking color schemes, and some have kitchenettes. There's also a cozy terrace deck and courtyard Jacuzzi. Beach chairs and coolers are available.

Ocean Park

Ocean Park

◎ Top Sights
1 Playa Ocean Park.....................................B1

⊕ Activities, Courses & Tours
2 Ashtanga Yoga Puerto Rico.................C2
3 Tres Palmas...B2

⊜ Sleeping
4 Andalucía Guest House..........................C2
5 Casa Isabel B&B......................................A1
6 Dream Inn...C2
7 Numero Uno..C1

8 The Dream Catcher................................C1

⊗ Eating
9 Acapulco Taqueria Mexicana.............C2
10 Cocobana...C2
11 El Chifrijo Food Truck..........................A2
12 Kamoli Kafé Butik................................A2
13 Kasalta...C2
14 Mere Pescao..B2

⊜ Drinking & Nightlife
15 El Bar Bero..A2

Casa Isabel B&B　　　　B&B **$$**
(Map p77; ☑787-529-8825; inmobiliariaurbanapr@
gmail.com; 65 Krug, Ocean Park; r incl breakfast
$135-165) A completely renovated 1930s Span-
ish revival home, Casa Isabel has six cozy but
modern rooms, all with private bathrooms.
Guests share several common areas – a bal-
cony, patio and a couple lounges – much of
it with gorgeous original tile floors and iron-
work. A full breakfast is served daily. Located
on a quiet street, just steps from Ocean Park
beach.

⊨ Isla Verde

Boriquen Beach Inn　　　　HOTEL **$**
(Map p72; ☑866-728-8400, 787-728-8400; www.
boriquenbeachinn.com/bbinn; 5451 Av Isla Verde,
Isla Verde; r $90-95; [P][❄][🛜]) It may look run
down but this old-school inn is one of the
best budget deals in town. Rooms lack
any hint of charm but are clean with good
beds, strong air-con and decent bathrooms.
There's a spacious kitchen for guest use and

free parking on-site. Best of all, you can hear
the waves from reception.

El Patio Guesthouse　　　　GUESTHOUSE **$**
(Map p72; ☑787-726-6953; 23 Ext Villamar Mar
de Bering, Isla Verde; s/d/tr $65/75/80; [❄][🛜][🖥])
In the cheaper price bracket, this little Isla
Verde place doesn't have much charm but is
still a solid option. It's walking distance to
the beach and other attractions, and is run
by a kind woman who bends over backwards
to make sure that the rooms are spick-and-
span. There's a guest kitchen and laundry,
and rooms have TVs and fridges.

La Playita　　　　INN **$$**
(Hotel La Playa; Map p72; ☑787-791-1115; 6 Amapola,
Isla Verde; r $110-120; [❄][🛜]) ✎ Yes, you can stay
oceanfront in Isla Verde without breaking
the bank. And be green about it – La Playita
has solar hot-water heaters, low-power air-
con units and a 2000-gallon water-catchment
system. A small garden leads to modern
rooms with tasteful beachy decor. The breezy

restaurant opens directly onto the water – a million dollar view (perfect for breakfast!).

InterContinental San Juan Resort & Casino RESORT $$$

(Map p72; ☑787-791-6100, 877/721-0185; www.icsanjuan.com; 5961 Av Isla Verde; r $265-305, ste $315-465; P❋@🛜🏊) The InterContinental offers a full-on luxury beachside resort experience with all of the usual extras you'd expect. The nearly 400 rooms and facilities are spiffy enough, though other resorts in the area may have more character and panache. Some rooms have views of the airport, located a highly efficient 10-minute ride by taxi.

Water Beach Club Hotel HOTEL $$$

(Map p72; ☑888-265-6699, 787-728-3666; www.waterbeachhotel.com; 2 Tartak, Isla Verde; r from $290; P❋@🛜🏊) One of Puerto Rico's trendiest boutique hotels, the Water Beach Club has a reception area straight out of a design magazine; elevators sport glassed-in waterfalls and hallways have black lights and neon signage. A hopping rooftop bar and plunge pool make this a popular spot with the jet set. The minimalist rooms are artfully designed, many with spectacular beach views.

El San Juan Hotel RESORT $$$

(Map p72; ☑888-579-2632, 787-791-1000; www.elsanjuanhotel.com; 6063 Av Isla Verde, Isla Verde; P❋@🛜🏊) A five-star beauty fronting palm-lined Isla Verde Beach, this iconic hotel was closed for a lavish restoration at the time of research. It was set to reopen in mid-2017. Once completed, the resort will likely be one of the most luxurious in town.

✖ Eating

Few would dispute that San Juan offers some of the best eating in the Caribbean. From contemporary takes on traditional fare to cafes serving exquisite locally grown coffee to restaurants run by renowned chefs and food trucks serving up international eats, you'll be spoiled for choice.

✖ Old San Juan

★Antojitos del Callejón PUERTO RICAN $

(Map p56; ☑787-721-6227; cnr Tanca & Norzagaray, Old San Juan; meals $3-8; ⊗8am-10pm; 🚍Fort) A hole-in-the-wall on a small pedestrian street, this local favorite is known for its delicious *criollo* dishes and *antojos* (finger foods, typically fried). Plastic tables are set up in front, in an empty lot carpeted in astroturf, with

a view of ocean just beyond. Service is efficient and friendly and the Medalla beer ice cold. Come dark, the salsa music begins and diners move their tables to the side and get up to dance.

★Cafeteria Mallorca PUERTO RICAN $

(Map p56; ☑787-724-4607; 300 San Francisco, Old San Juan; mains $5-15; ⊗7am-6:30pm; 🚍El Morro) If you're looking for a classic Puerto Rican eating experience, get back to the basics with a cup of coffee and breakfast in this cozy, timeless nook on San Francisco. Cheap and simple, the Mallorca is where all-night ravers share pick-me-ups and American journalists sift through their travel notes. No frills, but plenty of warm familiarity.

★La Bombonera PUERTO RICAN $

(Map p56; ☑787-705-3370; 259 San Francisco, Old San Juan; $5-17; ⊗7:30am-5pm Tue-Sun; 🚻; trolley City Hall, El Morro) This historic diner shines with a recent renovation including Tiffany stained-glass windows, marble-top tables and a gleaming bronze coffee machine. Even the wait staff is gussied up in bow ties and bolero jackets. *Mallorcas,* pastries and steaming cups of coffee are the favorites here but tasty breakfasts and daily specials make it easy to come for more.

Old San Juan Farmers Market MARKET

(Map p56; www.mercadoagricolanatural.com; Museo de San Juan, 150 Norzagaray, Old San Juan; snacks from $2; ⊗8am-1pm Sat; 🚻; trolley Fort, El Morro) 🍃 Stop by the courtyard of the Museo de San Juan to pick up some organic local produce or coffee, nibble on homemade chocolate, bread or cheese, peruse the handcrafted gifts or tuck into an inexpensive brunch.

Manolín PUERTO RICAN $

(Map p56; ☑787-723-9743; www.cafemanolinoldsanjuan.com; 251 San Justo, Old San Juan; mains $5-12; ⊗6am-4:30pm Mon-Fri, 7am-4:30pm Sat, 8am-5pm Sun; trolley City Hall, El Morro) Elbow in with the local office workers at this snaking grill and fill up on excellent *mofongo* (mashed plantains) and *churrasco a la parrilla* (skirt steak). Other all-star local fare on the menu includes garlic shrimp, pork chops and the delectable pistachio pudding. Breakfasts, especially the fluffy omelets, are worth crawling out of bed for – just get there by 10:30am.

St Germain Bistro & Café FRENCH $

(Map p56; ☑787-725-5830; www.solycruz.com/stgermainpr; 156 Sol, Old San Juan; dishes $8-15; ⊗11:30am-4pm & 6-11pm Tue-Fri, 11:30am-11pm

DON'T MISS

SANTURCE'S STREET ART

Santurce is the heart of San Juan's vibrant street-art movement with spectacular murals, some as high as 50ft, that stop you in your tracks. Courtesy of an international urban art festival, *Los Muros Hablan* (The Walls Speak), these works of art have helped transform a gritty no-go neighborhood into one of the city's most dynamic districts.

Fanning out from **La Placita de Santurce** (p84), these murals offer insight into Puerto Rican culture. Look for the farming scene of a bison hauling off a cart piled high with fast food; a recumbent Taíno Indian, a cloth draped over his head, being reclaimed by nature; a fat iguana (iguanas are big pests on the island) squatting down the length of one building; and a group of crabs (Santurce is reclaimed swampland and was once infested with crabs) clustering around a computer screen.

To make sense of these and many other murals, ask about tours with **Casa Sol** (p75). To find out about alternative arts events hereabouts, head to the neighborhood hangout, **Abracadabra Counter Cafe** (p82).

Sat, 10am-3pm & 6-11pm Sun; 🍴) Main-course salads are the stars at this casual, idiosyncratic and ultimately tasty French cafe. Light fare such as creative sandwiches and crepes are among the staples. The soup choice changes daily, while the homemade cakes are melt-in-your-mouth heavenly. The upstairs sibling bar Mezzanine (p83) is splendid for a drink.

Señor Paleta   ICE CREAM $

(Map p56; ☑787-724-2337; 153 Tetúan, Old San Juan; paletas $3.50-5; ☺10:30am-6pm Tue, to 8:30pm Wed-Sun) Hole-in-the-wall selling artisanal *paletas* (popsicles) made from fresh fruits, nuts and other tasty treats. Flavors range from coconut, melon and *guanabana* (soursop fruit) to cheesecake, amaretto and pumpkin spice. Look for the sidewalk queue that grows longer as the day becomes hotter. The cool relief is well worth the wait. Cash only.

Old San Juan Food Trucks   STREET FOOD $

(Map p56; Plaza de la Dársena, Calle Comercia, Old San Juan; $2-7; ☺2pm-3am Fri-Sun; trolley City Hall, Fort) For cheap eats, head to the food trucks that line Plaza de la Dársena. Vendors do a brisk trade in Puerto Rican and American staples like *alcapurrillas* (plantain-based fritters), *pinchos* (kababs) and *pastelillos* (turnovers) along with the likes of pizza, burgers and hotdogs. A dieter's nightmare but a budget munchie godsend. Weekends only.

Caficultura   CAFE $$

(Map p56; ☑787-723-7731; 401 San Francisco, Old San Juan; meals $7-20; ☺8am-6pm Mon-Thu, to 10pm Fri, to 8pm Sat & Sun; 🚋El Morro) Just assume you'll want to settle in at this atmospheric cafe – once you drink your *café con leche,* you'll surely want another. The gaslight era is evoked with its high ceilings and marble-topped tables. Watch the masses from sidewalk tables. Live music most Friday nights.

El Jibarito   PUERTO RICAN $$

(Map p56; ☑787-725-8375; www.eljibarito 1977.com; 280 Sol, Old San Juan; mains $10-27; ☺10:30am-9pm; 🍴) Welcome to the neighborhood, *hermano.* El Jibarito is the kind of mom-and-pop place you just know will serve a good and garlicky *mofongo* (mashed plantains) or *arroz con habichuelas* (rice and beans). Which it does. A favorite of local families and visitors, the meals are simple but hearty.

Pirilo   PIZZA $$

(Map p56; ☑787-721-3322; 207 Tanca, Old San Juan; ☺11am-midnight Sun-Thu, to 2am Fri & Sat; 🍴; trolley Fort) A spectacular 2nd-floor dining room – brick walls, 18ft ceilings, exposed wood beams, tall windows running its length – leaves no doubt you're in Old San Juan. Except that Pirilo is all about pizza. From classic to gourmet, you'll find the crust crispy on the outside, pillowy on the inside, the sauce perfectly balanced and the toppings super fresh.

Café Puerto Rico   PUERTO RICAN $$

(Map p56; ☑787-724-2281; Plaza Colón, 208 O'Donnell, Old San Juan; mains $12-24; ☺11:30am-3:30pm & 5:30-10:45pm Mon-Sat, noon-9pm Sun; 🍴; 🚋Fort) An old-school restaurant with wood paneling and landscape art, Café Puerto Rico is where locals send you for *mofongo* (fried and mashed plantain). In this town, that's saying something. Available in yucca, green or sweet plantain, the *mofongo* comes sculpted into a bowl and stuffed with your choice of protein. The chicken in creamy garlic sauce is a fave.

La Madre   MEXICAN $$
(Map p56; ☎787-647-5392; 351 San Francisco, Old San Juan; mains $15-25; ☻noon-11pm Mon-Wed, to midnight Thu, to 2am Fri, 10am-2am Sat, 10am-11pm Sun; trolley El Morro) Upscale Mexican cuisine is the theme at this hipster restaurant-lounge. Start with delectable tamarind margaritas or opt for fruity alternatives like *parcha* (passion fruit) or *acerola* (cherry). The food boasts creative twists while the entertainment changes nightly – everything from oldies to salsa. Videos of old cartoons may make some maudlin after their third mojito.

Carli's Café Fine Bistro & Piano   FUSION $$
(Map p56; ☎787-725-4927; www.carlisworld. com; 500 San Justo, Old San Juan; mains $18-38; ☻3:30-11pm Mon-Thu, to 1am Fri & Sat; ☒City Hall, El Morro, Fort) As much a place for a quiet cocktail or a night of excellent jazz as it is for its dining. Carli's has a wide menu of tapas and mains bring a Puerto Rican flair to continental classics. Tables out front on the small plaza are prized. In the evening, Carli Muñoz, the owner and noted jazz musician, often works the piano.

★Verde Mesa   CARIBBEAN $$$
(Map p56; ☎787-390-4662; www.verdemesa.com; 107 Tetuán, Old San Juan; mains $15-25; ☻6-10pm Tue-Sat; ☒) Hidden in plain sight on a bustling Old San Juan street, this little gem of a restaurant is lauded for its vegetarian and seafood fare. Take a break from *mofongo* and enjoy fresh and flavorful food. Many of the ingredients are sourced from local organic farms. Pressed-tin ceilings, antiques and mood lighting give meals a romantic patina. Don't miss the crème brûlée.

Marmalade   FUSION $$$
(Map p56; ☎787-724-3969; www.marmaladepr. com; 317 Fortaleza, Old San Juan; mains $18-44, tasting menu $65-85; ☻5-10pm; ☒) The personal vision of noted chef Peter Schintler, Marmalade was one of the first restaurants to bring real foodie recognition to Old San Juan more than a decade ago. The minimalist interior is decked out like the Korova Milk Bar in *A Clockwork Orange*. The food takes full advantage of local sourcing and dishes are prepared with an intense passion for detail.

Trois Cent Onze   FRENCH $$$
(Map p56; ☎787-725-7959; www.311restaurant pr.com; 311 Fortaleza, Old San Juan; mains $24-39; ☻6-10pm Mon-Thu, to 10:30pm Fri & Sat) This well-established French bistro evokes elegance, sophistication and romance with its billowing white curtains, flickering candles and delightful Moorish-Andalusian tiles. Order from a menu replete with scallops, duck and foie gras that also includes a few nods to the island (the Caribbean lobster is a treat). The wine list rivals any in France.

Aguaviva   SEAFOOD $$$
(Map p56; ☎787-722-0665; www.aguavivapr.com; 364 Fortaleza, Old San Juan; mains $24-42; ☻5-10pm Mon-Wed, to 11pm Thu & Fri, 4-10pm Sun, closed Sat; ☒El Morro) This high-profile SoFo restaurant has an underwater theme – all turquoise blues and brilliant whites and hanging lamps that look like jellyfish. The specialty is Latin-Caribbean seafood like lobster *mofongo* (mashed plantains) and coconut shrimp; many come for the oysters though, which are flown in daily. Be sure to pair your meal with a specialty drink – the watermelon sangria is a sure bet.

✖ Condado

Kabanas Food Truck   BURGERS, MEXICAN $
(Map p66; ☎787-969-2180; www.facebook.com/ kabanas413; 1014 Av Ashford, Condado; meals $7-12; ☻8am-10pm Mon-Thu, to 1am Fri-Sun) Condado on the cheap – it can be done, and done well. This food truck serves mouthwatering burgers with homemade *tostones* (fried banana chips), hefty tacos with parmesan-encrusted tortillas and breakfast options like waffles, eggs Benedict and açaí bowls. It can get busy, but the wait staff is friendly and efficient. Almost best of all – the ocean views while you eat!

El Mercado Urbano   MARKET
(Map p66; www.facebook.com/elmercado urbano; Parque La Ventana al Mar, Av Ashford, Condado; ☻9am-5pm first Sun of month; ☒D53, T21) A popular farmers market in the swanky Condado neighborhood, El Mercado Urbano is the place to find organic fruits and veggies, homemade baked goods and prepared foods to go. You can even grab a cocktail – perfect for an impromptu picnic on the beach. Look for the big white tents on Parque La Ventana al Mar on the first Sunday of every month.

Freshmart   MARKET, CAFE **$**
(Map p66; ☑787-999-7800; www.freshmartpr.
com; 1310 Av Ashford, Condado; snacks $2-9;
☺7am-10pm, deli open to 9pm; 🛜🖧🚹; 🚌D53,
T21) A Puerto Rican Whole Foods is what
you'll find at Freshmart. A market dedicated
to organic food and products, it also has a
mezzanine-level cafeteria with a great selection of vegetarian, vegan and gluten-free
dishes. Meat lovers, fear not – there are plenty of options for you too. Sandwiches, salads,
artisanal pizzas and more are prepared fresh
every day. Breakfast is a hit.

Pinky's West   CAFE **$**
(Map p66; ☑787-222-5615; 1104 Av Ashford, Condado; dishes $8-15; ☺7am-10pm) Break free of
hotel restaurants and come to Condado's
popular deli-cafe for breakfasts, smoothies,
sandwiches and wraps. A chance to make up
for all that delicious, rich Puerto Rican food
you've been eating and also an opportunity
to hit a laid-back local hang.

Alí Baba   TURKISH, MEDITERRANEAN **$$**
(Map p66; ☑787-722-1176; Av Ashford 1214, Con-
dado; meals $11-27; ☺4-10pm Tue-Sat, noon-10pm
Sun; 🖋; 🖧) Tucked into a tiny marketplace,
Alí Baba serves some of the best Turkish
food on the island. Traditional lamb dishes,
hummus and falafel plates, vegetarian and
meat musaka, and freshly baked *lavash*
bread are among the delights on the menu.
Dine in the colorful dining room with doz-
ens of mirrored lanterns, or outside in a
breezy walkway. Service is tops.

Pikayo   FUSION **$$$**
(Map p66; ☑787-721-6194; www.facebook.com/
pikayosanjuan; Condado Plaza, 999 Av Ashford,
Condado; mains $37-50; ☺6:30-10pm Sun-Thu,
to 11pm Fri & Sat) Wilo Benet is one of the
island's platoon of celebrity chefs. He's uncovered the soul of Caribbean cooking by
infusing colonial-era Puerto Rican cuisine
with various African and Eastern European
elements. This showcase restaurant is renowned not just for its menu of steaks and
seafood but also its polished service.

✕ Ocean Park

★Cocobana   VEGETARIAN **$**
(Map p77; ☑787-268-7758; 2000 Loíza, Ocean Park;
☺11am-5pm Mon-Sat; 🛜🖋) A mural of a cow
with a toothy smile and a flower behind its
ear will be the first sign that you've arrived
at one of the best vegetarian restaurants in
town. Cocobana has an extensive menu of

innovative sandwiches, wraps, salads and
smoothies – oh so many smoothies. Ingredients are fresh and local, prepared in an open
kitchen, the bustling chef in full sight.

Be sure to look beyond the menu though.
The daily specials, served cafeteria-style,
entice many meat eaters to the veggie side.
The special includes a *criollo* main, rice and
beans, salad, soup and a drink. All for ten
bucks. Swap in a smoothie for some extra
change.

★Acapulco Taqueria Mexicana   MEXICAN **$**
(Map p77; ☑787-727-5568; 2021 Loíza, Ocean Park;
meals $8-14; ☺11:30am-10pm Tue-Thu, to 10pm
Fri, 10:30am-10pm Sat, to 9pm Sun; 🖋) Hands
down, the best street tacos in town. Acapulco
is a purist – no cheese, no lettuce, no hard
shell. This is the real deal: a pair of stacked
corn tortillas, sizzling meat, cilantro, onion
and a squeeze of lime. Look for the *trompo*
(a vertical skewer of slow-cooked pork with
a pineapple on top) the heart of the classic
taco *al pastor*. Down it with a Negra Modelo.
Perfection.

El Chifrijo Food Truck   CENTRAL AMERICAN **$**
(Map p77; cnr Loíza & San Jorge, Ocean Park; mains
$7-8; ☺6-10pm) *Bienvenido a la comida
de la calle real* (welcome to the real street
food): this food truck might not stand alone
in its location near a fuel-station forecourt,
but it does stand pretty much alone in quality as far as the neighborhood's food trucks
go. Costa Rican and El Salvadorian food is
what's on offer.

Kamoli Kafé Butik   CAFE **$**
(Map p77; ☑787-721-4326; 1706 Loíza, Ocean
Park; $6-16; ☺7:30am-9:30pm Mon-Fri, 8:30am-
9:30pm Sat & Sun; 🖋) An urban boho eatery
with a boutique on the side, Kamoli has an
eclectic menu, especially geared towards
breakfast and brunch. Classics like banana
pancakes share the limelight with dishes
like the Breakfast Salad (sunny-side-up eggs
on a bed of greens). A monster list of freshly
prepared juices include energizing, wellness
and detox concoctions.

★Kasalta   CAFE **$$**
(Map p77; ☑787-727-7340; www.kasalta.com; 1966
McLeary, Ocean Park; mains $5-25; ☺6am-10pm)
Oh the garbanzo (chickpea) soup! Tucked
into Ocean Park's residential enclave, Kasalta
is the sort of authentic Puerto Rican bakery
and diner that you'll find yourself crossing
town to visit daily. The coffee here is as leg-
endary as the sweets that fill a long glass

WORTH A TRIP

BEBO'S BBQ

Don't let the lines of people stop you from eating at **Bebo's BBQ** (Map p52; ☑787-791-7115; www.bebosbbqpr.com; 2352 Marginal Av Los Angeles, Carolina; meals $5-10; ⊙24hr) – it moves fast. And if it doesn't, it's worth the wait. Bebo's is a favorite eatery among the locals. This open-air cafeteria-style joint across from the airport serves up all manner of barbecued pork and chicken with sides of yucca, rice, beans and onions, at picnic-style tables.

display case and include everything from Danish pastries to iced buns.

Mere Pescao   FUSION $$
(Map p77; ☑939-338-1918; 1915 Loíza, Ocean Park; plates $8-14; ⊙2-10pm Wed-Sun; ☑T5) This neighborhood eatery serves up global-fusion dishes that deliver big, flavorful punches. Most have an Asian twist – burritos with kimchi rice, steamed buns stuffed with crab meat, pulled-pork sushi rolls – but you'll also find Puerto Rican takes on pierogies, gyros and fish 'n' chips. Servings are made to share, tapas-style, and tables are close together, creating a cozy, communal feel.

✖ Santurce

★**Santurce Food Trucks**   STREET FOOD $
(Map p66; cnr Av Ponce de León & Cerra, Santurce; meals $4-8; ⊙11am-11pm Wed-Sun) A set of upscale food trucks set up shop most days in an enclosed parking lot on Santurce's main drag. Meatballs. Dumplings. Tacos. Bagels. Gelato. It's a veritable international marketplace. Picnic tables are set up streetside for diners to eat side by side. Evenings bring twinkling lights, adding to the festive feel.

Abracadabra Counter Cafe   CAFE $
(Map p66; ☑787-200-0447; http://abracadabra countercafe.com; 1661 Av Ponce de León, Santurce; meals $7-10; ⊙8:30am-3pm Tue-Thu, to 10pm Fri, 9am-2pm Sat & Sun) As colorful as the neighboring street murals, this vibrant cafe draws in an eclectic crowd. Fresh juices, fine coffees, sublime breakfasts (served all day) and a variety of casual fare are reasons to drop by. A small stage provides a space for live music – typically jazz – on Friday night. The only downer is the service, which is hit or miss.

★**José Enrique**   BISTRO $$$
(Map p66; ☑787-725-3518; www.joseenrique pr.com; 176 Duffaut, Santurce; mains from $18; ⊙11:30am-10pm Tue-Fri, 6:30-10pm Sat) Though hidden in a pink house without a sign, you'll have no problems finding one of the western hemisphere's best restaurants – just follow the excited hordes in the know. Reservations aren't possible, so be prepared to wait on the sidewalk; your meal is definitely worth the minor inconvenience. The namesake chef is a multiple-award winner and he combines local ingredients brilliantly.

Santaella   PUERTO RICAN $$$
(Map p66; ☑787-725-1611; www.santaellapr.com; 219 Canals, Santurce; mains from $19; ⊙11:30am-11pm Tue-Fri, 6-11pm Sat) One of San Juan's best restaurants, Santaella buzzes with excitement, inspired by the superb drinks at the bar and the sensational Puerto Rican fare. Dishes range from tapas-small to full-size and include a varying lineup of simple creations that are a triumph of flavor. Although many are happy to wait in the alluring bar, those in the know book in advance.

✖ Isla Verde

Playa Papaya   BISTRO $$
(Map p72; ☑787/399-1007; Ocean Tower, 5757 Av Isla Verde, Isla Verde; meals $8-15; ⊙8am-3pm Mon-Thu, to 5pm Fri-Sun; ☑) This Tiki-inspired bistro serves up a mean breakfast – from coconut pancakes and Oreo waffles to steak and eggs with sweet papaya sauce. Looking for lighter fare? Check out the half dozen açaí bowls with ingredients like chia, bee pollen, hemp and agave. Or opt for a fresh fruit smoothie made to order. Service is hit or miss.

Yamiko Sushi   JAPANESE $$
(Map p72; ☑787-982-3322; www.yamikosushi.com; 5960 Av Isla Verde, Isla Verde; sushi $5-12, mains $11-20; ⊙3pm-1am Mon-Thu, to 4am Fri & Sat, to 3am Sun) What a genius move – late-night sushi! The decor is simple; people come for the warm hospitality and top-notch sushi with super-fresh ingredients, not fancy wall hangings. Yamiko also offers a full range of Japanese and Chinese mains. Free delivery for orders over $20.

Metropol   PUERTO RICAN, CUBAN $$
(Map p72; ☑787-791-5585; http://metropolres taurant.com; Av Isla Verde, Annexo Club Gallistico, Isla Verde; dishes $11-22; ⊙11:30am-10pm; ☑) Find this neighborhood favorite right next

to the cockfighting arena. It's well known for the plentiful portions and simple (but not plain) local and Cuban fare. The stuffed Cornish hen is popular – perhaps a casualty of the arena next door? There are several other locations around the island, though it's a family-run endeavor.

Ceviche House
PERUVIAN **$$**

(Map p72; ☑787-726-0919; 79 Av Isla Verde, Isla Verde; mains $18-30; ⊙11:30am-10pm Mon-Thu & Sun, to 11pm Fri & Sat) Though the ceviche here is grand, as one might expect, this casual Peruvian restaurant also cooks up delicious, juicy steaks and a full range of fresh seafood like whole red snapper or mussels with salsa. The friendly staff are attentive without being overbearing.

🍸 Drinking & Nightlife

San Juan is a late-night town and you'll find places to party across the city. Old San Juan is good for strolling the cobblestone streets from venue to venue, with lounges and dive bars tucked into colonial-era buildings, popular with both locals and travelers. Beachfront neighborhoods like Condado are known for their glitzy resort venues. Or you can go totally hipster in Santurce, where trendy places open (and close) regularly.

🍸 Old San Juan

⭐ La Factoría
BAR

(Map p56; ☑787-412-4251; www.facebook.com/lafactoriapr; 148 San Sebastián, Old San Juan; ⊙6pm-4am) You've gotta wedge your way in on weekend nights for DJs, acoustic guitars or sing-along sets. And that's just the start. The so-named *Hijos de Borinquen* (or 'Sons of Puerto Rico') has three speakeasies hidden inside – one a wine bar, another a salsa dance club, the last a snazzy lounge. Great craft cocktails throughout plus tapas for filler.

⭐ El Batey
BAR

(Map p56; ☑787-723-7657; 101 Calle del Cristo, Old San Juan; ⊙1pm-5am) If Hunter S Thompson's ghost wanted to relive his *Rum Diary* days, this is where you'd find him. Cool, crusty and unashamedly divey, the walls of this cavernous drinking joint are covered in graffiti, while the low-key lighting will have you groping in your pockets for spare change to light up the suitably retro jukebox.

El Batey is a place to down shots, shoot pool and ramble soulfully about when Elvis was king and the Bacardí bottles still came from Cuba.

La Taberna Lúpulo
BAR

(Map p56; ☑787-721-3772; 150 San Sebastián, Old San Juan; ⊙noon-2am Sun-Thu, to 4am Fri & Sat) This beautiful old corner bar has been updated with Puerto Rico's best selection of microbrews. The lineup on the 50 taps is ever-changing and includes some of America's best and most unusual brews. Windows are open to the street on both sides and the neighborhood has a relaxed, leafy charm.

Mezzanine
COCKTAIL BAR

(Map p56; ☑787-724-4657; www.themezzaninepr.com; 156 Sol, Old San Juan; ⊙noon-midnight Tue & Wed, to 2am Thu & Fri, 10am-2am Sat, 10am-midnight Sun; 🛜) A perfectly raffish 2nd-floor lounge, Mezzanine has a raggedly refined atmosphere that seems timeless. The cocktails are inventive, the wine list good and the tapas dishes go down smoothly. There's live jazz some nights. Four-dollar drinks every night from 4pm to 8pm. It's on the floor above the very popular St Germain Bistro (p78).

Finca Cialitos
COFFEE

(Map p56; ☑939-207-9998; www.fincacialitos.com; 267 San Francisco, Old San Juan; snacks from $3; ⊙7:30am-4:30pm Tue-Fri, 8am-5pm Sat & Sun) Your best cup of San Juan Joe is at this cavernous yet cozy find. Beans for the brews here come from the family's coffee estate in the nearby lush hills and are roasted on-site. Friendly baristas, freshly baked pastries, simple sandwiches and comfy chairs will convince you to linger away a morning.

Café Cola'o
COFFEE

(Map p56; ☑787-725-4139; www.prcafecolao.com; Pier 2, Av La Marina, Old San Juan; snacks from $3; ⊙6:30am-6pm Mon-Fri, 9am-7pm Sat & Sun; 🚌City Hall, El Morro) Café Cola'o is known for the outstanding handpicked coffee it serves from various small farms in Puerto Rico's Central Mountains. Ask baristas for recommendations – they have an encyclopedic knowledge of all things java. Pair your caffeine fix with a hot panino or a classic *mallorca*. Cozy indoor and outdoor seating, most with views of the bay.

Café Cuatro Sombras
COFFEE

(Map p56; ☑787-724-9955; www.cuatrosombras.com; 259 Recinto Sur, Old San Juan; snacks from $3;

7am-8pm Mon-Thu, to 9pm Fri-Sun; 🛎; trolley City Hall) Those desperate for exquisitely served caffeine can tiptoe here from the cruise-ship port; others will be drawn in by the cozy-meets-hipster look, which feels more like a craft brewery than a coffee emporium. The beans are locally grown and roasted. In the morning enjoy their iconic toast with guava butter.

🍷 Condado & Ocean Park

La Concha Lobby Bar   BAR, CLUB
(Map p66; 📞787-721-7500; www.laconcharesort. com/bars-lounges; La Concha Resort, 1077 Av Ash-ford, Condado; ⊙noon-late) Take your rightful place with the beautiful people at the un-disputed hot spot of San Juan. On weekend nights, the lobby bar explodes with activity while chic cocktail-bearing waitresses in space-age outfits and wedge heels do their best to swivel through. Things get progres-sively wilder as the night turns to morning, with dancing to DJs and live music.

El Bar Bero   BAR
(Map p77; 📞787-473-8161; www.facebook.com/ elbarberopr; 1507 Loíza, Ocean Park; ⊙7pm-2am Wed-Sat) Barbershop by day, bar by night. El Bar Bero (*barbero* means barber) is a light-hearted local spot. Talented mixologists rule this roost with a spectacular list of house cocktails, many with hair-related names like El Mullet or El Goatee. Opt for one with house-made ginger beer. Old-school barber stools serve as seating at the bar.

Oceano   BAR
(Map p66; 📞787-724-6300; www.oceanopr.com; 2 Vendig, Condado; ⊙noon-10pm Mon-Thu, to midnight Fri & Sat, 11am-10pm Sun) Cruise the three bars and pick your poison: chilled-out lounge, open-air beach bar or dress-to-impress rooftop. Gay and straight folks alike come for elegant eats, craft cocktails and top DJs. Tuesday is salsa night – free dance classes start the evening off.

🍷 Isla Verde

El San Juan Hotel Lobby Bars   CLUB
(Map p72; 📞787-791-1000; www.elsanjuanhotel. com; 6063 Av Isla Verde, Isla Verde; ⊙8pm-2am) El San Juan Hotel's three lobby bars are among the most glamorous around with chande-liers, leather seating, tropical wood details and live music. Enjoy a casual drink Mon-day or Tuesday with a background of clas-sical piano and guitar; Wednesday through Sunday come for a more lively scene when salsa, merengue and flamenco bands get the crowd moving.

Club Brava   CLUB
(Map p72; 📞787-791-2781; www.bravapr.com; El San Juan Hotel, 6063 Av Isla Verde, Isla Verde; cover $20; ⊙10pm-late Thu-Sat) This club inside El San Juan Hotel, gets packed with 'beautiful people' and garners rave reviews from all-night clubbers. A mix of house, reggaetón and salsa fills the small, two-level club, and the atmosphere is electric. Dress up, bring your credit card and get ready to get down to what's touted as the best sound system in the Caribbean.

🍷 Santurce

★La Placita de Santurce   STREET PARTY
(Map p66; Calle Dos Hermanos, Santurce; ⊙5pm-late Thu-Sat; 🚍T3, T5) Santurce's famous mar-ket – La Placita – is known as the hub of San Juan's hottest nightlife scenes. Especially good on Thursday and Friday nights, the historic market plaza and its surrounding streets host what becomes a veritable street party: people meeting up, drinking, eating and, as soon as the salsa band warms up, dancing until the wee hours.

Circo Bar   GAY
(Map p66; 📞787-517-6667; 650 Condado, San-turce; ⊙9pm-late) A video bar – with a ka-raoke detour on Thursday and drag shows that get mixed reviews – this place turns sweaty and snug after midnight and on

weekends, when high-energy dancing gets everyone up close and personal. Amid the flashing TV screens you'll find a youngish male crowd wriggling to house beats or chilling out on the walk-through smoking patio. No cover.

Scandalo The Club　　　　GAY
(Map p66; ☑787-485-1934; 613 Av Condado, Santurce; cover $5; ☺9pm-late) Don't let the bars on the windows turn you off, Scandalo is a popular gay club in the heart of Santurce. DJs play house and Latin music, keeping the small dance floor busy while bartenders pour strong drinks. Drag shows on Thursday and strippers on Sunday liven things up even more.

Hacienda San Pedro Coffee Shop　　COFFEE
(Map p66; ☑787-993-1871; https://catehsp. com; 318 Av de Diego, Santurce; snacks from $3; ☺6:30am-6pm Mon-Fri, 8:30am-4pm Sat, 9am-3pm Sun; ☎; ☑T5, T21) An example of why San Juan has become a coffee mecca: beans grown and roasted locally are used in a fab range of coffee drinks, most at prices you won't find in touristy areas. Pastries are excellent and it's easy to let the hours slip by in the sleek surrounds or outside on the breezy back patio.

☆ Entertainment

San Juan has an eclectic entertainment scene. From salsa performances in backstreet bars to the symphony at Bellas Artes. Resort hotels also have live entertainment most nights and Santurce's galleries and artsy cafes offer up indie films, performance art and live music.

A number of the resort hotels have live salsa music in their lobbies in the evening, usually on weekends: the InterContinental (p78) and the **Marriott Resort** (Map p66; ☑787-722-7000; www.marriott.com; 1309 Av Ashford, Condado; r $250-390, ste $415-665; P✳@☎☒) are sure bets. Old San Juan's plazas – especially Plaza de Armas (p60) – are also popular spots for organized and impromptu *bomba* concerts and dancing.

★Nuyorican Café　　　　LIVE MUSIC
(Map p56; ☑787-977-1276; www.nuyorican cafepr.com; 312 San Francisco, Old San Juan; cover $5; ☺8pm-late) If you came to Puerto Rico in search of sizzling salsa music, you'll find it at the Nuyorican Café. San Juan's hottest nightspot – stuffed into an alley off Fortaleza, opposite a nameless drinking hole – is a congenial hub of live

Latino sounds and hip-gyrating locals. Six-piece salsa bands usually get hopping around 11pm.

La Respuesta　　LIVE MUSIC, PERFORMING ARTS
(Map p66; 1600 Av Fernández Juncos, Santurce; ☺hours vary) This art hub is known for hosting a wide range of live music shows (from R&B to heavy metal), alternative films and poetry readings. It also has occasional exhibits from up-and-coming artists. Check the Facebook page to see what's on.

El Centro de Bellas
Artes Luis A Ferré　　　　THEATER
(Bellas Artes; Map p66; ☑787-724-4747; www.cba. gobierno.pr; 22½ Av Ponce de León, Santurce; ☺box office 10am-6pm Mon-Sat, to 4pm Sun; ☑T3, T5) Built in 1981, this center has more than 1900 seats in the festival hall, about 750 in the drama hall and 200 in the experimental theater. The Puerto Rican Symphony Orchestra holds its weekly winter performances at the complex's newer 1300-seat Pablo Casals Symphony Hall. International stars perform here and it's the major host of the annual Festival Casals (p74).

Teatro Tapia　　　　THEATER
(Map p56; ☑787-480-5000, 787-721-0180; Plaza de Colón, Fortaleza, Old San Juan; tickets $10-30; ☺box office 9am-6pm Mon-Fri, to 5pm Sat & Sun) A city landmark, the Teatro Tapia on the southern side of Plaza Colón is an intimate neoclassical theater designed in the Italian style with three-tiered boxes and an elegantly decorated lobby. Dating from 1832, the building has long been a nexus of the island's rich cultural life; it hosts big names in opera, stage and ballet from around the world.

Amigos del Corralón　　　　THEATER
(Map p56; ☑787-529-3668; San José 109, Old San Juan; ticket prices vary; ☺hours vary) This great venue is housed in a grand three-story building dating to the 18th century. Theater, dance and music can be enjoyed on a rotating schedule and there are frequent art exhibits in the gallery spaces. It's worth entering, at least for a peek, to look at the colonial-era floor tiles and the courtyard performance space.

Cinemas
Movie theaters can be found in Santurce and in most of San Juan's major shopping centers. Check www.caribbeancinemas.com for most theaters and showtimes island-wide. Movie buffs should check out the city's annual

DENNISVDW/GETTY IMAGES ©

1. Architecture, Old San Juan
There are 400-plus historically listed buildings in Old San Juan.

2. Old San Juan
Historic Old San Juan is home to a wealth of Unesco treasures.

3. San Juan
In addition to its collection of well-polished, colonial-era artifacts, San Juan is a mosaic of colorful, ever-evolving neighborhoods.

4. Dos Hermanos Bridge
Dos Hermanos Bridge divides Laguna del Condado from the Atlantic Ocean.

DENNIS VAN DE WATER/SHUTTERSTOCK ©

DON'T MISS

WINTER BASEBALL

From November through January, winter baseball is one of Puerto Rico's favorite pastimes. Top teams play during the winter, when major league action in the US is dormant, and many famous players got their starts playing here. However, the tight economics of the local baseball league mean that wages are small and post-game victory banquets are lean. Players are there for the love of the game or in the hopes of being spotted by a scout.

Going to a game is a great way to meet locals – and it's priced for the masses. Seats range from $5 to $18 (kids get in half-price) and large stadiums mean you don't normally need to buy tickets in advance. Vendors wander the stands selling cold beer and mixed drinks (think watery piña coladas) for $3; Puerto Rican snacks and traditional ballpark fare also are available.

Teams have fervent support from loyal fans and games can be raucous. In San Juan, two teams worth watching are the **Cangrejeros de Santurce** (Santurce Crabbers) and **Gigantes de Carolina** (Carolina Giants). Learn more about the teams and the schedules of winter league baseball at www.mlb.com/mlb/events/winterleagues.

international cinema festival (p74) as well as the popular Puerto Rico Queer Filmfest (p74).

Fine Arts Miramar   CINEMA
(Map p66; ☑ 787-721-4288; www.caribbeancine
mas.com; 654 Av Ponce de León, Miramar; adult/
child $7.75/5.75; ☐ T3, T5) This art-house cin-
ema was once a sanctuary for adult-only
movies. These days it shows independent
films from around the world, as well as
Hollywood blockbusters.

Metro Cinemas   CINEMA
(Map p66; ☑ 787-722-0465; www.caribbeancine-
mas.com; 1255 Av Ponce de León, Santurce; adult/
child $6.25/4.25; ☐ T3, T5) This classic restored
cinema is in Santurce, edging towards Miramar. It shows a mix of popular and arty
films.

Casinos

San Juan has a reputation for being a Las-
Vegas-on-the-sea, a mantle it stole from
Havana when Castro threw the mob and
their gambling syndicates out of Cuba in
1959. As a result, many travelers and islanders come to town purely for the action. All of San Juan's large resort hotels
have casinos; the most popular are El San
Juan Hotel (p78), the San Juan Marriott
Resort & Stellaris Casino (p85) and La
Concha (p76).

Most offer Caribbean Stud Poker, Let It
Ride, Pai Gow Poker and the Big Six Wheel,
as well as the standard blackjack, roulette,
craps, baccarat and minibaccarat. Casinos
typically open between noon and 4pm, and
8pm and 4am. Some are 24-hour, such as the
Marriott, La Concha and the Ritz-Carlton.

Sports

Baseball is hugely popular in Puerto Rico;
watching a game in San Juan is great fun
and a good way to get a taste of the local
culture.

Hiram Bithorn Stadium   STADIUM
(Map p52; ☑ 787-725-2110; cnr Av Franklin D Roosevelt & Nemesio Canales, Hato Rey) This baseball stadium seating 18,000 is home to the
Cangrejeros de Santurce. It's named after
the first Puerto Rican to play in the Major
Leagues (Chicago Cubs, 1942). Concerts are
held here too.

Roberto Clemente Coliseum   STADIUM
(Map p52; ☑ 787-294-1037; Av Franklin D Roosevelt,
Hato Rey) Roberto Clemente Coliseum is
named after the baseball hall of famer who
died tragically in a plane crash in 1972. This
indoor arena is used mostly as a sports and
concert facility.

🔒 Shopping

Popular Puerto Rican souvenirs include
santos crafts, domino sets, *vejigante* masks,
cigars, rum and coffee. The best arts and
crafts shopping is in Old San Juan, though
most of the schlocky T-shirt shops are there
too. San Francisco and Fortaleza are packed
cheek-by-jowl with shops while Calle del
Cristo is home to many of the old city's more
chic establishments.

For designer clothes and high-end jewelry,
make a beeline for Condado. The shops facing
Parque la Ventana al Mar are especially luxe –
you'll have no problem dropping your casino
winnings here.

If haggling is more your style, make time for the bustling Mercado de Río Piedras (p69), where you'll find everything from plantains to pantyhose.

★ Puerto Rican Art & Crafts   ARTS & CRAFTS

(Map p56; ☑ 787 725 5596; www.puertorican art-crafts.com; 204 Fortaleza, Old San Juan; ☺10am-6pm Mon-Sat, noon-5pm Sun; 🚋 City Hall) A large shop specializing in Puerto Rican folk art, paintings and jewelry. Items come from artist workshops found throughout the island. The prices are on the high end, but so is the quality.

★ Santurce POP   SHOPPING CENTER

(Map p66; www.santurcepop.com; 1116 Av Ponce de León, Santurce; ☺10am-6pm Tue-Sat; 🚋T3, T5) In the heart of Santurce, this boho design mart has several booths of handcrafted and locally sourced goods. You'll find everything from hipster T-shirts and unique jewelry to fine leather goods and smoking accessories. Oftentimes the designers themselves are on hand to answer questions. The vegetarian and vegan eatery here is a perfect fit.

★ Olé   CLOTHING

(Map p56; ☑787-724-2445; www.olepuertorico. com; 105 Fortaleza, Old San Juan; ☺10am-6:30pm Mon-Sat; 🚋City Hall) Although it's beloved by tourists, this old-school hat shop is no tourist trap. As he has for generations, Guillermo Cristian Jeffs will custom-fit you for a truly authentic handwoven Panama hat (from $60) – not some machine-made knockoff.

Artisans Fair   MARKET

(Map p56; Paseo de la Princesa, Old San Juan; ☺noon-8pm Fri-Sun) On weekends, head to Paseo de la Princesa for Puerto Rican folk art – ceramics, leather goods, jewelry – peppered with tourist schlock. When there's a cruise ship in port, the fair extends east to Plaza de la Dársena.

Galeria Botello   ART

(Map p56; ☑787-723-9987; www.botello.com; 208 Calle Cristo, Old San Juan; ☺10am-6pm Mon-Sat) This labyrinthine gallery showcases the work of Ángel Botello, considered one of Latin America's greatest post-modern artists. Works by other international superstars – including the likes of Salvador Dalí – are also sold. An easy place to drop that extra $10k in your pocket.

Butterfly People   ARTS & CRAFTS

(Map p56; ☑787-723-2432; www.butterflypeople. com; 257 Cruz, Old San Juan; ☺11am-6pm Mon-Thu, noon-5pm Sat & Sun; trolley City Hall) Specializing in butterfly art – as in real butterflies – this shop sells artful displays and jewelry made from these winged creatures. Though not for everyone, the items definitely make a striking, if somewhat morbid, impression. Custom orders can be arranged.

Librería Instituto de Cultura
Puertorriqueña   BOOKS

(Librería ICP; Map p56; ☑787-721-5105; https:// tienda.icp.gobierno.pr; cnr Calle del Cristo & Beneficiencia, Old San Juan; ☺10am-5pm; 🚋El Morro, Fort) This well-stocked bookstore carries a good range of *Boricua*-focused books, all published by the Institute of Puerto Rican Culture. You'll find everything from history and poetry to novels and children's fiction. The shop also has a small section of high-end religious art, locally made jewelry and posters.

Pure Soul   FASHION & ACCESSORIES

(Map p56; ☑787-723-2800; www.puresoulbou tique.com; 258 Tetuán, Old San Juan; ☺10am-6pm; 🚋City Hall, Fort) This corner boutique oozes tropical chic with flowing dresses, linen wear and an assortment of handcrafted shoes and purses. Many of the items are made by local designers, though some of the textiles come from as far away as Oaxaca and the Guatemalan highlands. A small but impressive jewelry case is worth a peek.

Cigarros Antillas   CIGARS

(Map p56; ☑787-725-5481; Juan A Corretjer, Old San Juan; ☺9am-5pm; trolley City Hall, Fort) Cigar fans should stop by the open storefront of Cigarros Antillas to see workers roll by hand. The shop specializes in medium cigars, sold in a variety of styles. Find it near Old San Juan's bus terminal.

Plaza Las Américas   MALL

(Map p52; www.plazalasamericas.com; 525 Av Roosevelt, Hato Rey; ☺9am-9pm Mon-Sat, 11am-7pm Sun; Ⓜ Hato Rey) This massive mall is the Caribbean's largest with over 300 stores, 40 eateries and 13 movie screens. Located near the Hato Rey metro station.

ⓘ Information

DANGERS & ANNOYANCES

Safety-wise, San Juan is comparable with any big city in mainland US. Though you'll hear stories of muggings and thefts, the worst most visitors will face is tripping up over an uneven sidewalk. Take all the usual precautions and you'll minimize any risk of trouble.

Never leave your belongings unguarded on the beach, don't leave your car unlocked and don't wander around after dark in deserted inner-city areas or on unpoliced beaches. Also hold off from wearing flashy jewelry or watches. Areas to avoid at night include Puerta de Tierra, parts of Santurce (especially around Calle Loíza) and the Plaza del Mercado in Río Piedras.

Old San Juan is relatively safe and well policed. However, the enclave of La Perla just outside the north wall is known for its drug-related crimes and can be unsafe at any time.

EMERGENCY

In any kind of emergency, call ☑911.

INTERNET ACCESS

Almost all lodgings have wi-fi, though many in common areas only. A number of plazas in Old San Juan have free hot spots.

MEDICAL SERVICES

San Juan has a well-regarded hospital and drugstore chains like Walgreen's are ubiquitous. **Ashford Presbyterian Community Hospital** (☑787-721-2160; www.presbypr.com; 1451 Av Ashford, Condado; ⊘24hr; ☐T21) El Presby is the best-equipped and most convenient hospital for most travelers.

MONEY

ATMs are found everywhere, most associated with full-service banks.

Banco Popular (www.popular.com; 206 Tetuán, Old San Juan; ⊘8am-4pm Mon-Fri) is the most, well, popular bank in town. Full-service locations and ATMs are found in most neighborhoods, including Condado, Santurce, Ocean Park and Isla Verde.

POST

Old San Juan Post Office (Map p56; ☑787-724-2098; www.usps.com; 100 Paseo de Colón, Old San Juan; ⊘8am-4pm Mon-Fri, to noon Sat; ☐city hall) Most convenient branch for travelers.

TOURIST INFORMATION

Puerto Rico Tourism Company (PRTC; ☑800-223-6530, 787-721-2400; www.seepuertorico.com; ⊘9am-5pm Mon-Fri, 10am-1pm Sat & Sun) distributes information in English and Spanish at two venues in San Juan: the **Luis Muñoz Marín International Airport** (PRTC; Map p52; ☑787-791-1014, 800-866-7827; www.seepuertorico.com; Terminal C, LMM airport; ⊘9am-8pm) and near the cruise-ship terminal

in **Old San Juan** (PRTC; Map p56; ☑800-866-7827, 787-722-1709; www.seepuertorico.com; Edificio Ochoa, 500 Tanca, Old San Juan; ⊘8am-4pm Mon-Fri, 9am-5pm Sat; ☐City Hall, Fort, El Morro).

❶ Getting There & Away

AIR

International flights arrive at and depart from San Juan's busy **Luis Muñoz Marín International Airport** (SJU, LMM Airport; Map p52; ☑787-253-2329; www.aeropuertosju.com; off Hwy 26, Isla Verde; ⊘24hr), which is about 8 miles east of Old San Juan. Daily direct flights arrive from Miami, Atlanta, Dallas, New York City and the US Virgin Islands. Within the Commonwealth, flights from San Juan include Ponce, Aguadilla and Mayagüez. Several airlines serve Luis Muñoz including United, Delta, JetBlue and **Seaborne Airlines** (☑866-359-8784, 787-946-7800; www.seaborneairlines.com; Luis Muñoz Marín International Airport).

Private aircraft, charter services and many of the commuter flights serving the islands of Culebra and Vieques arrive at and depart from San Juan's smaller **Isla Grande Airport** (SIG, Fernando Luis Ribas Dominicci Airport; Map p52; ☑787/729-8790; www.prpa.gobierno.pr; Calle Lindbergh, Isla Grande, Miramar), on the Bahía de San Juan in the city's Miramar district. Airlines include Vieques Air Link, Air Flamenco and Cape Air.

CRUISE SHIP

Almost 20 cruise lines call on San Juan, with many cruisers starting and ending their voyages here. It's the second-largest port for cruise ships in the western hemisphere, serving nearly two million passengers each year. Most ships dock at the piers along Calle La Marina near the Customs House, just a short walk from the cobblestoned streets of Old San Juan; others dock at the Pan American Pier on nearby Isla Grande. Popular cruise lines serving San Juan include Royal Caribbean and Viking Ocean Cruises.

PÚBLICO

While there's no island-wide bus system, *públicos* (public vans) offer an alternative option, providing an inexpensive though often time-consuming link between San Juan and other major towns like Fajardo, Ponce or Mayagüez.

In San Juan, *público* centers include LMM international airport and the **Terminal de Carros Públicos** (Terminal de Carros Públicos de Río Piedras; Map p52; ☑787-294-2412; cnr Arzuaga & Vallejo, Río Piedras) in Río Piedras. Vans leave once they're full and make frequent stops, dropping off and picking up passengers along the way. Service runs Monday through Saturday. Cash only.

ⓘ Getting Around

TO/FROM THE AIRPORT

Luis Muñoz Marín International Airport
Fixed-price taxis cost per carload (with up to five passengers) $10 to Isla Verde, $15 to Condado and Ocean Park, and $19 to Old San Juan. Add $1 for each piece of luggage, and $1 between 10pm to 6am. Taxis line up outside of baggage claim areas, where taxi touts hustle passengers into cabs in a remarkably efficient way. Rates are visibly posted. If you find others going your way, consider splitting the cost – just agree on a final destination (ie only one stop per cab).

The **bus** is the cheapest option into town at $0.75 a ride. Look for the 'Parada' sign outside the arrivals concourse. The D53 and T5 buses serve Old San Juan. The prior via Isla Verde, Ocean Park and Condado; the latter via Isla Verde and Santurce.

BICYCLE

With its unpredictable road conditions and drivers, San Juan can be a tough place to cycle. However, cyclists can navigate a pleasant and safe cross-city route by following the shoreline from Old San Juan through Condado and Isla Verde as far as Piñones (the last part is on a designated bike lane).

San Juan Bike Rentals (🖉 787-554-2453; www.sanjuanbikerental.com; rentals per day $30; ⊘7am-6pm Mon-Fri, 9am-4pm Sat) Rents a variety of well-maintained bikes, including mountain, road, hybrid and cruisers. All come with helmet, lock and bar bag. Free delivery and pick-up in metro San Juan.

BUS

AMA Metrobus (Autoridad Metropolitana de Autobuses, Metropolitan Bus Authority; 🖉 787-294-0500; http://ati.pr; fare $0.75, coins only; ⊘ most routes 5am-8pm Mon-Sat) operates San Juan's public buses. The buses are clean and air-conditioned, but the system itself is not easy for visitors. Route maps and information are hard to find and few bus stops have any indication of what buses stop there. Service can also be erratic, with wait times between 30 and 60 minutes. Your best bet is to ask around, especially at bus stops, where veteran riders will offer advice.

The routes taken most often by visitors (bus numbers are followed by associated route descriptions) include:

T3 Old San Juan, Puerta de Tierra, Av Ponce de León (Miramar/Santurce), Sagrado Corazón (Tren Urbano station)

T5 Old San Juan, Puerta de Tierra, Av Ponce de León (Miramar/Santurce), Isla Verde (via Loíza), Luis Muñoz Marín International Airport

T9 Old San Juan, Puerta de Tierra, Convention Center, Av Fernández Juncos (Miramar/Santurce), Sagrado Corazón (Tren Urbano station), Río Piedras

T21 Old San Juan, Puerta de Tierra, Av Ashford (Condado), Av Ponce de León (Santurce), Sagrado Corazón (Tren Urbano station)

C35 Convention Center, Av Ponce de León (Miramar/Santurce), Sagrado Corazón (Tren Urbano station), Av Fernández Juncos (Miramar/Santurce)

D45 Sagrado Corazón (Tren Urbano station), Isla Verde, Piñones, Loíza

D53 Old San Juan, Puerta de Tierra, Condado, Ocean Park (via McLeary), Isla Verde, Luis Muñoz Marín International Airport

CAR

Try to avoid driving in the city. Roads can be in poor condition, while haphazard local driving habits may jangle your nerves or crinkle your fender.

Parking in Old San Juan is scarce. Look for the large parking garages along Recinto Sur; rates are modest (from $1.25 per hour). Parking in the rest of metro San Juan – either on-street or in garages – is easy to find.

All major car-rental firms have offices at LMM International Airport and most also have offices in resort and tourist areas.

FERRY

AcuaExpreso (Cataño Ferry; Map p56; 🖉 787-494-0934; Pier 2, Calle La Marina, Old San Juan; per trip $0.50; ⊘ 6am-7pm Mon-Fri, 8am-8pm Sat & Sun) ferries connect the northern and southern sides of Bahía de San Juan via Old San Juan and Cataño. Boats run every 15 to 30 minutes. The trip across the bay is typically calm and pretty, lasting less than 10 minutes. In Old San Juan, the ferry dock is at Pier 2, near the tourism office.

METRO

Tren Urbano (p93) connects Bayamón with downtown San Juan as far as Sagrado Corazón on the southern side of Santurce. Modern trains run every eight to 16 minutes, serving 16 stations. The line, which mixes elevated and underground tracks, is useful for visitors traveling to destinations such as the Mercado de Río Piedras, UPR's Botanical Garden and the **Museo de Oller** (p92).

TAXI

Taxi fares are set in the main tourism zones. From Old San Juan, trips to Condado, Ocean Park or Isla Grande Airport cost $12, and $19 to Isla Verde and Luis Muñoz Marín International Airport. Journeys within Old San Juan cost $7. You'll also pay a $2 gas surcharge per trip plus $1 for each piece of luggage; add a $1 surcharge between 10pm and

6am. There's also a $1 reservation charge. And if there's more than five passengers, $2 per person is added.

Outside of the major tourist areas, cab drivers are supposed to use meters, but that rarely happens. Insist on it, or establish a price from the start.

Taxis line up at the eastern end of Calle Fortaleza in Old San Juan; in other places you will likely need to call one. Try **Metro Taxi** (☑787-725-2870; ☺24hr) or **Rochdale Radio Taxi** (☑787-721-1900; www.taxiprrochdale.com; ☺24hr).

A growing alternative is to use drive-share services like Uber (www.uber.com), a private car service offered by freelance drivers. Fares are cheaper than taxis and the service reliable; all fares are paid by credit card, using an app. In San Juan, the only places these drivers can't pick up passengers are the airports and hotels. They can drop off anywhere.

TROLLEY

A useful, if painfully slow, free **trolley service** (☺Fort (Green) line 9am-6pm daily, El Morro (Blue) & City Hall (Red) lines 7am-7pm Mon-Fri, 9am-7pm Sat & Sun) links more than two dozen sights in Old San Juan. The three routes are served by buses styled like open-air trolleys, allowing you to hop on and off at the 26 stops. All routes pass by Pier 4 of the cruise-ship terminal along Calle La Marina.

AROUND SAN JUAN

Cataño & Bayamón

POP 199,000

Not too far from downtown San Juan, both these suburbs make for worthwhile day trips. Bayamón, the furthest, is all about museums. Its town center is a charming collection of colonial-era buildings mixed with modern-day structures; it has two great art museums as well as tours of emerging artists' studios. A five-minute drive away, Parque de las Ciencias – a hands-on museum and exhibition complex – is a hit with families.

The neighboring municipality of Cataño is heavily industrialized and is home to the Bacardí Rum Factory. Overlooking San Juan Bay, the factory has an extensive verdant campus and daily tours. Nearby Isla de Cabras offers a windswept escape from the city with rocky beaches, footpaths and enviable views of Old San Juan.

⊙ Sights

★Espacio Emergente   MUSEUM

(Map p52; ☑787-785-6010; 18 Manuel Rossi, Bayamón; ☺8:30am-4pm Mon-Sat; Ⓜ Bayamón) **FREE** This modern museum features thought-provoking work from emerging artists in Puerto Rico and beyond. Mediums include, among others, painting, sculpture and installation art. Espacio Emergente also hosts several artists in residence; free tours of their studios including meet-and-greets with the artists themselves are offered twice a month. Call for the schedule and to reserve a spot.

Museo de Oller   MUSEUM

(Map p52; ☑787-785-6010; Plaza de Bayamón, 13 Degetau, Bayamón; ☺8:30am-4pm Tue-Sat; Ⓜ Bayamón) **FREE** Located in the former city hall on the plaza of Bayamón's charming historic district, this art museum pays tribute to native son Francisco Oller (1833–1917), one of Latin America's most celebrated Impressionists. Many of Oller's great works are displayed elsewhere, but the restored neoclassical building is worth a peek and the collection includes good Oller portraits, as well as paintings and sculptures by other well-respected Puerto Rican artists. The museum also has temporary exhibits, which change every few months.

Parque de las Ciencias Luis A Ferré   MUSEUM, AMUSEMENT PARK

(Sciences Park; Map p52; ☑787-799-1898; www.parquedelasciencias.org; Av Comerio, Bayamón; adult/child $10/8; ☺9am-5pm Mon-Fri, 10am-6pm Sat & Sun; ⊞) A veritable smorgasbord of family-friendly museums and exhibits plus a minizoo are housed in the expansive Parque de las Ciencias. Kids learn about aerospace and archeology, transportation and communication, plant life and the world's oceans. There's a planetarium and an art museum featuring work by some of Puerto Rico's best-known artists.

Isla de Cabras   ISLAND

(Map p52; ☑787-788-0440; Hwy 870, Cataño; parking $4; ☺8:30am-5:30pm Wed-Sun; Ⓟ ⊞) **FREE** Isla de Cabras is a pleasant seaside park, popular with local families and perfect for travelers craving off-the-beaten-track experiences. It has grassy areas, tall palm trees, picnic areas, a rocky seashore and waves. You can fish, but offshore currents are too dangerous for swimming. The views of El Morro (p54) across the channel are spectacular. On the island's southern end, the ruins of **Fuerte del Cañuelo** date from 1610. The fort once worked in tandem with El Morro to protect Bahía de San Juan.

Casa Bacardí Rum Factory   DISTILLERY, MUSEUM
(Map p52;   ✆787-788-8400;   www.visitcasa
bacardi.com; Km 6.2, Hwy 165, Cataño; tours $15-45; ☺tours 9am-4:30pm Mon-Sat, 10am-4:30pm Sun; Ⓟ) Called the 'Cathedral of Rum' because of its six-story distillation tower, the Bacardí Rum Factory sits on 127 acres near the mouth of the Bahía de San Juan, across from Old San Juan. The world's largest, most famous rum-producing family started their business in Cuba more than a century ago and began moving their operation here in 1936. Today the distiller produces some 100,000 gallons of rum per day and ships 21 million cases per year worldwide.

Three signature tours (every 30 minutes, lasting about one hour) are offered throughout the day.

❶ Getting There & Away

Take the **AcuaExpreso ferry** (p91) from Old San Juan to Cataño and enjoy a quick harbor tour along the way. Taxis typically line up at the dock, to take you wherever you're headed.

The **Tren Urbano** (Urban Train; ✆787-294-0500; http://ati.pr; fare $1.50; ☺5:30am-11:30pm) also links San Juan to Bayamón. From Old San Juan or Condado, catch bus T21 to the Sagrado Corazón station in Santurce, which is the first stop on the metro line.

Piñones

Head east from modern San Juan and you'll find pleasantly windswept Piñones, a series of natural beaches, forest walks in Bosque Estatal de Piñones, and lively seaside hangouts. Do as weekending *sanjuaneros* do and saunter Piñones' sandy curves backed by pine groves, swim in the reef-protected waters, nosh on seafood snacks and down *coco frío* (ice-cold coconut milk) at music-filled roadside stands.

Follow Rte 187 out of San Juan as it parallels the ocean and you'll know you're heading in the right direction at Punta Cangrejos, a small bridge marked by a sign saying *'Bienvenidos a Boca de Cangrejos'* (Welcome to Crabmouth Point).

After the sign, you can veer off to the left to the top of the cliff overlooking the ocean; this is a popular drinking spot with fabulous views, especially at sunset. This also kicks off the run of restaurants and *friquitines* (also known as *buréns* in Piñones) – the food kiosks of all sizes that line the coastal road.

History

In the 16th century most of this fertile low-lying coastal region east of San Juan was farmed by local people. When the Spanish took over in 1719, they converted the land into huge sugarcane plantations. Captured natives were forced to provide labor, although they resisted mightily. Unable to prevent farmhands from disappearing into nearby mountains, plantation owners began shipping in slaves from West Africa and sometimes stealing them from other Caribbean islands. Most of the 30,000 residents living in the area today are descendants of these Yoruba slaves and remain proud of their Afro-Caribbean heritage.

◎ Sights & Activities

Paseo de Piñones, a 5-mile long, first-rate nature trail and bike path, runs along the beach and through the forest reserve (Bosque Estatal de Piñones).

To see a patch of the rarely viewed coastal wilderness, rent a kayak and explore the Laguna la Torrecilla (p70), with its fish, birds and occasional manatees.

If it's a good surfing day at Piñones, you'll spot rows of cars with board racks parked by the good breaks. Or check ahead with one of the San Juan surf shops before you go.

**Centro Cultural
Ecoturístico de Piñones**   CULTURAL CENTRE
(Map p52; Km 4.2, Hwy 187, Boca de Cangrejos, Piñones-Loíza; ☺9am-5pm) This center hosts a number of cultural activities, many promoting Afro-Caribbean music and dance. It also houses the Corporación Piñones Se Integra, a nonprofit offering alternative self-guided kayak tours of nearby mangroves. Look for the yellow building with *bomba* dancers painted on the front.

Corporación Piñones Se Integra   KAYAKING
(COPI; Map p52; ✆787-253-9707; www.copipr. com; Km 4.2, Hwy 187, Boca de Cangrejos, Piñones-Loíza; kayaking per 80min $15; ☺9am-5pm) This community-based nonprofit is focused on improving living conditions in Puerto Rico's poorer *barrios,* particularly Loíza. Headquartered at the Centro Cultural Ecoturístico de Piñones, it also works to protect San Juan's environment, including the adjacent

WORTH A TRIP

FUN FOR THE KIDS

Kids go to town at the **Museo del Niño de Carolina** (Map p52; ☎787-257-0261; www.museodelninocarolina.com; Av Campo Rico, Carolina; adult/child $10/6, mini-zoo extra $2/1, go-karts $5; ☺9am-5pm Wed-Fri, 10am-6pm Sat & Sun; ⓟ♿), a hands-on museum in the suburb of Carolina. Inside, interactive and fun displays get kids thinking about things like volcanoes, electricity and music. Dress-up areas, a minicity and construction sites let them play at being grown up. Outside, an MD-82 American Airlines plane is perfect for exploring. A small petting zoo and go-karts also are big hits. Worth the short trip to the 'burbs, especially on a rainy day.

Laguna Torrecilla, where it offers self-guided kayak tours.

🏖 Beaches

Piñones' wild beaches contrast sharply with the well-raked expanses of Isla Verde not 2 miles to the west. Beaches run almost continuously along Rte 187, though the most picturesque, deserted ones start at around Km 9.

For swimming, avoid the coral reefs at the western end of the strand of beaches, near where the bus from San Juan stops. This is also where many of the food stands are. Instead, walk further east along the pleasant hiking and biking path.

🍴 Eating

The ocean vistas and open-air seating make the food kiosks terrific places to kick back with a *coco frío* or beer. At dusk, your mouth will water from the smoky smells of roadside barbecue stands.

Piñones has countless restaurants, bars and beach shacks, and places come and go. See where your senses carry you.

La Comay PUERTO RICAN **$**
(Km 8, Hwy 187; mains $8-15; ☺11am-8pm Sat & Sun) Luz cooks up all manner of fried Puerto Rican goodies (such as crab *alcapurrias* and regular *alcapurrias)* on weekends. Look for the kiosk on the inland side of Rte 187, almost to the town of Loíza. Cash only.

★**El Nuevo Acuario** PUERTO RICAN **$$**
(Map p52; ☎787-662-8258; Km 4.4, Hwy 187; mains $11-28; ☺noon-12:30am Fri-Sun, to 11pm Mon & Thu; 🚌D45) Sitting in a crowd of beachfront eateries, there's nothing about El Nuevo Acuario that stands out. Open air: tick. Plastic tables and chairs: tick. A view of the ocean: tick. The food, however, is in a class of its own. Creative takes on Puerto Rican seafood, refined flavors, gourmet presentation and service that makes you feel like a regular.

Mi Casita Seafood SEAFOOD, PUERTO RICAN **$$**
(Map p52; ☎787-791-1481; Km 4, Hwy 187; meals $10-28; 🚌D45) Mi Casita serves up bellywarming comfort food, Puerto Rican style: whole fried red snapper, *churrasco con tostones* (skirt steak with fried plantains), fried pork with *mofongo* (fried and mashed plantain) etc. Like at the neighboring restaurants, diners sit on an outdoor patio. Service can be slow and the silverware is plastic – small prices to pay for a great meal.

❶ Getting There & Away

The D45 bus stops on Av Los Gobernadores near the traffic circle at Av Isla Verde in the Isla Verde neighborhood (connect with T5 or D53 for the rest of San Juan) and travels past the western end of the Piñones beaches to the town of Loíza. You can also cycle between San Juan and Piñones on a dedicated bike path.

Loíza

POP 28,000

After Piñones, Rte 187 breaks out of the forest and crosses a bridge spanning the island's largest river, the Río Grande de Loíza, bringing you to the town of Loíza. Beyond the administrative center (called Loíza Aldea), the municipality is largely rural, technically including Piñones along with five other wards.

A Taíno village when the conquistadores arrived, the area was named after Loaíza, the female *cacique* (chief) who ruled over it. As the Taínos were decimated by hard labor, brutality and disease, slaves from West Africa were brought to replace them in the sugarcane fields. As time passed, emancipated slaves were relocated here to help defend against intruders and, eventually, the area became a haven for escaped slaves. By 1719, the village had grown large enough to be declared an official town. Today Loíza has one of the highest concentrations of Afro-Puerto Ricans on the island, descendants of the Africans brought to these shores long ago. The town is known for its cultural richness and African influences in its food, music, dance and art.

◎ Sights

**Iglesia del Espíritu Santo y
San Patricio**   CHURCH
(Church of the Holy Ghost & St Patrick; ☑ 787-876-2229; Plaza de Loíza, Calle Espíritu Santo, Barrio Loíza Aldea; ☺ 8am-4pm Mon-Fri) At the northern end of Plaza de Loíza, the neoclassic Iglesia del Espíritu Santo y San Patricio stands proudly above the surrounding modest modern buildings. It dates from 1645 and takes its name from the patron saint of Ireland to honor Puerto Rico's famous Irish mercenaries, who designed many of Old San Juan's fortifications. It is one of the oldest Catholic churches on the island.

✪ Festivals & Events

★ Fiestas de Santiago Apóstol   CULTURAL
(Saint James Festival; ☺ Jul) Puerto Rico's African soul is unveiled for five days every July during the Fiestas de Santiago Apóstol, a cultural extravaganza of drums, masks and hybrid religious iconography in honor of Saint James, the town's patron saint. Street food, arts and crafts booths and dance performances are woven throughout the celebration.

Starting on July 25, the festival is marked by three religious processions for Saint James: *Santiago de los Hombres* (Saint James of the Men), *Santiago de las Mujeres* (Saint James of the Women) and *Santiago de los Niños* (Saint James of the Children). On three consecutive days, statues representing these different versions of Saint James are carried through town to the historic Iglesia del Espíritu Santo y San Patricio, on the central plaza in Barrio Loíza Aldea. During the processions, locals dress in bright costumes and coconut masks representing different characters from Saint James' times: *caballeros* (knights), *vejigantes* (demons or Moors), *locas* (crazed women) and *viejos* (old men).

🛍 Shopping

Handmade *vejigantes* (Puerto Rican masks) carved by local artisans are widely available in Loíza and are generally of higher quality and less expensive than those sold in San Juan. Wander the town center and you'll see plenty of colorful creations.

★ Artesanías Castor Ayala   ARTS & CRAFTS
(☑ 787-564-6403; arioayala01@yahoo.com; Km 6.6, Hwy 187, Barrio Medianía Alta; ☺ 10am-6pm) This family-run shop sells some of the best *vejigantes* (Puerto Rican masks) on the island. The patriarch, Castor Ayala, began making and selling the coconut masks in the 1950s. He taught his craft to his children, one of whom – Raul Ayala – continued the business. The shop still runs out of the original yellow clapboard building, complete with tropical murals.

★ Estudio de Arte Samuel Lind   ART
(☑ 787-876-1494; http://samuel-lind.artistweb sites.com; off Km 6.6, Hwy 187, Barrio Medianía Alta; ☺ 9am-5pm Wed-Sun, or by appointment) This studio showcases the spectacular artwork of Samuel Lind, a master artist whose work is inspired by the culture and natural beauty of Loíza. Lind walks visitors through the two-story studio, explaining the history and ideas behind different paintings, sculptures and serigraphs. His work can also be enjoyed in the Caguas Botanical Garden as well as businesses around the island.

It's best to call ahead if you plan to stop by, to be sure the studio is open.

❶ Getting There & Away

The D45 bus picks up passengers on Av Los Gobernadores near the traffic circle at Av Isla Verde in the Isla Verde neighborhood. From there, the bus travels east past the Piñones beaches to the central plaza in Loíza Aldea. Bussing it is recommended during the **Fiestas de Santiago Apóstol**, when traffic and parking can be terrible.

Públicos (public vans) run between Río Piedras in San Juan and Loíza's central plaza. On the return, *públicos* leave Loíza from a terminal three blocks south of the plaza. The schedule is erratic – prepare to wait if taking this option.

El Yunque & East Coast

Includes ➡

El Yunque 98
Luquillo & Around 105
Fajardo & Around 107
Naguabo & Around 111
Yabucoa & Around 114

Best Places to Eat

➡ Luquillo Beach Kiosks (p106)

➡ Pasta y Pueblo (p107)

➡ Mi Vida Café & Burger (p104)

➡ La Estación (p111)

➡ Bistro del Mar (p110)

➡ Kiosko El Limón (p113)

Best Places to Sleep

➡ Casa Flamboyant (p104)

➡ El Hotelito (p103)

➡ Barefoot Travelers Rooms (p113)

➡ Caribe Playa Beach Resort (p114)

Why Go?

The east coast is Puerto Rico shrink-wrapped; a tantalizing taste of almost everything the island has to offer squeezed into an area you can drive across in a couple of hours. Sodden rainforest teems with noisy wildlife and jungle waterfalls at El Yunque National Forest, the Commonwealth's tropical gem. Down at sea level, beach lovers bask on the icing-sugar sand of Playa Luquillo.

Unvarnished Fajardo is the island's uncrowned water-sports capital, where adventurers kayak, dive, snorkel and fish, and yachters park their sailboats. Golfers and those craving a one-stop holiday will find delight in the highest concentration of large, upscale resorts outside San Juan.

Cutting through the region like a thin, green ribbon is the Northeast Ecological Corridor, a slender tract of undeveloped and endangered pristine land featuring one of Puerto Rico's stunning bioluminescent bays at Las Cabezas de San Juan Reserva Natural.

When to Go

Along the coast your best timing depends on your priorities: peak winter season (December to February), summer and weekends see the most places open (especially locally beloved food kiosks). But other times you'll enjoy a solitude that grows with your distance from San Juan.

Note that hurricane season – June through late November – can bring sodden conditions to El Yunque, with the possibility of trails being closed due to mudslides and flooding.

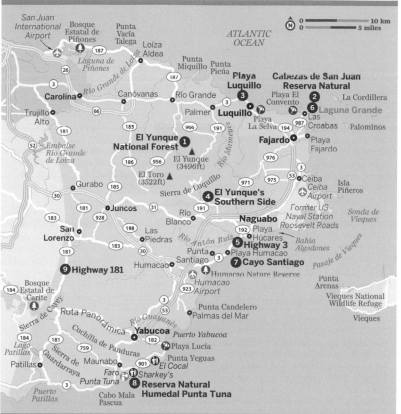

EL YUNQUE & EAST COAST

El Yunque & East Coast Highlights

❶ El Yunque National Forest (p98) Hiking on lush rainforest trails with views of the ocean beyond.

❷ Cabezas de San Juan Reserva Natural (p107) Exploring seven ecosystems with expert guides and naturalists.

❸ Playa Luquillo (p105) Surfing the local break and swimming at one of the island's best beaches.

❹ El Yunque's Southern Side (p102) Swimming in hidden waterfall pools and admiring petroglyphs on El Yunque's quiet southern side.

❺ Highway 3 (p112) Enjoying the low-key beaches, villages and great eats on this two-lane road south of Playa Húcares.

❻ Laguna Grande (p110) Taking in the glow of Fajardo's glowing bioluminescent bay.

❼ Cayo Santiago (p112) Kayaking to this tiny island, home to over a thousand rhesus macaque monkeys.

❽ Reserva Natural Humedal Punta Tuna (p114) Strolling through dense mangrove forests and along an untouched coastline – and learning a bit too – on interpretive trails.

❾ Highway 181 (p115) Journeying back in time on this verdant corkscrew road dotted with mountain villages and breathtaking vistas.

History

Much of this region was once covered with lighter variations of the dense foliage now found only in El Yunque, but native Taíno successfully farmed the fertile land around the low-lying coasts. All that changed when the Spanish arrived en masse around 1700. The tremendous wealth of natural resources in El Yunque – lots of fresh water and timber, for example – attracted settlers, who quickly turned existing farmlands into massive sugarcane plantations.

A small gold rush added to the need for a strong labor force, and after most of the indigenous population was wiped out by disease or forced deep into the mountains, the Spanish brought in West African slaves in considerable numbers. Descendants of those Yoruba people make up the bulk of the 30,000 residents who live in the municipalities around El Yunque today.

The next wave of colonization came when the US took control of the island in 1898, at the end of the Spanish-American War, eventually setting up the commonwealth status that continues to this day. A region around a US military base near Fajardo that closed in 2003 has been the focus of developments like windpower farms.

❶ Getting There & Around

Most of the east coast is traversable via Hwy 3 or Hwy 53. Once you leave San Juan, be it on Rte 187 (the scenic route via Piñones and Loíza) or on the main drag of Hwy 3, be prepared for bursts of commercial development (fast-food chains and strip malls) along with distant views of El Yunque and glimpses of the ocean.

Públicos (public vans) run between Fajardo and San Juan (Río Piedras, actually), but to penetrate further into the countryside, a car or bike is necessary. It is easy to organize a tour into the El Yunque rainforest. The driving trip from San Juan to Fajardo takes around 75 to 90 minutes. From San Juan to Yabucoa, the timing is about the same if you cut through the middle of the island on Rte 52. Of course, rush-hour traffic can muck up the timings, especially in San Juan.

With its high concentration of cars, the northeast is not the most pleasant part of Puerto Rico in which to cycle. But stay off the main arteries of Hwys 3 and 66 and two-wheeled transport is possible.

Finally there are some beautiful drives through the lush mountains and hidden villages, including one along Hwy 181 (p115).

El Yunque

El Yunque National Forest is one of Puerto Rico's crown jewels. It boasts nearly 29,000 acres of lush mountainous terrain, with waterfalls dotting the landscape, rushing rivers and gurgling brooks, bromeliads clinging to towering trees, and bamboo groves opening to spectacular ocean views.

The only rainforest in the US National Forest System, El Yunque (named after the Taíno god, Yúcahu) has 37km of trails, some short and paved, others long, steep and barely there. Almost all gain some elevation; one of the toughest is to El Yunque's peak, El Toro, almost 1100m above sea level. Both casual and experienced hikers are sure to find rewarding trails.

El Yunque has two entrances. The northern side, 40km east of San Juan, receives the majority of visitors. The southern side, near Naguabo, retains a wild pristine feel. Several guesthouses here have private trails leading into the El Yunque, making it easy to hike an entire day and not see a soul.

◉ Sights

Once you've entered El Yunque National Forest's northern entrance, the forest's visitors center (p104), major attractions, trailheads and picnic areas appear as Hwy 191 twists, turns and climbs steeply on its way south toward the summit. (It's also possible to follow Hwy 186 along the western side of El Yunque, but to experience the forest's heart, Hwy 191 is the road to take.)

In addition to short and long hiking trails in El Yunque, there are highlights directly accessible by road within the forest.

★ El Yunque
National Forest   NATURE RESERVE
(☎ 787-888-1880; www.fs.usda.gov/elyunque; Northern Entrance, Km 4, Hwy 191; adult/child $4/free; ⏱ 7:30am-6pm; 🅿 ♿) The only rainforest in the US National Forest System, El Yunque is a highlight of any visit to Puerto Rico. Visitors enjoy access to the lush, verdant forest along 37km of paths, often passing waterfalls and rivers along the way. El Portal Visitors Center (p104), near Luquillo, is a good place to get your bearings before setting out to explore. The park has two entrances, both off of Hwy 191 – one on the northern side of the island (near Luquillo), the other towards the southern side (near Naguabo).

The northern side is much more visited and has lots of well-marked trails and parking areas; the southern side is wilder and less developed, making for beautiful off-the-beaten-track experiences. Note: Hwy 191 does not cut through the park – mudslides closed the middle section of the road years ago. Unless on foot, visitors must take Hwy 3 (which becomes Hwy 53) to access both sides of El Yunque.

EL YUNQUE'S FLORA & FAUNA

More than 240 species of tree and 1000 species of plant thrive in this misty, rain-soaked enclave, including 50 kinds of orchid. El Yunque is also the island's major water supply, with six substantial rivers tracing their sources here. The fauna is characterized by the presence of the critically endangered Puerto Rican parrot (*el higuaca*) and more than 60 other species of bird, nine species of rare freshwater shrimp, the coquí frog, anole tree lizards and the 7ft-long Puerto Rican boa. Night visitors can search for any of seven types of bioluminescent fungi, otherwise known as glow-in-the-dark mushrooms!

Four forest zones define El Yunque:

Tabonuco Forest Below 2000ft and receives less than 100in of rain. Features tall, straight trees and palms, orchids, flowers and aromatic shrubs.

Palo Colorado Forest Above 2000ft in the valleys and on gentle slopes. Annual rainfall averages as much as 180in. This area is lush with trees more than 1000 years old, laden with vines and orchids.

Palma Sierra Forest Above 2500ft along streams and on steep valley slopes. The mountain palm tree dominates with ferns and mosses growing beneath.

Cloud Forest Grows above the Palma Sierra Forest and gets up to 200in of rain per year. Trees are twisted from strong trade winds and are less than 12ft tall. Mosses and lichens hang from trees and cover the forest floor, accented by red-flowering bromeliads.

La Coca Falls
WATERFALL

(Km 8.1, Hwy 191; **P**) The first spectacular natural feature you see as Hwy 191 climbs south toward the forest peaks is an 85ft cascade as the stream tumbles from a precipice to the right of the highway onto boulder formations.

Yokahú Tower
VIEWPOINT

(Km 8.8, Hwy 191; **P**) This 65ft, Moorish-looking stone tower was built as a lookout in 1962. It's the first good place for vistas of the islands to the east, but there are better vantage points higher up on the mountain. The tower often gets crowded with tour groups. Pass it by unless you have extra time.

La Mina Falls
WATERFALL

(Km 11.7, Hwy 191; **P**) To marvel at these falls, or to take a splash in some water, take the steep 30- to 45-minute hike (1.1km) from the Palo Colorado information Center (p104) down the mountain to the base of the falls. Here you'll find the 35ft water cascade, quite stunning in its natural beauty. The hike is lush and slippery – be sure to be wear sturdy walking shoes. This is a popular spot with families and groups, so come early for tranquility.

Baño Grande & Baño de Oro
VIEWPOINT

(Km 11.8, Hwy 191; **P**) Baño Grande, a former swimming hole built during the Depression by the Civilian Conservation Corps, lies across Hwy 191 from the Palo Colorado Information Center (p104). About 50yd up the road, Baño de Oro is another former swimming hole that is now a popular spot for photo opportunities. This water hole takes its name from the Río Baño de Oro, which feeds the pool. Meaning 'bath of gold', Spaniards gave the river this name because they mined it for gold during the 16th century.

El Hippie Petroglyphs
ARCHAEOLOGICAL SITE

(off Km 28, Hwy 191) Several Taíno petroglyphs can be seen along the Río Blanco in the foothills of El Yunque. Located just south of a swimming hole known as 'El Hippie,' they're carved on two huge rocks along the river. Travelers can access the site on their own or, for a richer experience, hire a local guide (p103) to receive detailed historical explanations about the pre-Columbian symbols.

To access the site on your own, follow the turnoff after the small bridge on Hwy 191. Follow the signs that read 'Rio Hippie.' At the next bridge, take a left and follow the road towards its end. A local family offers parking ($5) on their property and easy access to the petroglyphs. A sign is prominently displayed on their fence.

🏃 Activities

With more than 23 miles of well-maintained trails and plenty of rugged terrain, El Yunque has a plethora of easy day hikes. Come prepared (water bottle, good walking shoes

El Yunque

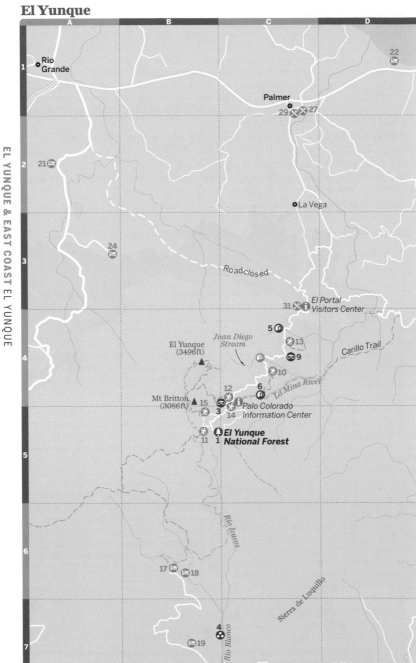

El Yunque

◎ Top Sights
1	El Yunque National Forest	B5
2	Playa Luquillo	E1

◎ Sights
3	Baño Grande & Baño de Oro	C4
4	El Hippie Petroglyphs	B7
5	La Coca Falls	C4
6	La Mina Falls	C4
7	Las Paylas	E3
8	Playa Azul	F1
9	Yokahú Tower	C4

⊕ Activities, Courses & Tours
10	Big Tree Trail	C4
11	El Toro Trail/Trade Winds National Recreation Trail	B5
12	El Yunque Trail	C4
13	La Coca Trail	C4
14	La Mina Trail	C5
15	Mt Britton Trail	B5

⏾ Sleeping
16	Balneario La Monserrate	E1
17	Casa Cubuy Ecolodge	B6
18	Casa Flamboyant	B6
19	Casa Picaflores	B7
20	El Hotelito	F4
21	Hacienda Siesta Alegre Inn	A2
22	Hotel Yunquemar	D1
23	Luquillo Sunrise Beach Inn	E1
24	Rainforest Inn	A3

⊗ Eating
25	Aromas Coffee & Crepes	E1
26	Boardriders Surf Bar & Grill	F1
27	Lluvia	C1
28	Luquillo Beach Kiosks	E1
29	Mi Vida Café & Burger	C1
30	Pasta y Pueblo	E1
31	Yuquiyú Delights	C3

and rain poncho), remembering there are few places to buy snacks and use restroom facilities.

It's a good idea to check in at the visitors center (p104) for the latest weather update before heading out for a trek. El Yunque's weather reflects its wet ecosystem: sudden surges of light rain can occur anytime during the year in this dense rainforest, so throw on some protective gear and get on with your day. During hurricane season El Yunque can get drenched; some trails might be closed due to mudslides and streams swell enormously. Winter nights in the Luquillo mountains can be damp and a little chilly.

EL YUNQUE & EAST COAST EL YUNQUE

EXPLORE EL YUNQUE'S SOUTH SIDE

For pure off-the-beaten-path joy, skip the northern side of El Yunque and head to the region's alternative entrance off the southern portion of Hwy 191, just west of the town of Naguabo. Since mudslides closed the central section of the road in the 1970s, the southern expanse of the rainforest has remained relatively isolated and unexplored.

Spend the night at one of the wonderful southern-side lodgings up the precipitous and winding Hwy 191. From there, you can procure directions to a number of nearby hiking and swimming spots, or hire a local expert to guide you to some of the area's highlights including hard-to-reach waterfalls and Taíno petroglyphs (p99).

★ El Yunque Trail
HIKING

(Km 11.7, Hwy 191) On a clear day, never-ending views extending to Vieques and Culebra reward hikers who tackle the almost 1500ft of elevation gain on this trail. This is the main event for most hikers, taking you to the top of El Yunque (3496ft) in 1½ hours or longer. It starts opposite the Palo Colorado Information Center (p104).

The 3.8km trail is mostly paved or maintained gravel as you ascend past mountain palm trees and waterfalls to the cloud forest (with its stunted or 'dwarf' trees) to the observation deck, which is surrounded by microwave communication towers that transmit to the islands of Culebra and Vieques. If you want a rock scramble from here, take Los Picachos Trail (0.17 miles) to another old observation tower and feel as if you have crested a tropical Everest. You can return via a different route by descending down a service road to the Mt Britton Trail and then down a dirt track to Rte 191 and back to your starting point.

Big Tree Trail
HIKING

(Km 10.4, Hwy 191) About half an hour each way, this trail through tabonuco forest to La Mina Falls contains bilingual interpretive signs that highlight sights such as a 300-year-old ausubo tree. This short 0.86-mile trail is moderately difficult; its name comes from the size of the vegetation along the way. It's probably the most popular trail in the park; combine it with La Mina Trail.

La Mina Trail
HIKING

(Km 11.7, Hwy 191) The forest's newest trail was opened in 1992 as an extension of the Big Tree Trail, though it can also be done in isolation from its starting point at the Palo Colorado Information Center (p104). The trail heads downhill through palo colorado forest to La Mina Falls and an old mine tunnel. Mostly paved, it's an easy though often slippery 1.1km walk down, and a steep hike back up. The payoff are the falls, which drop 35ft into a perfect natural swimming pool. Take your bathing suit to cool off after the intense walk.

La Coca Trail
HIKING

(Km 8.5, Hwy 191) To get off the beaten path, try this short but challenging trail. Wilder and less maintained than some of the more popular forest rambles, this 2.9-km (one-way) hike descends through thick tabonuco forest and enormous ferns and crosses several rocky streams. Most visitors take three to four hours for this out-and-back trek because of the slippery terrain and tempting swimming.

El Toro Trail/Trade Winds National Recreation Trail
HIKING

(Km 13, Hwy 191) Although it's often closed, this trail is El Yunque's best backcountry adventure. The 12.6km round-trip to El Toro (3522ft) and back is challenging due to wet conditions, thick mud and poorly maintained paths. It's an all-day excursion for most hikers (some parties even camp out overnight).

El Toro is El Yunque's highest point and the trail traverses dense jungle broken by intermittent views of both coasts. During the ascent you'll pass through all four forest zones, ending in the cloud forest at 3000ft. This haunting dwarf forest features ghostly epiphytes and ubiquitous mist.

The trailhead for the Trade Winds Trail is situated at Km 13 on Hwy 191, behind the gate where the road ends. The unpaved path climbs 6.3km to the summit of El Toro, from where you can either retrace your steps or continue west on the similarly vague El Toro Trail to Km 10.8 on Hwy 186 (3.4km from El Toro and 9.7km from Hwy 191). From here you'll need to return the way you came, or arrange for a car to pick you up.

Be sure to contact the forest visitors center (p104) for current road conditions and trail status.

Mt Britton Trail
HIKING

(Hwy 930) If you are short on time and want to feel as if you have really 'summited,' take the 0.8-mile (45-minute) climb up through the palma sierra forest into the cloud forest that surrounds this peak. It's named after the famous botanist, Nathaniel Britton, who identified several plant and tree species in the region in the 1920s.

👉 Tours

★ Kalichi Adventures
ADVENTURE SPORTS

(📞787-365-3401; www.kalichiadventures.com; tours from $175; ⊙tours 7am-2pm Wed-Sun) This well-run, safety-focused tour company leads physically challenging and gorgeous hikes on the southern side of El Yunque. You'll be rappelling, rock climbing, body rafting and even taking a 11m jump off a waterfall. Not for the faint of heart. The cost is totally worth it if you can swing it budget-wise. Hotel pick up in San Juan available.

★ AdvenTours
ADVENTURE

(📞787-530-8311; www.adventourspr.com; tours per person from $75; ⊙1-8pm Mon-Fri, tour schedules vary) AdvenTours offers a huge range of excursions including birdwatching tours and night hikes in El Yunque National Forest to spot nocturnal animals and bioluminescent fungi. You can also custom-design trips and arrange for pick up in San Juan.

Robin Phillips
HIKING

(📞787-874-2138; tours per person from $25) Longtime guide Robin Phillips leads visitors on off-the-beaten-track hikes through the southern side of El Yunque. Highlights include Taíno petroglyphs (p99), waterfalls and untamed rivers.

🛏 Sleeping

There are several inns, B&Bs and guesthouses along the edges of El Yunque – not actually within the national forest, but along its fringe, which still feels very wild. The proximity to the rainforest means lots of animal activity: the sound of chirruping coqui will send you to sleep and you'll wake to the song of tropical birds.

Some places are accessible near the northern section of Hwy 191, coming from Río Grande; Luquillo's beaches are only a few minutes away. Others are on the southern side, also near Hwy 191, the nearest town being Naguabo. (Due to mudslides in the '70s, the middle of Hwy 191 was shut down, creating two separate entrances to El Yunque.) The accommodations are good choices if you want to be in close proximity to day trips in and around Fajardo. Most properties have minimum two-night stays.

🛏 North Side

★ El Hotelito
INN $$

(📞787-980-7402; www.yunquehotelito.com; off Hwy 976; r incl breakfast $160; P🛜🏊) Located on a 25-acre tropical flower farm, this seven-room inn offers serenity and beauty. Once a private home, there's art, family heirlooms and loads of books in the welcoming common areas. A pool overlooks the rainforest. Rooms are upscale and artsy, all with private balconies with mountain or ocean views. Five kilometers of private trails lead directly to El Yunque.

★ Hacienda Siesta Alegre Inn
BOUTIQUE HOTEL $$

(📞787-887-7500; www.haciendasiestaalegre.com; Km 23.9, Hwy 186; r $165-185, ste $235, all incl breakfast; P❄🛜🏊) Colonial luxury meets mountainside beauty at this 30-acre horse ranch in the foothills of El Yunque. Nine rooms, all exquisitely and uniquely decorated, have antique canopy beds, vintage tubs, hardwood floors and fine art throughou; they also open onto tropical gardens. There's an elegant common living room, game room and library – all open air. A gorgeous pool is the cherry on the top.

This is a popular wedding site, especially on Friday and Saturday, which may result in late-night music and limited access to some areas of the property. Be sure to ask about events when booking.

Rainforest Inn
INN $$

(📞787-378-6190; www.rainforestinn.com; off Km 22.1, Hwy 186; r incl breakfast $165-170; P🛜) 🌿 Bordering the national forest, the Rainforest Inn – a former coffee estate plantation – has two two-bedroom units plus a suite with beautiful (and lovely smelling) reclaimed cedar beams and luxurious details such as a hanging bed, a claw-foot bathtub and antique mahogany furniture. Outside the property has views of El Yunque peak and a private path leads to a stunning waterfall pool. No children under 12.

🛏 South Side

Casa Picaflores   INN $$
(📞 787-874-3802; www.casapicaflores.com; off Km 28, Hwy 191; cabin or studio $160, 3-bedroom villa $425, all incl breakfast; P❄🐾📶🛏) 🍴 Spend the night in a well-appointed three-bedroom house, nestled into a cozy *casita* (small house) or in an open-air *cabaña* (cabin), surrounded by abundant fruit trees and majestic mahogany boughs. The lodgings feature organic linens, cleaning products are biodegradable and the grounds contain a compost fertilized vegetable garden.

Casa Cubuy Ecolodge   GUESTHOUSE $$
(📞 787-874-6221; www.casacubuy.com; Km 22, Hwy 191; r incl breakfast $120-135; P📶) 🍴 Co-cooned atop winding Hwy 191 on El Yunque's wild, isolated southern slopes, Casa Cubuy Ecolodge offers 10 simple rooms – not much luxe here – with jaw-dropping views of the rainforest. Sleep with the windows open to be surrounded by a symphony of frogs or take a private trail to a nearby waterfall and natural swimming pool.

★Casa Flamboyant   B&B $$$
(📞 787-559-9800;   www.casaflamboyantpr.com; Km 22.2, Hwy 191; r incl breakfast $230-295; P📶🛏) Tucked way up in the mountains with panoramic views of El Yunque, Casa Flamboyant makes the most of its breath-taking location. Three well-appointed rooms (two with private terraces), a cozy living room and an infinity pool are as elegant as Puerto Rico's rainforest gets. Private trails lead to gorgeous waterfalls and swimming holes, which guests often have to them-selves. Adults only.

ℹ CAMPING IN EL YUNQUE

There are no developed campgrounds or designated camping areas in El Yun-que, but wilderness camping is allowed along most roads and trails except areas that are closed. Tents must be located at least 30ft away from any trail or body of water and at least 50ft from roads and developed picnic sites.

Most importantly, campers need a free permit that must be obtained at least 14 days before your visit. Check the website (www.fs.usda.gov/elyunque) or at the visitors center for details.

🍴 Eating

Palmer, the colorful strip where Hwy 191 heads south from Hwy 3 towards El Yunque, has some attractive eating options. Inside the park, there are several cheerful roadside stands and the visitors center has a good cafe.

★Mi Vida Café & Burger   CAFE, BURGERS $
(📞 787-888-7356; 5 Principal, Palmer; burgers $3-12; ⏱10am-6pm; 🌱) This mom-and-pop cafe serves up some of the best burgers on the coast – some stuffed with chorizo – with pur-ple yam fries on the side. Swap out the bun for huge plantain or *mofongo* patties. Freshly made and well-stuffed *pastelillos* (turnovers) and all manner of wraps are great to go op-tions. Vegetarian choices abound.

★Lluvia   CAFE $
(📞 787-657-5186; www.lluviapr.com; 52 Princi-pal, Palmer; mains $5-12; ⏱7am-3pm Wed-Sun; 📶🌱📶) With a setting seemingly straight out of an IKEA catalogue, this contempo-rary cafe dishes up a range of creative meals, from excellent breakfasts to thick sandwich-es, salads, flatbread pizza and more at lunch. The orange juice is freshly squeezed and the coffee made from premium Puerto Rican beans.

Yuquiyú Delights   PUERTO RICAN $
(📞 787-396-0970; www.yuquiyudelightspr.com; Km 4, Hwy 191, El Yunque National Forest; mains $6-9; ⏱9am-4pm; 🌱📶) This modest eatery is lo-cated inside El Portal Visitors Center (p104). Choose from *comida criolla* (traditional Puerto Rican cuisine), burgers, baked goods, snacks and smoothies.

ℹ Information

El Portal Visitors Center (📞787-888-1880; www.fs.usda.gov/elyunque; Northern Entrance, Km 4, Hwy 19; adult/child $4/free; ⏱9am-5pm) Make this sprawling visitors center your first stop. There are interactive exhibits, a short overview film (in Spanish and English), a walkway through the forest canopy and a gift shop. Vending machines serve up drinks and snacks, plus there is a good small cafe. Pick up free basic maps and information, then admire some stunning tree ferns.

Palo Colorado Information Center (Km 11.8, Hwy 191; ⏱9:30am-5pm) It's worth enduring the switchbacks and steep road to get to this information center, which is the starting point for short and spectacular hiking trails. The picnic area – which includes a series of sheltered concrete platforms hidden in the jungle, overlooking a ravine of rushing water – is hard to match anywhere on the island.

ℹ Getting There & Away

As there's no public transportation to El Yunque, you will need to get here with private vehicle, taxi (from $85) or on a guided tour. Driving from San Juan, there will be signs directing you from Hwy 3 to Hwy 191. Turn south at Palmer and follow the signs to El Yunque National Forest.

Take note that some highway maps still show that you can traverse the forest on Hwy 191 (or access El Yunque from the south via this route). However, this section of Hwy 191 has been closed by landslides south of Km 13 for years; there are no plans for repair. Some road maps also suggest that El Yunque can be approached via a network of roads along the forest's western border. Don't try it: these roads are unmaintained tracks that often dead-end in serious jungle. Be sure to check the latest conditions of El Yunque's roads on the **forest service** (p98) website.

Luquillo & Around

POP 18,700

In many ways Luquillo is a typical Puerto Rican town: a coastal strip of magnificent beaches backed by a mishmash of condo towers, strip malls and urban sprawl. But here, in the island's busy northeastern corner, beauty easily outweighs the beast. Playa Luquillo, the mile-long crescent of surf and sand to the west of the town, is regularly touted as being the Commonwealth's finest *balneario* (public beach) and the proverbial home of Puerto Rican soul food. Because of Luquillo's popularity with *sanjuaneros* (people from San Juan), your best time to visit is on a weekday.

Luquillo traces its history to an early Spanish settlement in 1797 and its name to a valorous *cacique* (Taíno chief), Loquillo, who made a brave standoff against early colonizers here in 1513. These days the almost 20,000-strong town is bypassed by the arterial Hwy 3 which carries traffic to Fajardo.

🏊 Beaches

★ Playa Luquillo   BEACH
(Balneario La Monserrate; off Frontage Rd, Luquillo; parking $5; [P]) Luquillo is synonymous with the fabulous Playa Luquillo. Set on a calm bay facing northwest and protected from the easterly trade winds, the public part of this beach makes a mile-long arc to a point of sand shaded by evocative coconut palms. The beach itself is a plane of broad, gently

sloping sand that continues its gradual slope below the water.

With crowds converging here at weekends and during holidays, Luquillo has always been more about atmosphere than solitude. Many come just for the famous long strip of food kiosks (p106) at its western end. Umbrellas ($10) and beach loungers ($5) can be rented near the *balneario* (p106).

Playa Azul   BEACH
(off Calle Herminio Díaz Navarro, Luquillo; ⚓) To escape the crowds of famous Playa Luquillo, head for Playa Azul, east around the headland and in the town itself, directly in front of the condominium development of the same name. While the beach is more exposed to the trade winds and dangerous riptides, Playa Azul is just as broad, powdery and gently sloping as Luquillo.

You can join surfers in these waters at **La Pared** (the Wall) to catch a surf break. Or scramble over the stone jetty at the eastern end of the beach and follow a strand of beaches and bays that stretch over 5 miles to Playa Seven Seas in Las Croabas.

⊙ Sights & Activities

Benefiting from a fabulous beachside location and proximity to El Yunque National Forest, Luquillo is well-positioned for both aquatic and land-based adventures, including pockets of paradise to play golf.

★ Enchanted
Island Eco Tours   KAYAKING, HIKING
(📲 787-888-2887; http://ecotourspuertorico.com; tours from $58) Explore the rich life in and out of the water on trips along the coast, rivers and bayous. Numerous options are available including moonlight kayak tours and excursions to El Yunque. Guides are the epitome of professional, sharing interesting information on ecosystems while keeping it fun and safe.

★ Surfing Puerto Rico   SURFING
(📲 787-501-7873; www.surfingpuertorico.com; lessons from $60, surfboard rentals per half-day from $20; ⊙ 8am-6pm) National Surfing Champion and longtime instructor Brian Ramos leads personalized and fun surf classes on Playa Azul's La Pared. Sessions last two hours, including a 30-minute land prep to get your technique down and talk water safety. Geared towards beginner and intermediate surfers, this shop is especially popular with kids and teens.

EL YUNQUE & EAST COAST LUQUILLO & AROUND

Bahía Beach Resort & Golf Club GOLF
(☑787-809-8950; www.stregisbahiabeach.com; St Regis Bahía Beach Resort, Km 4.2, Rte 187, Rio Grande; greens fees $220-275; ☺7am-6pm) Designed by Robert Trent Jones Jr, this gorgeous 18-hole golf course runs along several lakes and dazzling beachfront, all with a view of El Yunque National Forest. Golf carts included in the rate and clubs are available for rent. Significant discounts on green fees after 3pm.

Las Paylas RIVER, WATERFALL
(Km 5.4, Hwy 983, Luquillo; admission $0.50, parking $5) A set of natural waterslides in El Yunque's foothills is popular with locals, especially on weekends. Las Paylas, as the 'slides' are called, are created by a series of small waterfalls running over smooth boulders, big and small, and ending in a crystal-clear swimming hole. The most confident slide down belly down, face first. Others enjoy the show from nearby rocks.

There's no public access to Las Paylas. Instead, homeowners charge a small fee for visitors to pass through their property or to park their cars. House No 6051 has the best access; look for a bright green affair on the western side of the highway. It even has a small gated parking area. A well-maintained path leads visitors directly to the waterslides.

🛏 Sleeping

Luquillo is a good option if you want easy access to great beaches and El Yunque. From here, you also can take easy day trips to San Juan and the bioluminescent bay in Fajardo.

Balneario La Monserrate CAMPGROUND $
(☑787-889-5871; Playa Luquillo, Luquillo; tent/powered sites $10/17, parking $4; ℗) The 30 campsites at this Playa Luquillo spot right on the sand are very popular in summer, but are pretty solitary during the winter. Toilets and outdoor showers ($1) available. Security is now provided 24/7 (muggings have occurred in the past), though sites closer to the main building tend to be safer, especially when it's slow. Lockers can be rented for your valuables.

Hotel Yunquemar HOTEL $$
(☑787-889-5555; www.yunquemar.com; 6 Calle 1, Luquillo; ste $225-260, all incl breakfast; ℗❄🛜🏊) The name Yunquemar sums it up. Lying in the shadow of El Yunque and within pebble-pitching distance of the *mar* (sea), you've got the best of both worlds here. A simple, family-run hotel with its own swimming pool and thin beach, and a pool

table and wide-screen TV tucked down in the enormous basement. It's a few minutes drive from central Luquillo.

Luquillo Sunrise Beach Inn HOTEL $$
(☑787-889-1713; www.luquillosunrise.com; Herminio Díaz Navarro, Luquillo; r incl breakfast $150-190; ℗❄🛜) The Luquillo Sunrise is caressed by cooling breezes in its 17 ocean-facing rooms. Each is very '80s tropical in decor – think Golden Girls – but comfortable nonetheless. There's a communal patio and all upper-floor rooms have large balconies overlooking Playa Azul. Luquillo plaza is two blocks away and the famous *balneario* is a 30-minute stroll along the beach.

🍴 Eating

★**Luquillo Beach Kiosks** PUERTO RICAN $
(Playa Luquillo, off Hwy 3, Luquillo; dishes $3-20; ☺hours vary, generally noon-10pm; 🏮) Luquillo's famous line of 60 or so beachfront *friquitines* (also known as *quioscos, kioskos* or just plain food stalls) along the western edge of Hwy 3 serve often-excellent food at very popular prices. It's a fine way to sample local food and snack culture, including scrumptious *surullitos* (fried cornmeal and cheese sticks).

Start by wandering past the dozens of choices to see what strikes your fancy. You'll find everything from outstanding *comida criolla* to top-notch burgers and Peruvian ceviche. All sell Medalla beer and most have full cocktail menus. The stalls themselves range from very basic to slightly stylish affairs. Most have kitchens on the parking side where you browse and tables on the beach side.

Recommended choices are **Terruño** (kiosk 20) for creative local fare, and upscale **La Parilla** (kiosk 2), where seafood is the specialty.

Boardriders Surf Bar & Grill CAFE $
(☑787-355-5175; www.boardriderssurfbar.com; Playa Azul, Herminio Díaz Navarro, Luquillo; dishes $7-22; ☺11am-midnight Mon-Thu, to 2am Fri, 10am-2am Sat, 9am-midnight Sun; 🍴) A beachside hipster hangout festooned with Christmas lights. Stash your board in Luquillo Surfshop next door and refuel on fish tacos, veggie wraps and burgers before your next set. Check out the action at the surf break in La Pared right in front. There's live music – typically reggae – on weekends.

Aromas Coffee & Crepes CAFE $
(☑787-335-6911; 60 Calle 14 de Julio, Luquillo; dishes from $4; ☺7am-7pm; ❄) Right on Luquillo's somnolent central square, this sprightly cafe

is one of the best breakfast and lunch places around. A range of coffee drinks add zest to the day; go local with the coconut-flavored latte. There are fresh baked goods and a menu that includes sweet and savory crepes and excellent eggs Benedict; hearty sandwiches hit the spot.

★ **Pasta y Pueblo**   ITALIAN $$
(☑787-920-8620; 14 de Julio, Luquillo; dishes $12-30; ☺4:30-9:30pm Tue-Sun; ☑) On a gravel lot with a skateboard ramp in front (for the chef's son), this unassuming little shack a half block from Playa Azul slings some plate-licking fabulous food. There's often a crowd waiting for one of the six tables to dine on pasta laced with seafood or more traditional sauces. The guava cheesecake gets rave reviews. BYO wine.

❶ Getting There & Around

Hwy 3 leads directly to Rte 193 (aka Calle Fernandez Garcia), which is the main artery of Luquillo.

Públicos (public vans) run from the **Río Piedras terminal** (p90) in San Juan to Luquillo's central plaza ($5) from Monday to Saturday. Trips take from 2½ to 3½ hours, depending on the traffic. If you're going to the beach, make sure you disembark next to the **food kiosks** (p106), a mile or so before Luquillo *pueblo*. Taxis cost $72 from San Juan each way.

The House of Coffee & Bike Rental (☑787-360-2487; 250 Fernandez Garcia, Luquillo; per hour/day $4/21; ☺7am-8pm Mon-Thu, to 9pm Fri & Sat, to 2pm Sun) rents decent mountain bikes per hour or day. (The cappuccino is pretty good too.) Helmet and lock included.

Fajardo & Around

POP 34,400

Fajardo sprawls like a scruffy suburb between the foothills of El Yunque and the sea. It has many personalities: downbeat ferry port for Vieques and Culebra, upscale yacht harbor, nature preserve and beautiful beach escape.

Fajardo also reigns as one of Puerto Rico's biggest water-activity centers. Around Fajardo you can do everything from diving in the waters of the coral-rich La Cordillera islands to kayaking one of Puerto Rico's three bioluminescent bays – the very popular Laguna Grande, which is part of the very worthwhile Las Cabezas de San Juan Nature Reserve. A few miles south, boaters

enjoy Puerto del Rey, one of the largest marinas in the Caribbean.

Downtown Fajardo itself, founded in 1760, has little to show for 250 years of history. Just north, though, the extended neighborhood of Las Croabas is a good place to start a visit. Besides the nature reserve, it features the beguiling beach, Playa Seven Seas.

◉ Sights

★ **Las Cabezas de San Juan Reserva Natural**   NATURE RESERVE
(☑787-722-5882; www.paralanaturaleza.org/cabezas-de-san-juan; off Hwy 987, Las Croabas; varies; ☺9am-4pm Wed-Sun, English tours 2pm; ℗♿) A 316-acre nodule of land on Puerto Rico's extreme northeast tip, the Cabezas de San Juan Reserva Natural protects the Laguna Grande bioluminescent bay (p110), rare flora and fauna, mangroves, lush rainforest, various trails and boardwalks, and an important scientific research center. It's popular but can only be visited as part of a tour booked in advance.

Despite its diminutive size, the reserve shelters seven – yes, seven – different ecological systems, including beaches, lagoons, dry forest, coral reefs and mangroves. Animal species that forage here include big iguanas, fiddler crabs, myriad insects and all kinds of birds. Such condensed biodiversity is typical of Puerto Rico's compact island status and Las Cabezas is highlighted as an integral part of the Commonwealth's vital threatened Northeast Ecological Corridor.

A historical highlight amid the natural beauty is the splendidly restored 1882 El Faro de las Cabezas de San Juan (p108), Puerto Rico's oldest lighthouse. With a well-conceived nature center and spectacular views of the north and east coasts, it's a highlight for many tours of the reserve.

There are about 2 miles of trails and boardwalks that lead through the park, but you can't follow them on your own: you must take a guided **walking tour** (adult/child $12/10). It lasts more than two hours and includes a short tram ride through the dry forest section. Tours depart through the day, but most are in Spanish; the English tour is usually at 2pm.

Other tours include a **bike tour** ($22) and a **birding tour** ($14). **Night tours** (adult/child $24/14) explore the grounds, lighthouse and bioluminescent bay. Reservations are required for all tours.

Fajardo & Around

Fajardo & Around

⊙ Top Sights
1 Cabezas de San Juan Reserva
Natural...B2
2 Playa Seven Seas.................................A2

⊙ Sights
3 El Faro de las Cabezas de San
Juan...B1

⊛ Activities, Courses & Tours
Bio Island......................................(see 6)
4 Captain Osva Fishing Charters...........B3
East Island Excursions.................(see 5)
5 Puerto del Rey.....................................A5
6 Pure Adventure...................................B2
Sea Ventures Dive Center...........(see 5)

⊟ Sleeping
7 El Conquistador Resort.......................B2
8 Fajardo Inn...A3
9 Moonlight Bay Hostel.........................B3
10 Playa Seven Seas Camping................B2

⊗ Eating
11 Bistro del Mar.....................................B2
12 La Estación...A2
13 Las Vistas...B2
14 The House of Pastelillos.....................B2

at times, it gets packed on weekends and during summer. Beach chairs, umbrellas, snorkel gear and kayaks can be rented from vendors on the beach.

For good snorkeling, follow the beach about a half mile to the northeast to off Hwy 987 (aka Hidden Beach); the reefs are just offshore. For a quiet spot, head west on the well-marked trail from Playa Seven Seas to the pretty Playa El Convento, where you'll likely have the beach to yourself.

El Faro de las
Cabezas de San Juan   LIGHTHOUSE
(☑787-722-5882; www.paralanaturaleza.org/cabe zas-de-san-juan; off Hwy 987, Las Croabas; varies; ☺9am-4pm Wed-Sun, English tours 2pm; ℗) Built in 1882, El Faro de las Cabezas de San Juan is Puerto Rico's oldest lighthouse. Adorned with rich neoclassical detail and topped by a distinctive Spanish colonial tower, it overlooks the peninsula's steep, craggy cliffs where the stormy Atlantic meets the Sonda de Vieques (Vieques Sound).

🏃 Activities

The Fajardo region is decidedly amphibi-an – life is as exciting in the water as it is on land. This coastal area is blessed with

You can get a glimpse of some of the reserve by simply walking east down the narrow beach from Playa Seven Seas. Better yet, take a kayak tour with a tour operator at sunset and explore Laguna Grande (p110) after dark for the blue-glowing, underwater 'fireworks' of bioluminescent micro-organisms.

★ Playa Seven Seas   BEACH
(☑787-863-8180; off Hwy 987, Las Croabas; parking $5.50) On the southwestern shore of the peninsula of Las Cabezas, Playa Seven Seas is a sheltered, coconut-palm-shaded, horseshoe-shaped public beach. Quiet and slow

many tiny islands (not to mention Culebra and Vieques) that provide fabulous opportunities for swimming, diving, fishing or just relaxing on a quiet beach. Good snorkeling sites abound.

East Island Excursions BOATING
(☑787-860-3434; www.eastwindcats.com; Puerto del Rey Marina, Km 51.4, Hwy 3; adult/child from $75/55, transport from San Juan $16; ⊘8am-5pm) These glass-bottomed catamarans are in high demand, so book early. All kinds of day trips to the La Cordillera islands are offered, and it even does quick runs over to St Thomas on high-speed cats. One boat has a slippery waterslide that launches you right into the ocean. A buffet lunch and free piña coladas seal the deal.

Bio Island BOATING
(☑787-422-7857; www.bioislandpr.com; Parque las Croabas, off Hwy 987, Las Croabas; tours from $52) Bio Island offers evening tours of the bioluminescent bay on an electric boat seating just six people, making for a mellow and educational trip.

Puerto del Rey MARINA
(☑787-860-1000; www.puertodelrey.com; Km 51.4, Hwy 3) Standing behind a breakwater in a cove 2 miles south of Fajardo and about 4.7 miles south of the ferry dock, this is one of the largest marinas (1100 slips) in the region. Many yachts stop here to take advantage of the marina's facilities. It's a hub for sailing, diving and fishing charters aimed at visitors.

Pure Adventure KAYAKING
(☑787-202-6551; www.pureadventurepr.com; Parque las Croabas, off Hwy 987, Las Croabas; bio bay tours from $48, snorkeling trips from $70, 1-/2-tank dives from $75/100; ⊘9am-6pm Mon-Sat) Owned and operated by two marine biologists, Pure Adventure offers a variety of excursions, including evening kayak tours of the bioluminescent bay, snorkeling in the rich waters off Playa Seven Seas and diving off the coast of Vieques. Trips integrate information about ecosystems, flora and fauna as well as the local culture and history.

Sea Ventures Dive Center DIVING, SNORKELING
(☑800-739-3483, 787-863-3483; www.divepuertorico.com; Puerto del Rey Marina, Km 51.4, Hwy 3; snorkeling trips from $60, 2-tank dive trips from $110) This five-star PADI-certified dive shop offers daily diving and snorkeling trips from Fajardo to local reefs, including near Palominos

and Icacos as well as Culebra and Vieques. Full-day trips to St Thomas are also offered. A full range of dive certification courses available too.

Fishing

From November to March dorado, wahoo, white marlin and sailfish are found, while from July to September it's all about blue marlin.

Captain Osva Fishing Charters FISHING
(☑787-547-4851; www.deepseafishingpr.com; Km 2.7, Hwy 987, Las Croabas; half-/full-day trips from $650/985) Offers half- and full-day deep-sea fishing charters on a 41ft boat for up to six people. Trips head to the Atlantic or Caribbean; all equipment, including bait, provided. Snacks, beer and soft drinks included too.

🛏 Sleeping

Moonlight Bay Hostel HOSTEL $
(☑787-801-1578; www.moonlightbayhostel.com; 478 Cometa; dm/r from $26/60; ✳🛜) Close to the ferry terminal for boats to Culebra and Vieques, this hostel is a real find. It has a fine rooftop terrace plus a modern kitchen where you can make free DIY pancake breakfasts. Details are well thought out with top-quality mattresses (memory foam!), a washer/dryer for guest use, linens and more. There's often a party vibe here, so light sleepers beware.

Playa Seven Seas Camping CAMPGROUND $
(☑787-863-8180; off Hwy 987, Las Croabas; campsites $10; 🅿) The campgrounds at one of Puerto Rico's loveliest beaches, Playa Seven Seas, fills up fast. Make sure you reserve in advance if you plan to come during summer or holidays. In the low season, it's only open on weekends. Showers and bathrooms are available and there's 24/7 security and an on-site cafe.

Fajardo Inn RESORT $$
(☑787-860-6000; www.fajardoinn.com; 52 Parcelas Beltrán; d/ste from $100/170; 🅿✳🛜🏊) 🏌 Perched on a hill overlooking Fajardo, this hacienda-style inn exudes an unhurried ambience. It has comfortable uncluttered rooms with a tropical theme, some with balconies with distant sea views. Its facilities are extensive – two restaurants, two pools, tennis court, huge gym, mini-golf and playground – though much could use some sprucing up. A solid option, especially for families.

DON'T MISS

LAGUNA GRANDE BIOLUMINESCENT BAY

One of the most popular sights in the east is Laguna Grande, a bioluminescent lagoon in the Cabezas de San Juan Nature Reserve (p107) that glows on moonless nights. One of three in Puerto Rico (the others are Bahía Mosquito (p131) on Vieques and La Parguera Bay in the south), Laguna Grande is especially popular because of its close proximity to San Juan.

It's a magical experience: by kayak you start off in a virtual cave of mangroves until you slowly break out into open sky where you are dazzled by millions of stars overhead. As your eyes adjust, look down! Below, a surreal blue glow follows the movement of your paddle as it moves through the water, fish outlined in blue as they dart past. The unreal and eerie glow is created by trillions of microscopic dinoflagellates reacting to movement in the water.

Options for seeing the glowing waters include (swimming is prohibited at all times, whichever way you visit):

Kayaking Guided kayak trips are the most popular way to experience the lagoon. They have the least impact on the dinoflagellates and get you closest to the glow. However, with several different agencies providing tours, it can get crowded. Add to that paddling through mangroves at night and mishaps can happen, slowing down the group.

Electric boat Glide across the waters with ecofriendly Bio Island (p109), which runs tours that last a little over an hour on a six-passenger boat. Guides explain the why behind the glow.

Walking tour Experience the glow on a nighttime walking tour offered at Cabezas de San Juan Reserva Natural (p107). You tour the grounds by foot and tram and then spend time at the lagoon walking along boardwalks. Tours end at the lighthouse (p108) where you contrast the bay's dim glow to the encroaching luminosity of civilization.

Tour reservations Be sure to book any tour of Laguna Grande as far in advance as possible as trips fill up quickly. Note: A full moon makes the water's glow hard to discern. The rainy season, from August to November, can result in murky runoff that also diminishes the experience. Finally, be sure to avoid rogue operators that use nonelectric boats, which can contaminate the water and kill the dinoflagellates.

El Conquistador Resort
RESORT $$$

(☎787-863-1000; www.elconresort.com; 1000 Ave El Conquistador; r/ste from $280/650; P❃@ ☎❧) A 900-unit mega resort that glitters along a steep coastal escarpment a few miles north of Fajardo, this mini-town boasts its own cove, cable car and a private fantasy island. Ideal for vacationers in search of golf, tennis, spa pampering, water sports and fine dining – with lots of company – this is the quintessential full-service holiday.

✗ Eating

★Bistro del Mar
FOOD TRUCK $

(☎939-269-1978; Parque las Croabas, off Hwy 987, Las Croabas; meals $3-15; ☉6-10pm Mon-Sat) This tiny food cart packs a taste bud punch with spectacular takes on Puerto Rican and Mexican eats. Order stuffed plantains, *mofongo,* tacos, ceviche, quesadillas and more. Be sure to order a side of coconut fries. Popular with folks returning from kayak tours on the bioluminescent Laguna Grande. Cash only.

The House of Pastelillos
PUERTO RICAN $

(☎787-268-2222; www.facebook.com/thehouseof pastelillos; Playa Seven Seas, off Hwy 987, Las Croabas; pastelillos $4-16; ☉10am-6pm Thu-Sun) This beach shack on Playa Seven Seas specializes in Puerto Rican *pastelillos,* flaky, hot turnovers stuffed with yummy goodness. At last count, The House of Pastelillos had over 20 varieties, including lobster, crab, corned beef, *mofongo,* spinach and Nutella. A long list of beers and smoothies makes this a perfect place to take a break from the beach.

Las Vistas
CAFE $

(☎787-655-7053; www.lasvistascafepr.com; 83 Calle No 2, Las Croabas; mains $8-15; ☉8am-2pm Thu-Mon; ☛) Beautiful fruit plates vie for your attention with the panorama at this rooftop terrace. The menu stresses brunch with eggs in all forms plus pancakes and some pasta dishes for those leaning towards the savory. Service is friendly and attentive. A perfect stop before or after some calorie-burning activity.

★ **La Estación** STEAK, SEAFOOD **$$**
(📞787-863-4481; www.laestacionpr.com; Km 4, Hwy 987; mains $18-30; ⊙5-10pm Thu, noon-10pm Fri & Sat, 4-10pm Sun, noon-10pm Mon; 🚗) Done up like an artist's loft, this playfully converted gas station has a 4WD dashboard bar on the patio and an open-air dining room hung with vintage bicycles. Creative fare includes a skirt steak, seafood and a few good veggie items. Watch for seasonal specials. Mains come served on heavy wooden pedestals, with delicious sauces and an eye-fluttering passion-fruit salad dressing.

ⓘ Information

HIMA Hospital San Pablo-Fajardo (📞787-655-0505; www.himasanpablo.com; 404 Av General Valero; ⊙24hr) The largest hospital along Puerto Rico's east coast, HIMA is your best option in an emergency.

Wash-n-Post (📞787-863-1995; 100 Calle 2; self-service from $5.50, drop-off service per pound $1.25; ⊙8am-7pm Mon-Sat, 11am-5pm Sun) Across the street from the Villa Marina Shopping Center, this UPS office doubles as a laundromat. Same day service available if you drop your threads off early. If you're doing it yourself, last wash is one hour before closing.

ⓘ Getting There & Around

AIR

José Aponte de la Torre-Ceiba Airport (RVR; 📞787-863-1011; off Hwy 53, Ceiba; 24hr parking $8.50; 🛜) The small Ceiba airport sits on what was once the Roosevelt Roads Naval Station. It primarily offers flights to Culebra, Vieques and San Juan. Local car-rental agencies typically provide pick up and drop off service to the airport.

A taxi from the airport to Fajardo's ferry terminal is fixed at $15 for up to three passengers; to San Juan it's $80.

BOAT

Ferries to both Vieques and Culebra leave from the modern **Autoridad de Transporte Marítimo** (p111) in the gritty Playa Fajardo/Puerto Real neighborhood, about 1.5 miles east of town. A taxi from San Juan costs $80 for up to five people.

Autoridad de Transporte Marítimo (ATM, Maritime Transportation Authority; 📞ext 2736 787-494-0934; https://ati.pr/rutas-y-mapas; Calle Playa; adult/child to Culebra $2.25/1, to Vieques $2/1) offers daily service to Vieques and Culebra on *lanchas* (passenger boats) and *ferries* (cargo boats). Tickets are sold immediately before departure; no reservations or advance sales accepted.

CAR

Sights in the region are dispersed and you'll really need a vehicle to see things. Most car-rental agencies are in Fajardo or near the José Aponte de la Torre-Ceiba Airport.

To get to the ferry terminal, take Hwy 195 from Hwy 3; follow signs that say 'Embarcadero' or 'ferry.' There's secure outdoor parking ($5 per day) near the ferry docks. Note that most rental-car contracts prohibit taking cars on the ferry to Culebra or Vieques.

For Cabezas de San Juan Reserve, Las Croabas and Playa Seven Seas turn north off Hwy 195 onto Hwy 987.

Avis (📞787-885-0505; www.avis.com; Escolastico Lopez, Ceiba; per day $45-125; ⊙8am-5pm Mon-Fri, 9am-1pm Sun) Located near Ceiba airport, Avis provides free shuttle service to/from the ferry terminal.

Enterprise (📞844-794-8594, El Conquistador Resort 844-874-6746; www.enterprise.com; 1000 Av El Conquistador; 4227 Marginal No 3; per day $45-100; ⊙8am-5pm) Enterprise has two locations in Fajardo. Both provide shuttle service to/from the ferry terminal. One-way rentals are also offered for an additional fee.

PÚBLICO

Públicos (public vans) running from the **Río Piedras terminal** (p90) in San Juan serve the ferry terminal ($26) and Fajardo *pueblo* ($5.50). Be sure to leave early – the travel time is three to four hours, depending on traffic. *Públicos* run Monday to Saturday only, the last one leaving at 3:30pm in either direction.

If you're headed to the ferry terminal and you're on a tight budget, consider getting off in town and walking the 35 minutes to the ferry – a straight shot on a decent road. A *público* trip to/from San Juan's international airport costs $10 to $30, depending on where you get off.

TAXI

You can always find taxis at the ferry terminal and Ceiba airport to take you to San Juan or its Luis Muñoz Marín International Airport ($80 to $90). For taxi service originating elsewhere, try **Fajardo Taxi** (📞787-513-7685; www.fajardotaxi.com; ⊙24hr).

Naguabo & Around

POP 24,900

There are two parts to Naguabo: the landlocked downtown area – an enclave of modest homes with a hair-pulling one-way street system – and the laid-back and appealing seaside community.

On the water, Playa Húcares offers gorgeous ocean views and lunch in its low-key seafood restaurants (though no beach, despite

CAYO SANTIAGO: MONKEY COLONY

There's a monkey colony about a kilometer off the coast thanks to a team of scientists who in 1938 decided to turn Cayo Santiago into a research area. Five hundred rhesus macaque monkeys were brought from India and let loose on the peaked, hazy island just offshore from Punta Santiago. Today 1200 descendants of these primates run rampant on the 39 tropical acres.

Only researchers from the Caribbean Primate Research Center are permitted on the island, but visitors can eyeball groups of monkeys living life – eating, climbing, fighting – from kayaks and boats (don't forget that monkeys can swim). There's decent snorkeling around a sunken ship not far from the shore – keep your eyes peeled for starfish. Recommended tour operators include Barefoot Adventures and Captain Paco.

its name). Heading south, a string of tiny seaside villages and windswept beaches lead to the Humacao Nature Reserve and, beyond that, to the vast Palmas del Mar resort area.

◉ Sights

There's nothing worth a detour into downtown Naguabo – it's a collection of modest homes and small businesses – but the seaside drive along Hwy 3 is very rewarding for its untouched beaches, simple eateries and nature reserve.

★ **Humacao Nature Reserve** NATURE RESERVE
(☑ 787-852-6088; gear rental 787-852-6058; Km 74.3, Hwy 3; bike/paddleboat/kayak rental per hour $7/10/15; ☺ concessions 7:30am-3:30pm Mon-Fri, 9am-4pm Sat & Sun; P ♠) FREE Almost 3200 acres once used for a sugarcane plantation have been given back to nature at this gem of a nature reserve. Mangroves and palm trees provide shade for lagoons that serve as havens for myriad birds and fish; turtles and iguanas are easily spotted too. Kayak the placid waters or bike or walk along the many nature paths.

Punta Santiago VILLAGE
(Hwy 3) The town of Punta Santiago is a local weekend and holiday hot spot. Its *friquitines* and kiosks offer lots of succulent treats such as *arroz con jueyes* (rice with crab

chunks), *pastelillos* (turnovers) and pork in all shapes, ways and forms. During the busy season it's fun and upbeat – a window into the local beach-town culture.

Playa Húcares VILLAGE
(Malecón de Naguabo; Hwy 3) One of the set locations for *The Rum Diary* movie, Playa Húcares doesn't actually have a beach – the waterfront is a long pleasant *malecón* (boardwalk) overlooking the bay and the surrounding hills. It does have dramatic views of Vieques, 10 miles out to sea, and Cayo Santiago, closer to shore. Playa Húcares is also worth visiting for a simple, slow, seafood lunch at one of its waterfront restaurants. Or come on a weekend evening to see the town lit up and alive with visitors and locals partying away the night.

Playa Naguabo BEACH
(Hwy 3) About a kilometer south of Playa Húcares, there's a 3km-long windswept beach known as Playa Naguabo. Here you can park anywhere along the two-lane road and enjoy quiet and lovely views out to sea and the islands. Sporadic stands sell ultra-fresh seafood at cheap prices during the day.

⚡ Activities

Most organized activities are based in the Palmas del Mar resort, though two local outfits offer excellent tours to Cayo Santiago.

★ **Barefoot Adventures** OUTDOORS
(☑ 787-850-0508; www.barefoottravelersrooms. com; Punta Santiago; kayaking/snorkeling excursions per person from $55, hang gliding flights from $200) The Barefoot Travelers Rooms guesthouse offers tandem hang-gliding flights in El Yunque. Its kayaking/snorkeling excursions to Cayo Santiago (aka Monkey Island) are very popular, particularly for the profusion of primate-spotting opportunities. Kayak rentals also available.

Captain Paco FISHING, SNORKELING
(☑ 787-316-0441; Km 66.8, Hwy 3, Playa Húcares) Captain Paco offers popular fishing or snorkeling excursions to Cayo Santiago aboard *La Paseadora,* a sturdy motorboat with sunshade. Prices are negotiable; start your bidding at about $45 per person.

Sea Ventures Dive Center DIVING
(☑ 787-863-3483, www.divepalmasdelmar.com; Palmas del Mar, Km 86.4, Hwy 3, Humacao; 2-tank dive incl gear rental from $120; ☺ 8am-6pm)

This popular dive shop organizes trips to almost three dozen sites near Palmas del Mar. Expect to swim through caverns and tunnels.

Rancho Buena Vista   HORSEBACK RIDING
(☑787-479-7479; www.ranchobuenavistapr.com; Palmas del Mar, Km 86.4, Hwy 3, Humacao; rides from $45) These large stables specialize in the Paso Fino, a breed local to Puerto Rico. Guides lead riders through the lush hills or along the beach (or both); rides typically run one to two hours in length.

🛌 Sleeping

There are a handful of guesthouses along this section of Puerto Rico's east coast. More than anything, condo rentals abound in the 2700-acre Palmas del Mar resort area; house-share websites have listings.

For those willing to leave the coast, several comfortable guesthouses are tucked into the southern side of El Yunque National Forest – a breathtakingly beautiful and tropical place to stay. All are easily reached from Naguabo.

Hostel Bahía del Paraíso   HOSTEL $
(☑787-874-6414; www.bahiadelparaiso.hostel.com; 182 Calle 9, Playa Húcares; dm $28, r with shared bathroom $75; ❈⊛) A converted house up the hill from the main drag, this hostel has a mixed dorm with three bunks and one private room; both have air-con and share a spacious bathroom. A fully equipped common kitchen plus a cozy living room make it easy to meet other travelers. The balcony has spectacular views of the bay.

★Barefoot Travelers Rooms   GUESTHOUSE $$
(☑787-850-0508; www.barefoottravelersrooms. com; cnr Calles 2 & 3, Punta Santiago; r with/ without bath $90/80; ❈⊛⊠) At this homey three-room guesthouse your detail-oriented hosts really do walk around shoeless – when they're not giving hang-gliding lessons or leading kayaking tours. Amenities include a fully equipped guest kitchen, a library and an airy living room with TV and DVD player. There's also an inviting pool with a sunny patio. Located in a gated community, just a block from the beach.

Casa Libre Puerto Rico   GUESTHOUSE $$
(☑787-874-6414; www.casalibrepr.com; 188 Calle 8, Playa Húcares; r incl breakfast $95-110; P❈⊛⊠) Set on a hill above the bay, this guesthouse has four colorful rooms, all with comfortable beds and soothing decor. The

Puerto Rican and Californian hosts make a tasty full breakfast, which is served on the expansive poolside deck. Reserve the purple room upstairs for breathtaking El Yunque and water views.

🍴 Eating

From Playa Húcares south through Punta Santiago, you'll find all manner of street food priced for the masses. Look for stalls – and crowds – along Hwy 3 as you drive. Comb the kiosks and holes-in-the-wall for great *empanadillas* (dough stuffed with meat or fish), *mojito criollo* (rum, mint and lemon) sauce on fresh fish, and tasty *surullitos*.

★Kiosko El Limón   PUERTO RICAN $
(☑787-850-7614; Doctor Vidal, Punta Santiago; dishes $4-14; ⊗10am-10pm Tue-Thu & Sun, to 2am Fri & Sat) A sprawling roadside stand, El Limón is a laid-back eatery, bar and hangout where you'll find everything from fishermen throwing back Medalla beers to families coming for fish dinners. Order at the counter and take a seat at one of the outdoor plastic tables. All manner of *frittangas* (fried food) call passersby from under heat lamps – perfect for grabbing and going to the beach.

★Restaurant Vinny   SEAFOOD, PUERTO RICAN $$
(☑787-874-7664; Malecón, Playa Húcares; mains $5-17; ⊗8am-7pm) Vinny does a bang-up lunch for $6 and the best lobster *pastelillos* (turnovers) on the island. As is typical for Playa Húcares, seafood is the main event. Diners enjoy their meals at long plastic picnic tables set outdoors in a communal style with the sea air for atmosphere.

Daniel's Seafood   SEAFOOD $$
(☑787-852-1784; 7 Marina, Playa Humacao; mains $11-25; ⊗11:30am-8pm Wed-Sun; ❈) Right on the waterfront, this longtime favorite is several cuts above the casual (aka roofless) standard for the area. Fresh seafood with sophisticated preparations is the norm here; many come just for the lobster-stuffed fish with garlic sauce. Dine in air-con comfort or on the open-air terrace.

ℹ️ Getting There & Around

This is car country. Though *públicos* prowl Hwy 3 from Naguabo to Humacao, none are on a specific schedule so you should be prepared to wait.

Hotel staff can help arrange transportation to and from San Juan's Luis Muñoz Marín

International Airport – about a 75-minute trip in normal traffic. During peak season, rates run $85 to $100.

Yabucoa & Around

POP 35,300

Surrounded by rolling hills on three sides and fringed by calm ocean waters on the other, Yabucoa sits on a tract of fertile land once used to grow sugarcane. The town itself holds little for visitors, but on the periphery, Yabucoa is the starting point for two dramatic drives: the famed Ruta Panorámica (Hwy 182) west into the hills, and the less heralded, but no less spectacular, Hwy 901 that tracks the coast between Playa Lucía and the Punta Tuna Lighthouse.

◉ Sights

The *balneario* (swimming hole) at **Playa Lucía**, near the junction of Hwy 901 and Hwy 9911 in Yabucoa, has great shade under its tall coconut trees and several little beach bar-restaurants just off its premises. Headed south, **El Cocal** is one of the few good surfing spots in the area (ask for directions at the *balneario*). Further still toward Maunabo is **Sharkey's**, another decent surf break where you're likely to have the waves to yourself.

Off Hwy 901 along the coast, you can ponder the ruins of **Hacienda de Santa Lucía**, an old sugarcane plantation a mile north of Playa Lucía. Although there are no must-see sights along this stretch, the windswept beaches glimpsed from the road are serene places for a stop. The Centro Educativo Amigos de las Tortugas Marinas offers interesting exhibits on the sea turtles on Puerto Rican shores.

From Hwy 901, take Hwy 760 toward the ocean. The coastal view from the base of the Faro Punta Tuna, the lighthouse just southeast of Maunabo, is worth the drive. The wetland reserve next door has well-maintained interpretive trails and serves as a nesting ground for leatherback and hawksbill turtles. At its northern end, a path leads down to the secluded **Playa Larga**.

★**Reserva Natural Humedal Punta Tuna**　　NATURE RESERVE

(Punta Tuna Wetland Nature Reserve; ☑787-861-0387; Km 4.2, Hwy 7760, Maunabo; ☺8am-5pm; ℗) FREE This lush wetland reserve spans 2.2km of coastline, just north of the Punta Tuna Lighthouse. Interpretive trails through

the mangrove and along the beach provide interesting information on the reserve's ecology, flora and fauna, and a lookout tower makes it easier to spot wildlife, especially in the mornings. The small visitors center has enthusiastic staff with in-depth knowledge about the area; guided tours are available upon request.

Unique among Puerto Rico's reserves, trails are outfitted to accommodate visitors who are vision- and physically challenged; features include phone apps that 'read' signage and trails that are wide and well maintained. Guides also can lead driving tours through the reserve.

The beach here, **Playa Larga**, is gorgeous in an untouched, secluded way. Be careful in the water – riptides make it dangerous for all but the strongest swimmers.

Faro Punta Tuna　　LIGHTHOUSE

(off Hwy 760, Maunabo; ☺9am-3:30pm Wed-Sun) FREE Named after the fruit-bearing *tuna* (prickly pear) cactus that once covered the area, this lighthouse makes for a scenic stop. Built in 1892, it juts out high above the ocean, with sweeping views of the dramatic coastline. The lighthouse itself is closed to the public. A small museum above the office has Taíno artifacts.

Centro Educativo Amigos de las Tortugas Marinas　　NATURE CENTER

(ATMAR, Friends of the Sea Turtle Educational Center; ☑787-469-3400; www.tortugasmaunabo.com; Hwy 901, Maunabo; ☺9am-2pm Mon-Thu, to 4pm Fri & Sat, to 3pm Sun; ℗) FREE A project of the nonprofit Amigos de las Tortugas Marinas, this one-room nature center is jam packed with exhibits on the various sea turtles that migrate to and nest on Puerto Rico. Skulls, shells and even unhatched eggs help to round out the detailed informational placards and videos. Bilingual staff guide visitors through the room, sharing facts and anecdotes.

🛏 Sleeping

★**Caribe Playa Beach Resort**　　INN $$

(☑787-839-6339; www.caribeplaya.com; Km 112, Hwy 3, Patillas; r $120-130; ℗❋☎≋) Tucked in a forest of slanting coconut trees, this mid-century modern inn pulls you right in. Recently renovated rooms are spacious and bright with a contemporary feel. All have microwaves and fridges; some have oceanfront balconies. Two immaculate pools – one adults only – are set along the beach. A natural pool

EXPLORE HIGHWAY 181 & THE RUTA PANORÁMICA

For a fine circle tour of the east, head south and to the coast from San Juan via Hwy 181, connecting to Hwy 182, which boasts the moniker *Ruta Panorámica* (Panoramic Route).

It's a beautiful and remote route that takes you to Yabucoa, and along this mostly narrow, bumpy and sharply curved road, you'll climb high into the tropical rainforest west of El Yunque. Expect to see thickets of bamboo arching over the road amid a plethora of verdant green and flame trees providing vivid orange contrast against the huge, elegant tree ferns. Simple hamlets dot the landscape.

Travel is slow – allow at least three hours – which is all the better when you round a blind bend and find a passel of chihuahuas in the road or a bunch of school kids riding ponies. Amid the dense foliage, you'll be dazzled by deep canyon glimpses and, eventually, views out to sea.

Once in Yabucoa, you can head back up the coast north and west to San Juan.

carved into the rocky coast makes for great snorkeling.

Hotel Lucía Beach HOTEL **$$**
(Lucía Beach Villas; ☑787-705-8734; www.tropical innspr.com; cnr Hwys 901 & 9911, Yabucoa; d incl breakfast $120-130; [P][❄][☎][☒]) Opened in 2015, this two-story hotel has 26 spacious and modern rooms that open onto a small pool, a manicured lawn and, beyond that, popular Playa Lucía. Each has a mini-fridge, microwave and coffeemaker. A casual on-site restaurant offers breakfast. Guests also enjoy access to the facilities at the more basic Parador Palmas de Lucía next door. All-inclusive packages available.

Parador MaunaCaribe INN **$$**
(☑787-861-3330; www.tropicalinnspr.com; Km 1.9, Hwy 901, Maunabo; d from $100; [P][❄][☎][☒]) One of the Tropical Inn's paradors, this oceanside option boasts an infinity pool and rooms with blonde wood furniture and a muted tropical flair. Unfortunately, the pastel-painted complex is somewhat saddled with a sterile cookie-cutter layout, but the many amenities, including a spacious restaurant and bar, more than compensate.

✖ Eating

In this less traveled part of Puerto Rico, you'll find few places to eat that are worth a detour. Often, your best bets are simple stalls in the towns.

★ **Calixto's Place** PUERTO RICAN **$**
(☑787-204-4282; Malecón de Patillas, off Km 118, Hwy 3, Patillas; plates $4-18; ⊗11am-8pm) Calixto's is a bustling restaurant-bar overlooking a pretty oceanfront park in Patillas. A huge deck is the weekend go-to for locals. Stuffed *mofongo* is the specialty, though if you just want some finger foods to go with your mojito, the freshly baked crab *pastelillos* (turnovers) and baskets of chicken wings are impossible to resist.

El Nuevo Horizonte PUERTO RICAN **$$**
(☑787-893-5492; Km 9.8, Hwy 901, Yabucoa; dishes $11-31; ⊗11am-8pm Wed, Thu & Sun, to 10pm Fri & Sat) The view rarely gets better than the one you'll enjoy from this place, perched high on the mountainside overlooking the Caribbean. At this simple restaurant you can smell the *asopao de langosta* (lobster stew) cooking 200yd before you get here. A cauldron will set you back about $30 and serves at least two people. Live music on weekends.

ℹ Getting There & Away

A rental car or taxi are the most reliable ways to get around this part of Puerto Rico; *públicos* are too sporadic to be dependable. A cab ride from Yabucoa to Maunabo costs around $20 and to San Juan's Luis Muñoz Marín International Airport $90 to $100.

If driving, stick to the scenic, oceanside Hwy 901; the short tunnel on Hwy 53 between Yabucoa and Maunabo can get backed up with traffic.

Culebra & Vieques

POP 10,350

Includes ➡

Culebra........................118
Vieques 128

Best Places to Eat

➡ Zaco's Tacos (p125)

➡ El Panino (p125)

➡ El Quenepo (p140)

➡ Coqui Fire Cafe (p141)

➡ Horta's BBQ (p141)

Best Places to Sleep

➡ El Navegante de Culebra (p124)

➡ Villa Flamenco Beach (p124)

➡ The Lazy Hostel (p137)

➡ Casa de Amistad (p138)

➡ Hacienda Tamarindo (p139)

➡ Malecón House (p138)

Why Go?

Separated from mainland Puerto Rico by an 13km stretch of choppy blue water, the two bejeweled Caribbean havens of Culebra and Vieques have an irresistible charm thanks to mellow locals, laid-back expats and itinerant sailors.

Disembark for a few days and you'll uncover a wealth of surprises – horses roaming free in Vieques, endangered turtles in Culebra – and people who reclaimed their prized islands from the US Navy in 1975 (Culebra) and 2003 (Vieques) after more than 50 years of military occupation.

But it's the beaches that will have you purring with delight. Between them, the two members of the Spanish Virgin Islands may have the greatest variety of truly superb beaches in the Caribbean. Many are deserted, giving you the chance for boundless frolic. Best of all, these two islands have yet to attract mass tourism, so there's nary a golf course, casino or huge resort.

When to Go

The spring shoulder season (April through June) brings picture-perfect weather and fewer travelers. There aren't many discounts on lodging but you'll have less company on the beach; some days, it may just be you and the birds.

The best viewing of the bioluminescent bay in Vieques is during the new moon; some operators don't go out when it's full. From April through June, wildlife fans can volunteer for a turtle-egg protection project on Culebra.

The famous Caribbean trade winds gently buffet these two islands, but it's still warm and balmy just about every day of the year.

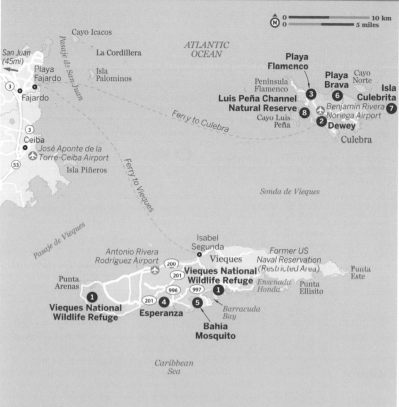

Culebra & Vieques Highlights

❶ Vieques National Wildlife Refuge (p129) Reveling in some of the best beaches in the Caribbean where you can find a patch of sand ideal for you.

❷ Dewey (p118) Bar-hopping with sailors between the trio of popular nightspots in Culebra's town.

❸ Playa Flamenco (p120) Wandering the long crescent of sand at this paradisial place, where memories of a

military past dissolve in the beautiful waters.

❹ Esperanza (p130) Eating, drinking or just chillaxing on the colorful yet laid-back oceanfront 'strip'.

❺ Bahía Mosquito (p131) Seeing aquatic stars on a serene and distinctly surreal evening tour of Vieques' Bioluminescent Bay.

❻ Playa Brava (p121) Hiking through brush and low forest and being

rewarded with one of Culebra's picture-perfect beaches.

❼ Isla Culebrita (p118) Taking a water taxi to this idyllic island of white-sand beaches, tide pools and untouched reefs.

❽ Luis Peña Channel Natural Reserve (p120) Plunging in and snorkeling Culebra's vibrant reefs in this natural reserve, easily accessible from Playa Tamarindo.

History

Some 500 years ago the islands east of Puerto Rico, including Culebra and Vieques, were disputed territory between the Taíno and the Caribs. Groups from both tribes came and went from the islands according to the season – probably to hunt the turtles nesting here. Vieques had more fertile, flatter land for farming and therefore was the more popular island. The first real settlement came to Culebra during the early 16th century, when Taíno and Carib refugees from Borinquen gathered here and on Vieques to make peace with each other, pool their resources and mount a fierce (but ultimately unsuccessful) campaign to drive the Spaniards from the big island.

When Spain conceded Puerto Rico and her territories to the US following the Spanish–American War in 1898, both Culebra and Vieques became municipalities of the Republic of Puerto Rico. Residents are therefore recognized as US citizens (half of them are expat Americans, in any case).

❶ Getting There & Away

There's frequent air service from San Juan to both Vieques and Culebra. Much cheaper are the regular public ferries between Fajardo and the islands. In January, ferry passengers can sometimes spot humpback whales.

There are direct flights but no ferries between Vieques and Culebra; you can go by water on a costly boat charter.

Distances on the islands are fairly small, but wheels are needed to explore those alluring remote beaches.

Culebra

POP 1700

Long feted for its diamond-dust beaches and world-class diving reefs, sleepy Culebra is probably more famous for what it *hasn't* got than for what it actually possesses. There are no big hotels here, no golf courses, no casinos, no fast-food chains, no rush-hour traffic and, best of all, no stress. Situated 27km off mainland Puerto Rico, but inhabiting an entirely different planet culturally speaking, the island's slow pace can sometimes take a bit of getting used to. It's home to rat-race dropouts, earnest idealists, solitude seekers, myriad eccentrics and anyone else who's forsaken the hassles and manic intricacies of modern life. It's also home to a range of gorgeous natural areas, bays, snorkeling sites, hiking trails and all manner of fine beaches. Come, join the local vibe and explore one of Puerto Rico's most gorgeous destinations.

History

First hunting grounds for Taíno and Carib tribes, then a pirate stronghold during the days of the Spanish Empire, much of Culebra's

7000 acres has remained essentially the same ever since two-legged creatures took to walking its shores. The US Navy grabbed control of most of the island early in the 20th century and didn't cede its lands back to the locals until 1975.

Although development was threatened on the pristine lands after the military left, resident expats and native-born *culebrenses* (Culebra natives) combined forces to resist rampant growth. They've continued to work together to preserve the island's low-key vibe.

◉ Sights

Heading left away from the ferry dock will bring you to Calle Pedro Márquez, usually referred to as the 'main road,' which runs through Dewey, the island's principal settlement. Sights in town are modest at best.

★ Culebra National Wildlife Refuge   WILDLIFE RESERVE

(Map p119; ☏ 787-742-0115; www.fws.gov/caribbean/refuges/culebra) More than 20% of Culebra is part of a spectacular national wildlife refuge, which US President Theodore Roosevelt signed into law more than 100 years ago. Most of this land lies along Culebra's coastline and includes more than 20 cays. Containing three different ecosystems, the refuge serves as a habitat for endangered sea turtles and is also the largest seabird nesting grounds in the Caribbean. For visitors, it is a place for hiking, birdwatching and enjoying secluded beaches.

★ Isla Culebrita   ISLAND

(Map p119) If you need a reason to hire a water taxi, Isla Culebrita is it. This small island, just east of Playa Zoni (p121), is part of the national wildlife refuge. With its six beaches, tide pools, reefs and nesting areas for seabirds, Isla Culebrita has changed little in the past 500 years. The north beaches, especially the long crescent of **Playa Tortuga**, are popular nesting grounds for green sea turtles – you might even see them swimming near the reefs just offshore.

The Isla is also home to **Faro Culebrita**. Built in 1886, it was one of the oldest operating lighthouses in the Caribbean when it was shut down by the US Navy in 1975. Currently in ruins, it is earmarked for extensive repairs. A well-marked path leads you there – the lighthouse itself is off-limits but the vistas are picture postcard perfect.

Bring a lot of water, sunscreen and a hat if you head here – there's little shade here. And don't forget snacks and snorkel gear!

Culebra

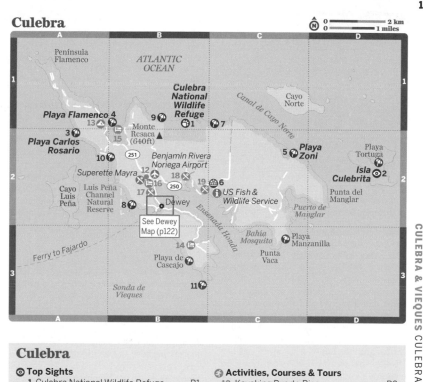

Culebra

◉ Top Sights

1	Culebra National Wildlife Refuge	B1
2	Isla Culebrita	D2
3	Playa Carlos Rosario	A2
4	Playa Flamenco	B1
5	Playa Zoni	C2

◉ Sights

6	Museo Histórico de Culebra	C2
7	Playa Brava	C1
8	Playa Melones	B2
9	Playa Resaca	B1
10	Playa Tamarindo	B2
11	Punta Soldado	B3

◈ Activities, Courses & Tours

12	Kayaking Puerto Rico	B2

⬛ Sleeping

13	Camping Culebra	A1
14	Club Seabourne	B3
15	Culebra Beach Villas	B2
16	Palmetto Guesthouse	B2
	Villa Flamenco Beach	(see 15)

✖ Eating

17	El Panino	B2
18	Susie's	B2
19	Tiki's Grill	B2

Round-trip water-taxi service costs around $50 per person, including beach gear, hammock and snorkel set.

◉ Dewey

Nestled on a thin knob of land between two glistening bays, Dewey is Culebra's diminutive main town and the launching pad for the island's rustic attractions. A languid settlement that awakes from its slumber for the arrival and departure of the ferry (p127), it's more of a rural backwater than delectable Caribbean idyll. Named after the US admiral who won the Battle of Manila Bay in 1898, it's a place where no one's in a hurry and where residents stop to chat about what hot commodities have turned up at the grocery store.

◉ Ensenda Honda

Sailboat masts sway like metronomes on Culebra's sheltered central bay. You'll find fine views of the waters from all sides, including from a few good shoreside restaurants and along Hwy 250. Watch for all

OFF THE BEATEN TRACK

EXPLORE CAYO LUIS PEÑA

Less visited than Isla Culebrita, Cayo Luis Peña is the island of peaks, rocks, forests and coves you'll pass just a few minutes before the ferry (p127) lands you at Culebra's dock. This island is a part of the Culebra National Wildlife Refuge (p118) and it has a collection of small sheltered beaches and snorkeling all around the island. Luis Peña is a short kayak or water-taxi trip from Culebra.

manner of fish – including small sharks – swimming through the crystal waters.

Museo Histórico de Culebra MUSEUM
(Culebra History Museum; Map p119; ☑ 787-742-3832; Hwy 250; admission $1; ⊘ 10am-3pm Fri-Sun; P ♿) Housed in the Navy's former munitions warehouse (*El Polvorín*), the Museo Histórico de Culebra is a compact little place jam-packed with interesting displays on the history of the island, its culture and ecology. Entire sections are dedicated to the presence of the US military, endangered sea turtles and the Taínos who once lived here. Displays themselves range from quite professional (Taíno artifacts and artillery shell casings) to science fair (the puffer fish with googly eyes is a stand out).

🏖 Beaches

Culebra's beaches offer wild natural beauty. Tourist facilities vary, with plenty at Playa Flamenco and blissfully few at Playa Zoni. Several beaches are only accessible by hiking in, increasing the possibilities of having a Caribbean beach to yourself, at least for a few hours. When venturing out to most beaches – on foot or with wheels – be sure to bring lots of water and snacks.

Isla Culebrita (p118) and **Cayo Norte** are two of the more popular cays off Culebra and are easily visited; there are 18 others surrounding the island.

★ Playa Flamenco BEACH
(Map p119; end of Hwy 251) Stretching for a mile around a sheltered, horseshoe-shaped bay, Playa Flamenco is not only one of Culebra's best beaches, it's also generally regarded as the finest in the Caribbean. Backed by low scrub and trees rather than craning palms, Flamenco gets very crowded on weekends, especially with day-trippers from San Juan.

Alone among Culebra's beaches, it has a range of amenities. Weekdays are good for a visit, when crowds are few.

In the winter months you'll feel like Robinson Crusoe contemplating the clarity of the water here; the name comes from the nearby lagoon, which attracts flamingos in winter. Services include a collection of kiosks (selling snack food, lunches, rum punches and beer, and renting beach gear), toilets, outdoor showers, lockers, lifeguards, picnic tables and an often jam-packed parking lot. Camping (p124) is allowed.

The iconic **rusting tank** is at the beach's western end, a legacy of when US troops practiced invasions here. Its swirling green and yellow stripes, the work of local artist Jorge Acevedo, represent a dancing fish.

Playa Flamenco is 4.5km from the ferry terminal (p127) and is a straight shot from Dewey. The main road leading out of town becomes Hwy 251, passes the airport and ends at the beach. By car, the trip takes about 15 minutes; by foot, plan on 40 minutes.

★ Playa Carlos Rosario BEACH
(Map p119; off Hwy 251) Remote Playa Carlos Rosario is a thin, white-sand beach with one of the best snorkeling areas in Puerto Rico. This is mostly due to a barrier reef that almost encloses the beach's waters; you can snorkel on either side of it by swimming through the boat channel – look for the floating white marker – at the right-hand side of the beach. But be very careful: water taxis and local powerboats cruise this channel, and swimmers have been hit.

To get to the beach, follow a path through an opening in a chain-link fence on the western side of the parking lot at Playa Flamenco. A 15-minute hike over the hill brings you to a tiny **no-name beach**. Continue north from here, crossing the narrow peninsula, and head down to the sandy basin and shade trees of Playa Carlos Rosario.

For truly spectacular snorkeling, continue working your way north along to the beach for about a half-kilometer to a snorkeling site called **The Wall**, which has 12m drop-offs, huge sea fans and rich colors.

Playa Tamarindo BEACH
(Map p119; off Hwy 251) Playa Tamarindo is all about snorkeling; it shares the fish-filled waters of the **Luis Peña Channel Natural Reserve**, making it a popular spot for independent travelers as well as organized tour groups. This often-overlooked beach is not

as flashy and fabulous-looking as others, but offers a good combination of sun and shade, gentle currents and lots of underwater life. Head to the extreme right or left of the beach for the easiest access to the colorful underwater life.

★**Playa Zoni** BEACH
(Map p119; off Hwy 250) Head to the eastern end of the island and you'll eventually run out of road at Playa Zoni. Many locals think this is a better beach than Flamenco and it's hard to argue. Zoni isn't quite as big and curving, but it certainly is stunning in its own right with soft sand, turquoise waters and idyllic views of Cayo Norte, Isla Culebrita (p118) and even Charlotte Amelie on the horizon. Do like the locals do and bring a cooler for a picnic.

Playa Resaca BEACH
(Map p119; off Hwy 250) A *resaca* is an undertow and a metaphor for a hangover, an allusion to the state of the water perhaps, or the way you will feel after climbing up and down 200m Monte Resaca to reach it. Not well maintained nor easy to find, the trail is a 40-minute hike that involves scrambling, but the reward is worth it – a gorgeous windswept beach you'll likely have to yourself. The beach lives up to its name and is unsafe for swimming.

The trailhead is not well marked. To get to it, take Hwy 250 east and turn north immediately after you pass the airport. Follow this road until it ends at a roundabout. Two paths begin here – follow the smaller one, marked with a huge rock and a sign indicating a turtle nesting zone.

Monte Resaca, the island's highest point, is characterized by an ecologically unique boulder-strewn forest on its upper slopes that harbors rare types of flora and fauna (mainly lizards). It's a tough (and sometimes prickly) climb. Bring lots of water and sturdy shoes.

Playa Brava BEACH
(Map p119; off Hwy 250) The beauty of Playa Brava lies in the fact that there is no road here; you *have* to hike about 30 minutes along a little-used trail that is often overgrown with sea grape and low scrub. The rewards are immense when you finally clear the last brush and are confronted with an isolated but stunning swath of sand that glimmers with a fierce but utterly enchanting beauty. Bring walking shoes and snacks. No need for snorkel gear – the water is too rough.

To get to the trailhead, take Hwy 250 east and turn north on the road immediately after the history museum. Follow it until the pavement ends and you come up against a chain gate near a few small houses. This is the entrance to a cattle farm, but it is also a public right-of-way; park your car or bike and head due north on the trail beyond the gate. The second half of the trail leads through a grove of trees that often attracts butterflies.

Punta Soldado BEACH
(Map p119; off Hwy 250; P) On the southwestern tip of the island, Punta Soldado has a rocky beach perfect for exploring. The water is calm

CULEBRA & VIEQUES CULEBRA

PENINSULA FLAMENCO'S MILITARY PAST

Up until the early 1970s, Flamenco was part of a live firing range used by the US Navy for target practice. First requisitioned by the military in 1902 to counter a rising German threat in the Caribbean, Culebra's beaches were used to stage mock amphibious landings and myriad ground maneuvers. In 1936, with WWII in the offing, the Flamenco peninsula yielded to its first live arms fire and the beach was regularly shelled.

Burgeoning decade by decade, the military operations reached their peak during the late 1960s at the height of the Vietnam War, with the navy simulating gun attacks and submarine warfare. When the US government hinted at expanding the Culebra base in the early 1970s, public sentiment quickly turned bellicose. In what would become a dress rehearsal for the Navy–Vieques protests 30 years later, a small committed group of Puerto Rican protesters – including Independence Party leader Rubén Berríos – initiated a campaign of civil disobedience that culminated in squatters accessing the beach and having to be forcibly removed by police. Despite arrests and imprisonments, the tactics worked. In 1975 the US Navy pulled out of Culebra and the beach was returned to its natural state.

Over 40 years later you can still find evidence of the war games that once pounded Flamenco's sands. At the beach's western end, contrasting rather sharply with the diamond-dust sand and translucent water, an incongruously brightly painted yet rusting tank is a ghostly reminder of past military maneuvers.

Dewey

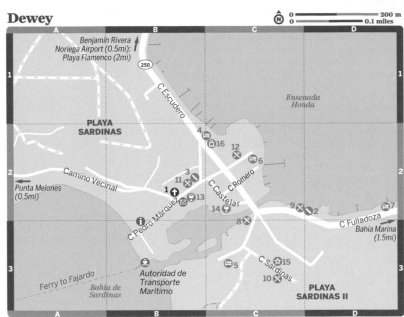

Dewey

◉ Sights
1 Iglesia Nuestra Señora Del
Carmen.................................... B2

⊙ Activities, Courses & Tours
2 Aquatic Adventures............................. D2
3 Culebra Snorkeling & Dive Center........ B2

🛏 Sleeping
4 Casa Ensenada............................... C2
5 Culebra International Hostel............... C3
6 El Navegante de Culebra..................... C2
7 Villa Fulladoza.............................. D2

✖ Eating
8 Colmado Milka.............................. C3

9 Dinghy Dock................................ C2
10 El Eden..................................... C3
11 Vibra Verde................................ B2
12 Zaco's Tacos............................... C2

⊙ Drinking & Nightlife
13 La Lobina.................................. B2
14 Mamacita's................................ C2

✪ Entertainment
15 Cine Culebra.............................. C3

🛍 Shopping
Artefango..............................(see 9)
16 La Cava Gift Shop........................ C2

and clear and filled with healthy coral, also making it a great spot for snorkeling – turtles and puffer fish are often sighted here. Enter the water towards the left-hand side of the beach for the best snorkeling; the reef is about 45m offshore.

Playa Melones   BEACH
(Map p119; Camino Vecinal) This is the closest beach to Dewey. This tiny strip of sand with some shade trees and a smattering of picnic tables is the best place to catch a sunset. The snorkeling is also decent at both ends of

its small bay. The beach name comes from the prevalence of melon cactus in this part of the island. Consider bringing shoes you can wear in the water; cacti line the seafloor.

🏃 Activities

Diving & Snorkeling
Despite reef damage from the US Navy testing era and endemic climate change pressures, Culebra retains some of Puerto Rico's most amazing dive spots, including sunken ships, coral reefs, drop-offs and caves.

Highlights include the *Wit Power* tugboat (which sank in 1984), the Geniqui Caves, El Mono boulders and the fish-filled water world of Cayo Ratón.

Good snorkeling sites can also be accessed from many beaches. Tamarindo (p120) is a good example of the bounty on offer: it teems with a spectacular variety of fish and features a 50ft wall of coral, all protected by the Luis Peña Channel Natural Reserve. Other good spots include Playa Carlos Rosario (p120) and Playa Melones.

Most dive shops rent snorkeling equipment and boat captains often will arrange snorkel tours.

★Culebra Snorkeling
& Dive Center   DIVING, SNORKELING
(Map p122; ☑787-435-3662; www.culebrasnorkelingcenter.com; Pedro Márquez, Dewey; ☉8:30am-5pm Mon-Thu, to 1:30pm Sun) This friendly shop offers excellent snorkeling excursions around the island where you're sure to see turtles, stingrays and all sorts of tropical fish. If DIY is more your thing, staffers will share snorkeling maps and tips and point you in the right direction. High-end snorkel gear, kayaks, underwater cameras, even rash guards are available for rent too.

Aquatic Adventures   DIVING, SNORKELING
(Map p122; ☑515-290-2310; www.diveculebra.com; Calle Fulladoza, Dewey; snorkeling/2-tank dives from $60/95; ☉9:30am-5pm) Located above Dinghy Dock (p125) (so handy for a post-dive cocktail), this fine shop leads five-hour dive and snorkeling tours that leave around 10:30am. Trips include lunch.

Boating
Excursions to Isla Culebrita (p118) and **Cayo Norte** are a gorgeous way to spend a day. Round-trip water taxis cost about $50 per person to Culebrita. Trips to Cayo Norte are generally combined with snorkeling and lunch, and start at $60 per person. Captain German (p127) and Captain Brad (p127) are reliable options for both. If they're booked, you'll often find captains along Dewey's waterfront.

★Culebra Sailing   BOATING
(☑787-435-9996; www.culebrasailing.com; per person from $150) It's hard to beat sailing in Culebra's turquoise blue waters in a classic 60ft wood schooner. Captain Mike Brown does just that on daily sailing trips. Limited to just six people, excursions include stops at the island's hidden beaches and cays as

well as snorkeling in waters rich with sea life. Sailing lessons also offered.

Pez Vela Charters   BOATING
(☑787-215-3809; www.culebracatamaran.com) Captain Bill Penfield offers popular catamaran and sailing trips around Culebra and its cays. Snorkeling and beach hopping are a given. Snacks, lunch and nonalcoholic drinks included too. Deep-sea fishing tours also available.

Kayaking
The usually placid waters of Ensenada Honda (p119) are ideal for a paddle; the beaches and small coves can also be fun.

Kayaking Puerto Rico   KAYAKING, SNORKELING
(Map p119; ☑787-742-0523; www.kayakingpuertorico.com; Hwy 251; 3hr tours from $55-60) These tours, cheerfully called 'aquafaris', combine kayaking and snorkeling the rich waters of the Luis Peña Channel Natural Reserve, ending with some time on Playa Flamenco. You can also start at Fajardo at the ferry port (p111) at 8am ($75, includes transfers). This outfit also rents gear (snorkel equipment, paddleboards and kayaks) at reasonable prices. Located across from the airport.

Cycling
With its hills, dirt trails and back-to-nature ruggedness, Culebra is an excellent place to bike – not just for exercise but also as a handy means of transportation.

Pedal Power   CYCLING
(☑603-479-7098; www.culebrabikerentals.com; bike rental per day/week from $20/17, flat-rate helmet rentals from $5) Pedal Power delivers good-quality mountain bikes to your door, ferry or flight. Look out for the VW van decked out in daisies.

Hiking
Rejoice! The island is your oyster. The 4.5km hike from Dewey to Playa Flamenco (p120) is along a paved road with some inclines, but the destination is idyllic. You can veer off to Playa Tamarindo (p120) from a junction just before the lagoon. Playa Carlos Rosario (p120) is reached via a trail that starts at the western end of Playa Flamenco (p120). The hike to Playa Brava (p121) begins at the end of a back road that cuts north from Rte 250 just past the island's graveyard. The trail rises to a ridge and then drops to the beach through thick scrub. The toughest hike on the island is the rough trail to Playa Resaca (p121) that traverses

LOCAL KNOWLEDGE

TURTLE WATCH

Two of Culebra's most isolated beaches – Resaca (p121) and Brava (p121) – are nesting sites for the endangered leatherback sea turtle, the world's largest living sea turtle (adults can reach 2m in length and weigh 1500lb). The nesting season runs from April through early June.

Each year a few volunteers are accepted by the Department of Natural Resources (p262) to monitor the delicate egg-laying process. Volunteers travel out to the beaches, where they count eggs, measure turtles and document the event for environmental records. Locals also close nesting beaches during this time from dawn to dusk. The rather smaller hawksbill sea turtle (up to 3ft long and 250lb) also lays eggs on Culebra's beaches.

the eponymous mountain; the trailhead is about 3km from Dewey.

🛏 Sleeping

Several guesthouses and inns are a short walk from the ferry dock (p127), though there are many options island-wide. Many have docks for boats.

🛏 Dewey

Culebra International Hostel　　HOSTEL **$**
(Map p122; ☑732-547-8831; www.culebrahostel.com; Calle Fulladoza, Dewey; dm $33, r $90; 🌣🛜) Once an auto-parts shop, this rambling hostel offers two spacious dorms (including one female-only) with good bunk beds and air-con. There's a simple kitchen and lots of outdoor seating, mostly in a wild garden of potted plants (over 350 at last count). Expat manager Tommy often cooks dinner for guests, served family style.

★ Villa Fulladoza　　APARTMENT **$$**
(Map p122; ☑787-742-3576; www.villafulladoza.wix.com/culebra; 350 Fulladoza, Dewey; apt $80-95; 🛜) Super-cute and vividly turquoise and salmon, unfussy Villa Fulladoza offers seven bright fan-cooled studio apartments with ocean breezes and plenty of room. The shared patio is shaded by a swaying mango tree, while many of the units have large terraces (get one upstairs for great views). If you are lucky enough to enjoy your own private water transportation, there's a boat dock.

★ El Navegante de Culebra　　INN **$$**
(Map p122; ☑787-568-1378; www.naveguest.com; Calle Pedro Márquez, Dewey; r $90-130; 🅿🌣🛜) A modern inn in the heart of Dewey, El Navegante's eight units are airy, with clean lines and a distinct beachy feel. Most have gorgeous views of the bay and a huge deck makes enjoying the vista easy. Lockers, big

enough for monster suitcases, are available for late check-out and early check-in.

Casa Ensenada　　GUESTHOUSE **$$**
(Map p122; ☑866-210-0709, 787-241-4441; www.casaensenada.com; 142 Escudero, Dewey; studio $125-150, 1-bedroom apt $175; 🌣🛜) This pleasant guesthouse just north of town on the waterfront at Ensenada Honda is handily placed. The inn has three units (accommodating two, four or up to six people) with kitchen or kitchenette, separate entrance and air-conditioning. Unexpected extras include free use of a kayak, free boat dock, beach towels, grill, hammocks and a spacious breezy patio.

🛏 Outside Dewey

Camping Culebra　　CAMPGROUND **$**
(Map p119; ☑787-742-0700; www.campingculebra.com; Playa Flamenco, Hwy 251; campsites from $30; 🅿) Famous Playa Flamenco (p120) is the only place where you can legally camp in Culebra. Campsites are in five zones: A is closest to the food kiosks while E is closest the beach (and therefore most popular). Outdoor showers have limited hours; bathrooms are open 24/7. The campground has on-site security and is quite safe. Reservations aren't typically necessary.

The campground office is located near the entrance to the parking lot. Camping gear can be rented from on-site vendors.

★ Villa Flamenco Beach　　APARTMENT **$$**
(Map p119; ☑787-742-0023, 787-383-0985; www.villaflamencobeach.com; off Hwy 251; studio $135-145, 1-bedroom apt $155-180; 🅿🌣🛜) Gentle waves lulling you to sleep, a night sky replete with twinkling stars and one of the best beaches on the planet just outside your window: this six-unit place is an absolute winner. Enjoy the getaway with self-catering kitchen facilities, inviting hammocks and little more than

palms, sand and turquoise waters for atmosphere. Closed October and November.

Culebra Beach Villas
APARTMENT $$

(Map p119; ☑877-767-7575, 787-767-7575; www.culebrabeachrental.com; off Hwy 251; apt $150-355; P☀❄🛜) The only visible building on Playa Flamenco (p120) is a three-story Caribbean villa at this condo complex. There are 33 self-catering apartments (each individually owned – and decorated) with kitchens for two to eight people. The setting is stunning, of course, though you'll want to stock up on provisions in Dewey. Minimum stays are two or more nights. Wi-fi in the reception area only.

Palmetto Guesthouse
GUESTHOUSE $$

(Map p119; ☑787-239-7779; www.palmettoculebra.com; off Hwy 250, Barriada Clark; r $100-130; ☀🛜) In the Barriada Clark neighborhood near the airport, the Palmetto has five rooms, all simple and clean though some are a bit cramped. There are two guest kitchens, equipped like home, and a garden with a deck. Beach chairs and coolers, a huge magazine pile, bug spray and other toiletries are there for sharing. Complimentary coffee available most mornings. A comfortable option, if a bit pricey for the location.

Club Seabourne
HOTEL $$$

(Map p119; ☑787-742-3169; www.clubseabourne.com; Hwy 250; r/villa incl breakfast from $185/280; P☀❄🛜🏊) This Caribbean-chic hotel offers relaxed luxury in a garden setting. Individual rooms and villas are tucked into a lush hillside, all with private balconies or decks with distant ocean views. The property has an outdoor bar, an upscale restaurant and a secluded swimming pool surrounded by tall palm trees. Kayaks and bikes available. Wi-fi in the main building only.

✖ Eating

✖ Dewey

★ Zaco's Tacos
MEXICAN $

(Map p122; ☑787-742-0243; www.zacostacos.com; 21 Pedro Márquez, Dewey; mains $6-9; ⊙noon-9pm Mon-Fri, 9:30am-2:30pm Sun; 🖐) This hip open-air restaurant dishes up ultra-fresh Mexican fare plus a smattering of tasty salads. If you're hungry, order a monster-sized burrito with all the fixins. Enjoy your meal in the clapboard dining room or on the shady back patio. Daily specials are worth a look.

★ El Panino
FOOD TRUCK, SANDWICHES $

(Map p119; ☑787-501-1441; Calle Escudero, Dewey; $8-12; ⊙8am-4pm; 🖐) Sitting in a gravel lot with a handful of other food trucks, El Panino is far and away the heavy hitter here. Gourmet sandwiches, served hot and gooey (like the breakfast melt made with chorizo, egg, and cheese) or cool and flavorful (try the roasted veggie sandwich with pesto and goat cheese), are mouthwatering good.

Vibra Verde
CAFE $

(Map p122; Pedro Márquez, Dewey; mains $6-12; ⊙8:30am-2pm Thu-Mon; 🖐) The menu of this great little eatery is a delight of healthy, organic fare. Granola breakfasts are joined by freshly made baked goods, eggs and fine coffee. Lunch includes a wealth of tasty sandwiches. Service, unfortunately, can be painfully slow. (Greatness takes time. Or at least a bigger staff.)

★ El Eden
CARIBBEAN $$

(Map p122; ☑787-617-8517; www.eledenculebra.com; 836 Sardinas, Dewey; dinner mains $18-29; ⊙dinner 6-9pm Wed-Sat, store 9am-9pm daily; ☀🖐) Though not remotely elegant – imagine plastic tables and chairs sharing space with a liquor store – the food at El Eden is simply remarkable. Dishes feature creative takes on seafood and pasta, and the desserts are legendary. Owners Richard and Luz greet everyone like they are long-lost friends. A special-occasion dinner choice for locals.

Dinghy Dock
SEAFOOD $$

(Map p122; ☑787-742-0233; Calle Fulladoza, Dewey; mains $11-30; ⊙11am-11pm; 🖐) It's easy to get mesmerized by the giant tarpon that swim right up to this open-air restaurant, just a couple of feet from diners. Seafood is the reason to come here – fresh catches such as swordfish and snapper are joined by octopus and shrimp salads. Steak makes a great alternative. All around, the flavors are refreshingly bold.

Colmado Milka
SUPERMARKET

(Map p122; ☑787-742-2253; off Calle Fulladoza, Dewey; ⊙7am-8pm Mon-Sat, to 1pm Sun) On the road to the library (p126), Colmado Milka is the island's second-largest supermarket, which means it's slightly smaller than the small 'large market' near the airport. Fresh items are hit or miss but scour the aisles for hidden gems of foodie joy.

✗ Outside Dewey

Tiki's Grill   FOOD TRUCK, BURGERS $
(Map p119; ☑787-742-0241; Hwy 250; $8-12; ☺9am-9pm Fri-Tue; 🖔) An eye-catching food truck – with a prime spot on Hwy 250 overlooking the bay – Tiki's Grill serves up big juicy burgers in 20 different ways. Think classic (cheese burger, bacon burger, chili burger) to creative (the 'Blue Moon' with gorgonzola and sauteed mushrooms or the 'Piono' with plantains and chilis). All patties come with hand-cut fries.

Susie's   FUSION $$
(Map p119; ☑787-742-1141; www.susiesculebra.com; Hwy 250; mains $15-23; ☺6-9pm Fri-Tue; ☑) Beautifully presented Puerto Rican–Asian fusion fare, this Culebra favorite curates a rotating collection of crowd-pleasing dishes, always including fresh fish such as grouper and snapper. Located just past the airport, the restaurant has a vague hacienda feel, albeit with outdoor dining and tiki torches.

🍷 Drinking & Nightlife

La Lobina   SPORTS BAR
(Map p122; ☑787-556-3971; 28 Pedro Márquez, Dewey; ☺8pm-midnight Sun-Thu, to 2am Fri & Sat) A hot spot for locals and expats, La Lobina has a huge outdoor deck opening onto the bay – perfect on warm nights – and an indoor lounge with a pool table and TVs tuned to the latest sporting events. Live salsa bands or DJs transform the deck into a dance floor most weekends.

Mamacita's   BAR
(Map p122; ☑787-742-0090; www.mamacitas guesthouse.com; 64 Calle Castelar; ☺4pm-midnight Sun-Thu, to late Fri & Sat) The after-dinner bar scene at this restaurant is sizzling. On weekends, locals, expats and yacht crews head here for its open-air deck and Friday-night DJ. *Bomba y plena* drummers get the patio bouncing every Saturday night, when everybody hits the dance floor. Happy hour starts at 4pm during the week.

☆ Entertainment

Cine Culebra   CINEMA
(Map p122; www.cineculebra.com; Sardinas, Dewey; adult/child $4/2; ☺7:30pm Tue & Fri) If you need a movie fix, Cine Culebra is as good as it gets: a converted shipping container with a huge flat-screen TV and theater seating. Not bad for four bucks! Films screened on Tuesday and Friday only.

🛍 Shopping

★Artefango   ART
(Map p122; www.artefango.com; Calle Fulladoza, Dewey; ☺11am-9pm, hours vary) Perched above the Dinghy Dock (p125), this inviting gallery is the creative expression of Jorge Acevedo, a local activist and artist. His works span many mediums and feature Culebra scenes often mixed with powerful messages for social justice; the T-shirts are affordable fashion statements. The affable artist is usually here.

La Cava Gift Shop   GIFTS & SOUVENIRS, WINE
(Map p122; ☑787-742-0566; 250 Escudero, Dewey; ☺9am-5pm) On the road leading into town, La Cava sells high quality beach- and swimwear, jewelry, souvenirs, even *República de Culebra* stickers. A section of the shop is wholly devoted to fine wines and gourmet treats.

ℹ Information

Few establishments have meaningful street addresses on Culebra; directions tend to be descriptive. Basic cartoon-style maps are handed out by hotels and car rental agencies. Almost all services are in Dewey, including several ATMs.

DANGERS & ANNOYANCES

Culebra breeds swarms of mosquitoes, especially during the rainy season (May to November). Some of the daytime species have been known to carry dengue.

EMERGENCY

Police Station (☑787-742-3501; Fulladoza, Dewey; ☺24hr) Located on the road headed out of Dewey, towards Punta Soldado.

INTERNET ACCESS

Most accommodations have wi-fi as does the **tourist information office** (p127), whose internet extends to the little park outside. The **Culebra Community Library** (☑787-309-9306; Sardinas, Dewey; ☺10am-2pm Mon-Sat; 📶🖔) also offers internet service ($1 per hour) on desktops and through wi-fi.

MEDICAL SERVICES

Despite its small population, Culebra has decent health services.

Culebra Health Clinic (☑787-742-3521; Calle Font, Dewey; ☺8am-5pm Mon-Sat) This Dewey clinic is staffed with resident doctors. It houses the only pharmacy on the island; prescription medications can be ordered and flown in from the mainland.

Hospital de Culebra (☑787-742-3511; Calle Font. Dewey; ☺24hr) Adjoining the health clinic, Culebra's hospital has a 24-hour emergency room. The island also keeps a plane on emergency standby at the airport for medical transport to the main island.

MONEY

Banco Popular (☑787-742-3572; www.popular. com; 9 Pedro Márquez, Dewey; ☺8am-3:30pm Mon-Fri) The only full service bank in Culebra; it has a 24-hr ATM.

POST

Post Office (Map p122; ☑742-3862; www. usps.com; 26 Pedro Márquez, Dewey; ☺9am-4pm Mon-Fri, to noon Sat) Super-efficient, well cooled and right in the center of town.

TOURIST INFORMATION

Try www.culebrainfo.com for good general information on the island. For backup, check out www.islaculebra.com or www.culebra-island.com.

Tourist Information Office (Map p122; ☑787-742-1033; Calle Pedro Márquez, Dewey; ☺8am-noon & 1-4:30pm Mon-Fri; ☎) Island-wide information can be found at this tourist information counter, a block from the ferry terminal. Wi-fi is free and extends to the shady plaza right outside its doors.

US Fish & Wildlife Service (Map p119; ☑787-742-0115; www.fws.gov/caribbean/refuges/culebra; off Km 4.2, Hwy 250; ☺7am-4pm Mon-Fri) This government agency is responsible for managing the Culebra National Wildlife Refuge. Stop by the office on the eastern side of Ensenada Honda for maps, information about the refuge, its flora, fauna and hikes, and permission to visit other sections of the refuge.

❶ Getting There & Away

TO/FROM THE AIRPORT

Most guesthouses and inns offer pickups from the airport or ferry dock for free or a small fee; otherwise, a taxi will get you just about anywhere on the island.

AIR

Culebra's **Benjamín Rivera Noriega Airport** (CPX; Map p119; ☑787-742-0022; Hwy 251) is a tiny affair with a snack bar, a couple of car-rental booths and check-in counters. There's frequent service from San Juan, Ceiba and, handily for island-hoppers, Vieques.

Airlines serving the airport include **Air Flamenco** (☑877-535-2636, 787-742-1040; www.airflamenco.net; Benjamín Rivera Noriega Airport, Hwy 251), **Vieques Air Link** (☑787-742-0254, 888-901-9247; www.viequesairlink.com; Aeropuerto Benjamín Rivera Noriega, Hwy 251) and **Cape Air** (☑800-227-3247; www.capeair.com; Benjamín Rivera Noriega Airport, Hwy 251).

Charter flights also can be arranged through **M&N Aviation** (☑787-791-7090, 877-622-5566; www.mnaviation.com; Aeropuerto Benjamín Rivera Noriega, Hwy 251).

The approach to Culebra's airport over Playa Flamenco and then between two peaks is one of the world's most spectacular.

FERRY

The most popular – and cheapest – way to Culebra from the mainland is on the **Autoridad de Transporte Marítimo** (ATM, Maritime Transportation Authority; Map p122; ☑787-494-0934; https://ati.pr/rutas-y-mapas; Calle Pedro Márquez, Dewey; one-way adult/child $2.25/1; ☺office open before sailings) ferry service from Fajardo on either passenger or cargo boats. The service is reliable, though past problems gave it a bad rep it's still trying to shake.

Get to the ferry terminal at least an hour early to buy your ticket (advance sales or reservations are not accepted). Schedules vary by day, but there are usually at least three round trips. Trip times run between one to two hours, depending on the boat (passenger boats are fastest). Check times locally or at tourist information websites.

On busy weekends, especially during the summer, travelers may get bumped by island residents.

❶ Getting Around

Arriving by ferry, you can easily walk to any point in Dewey proper, while another 45 minutes will take you to Playa Flamenco. Elsewhere you'll want your own transport (a bike or golf cart will do).

BOAT

Water taxis provide round-trip service to Culebra's nearby cays, including Isla Culebrita, Cayo Norte and Cayo Luis Peña. Fares range from $35 to $50 per person, depending on the destination. Try **Cayo Norte Water Taxi** (☑787-435-6546; per person $35-50) or **Water Taxi** (☑787-685-5815; amarog1281@hotmail.com; per person $35-50).

CAR & GOLF CART

Mainland rental companies forbid you to bring cars to Culebra on the ferry. Locally, rental agencies push 4WDs hard but there's no reason for these on Culebra's well-maintained paved roads. Golf carts are good alternatives.

Avis (☑787-742-0726; www.avis.com; 98 Escudero, Dewey; rental from $68; ☺9am-5pm) The only international car-rental agency on the island.

Carlos Jeep Rental (☑787-742-3514; www.carlosjeeprental.com; Hwy 250; golf cart rental from $28, 4WDs from $45; ☺5am-9:30pm)

Jerry's Jeep Rental (☑787-742-0587; www.jerrysjeeprental.com; Hwy 251; golf carts from $30, 4WD rental from $45; ☺8am-6pm Sat-Thu, 7am-7pm Fri)

PÚBLICO

Públicos (public vans) have one route on the island, from the ferry terminal to Playa Flamenco (per person $3). As long as there's room, passengers can flag them down anywhere along the route. The fare remains the same, regardless where you get on.

TAXI

There's a taxi service on the island, mostly *público* drivers supplementing their income. (You'll likely be picked up in a van.) Fares run from $5 to $20, depending on where you're headed on the island.

Raul Transportation (☑ 787-358-4816, 787-955-9238)

Willy's Transportation (☑ 787-449-0580, 787-449-0598)

Xavier Transportation Services (☑ 787-463-0475; cortes_xh@yahoo.com)

Vieques

POP 8650

Measuring 21 miles long by 5 miles wide, Vieques is substantially bigger than Culebra and distinctly different in ambience. Though still a million metaphorical miles from the bright lights of the Puerto Rican mainland, the larger population here has meant more choice of accommodations, swankier restaurants and generally more buzz. It's renowned for its gorgeous beaches, semi-wild horses and unforgettable bioluminescent bay.

Since the official withdrawal of the US Navy in 2003, Vieques has regularly been touted as the Caribbean's next 'big thing,' with pristine beaches and a coastline ripe for the developer's bulldozer. Fortunately, environmental authorities swept in quickly after the handover and promptly declared all of the former military land (70% of the island's total area) a US Fish & Wildlife Refuge. The measure has meant that the bulk of the island remains virgin territory to be explored and enjoyed by all. Development elsewhere has been slow and low-key. Understandably, Vieques' residents – many of whom are US expats – are fiercely protective of their Caribbean nirvana.

History

When Columbus 'discovered' Puerto Rico on his second voyage in 1493, Taíno people were living peacefully on Vieques, except for the occasional skirmish with Carib neighbors. With the expansion of Puerto Rico under Ponce de León, more Taíno fled to the island; Caribs joined them and the two groups mounted a fierce resistance to Spanish occupation. It failed. Spanish soldiers eventually overran the island, killing or enslaving the natives who remained.

Even so, Spanish control over the island remained tentative at best. In succeeding years, both the British and French tried to claim the island as their own. Vieques, however, remained something of a free port, thriving as a smuggling center.

Sugarcane plantations covered much of Vieques when the island fell to the Americans in 1898 as part of the spoils from the Spanish–American War, but during the first half of the 20th century the cane plantations failed. Vieques lost more than half its population and settled into near dormancy; the remaining locals survived as they always had, by subsistence farming, fishing and smuggling.

First requisitioned by the US military in 1941, Vieques was originally intended to act as a safe haven for the British Navy during WWII, should the UK fall to the Nazis. But after 1945 the US decided to keep hold of the territory to use as a base for weapons testing during the Cold War. Taking control of more than 70% of the island's 33,000 acres in the east and west, the military left the local population to live in a small strip down the middle while they shelled beaches and dropped live bombs on offshore atolls. On average the military bombed Vieques 180 days a year and in 1998 alone dropped a total of 23,000 explosive devices on the island.

The US military held onto it until May 2003 when, after four years of international protests, the land was ceded to the US Fish & Wildlife Refuge. In the years since, Puerto Rican, US and international developers have been salivating at the prospect of building mega hotels and more. For the time being, tourism, construction, cattle raising, fishing, ordinance clearing and some light manufacturing bring money and jobs to the island.

You can track the status of the navy's clean-up of the island at www.navfac.navy. mil/vieques.

◉ Sights

Vieques is considerably more populated than its sleepy sister island, Culebra. Consequently, it has two towns to Culebra's one. The main settlement, Isabel Segunda (Isabella II), is on the northern side where the ferry docks. It has lots of colorful clapboard houses and the views of the mainland aren't bad either.

Most people run through Isabel Segunda en route to Esperanza, on the Caribbean side.

Esperanza is on a lovely stretch of coast, with a public beach and a malecón (waterfront promenade) lined with numerous alluring restaurants and guesthouses.

No matter where you go, you'll likely encounter the island's semi-wild horses, who often canter down the road oblivious to the honks and demands of drivers.

Vieques National Wildlife Refuge

Lying within these protected confines are the best reasons to visit Vieques. This 18,000-acre **refuge** (Map p130; ☑ 787-741-2138; www.fws.gov/caribbean/refuges/vieques; Km 3.2, Hwy 997; ☺6am-6:30pm Oct-Mar, to 7:30pm Apr-Sep; ☑ 🚻) occupies the land formerly used by the US military. The 3100-acre western segment at the western end was used mainly as a storage area during the military occupation and is very quiet. The 14,700-acre eastern segment, which includes a former live firing range (still off-limits), has the island's best beaches along its southern shore.

The refuge protects vast tracts of largely pristine land containing four different ecological habitats: beaches, coastal lagoons, mangrove wetlands and forested uplands. It also includes an important marine environment of sea grasses and coral reefs. Many colorful species survive in these areas, including the endangered brown pelican and the Antillean manatee. Vieques' dwarfish thicket-strewn forest, which includes some indigenous cacti, provides one of the best examples of dry subtropical forest in the Caribbean.

Much of the refuge's land is still officially off-limits to visitors. A potentially dangerous no-go zone is Punta Este in the far east of the island, where a live ordinance is still being removed. Other restricted areas in the east include most of the north coast east of Isabel Segunda, along with the south coast east of Playa La Plata (p133). The most easily accessible area is the ribbon of land that abuts the road leading from Hwy 997 to La Plata.

Most of the hilly western part of the refuge is open for business and includes a lonely swath of colorful wildflowers and scores of (mostly sealed) cavernous military-style bunkers that were used to store ammunition.

Perhaps the finest **Giant Ceiba Tree** in Puerto Rico is situated on the right-hand side of the road as you head toward Punta Arenas (p135), adjacent to the **Mosquito Pier**, a popular snorkeling site. Rumored to be 400 years old, the tree resembles a gnarly

IT'S ALL IN THE NAME

The name 'Vieques' is a 17th-century Spanish colonial corruption of the Taíno name *bieque* (small island). The Spaniards also called Vieques and Culebra *'Las Islas Inútiles'* (the Useless Islands) because they lacked gold and silver. But over the centuries, residents and visitors who share affection for this place have come to call Vieques *'Isla Nena,'* a term of endearment meaning 'Baby Girl Island.'

African baobab, which is probably the reason why it was venerated so much by uprooted Afro-Caribbean slaves. The Ceiba is Puerto Rico's national tree.

Isabel Segunda

A small coastal town dotted over low hills on Vieques' north coast, nontouristy Isabel Segunda (Isabel II) is the island's administrative center and capital. Sometimes busy, sometimes quiet – depending on ferry activity – the town is more urban than anything on Vieques (though that's not saying much).

Named for the enigmatic Spanish queen who reigned between 1833 and 1868, the town is the island's oldest settlement, founded in 1843, and showcases a handful of historical sights.

Fortín Conde de Mirasol FORT, MUSEUM (Fuerte de Vieques; Map p133; ☑787-741-1717; 471 Fuerte, Isabel Segunda; donations accepted; ☺8:30am-4:15pm Wed-Sun; ☑) Beautifully renovated, this small fort sits on a hill above Isabel Segunda with sweeping views of the mainland and nearby islands. It is the last Spanish fort constructed in the Americas (1845). Although never completed, the fort has ramparts and a fully restored central building that houses a history and art museum; it's also home to Radio Vieques and the Vieques Historic Archives. Its gift shop has an extensive selection of books on the island's history.

El Faro de Punta Mulas VIEWPOINT (Map p133; F Anduce, Isabel Segunda; ☺hours vary) One of Puerto Rico's 16 historic lighthouses, this pastel-shaded monument stands on the hilly point just north of the Isabel Segunda ferry dock. Built in 1896 and beautifully restored in 1992, it contains a small museum with exhibits on the island's history. The lighthouse is only opened occasionally; the

Vieques

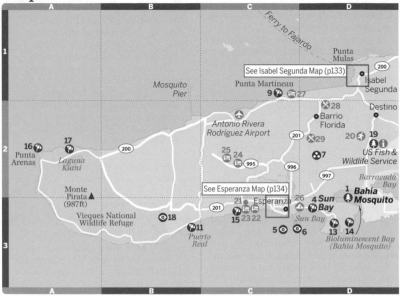

Vieques

◎ Top Sights
1	Bahía Mosquito	D3
2	Playa Caracas	E2
3	Playa La Plata	F2
4	Sun Bay	D3

◎ Sights
5	Cayo Afuera	C3
6	Cayo de Tierra	C3
7	Hombre de Puerto Ferro Archaeological Site	D2
8	Pata Prieta	E2
9	Playa El Gallito	C1
10	Playa Escondida	F2
11	Playa Grande	B3
12	Playa La Chiva	E2
13	Playa Media Luna	
14	Playa Navio	
15	Playa Negra	C3
16	Punta Arenas	A2
17	Starfish Beach	A2
18	Sugar Mill Ruins	B3
19	Vieques National Wildlife Refuge	D2

◎ Activities, Courses & Tours
20	Colón Horse Riding	D2
21	Island Adventures	C3

◎ Sleeping
22	Blue Horizon Boutique Resort	C3
23	Hacienda Tamarindo	C3
24	Hix Island House	C2
25	La Finca Vieques	C2
26	Sun Bay Campgrounds	D3
27	W Retreat & Spa	C1

◎ Eating
28	Horta's BBQ	D2
	Kiosko La Taina	(see 19)
29	Next Course	D2
	Sol Food	(see 19)

grounds are typically used for special events. Come here for the vista and sunset.

◉ Esperanza

Esperanza is the quintessential Caribbean beach town, a shabby-chic cluster of clapboard houses and colorful open-fronted restaurants that has lifted many a dampened mainland spirit. If you've been fighting your way through the traffic of San Juan, this could be your salvation: an exotic but laidback mélange of infectious Latin music and friendly streetside salesfolk peddling rum, reggae and bioluminescent kayaking trips.

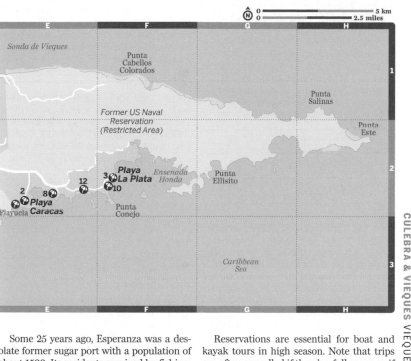

Some 25 years ago, Esperanza was a desolate former sugar port with a population of about 1500. Its residents survived by fishing, cattle raising and subsistence farming. But then a couple of expatriate Americans in search of the Key Largo, Bogart-and-Bacall life, started a bar-guesthouse called Bananas. Gradually, word spread among independent travelers and a cult following took root. Protected (rather ironically) by the presence of the US military on Vieques, Esperanza has managed to retain much of its rustic pioneering spirit and is a relaxed and fun place to visit.

★ **Bahía Mosquito** NATURE RESERVE
(Bioluminescent Bay; Map p130; off Hwy 997) Locals claim that this magnificent bay, a designated wildlife preserve approximately 2 miles east of Esperanza, has the highest concentration of phosphorescent dinoflagellates not only in Puerto Rico, but in the world. A trip through the lagoon – take a tour – is nothing short of psychedelic, with hundreds of fish whipping up fluorescent-blue sparkles below the surface as your kayak or electric boat passes by (no gas-powered boats are permitted – the engine pollution kills the organisms that create the phosphorescence).

Reservations are essential for boat and kayak tours in high season. Note that trips are often cancelled if there's a full moon or if the waters are rough.

Cayo Afuera ISLAND
(Map p130) A popular place to journey is the islet of Cayo Afuera, an uninhabited pinprick of land a few hundred meters across the bay from Playa Esperanza. It is part of the Mosquito Bay Reserve and many intrepid locals swim here (not advisable unless you're a strong swimmer and are visible to passing boats); others kayak to it on their own or on organized tours. There's great snorkeling here, both under the ruined pier and on the ocean side of the islet where a sunken sailboat languishes beneath the surface.

Cayo de Tierra ISLAND
(Map p130) A teardrop of land between the Malecón and Sun Bay reached by a slender sandspit (or by wading, if storms have washed it out), Cayo de Tierra has a few irregularly maintained trails that make for an interesting ramble. At the northern tip is a large hyper-saline lagoon teeming with birds, including ospreys and pelicans. The most direct route there is to walk east along the beach from the Esperanza pier.

🛈 YOU ARE A BIOHAZARD

Swimming in the bioluminescent Bahía Mosquito (p131) is illegal, and for good reason. Sunscreen and insect repellent are harmful to the dinoflagellates that light up the waters, and any immersion in the water has been banned, just as it has been in Fajardo's Laguna Grande (p110).

If you see anyone taking a dip, they are harming the water and violating the law, no matter what excuse they offer.

Vieques Conservation & Historical Trust   MUSEUM

(Map p134; ☑ 787-741-8850; www.vcht.org; 138 Flamboyán, Esperanza; donations accepted; ⊙9am-5pm; 🛗) 🖋 This trust, founded in 1984 to help protect the island's bioluminescent waters, operates a tiny museum, which contains intriguing exhibits on its ecological efforts, the island's natural history and its early Indian inhabitants. There's also a small aquarium with a rotating line-up of local sea creatures on display for a few weeks before they're returned to the ocean.

Pondering the range of exhibits can take longer than you'd think; the gift store has local info and artisan creations. Hiking and walking tours (p137) of the island also offered.

⊙ Elsewhere on Vieques

Sugar Mill Ruins   HISTORIC SITE

(Map p130; off Hwy 201) Abandoned in 1942 after the US Navy expropriated the land, this 19th-century sugar mill now lies in ruins, overtaken by the forest. Rusting machinery, crumbing brick walls and caved-in ceilings are all that's left. No set path runs through the site. Instead you'll find yourself pulling back vines and trudging through forest to see this historic site.

Hombre de Puerto Ferro
Archaeological Site   ARCHAEOLOGICAL SITE

(Map p130; off Km 6.5, Hwy 997; 🅿) **FREE** Big boulders identify the grave from which a 4000-year-old skeleton of a pre-Arawak known as the 'Hombre de Puerto Ferro' was exhumed. Little is known about the skeleton, but archaeologists speculate that it is most likely the body of one of Los Ar caicos (the Archaics), Puerto Rico's earliest known inhabitants; this racial group made

a sustained migration as well as seasonal pilgrimages to the Caribbean from bases in Florida. The remains are now on exhibit at the Museo de Historia, Antropología y Arte (p68) in San Juan.

🏖 Beaches

Vieques' beaches are as legendary as Culebra's – and there are a lot more of them. The beaches in the national wildlife refuge are among the best on the island. Elsewhere you'll find numerous strips of sand, including a gorgeous public one in the south, where days can easily pass into weeks.

Unfortunately many of Vieques' beaches are prone to petty theft. No matter how remote your beach, don't leave your valuables unguarded while you swim or snorkel, especially on the beach in downtown Esperanza – they'll be gone in a heartbeat.

🏖 Vieques National Wildlife Refuge

In one sense, the military occupation was a blessing in disguise, as it has left many of the island's more remote beaches in an undeveloped and pristine state. Now protected in the national wildlife refuge (p129), the beaches are clean, untrammeled and paradisal.

Others, encased in the former weapons-testing zones, remain closed off. Closed roads leading to contaminated areas are clearly marked as such, but if you have questions about whether an area is safe, check with the US Fish & Wildlife Service (p143).

Signage is excellent in the refuge, which makes finding even secluded beaches fairly easy. Best of all, you can hop from one to another, looking for your own ideal beach, which on weekdays you may have to yourself. Most of the roads are paved or well-maintained gravel.

Beaches at the western end have interesting views back to the mainland. Roads here can get muddy but all are usually car-capable.

★ Playa Caracas   BEACH

(Red Beach; Map p130; Vieques National Wildlife Refuge, off Km 3.2, Hwy 997, Southern Shore) Calm and clear Playa Caracas is reached on a paved road and has gazebos with picnic tables to shade bathers from the sun; there's excellent snorkeling – lots of healthy sea fans and underwater life – off the eastern side of the beach. Walking west, Playuela is a lesser-known cove with less shade,

Isabel Segunda

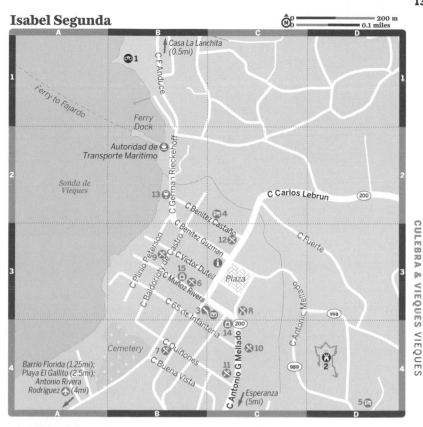

200 m
0.1 miles

Isabel Segunda

◎ Sights
1 El Faro de Punta Mulas B1
2 Fortín Conde de Mirasol D4

◎ Activities, Courses & Tours
3 Blackbeard Sports B3

◎ Sleeping
4 Casa de Amistad C2
5 SeaGate Hotel D4

◎ Eating
6 Conuco B3

7 Coqui Fire Cafe B4
8 Gray's Magic Coffee C3
9 Morales Supermercado B3
10 Panadería La Viequense C4
11 Shawnaa's C4
12 Taverna C3

◎ Drinking & Nightlife
13 Al's Mar Azul B2

◎ Shopping
14 Funky Beehive C4
15 Siddhia Hutchinson Gallery B3

meaning you'll find few people here and you can enjoy the view back to lovely Playa Caracas.

★ Playa La Plata
BEACH
(Silver Beach; Map p130; Vieques National Wildlife Refuge, off Km 3.2, Hwy 997, Southern Shore; ◎ 6am-6:30pm Oct-Mar, to 7:30pm Apr-Sep) Playa La Plata is as far east as you can go at present. This gorgeously secluded beach is on a mushroom-shaped bay and has sand like icing sugar and a calm sea that seems to shimmer in a thousand different shades of turquoise, cobalt and blue. The snorkeling is good towards the western side of the

Esperanza

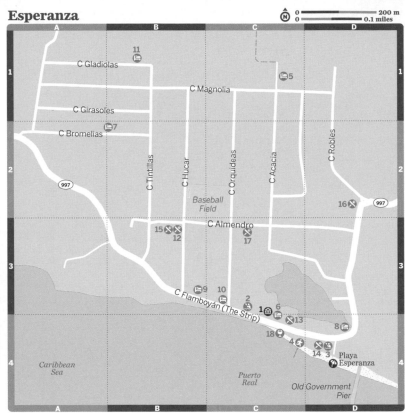

Esperanza

◎ Sights
1 Vieques Conservation &
  Historical Trust C3

✪ Activities, Courses & Tours
2 Abe's Snorkeling & Bio-Bay
  Tours C3
3 Fun Brothers.................................... D4
4 Marauder Sailing Charters C4
  Vieques Conservation &
  Historical Trust .... (see 1)

🛌 Sleeping
5 Acacia Guesthouse............................ C1
6 Bananas C4
7 Casa de Kathy B2
8 El Blok D4

9 Malecón House B3
10 The Lazy Hostel C3
11 Villa Coral Guesthouse B1

🍴 Eating
  Bananas.. (see 6)
12 Colmado Lydia B3
13 El Quenepo C4
14 Esperanza Food Trucks D4
15 La Dulce Esperanza B3
16 La Tienda Verde D2
17 Rancho Choli C3

🍸 Drinking & Nightlife
  El Blok Bar .... (see 8)
18 La Nasa C4
  Lazy Jack's .... (see 10)

beach. The road here is really very rough;
only a 4WD will get you close without
walking.

Playa La Chiva   BEACH
(Blue Beach; Map p130; Vieques National Wildlife Refuge, off Km 3.2, Hwy 997, Southern Shore;
⊙ 6am-6:30pm Oct-Mar, to 7:30pm Apr-Sep) **FREE**

Gorgeous Playa La Chiva, at the eastern end of the main road, is long and open with occasionally rough surf. It's easy to find your own large patch of sand and you can find shade in the shrubs. There's good snorkeling towards the eastern side of the beach just off a small island; park at spot No 5 through 10 for the best access.

Playa Escondida   BEACH
(Secret Beach; Map p130; Vieques National Wildlife Refuge, off Km 3.2, Hwy 997, Southern Shore; ☉ 6am-6:30pm Oct-Mar, to 7:30pm Apr-Sep) The deliciously deserted stretch of sand at Playa Escondida has absolutely no facilities – just jaw-dropping beauty. It faces Bahía Ensenada Honda, which is good for kayaking. The road here is very rough and is 4WD-only, especially after storms.

Pata Prieta   BEACH
(Map p130; Vieques National Wildlife Refuge, off Km 3.2, Hwy 997, Southern Shore; ☉ 6am-6:30pm Oct-Mar, to 7:30pm Apr-Sep) This gorgeous cove has a slender patch of sand and protected waters that are excellent for snorkeling. A steep gravel path leads to the beach.

Starfish Beach   BEACH
(Map p130; Vieques National Wildlife Refuge, off Hwy 200; ☉ 6am-6:30pm Oct-Mar, to 7:30pm Apr-Sep) On the northern side of Laguna Kiani is the best beach on Vieques for children, with gentle surf, crystal-clear waters and immense starfish lying all along the shore.

Punta Arenas   BEACH
(Green Beach; Map p130; Vieques National Wildlife Refuge, off Hwy 200; ☉ 6am-6:30pm Oct-Mar, to 7:30pm Apr-Sep) Punta Arenas is excellent for a quiet picnic, some family-friendly snorkeling and views of the mainland (note the wind farm) and El Yunque across the water. The strand here is not very broad and is punctuated with coral outcroppings, but there are plenty of shade trees. Snorkeling reefs extend for miles and you can expect to have this place pretty much to yourself, except on summer weekends, when a lot of yachts out of Fajardo come here on day trips.

🐠 Elsewhere on Vieques

★ **Sun Bay**   BEACH
(Balneario Sun Bay; Map p130; ☎787-741-8198; off Hwy 997, Parque Nacional Sun Bay; admission Wed-Sun only $4; ☉ 8:30am-5pm Mon-Thu, to 6pm Fri-Sun; 🅿 ♿) Part of Puerto Rico's national park system, Sun Bay is a long half-moon-shaped bay, less than a half-mile east of Esperanza. It's the island's *balneario* (public beach), with all the amenities you could hope for, including lifeguards and a cafe (11am to 5pm daily) serving up *criollo* treats. Measuring a mile in length, Sun Bay rarely seems busy – even with 100 people sunning and playing on it, it will still appear almost deserted. The surf is gentle.

Playas Media Luna & Navio   BEACH
(Map p130; Parque Nacional Sun Bay, off Hwy 997; admission Wed-Sun only $4; ☉ 8:30am-5pm Mon-Thu, to 6pm Fri-Sun) If it really is isolation you're after, head east on the sandy road that runs along Sun Bay and you'll enter a low forest. Go left at the fork in the road. In a couple of hundred yards, you'll stumble upon **Playa Media Luna**, a protected, shady beach that is excellent for kids. Beyond that is **Playa Navio**, where bigger waves are the domain of bodysurfers.

Playa Negra   BEACH
(Black Sand Beach; Map p130; off Hwy 201) Tired of all that powdery, blinding white sand? This beach lives up to its name with dark, sparkly sand derived from offshore volcanic rocks. It's rarely visited and has a nice line of craggy bluffs as a backdrop. Look for the sign on Hwy 201 as you head west from Esperanza; a short path along a dry riverbed leads you there.

Playa Grande   BEACH
(Map p130; off Hwy 201) Playa Grande has a long, narrow strip of golden sand and wave-tossed water that drops off very quickly (meaning it's not optimal for kids or weak swimmers). If you head west on Rte 996 from Esperanza to Rte 201, you'll eventually come to a dead end where you can park and hit the sand.

Playa El Gallito   BEACH
(Gringo Beach; Map p130; Km 3.8, Hwy 200) Playa El Gallito is a small beach with a great reef for snorkeling just 10yd offshore. Note, though, that between December and March, seas can get rough here due to trade winds that often blow from the northeast.

🏃 Activities

All manner of activities on land and sea are on offer on Vieques. Besides the Bioluminescent Bay, there are other small bays good for kayaking and paddleboarding, especially along the southern shore of

CULEBRA & VIEQUES VIEQUES

the national wildlife refuge. Snorkel sites abound and many of the best are accessible from shore.

Blackbeard Sports · DIVING

(Map p133; ☑787-741-1892; www.blackbeard sports.com; 101 Muñoz Rivera, Isabel Segunda; 2-tank dives from $120; ☺9am-4pm Mon-Sat, 10am-2pm Sun) Blackbeard offers PADI certification courses and dive trips to local reefs. Adventure tours – including biking, hiking and kayaking – are also available. Gear rentals are offered at reasonable daily rates (think snorkeling equipment, bikes and paddleboards to beach accessories, fishing and camping gear). There's a second location at W Retreat & Spa (p139).

Abe's Snorkeling & Bio-Bay Tours · KAYAKING, SNORKELING

(Map p134; ☑787-741-2134; www.abessnorkel ing.com; 136 Flamboyán, Esperanza; tours from adult/child $40/20; ☺9am-6pm) Abe's offers guided kayaking and snorkeling trips to the wildlife refuge, Cayo Afuera, Bahía Mosquito and other locations around the island. Its tours are particularly geared towards beginners and children; it even has kayaks that can accommodate families of three or four.

★ Vieques Paddleboarding · OUTDOORS

(☑787-366-5202; www.viequespaddleboarding. com; tours $65-125) This outfit leads informative and fun paddleboarding trips along Vieques' coast and its mangroves. Guides have deep knowledge about the local history and ecology and readily share it. Most excursions also include snorkeling. Bottled water, snack and photos included. All skill levels and ages welcome, including young children who can join as ride-alongs with an adult.

Fun Brothers · KAYAKING

(Map p134; ☑787-435-9372; www.funbrothers-vieques.com; Malecón, Esperanza; kayak/paddleboard/snorkel gear rental per day $50/60/12; ☺8:30am-5:30pm) Rents kayaks, snorkel gear, paddleboards, scooters and more. The cheery bros also run a popular bioluminescent bay tour in glass-bottom kayaks (from $55). Look for their beach shack at the eastern end of the *malecón*.

Marauder Sailing Charters · BOATING

(Map p134; ☑787-435-4858; www.maraudersailing charters.com; Malecón; sailing trips per person $150-230) Marauder runs excellent sailing excursions on a classic 34ft sloop with a stop for swimming and snorkeling. A gourmet lunch prepared onboard and beverages are included. Use of underwater camera, with free downloads, is available too.

Island Adventures · BOATING

(Map p130; ☑787-994-5020; www.biobay.com; Km 4.5, Hwy 996; adult/child from $50/35) See the Bahía Mosquito without paddling. Island Adventures offers 1½-hour group tours in an electric boat most nights, except when

---

VIEQUES BY BIKE

Free from the mainland's traffic jams and unforgiving drivers, Vieques has become a little-heralded biking center. While the main local roads are at times challenging, you can find quiet bike rides in the wildlife refuge (p129), although gravel roads mean it can be rugged and/or thrilling.

As well as renting out bikes, helmets, locks and child seats, the island's main bike outlets organize guided rides around the island. If you're up for going it alone, they can furnish you with maps, routes and insider tips.

Some of the best bicycling is along Hwys 995, 996 and 201, which wind through the countryside north and west of Esperanza and are light on traffic. The main road from Isabel Segunda to Esperanza is Hwy 997, but head west on Hwy 200 and then south on Hwy 201 and you'll find a quieter, more pleasant alternative route. Halfway along, you can detour up Hwy 995, another lovely country road.

The ultimate Vieques loop involves heading west out of Isabel Segunda on Hwy 200 all the way to Punta Arenas (the last section is unpaved). After some shore snorkeling and an idyllic picnic lunch, swing south through the old military bunkers to Playa Grande before linking up with Hwy 996 to Esperanza.

Blackbeard Sports (p136) and Vieques Adventure Company (p137) are good sources for rentals and tours.

there's a full moon. Be aware that schedules can change at the last minute.

Amity Fishing Charters   FISHING
(☑787-502-3839; half-day fishing trips from $350)
This local outfit offers fishing charters around Vieques. With a 600- to 5000ft drop just a mile offshore, the island's waters are rich with black-fin tuna, mahi-mahi, wahoo, kingfish, barracuda, bonito and blue marlin, among others.

★**Vieques Adventure Company**   ADVENTURE
(☑787-414-4101; www.viequesadventures.com; tours from $50; ☺hours vary) This outfit runs well-organized tours of the island, including hiking and historical tours, beach hopping and snorkeling excursions, and mountain bike trips. Groups are small. Gear rentals available too.

**Vieques Conservation
& Historical Trust**   WALKING, HIKING
(Map p134; ☑787-741-8850; www.vcht.org; 138 Flamboyán, Esperanza; tours from $20; ☺9am-5pm) The Vieques Conservation & Historical Trust offers a variety of hikes and walking tours around the island, including birdwatching, architectural tours and hikes to the Sugar Mill Ruins (p132).

Colón Horse Riding   HORSEBACK RIDING
(Map p130; ☑787-237-9236; off Hwy 997; tours per person from $60; ☺9am-6pm) Take a 1½-hour tour on horseback through Isabel Segunda to the countryside and along the coast... even in the ocean (wear pants you don't mind getting wet). Excursions are limited to small groups; all levels welcome.

Fishing

Fishing is sublime in Vieques. Imagine dispersed fisherfolk and enough bonefish, tarpon and permit to stock a miniocean. Fishing boats also allow you access to waters off still-closed stretches of coastline in the former military zone. Local operators also offer deep-sea and fly-fishing excursions in and around the waters of Vieques.

Caribbean Fly Fishing Company   FISHING
(☑787-450-3744; www.cffcinc.com; half-day fishing trips from $425) Book a bone-fishing excursion with Captain Franco, a knowledgeable and friendly guide with deep experience in Vieques' waters. Trips are on a custom-designed boat, kayak or even paddleboard. Two people max per trip. All gear and tackle included.

THE BEAUTIFUL INTERIOR

Yes, the coasts have beaches and nature preserves, but Vieques also has an often-beautiful tropical interior of lush forests, rolling green hills, marauding horses and idiosyncratic little places worthy of a pause.

The main road between Isabel Segunda and Esperanza, Hwy 997, is verdant and winding but is also busy by local standards. On your journeys around the island, try some of the roads less traveled such as Hwys 201 and 995. Around every – often sharp – bend you'll make a new discovery and Vieques is not so big that you'll need to spend more than an hour or two on these forays.

★**Festivals & Events**

★**Fiestas Patronales de Vieques**   CARNIVAL
(Carnaval de Vieques; Central Plaza, Isabel Segunda) In the third week of July, *Viequenses* party hard to celebrate the Vírgen del Carmen, patron saint of the sea, seafarers, fisherman. More a festival than a religious event, islanders gather in Isabel Segunda's central plaza, where food stands, band stands and amusement rides are set up; live music is a given. Parades of dancers, decked out in shimmering outfits and feathers, lead the way.

Look for folks carrying jugs of *bili* (a white rum, cinnamon and fruit concoction), popular during this fest.

Sleeping

Vieques is a rural island, so expect to hear chickens, dogs, cats, cattle and horses making barnyard noises day and night. Travelers will find a range of places to stay in both of Vieques' main towns, throughout its lush hills and on the beach (if you're up for camping). However, there are few true oceanfront properties, mostly because the wildlife refuge is off-limits to development. Most places have a minimum stay during high season.

Esperanza

★**The Lazy Hostel**   HOSTEL $
(Map p134; ☑787-741-5555; www.lazyhostel.com; 61a Orquideas, Esperanza; dm from $30, r from $75, all incl breakfast; ※⚲) Created from shipping containers, the two dorms (one female-only) at this hostel are surprisingly comfortable. Both have four bunks, each bed with priva-

cy curtain, power strip and night-light. Private rooms are simple and equally inviting. All have air-con and share spick- and-span bathrooms. An outdoor kitchen makes cooking (and saving a bit of dough) easy. Guest age limit is 'about' 50.

Adjoining a boisterous restaurant-bar (p141), prepare to party (or wear earplugs) on weekends and holidays. A valuable budget option close to some of the island's best beaches.

Bananas
GUESTHOUSE $

(Map p134; ☑787-741-8700; www.bananasvieques. com; 142 Flamboyán, Esperanza; r $80-100, 2-bedroom unit $140; ✳🛜) Totally updated in 2016, Esperanza's original budget guesthouse and restaurant and its seven rooms have an ultra-casual, cheerfully nautical feel. Rooms have air-con and screened-in private terraces and open onto a long hallway with armchairs – the only guest-only common area. Light sleepers should note that the house bar closes around 1am on weekends; otherwise, the place shuts down around 11pm.

Guesthouse office hours are 9:30am to 4:30pm only.

Casa de Kathy
APARTMENT $$

(Map p134; ☑787-741-3352; www.casadekathy.com; 367 Bromelias, Esperanza; studio $85, 2-bedroom apt $120-150; ✳🛜) A cheerful guesthouse, Casa de Kathy has two apartments at the top of a hill, just a few minutes walk from Esperanza's *malecón* (boardwalk). Both are wonderfully cozy and decked out with all the things you might need – from coffee-making facilities and board games to beach gear and tips on the best snorkeling sites. A large common balcony has sweeping ocean views.

Acacia Guesthouse
APARTMENT $$

(Map p134; ☑800-957-1728, 787-741-1059; www. acaciaguesthouse.com; 236 Acacia, Esperanza; apt $120-145; 🅿✳🛜🏊) Five airy apartments are housed in a three-story whitewashed building situated on a rise above Esperanza's beachside strip. From the 2nd- and 3rd-floor decks and rooftop patio you have spectacular views over hills and the Caribbean. Units are simply decorated but have full kitchens and comfortable furnishings. Air-con is only provided in studios; cooling breezes give comfort in other units.

Villa Coral Guesthouse
GUESTHOUSE $$

(Map p134; ☑787-741-1967; www.villacoralguest house.com; 485 Gladiola, Esperanza; r $90, 2-bedroom apt $160-185; 🅿✳🛜) At this Spanish-style charmer, the tranquil roof deck and pleasant bougainvillea-fringed front veranda dispel any lingering stress. Located in a quiet residential area a few minutes' walk from the action, the six units sport colorful contemporary textiles and bathroom sinks tiled like dreamy waves. All have fridges, microwaves and coffeemakers. Beach gear available too.

★Malecón House
INN $$$

(Map p134; ☑787-741-0663; www.maleconhouse. com; 105 Flamboyán, Esperanza; r $180-300, ste $325, all incl breakfast; 🅿✳🛜🏊) With its travertine floors, beautiful fabrics and light-wood furniture, this spacious 13-room upmarket inn is a gracious choice. Looking out over the water from a quiet section of the main street, two rooms have private seaside balconies, one has a four-poster mahogany bed and all have a clean and uncluttered feel.

El Blok
BOUTIQUE HOTEL $$$

(Map p134; ☑787-741-6020; www.elblok.com; 158 Flamboyán, Esperanza; r $200-250, ste $270; ✳🛜🏊) El Blok sits on the main drag but feels a world apart. Exuding an industrial-chic feel, it's built entirely in exposed cement, a stunning design that is sinuous and organic (and different from everything else around). A lacy sheath over three free-flowing floors allows its 22 rooms to catch the ocean breezes. The units themselves are luxurious, modern and spare, all with balconies.

🛏 Isabel Segunda

★Casa de Amistad
GUESTHOUSE $$

(Map p133; ☑787-741-3758; www.casadeamistad. com; 27 Benitez Castaño, Isabel Segunda; r $105-125; 🅿✳🛜🏊) Casa de Amistad is everything a great holiday guesthouse should be: welcoming, comfortable, well located, stylish and well priced. It fits the bill (and more) with eight mid-century-meets-Caribbean-chic rooms, all with air-con, modern bathrooms and flat-screen televisions. Some have balconies to enjoy the balmy air. The ferry is a five-minute walk and there are great restaurants close by.

A sitting room/library, sparkling guest kitchen, landscaped yard, swimming pool and a rooftop deck make relaxing or chatting with fellow travelers easy. Beach gear available for daily outings too.

SeaGate Hotel
GUESTHOUSE $$

(Map p133; ☑787-741-4661; www.seagatehotel. com; off Calle Antonio Mellado, Isabel Segunda; r incl breakfast $100-205; 🅿✳🛜) On a hill high above the town, the SeaGate is a hike from the ferry dock. Horses roam freely in the surrounding grounds, lush vegetation fills the garden, and views of the surrounding countryside and ocean are panoramic. Basic rooms have fridges and microwaves; for a little more you get sea views and a private balcony. Decor is deeply '80s.

🛏 Elsewhere on Vieques

Sun Bay Campgrounds CAMPGROUND **$**
(Map p130; ☎787-741-8198; off Hwy 997; campsites $10; P) Pitch your tent on one of the prettiest beaches on Vieques. Sun Bay campsites have individual grills and 24-hour access to bathrooms. Nighttime security is on hand too. Be sure to make reservations during the summer, weekends and holidays.

La Finca Vieques GUESTHOUSE **$$**
(Map p130; ☎787-741-0495; www.lafinca.com; Km 2.2, Hwy 995; r $110-160, houses from $175; P🐾🗣✉) 🐾 Finca Caribe is Vieques personified. Sitting high up on a mountain ridge seemingly a million miles from anywhere (but only 3 miles from either coast), it's the kind of rustic haven stressed-out city slickers often dream about. Its back-to-nature hippy-chic facilities – shared outdoor showers, communal kitchen and hempish decor – attract a devoted following.

★Hacienda Tamarindo GUESTHOUSE **$$$**
(Map p130; ☎787-741-8525; www.haciendatamarindo.com; Km 4.5, Hwy 997; r $200-265 ste $250-315, 2-bedroom villa $375; P✻🗣✉) Perched on a hill looking out to a fine Caribbean vista, this 17-room guesthouse has lashes of style leavened by a relaxed island vibe. Rooms have a decidedly Caribbean *luxe motif* – tropical wood furnishings, elegant doors, wrought-iron balconies, colorful textiles and fine art – while the manicured grounds enjoy bursts of bougainvillea and hammocks strung here and there.

Large and delicious breakfasts are served under the namesake tamarind tree. A dip in the pool afterwards is a great way to start the day. (And a dip into the honor bar is a great way to close it.) Children 15 and over only.

W Retreat & Spa RESORT **$$$**
(Map p130; ☎787-741-4100; www.wvieques.com; Km 3.2, Hwy 200; r from $410, ste from $740; P✻🗣✉) Trendy and uber-chic, Vieques' only large chain resort makes a bold statement with bursts of color and texture from striped rugs to furry pillows. All 156 rooms

(not all oceanside) have open bathrooms with washing-board-style tubs. Other features include a full spa, a top-end organic restaurant, a beachside fire pit and two beaches (where the surf can get rough).

Blue Horizon Boutique Resort BOUTIQUE HOTEL **$$$**
(Map p130; ☎787-741-3318; www.bluehorizonboutiqueresort.com; Km 4.3, Hwy 997; r $235-500; P✻🗣✉) One of the island's few beachside resorts, the Blue Horizon has only 10 rooms, each harbored in separate bungalows on a stunning oceanside bluff. The sense of casual elegance – both natural and created – is imbued in the place. The feel extends to its three on-site restaurants and a cozy lounge, which overlooks an Italiante infinity pool fit for a Roman emperor. Adults only.

Hix Island House APARTMENT **$$$**
(Map p130; ☎787-741-2302; www.hixislandhouse.com; Km 1.5, Hwy 995; studio incl breakfast $180-330, apt incl breakfast $340-440; P🗣✉) 🐾 Off-the-grid, minimalist and austere, this unique guesthouse consists of four industrial concrete blocks that arise out of the surrounding trees like huge granite boulders (or fittingly, abandoned navy bunkers). The 13 luxurious rooms are completely open on two sides, most with outdoor showers, giving you the feeling that you are actually living in the forest. Designed by cutting-edge Canadian architect John Hix.

🍴 Eating

Good food in a variety of cuisines and price ranges can be found across the island, though seafood figures prominently. In Esperanza, most eateries are on Calle Flamboyán (aka *el malecón*) with enviable views over the turquoise water to Cayo de Tierra. Meanwhile, Isabel Segunda's restaurants dot the town; come here for the best selection of Caribbean cuisine on the island. Most places are casual, but be sure to reserve in high season for more upscale restaurants.

🍴 Esperanza

La Dulce Esperanza BAKERY, BREAKFAST **$**
(Map p134; ☎787-741-0085; Calle Almendro, Esperanza; pastries & breakfasts $2-6; ⏱7-11am) The sweet aroma from La Dulce Esperanza will surely lead you to its door. Esperanza's best bakery, it sells all types of sweet breads and cakes. Almost best of all are the budget breakfasts to-go – everything from eggs and

---

DON'T MISS

THE ISLAND'S BEST FOOD TRUCKS

The second-best reason to turn off Hwy 997, the country road linking Isabel Segunda and Esperanza, are two food trucks that are the finest on the island (the best reason are the amazing beaches along the southern shore of the Vieques National Wildlife Refuge). In fact, these two trucks straddle the entrance (which sometimes goes by its old name 'Garcia Gate') to the refuge and can provide you with a picnic of your dreams.

Foremost is **Sol Food** (Map p130; Km 3.2, Hwy 997; mains $5-7; ☺11am-3pm Sat & Sun; ⚐) which sells succulent *carnitas* soft tacos that will have you making cooing noises between bites (don't miss the corn with lime butter). Nearby, **Kiosko La Taina** (Map p130; Km 3.2, Hwy 997; mains $6-8; ☺11am-3pm Mon-Fri) has a killer fresh-fish sandwich and *pastelillos*.

---

ham to hot-off-the-griddle pancakes – most for under $4. Get there before 10am – the place typically sells out.

Rancho Choli PUERTO RICAN $
(Map p134; ☑787-698-4464; Calle Almendro, Esperanza; $6-11; ☺10am-10pm; ⚐) Down home cooking is what you'll find at this casual restaurant. The menu changes daily but prepare to be delighted by mouthwatering plates of stuffed *mofongo, lechón asado* (roast pork) and freshly caught whole lobster. Order a side of *tostones* and wash it all down with a glass of tamarind juice. Just a block from the main drag.

Esperanza Food Trucks FOOD TRUCKS $
(Map p134; Calle Flamboyán, Esperanza; meals $3-8; ☺noon-6pm Fri-Sun) Every weekend, food trucks set up shop in the parking lot facing Playa Esperanza at the eastern end of town. You'll find cheap, delicious eats including *criollo*, tacos and, of course, *fritangas* (fried food) – it wouldn't be street food if there weren't a few artery-blocking goodies. Enjoy your meal on the beach.

Bananas AMERICAN, CARIBBEAN $
(Map p134; ☑787-741-8700; www.bananasvieques. com; 142 Flamboyán, Esperanza; mains $11-20; ☺11am-late; ⚐) The ultra laid-back open-air restaurant at Bananas guesthouse (p138) weighs in with hearty salads, sandwiches and

criollo dishes. It sits on Esperanza's main street, facing the ocean, so it's a great spot to have a drink and watch the sunset (or the world go by). Happy hour is celebrated twice a day starting at 11am and 4:30pm year-round.

★**El Quenepo** SEAFOOD $$$
(Map p134; ☑787-741-1215; www.elquenepo vieques.com; 148 Flamboyán, Esperanza; mains $26-34; ☺5:30-10pm Mon-Sat) Upscale El Quenepo has a lovely interior and an equally delectable menu. The food is catch-of-the-day fresh – a family of seven brothers supplies the seafood – and the decor is contemporary. Specialties include whole Caribbean lobsters, *mofongo* (mashed plantains) made with breadfruit grown in the backyard and delicately pan-seared scallops with coconut crème fraiche and caviar. Be sure to book ahead.

Colmado Lydia MARKET
(Map p134; ☑787-741-8678; cnr Almendro & Hucar, Esperanza; ☺7am-6pm Mon-Sat) Near the baseball field, this small market is a good place to supplement any supplies you can't find at the town's **other grocery store** (Green Store; Map p134; ☑787-741-8711; cnr Hwy 997 & Robles, Esperanza; ☺9am-9pm).

🍴 Isabel Segunda

★**Panadería La Viequense** BAKERY $
(Map p133; ☑787-741-8213; 352 Antonio G Mellado, Isabel Segunda; mains $3-11; ☺6am-4pm) If it's breakfast you're after, this is the place for early eggs or hangover-obscuring coffee. If you miss the 11am cutoff, you can feast instead on decent baked goods and sandwiches. Service is no-nonsense and fast, the decor clean and modern, and the clientele local with a smattering of in-the-know tourists. Don't miss its photo gallery of early 20th-century Vieques.

Gray's Magic Coffee SANDWICHES, COFFEE $
(Map p133; ☑787-741-1107; 370 Antonio G Mellardo, Isabel Segunda; sandwiches $5-9; ☺8:30am-5pm, closed Wed & Sun; ☏) Set in a glammed-up clapboard house near the central plaza, Gray's serves delicious espresso drinks and simple sandwiches. While you wait, the owner entertains customers with wand tricks and sleights of hand.

Shawnaa's PUERTO RICAN $
(Map p133; ☑787-741-1434; 327 Antonio G Mellado, Isabel Segunda; mains $6-8; ☺10am-2pm Mon-Fri) Be sure to bring a big appetite to Shawnaa's cafeteria-style buffet. It's full of superb *comida*

criolla (traditional Puerto Rican cuisine) dishes that you can take out onto the patio or enjoy in the shaded interior. Arrive early to get the best selection of eats. Don't miss the *mofongo*.

★**Coqui Fire Cafe**   MEXICAN **$$**
(Map p133; ☑787-741-0401; 421 Quiñones, Isabel Segunda; $12-25; ☺5-9pm Mon-Fri) Sitting on a quiet corner in Isabel Segunda, Coqui Fire lights up the foodie scene with delicious Mexican dishes served with flair. Try the *carnitas* (pork shoulder braised in chilies and papaya juice) or go big with the blackened shrimp served with *mole*. The signature margarita is a hit, prepared with a dash of homemade heat. Reservations recommended.

Taverna   ITALIAN **$$**
(Map p133; ☑787-438-1100; 453 Carlos Lebrun, Isabel Segunda; mains $11-28; ☺5:30-9pm Thu-Mon; ✲) As understated as a delicate wine, this simple eatery has a brick-lined dining room and superb thin-crust pizza. Try the pesto version or opt for seafood. The wedge salad is a winner, while the pasta options include fettuccine Alfredo. End the meal with the lavender and crème brûlée. Come for the great food, not the decor.

Conuco   PUERTO RICAN **$$**
(Map p133; ☑787-741-2500; www.restaurante conuco.com; 110 Muñoz Rivera, Isabel Segunda; mains $15-26; ☺5:30-9:30pm Tue-Sat) Enjoy a modern take on Puerto Rican cuisine at this cottage-styled place named for Taíno garden plots. Standouts include the *bacalaítos* (cod fritters), mahi-mahi with passion fruit and coconut sauce, and the *pionono* (sweet yellow plantains stuffed with ground-beef stew). Romantic and refined, this is one of the northern side's best spots for a dinner date. Try the guava cocktails. Service is hit or miss.

Morales Supermercado   SUPERMARKET
(Map p133; ☑787-741-6701; 15 Baldorioty de Castro, Isabel Segunda; ☺6am-9pm Mon-Sat, to 6pm Sun) This grocery store has the widest (albeit narrow) selection of goods on the island. A second location is 1 mile west of town on Hwy 200 towards the airport.

✗ Elsewhere on Vieques

★**Horta's BBQ**   BARBECUE **$**
(Map p130; ☑787-741-2548; Km 1.7, Hwy 200; $6-17; ☺5-10pm Wed-Mon) A roadside stand turned hopping open-air eatery, Horta's BBQ serves up some of the best ribs on the island. Orders

come from quarter to full rack, always fall-off-the-bone tender and covered in traditional or guava sauce. Other grilled options – shrimp, chicken, skirt steak – are available if pork isn't your thing.

Next Course   FUSION **$$$**
(Map p130; ☑787-741-1028; Hwy 201; mains $25-44; ☺5:30-10pm Fri-Tue) Cocooned away on Hwy 201 in the hills north of Esperanza and serenaded by a throaty chorus of frogs, this upscale place offers 'cuisine inspired by travel'. Influences come from Thai, Mexican and Persian kitchens, with an emphasis on fresh local food (some of its fruit is grown on-site). After dark, orient yourself by its tiki torches and strings of patio lights.

🍸 **Drinking & Nightlife**

★**La Nasa**   BAR
(Map p134; ☑787-930-0031; 107 Flamboyán, Esperanza; ☺11am-late Fri-Sun) A drinking shack right on the water, La Nasa is where it's at for locals. The beers are cheap, the chatter cheerful and the dance floor packed. Live bands occasionally play on weekends.

Lazy Jack's   BAR
(Map p134; ☑787-741-1447; 61a Orquideas, Esperanza; ☺noon-1am Sun-Thu, to 2:30am Fri & Sat) There are music jams most nights of the week at the hardest-core of the *malecón* bars. Depending on the day, you can play at an open jam session, kick back with a thin-crust pizza while grooving to a reggae band, or shake your tail feathers at the Saturday night dance party. It's also the island's go-to sports bar for big games.

El Blok Bar   BAR
(Map p134; ☑787-741-6020; www.elblok.com; El Blok Hotel, 158 Flamboyán, Esperanza; ☺4:30-10pm) For a bit of urban chic in the middle of the laid-back Esperanza strip, head to the rooftop bar at El Blok (p138). The modern architecture and upscale surrounds make sunsets that much more breathtaking. Cocktails are top shelf and the crowd decidedly hip.

Al's Mar Azul   BAR
(Map p133; ☑787-741-3400; www.facebook.com/alsmarazulbar; 577 German Rieckehoff, Isabel Segunda; ☺11am-late) Al's is a total dive bar and nexus of local gossip. Locals come to play pool and expats come to drink...and drink. Visitors teeter somewhere in between. Karaoke crooners fill the place on Saturday night. Those in the know head to the narrow deck out back for sunset and stars. Food is greasy and filling.

🛍 Shopping

Funky Beehive   ARTS & CRAFTS, CLOTHING
(Map p133; ☑ 787-342-1438; Antonio G Mellado, Isabel Segunda; ⊙ 10am-5pm Mon-Sat, to 1pm Sun) A boutique with flair that mixes high-end souvenirs with quality beachwear and artisanal products. A good place to find a memento or gift.

Siddhia Hutchinson Gallery   ART
(Map p133; ☑ 787-741-1343; www.siddhiahutchinson gallery.com; 123 Muñoz Rivera, Isabel Segunda; ⊙ 10am-4pm Mon-Sat, 11am-3pm Sun) The gallery of artist Siddhia Hutchinson exhibits her first-class paintings of colorful tropical scenes. It also features pottery, jewelry and sculpture of other artists – local and far off.

ℹ Information

While some actual street addresses exist on Vieques, citizens and businesses rarely use them.

DANGERS & ANNOYANCES
Dial ☑ 911 for emergencies.

Vieques has a petty-crime problem. Car theft happens often, especially at isolated beaches in the wildlife refuge. Leave nothing in your car and even consider leaving the doors unlocked to prevent damage to the vehicle by break-ins. Also, belongings left on the beach vanish quickly. Bring as little as possible so you can worry about sun exposure rather than thievery.

INTERNET ACCESS
Wi-fi is available at most inns and guesthouses. There's also a free hot spot in Isabel Segunda's central plaza, right in front of city hall. The **Vieques Conservation & Historical Trust** (☑ 787-741-8850; www.vcht.org; 138 Flamboyán, Esperanza; donations accepted; ⊙ 9am-5pm) has half a dozen old-school computers available to visitors, along with a printer.

MEDIA
Vieques Insider (www.viequesinsider.com) magazine is a good resource on everything Vieques. It's published monthly and available for free at the tourist office. The online version is just as good.

MEDICAL SERVICES
Farmacia San Antonio (☑ 787-741-8397; 52 Benítez Guzman, Isabel Segunda; ⊙ 8am-6pm Mon-Fri, 9am-noon & 1:30-6pm Sat)
Hospital Susan Centeno (☑ 787-741-2151; Km 0.4, Hwy 997; ⊙ clinic 7am-4pm Mon-Fri, emergency 24hr)

MONEY
Isabel Segunda has several ATMs as do Esperanza's two grocery stores.
Banco Popular (☑ 787-741-2071; www.banco-popular.com; 115 Muñoz Rivera, Isabel Segunda;

THE WILD HORSES OF VIEQUES

A family of horses grazing along a country road. A mare walking beside her foal, its knees wobbly. A handful of horses standing in a grove of palm trees on a white-sand beach. These are everyday scenes in Vieques, where horses are as much a part of the fabric of the island as the sea air.

Vieques' wild horses are descendants of those brought by the Spaniards hundreds of years ago. Their breed, Paso Fino, has been developed since then, a blend of Barb, Spanish Jennet and Andalusian horses. Known for their elegant gait (*paso fino* means 'refined step'), Paso Finos always have three hooves touching the ground, which makes for a smooth ride.

Despite the moniker, the majority of Vieques' horses aren't wild. In fact, most have owners and many are branded. Nevertheless, privately owned horses have freely roamed the island for decades, primarily to give them access to public grazing lands. Today there are well over a thousand 'free range' horses on Vieques, due mostly to equine reproduction having gone largely unchecked.

The growing number of horses has caused some islanders to worry about equine health and safety. Concerns include untreated injuries from traffic accidents involving horses and malnutrition during droughts. Also, destruction of private property caused by horses foraging for food in gardens and garbage bins is a reality.

In 2016, the island's mayor invited the Humane Society of the US (HSUS) to help. HSUS workers installed freshwater troughs around the island, focusing on areas with few inhabitants, to encourage horses to graze where they'd be less likely to cause accidents and property damage. In early 2017, the HSUS began administering contraceptive vaccines to mares.

Properly cared for, Vieques' 'wild' horses will remain a unique and memorable part of the island landscape. To be sure, there are few sights more striking than a herd of horses galloping along a Caribbean seashore.

8am-3:30pm Mon-Fri) Fully operating bank with ATM.

Cooperativa de Ahorro y Crédito Roosevelt Roads (☑787-741-8430; www.cooprr.com; 112 Muñoz Rivera, Isabel Segunda; ⊘8:15am-4:30pm Mon-Fri, to noon Sat) Has an ATM.

POST

Post Office (Map p133; ☑787-741-3891; www. usps.com; 97 Muñoz Rivera, Isabel Segunda; ⊘8am-4:30pm Mon-Fri, to noon Sat) The island's only post office.

TOURIST INFORMATION

Good websites for directories of island businesses, services and accommodations include www. enchanted-isle.com and www.vieques-island.com.
Puerto Rico Tourism Company (PRTC; Map p133; ☑787-741-0800; www.seepuertorico. com; Central Plaza, Calle Carlos Lebron, Isabel Segunda; ⊘9am-4pm Mon-Fri) Friendly, helpful and bilingual staff on hand to give out information, brochures and Vieques maps. Located inside the *alcaldía* (city hall).
US Fish & Wildlife Service (Map p130; ☑787-741-2138; www.fws.gov/southeast/maps/vi.html; Km 3.2, Hwy 997; ⊘8am-noon & 1-3pm Mon-Fri) Maintains a visitors center located at the Vieques National Wildlife Refuge's eastern side, which is manned by knowledgeable staff.

❶ Getting There & Away

AIR

Vieques' tiny **Antonio Rivera Rodríguez Airport** (VQS; Map p130; ☑787-729-8715; Hwy 200, Km 2.6; 🖱) has frequent service from San Juan, Ceiba and, handily for island-hoppers, Culebra.

Airline options include **Air Flamenco** (p127), **Air Sunshine** (☑787-741-7900, 800-327-8900; www.airsunshine.com; Antonio Rivera Rodríguez Airport), **Cape Air** (p127) and **Vieques Air Link** (p127).

Charter flights also can be arranged through **M&N Aviation** (☑787-791-7090, 877-622-5566; www.mnaviation.com; Antonio Rivera Rodríguez Airport).

Check bag size and weight limits before flying. Typically, medium-sized suitcases meet the requirements but airlines limit baggage weight, including carry-ons, to 30lb.

Públicos (public vans) greet most flights and will take you anywhere you want to go on the island.

FERRY

By far the cheapest way to and from Vieques and the mainland (Fajardo) is by ferry (adult/child $2/1, 75 minutes). Though the service suffers from a bad reputation, it's relatively reliable. Arrive at the **ferry terminal** (ATM, Maritime Transportation Authority; Map p133; ☑787-565-2717;

https://ati.pr/rutas-y-mapas; German Rieckehoff, Isabel Segunda; adult/child $2/1; ⊘ office open before sailings) at least an hour early and buy your ticket; advance sales and reservations are not accepted. Sometimes there are delays but rarely longer than an hour. Note that on summer weekends, the ferry from Fajardo can sell out, in which case residents are given priority.

Schedules vary by day but there are usually three round trips. Check times locally or at tourist info websites.

❶ Getting Around

BICYCLE

Vieques can be good for for cycling; Hwy 997 across the island from Isabel Segunda to Esperanza is less than 6 miles in length and has a few hills. However, traffic on the island's narrow roads can be a problem for casual riders. The best places are the quiet roads in the wildlife refuge, although these can be rugged in places.

CAR & SCOOTER

Cars are highly useful for exploring Vieques, as the island is large and most of the best beaches are off the main routes. Expect to pay about $55 to $85 a day for a small car or 4WD. The latter are useful to get to the outer beaches in the wildlife refuge.

Coquí Car Rental (☑787-741-3696; www. coquicarrental.com; German Rieckehoff, Isabel Segunda; per day from $60; ⊘8am-6pm) Renting 4WD and vans. Add-ons like beach gear and gourmet lunch baskets available. Offices are near the ferry terminal and at Blue Horizon Resort.
Maritza's Car Rental (☑787-741-0078; www. maritzascarrental.com; Km 2, Hwy 201; per day $55-110; ⊘8am-6pm) Everything from small cars to monster SUVs are available here. Free pickup and drop-off available.
Scooters for Rent Vieques (☑787-741-7722; www.scootersvieques.com; 346 Antonio G Mellado, Isabela Segunda; per day rental from $50; ⊘8am-6pm) The business name kinda says it all. Helmets included. Located a short walk from Isabela Segunda's ferry terminal.

PUBLIC TRANSPORT

Público typically greet both ferries and airplanes – they read '*Vieques y Sus Barrios*' (Vieques and Its Neighborhoods) on the windshields. These vans cover the entire island. The trip between Isabel Segunda and Esperanza costs $3, with *públicos* running regularly from 7am to 11pm. Sometimes there's an additional $0.50 charge per bag.

TAXI

A fare of $10 to $20 should get you anywhere on the island. Try **Coqui Ayala** (☑787-374-6820), **Edna Robles** (☑787-630-4673), **Nate** (☑787-364-5911) or **741 Taxi** (☑787-741-8294; www. 741taxi.com; ⊘24hr).

Ponce & South Coast

POP 485,000

Includes ➡

Ponce 146
Guayama & Pozuelo ... 155
Bahía de Jobos 157
Playa Salinas 158
Coamo 159
Yauco & Around 162
Guánica & Around 163
La Parguera 166

Best Places to Eat

➡ El Negocio de Panchi (p152)

➡ El Vejigante (p152)

➡ La Casa de Los Pastelillos (p156)

➡ Restaurante La Guardarraya (p163)

➡ Alexandra (p165)

➡ Moon's Bar & Tapas (p169)

Best Places to Sleep

➡ Mary Lee's by the Sea (p165)

➡ Copamarina Beach Resort (p165)

➡ La Jamaca (p169)

➡ Hotel Bélgica (p151)

Why Go?

The Caribbean-facing south coast offers the opportunity to unplug, escape the cruise-ship crowds and take a DIY journey into Puerto Rico's tempestuous, rough-and-tumble piratical past.

Even the proud southern capital of Ponce – the so-called Perla de Sur (Pearl of the South) – stands in elegant disrepair, where haute eateries and mesmerizing museums neighbor slouching colonial-era facades. Along coastal Hwys 2 and 3, the dilapidation increases, with crumbling chimneys of sugar mills standing beside their graying industrial replacements – chemical and pharmaceutical factories. But for all these dichotomies, unpolished charm abounds in the towns and the tatty beaches get increasingly magical as you progress west through mazes of mangroves, ethereal dry tropical forest and, finally, the surreal glow of the Bahía de Fosforescente alongside some of the Caribbean's most captivating diving.

When to Go

With some of the most consistent weather in the world, the dry, sunny climate is enticing, though June through August can be blisteringly hot.

During summer school holidays (August), Puerto Rican families fill the sun-washed plazas, wander through colonial-era buildings and enjoy alfresco dining at the ubiquitous seafood shacks. Book accommodation in advance at this time – and in Ponce, during its many festivals.

Although the arid, breezy atmosphere doesn't change much in winter, the typically languid pace slows to a crawl between September and May, picking up only for local festivals. October and November can be particularly dead months in tourist-dependent places like La Parguera, with facilities closing up almost completely.

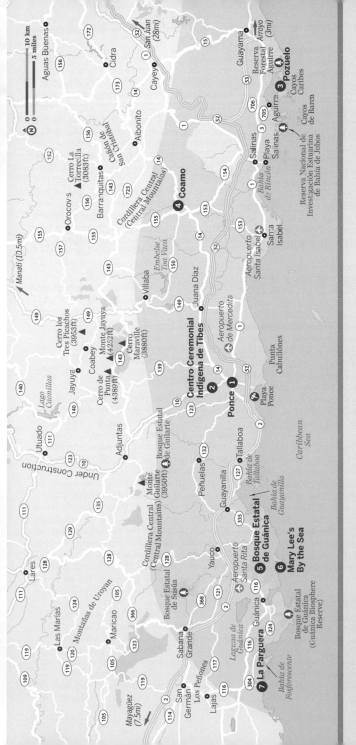

Ponce & South Coast Highlights

1 Museo de Arte de Ponce (p147) Falling in love with *Flaming June* in the cultural hot spot of Ponce.

2 Centro Ceremonial Indígena de Tibes (p154) Connecting with the mysterious Taíno past at the island's largest archaeological site.

3 La Casa de Los Pastelillos (p156) Swaying on a hammock while lunching on golden, octopus-stuffed pastries in Pozuelo.

4 Baños de Coamo (p159) Soaking in waters once thought to be the fountain of youth.

5 Bosque Estatal de Guánica (p163) Hiking the birding trails of one of this amazing subtropical dry forests.

6 Mary Lee's By The Sea (p165) Checking in to this tranquil place and spending your days paddling out to the nearby cays.

7 The Wall (p168) Taking the plunge with world-class diving in La Parguera.

History

The rolling foothills and broad coastal plains of the south coast were home to a number of indigenous tribes; they were later colonized by Spaniards, who raised cattle and horses here for the colonial expeditions across Latin America during the 16th century. In 1630 they built the hamlet that would eventually become Ponce on a port between the mountains and the coast.

For more than a century, goods and materials flowed through the welcoming harbors. Ostensibly the port of Ponce was open only to Spanish vessels trading directly with Spain, but the watchful eyes of the island governor were far away in San Juan, and free trade flourished, bringing with it goods, currencies and people from across the New World and Africa.

When slave revolts erupted in the neighboring French-held island of Saint-Domingue in the 1790s and in South America between 1810 and 1822, many wealthy refugees fled to the south coast of Puerto Rico, buying land to grow coffee and sugarcane. Soon they imported former slaves from Caribbean colonies to meet the ever-increasing American appetite for sugar, coffee and rum. Production and profits from agriculture skyrocketed throughout the 19th century, when sugar barons built cities with elegant town squares, neoclassical architecture and imported French fountains.

The Spanish-American War ended the freebooting days, bringing with it military occupation, uniformly enforced trade laws and economic freefall. Hurricanes devastated the coffee industry, sugar prices fell and the US government decided to develop San Juan, not Ponce, as a strategic port. When the Depression hit in the 1930s, the region went into an economic hibernation. These days the south limps along littered with contradictions between the past and the future.

❶ Getting There & Around

Ponce's **Aeropuerto Mercedita** (Hwy 1) serves a couple of US cities direct (including New York and Orlando, Florida). The main transport artery in and out of the region is Hwy 52 from San Juan to the northeast. This road continues to Ponce, after which, in a new guise at Hwy 2, it trundles on towards the West Coast. Things get slower as you head west.

Ponce

POP 160,000

Ponce es Ponce (Ponce is Ponce), runs a simple yet telling Puerto Rican saying: the explanation given as to why the nation's haughty second city does things, well, uniquely – and in defiance of the capital. Native son and author Abelardo Díaz Alfaro went further, calling Ponce a *baluarte irreductible de puertorriqueñidad* – a bastion of the irreducible essence of Puerto Rico. Strolling around the sparkling fountains and narrow architecturally ornamented streets of the historic center certainly evokes Puerto Rico's stately past. Unfortunately, the neighborhoods that surround the central square exhibit woeful characteristics of Puerto Rico's present: irreducible snarls of congested traffic, economic stagnation and cookie-cutter urban sprawl.

If you stick to the centre with its outstanding colonial-era architecture and the city's dozen or so museums (many ranking among the island's best) and the area 5km south at the seashore-hugging restaurant-lined boardwalk of La Guancha Paseo Tablado, you only need experience Ponce's elegant side.

History

History is better preserved in and around Ponce than almost anywhere else in Puerto Rico – both the colonial past (found downtown) and the indigenous past (just outside at the island's largest and most educational archaeological site, the Centro Ceremonial Indígena de Tibes).

The earliest European settlement saw numerous scuffles between Spanish conquistador Ponce de León (from whom the town gets both its name and one of its nicknames, 'City of Lions') and the Taíno tribes, but the region was claimed for the Spanish Crown in 1511. The city was established around 1630, when the Spaniards built the first incarnation of the current cathedral and named it for the patron saint of Mexico, la Virgen de Guadalupe.

Ponce grew fat off the rewards of smugglers in the late 1600s. By the mid-1700s Ponce's bourgeois society wanted at least a patina of respectability and poured resources into legitimate enterprises such as tobacco, coffee and rum. Sugar, too, became an important business and entire plains (the same denuded ones you see today) were removed of greenery and replaced with silky, lucrative sugarcane. The added wealth and polyglot mixture of Spanish, Taíno, French and West Indian peoples helped establish Ponce as the island's earliest artistic, musical and literary center. Working-class areas pulsated to the rhythm of boisterous strains of *bomba y plena,* two distinct yet often associated types of folk music; the parlors of the bourgeoisie resonated to *danza* (a more elegant ballroom dance).

That golden age ended in 1898 when Spain rejected America's demand to peacefully observe Cuban independence. This instigated the Spanish-American War, which included an American invasion of Puerto Rico that landed in Guánica. Under subsequent American rule, Puerto Rico's economy was drastically transformed and Ponce's sugarcane fields were found lucrative for industrialized investors. In 1899, however, a pair of hurricanes devastated the sugar fields and Ponce's industry never fully recovered.

Decline began and Ponce became a hotbed of civic unrest. It boiled over during the Ponce Massacre of 1937, which politically alienated Ponce from the rest of the island. Ponce was already on its knees by the time the Americans' Operation Bootstrap, an ambitious island-wide industrialization project, dealt the region a near-fatal blow by favoring the development of ports on the north coast.

Having limped along through the latter half of the 20th century through textile and cement production, tourism has recently helped turned much of the area's fortunes around, along with rum and pharmaceutical production.

◉ Sights

Should you ever get lost in Ponce, just look to the skies for a sign from God: the town's two infallible landmarks are the towering steeples of the Catedral Nuestra Señora de Guadalupe, which sits regally at the center of the lovely Plaza Las Delicias, and an enormous concrete-and-glass cross, El Vigía, which overlooks the town to the north.

As you navigate your way through the outskirts of Ponce, the first impression, characterized by traffic jams and minimalls, is uninspiring. But the soul of Ponce is its idyllic Spanish colonial plaza and the surrounding grid of streets replete with picturesque historic buildings.

❶ PLAN YOUR TRIP

➜ Book a tour in advance for a visit to the Hacienda Buena Vista (p154).

➜ Ensure you book a hotel room ahead of time: while elsewhere in Puerto Rico rooms sit vacant year-round, in Ponce they fill up fast.

➜ Look at the www.seepuertorico.com website for information on visiting one of the south's famous festivals.

★ **Museo de Arte de Ponce**　　GALLERY
(MAP; ☑787-848-0505; www.museoarteponce.org; 2325 Av Las Américas; adult/concession $6/3; ⊙10am-5pm Wed-Sat & Mon, noon-5pm Sun) *Brush Strokes In Flight,* a bold primary-colored totem by American pop artist Roy Lichtenstein, announces the smartly remodeled MAP, where an expertly presented collection ranks among the best in the Caribbean. It is itself worth the trip from San Juan. A $30-million renovation celebrated the museum's 50th anniversary and the smart curation – some 850 paintings, 800 sculptures and 500 prints presented in provocative historical and thematic juxtapositions – represents five centuries of Western art.

The greatest-hits collection of Puerto Rican painters is stirring; look for the wall-sized *Ponce* by Rafael Ríos Rey at the rear of the museum. The building's blanched edifice, winged central stair and hexagonal galleries were designed by architect Edward Durell Stone, who created Washington DC's Kennedy Center. The exceptional pre-Raphaelite and Italian baroque collections are offset by impressive installations and special exhibits (which occasionally cost a small extra fee).

A complete tour of the museum takes about three hours, but if you only have time for a quick peek, spend some time sitting in awe of Edward Burne-Jones's ghostly, half-finished *The Sleep of Arthur in Avalon* (look for the unfinished, blank eyes of the attending queens) and Lord Leighton's erotic *Flaming June,* the museum's sensual showpiece. Set across from the Universidad Católica, the MAP is about 10 blocks to the south of Plaza Las Delicias.

Plaza Las Delicias　　SQUARE
Within this elegant square you'll discover Ponce's heart as well as two of the city's landmark buildings, Parque de Bombas (p149)

PONCE & SOUTH COAST PONCE

Ponce

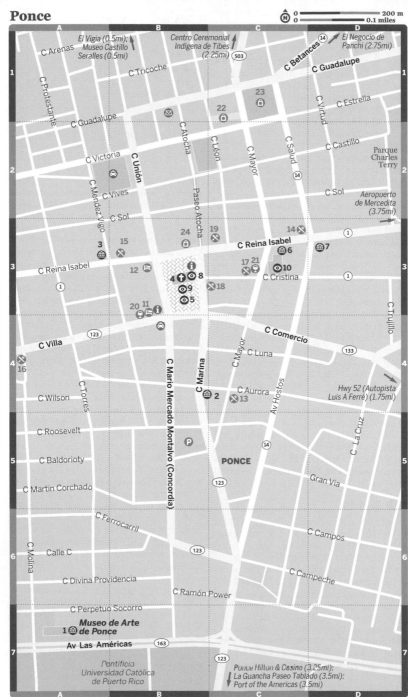

N 0 — 200 m
0 — 0.1 miles

El Vigía (0.5mi);
Museo Castillo
Seralles (0.5mi)

Centro Ceremonial
Indígena de Tibes
(2.25mi) 503

14 El Negocio de
Panchi (2.75mi)

C Arenas
C Tricoche
C Betances
C Guadalupe

C Protestante
C Guadalupe
23
22
C Atocha
C Léon
C Mayor
C Salud
C Virtud
C Estrella
C Castillo
Parque Charles Terry

C Victoria
C Unión
C Méndez Vigo
C Vives
C Sol
14
C Sol
Aeropuerto de Mercedita (3.75mi)

24
19
C Reina Isabel
14
6
7
1
3
15
C Reina Isabel
12
4 8
9
17 21
10
18
C Cristina
1
20 11
5
C Trujillo

C Villa
123
C Comercio
133

16
C Wilson
C Torres
C Mario Mercado Montalvo (Concordia)
C Marina
C Mayor
C Luna
Av Hostos
Hwy 52 (Autopista Luis A Ferré) (1.75mi)

C Roosevelt
2
C Aurora
13
PONCE

C Baldorioty
14
C La Cruz

C Martin Corchado
P
123
Gran Via

C Molina
Calle C
C Ferrocarril
123
C Campos

C Divina Providencia
123
C Campeche

C Ramón Power
C Perpetuo Socorro

1 Museo de Arte de Ponce
Av Las Américas
163

Pontificia
Universidad Católica
de Puerto Rico

123

Ponce Hilton & Casino (3.25mi);
La Guancha Paseo Tablado (3.5mi);
Port of the Americas (3.5mi)

Ponce

◉ **Top Sights**
1 Museo de Arte de Ponce.....................A7

◉ **Sights**
2 Casa de la Masacre de Ponce.............B4
3 Casa Wiechers-Villaronga...................A3
4 Catedral Nuestra Señora de
  Guadalupe.......................................B3
5 Fuente de los Leones........................B3
6 Museo de la Historia de Ponce...........C3
7 Museo de la Música
  Puertorriqueña.................................D3
8 Parque de Bombas............................B3
9 Plaza Las Delicias.............................B3
10 Teatro La Perla.................................C3

⊜ **Sleeping**
11 Hotel Bélgica....................................B3
12 Ponce Plaza Hotel & Casino...............B3

⊗ **Eating**
13 Café Café...C4
14 Campioni..C3
15 Chef's Creations...............................B3
16 El Barril de la Mulata..........................A4
17 El Vejigante......................................C3
18 King's Cream.....................................C3
   Melao.......................................(see 12)
19 Sabor y Rumba.................................C3

◉ **Drinking & Nightlife**
20 Studio 124..B3
21 Taska Gau...C3

⊜ **Shopping**
22 Mercado Juan Ponce de León............C1
23 Nueva Plaza del Mercado...................C1
24 Utopia..B3

and Catedral Nuestra Señora de Guadalupe. The smell of *panaderías* (bakeries) follows churchgoers across the square each morning, children squeal around the majestic fountain under the midday heat, and lovers stroll under its lights at night. The **Fuente de los Leones** (Fountain of the Lions), a photogenic fountain rescued from the 1939 World's Fair in New York, is the square's most captivating attraction.

Even as the commercial banks and the fast-food joints encroach around the edges, reminders of the city's prideful history dominate the plaza's attractions. Watch out for marble statues of local *danza* icon Juan Morel Campos and poet/politician Luis Muñoz Marín, Puerto Rico's first governor, amid more artsy ones of lions (the city's symbol, which doesn't take too long to realize). These days the square has free wi-fi too.

Catedral Nuestra Señora de Guadalupe   CATHEDRAL

(Our Lady of Guadalupe Cathedral; Plaza Las Delicias; ⊙7am-7pm) The twin bell towers of this striking cathedral cast an impression of noble piety over Ponce's Plaza Las Delicias. It was built in 1931, in the place where colonists erected their first chapel in the 1660s, which (along with subsequent structures) succumbed to earthquakes and fires. Its stained-glass windows and interior are picturesque. There are several services daily.

Parque de Bombas   NOTABLE BUILDING

(⟨☎⟩787-840-1045; ⊙9am-5pm) **FREE** *Ponceños* (people from Ponce) say that the eye-popping Parque de Bombas is Puerto Rico's most frequently photographed building, which is not too hard to believe as you stroll around the black-and-red-striped, Arabian-style edifice and make countless unwitting cameos in family photo albums. Since 1990, the landmark has been a tourist information center (p154), where pleasant, bilingual staff will sell you tickets for a trolley and direct you to local attractions.

Originally constructed in 1882 as an agricultural exhibition hall, the space later housed the city's volunteer firefighters, who are commemorated in a small, tidy exhibit on the open 2nd floor. The many-coloured lions are a reference to the man who gave the city its name: Juan Ponce de León y Loayza (*leon* in Spanish means lion).

Museo de la Música Puertorriqueña   MUSEUM

(⟨☎⟩787-848-7016; cnr Reina Isabel & Salud; ⊙8:30am-noon & 1-4:30pm Wed-Sun) **FREE** This spacious pink villa designed by Juan Bertoli Calderoni, father of Puerto Rico's neoclassical style, offers one of Ponce's best museum experiences. A guided tour showcases development of Puerto Rico's sound, allowing hands-on demonstrations of indigenous instruments. The collection of Taíno, African and Spanish instruments – especially the handcrafted four-string guitar-like *cuatros* – and careful explanation of Puerto Rican musical traditions are highlights.

The museum also hosts a three-week seminar on drum building in July, and holds concerts in its courtyard.

Casa Wiechers-Villaronga   HISTORIC BUILDING

(cnr Reina Isabel & Mendez Vigo; ⊙8:30am-noon Wed-Sun) **FREE** Perhaps the most grand of Ponce's historic homes, this mansion was designed by Paris-educated *ponceño* architect

Alfredo Wiechers. The carefully preserved Victorian details – such as the multidirectional pipeworks of the ancient shower and the hand-carved bedroom furniture – speak to the grand lifestyle of its former residents. Tours begin by request (better in Spanish, though possible in English). A twisting iron staircase ascends to the neoclassical rooftop gazebo for a bird's-eye perspective of the neighborhood.

Teatro La Perla · NOTABLE BUILDING

(Pearl Theater; ☑ 787-843-4322; cnr Mayor & Cristina; ⊙ lobby 8am-4:30pm Mon-Fri) FREE The restored 1000-seat Teatro La Perla was designed by Juan Bertoli Calderoni, father of Puerto Rico's neoclassical style, and completed in the 1860s. It took 20 years to rebuild following a 1918 earthquake, but it has since played a crucial role in the city's performing arts world, underscored by the nearby Instituto de Musica Juan Morel Campos, an affiliated music conservatory.

La Guancha Paseo Tablado · WATERFRONT

Commonly known as 'La Guancha,' this rebuilt public boardwalk is around 5km south of the city center near the relatively lonely Ponce Hilton and the Port of the Americas. Refurbished in the mid-1990s, it's a haven for picnicking families and strolling couples. Its chief points of interest include a concert pavilion, a well-kept public beach and a humble observation tower. It's also the launch point for ferries to Isla Caja de Muertos.

There's a handful of open-air bars, food kiosks and fine-dining restaurants. The place picks up with a breezy, festive atmosphere on weekends.

Museo de la Historia de Ponce · MUSEUM

(51-53 Reina Isabel; ⊙ 8am-4pm Tue-Sun) FREE Ponce's history museum is extensive for a city of fewer than 200,0000 people – evidence of the city's reverence for history. Located in the Casa Salazar (built 1911), the museum has 10 galleries displaying centuries of the city's history in ecology, economy, education, architecture, medicine, politics and daily life. A refreshingly Ponce-centric perspective on the development of Puerto Rican culture, the building itself is an architectural treasure that blends typical *ponceño criollo* detailing with Moorish and neoclassical elements.

El Vigía · VIEWPOINT

(☑ 787-259-3816; 17 El Vigía; adult/child $5.75/3, combo ticket incl Museo Castillo Serrallés $13.25/5.75; ⊙ 9am-5:30pm Tue-Sun) It doesn't really compare with the hilltop cross in Rio de Janeiro, but the 100ft reinforced-concrete Cruceta del Vigía looking over Ponce is one of the city's more reliable points of orientation and offers a cracking view from its upper echelons. During the 19th century the site was used by lookouts for the Spanish Crown, watching for signs of smuggling along the coast. Today it shares grounds with a scrubby Japanese garden, included in the admission price.

Museo Castillo Serrallés · MUSEUM

(Serrallés Castle Museum; ☑ 787-259-1770; www.castilloserralles.org; 17 El Vigía; adult/child $8.75/4.50, combo ticket incl El Vigía $13.25/5.75; ⊙ 9am-5pm Tue-Sun) On the same property as the mammoth El Vigía, Museo Castillo Serrallés was

---

THE PONCE MASSACRE

In the turbulent 1930s, Puerto Rico's troubled economy ignited revolutionary fervor across the island, but it was in Ponce, with its large student population and reputation for culture and sophistication, that a march for independence went terribly wrong.

The marchers had a parade permit for the demonstration, which was staged in the Plaza Las Delicias on Palm Sunday, March 21, 1937, but at the last minute the governor of Puerto Rico withdrew permission.

Angered, the nationalists defied the prohibition and marched anyway. Slightly fewer than 100 young men and women faced off with 150 armed police near Plaza Las Delicias. When the nationalists started singing *La Borinqueña* – the national anthem – a shot was fired and the entire plaza erupted in gunfire. Seventeen marchers and two police officers died. Not one civilian carried a gun and most of the 17 marchers died from shots in the back. While the US government chose not to investigate, the American Civil Liberties Union did, and confirmed that the catastrophe warranted its popular name, 'Masacre de Ponce' (Ponce Massacre). Now a small museum appropriately called the Casa de la Masacre de Ponce (cnr Marina & Aurora; ⊙ 1-3pm Wed-Sun) FREE is housed in the building that held the offices of the Nationalist Party in 1937, keeping the memory alive.

the home of Ponce's rum dynasty, the Serrallés family. Docents lead bilingual walking tours through the lovely Moorish-style castle. When the somewhat exhausting hour-plus tour ends, you can order snacks and drinks at the cafe. Relax on the terrace under the red-tiled roof and enjoy a view of the city below and the quiet burble of the garden's fountains.

Combo ticket options with El Vigía are available and are perhaps worth getting as they allow entry into everything at the Castillo Serallés tourist complex, including some Japanese gardens and a butterfly sanctuary.

✨ Festivals & Events

Carnaval
CARNIVAL

Ponce's Carnaval is a time of serious partying. Events kick off on the Wednesday before Ash Wednesday with a masked ball, followed by parades, a formal *danza* competition and the coronation of the Carnaval queen and child queen. The party ends with the ceremonial burial of a sardine (the traditional significance of which has been washed away by booze) and the onset of Lent.

Each parade and all of the critical activities take place in Plaza Las Delicias in front of Casa Alcaldía. If you're planning to visit Ponce during Carnaval, make your hotel and transportation reservations at least three months in advance.

Semana de la Danza
DANCE, MUSIC

(☉ mid-May) Held in mid-May, this 'Week of Dance' has parades and dance events. The (humorously stuffy) Ponce Municipal Band performs in Plaza Las Delicias as well-groomed couples offer postured examples of the form of dance that accompanies 'Puerto Rico's classical music.'

Ponce is a very appropriate venue: the city was home to the high society and composers who made *danza* a distinctive art form at the turn of the 19th century.

Fiesta de Bomba y Plena
MUSIC, DANCE

(☉ Aug) Drummers and *pleneros* (*plena* singers) arrive from all over the island to participate in this festival of *bomba y plena*, the singing, dancing and drumming style that evolved in Ponce among citizens of African descent who came en masse to work the cane fields.

Los Reyes Magos de Juana Díaz
RELIGIOUS

(☉ Jan 6) Puerto Ricans arrive from all over to celebrate epiphany in the small town of Juana Díaz, 15km northeast of Ponce.

There's a large procession and people come dressed as one of the shepherds or the three wise men who arrived late to see baby Jesus.

🛏 Sleeping

It's best to make your bed at one of the hotels surrounding Plaza Las Delicias, rather than one of the lackluster resorts outside the city center. The sterility of the Hilton and Holiday Inn might comfort the most cautious gringo, but local flavor is nil and prices soar for accommodations that are only questionably more comfortable. Beware: accommodation is costly here as there are, incredibly, no good options besides hotels.

★ Hotel Bélgica
HOTEL $

(☏ 787-844-3255; www.hotelbelgica.com; 122 Villa; r $75-100; ❈ 🛜) Just off the southwest corner of Plaza Las Delicias, this traveler-favorite has a creaking colonial-era ambience, with 15ft ceilings and wrought-iron balconies. The hallways are a bit of a maze and dimly lit, but the place is charming, with delightful old furniture in many of the 20 rooms.

Rooms near the front allow you to stare out over the plaza from private balconies, but be prepared for noise on weekend nights. The wi-fi is spotty.

Howard Johnson
HOTEL $$

(☏ 1-800-221-5801, 787-841-1000; www.wyndham hotels.com; cnr Hwy 1 & Calle Curva Turpo; d $95-150; 🅿 ❈ 🛜 ≋) While there's not much personality, the Howard Johnson is abundant in chain-hotel comforts including wi-fi, an exercise room, a game room and a terrific pool. A pristinely clean if slightly motel-like option very close to the airport.

Ponce Plaza Hotel & Casino
HOTEL $$

(☏ 787-813-5050; www.ponceplazahotelandcasino. com; cnr Reina Isabel & Unión; d from $110; 🅿 ❈ 🛜 ≋) Standing grandly over a corner of the plaza, this building's lemon-yellow colonial-era facade has emerged from the scaffolding after years of preservationist dispute. The historic building, location and clutch of amenities, and mix of classic colonial and modern rooms, keep it among the top options in the city center.

Of the two connected buildings, the best rooms (the colonial ones) face the square, with black-and-white-tiled floors and balconies; those in the back are clean but have little by way of atmosphere. The courtyard pool is tiny, but with two class eateries in the Lola restaurant (patronized by the city elite)

PONCE & SOUTH COAST PONCE

and **Melao cafe** (www.facebook.com/melao coffeeshop; snacks from $3; ◷7am-10pm; 🖶), chic design elements and an open-air bar, it's well worth a stop.

Ponce Hilton & Casino RESORT $$$

(☑787-259-7676; www.hilton.com; 1150 Av Caribe; r from $190; P🌢@🛜🌊) The 153-room Hilton stands within a gated area 6km south of town, near the La Guancha boardwalk (p150) on the Caribbean. It's the most deluxe option in Ponce, with well-manicured grounds, on-site golf, a nightclub, enticing pools, restaurants and a casino. However, it suffers from a lack of local flavor; sun-pink golfers are wont to gripe about their last round and the quality of the buffet.

All that said, it's still the only hotel in Ponce with ocean views (for which you pay higher-end prices; cheapest rooms have pool views only). For breakfast it's about $10 extra per night; check the website for the latest deals.

✖ Eating

A crop of creative chefs working in Ponce's city center are masterminding an unheralded, but varied, eating scene. For something cheap on-the-go, head to the carts around Plaza Las Delicias.

Also, if you're in town on the third Friday of the month, check out Ponce Fest, a culinary festival right on Plaza Las Delicias.

★ El Vejigante CARIBBEAN $

(www.facebook.com/elveji; cnr Cristina & Mayor Canera; mains $8-15; ◷midday-1am) A diminutive, cool, cozy little joint perfect for pre- or post-theatre dinner and drinks since Teatro La Perla (p150) is just around the corner. El Vejigante is far-reaching in its wine list, innovative in its food (Caribbean and Latin American fusion) and impeccable in its service. The walls are decorated with *vejigantes* (masks) and creations from the Ponce carnival.

Sample the homemade salsas (the tamarind salsa is delicious), accompanying staples like grouper ceviche with root veg mash. This place stays open during holidays and at such times feels like a true oasis in an otherwise closed-up city.

Sabor y Rumba CARIBBEAN $

(Reina Isabel 66; mains $10; ◷11am-11pm) An otherwise run-down courtyard has been spruced up to provide one of Ponce's best-value restaurants. There are outside tables and generous portions of *mofongo*

or *cerdo relleno* (stuffed pork). Read the electric scoreboard to find out what's cooking. There's also music classes, regular live music, an espresso machine and graffiti. Simple – and yet an engine of inspiration.

Café Café CAFE $

(☑787-841-7185; www.cafecafeponce.com; cnr Mayor & Aurora; mains $9-16; ◷11am-3pm Mon-Sat) 🍃 For the best coffee in Ponce and an excellent brunch or lunch, start at this art-filled, bilingual cafe, where the clientele ranges from businesspeople to skiving students. The coffee beans couldn't be fresher – they're roasted next door. For lunch, try the *mofongo* (mashed plantains) '*a caballo*,' stuffed with corned beef and topped with a fried egg.

King's Cream ICE CREAM $

(9223 Marina; cones $1-3; ◷8am-midnight) On warm evenings, lines stretch down the sidewalk of this institution, located across from Parque de Bombas. And for good reason: smooth-blended tropical licks overflow with fruit. There are other snack stalls nearby, but none matches the cones at this joint.

El Barril de la Mulata PUERTO RICAN $

(www.facebook.com/elbarrildelamulata; 151 Villa; mains $5-15; ◷noon-5pm Sat & Mon-Thu, to 10pm Fri) For hearty, beautifully cooked Puerto Rican fare come lunch time, don't look any further than this unpretentious restaurant three blocks west of Plaza Las Delicias. The steak and fish options are always different to the standard and the different rices served are more varied than anywhere in the city. The menu changes daily. There's dancing on Friday (sometimes).

Campioni PIZZA $$

(☑787-651-6263; www.facebook.com/campionipr; Reina Isabel 42; pizzas $15-30; ◷11:30am-midnight Sun-Thu, to 2:30am Fri & Sat) Probably the south coast's best take on traditional Italian fare, this refined colonial-era mansion with several different dining rooms has a good wine selection but spreads itself quite thin, concentrating on tapas and late-night cocktails, when perhaps deciding what sort of restaurant it wants to be might be wiser. Staff are eager to please, though, and portions are large (the pizzas are enormous).

El Negocio de Panchi INTERNATIONAL, FUSION $$

(☑787 848 4788; www.facebook.com/el depanchi; cnr Hwy 14 & Pichachos; mains $15-35; ◷4-11pm) Opposite an out-of-town shopping center

ISLA CAJA DE MUERTOS

The name Isla Caja de Muertos (return trip $28) – which translates to Coffin Island – could have been taken straight from the script of a swashbuckling adventure flick, but the big lizards here run a lazy show, trotting across dusty, cacti-lined trails and over the mangrove marsh. The morbid moniker is thought to have come from an 18th-century French author's observation that the island's silhouette looked like a casket.

There's not much to see here, but the opportunity to take a day trip from Ponce's congestion can be pleasant. It hosts some of the best snorkeling around and plenty of tranquil, if somewhat rocky, stretches of beach. Hikers wander past endangered plants and reptiles that thrive in the climate, as well as a regal 19th-century lighthouse that is occasionally used as a station for biologists. If you need more action, try a low-impact trip to scuba dive at the 40ft wall, just offshore. The only way to make the trip is through Island Ventures Water Excursions (☑787-842-8546; www.islandventurepr. com; round-trip $28).

lies the very antithesis: El Negocio de Panchi, a time-lost esoteric wooden house with a handful of tables inside, serving excellent culinary creations like mushrooms stuffed with manchego, lamb shank with root mash or puff-pastry escargots. It's 5km northeast of the city center but worth the drive to sample one of Ponce's best eateries.

Chef's Creations   FUSION $$
(☑787-848-8384; 100 Reina Isabel; mains $15-29; ⊙11am-2pm Mon-Wed, 6-10pm Thu, 6-11pm Fri & Sat) At quiet, classy Chef's Creations, the daily-changing menu leans toward international fusions of local fare such as *paella con tostones* (heading in a Spanish direction) or IPA-battered local fish and chips (heading in a British one). And if you can try the clams, do.

Pito's Seafood   SEAFOOD $$
(☑787-841-4977; Hwy 2, Sector Las Cucharas; mains $15-35; ⊙noon-10pm Sun-Thu, to midnight Fri & Sat) Pito's serves fish so fresh they practically swim up to your plate; it also has one of the city's best wine cellars, making a trip to its slightly inconvenient location worth it. To get here, head west on Hwy 2 from the center for about 4 miles and you'll see it on the left after Laguna de las Salinas.

🍸 Drinking & Nightlife

Ponce nightlife is at the mercy of capricious college crowds who pack into little restaurant-cum-bars around the plaza to slam drinks and grind to reggaeton. Hot spots change often and last as long as some celebrity marriages. The scene at La Guancha (p150) is also spirited; arrive too early however and you'll find it will be more family-focused.

The best casino is at the Hilton where there's a semblance of out-of-town nightlife that's about as Puerto Rican as Minnesota.

Taska Gau   CRAFT BEER
(Mayor cnr Cristina; beers from $3; ⊙4pm-3am Wed-Sat) Ponce now has this tucked-away little artisan-beer bar right opposite the Teatro La Perla as one of its standout bars, casting a whole new light on the nightlife on the surrounding blocks.

Studio 124   COCKTAIL BAR
(www.studio124pr.com; Villa 124) In the ever-changing world of Ponce's central bar scene, here's a place that seems set to stay popular due to its suave ambience and superbly mixed cocktails.

🛍 Shopping

Paseo Atocha, just north of the plaza, is closed to traffic, serving as a busy pedestrian marketplace with food stands, cheap goods and street stands of suspiciously affordable designer wear.

Nueva Plaza del Mercado   MARKET
(cnr Mayor & Estrella; ⊙6am-6pm Mon-Sat) Winding through crowds of shoppers on Paseo Atocha will lead you to Ponce's most exciting indoor market, four blocks north of Plaza Las Delicias. The selection of produce – freshly hacked off the vine – is just marvelous.

Mercado Juan Ponce de León   MARKET
(⊙8am-6pm Mon-Fri) Just west up the block from Nueva Plaza del Mercado, bustling Mercado Juan Ponce de León has stalls hawking pan-religious voodoo charms and salsa tunes on vintage vinyl.

WORTH A TRIP

DAY TRIPS FROM PONCE

On the fringes of Ponce the countryside conceals some important testaments to its history which make for some extremely worthwhile half-day trips (both are in a similar direction, heading north of the city towards the Central Mountains, and could be factored into one full-day trip).

Centro Ceremonial Indígena de Tibes (Tibes Indian Ceremonial Center; ☏787-840-5685; http://ponce.inter.edu/tibes/tibes.html; Km 2.2, Hwy 503; adult/child $3/2; ☺9am-3:30pm Tue-Sun, closed major holidays) This is the island's (and probably the Caribbean's) most mesmerizing indigenous site, and is in a spectacularly well-preserved state. The highlight, visually speaking, are the seven *bateyes* (Taíno ball courts) and two ceremonial plazas which have since their discovery yielded intriguing information about not only the Taíno, but also the pre-Taíno civilizations, like the Igneris. The historical pedigree is backed up by a really good museum and guided tours which illuminate the Puerto Rico that existed before Columbus like very few other places can.

Hacienda Buena Vista (☏787-284-7020, Ext 4 787-722-5888; Km 17.3, Rte 123; tour $12; ☺Wed-Sun by reservation) This lovingly restored coffee hacienda is a great opportunity to get under the skin of Puerto Rico's coffee-growing legacy. It's less a working coffee plantation (there are plenty of those in the Central Mountains) and more a riveting historical insight into life on a 19th-century coffee plantation – and it offers a tranquil woodsy escape from the downtown bustle of Ponce.

Utopia GIFTS & SOUVENIRS
(6953 Calle Isabel, Muñoz Rivera; ☺7am-6pm Mon-Fri, 8am-6pm Sat, 11am-6pm Sun) Selling colorful *vejigantes* (Puerto Rican masks), *santos* (small carved figurines representing saints) and trinkets, Utopia is the nicest souvenir shop on the square. The bonus? The little bar up front serves decent coffee and will sell six-packs of beer to go: hooray!

❶ Information

INTERNET ACCESS

The **Plaza Las Delicias** (p147) has free wi-fi and all accommodation options and even some restaurants have wi-fi too.

Mariana Suarez de Longo Biblioteca (☏787-812-3004; https://bibliotecaponce. wordpress.com; cnr Marginal & Av Santiago de los Caballeros; ☺8am-9pm Mon-Thu, to 6pm Fri, plus 10:30am-6pm Sat Jun; ☏) also has computers, laptop stations and wireless access.

MEDICAL SERVICES

Hospital Manuel Comunitario Dr Pila (☏787-848-5600; 2445 Av Las Américas) A hospital with a 24-hour emergency room.

Walgreens (☏787-812-5978; Km 225, Rte 2; ☺24hr) The only pharmacy that can accommodate a late-night need for aloe.

MONEY

Banks line the perimeter of Plaza Las Delicias so finding a cash machine is no problem. Most of the banks are open from 9am to 4pm weekdays, plus Saturday mornings.

POST

Post Office (93 Atocha; ☺8:30am-3:30pm Mon-Fri, to noon Sat) This is the most central of the city's four post offices.

TOURIST INFORMATION

Porta Caribe Regional Tourist Information Office (☏787-290-2911; Villa 122; ☺8am-4:30pm Mon-Fri) This office has insightful information on the entire south-coast region.

Puerto Rico Tourism Company (PRTC; ☏787-284-4141, 787-840-1045; Parque de Bombas, Plaza Las Delicias; ☺9am-5:30pm) You can't miss the big red-and-black structure in the middle of Parque de Bombas, where friendly, English-speaking members of the tourist office are ready with brochures, answers and suggestions.

❶ Getting There & Away

AIR

Seven kilometers east of the town center off Hwy 1, the **Aeropuerto Mercedita** (p146) looks dressed for a party, but is still waiting for the guests to arrive. **JetBlue** (☏787-651-0787, 800-538-2853; www.jetblue.com; Aeropuerto Mercedita), the only airline currently serving the airport, has services to New York and Orlando, but no domestic flights.

CAR

Swooshing down to Ponce from San Juan is easy on the smoothly paved Hwy 52, a partially toll-controlled highway called the Autopista Luis A Ferré. You'll know you've arrived when you pass through the mountains and drive through the towering letters by the roadside reading 'P-O-N-C-E.' The city center is about 5km from the south shore and the same distance again from the foothills of the Central Mountains to the north.

You don't have to drive through the center of town to get through Ponce – two bypass roads circle the city to the south. The inner road is Av Emelio Fagot/Av Las Américas (Hwy 163). The faster route is the outer road, Hwy 2, called the 'Ponce Bypass,' which hosts the town's biggest mall and loads of American chain stores. Hwys 52 and 2 merge in the southwest of Ponce; the road is known as Hwy 2 to the west of the city.

To reach the port, take the freshly paved route just east of the square, Rte 12. It becomes a divided highway south of the Ponce Bypass. Follow the signs to La Guancha Paseo Tablado.

CRUISE SHIP
A new cruise-ship terminal has been constructed 5km south of central Ponce, the **Port of the Americas** (Muelle de Ponce), and some cruises already stop here.

PÚBLICO
There's a nice, new **público terminal** (cnr Victoria & Unión) three blocks north of the plaza, with connections to most major towns, including San Juan. Pack unlimited patience for the indefinite wait.

① Getting Around

TO/FROM THE AIRPORT
Taxis tend to gravitate to the Plaza Las Delicias. Expect to pay $15 for the 4-mile taxi trip to or from the Mercedita Airport.

CAR
While driving in central Ponce is a nightmare and parking is little less of a headache, navigating the area in depth requires a car. Central blocks charge for parking. Rental-car agencies, including **Budget Car Rental** (⌨787-848-0907; Aeropuerto Mercedita; ◷8am-5pm Mon-Fri, noon-5pm Sat & Sun), are located at the Aeropuerto Mercedita.

TAXI
Hailing a cab at the Plaza Las Delicias is much quicker than calling for one, but if you do need to call, try **Ponce Taxi** (⌨787-840-0088; Plaza Las Delicias). It's $1 to drop the flag and roughly $1 per kilometer, but meters are used infrequently, so ask about the price before you get an unpleasant surprise. From the Plaza Las Delicias to the La Guancha boardwalk is $7; from the center to the Aeropuerto Mercedita, it's around $15.

TROLLEY
The city tourist office operates a trolley service ($2) for visitors, which is an informative and entertaining way to get to grips with attractions here. The trolley stops at key sights in central Ponce, allowing passengers to get out and snap photos.

There are supposed to be regular trips between 9am and 4:30pm, but drivers seem to change the schedule and routes on a whim and there are occasional breakdowns. They all leave and return to the **stop** in front of the Casa Armstrong-Poventud, on the western side of Plaza Las Delicias. Theoretically leaving at 10am, a long-distance trolley also takes in the more distant sights of El Vigía and Centro Ceremonial Indígena de Tibes.

Inquire at the tourist desk in Parque de Bombas before planning your day around a ride.

Guayama & Pozuelo

POP 44,000

A few kilometers up the hill from the Caribbean coast is Guayama, which has shared a rivalry with nearby Arroyo since colonial days when the shadowy brokering of Arroyo's ports fattened the wallets of Guayama's society families.

However, where Arroyo is charming and decrepit, Guayama seems sterile and modern. Today, Guayama's residents are mostly employed at pharmaceutical factories that lie west of town. The place once called the 'City of Witches' (a result of Santería worship brought here by African laborers) suffers from the contemporary spells of hasty development and heavy traffic.

During the first weekend of March the upscale Feria Dulce Sueño draws equestrian zealots for a Paso Fino horse race. Otherwise, there are a couple of impressive cultural diversions in town and some great eateries in the dreamier nearby fishing village of Pozuelo, which you'll find on a little peninsula rimmed by mangroves and pretty decent beaches.

◉ Sights

Centro de Bellas Artes GALLERY
(⌨787-864-7765; Km 138, Rte 3; ◷9am-4pm Tue-Sun) **FREE** This fine-arts center stands west of town in the former home of the Puerto Rican High Court. The collection focuses on emerging and established Puerto Rican artists (including a somewhat humorous set of reproductions). The works are engaging in themselves but the enthusiastic tour (available in English) is worth taking for the

snippets of insight into the culture that the art is themed around.

Museo Casa Cautiño
HISTORIC BUILDING

(☎787-864-9083; cnr Palmer & Vicente Palés Matos; ⊙8am-4:30pm Tue-Sun) FREE On the northern side of the plaza, this museum was built as a *criollo*-style town house in 1887 to house the wealthy Cautiño family, who profited from cane, cattle and tobacco. Almost 100 years later, the government claimed the property for back taxes (a common event on the island, which has saved many heirlooms).

Now the house has been restored to its dignified Victorian state, with Oriental carpets and period furnishings. It's one of those places that seems to open and close at whim, but well worth a look if you can.

★ Festivals & Events

Feria Dulce Sueño
SPORTS

(Fair of Sweet Dreams; ⊙Mar) The big day in the Guayama calendar is this Paso Fino horse race in March.

☷ Sleeping & Eating

Guayama's sleeping choices aren't good. If it's late and you're tired, consider pulling in here, but better sleeping options abound to the east.

For eats, there's inexpensive fare in the cafeterias by the central plaza, but the best food is a few kilometers down the road in Pozuelo.

Hotel Brandemar
HOTEL $$

(☎787-864-5124; www.brandemar.com; end of Rte 748; s/d $75/100; P❄☀) Following a twisting road through a residential neighborhood just outside of town, you'll come to the Brandemar, a just-adequate family-run hotel with no-frills rooms situated around a pool, with a restaurant across the way serving fresh seafood. There's a small beach just paces away, but it's no good for swimming.

★ La Casa de Los Pastelillos
SEAFOOD $

(Km 4, Rte 7710; pastelillos $3-7, mains $8-24; ⊙10:30am-6pm Mon-Thu, to 9pm Fri-Sun) After seeing the sorry excuse for what passes for

THE PRE-TAINO PEOPLE

Much like the Inca in Peru, the Taíno in Puerto Rico rather dominate discussions about the region's pre-Columbian peoples. But the Taíno actually appeared late in the day (around 1200 AD) and there is evidence of civilizations existing here for over four millennia before this date.

The island's first inhabitants are known as the pre-Ceramic people, a possibly nomadic population of hunter-gatherers whose presence in Puerto Rico can be traced to 3000 BC. Traces of their culture have been unearthed at sites such as Barceloneta, on the north coast.

By about 300 BC the Igneris were establishing themselves; heralding originally from the Orinoco region of Venezuela, they were significantly more advanced than their predecessors on the island. One important characteristic of the Igneris was their pottery, elaborate for this era, sometimes combining carvings and multiple colours. Other hallmarks of Taíno culture, such as *cemíes* (deities and the structures built to house them) and the devices used to inhale hallucinogens facilitating communication with the supernatural world, have also been discovered at Igneris sites. The Igneris were also horticulturalists, successfully farming vegetables such as the manioc, which became a staple for subsequent pre-Columbian peoples here.

Whilst the Igneris culture appears to have been a basis of sorts for later cultures in Puerto Rico, many ways in which the Igneris were developing have led historians to refer to these people as the pre-Taíno after approximately 600 AD. There were two main groups: the Elenoid, who occupied the east, and the Ostionoid, who lived in the west. Intriguingly, the Centro Ceremonial Indígena de Tibes (p154) occupies a site directly in between where these two groups lived. Excavated religious items dating from the pre-Taíno period are larger and more complex than those of the Igneris period, indicative of a more advanced society. The discovery of large *bateyes* (ball courts) for ceremonial purposes within pre-Taíno communities suggests this culture popularized the ball games the Taíno became famous for.

By the time the Taíno came along in 1200, many cornerstones of their culture, ranging from ceramics to living spaces to food, were already in place.

pastelillos (fried dumplings) elsewhere, you might not recognize the namesake of this seaside patio restaurant. The ambitious variations of the fried staple (shark? octopus? pizza?) are made to order, arriving as greasy, seafood-stuffed slices of heaven. More ample, healthful options are also lovingly made, based around fresh catches.

Add the view of crashing waves and dreamy hammocks tied between palms, and this is the south coast's best lunch spot.

Rex Cream ICE CREAM $
(24 Derkes; cones $1-3; ⊙9:30am-10:30pm) Exquisite ice cream made with seasonal fruit.

El Suarito CARIBBEAN $
(cnr Derkes & Hostos; mains $2-5; ⊙6am-7pm Mon-Sat) Popular with local wags, this cafeteria serves up eggs and toast, cheap pork chops and beer. The paintings on the walls are by regular Carlos Jun Vega and are based on El Suarito's clientele.

❶ Getting There & Away

If coming by car, you can't miss Guayama, which fans out from the junction of Hwy 3 and the Hwy 53 toll road. Guayama is 60km east of Ponce. To get to Pozuelo, where almost all of the charm of the Guayama region lies, drive 10km southwest of Guayama on Rte 7710.

Bahía de Jobos

The sprawling Reserva Nacional de Investigación Estuarina de Bahía de Jobos fans along the northern shores of the islet-spotted Bahía de Jobos, famous for its regular sightings of manatees. This area has a quiet, quaint and half-forgotten location south of the south coast's highways. Hiking trails cross creaking boardwalks among a labyrinth of mangrove canals. The marshy reserve borders a near-abandoned sugar town, Aguirre, another compelling detour from Hwy 3.

◉ Sights & Activities

Reserva Nacional de Investigación Estuarina de Bahía de Jobos NATURE RESERVE
(Km 2.3, Hwy 705) Bursting with wildlife, the National Estuarine Research Reserve at Bahía de Jobos is an enormous protected mangrove bay, one of Puerto Rico's largest and least visited patches of coastal wilderness. The Bahía de Jobos covers almost 3000 acres of brackish water, including associated coastal wetlands and 15 offshore mangrove cays known as Los Cayos Caribes. Though the low-lying mangrove marsh won't impress like the overwhelming natural beauty of El Yunque, it's an excellent place for birdwatching and those seeking wilderness isolation.

Start at the reserve's **Lab & Visitors Center** (☎787-853-4617; ⊙7:30am-noon & 1-4pm Mon-Fri, 9am-noon & 1-3pm Sat & Sun), a great educational nature center where you can learn about the star billing here: brown pelicans, great blue herons, snowy egrets, ospreys, peregrine falcons and American oyster catchers. Over 100 manatees feed here too, but far from shore so you'll rarely see them from land.

You can go on a superb short hike along the **Jagueyes Forest Interpretive Trail**, which twists around mangroves, wetlands and salt flats for about 30 minutes. The path, mostly on boardwalks, can be reached from the visitors center.

Another short hike heads through mangroves direct from the visitors center, skirting the ruins of old Aguirre.

Signage is scant after vandalism, but both paths are good. The mangroves also make an excellent kayaking route. The only problem currently? No kayak rental.

Aguirre HISTORIC SITE
(Hwy 705; ⊙24hr) Crumbling monuments to the sugar industry are evident everywhere in Puerto Rico's southeast, but there's no more heartbreaking reminder of departed 'King Sugar' than sleepy Aguirre, which abuts the Bahía de Jobos and is so far off the beaten path that it doesn't appear on many tourist maps. The moldering sugar town was booming in the early 20th century, complete with a mill, company stores, hospital, theater, hotel, bowling alley, social club, golf course, marina, executive homes and narrow-gauge railroad.

This was the planned private community of the Central Aguirre Sugar Company, and at its zenith around 1960, it processed 12,500 tons of sugarcane per day. Declining prices of sugar, foreign competition and escalating production costs drove the company under in 1990 and Aguirre became a virtual ghost town, which nevertheless makes for preposterously bizarre sightseeing. The community's rusting train tracks remain, as does a weedy **golf course** (☎787-853-4052; Km 1.6, Rte 705; fees weekdays $20-25, weekends $30-35; ⊙7am-6pm Tue-Sun).

PONCE & SOUTH COAST BAHÍA DE JOBOS

ℹ️ Getting There & Around

The only way to visit the Reserva Nacional de Investigación Estuarina de Bahía de Jobos and Aguirre is by car; Hwy 3 between Guayama and Salinas is the access road. Take Hwy 705 south from Hwy 3. Watch closely for the barely visible sign pointing to 'Historic Aguirre' opposite a closed fuel station: this brings you to the reserve entrance as well as to Aguirre.

Playa Salinas

Salinas proper, the town at the center of the south coast's agricultural economy, lies about 1.5km north of the coast and 1.5km south of the highway. Though it's the birthplace of baseball legends Roberto and Sandy Alomar as well as a pair of Miss Universe queens, the town itself isn't so easy on the eyes.

The coastal *barrio* of Playa Salinas fares far better. The name is a misnomer since there's no actual sand, but the geographical features of its harbor make it an important Caribbean port. The presence of a marina, attracting lots of retired American and European yachties, together with some offshore mangrove-fringed cays, means water-themed activities are readily available. Still more visitors are drawn by the seafood restaurants here beside an attractive waterside promenade.

◉ Sights & Activities

Malecón   VIEWPOINT
(Playa Salinas; ⊘24hr) This is the latest attraction for Salinas, a new seaside promenade running alongside the strip of seafood restaurants. Along its length, there are public gardens, restrooms and a stage for performances.

Marina de Salinas   WATER SPORTS
(☑787-824-3185; www.marinadesalinas.com; Rte 701, cnr Calles A & Chaplin; kayak rental per half day $20) Even if you're not staying at the marina's **Posada El Náutico** (☑787-824-3185; www.marinadesalinas.com/marinapr.html; r $95-175; P❋@⚲✹), most activities in the water are available through the front desk of the Marina de Salinas, where you can rent kayaks or organise day trips, deep-sea fishing expeditions and jaunts to the local cays.

The marina is right at the end of Rte 701 (known at various points as Calle A) at the intersection with Calle Chaplin.

🛏️ Sleeping & Eating

Manatee Eco Resort   HOTEL **$$**
(☑787-824-6688; Calle A Sector Playita No 286; r $80-110; P❋✹) It's not clear what efforts this self-defined 'eco' hotel makes for the environment, but it is Playa Salinas' best, most reasonable accommodation, so who's complaining? It's located across the harbor from the Marina de Salinas. The rooms are a bit dark and motel-like, but have tiled floors, mini-refrigerators and microwaves. The restaurant here, the Loco Pelicano, has a reputation for good seafood and dramatic sunset views.

You can rent kayaks ($40 per day) to navigate the bay where you might be lucky enough to see manatees.

★ Ladi's Place   SEAFOOD **$$**
(☑787-824-1900; www.ladisrestaurant.com; Calle A 86; mains $14-50; ⊘11am-9pm Sun-Thu, to 11pm Fri & Sat) From the road, this looks like the Playa Salinas restaurant strip's least appealing option, but from inside, you'll be surprised. Ladi's strives to offer the ideal eating and drinking environment: there's succulently cooked seafood here (fresh crab, mmmm) and it's also an atmospheric bar.

Additionally – thank goodness – the owners have realized that an open-sided bar-restaurant on the coast is a better idea than sequestering their clients away at the mercy of Arctic air-con.

It's the oldest eating joint in Playa Salinas, and claims to have invented Salinas' famous *mojo isleño* (a thin tomato-based sauce). The song list seems calibrated to please gringo sailors and things get lively come nightfall.

El Balcón de Capitan   SEAFOOD **$$**
(☑727-824-6210; Calle A 54, Hwy 701; mains $10-30; ⊘10:30am-10:30pm Mon-Sat, to 9:30pm Sun) Although the slow economy has shuttered many Playa Salinas restaurants, the Capitan soldiers on, earning its Mesón Gastronómico status through fresh plates of red snapper, a good seafood-stuffed *mofongo* and tangy *mojo isleño*. Eat in a dining room often frigid with air-conditioning or on the open-air patio.

ℹ️ Information

Tourist Office (☑787-824-4077; cnr Hwy 701 & Calle B; ⊘8am-6:30pm) Playa Salinas' tourist office can be found alongside a statue of toiling fishermen, known as Monumento al Pescador.

SOUTH COAST ROAD TRIP

Since the south coast offers visitors a chance to soak up the charms of Puerto Rico's Caribbean coast at a leisurely pace, it's crucial to get off the highways and travel on the older system of back roads, Hwy 1 and Hwy 3. Weaving your way through scrappy coastal towns, you can break at the roadside kiosks for a smoky plate of pork and join the weathered codgers for a few cold Medallas and a few bets on the mechanical horse races, known as *picas*. Don't expect much by way of beaches – the only place for any kind of quality hidden swim in the area is off Hwy 333, near Guánica – but for a deep dive into the essence of the region, you have to get off the highway.

You'll see plenty of the crumbling-brick smokestacks of former sugar refineries east of Ponce. Tiny dots on the map such as Arroyo and Aguirre (an actual ghost town) are largely abandoned, standing in picturesque disrepair. It may not match the postcard vision of the Caribbean, but there's no chance of suffering the tourist mobs of the north.

ⓘ Getting There & Away

Arriving from the east, Hwy 3 becomes Hwy 1 as it passes through Salinas. From Ponce, drivers should take Hwy 1 east or the Hwy 52 toll road to Hwy 1 south.

The mess of streets leading from Salinas to Playa Salinas is confusing to navigate, but Rte 701 leads to the small district of Playa Ward. From here, you are essentially in Playa Salinas and can continue around the bay via largely unmarked roads. As Rte 701 continues towards its end at the Marina de Salinas, it is also known as Calle A.

Coamo

POP 10,500

Ponce de León's obsessive search for the fountain of youth – which, according to some historians, was sought in hopes of curing sexual impotence – led not only to the discovery of North America, but perhaps also to the founding of this city, still famous for its thermal springs. León's lagging libido might be responsible for making Coamo one of the oldest colonial settlements on the island, a place that also staged a decisive battle of the Spanish-American War.

The main draw for travelers are the *baños* (baths) south of town, but Coamo's plaza also sports one of the island's more interesting churches, the Iglesia San Blas.

◉ Sights & Activities

Iglesia San Blas   CHURCH
(Plaza de Recreo) On the plaza in central Coamo is one of Puerto Rico's more interesting provincial churches. This Catholic church contains paintings by island masters Campeche and Oller, including a painting of one of Oller's girlfriends being tortured in purgatory.

Baños de Coamo   THERMAL BATHS
(Coamo's Baths; Rte 546; adult/child $3/1.50; ⊘6am-10pm Mon-Fri, 7am-10pm Sat & Sun) Following an extensive refurbishment, the centuries-old Baños de Coamo have the air of a modern spa, with handsome changing rooms, piped-in jazz and a small cafe. It's doubtful you'll have a tranquil soak due to the close quarters, but for thermal waters aficionados it is certainly worth a detour. Swimsuits are required – bathing au naturel isn't tolerated.

The upper pool has thermal water at about 110°F; the lower one is cooler. It's a very agreeable spot to soak away the stress of driving Puerto Rico's roads. Custodians will stress that you shouldn't spend above 15 minutes at any one time in the hot pools – after this period, you should take a break to cool off.

The thermal baths are found by following Rte 546 down from Hwy 153 to its end by a small river.

🛏 Sleeping & Eating

You'll pass loads of kiosks on the roads around Coamo, many of them roasting pork and seafood, and dishing out lunches for about $5.

Parador Baños de Coamo   HOTEL $
(☏787-825-2186; Hwy 546; r $80-90; [P][❄][≋]) The most recent incarnation of the hotels that have stood on this site for 150 years, Parador Baños de Coamo has been here since the 1970s. Lizards scurry around the grounds and guests enjoy an open-air bar and a series of thermal pools. Rooms are

DENNIS VAN DE WATER/500PX ©

1. El Yunque (p98)
The only rainforest in the US National Forest System, El Yunque National Forest boasts nearly 29,000 acres of lush mountainous terrain.

2. Culebra (p118)
Culebra is home to one of the greatest varieties of truly superb beaches in the Caribbean.

3. Playa Crash Boat (p211)
One of the best surfing spots on Aguadilla's coast, Playa Crash Boat got its name because the air force used to keep rescue boats here to pick up crews from bombers that didn't make the runway.

OLEG MOISEYENKO/GETTY IMAGES ©

modern, if a little worn. Things are quiet in low season.

Nonguests can use the hotel's swimming and thermal pools (adult/child $7/5) between 10am and 5:30pm.

La Ceiba
MEXICAN, PUERTO RICAN $

(www.restaurantelaceiba.com; Km 13, Rte 153; mains $5-20; ⊙10:30am-10:30pm Mon-Thu, to 11pm Fri & Sat, 11am-10pm Sun; 🤚) After a morning at the Baños de Coamo, this breezy, brightly painted, open-air Mexican spot is a great roadside stop. It has daily specials of Puerto Rican pork, rice and beans, and passable Mexican standards, such as grilled chicken or steak burritos. This is the exception to the rule that you should never trust a restaurant with pictures of the food on the menu.

🛈 Getting There & Away

Coamo itself sits inland, 38km northeast of Ponce and 17km north of the nearest coast at Playa Salinas.

To get to the baños from Ponce, take the Coamo turnoff on Hwy 53 and head north for about 4km along Hwy 153 and then look for the sign that points off to the left (west) to the Parador Baños Coamo, which is Rte 546. Go straight on from this point to get to Coamo town or down Rte 546 to get to the baños. You'll pass a number of condo developments and a golf course, before coming to Parador Baños Coamo and then the baños lower down the hill.

Yauco & Around

POP 16,000

Yauco is Puerto Rico's coffee capital, where well-scrubbed public squares and a hillside of brightly painted houses stand in contrast to the ragged little burgs that dot the southwest highway. Hidden up in the hills, the city was founded in 1758 by merchants tired of pillaging pirates. Now, the so-called 'Ciudad del Café' ('City of Coffee'), gleaming with a trove of colonial-era and Creole architecture, is a perfect supply stop before heading into one of the lonely, lovely forest reserves that characterize the hilly terrain hereabouts – Bosque Estatal de Susúa to the north or Bosque Estatal de Guánica to the southwest. The region can be explored in a day trip from Ponce.

◉ Sights

Plaza de Recreo
SQUARE

On the laid-back Plaza de Recreo, the massive Iglesia Católica Nuestra Señora del Rosario casts a long shadow over domino players and strolling lovers. The plaza sits just east of a bustling stretch of shops on Calle Comercio, where a number of jewelers will make gold pendants with your name on them – a good take-home souvenir.

Centro de Arte Alejandro Franceschi
MUSEUM

(cnr 25 de Julio & Betances; ⊙8am-3pm Mon-Fri, 9am-2pm Sat & Sun) FREE Yauco's immaculate little art museum is housed in a 1907 building chock-full of Victorian oil paintings and gilded frescoes. It's on the eastern side of Parque Arturo Lluberas.

Casa Museo de la Música
HISTORIC BUILDING

(15 Calle Santiago Vivaldi; ⊙8am-4pm Mon-Fri) FREE Musicians might find a bit of diversion in this former home of local composer Amaury Veray Torregrosa, though the wilting creole house has little inside except some faded sheets of music and old photos.

Volkylandia
MUSEUM

(📞787-267-7774; www.thevolkyland.com; Km 13.2, Hwy 121; admission $10; ⊙9am-3pm Sun) This museum has the largest private collection of VWs in the world. The staff are very passionate about their subject, and it is the classic VW Beetle, last produced in Mexico in 2003, that forms the bulk of the exhibition.

Bosque Estatal de Susúa
FOREST

(Calle el Tamarindo, Km 2.1, off Rte 368) This mysterious, mist-shrouded forest strewn across hills north of Yauco is just 3300 acres and practically deserted year-round. Ambitious hikers and mountain bikers will love its challenging, out-of-the-way trail network. The DRNA booth, picnic tables, toilet, campsites ($6 per tent) and few cabins ($40) are the sole facilities at Km 2.1 on Rte 368.

The campsites and cabins are maintained by the DRNA (Department of Natural Resources; 📞787-999-2200; www.drna.gobierno.pr; Km 6.3, Rte 8838, Río Piedras; ⊙8am-noon & 1-4pm Mon-Fri; Ⓜ Cupey) in San Juan and you should contact them at least 15 days in advance if you want to stay over here. It's advisable to call ahead anyway to find out what trails are open.

As even the main facilities in the forest have no staff, opening hours are for practical purposes from dawn until dusk.

Lago Luchetti
LAKE

(Rte 128; ⊙6:30am-6:30pm Tue-Sun) This man-made lake stretches its tentacled inlets deep into the surrounding hills just 9km north of

Yauco at the end of Rte 128. The lake is actually a reservoir, constructed in 1952, and is a popular fishing destination.

🛏 Sleeping & Eating

Hotel El Cafetal   MOTEL $
(📞 787-856-0946; Km 10, Rte 368; r $65-105; 🅿 ❄) This bizarre-looking and frankly sombre accommodation option is unfortunately your sole option. The approach is a steep, twisting drive on a hill outside town overlooking the mountains. It's no longer one of Puerto Rico's 'hourly rate' motels, but rooms are still the boggiest of bog standard. Try the half-decent restaurant here, if you can navigate the labyrinthine stairs and corridors to discover it.

Pay $5 more to get a room with a window and, if you're lucky, a view. There's a nice pool and – incredibly – room service.

⭐ Restaurante
La Guardarraya   PUERTO RICAN $
(📞 787-856-4222; www.laguardarraya.com; Km 6, Rte 127; mains $7-16) You'll see the signs announcing *chuletas can can* island-wide, but this 1957 institution, on stilts in a tropical forest clearing outside Yauco, is the place that invented the dish. What is it? A slab of pork, with the ribs and fat left on, prepared with delicate cuts so the fat blossoms when deep-fried to resemble the underskirt of a cancan dancer.

Sided with rice, beans and plantains, *chuletas can can* makes for an amazing (if decadent) meal, and the historical ambience of the restaurant with its well-groomed waiters ensures this is among Puerto Rico's best dining experiences. It roasts its own coffee on-site too.

El Café de Marta   CAFE $
(Fernando Pacheco, cnr Av Antonio Vivaldi; breakfast $5; ⏰ 6am-2:30pm Mon-Fri) Where is all that coffee in the 'city of coffee'? At this little place, apparently. It's in the unlikely environs of the *público* terminal, and has retained enough of Yauco's celebrated export to act as local ambassador of feisty caffeinated brews. Delicious, but the place still can't shake the island's Styrofoam cup syndrome.

ℹ Information

Tourist Office (📞 787-267-0350; cnr 25 de Julio & Betences; ⏰ 7:30am-3pm Tue-Sun) Yauco's tourist office is a friendly place with information about local indigenous and precolonial ruins, as well as things to do in the

'Ciudad del Café' (City of Coffee). It's in the basement of the brightly painted **Centro de Arte Alejandro Franceschi**, an art museum.

ℹ Getting There & Away

To get here from Ponce or from locales to the west, exit Hwy 2 on Hwy 359, which feeds north into Rte 127. Turn west (left) on Rte 127 and this road becomes Yauco's main drag, Calle 25 de Julio, which runs alongside Parque Arturo Lluberas.

The Bosque Estatal de Susúa is best accessed from Yauco by driving west on Rte 368 about 8km beyond Hotel El Cafetal.

Guánica & Around

POP 18,750

Not much happens in underwhelming Guánica itself, but international travelers are enticed by some of the south coast's most idyllic accommodation options southeast of town, an astounding swathe of bays and beaches, and the wilderness that links the whole region together, the stunning Bosque Estatal de Guánica, perched in hills above the sea. Guánica is 6km south of Hwy 2 on Rte 116.

◉ Sights & Activities

Bosque Estatal de Guánica   NATURE RESERVE
(📞 787-821-5706; Hwy 334 & Hwy 333; ⏰ 7am-4pm) The immense 10,000-acre expanse of the Guánica Biosphere Reserve is one of the island's great natural treasures. Located in two wonderfully untrammeled sections just east and west of Guánica, this remote desert forest is among the world's best examples of subtropical dry forest vegetation, containing extraordinary flora and fauna as a result. In the larger, more tourist-friendly eastern portion, numerous trails intersect this astonishing ecosystem, lending themselves well to mountain biking, birdwatching and hiking.

Scientists estimate that only 1% of the earth's original spread of dry forests of this kind remain, and the fact that there is such a vast acreage here renders this a rare sanctuary.

Over 700 varieties of plants, many near extinction, thrive in the reserve. Some of the unusual species here include the squat melon cactus with its brilliant pink flowers that attract hummingbirds. Another plant, with the unseemly name of the Spanish dildo cactus, grows into huge treelike shapes near the coast and attracts bullfinches and bats. Of

Guánica & Around

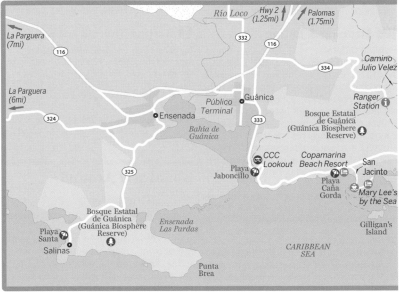

the fauna, nine of Puerto Rico's 14 endemic bird species can be found here, including the Puerto Rican woodpecker, the Puerto Rican emerald hummingbird and – the ultimate prize for birdwatchers – the exceedingly rare 'prehistoric' Puerto Rican nightjar, of which there are estimated to be as few as 1500.

When out hiking or biking, the 50-odd kilometers of trails hammer you with contrasts at every turn, alternating between arid, rocky, scrub-covered highlands and almost 20km of remote, wholly untouched coast.

Several trails sally forth from the Bosque Estatal de Guánica's Ranger Station (p166) and are of varying lengths and difficulty. **Camino Ballena** perhaps best demonstrates the contrasting topography of the reserve, while the most exhilarating route of all is the reserve's coastal hike, the **Vereda Meseta**. Most of the trails here are wide and at least a little metaled, making for great mountain biking as well. Nothing technical, but superb scenery and deserted routes.

There are two main routes into the eastern section of the reserve: Hwy 334 climbs from Guánica to the reserve's Ranger Station and the nexus of the majority of the trails, while Hwy 333 traverses the eastern reserve's coast to Bahía de la Ballena and further hikes.

Playa Ballena   BEACH

(Hwy 333) The lovely Bahía de la Ballena represents the end of the road and a rare opportunity to park your car and rely on two legs rather than four wheels. This is the first beach you come to on the bay, with parking places and a mix of rock and tawny sand from which you can swim.

Playa Tamarindo   BEACH

(Hwy 333) Follow Hwy 333 around to its conclusion at the Bahía de la Ballena and you'll find that the charming little access route to Playa Tamarindo is blocked off from vehicle access because it's a spawning ground for a rare type of Puerto Rican toad, the *sapo concho*. The victory of nature over mankind sets the tone nicely for the arc of sand beyond, one of the south coast's most splendidly remote beaches. It's perfect for swimming or hiking on the Vereda Meseta trail.

Behind the beach rears the wild Bosque Estatal de Guánica (p163).

Playa Caña Gorda   BEACH

(Stout Cane Beach; Hwy 333, Km 6.2; parking $4; ☉9am-5pm Tue-Sun) Playa Caña Gorda is the *balneario* on the southern edge of the dry forest on Rte 333. Locals come here to grill fresh fish, play volleyball and lie around in the shade. The modern facilities are

the most developed in the area, including a small shop with cold soda and sunblock. It's also right next to Copamarina Beach Resort.

Gilligan's Island BOATING

(return ferry $8.50; ⊙ferry 9am-5pm Tue-Sun) Gilligan's Island and nearby Isla Ballena (Whale Island) are all part of the same set of small mangrove islands off the tip of the Caña Gorda peninsula and are technically part of the dry-forest reserve of Bosque Estatal de Guánica (p163). Neither is too sandy, but both offer good sunbathing and passable snorkeling, and both get quite popular with day-trippers.

The ambitious can reach both islands via kayak; rentals are available at the Copamarina Beach Resort and Mary Lee's by the Sea for $15 per hour or about $35 per day, or you can catch the ferry in front of Restaurante San Jacinto every hour, barring bad weather.

If Gilligan's is packed, pony up a couple more dollars to the captain and try the less-visited isles of Ballena. The isles are closed to the public on Monday – apparently to give them a chance to recover from the influx of tourists over the previous week.

🛏 Sleeping & Eating

A community of vacation houses and guesthouses called San Jacinto dominates the highlands of the small Caña Gorda peninsula on the southern shore of Bosque Estatal de Guánica and southeast of Guánica. If you're looking for a cheap stay, drive up there and poke around, as some houses rent rooms.

★ Mary Lee's by the Sea APARTMENT $$

(☑787-821-3600; www.maryleesbythesea.com; 25 San Jacinto; studios $130-300; P❋) This charismatic guesthouse run by Mary Lee Alverez is one of the island's most isolated, idiosyncratic stays. Set on a steep hillside overlooking the mangrove cays and the Caribbean, guests have little choice but to unplug (limited wi-fi, no TVs) and relax. Each apartment is appointed with bright marine-themed furnishing and many have private decks, hammocks and barbecue facilities. One room even has a bathroom that opens out to a private garden shower.

Mary Lee herself is a character, an attentive host who came here to dive 50 years ago and never left. There are stairs that descend to a dock where you can relax by the water, or rent kayaks (per hour/day $15/35) to paddle out to nearby cays such as Gilligan's Island.

Copamarina Beach Resort RESORT $$$

(☑787-821-0505; www.copamarina.com; Hwy 333, Km 6.5; r $165-205, ste from $450, villas from $1100; P❋@❋❋) This full-service resort is the most upscale vacation retreat on the southwest coast of Puerto Rico, just east of the Playa Caña Gorda *balneario* on a shallow bay. It's relatively pricey but worth it: the immaculate grounds include a pair of beautiful pools, tennis courts and two upscale restaurants, one of which is Alexandra. There's also an on-site dive shop and a 24-hour service desk.

Most of the plush, elegantly outfitted rooms open to ocean breezes and swaying palms, making it idyllic for honeymooners, who drag beach chairs into the shallow waters under the shade of the palm trees. The only drawback is the resort's isolation but, for those who enjoy peace and quiet, this can also be its greatest asset.

Alexandra FUSION $$$

(☑787-821-0505; www.copamarina.com; Hwy 333, Km 6.5; dishes $24-39; ⊙6-10pm Sat & Sun) If one dish could represent the menu at this restaurant at Copamarina Beach Resort, it'd be lobster tail in mango and mustard sauce. Savory, inventive and decidedly upscale, the fusion Caribbean and New American dishes here are as elegant as the linen-draped dining room. Couples toast special occasions, and the waiters dote. Reservations recommended.

ℹ Information

Ranger Station (☑787-821-5706; ⊙7am-4pm) A solitary ranger is usually in evidence at this small center next to the main parking area at the end of Hwy 334 in the eastern portion of the Bosque Estatal de Guánica.

ℹ Getting There & Away

If you're driving to Guánica from either direction along the expressway, Hwy 2, turn off on Hwy 116 from where it's 6km south. You can get between Guánica and La Parguera via a 20km drive on the coast road, Hwy 324, or the slightly more circuitous but swifter Hwy 116.

The Bosque Estatal de Guánica can be reached from Guánica via two main routes. To get to the eastern section of the reserve and the **Ranger Station** (p166), follow Hwy 116 northeast from Guánica towards Hwy 2 and then turn right onto the narrow Hwy 334 to wind up to the reserve entrance. The southern extent of the eastern section of the forest – including the ferry to Gilligan's Island and Guánica's plushest accommodation possibilities – is also accessible by Hwy 333, to the southeast of Guánica.

La Parguera

POP 1000

La Parguera is a strange place. Here is a seaside tourist town with no appealing coastline, a town that invested millions on a smart new seaside *malecón* but still appears deserted, a town that hauls in visitors to witness its bioluminescent bay, and in ferrying them to see it, is slowly degrading its main attraction through motorboat-oil pollution.

This lazy locale is so laid back it's practically asleep. Its chief aficionados are vacationing Puerto Ricans and US expats who spend most of the morning in bed and most of the day sampling the world-class fishing and diving. But at night the same folks will be popping open cans of Medalla at a string of bars which erupt out of the daytime languor.

The ramshackle mix of old and new buildings has a chaotic charm, from the houses on stilts over the water to condo developments on the upland fields.

◉ Sights

Malecón SQUARE
La Parguera is one of the lucky towns in Puerto Rico to have benefited from a rejuvenation themed around making its center more conducive to walking around. The *malecón* in La Parguera is an ambitious development incorporating a waterfront walkway, plaza and a pedestrian-only street.

Having been accustomed to a grotty high street before that, residents are still getting used to the *malecón*, which has utterly changed the face of central La Parguera and left it looking, well, quite pleasant. There is a little coffee shop, an ice-cream stand and plenty more bars and restaurants thronging along the northern side.

Bahía de Fosforescente NATURE RESERVE
The once-glittering waters of Bahía de Fosforescente remain La Parguera's biggest draw, but the environmental impact of boat tours and developments has dimmed the spectacular show. Still, it can be interesting for those who have never seen the phenomenon. Boats visit the Bahía Monsio José and Bahía La Parguera, east of town, both of which are reached via narrow canals through the mangrove forest. If you visit at night bioluminescent microorganisms in the water put on a surreal light show.

The ride on the Fondo de Cristal (p168) is the least expensive way to witness this glowing water in Puerto Rico. But if you're ecologically minded, skip this bay for a place where nonpolluting kayaks or electric boats are used exclusively (and tell motorized-boat operators why you're saying no) or only come out here with an operator that uses kayaks.

Isla Mata la Gata & Isla Caracoles ISLAND
These two mangrove cays lie less than half a mile offshore from La Parguera and are worth a visit after the other dusty sights nearby. The sandy strands on the seaside are really the only places in La Parguera to spend a traditional day at the beach, but both are overused and the sand is not spectacular. You can come here with a rental boat or kayak, or with the boat operators ($10 per person for a round-trip) at the **Town Dock** (La Parguera Malecón).

Isla de Magueyes & Isla de Monos ISLAND
About 20yd south of La Parguera's Town Dock is Magueyes Island, which is used as a marine science station. The island

La Parguera

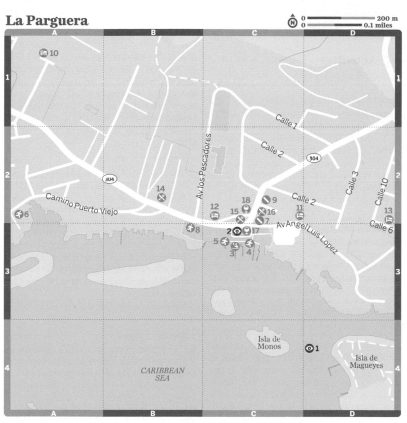

La Parguera

◉ Sights
1 Isla de Magueyes & Isla de
   Monos..D4
2 Malecón...C3

✪ Activities, Courses & Tours
3 Aleli Tours.......................................C3
4 Fondo de Cristal.............................C3
5 Gina's @ Johnny's Boats................C3
6 Parguera Fishing Charters A2
7 Paradise Scuba & Snorkeling
   Center..C2
8 PRKBC..B3
9 West Divers.....................................C2

🛏 Sleeping
10 La Jamaca......................................A1
11 Nautilus Hotel C2
12 Parguera Plaza Hotel.....................C2
13 Turtle Bay Inn.................................D2

✗ Eating
14 La Empanadilla...............................B2
15 Isla Cueva Beer & Burger Bar.........C2
   La Jamaca Restaurant.............. (see 10)
16 Moon's Bar & Tapas........................C2

◉ Drinking & Nightlife
17 Mar y Tierra....................................C3
18 Yolanda's..C2

was formerly a zoo and is now overrun by frighteningly large iguanas, many of which originally arrived from Cuba. Monkeys held for research on Isla de Monos (Monkey Island), around a mile to the west, have also escaped and are breeding ashore – pests to local farmers, but amusement for children and tourists.

PONCE & SOUTH COAST LA PARGUERA

Boat trips ($10 or less per person) head to these two neighbouring islands from the Town Dock.

🏃 Activities

⭐ Paradise Scuba & Snorkeling Center
DIVING

(☑787-899-7611; www.paradisescubasnorkeling pr.com; cnr Hwy 304 & Malecón; 2-tank dive $95) This slickly professional operator is a breath of fresh air in La Parguera water-sports scene, and are our top choice for diving or snorkeling in the vicinity. Their gear selection is extensive and their knowledge of the dive sites more so. The top dive destination is to The Wall, a few kilometers offshore.

West Divers
DIVING, SNORKELING

(☑787-899-3223; Km 3.1, Rte 304; kayak rental per person per day $40, snorkeling trip from $65, 2-tank dive trip $130; ⊗9am-7pm) West Divers has been around for years, but its prices are high and its customer service could be better. They offer three-hour snorkeling trips and half-day two-tank trips to the Wall. If you're in a party smaller than three, call ahead to inquire about joining another group.

Aleli Tours
KAYAKING

(☑787-300-6086; www.alelitours.com; Bahía de Fosforescente kayak tour per person $50) Down at La Parguera's Town Dock, Aleli Kayak Rental is the most ecologically responsible way to see the magical waters of the Bahía de Fosforescente. It is also the go-to place for paddleboard and snorkeling excursions. For any tours or rentals, call ahead, as opening hours vary.

PRKBC
WATER SPORTS

(Puerto Rico Kiteboarding Club; ☑747-646-6777; cnr Hwy 304 & Av Los Pescadores; kiteboarding per 2hr from $100) Not only kiteboarding, but also wakeboarding and night kayaking (the latter to see the famous Bahía de Fosforescente) are available at this popular operator. Prices vary depending on group size.

Gina's @ Johnny's Boats
BOATING

(☑787-460-8922; Town Dock; boat trips per person from $10, kayak/boat rental per hour from $15/35; ⊗8am-10pm) This obliging company offers the usual range of local tours, including to nearby Isla Mata la Gata, plus independent kayak and boat rental. Boat trips are cheapest if you go in a group at the scheduled departure times. Perhaps what makes this outfit stand out from its competitors is that they are almost always open, even outside of their official hours.

Based in a little shack at the other end of the malecón from the Town Dock.

Fondo de Cristal
BOATING

(☑787-899-5891; per person $10; ⊗8am-5pm) Fondo de Cristal offers glass-bottom boat tours to the Bahía de Fosforescente.

Parguera Fishing Charters
FISHING

(☑787-382-4698; www.puertoricofishingcharters. com; Camino Puerto Viejo; half/full-day charter from $550/950, up to 6 pax) Parguera Fishing Charters runs trips on its 31ft Bertram from

---

DIVING THE WALL

Although landlubbers can have plenty of fun in Parguera, divers know the real draw – the underwater treasure hidden 6 miles offshore.

The Wall (advanced dive, 50ft to 125ft) features a 'swim-through' at the base of an immense reef that has a sheer 60ft drop. Plenty of good diving takes place above that mark, but the real treat is wiggling in and out of the 'swim-through' hole and checking out the impressive reef structure at 80ft and below. Divers have reported seeing manatees, dolphins, manta rays and much, much more.

Other diving highlights near La Parguera:

Motor (novice, 55ft to 75ft) An unclaimed airplane motor adds mystery to a reef.

Barracuda City (novice, 60ft to 70ft) You'll get the hairy eyeball from big silver predators.

Super Bowl (intermediate, 55ft to 75ft) Swim-throughs and overhangs.

Chimney (intermediate, 55ft to 75ft) A north-facing ledge honeycombed with holes.

Black Wall (intermediate, 60ft to 130ft) A smaller version of the big coral wall.

Two for You (advanced, 55ft to 120ft) This reef looks like an underwater flower shop.

Fallen Rock (advanced, 65ft to 120ft) A magnet for abundant coral and bright-blue fish.

TOP CARIBBEAN VIEWS

Fuerte Caprón (Hwy 334, Bosque Estatal de Guánica) A hike through the brushy hills of Puerto Rico's bizarre dry forest brings you to a fort overlooking the turquoise horizon.

El Vigía (p150) This huge concrete cross on a Ponce hilltop takes in the Pearl of the South and the sea.

Rte 333 After a white-knuckled drive around Guánica, pull over to chill out on tiny beaches hidden by mangroves.

La Guancha Paseo Tablado (p150) Watch the ships roll in and out of the port at this boardwalk observation deck in Ponce.

La Casa de Los Pastelillos (p156) Swing on a hammock between palm trees and enjoy endless views at this hidden-away lunch favorite in Guayama.

a well-marked dock at the western end of town. Fishing in these waters is extremely good and the chances of a good day's catch are high.

★✦ Festivals & Events

Fiesta de San Pedro PARTY
(⊙ Jun) Named after the abundant pargo fish, La Parguera hosts the Fiesta de San Pedro to honor the patron saint of fishermen in June. The party takes over the main street, with live music, food kiosks, children's activities and vendors who pour untold gallons of Medalla.

🛏 Sleeping

Nautilus Hotel HOTEL $
(☎ 787-899-4565; www.nautiluspr.com; 238 Av Angel Luis Lopez; d $85-115; [P][❄][🛜][≋]) Just east of the town center, the Nautilus is a well-appointed modern place with 18 rooms. It's about the best deal in town and surprisingly, given the rock-bottom rates, not at all dreary.

★La Jamaca INN $$
(☎ 787-899-6162; www.lajamacapr.com; Reparto Lo Borde, off Hwy 304; r from $100; [P][🛜][≋]) Ah, imagine. *Jamacas* (hammocks) swinging in a breezy location on a verdant hill above town, amid a courtyard replete with plenty of plants and a pool. La Jamaca has been dishing out little pieces of paradise to its guests for a quarter of a century. It's nothing fancy, but it is blissful.

The nautically painted blue wooden exterior and the clean, chirpy rooms are a pleasure to guests. There's also a decent on-site restaurant (p170), as well as a small gift shop.

Parguera Plaza Hotel HOTEL $$
(☎ 787-920-4275; www.pargueraplaza.com; Hwy 304, Km 3.2; r $135-150; [P][≋]) La Parguera's newest hotel is its best. It has 25 comfortable

rooms, set back along wide, quiet corridors and decked out in blue and white maritime hues. Its other assets include a long, shadeless pool, a cute coffee and wine bar, the Brújula restaurant and a surf shop.

Turtle Bay Inn INN $$
(☎ 787-899-6633; www.turtlebayinn.com; 153 Calle 6; r/ste incl breakfast from $115/130; [P][❄][🛜][≋]) 🍃 This obtrusively yellow building has an inconvenient location a few blocks away from the waterside action, but the 12 rooms here are very comfortable and rates include a continental breakfast. The whole place is powered solely by solar panelling.

🍴 Eating

In this tourist-dependent town, many places close in October and November, the low season.

Moon's Bar & Tapas TAPAS $
(Hwy 304, Km 3.2; tapas $3-10; ⊙ 3pm-midnight Thu-Sun, to 2am Fri & Sat) This intimate, open-air spot serves decent tapas, bruschetta, scrumptious thick soups and homemade hamburgers. Or you can perch at the bar and enjoy a cocktail or maybe (not so common hereabouts) a glass of good wine.

La Empanadilla CAFETERIA $
(cnr Hwy 304 & Camino Puerto Viejo; empanadas $2; ⊙ 7am-3pm Mon-Fri) The best place for cheap empanadas in town – take away, or sit in a simple but agreeable interior that has a good buzz thanks to the animated locals conversing over their greasy purchases. The empanadas with *pulpo* (octopus) are the best.

Isla Cueva Beer & Burger Bar BURGERS $
(www.facebook.com/islacueva; Hwy 304; salads & burgers $6-14; ⊙ noon-midnight) As Hwy 304 bends around onto La Parguera's new

malecón, this is the first bar you'll come across and it's also the liveliest. Its range of beers is fantastic (the most local are the Boquerón Brewing Company range) but most customers seem to come for the varied range of burgers. The chorizo and sweet plantain burger is divine.

La Jamaca Restaurant   PUERTO RICAN **$**
(☑787-899-6162; www.lajamacapr.com; Reparto Lo Borde, off Hwy 304; mains $10-20; ⊘8am-8pm) The restaurant in La Jamaca is worth the short additional jaunt outside the center of La Parguera to eat at tables prettily positioned around a pool where you can cool off afterwards. The *mofongo* is delicious and the cocktails superb. Specials are chalked up daily on a blackboard. The food is good, but the location special.

🍷 Drinking & Nightlife

The streets might be empty during the day but at night the place parties hard despite its diminutive population. The action is concentrated around a raucous network of bars around the town's new *malecón* (p166) and is mostly a 50-50 mix of locals and vacationing Americans. People drink, eat and stroll from one end of the waterfront to the other.

Yolanda's   BAR
(Carretera 304, Km 3.2; ⊘noon-midnight) The high-pitched roof and wood trim give raucous Yolanda's a South Seas atmosphere. In the evening the patio makes a great place to party. It serves food to soak up the stiff drinks.

Mar y Tierra   BAR, POOL HALL
(Carretera 304; ⊘4pm-midnight, later on weekends) Mar y Tierra stands out among the cluster of bars packed along the main street and the docks – primarily because of the eardrum-busting Latin rock and salsa it pumps out. Go shoot some pool while you're at it.

❶ Getting There & Away

The fastest way here is off Hwy 2, on Hwy 116 from Guánica (20km) or on Hwys 101 and 116 from San Germán (15km). On either approach, follow the signs for the last few kilometers on Hwy 304.

Rincón & West Coast

POP 260,000

Includes ➡

Rincón........................173
Mayagüez....................182
Cabo Rojo Area..........186
Playa de Joyuda.........186
Boquerón...................188
El Combate...............190
Refugio Nacional
Cabo Rojo...................191
San Germán................192
Isla Mona...................195

Best Places to Eat

➡ Chateau Rose at the Horned Dorset Primavera (p180)

➡ La Copa Llena (p180)

➡ La Rosa Inglesa/English Rose Inn Restaurant (p180)

➡ Mangia Mi (p180)

➡ Annie's Place (p190)

Best Places to Sleep

➡ Tres Sirenas (p178)

➡ Blue Boy Inn (p179)

➡ Dos Angeles del Mar Guesthouse (p179)

➡ Surf 787 Guest Villa/B&B (p178)

➡ Horned Dorset Primavera (p178)

Why Go?

West is best – at least as far as those quintessential snapshots of Puerto Rico go. Here the azure ocean assumes a visceral palpability because this is the place to get in it: paddling to catch a ride on one perfect wave after another, or swimming off sandy strands that regularly grace 'world's best beach' lists.

The region's pièce de résistance is Rincón, a surfin' safari outpost (named in a Beach Boys song, for goodness' sake!) where beach bums catch waves in the salty dawn, then fuel up in the area's eclectic eateries or mingle around beach bonfires. Meanwhile in its set-piece wilderness, Refugio Nacional Cabo Rojo, every ounce of this land's seaside seductiveness – its stormy shorelines, beguiling beaches and down-to-earth coastal villages – gets showcased.

Bite down on a conch fritter and prepare to brave the waves, bask in the sunsets and absorb the mellow spirit of slacker independence.

When to Go

Welcome to the endless summer: the west coast is pleasantly hot all year round. It gets heavy rain in late summer and early fall, but otherwise, expect it to be sunny, breezy and around 80°F nearly every day.

If you're here to surf, winter is an ideal time to visit, although surfing competitions kick off from mid-October. Around this time cold fronts bring big waves to the western beaches, when average crests of 5ft or 6ft can grow as large as 25ft. In December and February, you may also spot migrating whales offshore.

Those who aren't here to ride the waves will find the calmer waters more inviting for swimming and deep-sea fishing in summer.

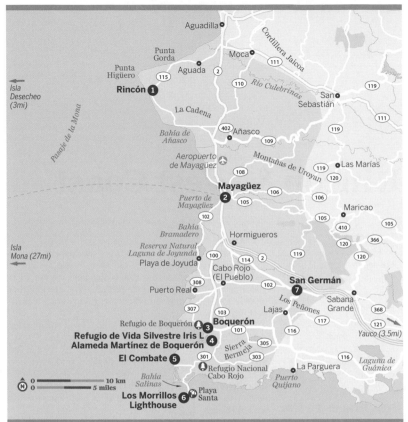

Rincón & West Coast Highlights

1 Rincón (p173) Surf beside beach bums and vacationing businessmen on the legendary breaks here.

2 Fido's Sangria Garden (p185) Get giddy on Sangria de Fido, the local punch of Mayagüez.

3 Cycling Cabo Rojo (p189) Hire a bike at the west's best bike shop in Boquerón, then pedal the beach-hugging byways of the Cabo Rojo area.

4 Refugio de Vida Silvestre Iris L. Alameda Martínez de Boquerón (p188) Meander mazes of mangroves in this mysterious forest.

5 Annie's Place (p190) Chow down on conch fritters at one of Puerto Rico's most idyllic beach bars in hidden-away El Combate.

6 Los Morrillos Lighthouse (p192) Peer at the endless sea from the top of the lighthouse overlooking idyllic Playa Santa, then cool off with a swim.

7 San Germán (p192) Play colonial adventurer on the labyrinthine historic streets and enjoy some of the west's best food.

History

The consensus is that Columbus first arrived in Puerto Rico in November 1493 and docked somewhere off the west coast (though there is some dispute as to actually *where*). Fifteen years later he was followed by Juan Ponce de León, who landed near Cabo Rojo before heading off east to found the settlement of Caparra close to San Juan. San Germán, the island's second-oldest city, was founded near Mayagüez in 1511, and moved to its present site in 1573.

More recently, the west has reared many great liberal thinkers including Dr Ramón Emeterio Betances, the inspiration behind the revolutionary Grito de Lares in 1868. The details of this abortive rebellion were fine-tuned in a series of safe houses near Mayagüez.

Mayagüez enjoyed an early 20th-century golden era in which it became renowned throughout the Caribbean as an early capital of cinema, with Teatro Yagüez known as a beacon of the arts. However, it was surfing that became the west's best-known pastime, after the 1969 World Surfing Championships were held in Rincón.

🛈 Getting There & Away

Mayagüez is the regional hub and has its own airport (yet currently receives flights from San Juan only). You can fly direct from the US into Aguadilla's **Rafael Hernández Airport** (p199) 30 minutes northeast of Rincón.

The island's ring road, Hwy 2, leads into the region from Arecibo on the north coast, or Ponce on the south coast, and is the main means by which people arrive.

The Cabo Rojo area southwest of Hwy 2 has Puerto Rico's best cycling: undulating, blissfully traffic-free roads and a top **bike shop** (p189).

Rincón

POP 14,000

You'll know you've arrived in Rincón – 'the corner' – when you pass the sun-grizzled gringos cruising west in their rusty 1972 Volkswagen Beetle with surfboards piled on the roof. Shoehorned in the island's most remote corner, Rincón is Puerto Rico at its most unguarded, a place where the sunsets shimmer scarlet and you're more likely to be called 'dude' than 'sir.' This is the island's surfing capital and one of the premiere places to catch a wave in the northern hemisphere.

For numerous Californian dreamers this is where the short-lived summer of love ended up. Arriving for the Surfing World Championships in 1968, many never went home. Hence Rincón became a haven for draft-dodgers, alternative lifestylers, back-to-the-landers and people more interested in riding the perfect wave than with bagging $100,000 a year, living in a Chicago suburb.

Rincón's town center has been revitalized recently and now boasts great bars and restaurants.

History

Rincón traces its history to the 16th century and a few low-key sugarcane plantations. The municipality is actually named after one of the area's original planters, Don Gonzalo Rincón. For most of its history, the town survived on cane farming and cattle raising.

Things changed when the World Surfing Championships arrived in 1968. Glossy images of Rincón were plastered over international media – the word was out. Every year since then has seen successive generations of wave riders make the pilgrimage. And while they pursued an endless summer, they began to invest in the community, building their own restaurants, guesthouses and bars. Eventually, Rincón's perfect surf and permanent beach bums lent the place the vibe it retains today, something similar to a Hawaiian surfing outpost.

◉ Sights

Rincón is more of a region than a town, encompassing a municipal center surrounded by clusters of commercial areas. The municipal center is only about four square blocks, encircling the Catholic church and the Presbyterian church that face each other across the revitalized and animated Plaza de Recreo. This core has experienced a renaissance of recent years and has essential services, but nevertheless most inns, restaurants and beach attractions lie north or south.

The best swimming beaches are south of the village, as are many of the larger hotels. A number of different snorkeling and surfing sites lie north and west of town, along Hwy 413. Moving further north, Hwy 413 climbs into steep hills similarly scattered with eating and sleeping options, that may turn eyes away from the swell (for a while at least).

Though Rincón is crawling with American expats, the tourist/local divide is more seamless and less exclusive than in the resorts out east.

★**Plaza de Recreo**　　　SQUARE
The Plaza de Recreo deserves a lot of plaudits for having spruced itself up in recent years. It's now once again surrounded by bustling restaurants, bars and even an inn; it becomes positively cacophonous on Thursday evenings with its popular **art walk**. Its pleasantly designed amphitheater and general leafiness render it one of Puerto Rico's nicer central squares.

Rincón & Around

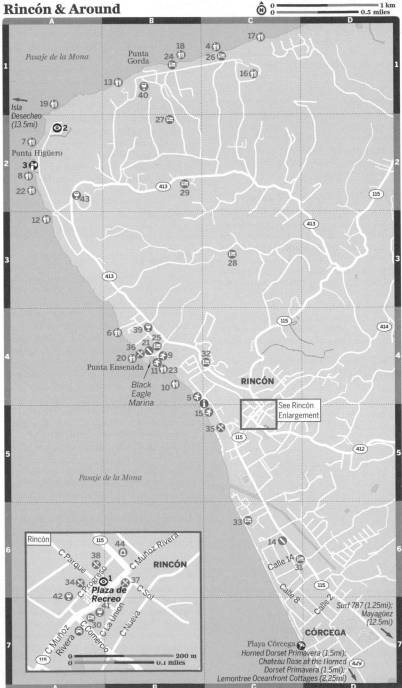

0 ——— 1 km
0 ——— 0.5 miles

Pasaje de la Mona

Punta Gorda

Isla Desecheo (13.5mi)

Punta Higüero

Punta Ensenada

Black Eagle Marina

RINCÓN

See Rincón Enlargement

Pasaje de la Mona

Rincón

RINCÓN

C Parque

C Muñoz Rivera

Plaza de Recreo

C Progresso

C Sol

C La Union

C Nueva

C Muñoz Rivera

C Comercio

0 ——— 200 m
0 ——— 0.1 miles

Playa Córcega

CÓRCEGA

Horned Dorset Primavera (1.5mi);
Chateau Rose at the Horned
Dorset Primavera (1.5mi);
Lemontree Oceanfront Cottages (2.25mi)

Surf 787 (1.25mi);
Mayagüez (12.5mi)

Calle 14

Calle 8

Calle 2

Rincón & Around

◎ Top Sights
1 Plaza de Recreo A6

◎ Sights
2 Bonus Nuclear Power Plant A2
  Parque Pasivo El Faro .... (see 3)
3 Punta Higüero Lighthouse.................... A2

◎ Activities, Courses & Tours
4 Antonio's.. C1
5 Capital Water Sports............................ B4
6 Dogman's... B4
7 Domes.. A2
8 Indicators... A2
9 Katarina Sail Charters.......................... B4
10 Little Malibu... B4
11 Makaira Charters.................................. B4
12 Maria's... A3
13 Pools.. B1
14 Puerto Rico Technical
   Divers.. C6
15 Rincón Balneario.................................. C5
16 Rincon Surf School............................... C1
17 River Mouth.. C1
18 Sandy Beach B1
19 Spanish Wall.. A1
20 Steps.. B4
21 Taino Divers.. B4
22 The Point.. A2
23 Tres Palmas... B4

◎ Sleeping
24 Beside the Pointe................................. B1
25 Blue Boy Inn... B4

26 Casa Isleña.. C1
27 Dos Angeles del Mar
   Guesthouse....................................... B2
28 La Rosa Inglesa/English Rose
   Inn B&B.. C3
29 Lazy Parrot Inn B2
30 Que Chévere A7
31 Rincón Inn Hostel................................. C6
32 Rincón Surf Hostel................................ C4
33 Tres Sirenas... C6

◎ Eating
34 Cafe 413... A6
35 La Cambija.. C5
36 La Copa Llena B4
  La Rosa Inglesa/English
   Rose Inn Restaurant .... (see 28)
37 Mangia Mi... B6
  Mi Familia's Pizzeria.................... (see 29)
38 Rincón Cash & Carry............................. A6

◎ Drinking & Nightlife
39 Carta Buena B4
  Lucky 13 BBQ............................... (see 31)
40 Pool Bar & Sushi................................... B1
41 Rincón Beer Company........................... A7
42 Roots.. A6
  Tamboo Tavern............................ (see 24)
43 The Beach House A2

◎ Shopping
  Parrotphernalia .... (see 29)
44 Uncharted Studio................................. B6

Punta Higüero Lighthouse   LIGHTHOUSE

FREE Nicknamed El Faro, the Punta Higüero Lighthouse dates from 1892 and rises almost 100ft. It was restored in 1922 after being severely damaged by a tsunami set off by the devastating 1918 earthquake. The 26,000-candlepower light has been automated since 1933 and still helps ships navigate the Pasaje de la Mona. The principal reason to come here, however, is the view. Five great surf breaks are nearby and sometimes humpback whales come within 100 yards of the coast.

The small museum in the base of the lighthouse has not been open for several years, but the lighthouse building crowns **Parque Pasivo El Faro** (◎6am-6pm).

Bonus Nuclear Power Plant   LANDMARK

(Hwy 4413) A curious landmark, this green dome poking out from behind the palm trees north of Rincón town behind the Punta Higüero Lighthouse once housed the Caribbean's first nuclear-powered electricity-generating facility. Back when the Beach Boys led the surfin' safari, the Boiling Nuclear Superheater Plant (known half-sarcastically by the acronym of Bonus) was a prototype of the superheater reactor. In its short life from 1960 to 1968, it suffered a reactor failure and drew scorn from environmentalists.

The US government tried converting the building into a museum, only to discover – shocker – that a failed nuclear power facility wasn't popular with tourists.

Subsequently Bonus became a rusting relic of the nuclear age and a favorite canvas for graffiti artists, who scrawl slogans to vilify nukes or praise marijuana. Locals named a surf break after it: Domes (p176), one of Rincón's most consistent breaks. The power plant currently opens only by appointment through the **Puerto Rican Electric Power Authority** (Autoridad de Energía Electrica; Map p52; ☑787-521-3434; www.aeepr.com; Rte 8838, cnr Hwys 1 & 52, San Juan).

RINCÓN & WEST COAST RINCÓN

🏃 Activities

Surfing

Surfing is the prime attraction, so if you're arriving in high season, make arrangements for rentals or lessons as early as possible. If you're just looking for a casual arrangement, there are shacks with boards to rent by the major surfing areas for around $25 per day. There are numerous surf schools: some great, many poor. Surf schools will also have gear rental.

Rincón Surf School   SURFING, YOGA
(☑ 787-823-0610; www.rinconsurfschool.com; 3-hour group lessons $95) Rincón Surf School often does lessons at Sandy Beach and is a good option for beginning adults. Also on offer are surf-and-yoga combo packages and lessons specifically for women.

Surf 787   SURFING
(☑ 787-448-0968; http://surf787.com; Hwy 115 Km 8.3, Behind Spyce Bar Restaurant; group surf lessons from $70) The coolest kid on the block, Surf 787 has a suite of packages, all-inclusive surf vacations, adult getaways and a kids surf camp. The instructors here, who are all CPR- and water-safety certified, also offer lessons for couples and small groups as well as private tuition.

Diving & Snorkeling

Because of the rough water this is not a great place for snorkeling, but snorkelers will fare much better in summer, when water is calmer. Head for either Playa Shacks (p207) near Isabela, or the beach by Steps (p176) near Black Eagle Marina for the best of what the Rincón beaches have to offer.

SURF BEACHES

As far as surfing folklore goes, Rincón wins the ultimate accolade: it's mentioned in a song by the Beach Boys. Released in 1962, *Surfin' Safari* names Rincón as the place where 'they're walking the nose,' surfer slang for moving forward on the board toward the front. For walking the nose or simply taking in the action from shore, here's a guide to Rincón's hottest surf beaches (running south to north):

Little Malibu Just north of the marina. OK in winter, with easy 4ft breaks. Good for beginners.

Tres Palmas The big kahuna, with breaks of up to 25ft. Requires *bon courage* and a long paddle out. Handle with care.

Steps Also known by its Spanish name, *Escalera,* this is the 'inside' break to Tres Palmas' 'outside' break. Good snorkeling spot when it's calm.

Dogman's A local favorite that is anything but predictable. Expect waves that are high and hollow.

Maria's A good right, but needs a decent swell. Three times a year the waves break big, but otherwise it's average.

The Point Just south of the Punta Higüero Lighthouse, this one is not for amateurs. Waves can break big here while Maria's is lying flat.

Indicators Good powerful rights, but a rock and coral bottom to watch out for.

Domes This classic surf spot, probably the most consistent overall in the Rincón area, is named after the nearby former nuclear facility. It sports good rights and the occasional left: watch out for a strong undercurrent.

Spanish Wall A beautiful secluded spot only reachable by a rough path, this place gets up in winter and can be particularly fabulous after a cold front.

Pools Offers a few shallow reef-break peaks that can occasionally barrel.

Sandy Beach Good beginners beach with decent waves when the swell is right.

Antonio's Used heavily during the 1968 Surfing World Championships, this has a right wall with a shorter left. Two take-off points spread the crowd.

River Mouth Gentler, with tidal pools, but wrongly overlooked as surfing can be great when the swells roll.

Rincón has many dive shops, thanks to the popularity of diving the pristine reefs around Rincón and Isla Desecheo.

★ **Puerto Rico Technical Divers**   DIVING
(☑787-477-3368; www.facebook.com/Prtekdiving center; Hwy 115 km 12; ⊗8am-5pm) This is one of the island's best-equipped dive facilities, specializing in shore diving around Rincón, Aguadilla and Isabela. They have a comprehensive range of gear to buy and to rent, too. It's a bit hard to spot from the road: look for the Vacas Gauchas *parrilleria* (grillhouse) and you'll know you're close.

Taino Divers   DIVING, SNORKELING
(☑787-823-6429; www.tainodivers.com; Black Eagle Marina; 2-tank dive $99-120, snorkeling $50-95) ✆ Located inside the little Black Eagle Marina north of Rincón, this is probably the best outfit on the west coast; the guides here are consistently responsible, professional and environmentally aware. It does almost daily runs to Isla Desecheo (8am to 2pm) and shorter trips to nearby reefs (8am to noon).

Swimming

The surf is often too rough for swimming at many sites along the coast. Fortunately, there's the safe and recently renovated Rincón Balneario (public beach) less than a kilometer from the Plaza de Recreo. Here you'll find restrooms, showers, some temporary food shacks and a new mall, which contains the tourist office, harbor restaurant and lookout tower.

Many of the hotels and guesthouses on the water south of the town center have decent swimming from the thin, thin stretch of strand out front.

Kayaking & Cruising

Capital Water Sports   WATER SPORTS
(☑787-718-7771; http://rinconxtreme.com; Sunset Village, Rincón Balneario; kayak rental from $25 per hr) You can rent kayaks from Capital Water Sports for approximately $25 an hour for use around the Rincón Balneario.

Katarina Sail Charters   CRUISE
(☑787-823-7245; www.sailrinconpuertorico.com; Black Eagle Marina; 3hr snorkel/sail adult/child $80/40) How about enjoying the wide skies and drop-dead gorgeous sunsets from the waters abutting Rincón a little less frenetically than if you were surfing? The Katarina offers several such possibilities. Even on the three-hour cruise you'll get the chance

to snorkel, sunbathe, spot manatees (and whales in season) and cast a line for a fresh fish lunch.

Fishing & Whale-watching

Several outfitters in the Rincón area run recommended fishing excursions: try Makaira Charters (☑787-299-7374; www.fishrinconpr.com; 1-4 people half/full day $575/850), who specialise in fishing charters.

Taino Divers runs responsible whale-watching tours (about $55 per person for a two-hour tour). Boats are required to keep a minimum distance from the gentle giants, but less scrupulous operators don't always adhere to that rule. Whale-watching is also possible from the Punta Higüero Lighthouse (p175) in December.

✯ Festivals & Events

Rincón International Film Festival   FILM
(www.rinconfilm.com; ⊗Mar) In late March and early April, Rincón reveals its cultural side in flying colors with its famed film festival that, within certain categories, rivals San Juan's big-screen bonanzas. Yes, surfing is one of those categories. But for comedy, short films and feature films, this catchy fest turns heads well away from the breaks for a week.

Rincón Triathlon   SPORTS
(http://trialorincon.com; ⊗Jun) This triathlon has been going since 1982, which is pretty much ancient history in the triathlon world. Held every June, it's a classic ironman contest that's starting to draw some quality international athletes – it makes for a serious fiesta for spectators.

🛏 Sleeping

With the exception of Que Chévere, a new inn which is conveniently on Plaza de Recreo, accommodation is either south of town (marginally better-connected to the center) or north of town via Hwy 413 (where steep hills and twisting lanes give an extra degree of isolation and add several premature gray hairs to drivers' heads). Several lanes branch off Hwy 413 to the properties on the north-facing beaches.

🛏 In Town

Que Chévere   INN $$
(☑787-823-6452; http://quecheverepr.com; 17 Muñoz Rivera; r $75-125) "Que Chévere!" is how most Latin Americans say 'how cool'

and when you see what you get for your money at this clean, tasteful new inn on Rincón's Plaza de Recreo, you might want to utter the same words. This is a new concept for the town: its first bang-in-the-center accommodation and its first backpacker hotel.

The only thing backpacker-like about Que Chévere really, however, is the price (in low season rooms can cost as little as $75) because the spacious doubles with their intriguing artwork (ask the owner for the stories behind the paintings) are as good as most guesthouses. An impressive cast-iron spiral staircase corkscrews up to a roof terrace which, incidentally, is as high above the ground as you will get in the town center.

The staff are very knowledgeable about the area.

South of Town

Tres Hermanos Camping CAMPGROUND **$**
(787-826-1610; Hwy 115 Km 5; campsite $17, RV site $25-40) The nearest tent camping to Rincón is at this public beach off Hwy 115 just west of the town of Añasco and 5 miles south of Rincón. The shaded sites are steps from a lovely beach. There's showers and toilets and RVs are welcomed. There is an additional vehicle parking charge of $3 to $5 depending on the size.

Rincón Inn Hostel HOSTEL **$**
(787-823-7070; www.rinconinn.com; Hwy 115 Km 11.6; r $45-75;) Here it is – the cheapest accommodation in the west shy of camping or dossing on the beach. This is a slightly dim, but perfectly clean, little place with a self-catering kitchen. It's a block back from the water and around 1.5km south of the center. After a renovation prices have gone up but it's still about the best deal around.

Tropical Treehouse CABAÑAS **$$**
(787-245-7396, 541-499-3885; www.tropical-treehouse.com; cnr Rte 412 & Carretera El Coqui; d $110-135;) ✎ Built on 25 acres of bamboo forest above the Rincón shore, this cool ecoretreat lets you experience sleep in one of two Swiss Family Robinson–style treehouses (or 'hooches'), built with woven bamboo, screened in with mosquito netting and perched high off the ground. They have bamboo furniture, basic kitchen facilities and a sustainable ethos (they're even solar-powered).

Surf 787 Guest Villa/B&B VILLA **$$**
(787-448-0968; http://surf787.com; Hwy 115 km 8.3, Behind Spyce Bar Restaurant; r $110-160, 6-bedroom vila from $595;) This surf school also has a serendipitous accommodation option tucked away on its premises in the forested hills southeast of Rincón. There is a wonderful villa that accommodates up to 16 people, depending on how much you wish to rent, and bed-and-breakfast on a per-room basis from October to April: both are great value for the location and facilities.

★ **Tres Sirenas** B&B **$$$**
(787-823-0558; www.tressirenas.com; 26 Sea Beach Drive; d inc breakfast from $190-295;) This is Rincón's best guesthouse and probably one of the Caribbean's finest. A stone's throw from two of the bigger, more luxurious hotels, true indulgence beckons at this tranquil end-of-street detached house, from the freshly brewed coffee in your room to the lovingly prepared breakfasts served to all guests at their private terraces (with views out to the glimmering ocean).

★ **Horned Dorset Primavera** RESORT **$$$**
(787-823-4030; www.horneddorset.net; Hwy 429 Km 0.3; garden/oceanfront ste from $470/870;) Undoubtedly the best small resort in Puerto Rico and perhaps the Caribbean, this place rightly claims to offer the 'epitome of privacy, elegance and service'. There are 30 suites in private villas furnished with hand-carved antiques and with their own private plunge pools (in case you get bored of the communal infinity pool, which overlooks the setting sun).

Lemontree Oceanfront Cottages APARTMENT **$$$**
(787-823-6452; www.lemontreepr.com; Rte 429; apt $220-235;) Large, oh-so-quiet isolated apartments away from the downtown clamor, this gaggle of beach-abutting cottages are self-contained units with well-stocked kitchens and furnishings that have a lot of TLC rubbed into them. Come here for a true escape, but be aware you're 7km south of central Rincón here.

North of Town

Rincón Surf Hostel HOSTEL **$**
(678-744-8556; www.rinconsurfhostel.com; Hwy 413 km 0.5; dorm/s/d $25/70/80) This hostel is a particularly tempting option for surfers and beachgoers, one block back from the beach on the northwestern side of Rincón. Clean

dorms and small private rooms, a communal kitchen and a little takeaway coffee shack out front make this a good stopover for those on a budget.

**Dos Angeles del
Mar Guesthouse** GUESTHOUSE $$
(📞787-823-1378; http://dosangelesdelmar.com; off Hwy 413; r $129-169; 🅿 ❄ 🛜 🌊) The hardworking hosts at Dos Angeles del Mar strive to make your stay as wonderful as it could be. There are five immaculate rooms in a lofty house surrounded by Puerto Rico's loveliest garden. The sea's a way off, but the top-floor rooms have spectacular views from the balconies and are impeccably kept.

Beside the Pointe HOTEL $$
(📞787-823-8550; www.besidethepointe.com; r $110-175, apt $185-210; 🅿 ❄ 🛜) The social centerpiece of Sandy Beach, this guesthouse has a happening bar and restaurant (Tamboo Tavern; p180), rooms that are outfitted like small apartments and lots of unpretentious elegance. Despite the seafront location not all rooms have good views, but all have nice tiled floors, flat-screen televisions, coffee makers and fridges. And, of course, you're right near that surf.

Lazy Parrot Inn HOTEL $$
(📞787-823-5654; www.lazyparrot.com; Hwy 413 Km 4.1; r $120-195; 🅿 ❄ @ 🌊) Claiming the middle ground between high quality and high quirky, the Lazy Parrot is a venerable inn crammed full with all kinds of parrots – including real ones, carved ones, inflated ones and stuffed ones. It occupies the high country above Rincón. Rooms are comfortable and the more expensive ones very spacious, but not flashy. There's an inviting pool, too.

**La Rosa Inglesa/English
Rose Inn B&B** B&B $$
(📞787-823-4032; www.larosainglesa.com; follow signs from Hwy 413 interior; r incl breakfast $125-200; 🅿 ❄) High in the hills, this B&B meets an equally high standard of cleanliness and comes with the best breakfast in town (you can get cheaper rates without the breakfast, but trust us, you don't want to miss out on the breakfast).

Casa Isleña HOTEL $$
(📞787-823-1525; http://casaislena.com; Hwy 413 Interior Km 4.8, Beach Rd; r $155-195; 🅿 ❄ @ 🛜 🌊) A high-class option in the thick of Rincón's best surfing at Sandy Beach (p176), Casa

ⓘ ADDRESSES IN RINCÓN
·····································

Many of the accommodations (as well as restaurants and pubs) do not have street addresses per se and are a nightmare to find even on GPS; a good old-fashioned phone call before you set out to confirm directions is always prescient.

Isleña is an elegant, Mediterranean-style guesthouse on a magnificent, moody stretch of ocean. It's a magnet for discerning jet-setting surfers; guests work out the sore muscles at morning yoga under palms and navigate the walled-in gardens to nine large, lovely sea-view rooms.

Blue Boy Inn B&B $$
(📞787-823-2593; www.blueboyinn.com; 556 Black Eagle Rd; r $185-245; 🅿 ❄ 🛜 🌊) This elegant little inn near the Black Eagle Marina (p177) is an excellent option with very private rooms. This isn't a good place for families (it suggests no children under 12), nor is it ideal for avid surfers (the best breaks are further north of town), but the tiled terraces are hidden among leafy gardens and exude a romantic, secluded atmosphere.

In the evening guests can cook in the outdoor kitchen near the lovely pool or sit around the crackling fire pit before retiring to their rooms, where high-thread-count sheets cover sleigh beds.

🍴 Eating

Outside of San Juan, Rincón's varied eating options are almost without equal on the island, and it's something of a spawning ground for brave new culinary ventures.

Self-caterers can shop at **Rincón Cash & Carry** (cnr Progreso & Benjamin Gomez; ⏰10am-6pm Mon-Sat, to 4pm Sun), in the town center, across from the Plaza de Recreo.

A lot of Rincón's guesthouses and hotels also serve food.

La Cambija PUERTO RICAN $
(Cambija 17; $4.50-12; ⏰noon-10pm Wed-Mon) In a town where so many successful restaurants are expat–owned, it's nice to see Puerto Rican–helmed La Cambija doing well. Locals and tourists mix around the bar, or at the informal, open-air tables, feasting on *pinchos* (marinated pork and plantain kebabs, mmm) or a fillet of mahimahi. It's packed in the evenings, with a bubbly Puerto Rican feel.

La Rosa Inglesa/English Rose Inn Restaurant BREAKFAST **$**
(☑787-823-4032; www.larosainglesa.com; follow signs from Hwy 413 interior; dishes $4.50-12; ☺8am-noon Wed-Fri, 8am-1:30pm Sat & Sun) The trick to this exceptional breakfast place are the crusty homemade breads and savory home-stuffed sausage, which turn the egg dishes into a real event. Upscale surfers shovel down breakfast burritos and poached eggs after surfing the morning away. It's kind of a pain to get here, situated as it is up in the hills above town, but the town's best breakfast and great views are ample reward.

Mangia Mi ITALIAN **$**
(☑787-823-4812; www.facebook.com/mangiami rincon; 4 Muñoz Rivera, cnr Sol; mains $13-18; ☺4:30-10pm Wed-Mon) Exploding onto the eating scene in central Rincón in 2016, Mangia Mi with its oak floors, vaulted ceilings and stone walls evokes the classically understated look of a restaurant in a well-to-do countrified corner of Tuscany. Award-winning chefs create delightful Italianate fare fresh every day for very reasonable prices (with the open kitchen, the creation in itself is theater).

Cafe 413 CAFE **$**
(157 Progreso; lunch $3-9; ☺8am-midnight Mon & Thu, to 2am Fri & Sat) Cafe 413 could have coined the phrase 'surfer chic': you would think it, to look at their no-expenses-spared decor, where surfboards and VW camper vans jostle for wall space with the typical ethereal-looking photos of surfers practicing their art. But the design is modern and pretty cool, and service almost as bright. The coffee is strong and the lunches enticing.

The menu has a healthy bent, where salads incorporate such ingredients as hemp seeds and sprouts. Sandwiches, omelets, burgers and the like are also available.

Mi Familia's Pizzeria PIZZA **$**
(☑787-823-5654; www.lazyparrot.com; Hwy 413 Km 4.1, Lazy Parrot Inn; pizza & pasta $7-20; ☺11:30am-10pm) Sometimes the best things in life are the simple ones and this Italian restaurant, located poolside at the Lazy Parrot Inn (p179) but masterminded by different people, is one of our favorite pizza stops on the island. Pizzas are straight out of a wood-fired brick oven and prepared with bundles of TLC.

★**La Copa Llena** INTERNATIONAL **$$**
(☑787-823-0896; http://attheblackeagle.com; Black Eagle Marina; mains $20-40; ☺3-9:30pm Wed-Sat, 11am-9:30pm Sun) Is your glass half empty or half full? It's hard not to look on the bright side of life at La Copa Llena (the full cup). Down by the Black Eagle Marina (p177), this is one of the best restaurants in Rincón, for the elegantly understated interior and huge sea-fronting patio but mostly for the innovative food.

Chateau Rose at the Horned Dorset Primavera FUSION **$$$**
(☑787-823-4030; http://chateauroserincon.com/; Hwy 429 Km 0.3; 3-course dinner $65-110; ☺7-9:30pm Wed-Mon) Elegant and exclusive, the Chateau Rose restaurant at the Horned Dorset Primavera (p178) is among Puerto Rico's best fine-dining options – fitting for a hotel that's also one of Puerto Rico's best. You climb the sweeping staircase to the black-and-white-tiled dining room of billowing lined drapes and an atmosphere right out of a colonial Caribbean culinary dream.

🍸 Drinking & Nightlife

Rincón's nightlife is varied, but there are few 'bars' per se: many restaurants rather become animated places come nighttime. Some focus more on drinking, some on eating, but it's invariably done under the same roof.

★**Rincón Beer Company** BREWERY
(http://rinconbeerco.com; 15 Muñoz Rivera; ☺4-11pm Sun-Mon & Wed, to midnight Thu & Fri, to 1am Sat) This cracking new brewpub has enlivened the Plaza de Recreo (p173) in central Rincón. It offers a great selection of Puerto Rico brews and it's preparing to concoct its own, too. San Juan's Old Harbor Brewery and Cabo Rojo's Boquerón Brewing Company are among the island breweries guest-starring at the most exciting new show on the local drinking scene.

Tamboo Tavern BAR
(www.besidethepointe.com; Sandy Beach; meals $3-10; ☺noon-midnight Sun-Thu, to 2am Fri & Sat) The patio bar of the Beside the Pointe guesthouse (p179) overlooks some of the best sand in Rincón. With a congenial après-surf scene and a young and vivacious local crowd who drink a little too much and dance a little too close, it was shortlisted by *Esquire* among the best bars in America, and it's easy to see why.

Roots
COCKTAIL BAR

(cnr Progreso & Comercio; ◷5pm-midnight Sun-Thu, until 2am Fri/Sat) Rincón's latest bar is all about serving incredible cocktails with none of the pretension, and with the gimmick that you can select your own ingredients for your chosen tipple (with a little guidance from the bartenders, of course). Very much a choose-your-own-adventure of a drinking session.

The Beach House
BAR

(www.thebeachhouserincon.com; Hwy 413 km 2.4; ◷7am-midnight Sun-Thu, to 2am Fri & Sat) It's not that the Beach House doesn't do food; it's that everything about its vibe and layout shouts 'drink'. It's an upmarket surfers hangout, open to the sun-drenched views down a few hundred meters to a bunch of top surf spots like Maria's (p176). Hummus and bean stuffed pitas, quesadillas and catch of the day with asparagus are in the $10 to $20 range.

Lucky 13 BBQ
BAR

(Hwy 115, cnr Calle 14; mains $13-32; ◷9am-2am, food to 10pm) Starting early and staggering home late, you could spend your entire day in Lucky 13. In fact, many people seem to. By the time breakfast is done it's time for the midday cocktails, after several of which a slather of slow-smoked barbecued meat seems the most natural choice in the world.

It's colorful, it's popular and its unappealing location, right on the main road into Rincón, puts no one off whatsoever.

Pool Bar & Sushi
BAR

(☑787-823-2583; http://poolbarsushi.com; off Hwy 413; sushi $5-21; ◷5pm-late) This bar is exactly what it says on the tin: has a pool, is a bar and serves sushi. It often shows surf films on a big screen. It's just back from Pools (p176) beach. Take the first left-hand turn off Hwy 413, then immediately bear left again and follow the road downhill, asking directions where you can.

★Carta Buena
JUICE BAR

(www.cartabuena.com; Hwy 413 Km 1.2; snacks & juices $3-7; ◷8am-4pm) ✐ Good coffee and better smoothies are served from a bright orange booth that waylays you as you head out from Rincón towards the Punta Higüero Lighthouse (p175). The incredible thing about Carta Buena is that everything you consume here is 100% natural (as in growing naturally on Puerto Rico) and grown in the surrounding garden.

🛍 Shopping

Rincón can be a good place to pick up an original souvenir and not just surfing-related items, either. Start your browse for a unique take-home gift at the Rincón Art Walk (p173) on Thursday evenings.

Uncharted Studio
ART, CLOTHING

(www.theunchartedstudio.com; 6 Sol, Plaza de Recreo; ◷11am-5pm) ✐ This hip gallery, right on the Plaza de Recreo (p173), sells the work of local artists, as well as cool custom T-shirts and surfwear. It also has environmentally friendly silk-screen prints that use natural solvents and paintings.

Parrotphernalia
GIFTS & SOUVENIRS

(www.lazyparrot.com; Hwy 413 Km 4.1, Lazy Parrot Inn; ◷9am-6pm) In the Lazy Parrot Inn (p179), this shop is a must-stop for parrot lovers. You will see handmade sea-glass jewelry here, which makes for one of Puerto Rico's more unique souvenirs.

❶ Information

EMERGENCY

The **local cops** (☑787-823-2020; cnr Nueva & Nueva Final) are based in the southeast corner of central Rincón, off Nueva.

INTERNET ACCESS

Almost every place to stay and many restaurants have free wi-fi.

MEDICAL SERVICES

In Rincón town, this **health center** (☑787-823-5555, 787-823-5500; www.costasalud.com; 28 Muñoz Rivera, cnr Calle A; ◷clinic 8am-4pm Mon-Fri, emergencies 7am-11pm Mon-Fri) is a block south of Plaza de Recreo.

MONEY

There are ATMs in the lobby of almost every hotel and in many bars, so finding cash won't be a problem. The nearest ATM to Plaza de Recreo is **Cooperativa de Ahorro y Credito** (cnr Calle B & Muñoz Rivera; ◷8:15am-4pm Mon-Fri, 8am-11:30am Sat).

POST

The **post office** (Hwy 115; ◷7:30am-4:30pm Mon-Fri, 8:30am-noon Sat) is 600m north of the Plaza de Recreo on Hwy 115.

TOURIST INFORMATION

The **tourist office** (☑787-823-5024; Sunset Bldg, Cambija s/n; ◷8am-4:30pm Mon-Fri) is in the Sunset Building adjacent to Rincón public beach.

RINCÓN & WEST COAST RINCÓN

The Rincón Tourism Association (www.rincon.org) puts out a great, amusing map, complete with site descriptions and essential phone numbers (it's completely not to scale). You can get one from your innkeeper: sometimes free, sometimes for $1.

ⓘ Getting There & Away

Rincón doesn't have its own airport, but there are two in the area. If you are coming from San Juan, fly into Mayagüez.

If you're making a beeline to Rincón direct from overseas, Aguadilla's Aeropuerto Rafael Hernández generally has a couple of flights a day from the US.

The easiest way to approach the town is via Hwy 115, which intersects Hwy 2 both at the northern end of the Rincón peninsula near Aguadilla and the southern end, not far north of the Mayagüez airport, **Aeropuerto Eugenio Maria de Hostos** (p186). As Hwy 115 sweeps into town, it becomes Calle Muñoz Rivera.

ⓘ Getting Around

Rincón – despite its mantle as an 'alternative' beach haven – has little provision for nonmotorized transport. The spread-out community with minimal public transport has few sidewalks and almost no facilities for bicycles.

The only reliable way to get around the area is by rented car, taxi, irregular *públicos* or – if you're energetic and careful – walking. Car rentals can be found at **Angelos** (☑ 787-823-3438; Hwy 115 Km 12) in central Rincón. The **público stand** (cnr Muñoz Rivera & Comercio, Plaza de Recreo) is just off Plaza de Recreo on Nueva. However, you're here in Rincón for the wild coastal scenery and it must be emphasised this is a pretty miserable way of getting about.

You will pay around $40 for a taxi from either the Aguadilla or Mayagüez airports. Car rentals can be found at both of these destinations, as well as in Rincón itself.

Mayagüez

POP 83,000

It takes some digging to discover the charm of Mayagüez. The 'Sultan of the West' is largely a transportation point for visitors en route to the far west in Rincón. The Commonwealth's third-biggest city, behind San Juan and Ponce, has few comparable attractions. Still, there's abundant vibrancy here, mostly thanks to a scattering of singular restaurants, some ambitious restoration projects and a hard-partying student population.

Mayagüez boasts a large university over 13,000 students strong, the west's most impressive arts museum, various historic buildings (including delightful Teatro Yagüez), Puerto Rico's only zoo, and a lovely central plaza.

But its gastronomy and drinking scene alone would be reason enough to stop by. Local treats include *brazo gitano* (gypsy's arm; Puerto Rico's unique take on a jam sponge cake) and a sweet rum-and-wine cocktail known as Sangria de Fido. When night falls, students descend Thursday through Saturday on a buoyant bar scene.

History

Founded in 1760 by émigrés from the Canary Islands, Mayagüez started inauspiciously, getting by on fruit production and agriculture. Even today the city remains noted for the sweetness of its mangoes. In the mid-19th century Mayagüez developed a contrarian nature and sheltered numerous revolutionary thinkers including Ramón Emeterio Betances, architect of the abortive Grito de Lares. Disaster struck in 1918 when an earthquake measuring 7.6 on the Richter scale all but destroyed the central business district, but the city rose from the rubble.

⊙ Sights

★ Museo de Arte   GALLERY
(MUSA - UPRM; ☑ 787-832-4040; http://musa.uprm.edu; Av Laureles, Recinto Universitario de Mayagüez; ⊙ 10am-4:30pm Tue-Wed & Fri, to 7:30pm Thu) **FREE** This brilliant, bold new art space is the best museum west of Ponce. Opened in 2016, it focuses on work by Puerto Rican artists from the 20th century onwards, including greats such as Lorenzo Homar and Rafael Tufiño, besides the Mayagüez painter and printmaker Marcos Irizarry. It's well deserving of a look to throw a light on the island's thriving contemporary arts. It's located on the Mayagüez university campus, just west of Estación Experimental Agrícola Federal (p184).

**Catedral de Nuestra
Señora de la Candelaria**   CHURCH
(Plaza Colón; ⊙ 6:30am-5:30pm Mon-Fri, 7:30am-7:30pm Sat, 6:30am-6:30pm Sun) Consecrated in 1760, Mayagüez' original Catholic church was replaced by the current model in 1836. The cathedral suffered many blows over the subsequent 80 years, culminating

Mayagüez

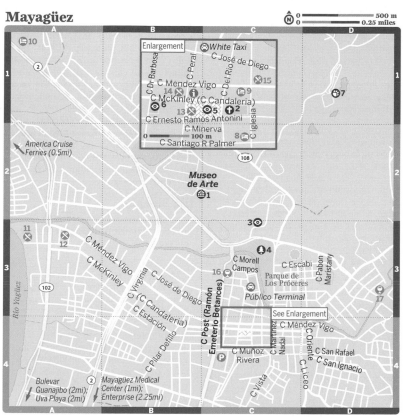

RINCÓN & WEST COAST MAYAGÜEZ

Mayagüez

⊙ Top Sights
1 Museo de Arte.................................B2

⊙ Sights
2 Catedral de Nuestra Señora de la
    Candelaria.................................C1
3 Estación Experimental Agrícola
    Federal.....................................C3
4 Parque de los Próceres.................C3
5 Plaza Colón.................................C1
6 Teatro Yagüez.............................B1
7 Zoológico de Puerto Rico.............D1

⊜ Sleeping
8 Hotel Colonial.............................C2

9 Howard Johnson Downtown
    Mayagüez.................................C1
10 Mayagüez Resort & Casino...........A1

⊗ Eating
11 Costa...A3
12 E Franco & Co.............................A3
13 Friends Cafe...............................B1
14 Rex Cream.................................B1
15 Ricomini Bakery..........................C1

⊜ Drinking & Nightlife
16 El Garabato................................C3
17 Fido's Sangria Garden..................D3

in the 1918 earthquake. Despite ambitious schemes, full refurbishment wasn't actually completed until 2004. The cathedral now sparkles afresh and survives as one of Puerto Rico's most evocative ecclesial monuments, with gilded scenes from the life of Christ behind the altar.

Plaza Colón · SQUARE

(cnr Candelaria & Del Río) The central plaza of Mayagüez is one of Puerto Rico's most attractive squares, shaded by the Catedral de Nuestra Señora de la Candelaria (p182) on its east side. It's a leafy place to sit and watch the city go by, and right in the middle is the city's best cafe, **Friends Cafe** (snacks $1-4; ☺8am-midnight; 🛜).

Parque de los Próceres · PARK

(☺6am-6pm) Mayagüez can boast not just one but two of Puerto Rico's most alluring urban parks, and this serene green space, a few blocks northeast of Plaza Colón, is replete with walkways, pools and gazebos. The Río Yagüez flows across the southwestern edge, while just to the north across Hwy 65 in a further area of manicured greenery is Estación Experimental Agrícola Federal. From the centre, Calle Martinez Nadal, two blocks east of Plaza Colón, leads north into the park.

Estación Experimental Agrícola Federal · AGRICULTURAL CENTER

(☎787-767-9705; Av Paris; ☺7am-4pm) 🆓 Wandering through the Estación Experimental Agrícola Federal, the tropical agricultural research station of the US Department of Agriculture, is a bit like wandering through a geeky botanical garden, what with the neatly labeled plantations of yams, plantains, bananas and imported tropical 'cash crops' such as cinnamon trees from Sri Lanka. Today, the station also throws many of its federal grants behind biofuels and tropical medicine. It's about 200m north up Av Paris from Hwy 65.

The adjacent city park known as Parque de los Próceres, on the south side of Hwy 65, also has verdant walkways and together these make an interesting stroll. These grounds lie just southeast of the university campus.

Zoológico de Puerto Rico · ZOO

(☎787-832-6330, 787-834-8110; Camino Zoológico, Bario Miradero, Hwy 108 interior; adult/child $16/11; ☺8:30am-5pm Wed-Sun; 🅿) The only real zoo on the island, with a recent multimillion-dollar top-to-bottom renovation, boasts over 600 species of reptiles, birds, amphibians and mammals. The highlight is the brightly polished arthropod and butterfly house, where kids squeal at glass enclosures of giant tropical cockroaches and colorful butterflies that flutter about. The latest thing are zoo nights, giving visitors the chance to observe the nocturnal behavioral patterns of animals.

Teatro Yagüez · THEATER

(Yagüez Theater; cnr Candelaria & Dr Basora; ☺8am-4:30pm Mon-Fri) 🆓 This elegant edifice, originally dating from 1909 and rebuilt following a fire in the 1920s, was the brainchild of Francisco Maymón Palmer, who had established himself as one of the Caribbean's early pioneers of cinematography. He ensured the theater became, over the ensuing decades, a leading center of the arts for its day. Now fully restored, it attracts regular performances and stands as one of Puerto Rico's most brilliant and talismanic old theaters with its colonnaded entrance and central cupola.

🛏 Sleeping

The options are poor for a city of this size and clout: limited to smart but bland business hotels.

Hotel Colonial · HOTEL $

(☎787-833-2150; www.hotelcolonial.com; 14 Calle Iglesia; s/d incl breakfast from $59/69; 🅿❄@🛜) With negotiation, these 29 rooms can be an affordable option in Mayagüez city center. Rooms are a bit bleak, but retain some haughty 'colonial' dignity. Anyway, it's under half the price of any other overnight option. There's local charm in the long staircases and Moorish tiling of these historic digs, especially considering the building was once a home for nuns.

A renovation in 2014 tarted things up somewhat.

Howard Johnson Downtown Mayagüez · HOTEL $$

(☎787-832-9191; www.hojo.com; 70 Méndez Vigo; d $100-143; 🅿❄🛜🏊) This place was once a monastery but any spirituality here has long been superseded by rampant capitalism: the hotel is firmly geared towards the business traveler. Rooms get corresponding facilities such as desks, mini-refrigerators and flat-screen televisions. Perks include a small courtyard pool and an on-site bar/restaurant. For multiple discounts, book online.

Mayagüez Resort & Casino · CASINO HOTEL $$$

(☎787-832-3030; www.mayaguezresort.com; Rte 104 Km 0.3; s/d/ste $195/215/365; 🅿❄@🏊) This hotel-and-casino combo is the plushest option in town and locals pack into the casino to drink and play slots. Located off Hwy 2 north of town, this 140-unit property, with tennis courts and pool, stands on 20 lovely acres of tropical gardens – actually an adjunct to the nearby agricultural research station, Estación Experimental Agrícola Federal.

✖ Eating

The restaurants don't lack for quality here, but they are spread over a wide area. Besides downtown, many other highly regarded eateries and beach bars can be found on the Bulevar Guanajibo (⊙24hr).

★ E Franco & Co   BAKERY, CAFE $
(🖸787-832-0070; www.brazogitano.net; Méndez Vigo Oueste No 276, cnr with Manuel Pirallo; dishes $7-16; ⊙7am-5pm Mon-Sat, 7:30am-5pm Sun) This salt-of-the-earth grocery-store-cum-cafe, stocked with fresh-baked goods and opulent hampers, has been here in Mayagüez for over 150 years and is still drawing in punters from as far away as San Juan for a monthly stock up. Cocooned in the waterfront warehouse district, Franco's is an upmarket place with tables scattered around a deli counter reminiscent of an old English tearoom.

Ricomini Bakery   BAKERY, CAFE $
(101 Méndez Vigo; dishes $2-8; ⊙5am-midnight) The Ricomini bakery and deli has been on this corner for well over a century. With a lunch counter, some tables and basic groceries, this is a de facto social hub of downtown Mayagüez: deals are made, relationships forged (and broken) and gossip boisterously exchanged.

Roll up for steaming coffee, scrambled eggs, a slice of the famous local sweet treat *brazo gitano* or a delicious toasted Cubano sandwich, stacked with ham, roasted pork, cheese and pickles.

Uva Playa   SEAFOOD $
(🖸787-652-3266; Bulevar Guanajibo 552; mains $11-15; ⊙5-11pm) Wholesome, no-nonsense seafood and grills, all dished up in friendly, modern environs with a deck overlooking the sea: it might sound an easy enough concept on a coast-abutting boulevard known for its dining, but Uva Playa pulls off a cracking eating-out experience time and time again.

Rex Cream   ICE CREAM $
(cnr Candelaria & Peral; cones $1-3) Rex is a small Puerto Rican ice-cream chain that was founded in Mayagüez in the 1960s by Chinese immigrants who came to the island via Costa Rica. Frequenting this signature store near Plaza Colón is still very much a local

tradition, particularly on public holidays. Among the numerous weird and wonderful flavors you can sample are corn sherbet and tamarind.

Costa   INTERNATIONAL $$
(🖸787-519-6647; Plaza de las Banderas, mains $19-36; ⊙11am-11pm; ✢) Right by the sea, Costa is a jewel in an otherwise underwhelming Mayagüez waterfront. Affluent residents chill in a minimalist space buffeted by icy air-con that wouldn't look amiss in a New York contemporary-art museum. There's a large patio with an open-air bar and select cool-sounding (and pretty good-tasting) dishes like *filet mignon* of Angus.

🍺 Drinking & Nightlife

The Mayagüez Resort & Casino is a sure-fire bet for upscale entertainment. The nightlife scene is animated, yet at the same time notoriously hard to pin down, with the city's huge student body regularly switching allegiances between here-today-gone-tomorrow bars and clubs. The only way you are going to gauge the latest scene is by asking locals. Things really get going from Thursday to Sunday.

★ Fido's Sangria Garden   BAR
(75 & 78 Calle Dulievre, off Hwy 106; ⊙11am-midnight Wed-Sat, to 7pm Sun) Wilfrido 'Fido' Aponte became a local legend for his potent sangria – a blend of Bacardí 151 and extraordinarily sweet tropical fruit juice. The drink garnered such a cultish following that, according to locals, Bacardí offered a king's ransom for the recipe, which Fido refused. His heirs still produce several varieties of the 'wine cocktail' and sell them out of a garage in a residential neighborhood of Mayagüez.

El Garabato   BAR
(cnr Ramón E. Betances & Morrel Campos; ⊙2pm-2am) El Garabato is more of a typical pub than a club. Here students swing by for a quick one between classes or stop to play dominoes with the regulars; wild nights are saved for Red Baron Pub, the city's classic dance club, which is upstairs in the same building.

ⓘ Information

Mayagüez Medical Center (Hospital Dr Ramón Emeterio Betances; 🖸787-652-9200; www.mayaguezmedical.com; Hwy 2, cnr Carolina) A hospital in Mayagüez. It's on Hwy 2 which, at this point, is also known as Avenida Hostos.

RINCÓN & WEST COAST MAYAGÜEZ

Tourist Information Office (☑787-833-1650; cnr Candelaria & Peral; ☺8am-Sat) On the main square, **Plaza Colón** (p184), Mayagüez tourist office is well stocked with local maps.

ⓘ Getting There & Away

AIR

The **Aeropuerto Eugenio María de Hostos** (Camino Aeropuerto, off Hwy 2) is about 5km north of town, just off Hwy 2. **Cape Air** (☑1-800-227-3247; www.capeair.com) currently has three to four flights daily to and from San Juan, but there were no international flights at the time of writing.

CAR

The city sits 23km south of Rincón and 158km west of San Juan.

Hwy 2, part of the island's nominal ring road, brings you in from the north or south. While this is a four-lane road, it is plagued by traffic lights.

Parking in central Mayagüez is not great, but a piece of cake if you've navigated Old San Juan or Ponce unscathed.

Hwy 105 (which actually runs along the north side of Plaza Colón under the guise of Calle Candelaria) is the west end of the Ruta Panorámica, which leads from Mayagüez into the mountains and to Maricao.

PÚBLICO

The **público terminal** (cnr Peral & Dr Nelson Perea) is in Barrio Paris, about four blocks north of Plaza Colón. Aguadilla and Rincón are common destinations, when there are any vehicles leaving. San Juan is also served.

ⓘ Getting Around

A few taxis usually show up at the airport when the flights arrive from San Juan; if none are there, or if you need to get to the airport, call **White Taxi** (☑787-832-1115, 787-832-1154; cnr José de Diego & Peral). The one-way fare to town is about $8.

To rent a car, try **Enterprise** (☑1-844-794-8596; Hwy 2 Km 158.9; ☺7:30am-5pm Mon-Fri, 9am-noon Sat).

One of Puerto Rico's fairly regular street renamings can confuse those who need to orientate themselves: Calle McKinley, which traverses the north side of Plaza Colón, is now called Calle Candelaria.

Cabo Rojo Area

Cabo Rojo (Red Cape) is the name of both a small administrative town (15km south of Mayagüez and 12km west of San Germán)

and the wider, infinitely more enticing municipality that surrounds it. To add to the confusion, it is also the name used to describe the rugged coastline that constitutes Puerto Rico's extreme and rarely traveled southwestern tip. Got it?

Cabo Rojo (El Pueblo) – Cabo Rojo the town, that is – is the only bland part of what is otherwise a fascinating region. It sprawls haphazardly around Hwy 2 and acts as a supply center for the sparsely populated, mangrove-fringed coast outside town. The only reason to stop is an office of the Puerto Rico Tourism Company.

ⓘ Information

For information on the entire Cabo Rojo area, the Porta del Sol branch of the **Puerto Rico Tourism Company** (PRTC; ☑787-721-2400; www.seepuertorico.com; Hwy 100 Km 6.6, Galeria 100 mall next to El Mesón restaurant; ☺8am-4pm Mon-Fri) is located in Cabo Rojo (El Pueblo).

ⓘ Getting There & Away

Busy Hwy 2 cuts inland between Mayagüez and Yauco, leaving this rather isolated corner of the island refreshingly untrodden. There's an extensive patchwork of wildlife refuges here, along with trails to hike, some unusual birds and mammals to spot and a quiet network of country roads that make for excellent cycling (the best bike hire is **Puerto Rico Bike Adventures** (p189) near Boquerón).

Taking Hwy 102 from San Germán to Cabo Rojo town is the best means of arrival here. From Cabo Rojo town, Hwy 100 leads to Boquerón and other locales further south whilst Hwy 102 goes northwest to Playa de Joyuda.

Playa de Joyuda

South of Mayagüez and just north of Boquerón, little Playa de Joyuda is a dining destination – famous for its string of seafood restaurants and known islandwide as the Milla de Oro del Buen Comer (Gourmet Golden Mile). It might be a bit generous to call these places 'gourmet,' but the seafood is very fresh, and there are more than a dozen family-owned establishments that line a 3-mile oceanfront stretch of Hwy 102, and specialize in oysters, crab and shrimp. Often, you can get a seat right over the water and look down at startlingly large carp who loll up to lazily beg for table scraps.

While Playa de Joyuda isn't a beach haven, there are plenty of accommodation

RINCÓN & WEST COAST CABO ROJO AREA

options in this idiosyncratic west-coast outpost, and with a couple of decent sailing and dive operators and a nearby nature reserve, there's enough outdoor adventures to work up an appetite for an evening of shellfish.

◉ Sights

**Reserva Natural
Laguna de Joyuda** NATURE RESERVE

(Hwy 102; ☺24hr) The heart of Playa de Joyuda's 300-acre Reserva Natural Laguna de Joyuda is a sizeable saltwater lagoon with a depth that rarely exceeds 4ft. The sanctuary is of great importance to waterfowl and other migratory birds that come here to prey on more than 40 species of fish. Humans come here for the same reason.

The reserve is also home to one of Puerto Rico's famous bioluminescent bodies of water, like those in La Parguera and Vieques, but is free of commercial tourism. After dark, microorganisms give the dark water a green glow. Travelers with access to a kayak can launch a nighttime exploration of the lagoon; watch for the access road off Hwy 102 near **Parador Perichi's** (☑787-851-3131; www.hotelperichi.com; Rte 102 Km 14.3; s $85-108, d $90-117; 🅿❄🛜🏊).

Adventures Tourmarine are the outfit to ask about renting kayaks to go out on the laguna, with costs around $20 per hour or $40 for the day. They also run a host of trips around the area on a 33ft lobster boat, including out to Isla Mona...if you can get a permit.

Isla de Ratones ISLAND

Just offshore, the tiny Isla de Ratones has a white sandy beach and is great for snorkeling. All local operators, including Adventures Tourmarine, will run trips here if asked.

🏃 Activities

Adventures Tourmarine BOATING

(☑787-375-2625; Rte 102 Km 14.3; tours $40-100) For trips or tours around the area on a 33ft lobster boat, try this operator. If you've got a big enough group (10 or more people), the owner will arrange trips to Isla Mona (p195), 80km offshore to the west, for approximately $100 per person. There are also snorkeling trips offered around the nearby cliffs ($60 without equipment).

You could also try your hand at deep-sea fishing in the Pasaje de la Mona ($250 per half-day charter) and diving off Isla Desecheo (about $100 per person). There

are kayaks for hire here, too (from $20 per hour).

🛏 Sleeping & Eating

Hotel Costa de Oro Inn HOTEL $

(☑787-851-5010; Rte 102 Km 14.7; r $55-85; 🅿❄) A tiny pool and spotless rooms make this little guesthouse the best value within miles. There are no big luxuries on the property, but you'll be comfortable enough. There's also a small cafeteria on-site where mains come for as little as five bucks.

Parador Joyuda Beach HOTEL $$

(☑787-851-5650; www.joyudabeach.com; Hwy 102 Km 11.7; d $99; 🅿❄🏊) Up the road from the Joyuda Plaza, this hotel is actually *on* a narrow strand of beach. Snorkeling right offshore is OK, as long as the wind stays southerly. The hotel has a restaurant, a swimming pool and 41 unsurprising rooms with those ubiquitous flowery bedspreads, terracotta-tiled floors and fussy grandmotherly feel.

★**Vista Bahía** SEAFOOD $$

(☑787-851-4140; Hwy 102 Km 14.1; mains $10-30; ☺11am-10pm Tue-Sun) The Vista Bahía (View of the Bay) lives up to its name: this restaurant, cheery from the word go, has a smart decking area at the rear whose ocean vistas cannot be bested by any of Playa de Joyuda's other restaurants. Staff try hard to please. Fresh conch with garlicky yucca chunks is a good bet for a main.

Island View SEAFOOD $

(☑787-851-9264; Hwy 102 Km 13.7; dishes $11-30; ☺11am-10pm) Great views of the few small cays that dot the water off the coast and big steaming dishes of seafood specialties, such as rice and crab, have made Playa de Joyuda's Island View (the sophisticated diner's choice) very popular, even if it's a tad staid in its atmosphere. Try the red snapper stuffed with shrimp.

El Gato Negro SEAFOOD $

(☑787-851-2966; Hwy 102 Km 13.6; dishes $15-25; ☺11am-10pm) El Gato Negro is one of Playa de Joyuda's most locally popular joints and chowing down on the seafood here feels somehow like a very authentic Puerto Rican experience, thanks no doubt to the patrons: everyone from gossiping old *abuelas* (grandmothers) to weekending families from San Juan. Stewed conch is a solid choice.

Like most of the restaurants on this foodie strip, El Gato Negro has a balcony with dreamy ocean views.

ℹ Getting There & Away

Playa de Joyuda is 12km south of Mayagüez and 13km north of Boquerón.

When driving around these parts, remember that they can also be negotiated by bicycle (the nearest bike hire is at **Puerto Rico Bike Adventures** near Boquerón).

Boquerón

POP 2000

Boquerón is the wild child of the west-coast fishing towns, a place of colorful characters who wander among wooden-shack restaurants and open-air food stalls. It boasts a well-regarded *balneario* and a marina, but the best diversions lie out of town: either diving or paying a visit to the verdant patchwork of wildlife reserves.

Back in the day (maybe the early '90s) Boquerón was the place to hang hereabouts, but those days are gone. It lacks El Combate's comparatively untouched charms or Rincón's world-class watersports and the overall feel is of a once-hip village surfing on the back of its past reputation.

But it does attract travelers of all types, from wealthy yachters to brightly dressed Rastafarians, having the area's best array of accommodation and a lively nightlife. And the party could yet get more manic, once dust settles on the construction work to complete the town's new *malecón* (waterside promenade).

⊙ Sights

★**Refugio de Vida Silvestre Iris L. Alameda Martínez de Boquerón** FOREST
(Refugio de Aves; ☑ 787-851-4795; Hwy 301 Km 1.1; ☺ 7:30am-2pm) Drive south from Boquerón along Hwy 301 and you will arrive at the main entrance to this reserve at Km 1.1, an extent of beguiling mangrove forest with a visitor center, and well-maintained boardwalk trails. There are routes for mountain bikes, too. The proximity of the mangroves renders the walkways like tunnels through the dense, otherworldly vegetation.

In hunting season, October to December, trails are closed on certain days. The intrepid can plan a hike or bike along trails here all the way to Boquerón through the Bosque Estatal de Boquerón (a separate reserve) if they so choose.

Another portion of Refugio de Vida Silvestre Iris L. Alameda Martínez de Boquerón

lies further east along Hwy 101, around **Laguna Cartagena** (cnr Hwys 101 & 306).

Refugio de Boquerón NATURE RESERVE
(Rte 101 Km 1.1; ☺ 7:30am-4pm) The Refugio de Boquerón is the western outpost of the Bosque Estatal de Boquerón, a 400-acre patch of mangrove wetlands that mostly spreads south of Boquerón town and immediately east of the Balneario Boquerón. This is an excellent area for birdwatching; more than 60 species are commonly sighted, including migratory ducks, ospreys and mangrove canary.

The Refugio de Boquerón is the best and easiest part of the Bosque Estatal de Boquerón to visit, as it's right next to town, the entrance being a little further north along Rte 101 from **Galloway's Bar & Restaurant** (Calle José de Diego; mains $12-24; ☺ noon-11pm).

The **main office** (☑ 787-851-7260, 787-851-7258; Rte 101 Km 1.1, Boquerón; ☺ 7:30am-4pm) can provide information on the *refugio* and has a 700ft walkway leading into the mangroves. Or stop at Km 1.1 just off Rte 101 and start walking along the trail you see there. Insect repellent is a must-carry, as is water, and always watch where you put your feet; tiny crabs scuttle about.

An excellent way to get a different perspective on this sanctuary is to rent a kayak and paddle south across Bahía de Boquerón (Boquerón Bay), where lovely views of the coastal side of the *refugio* open up.

🏖 Beaches

Balneario Boquerón BEACH
(parking $5; 🅿) Fanning out immediately south of Boquerón town, the Balneario Boquerón ranks among the best public beach facilities in Puerto Rico. The 2km-long arc of sand gets insanely busy on high-season weekends, but it's still big enough to carve out a relatively quiet space, and the beach area is backed by coconut palms and ample grassy lawns and showers, changing rooms, toilets and picnic tables.

Playa Buyé BEACH
(Camino Buyé) Playa Buyé is a small palm-fringed beach that's about 5km north of Boquerón off Hwy 307. It's got a distinctly more wild, timeless and paradisaical feel than the manicured Balneario Boquerón.

🏃 Activities

Along Calle José de Diego, there are a number of vendors renting kayaks and other gear to get in the water. This is a great option if you want to explore the mangroves east of town.

Puerto Rico

Adventure Water Sports WATER SPORTS
(☑787-567-4386; Balneario Boquerón; Jet Ski hire per 30 mins $50, kayak hire per hr $20; ◷9am-6pm) Located at the north end of the Balneario Boquerón beach, just across the bridge from the main part of Boquerón, these guys specialize in Jet Ski and kayak trips. It's probably the most adrenaline-packed fun you can have in town. Boat tours along the coast and paddleboard rentals are other options.

Puerto Rico Bike Adventures CYCLING
(☑787-381-4596; www.facebook.com/puertorico bikeadventures; Hwy 301 Km 3; bike hire from $40 per day) 6km southeast of Boquerón, this outlet offers mountain-bike hire, or guided daily mountain bike tours ($60) of the gorgeous coastal scenery hereabouts. The Refugio de Vida Silvestre Iris L. Alameda Martínez de Boquerón is right on the doorstep.

🛌 Sleeping

Blue Ocean Apartments APARTMENT $
(☑787-851-2637; www.blueoceanboqueron.com; cnr Hwy 101 & Barbarosa; apt $70-95; ❋☷) These recently refurbished, central apartments accommodating from two to 10 guests are probably Boquerón's best choice if you factor in the price (low) and the quality of the rooms (quite high). Apartments have neat little kitchens. At the time of writing, only the pool area has wi-fi.

Buyé Beach Resort CABIN $
(☑787-255-0358; Camino Buyé, off Hwy 307 at Km 4.8; cabin from $75; ⓟ❋☷) Located on the popular Playa Buyé (p188) beach north of Boquerón, this clean and simple operation has 16 cinder-block-and-tile cabins on the beach. Each one accommodates three to four people and includes a private bathroom and kitchen. There is a coin laundry here, too. Parking is $3 (refunded if you are a guest).

Centro Vacacional Boquerón CABIN $$
(☑787-851-1900, reservations 787-721-2800; www. facebook.com/centrovacacionalboqueron; Balneario Boquerón; cabin from $65, villa from $119) This excellent, enormous government-operated complex is the best of its kind in Puerto Rico – a sprawling village of basic apartments by the well-groomed Balneario Boquerón (p188) that hold six people and have a bathroom, kitchen, bunk beds and ceiling fans.

ⓘ A NIGHT AT THE BEACH

Camping on Puerto Rico's beaches is illegal, but some of the large, developed facilities at public beaches around the island, including Balneario Boquerón, have government-operated cabañas to rent. These facilities vary in quality – some are little more than cinder-block apartments with a kitchenette and a grill, others are a bit more plush, with balconies and barbecue grills. Still, they make an affordable way to stay on the beach. Here's the catch: since they are mostly for Puerto Rican families, they are poorly marketed to tourists, and guests have to bring their own linen. Contact the Centro Vacacional Boquerón.

They come in two classes – cabins (a basic option with no air-con) and villas (more modern with air-con).

Cofresí Beach Hotel HOTEL $$
(☑787-254-3000; www.cofresibeach.com; 57 Calle Muñoz Rivera; 2-bedroom apt $165; ☷) For families this apartment complex, conveniently located in the town of Boquerón, is a nearly uniform recommendation – each unit is fully equipped with a microwave and TV, and its position in a residential neighborhood is nicely removed from the downtown craziness. There's a limited maid service available by prior arrangement and a view of the bay from the pool.

🍴 Eating & Drinking

The cheapest eats are from the kiosks along Calle José de Diego, where vendors stand proudly beside piles of oysters and clams, which are shucked open, juiced with fresh lemon or hot sauce and slurped down on the spot. *Pinchos* (kebabs with grilled chicken, pork or seafood) are another option. None of it is above $4.

★ Pelican's INTERNATIONAL $
(www.pelicansboqueron.com; Hermogenes Pou 20; mains $10-20; ◷noon-10pm Mon & Wed-Fri, 8am-10pm Sat & Sun) A breath of fresh air in the Boquerón eating scene is this fun-loving, laid-back wooden house, where great pizzas and extraordinary burgers headline a menu also featuring more classically Puerto Rican dishes such as grilled red snapper or *mofongo*. With its turqoise-painted interior

decorated with models of parrots and palm trees, it's a wacky but wonderful place to fill your belly.

Terramar
ITALIAN $

(Cnr Calles José de Diego & Hermogenes Pou; mains $7-20; ⊙ 11am-10pm) A great option in central Boquerón, on the small back road looping off the main drag from next to Los Remos Restaurant & Beach Club. Terramar has the vibe of a cozy Madrid tapas bar and Italianesque fare almost unequaled in western Puerto Rico. Service is slow but the results are impressive. The stand-out dish? Possibly the stuffed jalapeños.

Pika-Pika
MEXICAN $$

(✐ 787-851-2440; 224 Calle Estación; mains $12-25; ⊙ noon-10pm Wed-Sun, 4-10pm Mon; ✐) Although discerning fans of Mexican cuisine might be a bit underwhelmed by the cheese-covered Puerto Rican/Tex-Mex fusions, this high-class cantina located on the road in and out of Boquerón is a place to escape the thumping. Here for donkey's years, it's decked out in dark wood, dimly lit and cool, and patronized by families and groups of friends.

Los Remos Restaurant & Beach Club
BAR

(Calle José de Diego; mains $11-20; ⊙ 8am-midnight Thu-Sun) Los Remos is symptomatic of a place that opens with the best intentions but tries to do everything from breakfast to late night drinks and consequently falls short. Plopped right in the center of the bar strip, it opens up onto the water out back, and the cocktails and nightlife generally can't be bettered in Boquerón.

❶ Getting There & Away

If you're driving from the town of Cabo Rojo or Mayagüez, follow Hwy 100 south to Hwy 101 and turn right (west). Driving from San Germán, it's a straight shot west on Hwy 101, south of Lajas.

El Combate

Remember that saying about first appearances being deceptive? Thus it is with El Combate. Named after a 1759 colonial turf war to control the lucrative salt flats to the south, El Combate (The Battle) is the last village heading south before the Los Morrillos Lighthouse at mainland Puerto Rico's

southern tip. As you skirt it, the community appears nothing more than a sprawl of backyard trailer camping sites and dreary condos. Alight in its tiny center, however, and a different feeling shines through. Here, the dreamy beach village vibe that Boquerón has long since lost lingers yet. Appropriately, you'll find one of western Puerto Rico's best beach bars, Annie's Place, a couple of tawdry guesthouses and a decent hotel, and the gorgeous 3-mile-long strip of sand that affronts the Pasaje de la Mona. This beach is perfect for swimming and is perennially popular with vacationing Puerto Rican families.

◉ Sights

Playa Combate
BEACH

This is the long golden strip of sand heading south from the Annie's Place restaurant at the point where Hwy 3301 hits the sea. Walk a short distance along and you'll invariably have a patch of beach to yourself. Behind the beach are a couple of sizeable lagoons you can walk or bike around.

🛏 Sleeping & Eating

Combate Beach Hotel & Restaurant
HOTEL $$

(✐ 787-254-2358; www.combatebeach.com; Hwy 3301 Km 2.7; r $109-199; P ❋ ☎) A favorite oasis in El Combate, this hotel is right behind the beach about 0.5km from all the development in town. The motel-style rooms are simple but clean, with private bathrooms. There is a nice, quiet pool, from where you can pick up a short trail to the beach, and a surprisingly well-stocked shop.

★ Annie's Place
PUERTO RICAN $

(Hwy 3301 Km 2.9; mains $5-23; ⊙ 10am-9:30pm Mon-Thu, to midnight Fri & Sat) Breezes from the ocean drift into mellow, open-walled Annie's, a bar-restaurant with sensational *empanadillas* (dough stuffed with meat or fish), lobster soup, fish salad and homemade burgers. Overlooking El Combate's long public beach, this has the most convivial atmosphere of the bars hereabouts and gets our vote as one of the best in Puerto Rico's west for dinner or drinks.

❶ Getting There & Away

Arriving by car, El Combate is at the end of Hwy 3301. Go west at the turnoff from Hwy 301. The town is 13km southwest of Boquerón.

Refugio Nacional Cabo Rojo

Rolling hills tumble into mangroves and crystalline salt pans. Rust-red limestone cliffs fall precipitously away into the ocean or drop to beaches reckoned by many to be the epitome of Caribbean paradise. Quiet lanes and well-marked trails twist and turn tempting cyclists and hikers into blissfully car-free exploration, and interpretation centers leave travelers insightfully informed about what they're seeing. This is the Refugio Nacional Cabo Rojo, the southernmost extent of Puerto Rico, crowned by its iconic Los Morillos Lighthouse and the unsurpassed highlight of any trip to the island's southwest.

◉ Sights & Activities

Centro de Visitantes de Pesca y Vida Silvestre de Cabo Rojo   NATURE RESERVE
(Refugio Nacional Cabo Rojo; ☑ 787-851-7258; Hwy 301 Km 5.1; ⊙ 8:30am-4:30pm) The turnoff to this refuge is about 1km north of the Hwy 301 turnoff to El Combate. Its visitors center contains displays on local wildlife and wildlife-management techniques. Outdoors you will find birdwatching trails among the ruins of an old farmstead in the Valle de Lajas (Lajas Valley). The area around the plains and shores of Cabo Rojo is a major winter ground for migratory ducks, herons and songbirds, and over 130 bird species have been sighted here.

You can arrange guided hikes through the refuge at the Centro Interpretativos Las Salinas de Cabo Rojo.

Corozo Salt Flats   NATURE RESERVE
(Hwy 301) FREE Vast salt flats surround the rocky, dramatic narrow peninsula which heralds your approach to the southwestern tip of Puerto Rico. These are truly captivating, although not without a whiff of desolation. As you head south along the dirt road toward the Los Morillos Lighthouse, you'll pass pools of evaporating brine and mounds of salt waiting to be shipped to market.

This can be a bizarre, picturesque and adventurous place to explore; a place where scrub forest gives way to an elevated headland surrounded by steep limestone cliffs and amazing views of the ocean.

The best place to get a handle on this salty domain is the Centro Interpretativo Las Salinas de Cabo Rojo.

There is also a small network of hiking and mountain-biking trails here (though no place to rent a bike; your nearest option is Puerto Rico Bike Adventures (p189) near Boquerón). These lead to a stretch of very long beach on the island's west side. This is not perfect sand – much of it is dotted with mangrove forest – but it is excellent for private swimming.

Centro Interpretativo Las Salinas de Cabo Rojo   NATURE CENTER
(☑ 787-851-2999; Hwy 301 Km 11; ⊙ 8:30am-4:30pm Thu-Sat, 9:30am-5:30pm Sun) A small center located along Hwy 301 as it approaches Los Morillos Lighthouse explains the geology and ecology of the salt pans of the Corozo Salt Flats, which dominate the scenery across Refugio Nacional Cabo Rojo. It is staffed by knowledgeable, ecosensitive guides who give thorough explanations of local flora and fauna, in the context of, ahem, salt. Opposite is a three-story wooden lookout tower that offers a bird's-eye view of the salt pans, a major bird migratory corridor.

SALT WARS

The saltpans that you'll see as you head out towards the Los Morillos Lighthouse (p192) at the wave-bashed tip of Refugio Nacional Cabo Rojo are part of the Corozo Salt Flats, and of a legacy many centuries old. Humans have been gathering salt on Cabo Rojo since AD 700. When the Spanish arrived they were quick to see the potential of the evaporation pools used by the Taíno people to make salt and they expanded the business. Salt production became such a lucrative force in the area that locals fought over it. The very name of the town on the edge of this wilderness, El Combate (aka The Battle) references a war between El Combate folks and factions from the nearby town of Lajas over control of the salt flats. Many of those heralding from El Combate may still refer to themselves as the *mata con hacha* (those that kill with axes) whilst Lajas citizens, who purportedly responded to the axes with stones, are often known as the *tira piedras* (stone throwers).

Los Morrillos Lighthouse   LIGHTHOUSE
(Hwy 301; ◷10am-6pm Wed-Sun, with seasonal variations) **FREE** From this smartly remodeled lighthouse at the bone-rattling end of Hwy 301, there's not much further you can go: you're as south as it gets in Puerto Rico. The lighthouse stands sentinel on the headland of Punta Jagüey, with some dramatic cliff formations right beyond the outer walls. An observation deck overlooks the surreal turquoise of the waters lapping Playa Santa and the expanse of the Caribbean behind.

If a volunteer is on hand at the lighthouse, they might offer a casual history of the Refugio Nacional Cabo Rojo area (largely revolving around the salt panned nearby).

The final stretch of unmetalled road is not passable for cars but a 10-minute walk from the parking lot will have you at the door.

★**Playa Santa**   BEACH
(Refugio Nacional Cabo Rojo) From the same parking space as that of Los Morrillos Lighthouse (or from another further on down the track bending left from the lighthouse approach track), you can follow the trails out to an immaculate crescent beach, where a protected bay makes excellent swimming for both humans and manatees. The beach here is touted as one of western Puerto Rico's best (and given greater accolades by some): one thing it most certainly has is a welcome feeling of isolation.

🛏 Sleeping & Eating

Grand Bahía Ocean View Hotel   RESORT $$
(☎787-254-1212; www.grandbahiaoceanviewhotel.com; Hwy 301 Km 11.5; d incl breakfast $138-165; P☀@🛜🏊) As if the location wasn't enough – rust-red cliffs, salt flats and an adjacent wildlife refuge – the rooms in this pretty, palm-shaded hotel have balconies, sleigh beds and tropical flowers. The serene grounds are immaculate too – drape-covered sun loungers and canopy beds look over an undisturbed stretch of ocean and an infinity pool framing some of the island's most spectacular sunsets.

❶ Getting There & Away

Whilst the main approach to the peninsula on which the lighthouse sits is via Hwy 301 from Hwy 100, there is a more adventurous option. For a lonely drive through undeveloped coastal plains or a cycling adventure, approach from La Parguera via Hwy 304, Hwy 305 and Hwy 303.

Then follow Hwy 301 south until it turns to dirt and stops.

The nearest towns to Refugio Nacional Cabo Rojo are El Combate (8km north) and Boquerón (15km north).

San Germán

POP 33,000

Puerto Rico's second-oldest city (after San Juan), San Germán is also one of its best preserved. For those interested in colonial Creole architecture, this little town can only be bested by Ponce and Old San Juan.

Yet despite its lavish architectural heritage and lofty listing on the National Register of Historic Places, San Germán is largely ignored (wrongly) by its modern inhabitants and by tourists. As a result, the classic four-square-block colonial center – laid out in an unusual irregular pattern – is a veritable ghost town after dark. The city's one downtown hotel sports cobwebs and few of the numerous historic buildings are open for public viewing.

But there are a clutch of excellent restaurants and, fortuitously, San Germán's semi-abandonment lends it an air of authenticity. And for history buffs, its narrow streets are far more absorbing to stroll around than those of any other town or city west of Ponce.

History

Founded in 1511 near present-day Mayagüez on the orders of Juan Ponce de León, the original coastal settlement was moved twice in its early life to escape the unwelcome attention of plundering French corsairs. The current town, which lies about 10 miles inland from the Cabo Rojo coast, was established in 1573 and once administered a municipality that encompassed the whole western half of the island. Downsizing itself over the ensuing four centuries, contemporary San Germán (named for Germaine de Foix, the second wife of Spain's King Ferdinand) is far more unassuming than the colonial capital of yore, although the historical buildings – some of which date from the 17th century – retain a quiet dignity.

◉ Sights

★Iglesia de Porta Coeli   CHURCH
(Heaven's Gate; Plaza Santo Domingo; ◷8-11:45am & 1-4:15pm Wed-Sun) This small, squat building might not look like much, but it is

San Germán

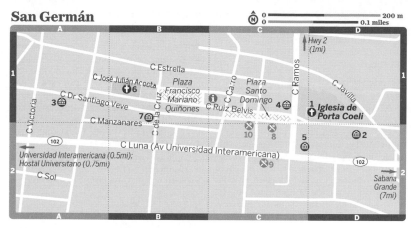

San Germán

◎ Top Sights
1 Iglesia de Porta Coeli............................D1

◎ Sights
2 Casa Acosta y Flores...........................D2
3 Casa de Lola Rodríguez de Tió............A1
4 Casa Morales.......................................C1
5 Casa Perichi...C2
6 Catedral de San Germán de
  Auxerre...B1
Iglesia de Porta Coeli
  Museum.......................................(see 1)
7 Museo de la Historia de San
  Germán...B1

⊗ Eating
8 De Lirious...C2
9 Ponto Frio..C2
10 Tapas Café..C2

actually one of the oldest surviving ecclesial buildings in the Americas. Originally constructed between 1606 and 1607 on the orders of Queen Isabella of Spain, it served as the chapel for a Dominican monastery that stood on this site until the 1860s. Atop a long, steep flight of steps overlooking Plaza Santo Domingo, the current structure dates from 1692.

The Porta Coeli has an interior with ausubo pillars and roof beams, and a ceiling made from palm wood, which is typical of construction in Puerto Rico during the 17th and 18th centuries. Inside, a small **museum** (admission adult/child $3/1) displays statues of the black Virgin of Montserrat, folksy carvings of Christ imported from the

early days of San Juan, choral books dating back 300 years and other curios.

**Catedral de San
Germán de Auxerre**   CHURCH
(Plaza Francisco Mariano Quiñones; ☺8-11:30am & 1-3pm Mon-Fri, 8-11am Sat) San Germán's cathedral, at the top (west) end of town is named for the town's patron saint and is noticeably grander than the diminutive Iglesia de Porta Coeli – its ecclesiastical counterpart at the opposite end of the town centre. Facing Plaza Francisco Mariano Quiñones, it dates back to 1739, but major restorations and expansions over the years (especially in the 19th century) have created a mélange of architectural styles, including colonial, neoclassical and baroque elements.

**Museo de la Historia
de San Germán**   MUSEUM
(www.mhisapr.org; cnr Dr Santiago Veve & De La Cruz; ☺10:30am-3:30pm Wed-Sun) **FREE** This salmon-hued building is one of the few, in San Germán where you can enter, look around and fully experience the local history. Here is a dedicated museum that attempts to explain the town's colorful past all in one location. Talks and events are regularly put on. Entry is free, but donations are accepted.

Universidad Interamericana   UNIVERSITY
(Luna) Founded in 1912, this university is now the largest private facility of its kind in the western hemisphere. The 267-acre campus just west of San Germán is probably the most attractive college setting in

Puerto Rico and it draws about 6000 students from all corners of the globe. There are branch campuses in San Juan, Arecibo, Barranquitas, Bayamón, Fajardo, Guayama and Ponce.

Historic Homes

Casa de Lola Rodríguez de Tió   MUSEUM
(☑787-892-3500; 13 Dr Santiago Veve) Built in 1843 in a neoclassical Creole style and said to be an excellent example of local 19th-century domestic architecture, this house is reputedly San Germán's most continually occupied residence. Its most famous resident was a 19th-century poet and patriot named Lola Rodríguez de Tió, who was exiled in the 1860s for her revolutionary activities. Lola's mother was a descendant of Ponce de León. The house is supposed to act as a museum, but is often closed. Phone ahead.

Casa Perichi   HISTORIC BUILDING
(94 Luna) Situated on the San Germán main drag, this 1920s estate has been on the National Register of Historic Places since 1986. Its eclectic architectural style featuring wraparound balconies and decorative wood trim has been called 'Puerto Rican ornamental artisan.'

Casa Morales   HISTORIC BUILDING
(38 Ramos) This Victorian-era house in San Germán was built soon after the American occupation in 1898. With its gables, porches and roof turrets, it is redolent of a Queen Anne–style structure from the plush neighborhood of a US mainland city. It's not possible to visit inside, but it makes for great pictures outside.

Casa Acosta y Flores   HISTORIC BUILDING
(70 Dr Santiago Veve) Built in 1917 in a crisscross of styles, this house to the east of San Germán's architecturally rich center exhibits elements of Creole, Victorian and art-nouveau architecture and looks like a wedding cake. It's somewhere to look at, not in.

🛏 Sleeping & Eating

Hostal Universitario   ACCOMMODATION SERVICES $
(☑787-264-2350, 787-264-1912; Luna, Universidad Interamericana; r $60-80) Adequate, clean accommodations at the Universidad Interamericana (p193) in San Germán. They're a step up from student digs and all rooms have private bathrooms. The campus on which they are located makes for very pleasant surroundings. Some rooms even have small kitchenettes.

★Tapas Café   SPANISH $
(48 Dr Santiago Veve; tapas $3-14; ⊙5-10pm Wed-Fri, 11am-10pm Sat & Sun) The food and atmosphere are both great at this cafe, which would effortlessly fit in among the Triana district of Seville. Flamenco drifts under the high ceilings, and bullfighting paraphernalia adorns the walls, while the kitchen turns out wondrous Spanish-influenced fare like *albondigas* (meatballs), *queso manchego* (Manchego cheese), *tortilla española* (Spanish omelet) and *jamon serrano* (cured Spanish ham).

Ponto Frio   CAFE $
(cnr Luna & Alfonso XII; sandwiches & salads $5-12; ⊙7am-8pm Mon-Fri, 9am-10pm Sat, 9am-8pm Sun) What do you do for refreshment in San Germán with the limited hours of the restaurants? The answer is that you gravitate here, to this chirpy modern cafe down on Luna, open throughout the day and serving healthy sandwiches and wraps, including gluten-free options, salads and pizzas. But the highlight are the açai bowls piled high with exotic fruits.

De Lirious   INTERNATIONAL $$
(55 Dr Santiago Veve; mains $10-30; ⊙5-10pm Wed-Fri, 1-11pm Sat, noon-8pm Sun) Given its refined ambience, delicious and originally prepared food, and consistent opening, this is one of San Germán's best choices for a meal. They kick you off with an array of delicious soups, such as Argentine sausage and plantain, then graduate you to enticing mains, such as the veal cutlets stuffed with apricots and cheese then drenched in cilantro sauce.

When the sun shines, there's a serene outside courtyard lending itself well to a glass of white wine. Like everywhere in town, it's often deserted.

ℹ Information

San Germán Tourism Office (☑787-892-3790; Plaza Francisco Mariano Quiñones, Viejo Alcaldía; ⊙8am-4pm Mon-Fri) has a spectacular location in the Vieja Alcaldía, but its opening hours are quite erratic.

ℹ Getting There & Away

San Germán lies just south of the Hwy 2 expressway, although signage from this road is not amazing. Mayagüez is 25km northwest on this road and Ponce is 60km east; if you are driving here from the west coast (Boquerón, Playa Joyuda), follow Hwy 102 from the town of Cabo Rojo.

Heading east from town, it's not very far at all (19km) to **Bosque Estatal de Susúa** (p162) via Hwy 2 and Rte 368.

Isla Mona

Few wilderness adventures in the Caribbean can compare with a trip to Isla Mona, a wild, deserted speck in the ocean some 80km to the west of the main island. And although few people ever visit, the 14,000-acre island looms large in the imagination. It's a place where the dramatic beauty of limestone caves and turquoise water coexists with the dangers of a rugged, isolated environment. Then there's the island's long, romantic history, told in Taíno petroglyphs and swashbuckling stories about sunken galleons, treasures of gold and skeletons of 18th-century pirates.

A nature reserve since 1919 and uninhabited for over 50 years, Mona is very difficult to visit. If you are considering a trip here, know it can take about four months of planning to secure permits and transportation.

The rangers and police detachment (at Playa Sardinera) can occasionally provide basic visitor assistance: beyond that, you are on your own.

History

Mona was first settled about 1000 years ago as pre-Columbian peoples migrated north through the Caribbean archipelago. Petroglyphs in some caves and the subtle ruins of *bateyes* (Taíno ball courts) are the chief remnants of the indigenous presence. Columbus stopped here on September 24, 1494 (at the end of his second New World voyage) and remained several days to provision for the long trip back to Spain. When the Spaniards returned in 1508, with an expedition led by Juan Ponce de León, Mona had become a sanctuary for Taíno people escaping slavery.

The Spanish eventually claimed the island to guard the ship traffic to and from the gold coast of the Americas, but abandoned it after two decades when they couldn't afford it. Uninhabited and defenseless, Mona was a haven for pirates by the late 1500s, when French corsairs used it as staging ground for their attacks on the Spanish colony at San Germán.

During the next 300 years, Mona became the refuge of a host of privateers, including Sirs Walter Raleigh and Francis Drake, John Hawkins, William Kidd and the Puerto Rican buccaneer Roberto Cofresí.

In the early 20th century it was mined for bat guano (exceptional agricultural fertilizer!) and it made headlines when a German submarine fired on the island, thinking it was a post for the Allies, in the early 1940s.

Following Civilian Conservation Corps (CCC) activities on the island, the comings and goings of treasure hunters, WWII and a scam to turn Mona into an airbase, the government of Puerto Rico slowly began to take seriously its duty to protect the island as a nature preserve, and eventually prohibited development. Finally, after almost a millennium of human interference, Mona returned to her wild state.

ISLA MONA WILDLIFE

Although the dry, semitropical climate might suggest an area with little variety in vegetation, Mona claims about 600 species of plants and 50 species of trees. Four of the plant species are endemic, unknown to the rest of the world. If you are exploring here, wear protective clothing. Mona has four types of venomous trees and bushes: indio, papayo, manzanillo and carrasco. Almost 3000 acres of the island consist of cactus thickets, while 11,000 acres are in scrub forest.

The biggest stars of the island's wildlife menagerie are the giant rock iguanas, *Cyclura stejnegeri* (similar to the iguanas at Anagada in the British Virgin Islands and Allan's Cays in the Bahamas), ferocious little beasts with sharp teeth and claws who charge when threatened.

Between May and October, Isla Mona's beaches are important nesting grounds for a number of species of marine turtle, including the chronically endangered Carey and Hawksbill turtles.

⚡ Activities

Isla Mona is almost a perfect oval, measuring about 11km from east to west and 6.5km from north to south. Most of the island's coastline is made up of rough, rocky cliffs, especially along the north side. The south side, meanwhile, has a number of narrow beaches that fringe the highlands. The most approachable of these beaches is **Playa Sardinera** (Isla Mona), where you will find toilets, showers and the concrete living quarters of the rangers and police detachment.

The island's terrain consists of a broad rim of coastal plain rising gently to a central mesa. Because the land is flat and overgrown, it is difficult to find landmarks on the horizon. More than a few people have gotten lost here – including the pirate William Kidd and a boy scout who died from dehydration and exhaustion in 2001. The basic photocopied map you get from the DRNA in San Juan is useless; the US Geological Survey (USGS), an agency of the US Department of the Interior, publishes a better map.

You will find spectacular 150ft visibility (or better) for diving in the waters around the island. There are excellent barrier and fringe-reef dives filled with lagoons and ruts on the south side of the island. Divers particularly enjoy the sharp drop-off along one reef that creates an overhanging wall; some fascinating creatures come to drift in its cool shadow.

Aside from diving, the only other activity is geeking out on the flora and the fauna.

❶ Getting There & Away

The only way to get to Isla Mona is by boat and it's almost impossible unless you are part of an organized trip. It is also extremely expensive; about $100 per person for minimum group sizes of 10 people (and, therefore, much more if you can persuade a captain to go with fewer passengers). If you are prone to seasickness, beware that the Pasaje de la Mona makes for a rough crossing.

One outfit with a proven track record in taking tourists out to the island – and offering water-based activities around its shores – is **Adventures Tourmarine** (p187). The company, based in Playa de Joyuda, only runs trips with a minimum of 10 passengers for around $100 per person. You could, of course, offer more money per person if you're eager to get out to Isla Mona but only have a small group.

North Coast

POP 650,000

Includes ➡

Dorado 199
Arecibo 201
Around Arecibo 203
Isabela & Around 207
Aguadilla 210

Best Places to Eat

➡ Mi Casa (p201)

➡ Eclipse (p210)

➡ TBC (p211)

➡ Blue Fin Food Truck (p212)

Best Places to Sleep

➡ Ritz-Carlton Reserve Dorado Beach (p200)

➡ TJ Ranch (p206)

➡ Villa Tropical (p208)

Why Go?

Veering from a manicured coast of plush golf resorts and posh surf spots, this region rears up into the less-visited vine-tangled crags of karst country, where landscapes seem positively prehistoric with yawning cave systems, *mogotes* (vegetated, steep-sided hillocks) and undulating spreads of forest.

However renowned the teeing in the east (Dorado) and the paddleboarding in the west (Isabela), don't make the mistake of forgoing what lies in-between.

The sights here have neither the untouched exotic character of El Yunque nor quite the rustic allure of the Central Mountains, but the north secretes a glut of DIY adventures, plus its own generous share of world-class diversions. Goggle at the world's largest radio telescope, climb one of its tallest statues, descend inside some of its largest caverns or simply strike out on forest trail to a hidden swimming hole – and still, should you wish, make your dinner reservation in San Juan.

When to Go

Outside of the island's rainy months (late summer to early fall), the north coast is generally sunny.

Big Atlantic storms can barrel in out of nowhere to whip the waves into white-capped frenzy. The arrival of low-pressure systems come late fall starts the big waves a-rolling and October's international surf tournament in Isabella starts drawing the surfers as surely as wasps to nectar.

Inland, the humidity increases, but on the shore the 80°F temperatures aren't at all oppressive. As there's only a difference of a few degrees between the coldest month, January, and the warmest, August, the region offers consistently sunny, breezy days year-round.

North Coast Highlights

❶ Birth of the New World Statue (p202) Gawking at the gargantuan statue that put Arecibo on the tourist map.

❷ Observatorio de Arecibo (p203) Immersing yourself in the heavens with an ascent to the world's largest radio telescope.

❸ Batey Zipline Adventures (p206) Swooping, paddling or galloping through the forests and rivers of karst country with an adventure outfit.

❹ Royal Isabela (p208) Getting into the swing of things with a round on one of the north coast's world-class golf courses.

❺ Playa Jobos (p207) Surfing the storied waves at this wonderfully dramatic beach.

❻ Playa Survival (p207) Walking a stretch of sandy north coast coastline along to this divinely deserted strip.

❼ TBC (p211) Sampling astonishing flavors to kickstart your day in one of Hwy 110's varied eateries.

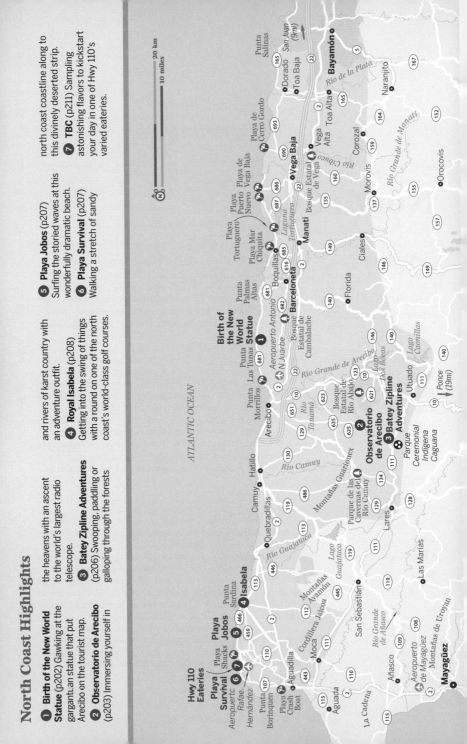

History

The north coast contains one of the island's largest and oldest Native American ceremonial sites near Utuado, an archaeological find offering dramatic proof that a well-organized Taíno culture thrived on the island before the arrival of the Spanish. Arecibo, the third-oldest city on the island, has made recent efforts to better showcase its own role in the island's history, and a Ruta del Taíno (Taíno route) now begins here at the Cueva del Indio, another sacred indigenous spot.

Glimpses into the island's 19th-century glory days can be had at the many old coffee haciendas in this neck of the woods such as Palacete Los Moreau near Isabela. The 20th century saw a burgeoning of San Juan's suburbs westward into satellite towns such as Vega Alta and Manatí. At the same time a concerted effort has been made to protect karst country through tree-planting projects and the formation of half a dozen forest reserves in the 1940s.

In recent decades, the region has endeavored to boost its economy through tourism. In 1955, Robert Trent Jones began designing the first of the north coast's many internationally renowned golf courses at Dorado, and the controversial arrival in 2016 of the tallest statue in North America, the 360ft Birth of the New World (p202) near Arecibo, sparked a concerted effort to regenerate the city.

❶ Getting There & Away

Aguadilla's **international airport** (Av Engineer Orlando Alárcon) is widely used by vacationers heading for the west coast beaches and scientists keen to study the stars at the Observatorio de Arecibo.

Hwy 22 and its continuation after Arecibo, Hwy 2, are the main arteries running the length of the region from San Juan to Aguadilla. Travel along the coast itself is therefore swift, if often congested, but up in the hills south of Arecibo karst country is a different story: rutted, twisting lanes and journeys of mere kilometers that can seem like hours.

Renting a car is easily the best option for getting around, although the Isabela region is also good for cycling.

Dorado

POP 12,000

For those who love golf, Dorado is pure gold, legendary for its exceptional courses. It boasts five championship-standard golf courses that are an international draw. If your interest in the fairways temporarily wanes, several stunning local beaches offer a welcome break from the clubhouse banter. If you're only interested in beaches, bypass Dorado for locales further west.

Away from the resorts, which include one of Puerto Rico's best, Ritz-Carlton Reserve Dorado Beach, a handful of really decent restaurants are hidden in this community's haphazard residential sprawl. The area's beaches are decent too, with a public beach in town and an even prettier free stretch of sand a few miles to the west at Playa de Cerro Gordo.

El Dorado's urban core is very spread out, and the route between PR 22 and the coast is almost entirely developed. Rte 165 turns into Calle Méndez Vigo, the town's central road.

History

Founded in 1842, Dorado first became a resort town in the early 1900s when the Rockefeller family started building a Caribbean Shangri-la. The venture went public in 1958 when Laurance Rockefeller, the well-known philanthropist and conservationist, opened up the region's first hotel, the Dorado Beach, a pioneering eco-resort where no building was taller than the surrounding palm trees. Although there have been some formidable resorts here over the years, many golfers today opt for time-shares and condo rentals. This has somewhat sapped the hotel scene of its once-ritzy image, although one of Puerto Rico's best big resorts, the Ritz-Carlton Reserve Dorado Beach (p200), is here.

◉ Sights

Dorado has a brace of small museums, neither of which is too remarkable, but a decent breather between golf rounds. The **Museo de Arte e Historia de Dorado** (306 Méndez Vigo, cnr San Francisco; ☺8am-4pm Mon-Fri, 9am-2pm Sat) **FREE** gives you the rundown on local history and archaeology and the **Museo y Centro Cultural Casa del Rey** (292 Méndez Vigo; ☺8am-4pm Mon-Fri) **FREE** is an old Spanish garrison displaying antique furniture. Admissions are free.

🏊 Beaches

★ **Playa de Cerro Gordo**   BEACH
(Hwy 690; parking $4; P) **FREE** Lying at the end of Hwy 690, this charming palm-dotted expanse of sand has had several million dollars

pumped into the expansion of its tourist facilities by the government. Restrooms, showers, fire pits and the like now complement the beach, but the place is nevertheless often deserted. Camping is possible here, and several hiking trails and a mountain bike route lead off from the eastern end of the beach.

Balneario el Ojo del Buey BEACH
(Calle 13; ⊙24hr; ℙ) FREE Calle 13 on the eastern side of Dorado terminates in a tan-colored stretch of tree-backed sand, and is freer from beach-goers than **Balneario Manuel Morales** (Rte 697; parking $4; ⊙8:30am-5pm Wed-Sun; ℙ) FREE to the west. The most interesting thing here, however, is the eroded rock formation of Ojo del Buey (Eye of the Bull), resembling a huge cow's head glaring out over the headland.

🏃 Activities

With expertly groomed holes, impeccably maintained greens and gentle Atlantic breezes, Dorado has the best golf courses in the Caribbean, period. There are five 18-hole courses here and all remain open despite the changes to the hotel that used to administrate them.

Dorado Beach Club GOLF
(Plantation Club; ☑787-626-1001; https://tpc.com/doradobeach; 500 Plantation Dr; ⊙7am-6pm) Four of the most famous courses at Dorado are now under the umbrella of the Dorado Beach Club, an upscale vacation facility housed partially in a former Hyatt. The famed **East Course** (☑787-626-1001; https://tpc.com/doradobeach; 100 Dorado Beach Dr; fees from $63) is the green jewel – Jack Nicklaus ranked its 540yd 4th hole, a double dogleg with a pair of ponds and amazing views, among the world's best. It's also listed among the planet's finest golf courses by *Golf Digest*.

Next door lies the equally famous 6975yd **West Course** (☑787-626-1001; https://tpc.com/doradobeach; 100 Dorado Beach Dr; fees from $63; ⊙7am-6pm), while nearer to the Dorado Beach Club clubhouse, known as the Plantation Club, you'll find the **Pineapple Course** (https://tpc.com/doradobeach; 500 Plantation Dr; fees from $63; ⊙7am-6pm) and **Sugarcane Course** (☑787-626-1001; https://tpc.com/doradobeach; 500 Plantation Dr; fees from $63), usually the most reasonably priced to play. Booking tee time at any of these can be done through the **Golf Pro Shop** (☑787-626-1001; https://tpc.com/doradobeach; 500

Plantation Dr; ⊙7am-6pm) at the Plantation Club or through its website.

Dorado del Mar GOLF
(☑787-796-3070; http://doradodelmargc.com; 200 Dorado del Mar Blvd; club rental $45, fees $100-125; ⊙7:30am-5pm) Dorado's fifth and newest course is the Chi Chi Rodríguez–designed Dorado El Mar at the Embassy Suites.

Goodwinds KITESURFING
(☑787-233-7862; www.kitegoodwinds.com; 100 Dorado Beach Dr; kitesurfing course $450) Goodwinds has established itself as one of the best kitesurfing outfits in Puerto Rico, and their full course familiarizes you with every aspect of the sport. Surfing lessons from beginner to advanced levels are also on offer.

🛏 Sleeping

Two huge resorts dominate the accommodation scene. If your budget doesn't stretch to these, your options come tumbling down to a couple of sketchy apartments and an often deserted **campground** (☑787-883-2515; campsites $13; ⊙beach 8am-6pm) near Playa de Cerro Gordo. Alternatively, stay in San Juan and come here for the day.

Embassy Suites by Hilton Dorado del Mar Beach Resort RESORT $$
(☑787-796-6125; http://embassysuites3.hilton.com; 201 Dorado del Mar Blvd; r incl breakfast $160; ℙ❄@🛜☀) Close to town amid a phalanx of gated communities, the Embassy Suites has a Chi Chi Rodríguez–designed golf course, business center, gym, tennis courts and specialty restaurants.

The open-plan lobby is a fountain-filled state-of-the-art extravaganza where smooth-talking salespeople in Hawaiian shirts leap from behind pillars and try to sell you time-shares. If you can survive this relatively innocuous form of initiation, you could be in for a good time.

⭐**Ritz-Carlton Reserve Dorado Beach** RESORT $$$
(☑787-626-1100; www.ritzcarlton.com; 100 Dorado Beach Dr; r $1100-4700; ℙ❄🛜☀) There's some wealthy types coming to Dorado, clearly, because the dreamy 1000-sq-ft-average Ocean Reserve rooms, with walk-in wardrobes and private balconies, are the modest accommodation option at this, Puerto Rico's most lavish place to stay. The hotel opened its doors in December 2012 as one of only a handful of Ritz-Carlton Reserve properties worldwide.

There are many more spacious apartments ('residences') offering anything from one to five rooms, graduating up to the pièce de résistance – an old plantation hacienda, converted into a sumptuous private villa with its own infinity pool.

Among several restaurants here, the stand-out is **Mi Casa** (tapas $5-15, mains $29-52; ⊘6-10pm Tue-Sat; 🕸).

✖ Eating

Dorado's guests mostly stay in time-shares and eat at the American fast-food restaurants lining the main roads, or inside the golf resorts. If you're here to golf and have a taste for something more adventurous, try the area by the public beach, where open-air snack bars sell lots of deep-fried delights and cold beer.

★**El Ladrillo**   SEAFOOD **$$**
(www.elladrillorest.com; 334 Méndez Vigo; dishes $15-35; ⊘5-10pm Tue-Thu, noon-11pm Fri & Sat, noon-10pm Sun; 🕸) El Ladrillo has been a culinary anchor of downtown Dorado for decades. It exudes old-world charm, with dark wood, exposed brick and thick steaks. Naturally, it serves seafood as well – everything from octopus salad to lobster *asopao* (an island specialty, a delicious thick stew). It also functions as a mini-art gallery; the walls are crowded with colorful local paintings.

Villa Dorada d'Alberto
Seafood Restaurant   SEAFOOD **$$**
(☑787-278-1715; Urb Costa de Oro, Calle E No 99; dishes $12-30; ⊘11am-9pm Tue-Thu & Sun, to 11pm Fri & Sat) With waiters in black ties and linen napkins, this classy joint serves seafood platters to a soundtrack of schmaltzy elevator music. On the weekends it's a scene as tables of locals buzz with date night, and it remains one of the only places around that draw vacationers from their all-inclusive slumber.

❶ Getting There & Away

Dorado lies 7km north of Hwy 22 and 30km west of San Juan.

Arecibo

POP 94,000

As you approach Arecibo in the crawl of traffic, it's hard to imagine that this sprawling municipality of nearly 100,000 people is Puerto Rico's third-oldest city. Founded

❶ BEWARE HIGHWAY TOLLS

If you're making the day trip across the north coast, don't forget to bring enough change for the tolls...in cash! There are five tolls along Hwy 22 between San Juan and Hatillo, each charging between $1.50 and $3, depending on which way you are headed. Staffed tolls have almost been phased out, meaning you'll need exact change as a rule. If you get caught without cash, you'll have to pull over, complete a pile of paperwork and find another toll booth to pay later a doubly unpleasant detour. Fines for non-payment at tolls can run to over $100 per violation.

The best option if you're hiring a car to travel around Puerto Rico for more than a few days is to pay your rental company the $10-odd one-off charge to activate the AutoExpreso tag, which means you can cruise straight through the automatic lane in tolls island-wide without stopping and frantically rummaging for small change.

in 1556, the original town was named after an esteemed *cacique* (Taíno chief). The city is endeavoring to restore its erstwhile glory days, with good new restaurants, a pleasant central plaza and a restored *malecón* (seaside promenade).

The major attraction outside of town, the colossal Birth of the New World monument, represents the explorer Christopher Columbus sailing for the Americas: it is one of the planet's tallest statues, around which a major adventure park is being planned. South of Arecibo rises a tract of forested karst country concealing more spectacular sights, including the world's largest radio telescope, the Observatorio de Arecibo.

Just west of Arecibo at Hatillo, the popular Hatillo Mask Festival in late December is one of Puerto Rico's most symbolic ceremonies.

◉ Sights & Activities

While central Arecibo has been spruced up, Hwy 681, heading east from Arecibo out to the Birth of the New World statue, is where most of the appeal for tourists awaits. Here, sandy beaches spill out along a coast dotted with some great restaurants more than 10km to the statue and beyond.

WORTH A TRIP

PLAYA MAR CHIQUITA

An anomaly among Puerto Rican beaches, Playa Mar Chiquita isn't alongside a main thoroughfare, has no long strand and isn't good for swimming or surfing. Still, the pure drama of this place makes it a favorite. Two rearing coral formations protect a small, shallow cove and tidal pools from the rage of the Atlantic, which sprays foam in unpredictable bursts. It's no undiscovered gem, however, and crowds do descend to knock back icy beer and to snack at the food stands.

There's a barely visible sign to the beach off Hwy 685, about 3km north of Manatí and just beyond the entrance to the town of Boquillas. If you miss the sign, go north on Hwy 648 (about 1.5km east of Boquillas). This road takes you over a steep hill to the beach.

Museo de Arte e Historia MUSEUM
(cnr Iglesias & Julian Sanchez; ⊘8am-4:30pm Mon-Fri, to noon Sat & Sun) FREE This well-refurbished colonial-era building displays modern art and a potted history of two of Arecibo's most famous products: rum and the playwright René Marqués.

★**Birth of the New World Statue** STATUE
(Estatua de Cristóbal Colón; www.terravistaparkland. com; Km 9.5, Hwy 681) Undeniably Puerto Rico's biggest, most bizarre new attraction, the 362ft (110m) likeness of Christopher Columbus (Cristóbal Colón) navigating towards the New World is the work of Russian sculptor Zurab Tsereteli and is the linchpin of the north coast's flashy new tourist development.

The statue, the tallest in North America and Puerto Rico's highest structure, stands astride a green rise overlooking an alluring expanse of beaches and mangroves: a wild area poised to become the TerraVista Park, a future adventure complex in which the statue will take centre stage. By 2020, there should be new hotels, restaurants, helicopter rides and 'mangrove adventure' activities such as kayaking and ziplining in this spot.

Officially opened in 2017, the statue is the first (and currently only) part of this megaproject. You can ascend to a viewing gallery about halfway up and imagine the crowds-to-be descending on this peaceful place.

The irony surrounding the statue is as much a talking point as the structure itself. First, that it should be raised within sight of an important ceremonial site for the Taíno whose culture was decimated following the explorer's arrival on these shores, and second that it should be raised at all with construction costs of millions of dollars to a heavily debt-saddled island. Many are also concerned about the statue's environmental impact in an ecologically sensitive area.

Love it or hate it, the statue exhibits some splendid workmanship and has launched a revival of this entire stretch of coast.

Cueva del Indio CAVE
(Km 8, Hwy 681; admission $5; ⊘9am-5pm; P) A stroll through coastal scrub brings you to cliffs where impressive formations have been chiselled and hollowed out by the elements. You can descend through a hole in the roof of one of the caves into a series of sea-bashed chambers, in one of which is a Taíno petroglyph. The site was certainly of extreme importance to the Taíno people.

Cueva del Indio is part of the area's future tourism megaproject, TerraVista Parkland, a massive adventure park, but for now it remains relatively tranquil.

**Faro y Parque
Histórico de Arecibo** AMUSEMENT PARK
(⊘787-880-7540; Rte 655; adult/child $12/10; ⊘9am-6pm Mon-Fri, 10am-7pm Sat & Sun) This gimmicky, overpriced theme park off Hwy 2 nevertheless offers a glimpse of the historic Arecibo lighthouse, and is a good place to break up the long drives across the north coast if you're traveling with kids, who will likely get into the pirate-themed stuff.

Perched on a headland on the hill at Punta Morrillos, east of Arecibo, the striking, whitewashed **Faro de los Morrillos** (Parque Histórico de Arecibo; adult/child $12/10, as part of Parque Histórico de Arecibo admission) dates from 1897. It has a museum and fantastic views of the Atlantic Ocean from the roof.

Balneario Morrillos BEACH
(parking $4; ⊘8:30am-5pm Wed-Sun; P) If you follow the road past the Faro de los Morrillos (p202) lighthouse for less than a kilometer, you come to the Balneario Morrillos. There is a big parking lot here and all the usual facilities. The beach boasts almost 1km of low dunes and white sand, and it usually gets

plenty of surf. Better beaches (although not necessarily with better facilities) lie further east along Hwy 681.

✨ Festivals & Events

Hatillo Mask Festival   CARNIVAL
(Festival de las Máscaras; ☺Dec 28) This carnival-style extravaganza remembers King Herod's Massacre of the Innocents, with masked performers dressed as Herod's soldiers. The celebration dates back to 1823, with the arrival on Puerto Rico of settlers from the Canary Islands.

🛏 Sleeping & Eating

★**Caño Tiburones**
Guest House   GUESTHOUSE **$$**
(☑787-378-5480; www.facebook.com/ctguest house; 158 Julian Sanchez; r/ste from $100/115; ✳🔃🛋) For the first time in many years, Arecibo has a decent central accommodation possibility. Decorated with photographs of the coastal scenery around town, this peaceful, sunny yellow residence has been kitted out with 10 sizable, spick-and-span tiled rooms, newly converted from a turn-of-the-century building. A somewhat shadeless pool awaits at the back. City center attractions are within easy walking distance.

Punta Maracayo Hotel   HOTEL **$$**
(☑787-544-2000; www.hotelpuntamaracayopr. com; Km 84.6, Hwy 2; r from $100; P✳🔃🛋) With excellent service, modern rooms and lots of colorful common spaces, Punta Maracayo is the best option along the dreary north-coast highways. Although the facility itself is a bit similar to a quality highway hotel in the US, it does well to dress things up with fresh tropical flowers in the lobby, wicker furniture and bold modern art.

The spacious pool area in the back is a great option for people traveling with children.

★**Salitre Meson Costero**   SEAFOOD **$$**
(☑787-816-2020; http://salitre.com; Km 3.8, Hwy 681; mains $14-32; ☺11am-9pm Sun-Thu, to 11pm Fri & Sat) A dining destination befitting the lofty standards Arecibo sets for itself these days, this smart seafood restaurant is one of several promising new places along Hwy 681 out towards the Birth of the New World statue. Huge platters of lobster, crab and octopus are served with style and there is a range of Creole soups and good pasta dishes.

ℹ️ Getting There & Away

Arecibo is accessible from San Juan (81km east) or Aguadilla (51km to the west) by the Hwy 22 expressway, or from Ponce by Hwy 10.

Arecibo's city center is trapped between Hwy 2 and the Atlantic Ocean – if you can successfully negotiate the bland strip malls and suburbs to get there. Most attractions lie either just east of center across the Río Grande de Arecibo on Hwy 681, or about 15 to 20 minutes' drive south of town in karst country, reached via Hwy 129 or Hwy 10.

Around Arecibo

South of Arecibo, its outlying suburbs tier upwards into the hills, then peter out entirely into swooping forested peaks and ridges, where the rock is riddled with cave systems. You can make the transition from coastal city clamor to mountainside calm in little more than a 20-minute drive, and this fact renders the region the most visited of any in the island's interior.

Headlining a string of blockbuster sights here is the world's largest and most sensitive radio telescope, the Observatorio de Arecibo. Harboring a fascinating museum and a view worthy of a futuristic James Bond film set, the observatory is open for public viewing and reigns as one of the island's most rewarding must-sees. There are also rugged forest parks, spectacular caverns, boat trips on lakes and a host of other adventures nearby.

👁 Sights

★**Observatorio de Arecibo**   NOTABLE BUILDING
(☑787-878-2612; www.naic.edu; Hwy 625; adult/child $12/8; ☺9am-4pm daily mid-Dec–mid-Jan, Jun & Jul, Wed-Sun rest of the year) Puerto Ricans reverently refer to it as 'El Radar.' To everyone else it is simply the largest radio telescope in the world. Resembling an extraterrestrial spaceship grounded in the middle of karst country, the Arecibo Observatory looks like something out of a James Bond movie – probably because it is (007 aficionados will recognize the saucer-shaped dish and craning antennae from the 1995 film *Goldeneye*).

The 20-acre dish, operated in conjunction with SRI International, is set in a sinkhole among clusters of haystack-shaped *mogotes,* like earth's ear into outer space. Supported by 50-story cables weighing more than 600 tons, the telescope is involved in the SETI

(Search for Extraterrestrial Intelligence) program and used by on-site scientists to prove the existence of pulsars and quasars, the so-called 'music of the stars.' Past work has included the observation of the planet Mercury, the first asteroid image and the discovery of the first extra-solar planets.

Top scientists from around the world perform ongoing research at Arecibo, but an informative visitors center with interpretative displays and an explanatory film provide the public with a fascinating glimpse of how the facility works. There's also a well-positioned viewing platform offering you the archetypal 007 vista.

To get to the observatory follow Hwys 635 and 625 off Hwy 129. It's only 9 miles south of the town of Arecibo as the crow flies, but the roller-coaster ride through karst country will make it seem more like 90.

Parque de las Cavernas del Río Camuy   CAVE

(☑787-898-8508; Km 18.9, Hwy 129; adult/child incl audio guide $18/13, parking $3; ⊙8am-5pm Wed-Sun & holidays) The beguiling network of stalagmite-ornamented caves at Río Camuy is the third-largest network of its kind in the world, formed by the soft karstic limestone that shapes the hills on this remarkable part of the island. This park is *big* – it's spread over 10 miles and has multiple entrances. A visit here can be an unearthly, slightly creepy diversion from the typically sunny shore, if you have the time and patience to put up with the terrible crowds.

Over the years, the caves have been shelters for indigenous people, home to millions of bats that help keep the island's insect population under control, and a source of fertilizer. But no modern explorers went to the trouble of making a thorough investigation of the caves until 1958. In 1986 the attraction opened as a tourist facility.

Call the park for local conditions (too much rain causes closures) and arrive before 10:30am to avoid the worst crowds or waits of upward of an hour standing in line. Don't expect much contact with the spectacular underground formations either. Your visit begins with a film at the visitors center and a trolleybus through the jungle into a 200ft-deep sinkhole to **Cueva Clara de Empalme** (Clear Cave Junction), where you take a 45-minute guided walk. Here you walk past enormous stalagmites and stalactites. At one point the ceiling of the cavern reaches a height of 170ft; at another

you can see the Río Camuy rushing through a tunnel.

After leaving the cave from a side passage, you take another tram to the **Tres Pueblos sinkhole**, which measures 650ft across and drops 400ft. Forty-two petroglyphs that you can now inspect have been found in **Cueva Catedral** (Cathedral Cave).

The last tour leaves at 2pm if you want to see all three areas. All told, the fun of the visit here depends on the size of the crowds, your patience and the tour guide (some of them seem bored stiff).

Parque Ceremonial Indígena Caguana   PARK

(☑787-894-7325; Km 12.4, Hwy 111; adult/child $3/2; ⊙8:30am-4:20pm) Like the archaeological site at Tibes near Ponce, this Taíno ceremonial site, off Hwy 111, has no monumental ruins; the power of the place comes from the natural botanical garden of ceiba, ausubo and tabonuco trees that shade the midslopes of the central mountains. There are 10 ceremonial *bateyes* (Taíno ball courts), dating back about 800 years.

Stone monoliths line many of the courts, and quite a few have petroglyphs, such as the famous Mujer de Caguana, who squats in the pose of the traditional 'earth mother' fertility symbol. Caguana is a place to walk and reflect, not to be thrilled by exhibits or enormous ancient monuments. Nevertheless, there is a small museum with artifacts and skeletons on the property, and a gift shop that sells inexpensive but attractive reproductions of Taíno charms, including the statues called *cemíes*.

Lagos Dos Bocas & Caonillas   LAKE

(Hwy 123; ⊙24hr) These two lakes – each more than 2 miles long – fill a deeply cleft valley at a point where karst country gives way to the jagged spine of the central mountains, east of Hwy 10 and north of Utuado. The lakes are the principal reservoirs for the north-central part of the island and they can provide a tranquil escape if the beaches are too congested.

In calm weather, you can ride Dos Bocas' free launch, which serves as a taxi service to the residents in the area. The **boat landing** (⊙8am-5pm Sat & Sun) FREE is on Hwy 123, on the western side of the lake. Boats leave almost every hour. You can disembark at restaurants around the lake or just sit back and enjoy the two-hour ride. You can similarly pick up the boat launch on the other side of

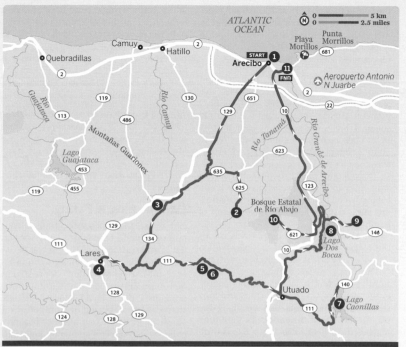

Driving Tour
Karst Country

START ARECIBO
FINISH FARO Y PARQUE HISTÓRICO DE
ARECIBO
LENGTH 95KM; FOUR HOURS WITHOUT
STOPS

Start in ❶ **Arecibo** (p201), a town perfectly situated to fuel up for the trip, and head south toward Lares, birthplace of the *independentista* movement. Take a scenic detour along the way to the ❷ **Observatorio de Arecibo** (p203), the world's largest radio telescope and a surreal sci-fi vision in the jungle. Afterwards, stop at the ❸ **Parque de las Cavernas del Río Camuy** (p204), where you'll find a network of dripping caves that can be a great place to cool off. Head south on Hwy 134 to Hwy 111. The circuit continues east from here, but it's worth taking the 6km detour west to Lares, where insurgents issued the short-lived Grito de Lares independence call in 1868. Here, refresh yourself with some of the Caribbean's most amazing (and aberrant) ice cream at ❹ **Heladeria El Grito** (p206). Backtrack on Hwy 111 and proceed east (up and down lots

of ridges) to encounter, in quick succession, ❺ **Tanamá River Adventures** (p206) (try your hand at kayaking or cave tubing!) and then ❻ **Parque Ceremonial Indígena Caguana** (p204), a quiet park that was once used for worship and ball games by indigenous Taíno people. After a quiet walk, follow signs toward Utuado, after which you can turn off for a detour to either of the stunning mountain lakes in the area, ❼ **Lago Caonillas** (p204) and ❽ **Lago Dos Bocas** (p204). Regular boats ply the lakes and ramshackle restaurants sell Puerto Rican favorites. You'll find serene accommodations just up from Lago Dos Bocas at ❾ **TJ Ranch** (p206).

On the way back towards Arecibo, you can divert down to Rte 621 and ❿ **Bosque Estatal de Río Abajo** (p206), where former lumber roads have been converted to trails. Leaving the park, head back north on Hwy 10 and, as it approaches the edge of Arecibo city, hook up with Hwy 681. This will bring you down to the ⓫ **Faro y Parque Histórico de Arecibo** (p202), where a picturesque lighthouse stands guard over the Caribbean.

the lake at the end of Hwy 612, about 3 miles beyond the Casa Grande Mountain Retreat. Along the shore there are several *comida criolla* (traditional Puerto Rican cuisine) restaurants, some of which hire kayaks.

Bosque Estatal de Río Abajo NATURE RESERVE
(☎787-880-6557; Hwy 621; ⊗8am-4pm) This 5000-acre forest just off Hwy 621, halfway between Arecibo and Utuado, sits amid some of the island's most rugged terrain. In the bosom of karst country, the forest's altitude jumps between 700ft and 1400ft above sea level. The steep sides of the *mogotes* (precipitous limestone hills) are overrun with vines and the forest features fine tropical hardwoods, including Honduran mahogany and Asian teaks, beside huge clumps of bamboo.

The remains of the lumber roads cut by the loggers and the Civilian Conservation Corps (CCC) workers have now become trails.

The first trail you'll encounter, starting from the currently defunct visitors center, is the **Visitors Center Trail**, a 500m-long stroll with three gazebos set up along the way, in the east of the park before the road reaches the DRNA office. Hwy 621 continues a few kilometers further into the forest to a camping, picnic and recreation area. Near this point, there is an aviary where the DRNA is working to reintroduce the Puerto Rican parrot and other endangered species. Several more trails begin here. Branching south off the access track to the aviary, the **Cueva del Agua Trail** is a 40-minute out-and-back route to a cave with a small lake inside. Longest is the **Río Tanama Trail**, a five-hour out-and-back route to a good swimming spot. The starting point is from the track leading to the aviary. Enquire at the DRNA office just inside the park boundary and you should be able to obtain a map and piece together a more substantial hike through this karst country.

To reach Bosque Estatal de Río Abajo from San Juan, take Hwy 22 west toward Arecibo. Turn south on Rte 10 toward Utuado. Turn west on Hwy 621 and continue to Km 4.4 and the park entrance.

🏃 Activities

★ Batey
Zipline Adventures ADVENTURE SPORTS
(☎787-484-3860; www.bateydelcemi.com; Hwy 111; All-inclusive tour per person $133) With a 150ft suspension bridge teetering above the Río Tanamá, seven different ziplines and an underground river cave to kayak to, an afternoon out at this adventure park is never dull. Horseback riding is also available. The best-of all-inclusive tour, including hiking, rappelling, caving and the ziplines, lasts 4½ hours.

The adventure park is located next to Parque Ceremonial Indígena Caguana (p204).

Tanamá River Adventures ADVENTURE SPORTS
(☎787-462-4121; www.tanamariveradventures. com; Hwy 111; tours $65-100) Hiking, canyoning, caving, cave tubing...you name it, and if it utilizes the karst- and river-riddled terrain of Puerto Rico's Central Mountains, this outfit obliges.

🛏 Sleeping & Eating

Out in wild karst country, finding a restaurant is understandably tough. Your best bet is at the attractions themselves (expect snack booths rather than fine dining), or at your accommodation. Casa Grande Mountain Retreat has a restaurant open to nonguests, but it could be a veggie buffet shared with a raucous meditation group. However, there is one shining beacon of culinary excellence hereabouts and that is the **Heladería El Grito** (2 Vilella, Lares; scoop from $1.50; ⊗10am-5pm Mon-Thu, to 9pm Fri-Sun) in Lares, a town that's been serving some of the Caribbean's best ice cream for generations.

★ TJ Ranch CABIN $$
(☎787-880-1217; http://tjranch.com; off Rte 146, Lago Dos Bocas; s/d $100/135; P ☲) A charming stop on any karst-country driving or cycling tour, TJ Ranch is a little-known Eden that's the best place to stay in the entire region. It harbors three beautiful, exquisitely decorated cabins surrounded by lush foliage up a corkscrewing track above Lago Dos Bocas.

Casa Grande
Mountain Retreat GUESTHOUSE $$
(☎787-894-3900/39; www.hotelcasagrande.com; Km 0.3, Hwy 612; r $130; P ☲☎) ✐ Materializing in the heart of Puerto Rico's gorgeous karst country, the Casa Grande is a great place to escape the daily grind. Nestled in its own steep valley, the ecologically congruous hotel stops you in your tracks and forces you to slow down. While there are no TVs or phones in any of the 20 rooms, there are daily yoga classes and a scrumptious on-site restaurant.

❶ Getting There & Away

Most of these sights lie a 15- to 25- minutes' drive south of Arecibo in karst country, all reached via either Hwy 129 or Hwy 10. Hwy 10 continues south to Ponce. The steep, twisting roads and the proximity of key attractions means this is a good region for exploring by bicycle as well as by car.

Isabela & Around

POP 42,000

Nicknamed 'Garden of the Northeast' for its local cheeses and elegant Paso Fino horses, Isabela and its surroundings boast an invitingly rugged coastline blessed with a handful of classic surfing beaches such as Jobos and Shacks that rival anything in Rincón, especially in winter when the breaks here are in fact often better. With accommodation and eating joints that now match Rincón, too, the 'scene' here begs to be checked out.

And surfing is not the only activity. Isabela now has one of the Caribbean's best golf courses and there is phenomenal horseback riding in the vicinity. You can also loll on the beaches, swim and snorkel to your heart's content. Isabela is great cycling country, too.

After the ghastly urban sprawl on Hwy 2, the miles of sand dunes, inlets and untrammeled beaches that lie sandwiched between the lashing Atlantic and a 200ft coastal escarpment are refreshing, resplendent respite.

◎ Sights

★ **Palacete Los Moreau**   HISTORIC SITE

(☑ 787-830-4475; Km 2.6, Hwy 464, Moca; ☺ grounds 9am-5pm, tours Thu-Mon) **FREE** Here's an intriguing diversion from the Isabela beach scene: a 19th-century tenderly restored French hacienda, exquisitely furnished within and with lush grounds to stroll about, usually open to the public and with enthusiastic tours of the property provided for free.

The serene two-towered mansion was frequented by one of Puerto Rico's most prolific writers, Enrique Laguerre, who wrote about the residence in his novel *La Llamarada,* and lies buried within the grounds. Phone ahead to secure a tour.

🏊 Beaches

To get some crashing waves and lonely sands to yourself, head 5km east of Isabela on Ave Noel Estrada. When you hit Hwy 2

at the carving of the *cacique* (Taíno chief) turn left then left again to reach the beach near the old Guajataca Tunnel. Swimming here can be dangerous: get local advice first.

Playa Jobos   BEACH

(Ⓟ) The wonderfully dramatic crescent of Playa Jobos is protected by a large headland of dead coral to the east, and the surf breaks pretty consistently off this point. The site of the 1989 World Surfing Championships, Jobos is a good place to surf or watch professional athletes doing their wave thing. There is also fine swimming off the eastern beach, where the point protects you from the surf.

The bar-restaurants on the southern side of the cove offer a laid-back après-surf scene, especially on weekends.

What locals refer to as Playa Jobos is actually one long coastline made up of different beaches – Jobos is the biggest one, at the intersection of Rtes 466 and 4466. That's also the beach where you will find the greatest number of hotels and restaurants.

Playa Shacks   BEACH

(Ⓟ) Playa Shacks lies less than a mile west of Playa Jobos, near Ramey Base on Rte 4466. There are good submarine caves here for snorkeling, while surfers take to the breaks further out.

★ **Playa Survival**   BEACH

Even the surfers rarely make it to remote Playa Survival, best reached by a 45-minute walk west from Playa Shacks. The narrow strip of sand found elsewhere on this section of coastline opens up into a wide sandy beach backed by hills and trees. It's a candidate for 'mainland' Puerto Rico's most beautiful beach.

🏃 Activities

Surfing

While Isabela might lack the surfer chic of Rincón, the waves here are just as legendary. Some say Playa Jobos has the best breaks on the island, but make sure you check out **Secret Spot** and **Shore Island** further east around the coast.

Isabela borders Aguadilla to the west, which means that, in practice, all the surf spots there are also easily accessible. Don't miss Table Top (p211), named for a flat, exposed reef that looks like a table with a round barrel coming up against cliffs); Surfer's Beach (p211), preferred location for local contests, with diverse breaks and strong northwestern swells; or Gas Chambers (p211), known as Puerto Rico's best 'right tube.'

To get the scoop on what's breaking and where, stop by **Wave Riding Vehicles** (☑787-669-3840; www.waveridingvehicles.com; Km 7.3, Rte 110; snorkeling gear $10, board rental $20, 2hr surf lesson $65; ☉10am-6pm) at Jobos Beach. Generally, October through to about April are the months with the best breaks.

Serious surfers will also find a number of custom board builders in the area. Of these, **MHL** (☑787-609-6198; www.liftfoils.com; Km 1.2, Rte 4466) has an impeccable reputation for handcrafted boards.

Hang Loose Surf Shop
SURFING

(☑787-560-0181; www.facebook.com/puertorico surfandbeachproducts; Km 1.2, Rte 4466; surf board rental per day from $30; ☉10am-5pm Tue-Sat, to 3pm Sun) Lots of international surfers come here to rent boards for their surfin' safari around Puerto Rico. This shop also sells a complete selection of gear, including boards. You can get lessons too.

Cycling

Hit the ocean road on or around Rtes 466 and 4466 for some of the best bike rides on the north coast, part of which is connected by – yep, really – an actual cycle lane.

Alternatively, the entire web of back roads south of Hwy 2, skirting the edge of karst country up as far as Bosque Estatal de Guajataca and Lago Guajataca in the San Sebastián region, make for great pedals.

Horseback Riding

★**Tropical Trail Rides**
HORSE RIDING

(☑787-872-9256; www.tropicaltrailrides.com; Km 1.8, Rte 4466; 2hr ride $55, private ride $90; ☉twice daily) You can take a ride along the fields, dunes and beaches with Tropical Trail Rides, which works out of stables near Playa Shacks. Private rides can be arranged to ratchet up the romantic experience further.

Golf

Royal Isabela
GOLF

(☑787-609-5888; www.royalisabela.com; 396 Av Noel Estrada; per day $250, caddie fee $90) Little touches, like a replicated Scottish burn (stream), a tee over an ocean inlet towards a cliff (supposedly shaped like a Taíno chief's face) and a finish playing around sugar plantation ruins, show indications of the creativity that went into the course design here. The course also conserves some important wildlife, including many rare butterfly species,

and there is a self-guided tour of the fauna you might spot.

Nonmembers must contact Royal Isabela in advance to see if there are available tee times. Sip a few cocktails in the elegant 19th hole, positioned to give the perfect course overview, or eat in the Moroccan-decorated La Casa restaurant afterwards.

🛏 Sleeping

In this northwestern nook of the island, Isabela is the best place to bed down. While the town itself has no options, the coast along Playa Jobos and Playa Shacks has several good hotels and apartments. An increasing number of cheaper, basic apartments are springing up, but finding budget accommodation is still not so easy.

Hotel Restaurante Ocean Front
HOTEL $

(☑787-872-0444; www.oceanfrontpr.com; Km 0.1, Rte 4466; r $85-150; P❋) Imagine a classic Caribbean-style beach hotel situated on a tempestuous stretch of sand popularly regarded by aficionados as being surfer heaven. That's the Ocean Front: small, compact and suitably modern, but not too flashy. Rooms have balconies and good views of the incoming surf and there's a popular onsite restaurant-bar that hosts occasional live music.

★Villa Tropical
APARTMENT $$

(☑787-872-7172; www.villatropical.com; 326 Bo Bajuras, Playa Shacks; apt $95-200; P❋🛜) Sea views hit you vividly from all sides at the impeccably designed Villa Tropical, where accommodation in huge, light, airy apartments will make you pinch yourself to check you're not teleported to an affluent Californian coastal enclave. Big balconies act as stages to watch the wicked surf action on a rarely traipsed stretch of sand just shy of Playa Shacks.

Villa Tropical's apartments also have remarkably well-equipped kitchens, making them ideal for families. For the best experience, grab a room in the end building, a block down from the reception, or rent out one of two apartments in the brand new Casa Soledad, with its own private swimming pool. There's a laundrette, snorkel-gear rental and a small shop on-site.

Parador Villas del Mar Hau
CABIN $$

(☑787-872-2045; www.paradorvillasdelmarhau. com; Km 8.3, Rte 466; cabins $180-210; P❋🖼) A clutch of brightly painted beach huts lie

WORTH A TRIP

ISLA DESECHEO

The island appearing alluringly on the horizon in spectacular northwest coast sunsets is Isla Desecheo, a 1-sq-mile knob of prickly cacti and bushy scrub situated 13 miles off Puerto Rico's northwest coast. One of four outlying islands making up the Puerto Rican archipelago (the others are Culebra, Vieques and Mona), Desecheo was 'discovered' by Columbus in 1493, but remained unnamed until Spanish explorer Nuñez Alvarez de Aragón passed through in 1517. Buccaneers and pirates frequented it during the 16th and 17th centuries to hoard booty and hunt the feral goats introduced by the Spanish; over the years it's been home to lizards, seabirds and a few monkeys, introduced for an adaptation experiment. From WWII to the early 1950s, Desecheo was – surprise, surprise – used as a bombing range by the US military who left behind a cache of unexploded ordnance, a fact that makes the island officially off-limits to visitors (trespassers will be arrested – or perhaps blown up).

But all is not lost. Thanks to its favorable position to the west of the geologically important Puerto Rican Trench, the waters around Desecheo are free from murky river runoff from the main island. As a result the sea here is unusually clear (visibility is generally 30m to 45m), making it one of the best spots for diving in the Caribbean. Desecheo was declared a US Fish & Wildlife Refuge in 1976 and a National Wildlife Refuge in 1983. Taíno Divers (p177) in Rincón offer diving trips to Isla Desecheo.

scattered like bucolic homesteads along a breathtaking beach where offshore coral islets create bathing lagoons: welcome to this rustic retreat run by the Hau family for nearly 50 years. Here you can ride a horse, go cycling, kayak, snorkel, hike the beach or sleep undisturbed under a palm tree.

Royal Isabela
RESORT **$$$**

(☎787-609-5888; www.royalisabela.com; 396 Av Noel Estrada; r from $500; [P][❄][🐾][⛱]) 🏌 Luxury melds with a strong environmental ethos at the Royal Isabela, the new golf resort that many are whispering is the superior of anything Dorado can offer for teeing, dining and – should your wallet stretch – staying. The vision of Stanley and Charlie Pasarell has risen out of former sugarcane plantation into an enticing tract of vegetated cliffs, rocky coves and undulating, copsefringed greenery.

The 20-odd idyllic *casitas* are cocooned away within the folds of this estate, so hidden that you can barely see one from the next. Needless to say, they're a soliloquy in style, with darkwood flooring, carved beds, walk-in four-jet showers and luxe toiletries. Each has its own private plunge pool and paths wind down to private alfresco dining areas – ideal for honeymooners.

As for the 19th hole, the vista across the grounds, sweeping to the sea, is magnificent. Next to the open-air bar is the terracottaroofed restaurant **La Casa** (http://royalisabela.

com/restaurant-at-la-casa; Av Noel Estrada, Royal Isabela; mains $30-50; ⊘noon-10pm).

Villa Montaña
RESORT **$$$**

(☎787-872-9554; www.villamontana.com; Km 1.2, Rte 4466; villas $275-650; [P][❄][@][⛱]) This resort is something of an anomaly in Puerto Rico: a high-end stay that works gracefully within its stunning environment. Here 48 brightly painted plantation-style villas look across the lawn to the tempestuous crash of Playa Shacks. Tucked away amid the tropical foliage, you'll find a tennis court, a gym, a spa and the highly regarded Moroccan-themed Eclipse (p210) restaurant.

✗ Eating

Hotel Restaurante Ocean Front
SEAFOOD **$**

(☎787-872-0444; www.oceanfrontpr.com; Km 0.1, Rte 4466; dishes $6-22; ⊘11am-10pm Mon-Thu, to 2am Fri & Sat) Tiny glowing lights and wavy green plants give this restaurant a relaxed, romantic atmosphere that complements the seafood dishes. The indoor setting is surprisingly formal, but the deck leaning out over the beach pulls casual surfers in for a drink. The owner is famous for his secret salmon recipe. Live music nightly. Rooms available.

★CLMDO
MEDITERRANEAN **$$**

(☎787-431-3098; www.clmdo.com; 114 Manuel Corchado Juarbe; mains $10-25; ⊘6-10pm Thu-Sun) Central Isabela finally has a restaurant it can be truly proud of – in fact, it may

---

DON'T MISS

HIGHWAY 110'S BIZARRE BUT BOUNTIFUL EATERIES

Somehow, inexplicably, where else-where main highways in Puerto Rico are the sorry domain of ubiquitous fast-food franchises, Hwy 110, which runs between Aguadilla's Aeropuerto Rafael Hernández and Hwy 2, has become a haven of varied world cuisines, hippy healthy-eating joints and bold new culinary ventures that will leave your palate feeling better about itself. Choose from Middle Eastern (Paprika; p212) and creative takes on your average supermarket (Reef; p212) or bakery (Levain; p211) or artisanal beer (**Beer Box**; www.facebook.com/beerboxpr; Km 8, Hwy 110; ⊘ 3-11pm Mon-Thu, to 1am Fri & Sat, to 9pm Sun).

---

just be the north coast's best. This crisply cheery modern space with its open kitchen opened its doors in 2013 with an innovative Mediterranean-influenced menu. The beef tagine and the crushed-chickpea and lemon couscous are popular dishes.

La Vista Smokehouse　　　　BARBECUE **$$**
(www.lavistasmokehouse.com; Km 6.3, Rte 466; mains $12-41; ⊘ 11am-10pm Wed-Sun) These guys make an art out of barbecue, but to sample it you'll have to go to a tad more effort than is the norm in Isabela, as this place is away from the coast, a kilometer up the hill from Playa Jobos. As for the grilled meats, think tender pulled pork or herb-infused brisket. The king of the dishes is the chargrilled rib eye with shrimp.

La Vista's 'pit master' is a passionate chap who has been grilling meat professionally for a good four decades. This is more a touristy hangout than a local place, but the quality is very, very high.

Eclipse　　　　FUSION **$$**
(⚡787-872-9554; www.villamontana.com; Km 1.2, Rte 4466; mains $14-34, 4-course dinner $55; ⊘ noon-10pm Sun-Thu, to 11pm Fri & Sat) The alfresco atmosphere – furious waves and gentle breezes, bright tropical flowers and elegantly rustic furniture – is nearly outpaced by the creative flavors of seafood and fresh, locally sourced vegetables at this on-site restaurant of Villa Montaña. Start with the fried brie and seaweed salad

or the octopus salad with golden plantains before moving on to mains of pan-Latin steak and seafood.

The menu changes daily. It's nice, but overpriced.

ⓘ Information

The regional information center is **Puerto Rico Tourism Company** (PRTC; ⚡787-890-3315; Aeropuerto Rafael Hernández Terminal Bldg, Aguadilla; ⊘ 8am-4:30pm Mon-Fri) at the Aguadilla airport on Ramey Base.

ⓘ Getting There & Away

The easiest way to access the region from San Juan is via the four-lane Hwy 22, which becomes Hwy 2 after Hatillo. Keeping anti-clockwise, Hwy 2 continues via the turnoff to Isabela (Hwy 113) to connect Aguadilla with the branch road to Rincón (Hwy 115), Mayagüez and eventually Ponce. From Isabela, Rte 466 continues west 7km to Playa Jobos and then past the turnoff to Playa Shacks to link up with Hwy 110 (notable for its restaurants).

Scheduled airline services to nearby Aguadilla's **Aeropuerto Rafael Hernández** (p199) change seasonally. Flights come in from New York and Newark (US) and the Dominican Republic about three times a week.

To really enjoy this region, you will need your own wheels to get away from the drab highways to where the best beaches are.

Aguadilla

POP 15,700

Occupying a small sliver of land wedged between Hwy 2 and the sea, Aguadilla is a ho-hum coastal city of surprising contradictions. Its world-class surf scene stands in vibrant contrast to its bland sprawl of Eisenhower-era tract housing and the nearby graying campus of a retired US Air Force base known as the Ramey Base.

It is a confusing place to navigate and the historic quarter has been largely abandoned in favor of generic out-of-town shopping malls along Hwy 2. Attractions in town are scant, although for practical considerations like the regional airport, shopping or car rental you may be obliged to stop by.

Surfers forge north to the unblemished beauty of beaches like Crash Boat, or continue to Isabela's beaches. Meanwhile, committed golfers beeline to the windy Punta Borinquen Golf Club, built for President Dwight Eisenhower. If neither activity appeals, bypass

Aguadilla altogether for Rincón (south) or Isabela (just northeast).

History

The early colonizers of Aguadilla (founded in 1780) were Spanish loyalists fleeing from the Haitian invasion of Spanish Hispaniola in 1822. By the late 19th century the settlement had become an important port, but in 1918 its fortunes changed for the worse when it was ravaged by the destructive San Fermín earthquake and subsequent tsunami.

🏝 Beaches

Get out of town and to the coastline, where beach after beach offers world-class surf.

Playa Wilderness   BEACH
(Hwy 107) Rough, lonely Playa Wilderness is a favourite with surfers. Off Hwy 107 to the left (west) as you follow the road north from central Aguadilla to the Ramey Base, you will see the golf course on your left and a road that heads west through the golf course. Follow this road to pass the ruins of an old lighthouse and reach the beach.

Playa Crash Boat   BEACH
(Rte 458; ☺ 24hr) This is the next must-go beach north up the coast from Aguadilla. An undulating road winds down to a car park, snack stands, a lively bar, a pier (off which you can swim) and a swathe of ocher sand. It got its name because the air force used to keep rescue boats here to pick up crews from the Strategic Air Command's bombers that didn't make the runway. It's on the looping Rte 458, which branches off Hwy 107.

🏃 Activities

Surfing

Table Top   SURFING
North of the Ramey Base and just northeast along the coast from Surfer's Beach, the land juts out into a flat, exposed reef that looks like a table (hence the name). Heading clockwise (northeast) around the coast from central Aguadilla, this is the last beach before you arrive in Isabela territory (where more great surf spots await).

Surfer's Beach   SURFING
On the northern side of the Rafael Hernández Airport and the Ramey Base is another one of Aguadilla's absolutely obscure hidden gems – at least if you like surfing. The preferred location for local surfing contests in the Aguadilla and Isabela area, this beach

has diverse breaks from multiple directions and strong northwestern swells.

Gas Chambers   SURFING
(Playa Crash Boat, Rte 458) Just north of Playa Crash Boat is one of the best surfing spots on Aguadilla's stretch of the north coast.

Cycling, Diving & Golf

Aquatica Dive & Surf   DIVING, CYCLING
(☑ 787-890-6071; www.aquaticapr.com; Km 10, Rte 110; dive incl gear from $85, bike rental per day $25; ☺ 9am-5pm Mon-Sat, to 3pm Sun) Outside Gate 5 of Ramey Base near the airport is one of Puerto Rico's best dive operators and bike-rental establishments. The staff here can also help you with route planning for your bike trip.

There are plenty of decent circuits in the Aguadilla and Isabela area that steer clear of main roads and incorporate some magnificent rural scenery, as well as a couple of moderately difficult single-track trails in the area.

Punta Borinquen Golf Club   GOLF
(Hwy 107; monthly membership $200) This golf course has a clubhouse full of history, having been built for President Dwight Eisenhower. It's a windy but popular course just west of Aguadilla's Ramey Base.

🍽 Sleeping & Eating

It's much more pleasant to continue a little further northeast to Isabela to sleep, although Aguadilla is where the regional airport is, so for practical reasons you may wish to sleep nearby.

★ TBC   BREAKFAST $
(The Breakfast Club; ☑ 787-464-3122; www.tbcfoodanddrink.com; Hwy 110, Km 8; breakfasts $4.50-12; ☺ 8am-3pm Sun-Mon & Wed-Fri, to 5pm Sat) Creativity and attention to detail are the fortes of this newcomer to the 110 eating scene, formerly operating near Shack's beach in Isabela. Ingredients like chia seeds, quinoa and house-made granola are thrown into the mix, to arrive at scrumptious dishes like chia pudding, quinoa and cinnamon porridge, spinach and feta scramble or caramelised onion and smoked-bacon omelet.

Levain   BAKERY $
(www.facebook.com/LevainArtisanBreads; cnr Hwy 110 & Wing Rd; snacks $2-12; ☺ 7am-7pm Mon-Fri, 8am-5pm Sat, 10am-2pm Sun) Puerto Rico's best bakery perches on the edge of the Aguadilla Ramey Base, tempting passersby with tasty

baked-on-the-premises bread, croissants and cakes. There are a few tables inside and more outside, and great coffee too.

Blue Fin Food Truck FAST FOOD $
(www.facebook.com/bluefinaguadilla; cnr Hwy 110 & Sabalo; meals $3-8; ⊗5-10pm Tue-Sun) The Blue Fin has risen to the top of the pile of the north coast's food-truck scene, whipping up delicacies like spicy crab, pulled pork, divinely seasoned chicken and sushi pizza from the Aguadilla Food Truck Park, just north of Hwy 110's intersection with Rte 4466 to Isabela. Taco Tuesday is a ball.

Paprika MIDDLE EASTERN $
(🖉787-658-6442; Km 9.8, Hwy 110; mains $8-15; ⊗5-9pm Sun-Tue & Thu, to 10pm Fri & Sat; 🖉) The owner here traces his heritage back to Egypt and Israel and it is from these roots the wonderful menu unfolds: dishes are bright with healthy ingredients, delicate seasoning and eye-catching presentation (Israeli fish balls, baba ghanoush, stuffed vine leaves) and there's craft beers to boot. There's often a party in the parking lot outside.

The Reef DELI $
(www.facebook.com/thereefgourmet; mains $9-14; ⊗11:30am-9pm Mon & Wed-Fri, 12:30-9pm Sat & Sun) The Reef is the latest upmarket deli to rise to prominence on the Hwy 110 strip, and delicious, well-prepared grub is a given here. As for the sit-down food, the burgers are the headline act, with everything from gorgonzola to spicy pepper burgers available. These guys do a good line in fresh fish too.

❶ Information

The regional information center is **Puerto Rico Tourism Company** (PRTC; 🖉787-890-3315; Aeropuerto Rafael Hernández Terminal Bldg, Aguadilla; ⊗8am-4:30pm Mon-Fri) at the Aguadilla airport on Ramey Base.

❶ Getting There & Away

Scheduled airline services to Aguadilla's **Aeropuerto Rafael Hernández** (p199) change seasonally. Flights come in from New York and Newark (US) and the Dominican Republic about three times a week.

Aguadilla occupies an easily accessible position on Hwy 2, 25km northwest of Rincón and 50km west of Arecibo. If you are driving between San Juan and the west coast (and want to avoid rush-hour traffic), consider taking the back road, Hwy 443, which breaks off Hwy 2 just east of Aguadilla, then rejoins it to the south.

Central Mountains

POP 575,000

Includes ➜
Caguas 215

Bosque Estatal
de Carite 216

Aibonito & Around 217

Barranquitas
& Around 218

Guavate 219

Reserva Forestal
Toro Negro 220

Jayuya 222

Adjuntas & Around 223

Maricao 224

San Sebastián
& Around 225

Best Places to Eat

➜ Orujo Taller de
Gastronomía (p215)

➜ El Rancho Original (p219)

➜ Casa Bavaria (p220)

➜ Restaurante Toro Verde
(p220)

➜ El Burén (p223)

Best Places to Sleep

➜ Las Casas de la Selva &
Tropic Ventures (p216)

➜ Hacienda Pomarrosa
(p222)

➜ Hacienda El Jibarito (p226)

Why Go?

Those who explore these winding roads gain a dramatically different perspective on the island and chances to commune with Puerto Rico's old soul. Best approached with a flexible agenda, this is a place of Taíno legends and sugarcane moonshine, muddy hillside towns and misty afternoons.

The whole thing is strung together by the Ruta Panorámica, a vine-covered ribbon of potholed blacktop that rolls like a roller coaster along the island's rugged spine. It meanders through ragged agricultural towns, humid patches of jungle and past cliff-edge vistas where birds of prey glide in lazy circles. Between fog-covered valleys and the sharp scent of fresh-roasted coffee beans, visitors catch a whiff of the endangered cultural essence of Puerto Rico.

For those requiring more definitive reasons to visit, they are manifold: the island's highest peaks, remotest hiking and best coffee haciendas – plus one of the world's most thrilling adventure parks near Barranquitas.

When to Go

Unlike the reliably sunny shores, the mountains catch all kinds of weather and are considerably cooler.

Cerro Maravilla in the Toro Negro forest records average temperatures 10°F to 15°F lower than San Juan. In winter, towns in the hills can be downright chilly, sometimes dropping to 45°F. There's no rainy season, per se, but the dampness gets into the bones, making layered clothing a must.

Mornings are clearer, making simultaneous views of the north and south coast possible, but the Ruta Panorámica will still often be blanketed in mist.

Central Mountains Highlights

❶ Caguas (p215) Study the stunning *retablos* of Edwin Báez Carrasquillo in the art museum's here.

❷ Guavate (p219) Join the spontaneous street party

hosted by *lechoneras* besides Bosque Estatal de Carite.

❸ Cañón de San Cristóbal (p217) Descend into the gaping gorges and crashing waterfalls.

❹ Toro Verde Nature

Adventure Park (p219) Hurtle through the treetops on some of the best ziplines.

❺ Reserva Forestal Toro Negro (p220) Forge along

off-piste trails yielding views of Puerto Rico's highest summit.

❻ Hacienda Pomarrosa (p220) Inhale the aromas and sample the brews of

homegrown Puerto Rican coffee.

❼ Gozalandia (p225) Cool off in some of the island's most magical waterfall plunge pools.

History

Legend has it that native Taíno survived here until the mid-19th century and, even today, Indian traditions run strong in the festivals and artisan workshops scattered along the Ruta Panorámica. In more recent times, notoriety has struck these mountains twice. In 1950 an unsuccessful uprising in Jayuya marked the death knell of the Puerto Rican independence movement as an effective political force. Further scandal erupted in 1978 when two young independence supporters were shot by police posing as revolutionaries on Cerro Maravilla in the Reserva Forestal Toro Negro, in an incident that uncovered corruption, ballot-box fraud and an alleged FBI cover-up.

ⓘ Getting There & Away

The Ruta Panorámica, a chain of 40 mountain roads, travels 165 miles across the roof of Puerto Rico – from Yabucoa in the east to Mayagüez in the west – crossing the whole of the Central Mountains. It is generally well-marked with distinctive brown road signs, and highlighted on almost all commercial maps of the island. If driving, be careful and never drive after dark.

Even major towns in the central region – Aibonito, Barranquitas, Jayuya and Adjuntas – are only accessible by car (or, should you have the time, bicycle), and without your own wheels, it will be impossible to see a fraction of what is hidden down the remote roads hereabouts.

Be warned that bikes can be precarious on the Ruta Panorámica, where drivers are famously erratic. Riders should stick to the wider link roads such as Rte 15 between Cayey and Guayama and listen to local advice.

Caguas

POP 77,000

Large, smart, modern Caguas, just a half hour's drive from San Juan, is a misleading introduction to Puerto Rico's central massif (which although large is neither smart nor modern). The thickly forested hills seem far away here, despite it being the best place to pick up supplies for mountainous sojourns such as Bosque Estatal de Carite. *La Ciudad Criolla* (the Creole City) is, however, a worthy half-day stop for its proud cultural scene, evidenced in a clutch of museums near leafy Plaza Palmer. This central square is where you will find the attractive cream-colored cathedral, dating from the 1930s and, amid the foliage, an intriguing floral clock and a statue of José Gautier Benítez, one of Puerto Rico's best-known poets.

⊙ Sights

★ **Museo de Artes Populares de Caguas** MUSEUM
(cnr Betances & Luis Padial; ⊙9am-noon & 1-5pm Tue-Sat) FREE A leading contemporary Puerto Rican artist, Edwin Báez Carrasquillo, specializes in creating *retablos,* three-dimensional scenes of Puerto Rican life full of fascinating minute detail, and his work forms the bulk of this riveting little museum. Subjects covered here range from the museum's founder in his study piled high with curios to the devastation of the 1918 hurricane.

Centro de Bellas Artes de Caguas ARTS CENTER
(⌨787-653-1511; www.bellasartesdecaguas.com; cnr Luis Padial & Segundo Ruiz Belvo; ⊙9am-5pm) FREE On the west side of Calle Luis Padial, spreading along a grand walkway replete with fountains and sculptures, the former premises of the General Cigar Company has been converted into an impressive three-tier cultural center, with artwork by Caguas artists and two dedicated performance spaces.

Museo del Tobacco MUSEUM
(Betances 87 cnr Luis Padial; ⊙9am-noon & 1-5pm Tue-Sat) FREE Puerto Rico's tobacco industry might be outshone by Cuba's, but the island produced plenty of its own tobacco back in the day, which was then often shipped to Cuba for manufacture into cigars. Tobacco growing, cutting, drying and processing was once an economic mainstay of Caguas and this museum provides a history of all of it.

✗ Eating

Orujo Taller de Gastronomía PUERTO RICAN $$
(80 Gautier Benítez; $12-30; ⊙5-10pm Tue-Sat, to 9pm Sun) Close to the centre, this spectacular restaurant offers surprises such as scallops or rib-eye skate, and has the neat touch of a screen so you can watch your food being assembled in the kitchen. A family ambience pervades, and for the thought that goes into the dishes the prices are reasonable.

ⓘ Getting There & Away

Caguas is 31km south of San Juan on a fairly swift Hwy 52.

The *público* terminal is two blocks northeast of Plaza Palmer on Calle Acosta. It's more useful than most *público* terminals in Puerto Rico, mainly because of its proximity to San Juan. Rio Piedras in San Juan is a 30-minute ride.

Bosque Estatal de Carite

Less than an hour south of San Juan, the **Bosque Estatal de Carite** (Carite Forest Reserve; ☑787-747-4510, 787-772-2009; Rte 184; ☺6am-6pm Tue-Sun) was created in 1935 to protect the watersheds of various local rivers from erosion and urbanization. Measuring 6000 acres in area, the mountain reserve is one of the first points of interest you will hit if you are traversing the Ruta Panorámica from east to west.

It can get crowded on weekends and during the summer when *sanjuaneros* (San Juan residents) come here to enjoy the 72°F temperatures, leafy shade and multiple *lechoneras* (restaurants specializing in smoky, spit-roasted suckling pig) that line Hwy 184 as it approaches the northern forest entrance in an area known island-wide as Guavate.

As with most Puerto Rican forest reserves, facilities are spartan and ranger stations are often unmanned. If you are intending to stay here, make arrangements in advance and bring water, insect repellent and food; no supplies are sold inside.

◉ Sights & Activities

Carite can be an incredible place for hiking, camping, fishing and cooling off in pools and streams, as long as you're up for some DIY adventure. There are 49 species of bird here – including the endangered native *falcón de sierra* (mountain hawk) – and a variety of trees.

Hurricanes have wreaked havoc on Carite's trails in the past and most paths have been destroyed. The only trail maintained by rangers is Charco Azul Trail, though with a bit of bushwhacking you can probably get through on the El Radar Trail and a couple of others that lead upstream from Charco Azul. It's best to phone ahead to check current conditions if you're a serious hiker, though you may well reach a park employee who knows nothing about the trails.

At Las Casas de la Selva, managers can provide information and guides for long hikes through Carite, many of which are suggested for experienced hikers only.

There are three main *areas recreativas* (recreational areas) good for a picnic: **Charco Azul** (Hwy 184; campsite $4; ☺6am-6pm; Ⓟ); near the southern entrance on Hwy 184), **Real Patillas** (Hwy 184; ☺6am-6pm; Ⓟ; also in the south on Hwy 184) and **Guavate** (Hwy 184; ☺6am-6pm Tue-Sun; Ⓟ; above the *lechoneras* in the north).

Charco Azul Trail   HIKING
After several storms destroyed trails in the Bosque Estatal de Carite, rangers decided to clear and maintain only this one, the reserve's most popular trail. It leads to a hazy blue swimming hole and camping/picnic area of the same name. It is an easy half-mile walk from Hwy 184, near the southeast corner of the forest.

El Radar Trail   HIKING
(Vereda Los Baldíos) The El Radar trailhead in the Bosque Estatal de Carite departs in a southwesterly direction off Hwy 184 near the northwest corner of the forest, and makes a steep, 2km climb to the peak of Cerro Baldíos. If you look beyond the ugly Doppler radar weather station, you'll be rewarded with vistas of the north and south coasts, and hills that roll off toward El Yunque.

🛌 Sleeping

★**Las Casas de la Selva & Tropic Ventures**   CAMPGROUND, CABINS **$**
(☑787-839-7318; www.eyeontherainforest.org; Hwy 184 Km 16.1; campsites $15, d $70; Ⓟ) This reserve is on the south slope of the Sierra de Cayey. Once a coffee plantation, it became a sustainable-growth tree farm 20 years ago

---

ⓘ **TAKING A HIKE**

Fine, we'll just say it: Puerto Rico can bedevil the ambitious hiker. Despite the lush natural areas and acres of natural reserves there's something about traipsing trails that just simply doesn't jibe with Puerto Rican culture – one park ranger suggested it was because people don't like getting their shoes dirty! Trails are often unmarked and poorly maintained and there are few reliable maps available locally. If you want to do a lot of hiking it's a good idea to order detailed topographical maps before you leave home, have no expectations for word-of-mouth route suggestions and arrive with an ample supply of patience.

and continues to be a leading institution for rainforest study. The 1000-acre reserve is mostly for ecological and environmental research and volunteers but, if there is space, visitors can come for a rustic vacation.

ⓘ Getting There & Away

The only way to enter the forest is by car: normally done via the forest's insanely popular northern entrance, at the restaurant strip of Guavate. The forest's northern gate (plus trails and camping access) is half a mile from here. The most popular way of seeing the mountains in their entirety is still a rental car.

From the north, take Hwy 52 to the Cayey Este exit to Hwy 184. You can also reach the forest from Patillas on the south coast via Hwy 184.

Aibonito & Around

POP 25,000

Once Puerto Rico's de facto capital, after Spanish Governor Romualdo Palacios González established residence here in 1887, Aibonito has long been a retreat for the island's political leaders and most wealthy citizens. The town is also the island's highest (at about 2000ft) and hosts an impressive flower festival. For these reasons, and because it's on the Ruta Panorámica, Aibonito is Puerto Rico's most visited mountain settlement.

The town has a euphonious name that suggests a Spanish exclamation meaning 'Wow, how beautiful,' but today, travelers should associate Aibonito with a very limited definition of beauty, with terrible traffic jams on the narrow streets and scant thought to urban planning.

Yet the extraordinary spectacle of Puerto Rico's deepest canyon, the Cañón de San Cristóbal, lying north of town in a deep volcanic rift, alone warrants a visit here. More serene views, this time from above, await at the Mirador La Piedra Degetau.

◎ Sights

★ **Cañón de San Cristóbal** CANYON
This canyon is so unexpected – both in location and appearance – that it may take your breath away. The deep green chasm seemingly drops out of nowhere, its rocky crags hiding a veil of falling water. Only 8km north of Aibonito and cutting more than 500ft down through the Central Mountains, it is bisected by the churning white waters of the Río Usabón – for adventurous outdoor lovers an exploration is truly a first-class thrill.

The highest waterfall on the island is here, where the river plummets down a sheer cliff into a gorge that is deeper, in many places, than it is wide.

To make the descent into the canyon, there are steep, slippery trails or you can make a vertigo-inducing technical descent – the latter recommended only for those with mountaineering experience.

Whilst you can catch a glimpse of the canyon from a distance by looking east from the intersection of Rte 725 and Rte 162, getting into the canyon is a bit trickier. One way is to take side roads off Rte 725 or Rte 7725 and then cross private land to approach the rim of the canyon. It's essential to get permission to cross private property. Cañón de San Cristóbal has sheer cliffs that are prone to landslides, and the trails into the canyon are a slippery death wish when they get wet (and it rains a lot around here).

The best way to visit the canyon is to plan ahead, make reservations and join an organized trek with **Go Hiking Puerto Rico** (☏787-857-2094, 787-857-3511; www.barranquitaspr.net/tours; half-day tours from $100 per person), run by local historian and geographer Samuel Oliveras Ortiz. Trips run on weekends and holidays and vary from a three- to four-hour basic tour ($100) to a five- to six-hour adrenalin-junkie fest with rock climbing and rappelling ($135 to $160 depending on number of people). Another outfit that comes recommended is **Montaña Explora** (☏787-516-6194; www.elyunquedaytrips.com; half-/full-day tour from $100/175 per person), with similar prices.

Wear secure shoes and layer appropriate clothing that you can take off at the canyon floor, where temperatures can be more than 10°F warmer than up on the brink. Of course, you will need water and snacks for the return trip up the canyon wall (where you get to climb up through a waterfall). You'll probably only see the canyon right as you approach its edge; the rift is so deep and narrow that the surrounding high-mountain plateau disguises it.

Mirador La Piedra Degetau VIEWPOINT
(Hwy 7718) This nest of boulders crests a hilltop alongside the Ruta Panorámica (Hwy 7718 here) at Km 0.7, just south of Aibonito. Once the 'thinking place' of Ponce-born writer Federico Degetau y González, this must have been a magical place in its day, with

its views of mountains, the Atlantic and the Caribbean. On a clear evening you can actually see cruise ships leaving San Juan over 20 miles to the north and the lights of Ponce glowing to the south.

Sadly, a lookout tower (that dwarfs the actual rocks), myriad picnic shelters, a playground and a paved parking lot hinder the lyrical ruminations of potential poets today. It's still an inspiring view, but one can't help feeling that Degetau must be turning in his grave.

✨ Festivals & Events

Festival de Flores FLOWERS
(☉Jun) Aibonito's Festival de Flores (Flower Festival) has grown into a major rite of summer during the last 30 years. Today it draws hundreds of commercial growers and amateur horticulturists, and tens of thousands of flowerlovers to see the town and surrounds ablaze with roses, carnations, lilies and begonias. There are food and craft stalls too, and the requisite beauty pageant.

✖ Eating

Restaurante
Asador Isla Bonita PUERTO RICAN $$
(☎787-735-8151; Hwy 162 Km 0.6, Barrio Cuyon; mains $10-25; ☉noon-4pm Fri-Sun) Location, location...come here for the 2700ft-high sublime views over the hilly greenery known as the Tetas de Cayey (the Cayey tits); the view is so good that it doesn't matter if the food, such as *mofongo* (mashed plantains with pork rinds) or *paella jíbara*, is only average. It's located off Hwy 162 near the junction Hwy 1: the penultimate right-hand turn before the junction if coming from Aibonito.

ℹ Getting There & Away

Aibonito is 41km southwest of Caguas. The quickest way to get here is by taking the Cayey exit off Hwy 52 and then continuing northwest via Hwy 1, then Rtes 7722 and 722.

Most drivers approach Aibonito via the Ruta Panorámica (Hwy 162 at this point). A less-traveled and yet more dramatic route (if you like hairpin turns) is to take Hwy 173 and Hwy 14 southwest from Cidra.

Barranquitas & Around

POP 50,000

Barranquitas is a diminutive, picturesque settlement clinging to the muddy slopes of the rain-lashed Cordillera Central. On the north side of the spectacular Cañón de San Cristóbal, the town is known as the Cuna de Próceres (Cradle of Great People) for its historical propensity to produce such notable figures as the legendary Muñoz clan, Puerto Rico's substitute 'royal' family.

Hurricanes and fires have repeatedly ravaged Barranquitas (the name translates to 'Place of Little Mud Slides'): the oldest structures date only from the 20th century. The charm here is less in the history and more in the tightly packed narrow streets that tumble into deep valleys from the pretty plaza. Indeed, the view as you descend into town from the mountains and the afternoon sun that sets the church tower ablaze are truly memorable.

The region's greatest range of restaurants awaits and, 20km northwest in Orocovis, Puerto Rico's best adventure park.

◉ Sights

Plaza de Recreo de Barranquitas PLAZA
(Calle Luis Muñoz Rivera, Barranquitas) Barranquitas' pretty central plaza is laced with wrought-iron railings and guarded by the **Parroquia de San Antonio de Padua**. The centerpiece of the plaza is a decorative wrought-iron gazebo adorned with distinctive art-nouveau flourishes, surrounded by four classical fountains.

Casa Museo Luis Muñoz Rivera MUSEUM
(Luis Muñoz Rivera 10, cnr Manuel Torres; admission $1; ☉8:30am-4:20pm Wed-Sun) This tin-roofed house honors the so-called grandfather of Puerto Rico's autonomy movement and the 20th-century architect of the Puerto Rican Commonwealth. This is where Luis Muñoz Rivera was born in 1859; it contains a collection of furniture, letters, photographs and other memorabilia, including his death mask.

The coolest thing on display is his 1912 Pierce-Arrow motorcycle, which carried him to his mausoleum.

Mausoleo Familia Muñoz Rivera MUSEUM
(7 Calle Padre Berrios; ☉8:30am-4:20pm Wed-Sun) FREE Just south of the plaza is a family tomb that holds the remains of Muñoz Rivera, his famous son Luis Muñoz Marín and their wives. Photographic displays at the tomb evoke the funeral of Luis Muñoz Marín, and the brightly colored frescoes on the walls are an aptly powerful testament to the man himself.

GUAVATE

A cherished place for traditional Puerto Rican cooking, Guavate is the spiritual home of the island's ultimate culinary 'delicacy,' *lechón asado* (whole roast pig), locally reared and turning on a spit. And, although the myriad of *lechoneras* that pepper the roadside might look a little rough around the edges (Styrofoam plates, Formica tables), appearances can be deceiving and the crowds tell another story. If it's the island's uninhibited soul you're after, look no further.

The best action is on weekend afternoons between 2pm and 9pm, when old-fashioned troubadours entertain crowds, and live salsa, *merengue* and *reggaetón* music summons diners to the makeshift dance floors for libidinous grooving. With over a dozen restaurants and stalls all offering similar canteen-style food and service, your best bet is to come hungry and follow the crowds. Standards include *arroz con gandules* (rice and pigeon peas), *pasteles* (mashed plantain and pork) and – brave, this one – *morcillas* (rice and pigs blood).

If you can't choose which lechonera, try **El Rancho Original** (Rte 184 Km 27.5; plates $6-10; ⊙10am 8pm Sat & Sun), where they serve consistently perfect pork that's heavenly, smoky and covered in crispy skin. But, truth be told, standards on the 'Ruta del Lechón' are very high and most places along the route have dedicated fans who swear their place is best.

To get to Guavate from San Juan, follow Expressway 52 to exit 31, halfway between Caguas and Cayey. Turn east onto Hwy 184.

🏃 Activities

⭐ Toro Verde
Nature Adventure Park   ADVENTURE SPORTS
(📞787-867-7020; www.toroverdepr.com; Hwy 155 Km 33, Barrio Gato, Sector Los Santiago, Orocovis; Zipline tours from $65; ⊙8am-5pm) This park was completed in 2010 and offers a suite of adventures among a striking belt of forest near the little town of Orocovis, 20km northwest of Barranquitas. The affordable, adrenaline-soaked zipline tours and single-track mountain-bike circuit make it the best facility of its kind on the island – and possibly in the Americas.

Although it's difficult to pick a highlight, 'El Monstruo' (the Monster) is a record-breaker as far as ziplines go.

There is also another 1.5km zipline, 'La Bestia' ($65), and combination tours involving other smaller ziplines and wildly swinging hanging bridges. Note that for the ziplines and bridges there are weight and age requirements (the youngest available for kids over 12) and that for all activities here you need to reserve in advance, as the park has cultivated a reputation far and wide and is immensely popular.

The 13km-long mountain-bike circuit ($25) is far and away the best maintained trail ride in the Central Mountains, designed by pro mountain-biker Marla Streb. Its single-track trails are challenging, with lots of tight lines and good drops.

The adventure park also has a shop and the well-regarded Restaurante Toro Verde (p220) using produce grown on the premises. Plans for a hotel to house weary adventurers are afoot.

El Monstruo   ADVENTURE SPORTS
(The Monster; 📞787-867-7020; www.toroverdepr.com; Rte 155 Km 33, Barrio Gato, Toro Verde Nature Adventure Park, Orocovis; $135 per person) You could not ask for a better thrill. Officially the longest zipline in the world, whooshing you almost 2.5km Superman-style over a lonely forest valley at speeds faster than you could achieve on any Puerto Rican road (95mph), this is the stunning highlight of the Toro Verde Nature Adventure Park.

🛌 Sleeping & Eating

Hacienda Margarita   HOTEL **$**
(📞787-451-1873; www.haciendamargaritahotel.com; Rte 152, Km 1.7, Barrio Quebrada Grande, Sector Tres Caminos; r/ste from $73/89; 🅿❄🛜🏊) Its destruction on several occasions is testimony to this hotel's lofty but exposed location on a hill crest 2.5km northeast of Barranquitas. Guests could not ask for more stupendous views, which look over the adjacent banana plantations to tumbling broccoli-green valleys stippled with gleaming white hamlets. There are 21 clean, modern rooms and suites here (complimentary bottled water and wi-fi).

CASA BAVARIA

You might not believe your eyes when you stumble upon **Casa Bavaria** (☑787-862-7818; www.casabavaria.com; Carr 155 Km 38.3, Barrio Perchas, Morovis; $5.50-19; ⊙noon-8pm Thu, Fri & Sun, to 10pm Sat), a German-Creole surprise of a restaurant perched 2105ft high in the mountains near Morovis in the center of the island. The menu mixes typical cuisine from the Bavarian region of Germany with meaty specialties of Puerto Rico. The outdoor seating and misty views draw bikers and road-trippers galore, and fans include President Bill Clinton, who stopped by in 2008 to order the schnitzel.

★**El Navideño** BOUTIQUE HOTEL **$$$**
(☑787-867-6900; www.facebook.com/fonday posadaelnavideno; Pedro Arroyo 3, Orocovis; r from $200; ✿) It's *Navidad* (Christmas) all year round at Puerto Rico's oddest boutique hotel, but once you've got over the festive songs and the *coquitos* (traditional rum-and-coconut drinks) being dished out at the bar, you'll find this place very comfortable, if OTT in almost every aspect (including the price).

The gaudy suites upstairs come with superplump beds, wi-fi, flatscreen TVs and DVD/Blu-ray players. Energy flow has been corrected by the same people who did Madonna's feng shui. Breakfast is served in an inviting central patio. El Navideño is in Orocovis, near Toro Verde Nature Adventure Park (p219).

Andante Fusion Culinaria PUERTO RICAN **$**
(☑787-477-4229; off Calle Nuevo Barranquitas, above Rte 152; mains $5-15; ⊙11am-11pm Wed & Thu, to midnight Fri & Sat, noon-11pm Sun) The Andante has been a gastronomic success since its opening in 2013, boasting imaginative food (chicken stuffed with spinach and guava sauce, for example) and drop-dead gorgeous views. It's up in what's become the most distinctive landmark hereabouts: the garish windmill above town, also accessible via a flight of some 320 steps from central Barranquitas.

★**Restaurante Toro Verde** INTERNATIONAL **$$**
(☑787-867-7020; www.restaurant.tororverdepr.com; Rte 155 Km 33, Barrio Gato, Sector Los Santiago, Orocovis; mains $17-42; ⊙11am-6pm Mon-Thu, 11am-9pm Fri-Sun) It's not so common to find fine dining *and* a fine view in the Central Mountains, but this restaurant at Toro Verde Nature Adventure Park (p219) will wow you on both counts. The marinated skirt steak in a cilantro, orange and chimichurri sauce is as wondrous as the location is dramatic.

❶ Getting There & Away

Barranquitas is 43km west of Caguas via Hwy 156. It's about a 20-minute drive out of Aibonito on Hwy 162 (or an even shorter detour off of the Ruta Panorámica via Hwy 143).

Reserva Forestal Toro Negro

Covering 7000 acres and protecting Puerto Rico's highest peaks, the Toro Negro Reserve provides a quieter, less-developed alternative to El Yunque. Bisected by some of the steepest, windiest parts of the Ruta Panorámica (Hwy 143 here), the area is often shrouded in mist and blanketed by dense jungle foliage. This is where you come to truly escape the tourist hotspots, but don't expect El Yunque's polish. Toro Negro's facilities – which comprise a campground, a few trails and a recreation area as deserted as the Mary Celeste – are spartan and sporadically staffed, and signage is rough.

Properly prepared, you can carve out memorable DIY adventures here on some of Puerto Rico's most intoxicating hikes. This appeal is augmented as the forest has on its western flank one of the island's most interesting coffee haciendas.

Cerro de Punta, at 4389ft, is the tallest point in the reserve and Puerto Rico's highest summit.

◉ Sights

★**Hacienda Pomarrosa** FARM
(☑787-844-3541; www.pomarrosacoffeelodge.com; Rte 511 cnr Hwy 143; 2-hour tour $20; ⊙11am Mon-Sat) Perhaps the best opportunity in Puerto Rico to discover what traditional coffee growing is like, plus the chance to learn about the entire bean-to-bag process, can be gleaned here at this tranquil coffee plantation west of Reserva Forestal Toro Negro and south of Jayuya.

Whilst other coffee plantations do tours, this is a more personal, in-depth and yet esoteric insight into Puerto Rico's coffee industry past and present. You can sample the beans grown here with a brew at the end of the tour. There is also an option to stay overnight in one of three charming villas (then, you'll get more delicious coffee for breakfast!). Reservations for tours are strongly advised; otherwise, if you just turn up it's possible no one will be there.

Cerro de Punta   MOUNTAIN

(Hwy 143) Rising to 4389ft, the summit of Cerro de Punta, Puerto Rico's highest mountain, lies in the western portion of the Reserva Forestal Toro Negro just off to the north above Hwy 143 (the Ruta Panorámica). The peak is crowned by communication towers, though the view north is stupendous – clouds permitting.

Hwy 143 passes the base of a narrow, unmarked, fairly treacherous cement road to the peak, and the best way to reach the top is to park here on the northern side of Hwy 143 and take the last 1.5 miles by foot, soaking up the sights and sounds of the surrounding jungle.

Area Recreativa Doña Juana   PICNIC AREA

(Hwy 143 Km 33) This is the area of about 5 sq km at the eastern end of the Reserva Forestal Toro Negro near the ranger station. It is here that would-be adventurers should sally forth from. The area has picnic sites, toilets, showers, camping areas and a half-dozen short trails branching off above Hwy 143 (to the left, as you approach from Barranquitas).

🏃 Activities

A decent network of trails exists, fanning out from around the Area Recreativa Doña Juana. The trail network is extensive, but complex, with paths in good nick but rarely marked. It's best to plan ahead and ask about current conditions at the DRNA in San Juan, as mudslides are common.

It's best to consult with the **ranger station** (☑787-867-3040; Hwy 143 Km 32.4; ⊘8am-5pm) for longer hikes. Out on the forest paths however, hikers may run into difficulty navigating with the basic maps available at the ranger station. They have photocopies of the reserve map marking key trails, however some of this material is extremely misleading. The trail map lacks useful detail and the compass rose has been rotated so north is not at the top of the page. You're not likely to get anything better in San Juan from the DRNA (p262), nor is it easy to get USGS maps on the island. Source a USGS map from map suppliers in the US, or mail-order one on the island.

Prepare properly: bring sufficient food and water, and insect repellent.

Camino El Bolo   HIKING

(Hwy 143) Across from the ranger station near Area Recreativa Doña Juana in Reserva Forestal Toro Negro, you'll spot a narrow trail heading uphill. That's El Bolo, a 4km jaunt taking you up to a mountain ridge with great southern views.

★ Vereda La Torre   HIKING

(Reserva Forestal Toro Negro) If you follow the Camino El Bolo trail up from the ranger station in Reserva Forestal Toro Negro, after about 5km you'll intersect with this trail, snaking up to an observation tower with superb views. You can return to the Area Recreativa Doña Juana, from where the ranger station is a short walk along Hwy 143, via Vereda La Piscina.

Vereda La Piscina   HIKING

(Hwy 143) This useful connector trail in the Reserva Forestal Toro Negro runs up through the camping area from Area Recreativa Doña Juana to link with the Camino El Bolo. It's a steep, muddy climb. Unfortunately, the swimming pool from which the trail takes its name is no longer functioning.

🧭 Tours

Acampa Nature Adventure Tours   HIKING

(Map p52; ☑787-706-0695; www.acampapr.com; 517 Ave Andalucia, San Juan; $143 per person) Offers one-day hiking/adventure tours to the Toro Negro rainforest. The excursion involves hiking/scrambling along the Quebrada Rosa River, rappelling off a 60ft cliff and ziplining 200ft across the treetops. Prices include transportation from San Juan, equipment and lunch. Note it's a six-person minimum.

🛏 Sleeping

Los Viveros   CAMPGROUND $

(Hwy 143 Km 32.5, Reserva Forestal Toro Negro; campsite per person $4) In Reserva Forestal Toro Negro, near the ranger station in Area Recreativa Doña Juana, this is a designated camping area with enough space for 14 tents. It's up above Hwy 143 by a defunct swimming pool that in its heyday made this a more appealing spot. Get a permit from the DRNA (p262) in San Juan. Apply 15 days in advance.

★**Hacienda Pomarrosa**　　FARMSTAY $$
(☎787-844-3541; www.pomarrosacoffeelodge.com;
Rte 511 cnr Hwy 143; r $125; [P]) ∕ Crickets
chirrup as you wake up cocooned within
an expansive working coffee estate replete
with bananas and breadfruit, and rimmed
by the pines that lend the coffee beans cul-
tivated here their unique taste. The three
tucked-away *casitas* (self-contained villas)
are touchingly decorated. Recline on the ve-
randahs in the hammocks, then wander up
to the restaurant for an exquisite breakfast.

❶ Getting There & Away

The Reserva Forestal Toro Negro lies in two
portions, east and west of Hwy 149. The forest
is traversed in its entirety by Hwy 143, the Ruta
Panorámica. All of the forest's public facilities lie
at the east part of the reserve around the Area
Recreativa Doña Juana at Km 33 on Hwy 143,
and at the ranger station a few hundred metres
along Hwy 143 to the west.

Jayuya

POP 16,000

Puerto Rico's unheralded mountain 'capi-
tal' lies a few kilometers north of the Ruta
Panorámica in an isolated steep-sided val-
ley overlooked by three of the island's high-
est peaks – Cerro de Punta, Cerro los Tres
Picachos and Cerro Maravilla. Verdantly
beautiful, the precipitous geography here
has protected many of the island's tradi-
tions. If you're bent on finding Puerto Rico's
last authentic *jíbaro* (country person), this
is a good starting point.

Steeped in Taíno legend, the original set-
tlement of Jayuya had little contact with the
rest of the island until 1911, when it was de-
clared a municipality. Efforts to keep Taíno
culture alive include several related sights
such as the quirky Museo del Cemí, plus a
festival of music, food, games and a Miss
Taíno pageant.

Jayuya has long had a reputation for cof-
fee production and, more recently, moon-
shine rum – visitors will have a chance to
sample both.

History

One of sleepy Jayuya's most notable mo-
ments was in 1950. Local nationalist leader
Blanca Canales led a revolt against US oc-
cupation known as the 'Jayuya Uprising.'
Rebels ransacked the police station and
declared a Puerto Rican republic from the
town square. The rebellion lasted just three
days before US planes bombed the town,
causing widespread destruction. Still, even
today, Jayuya is one of the island's most
un-Americanized towns.

◎ Sights

Pitorico Rum Distillery　　DISTILLERY
(☎787-828-1300; Rte 141 Km 0.7; ⊗9am-5pm Tue-
Sat) FREE It's certainly not Bacardi, nor even
Don Q, that does it for Jayuya folks – not
compared to their very own artisan rum,
which comes in delicious flavours like pas-
sionfruit and coconut. The amenable staff
here will give you a complimentary tour of
their distillery plus a few tastings.

RUTA PANORÁMICA

Traveling the Ruta Panorámica – the route devised by the Puerto Rico Tourist Board in
order to better promote the Central Mountains – can be a fun detour or a maddening
frustration. Here, distances suddenly become mysteriously elongated as the island
appears to double in size and you crawl along the curving lines of the map at a snail's
pace. Drives that would take 20 minutes on the coast turn into two- to three-hour
odysseys. Only a few brief glimpses of the faraway ocean remind you that you haven't
disappeared into the Amazonian jungle. First-timers beware: this is no Sunday-afternoon
dawdle. Maneuvering through dense rainforest and sleepy mountain villages, the Ruta's
roadsides are populated by posses of stray dogs, horse-riding *jíbaros* (country people)
and – most chillingly – the burnt-out wrecks of hundreds of abandoned cars. The latter
should be enough to remind wannabe speed freaks to steer carefully (never at more
than 25mph). Unfortunately, the locals aren't always so fastidious, often taking the pre-
carious hills and tricky chicanes at 35mph or more.

Drive defensively and be on your guard, and remember to sound your horn around blind
corners. And don't get ruffled if you can't find signs for the 'official' Ruta Panorámica –
signs are often obscured or moved by local business owners hoping to lure traffic.

★ **Hacienda San Pedro**   FARM
(☑ 787-828-2083; www.cafehsp.com; Rte 144 Km 8.4; ☺ 8am-6pm Mon-Fri, 10am-5pm Sat & Sun) San Pedro is a small, working coffee farm with an attached museum and cafe/tasting room where you can get a fascinating insight into the coffee-making process from green bean to dark-roast espresso. Tours are available on weekends at noon, 2pm and 4pm ($10). The gourmet blends served in its **Cafe La Finca** are some of the best brews you'll taste anywhere.

Casa Museo Canales   MUSEUM
(☑ 787-828-1241; Rte 144 Km 9.3; adult/child $1.50/1; ☺ 9:30am-4pm) In a small park in the *barrio* of Coabey, this reconstructed 19th-century coffee *finca* (rural smallholding) nestles in the shadow of the surrounding mountains. Replete with interesting antiques, it belonged to Jayuya's first mayor, Rosario Canales.

Museo del Cemí   MUSEUM
(☑ 787-828-1241; Rte 144 Km 9.2; adult/child $1.50/1; ☺ 9:30am-4pm Mon-Fri, to 3pm Sat & Sun) In the same park as Casa Museo Canales, in Coabey, this is perhaps the oddest building on the island. Designed by Río Piedras architect Efrén Badía Cabrera, the weird fish-like structure supposedly represents a gigantic *cemí* or native Taíno talisman. The exhibits inside are made up mostly of Taíno artifacts.

La Piedra Escrita   ARCHAEOLOGICAL SITE
(Hwy 144 Km 7.3; ☺ 24hr) Some of the island's best-preserved native petroglyphs are carved on a large rock in the middle of the Río Saliente just off Hwy 144 3km east of Jayuya. The stone forms a natural bathing pool, and it has become a popular stop-off for curious (and hot) travelers. There's a small car park and restaurant.

✴️ Festivals & Events

Jayuya Indigenous Festival   CULTURAL
(☺ Nov) Held in November, this festival remembers the region's Taíno heritage. How close the food, drink, music and 'Miss Taíno' contest come to a cultural insight into Jayuya's ancient indigenous population is open to debate.

🛏 Sleeping & Eating

There are a few very basic restaurants in town, and every place to eat out in the region is seemingly open Thursday through Sunday only. Jayuya's supermarkets therefore come in handy. For a coffee better than most San Juan can muster, head to Hacienda San Pedro or Hacienda Pomarrosa (p220) near the Reserva Forestal Toro Negro.

Hacienda Gripiñas   HOTEL $
(☑ 787-828-1717; Hwy 527 Km 2.5; s/d from $65/80; P ❄ 🛜 🏊) Ensconced in this beautifully restored coffee hacienda dating from 1858 and nestled in the shadow of Cerro de Punta, guests wander creaking floors through rooms furnished with antiques and historic coffee posters, and rock in wicker chairs on the breezy balconies.

★ **El Burén**   PUERTO RICAN $
(☑ 787-828-2589; Hwy 528 Km 5.4; mains $11-18; ☺ 2-8pm Thu, noon-8pm Fri & Sun, noon-9pm Sat) A host of Puerto Rican classics await you in an atmosphere reminiscent of a *jíbaro* ranch, but with the quiet confidence of an establishment that knows people know how well it cooks. Try *longaniza* (a chorizo with a vivid red hue from annatto seeds) and rice or seafood *mofongo*, and don't forgo the *sorullitos* (Puerto Rican corn fritters) to start with.

ℹ️ Getting There & Away

After all the zigzagging little roads up and down densely forested valley sides, it's a relief to halt for the night in Jayuya – an arduous 48km west of Barranquitas via Hwy 143 (aka the Ruta Panorámica) or 25km northeast of Adjuntas.

Adjuntas & Around

POP 18,000

Although calling Adjuntas the 'Switzerland of Puerto Rico' is a slight overstatement, the surrounding silhouetted mountains earn this agreeable agricultural hub a more accurate moniker: 'town of the sleeping giant.' After the discovery of copper near here in the 1960s, local community groups fought successfully to prevent their cool subtropical jungle haven from being turned into a huge open-cast mining pit. Instead, Adjuntas has become something of an environmental steward whose livelihood remains rooted in bananas, coffee and citrus fruits.

Situated where one of the island's major north–south arteries (Hwys 123 and 10) crests the Central Mountains, Adjuntas is a traffic bottleneck in the summer. The central plaza is a good place to wander while you cool the engine and there are several places on its periphery for refreshments.

The main draw hereabouts is the Bosque Estatal de Guilarte, with a peak to climb and remote, no-frills cabins.

◉ Sights

Hacienda Tres Angeles FARM
(📞787-360-0019; www.haciendatresangeles.com; Km 38.4, Hwy 129; Tours $15 per person; ⊘ Tours 8am-5pm Fri & Sat, 11am-5pm Sun) Adjuntas jousts with Jayuya for the accolade of being Puerto Rico's premier coffee region and this coffee hacienda is surely the most beautifully situated of any on the island. Tours here include a cuppa concocted with the beans grown in the grounds. It's a very nice visitor experience.

Bosque Estatal de Guilarte FOREST
(Rtes 518 & 131) This forest, 10km southwest of Adjuntas, consists of a number of parcels of land totaling about 5000 acres. Most is rainforest dominated by sierra palms. Coming from the northeast you first see Lago Garzas, a fishing site. West of this lake, the road rises toward the park's **ranger station** (📞787-829-5767, 787-772-2009; Rte 131; cabins from $20), near the intersection of Rtes 518 and 131. At the ranger station, there's a picnic area with shelters, cooking grills, toilets, cabins and a trail to the top of Monte Guilarte (3950ft).

The five cabins are maintained by the Departamento de Recursos Naturales y Ambientales (DRNA): sleeping up to six, with toilets and shower facilities. Cooking facilities are outdoors and there's no electricity. You must bring all your own gear, including bedding. Make your reservations 15 days in advance with the DRNA (p262) in San Juan. Camping is not permitted in Guilarte.

🛏 Sleeping & Eating

Adjuntas has a few basic eateries dotted around its central plaza, and Parador Villas de Sotomayor has a restaurant. Otherwise, stock up at the supermarkets in Adjuntas for picnic grub.

Parador Villas de Sotomayor CABIN $$
(📞787-829-1717; www.paradorvillassotomayor.com; Hwy 123/10 Km 36.3; cabins from $104; ☀) This campus of small cabins along a rock river is the best spot for families in the area, with an on-site horseback-riding stable, bright swimming pool, playground, basketball and tennis courts and plenty of space to run around.

There are 26 worn but decent villas and a well-regarded restaurant.

ⓘ Getting There & Away

Adjuntas is one of the easier places to reach in the Central Mountains, 25km north of Ponce and 50km south of Arecibo via the new Hwy 10, a road that – whilst a long way from fast – has nevertheless improved connections here no end. Fuel stations on Hwy 10 are few and far between compared to the roads on the coast.

Maricao
POP 5750

Fog-swathed Maricao is the minutest of Puerto Rico's main island municipalities, and a gem of a mountain retreat near the western end of the Ruta Panorámica. Commerce here is dominated by agriculture, and a coffee festival celebrating the most important local crop is the year's biggest event. Otherwise, this is a place of rushing streams, hair-raising switchback roads and weather so cool and damp that some houses have stone fireplaces to take the nip out of the air. Outside town lies resplendent mountain terrain and Puerto Rico's largest state forest, the Bosque Estatal de Maricao.

Maricao is just the kind of locale in which legends take root. Some claim it was the strong coffee cultivated here that woke up the devil on the island. Another story tells of 2000 Taíno that survived here into the 19th century, centuries after the last native Puerto Ricans were thought to have disappeared.

◉ Sights

Bosque Estatal de Maricao NATURE RESERVE
(Rte 120) This forest of more than 10,000 acres lies along the Ruta Panorámica south of Maricao: it's the largest of the island's state forests. The drive through is spectacular, with sharp curves snaking over ridges as the mountainsides fall away into sheer valleys. En route are several pull-offs at trailheads leading into the woods or down steep inclines, although most visitors just stop at the stone observation tower, La Torre de Piedra, as Rte 120 crests the mountaintop at 2450ft.

🎉 Festivals & Events

Festival del Acabe del Café FOOD & DRINK
(Coffee Festival; ⊘ Feb) In mid-February, Maricao's status as a hotbed of coffee production is highlighted in an entire festival dedicated

to the bountiful bean. Expect traditional coffee-making demonstrations, and crafts.

🛏 Sleeping

Parque Ecológico Monte de Estado en Maricao CABIN $
(☎787-873-5632, reservations 787-622-5200; Hwy 120 Km 13.1; campsite/cabin from $15/65; ᴘ🖭) Southeast of Maricao, this campground has 24 remodeled cabins sleeping between three and six, mostly with refrigerators, fireplaces and hot water. There are campsites too. The area also has a swimming pool, basketball courts, restrooms, showers and an observation tower. Expect cold, damp weather here because of the lofty altitude.

❶ Getting There & Away

You can approach Maricao from the east or west on the Ruta Panorámica, under the guise of Rte 120 as it heads through Maricao and the Bosque Estatal de Maricao. You can also connect to points north and south via Hwys 119 (to San Sebastián and thereafter the north coast) and 120 (to Sabana Grande, San Germán and then the coastline south or west) which involve a spectacular climb into the mountains on twisting roads.

San Sebastián & Around

POP 40,000

The day after orchestrating the Grito de Lares, an attempt to proclaim an independent Puerto Rico in the mountain town of Lares in 1868, insurgents moved on to nearby San Sebastián, where they were comprehensively defeated by government troops. Thus ended San Sebastián's most important moment in history, and Puerto Rico's one-day stint as a republic.

Today this small town is mainly known for its eccentric Friday market, which sells everything from rifles to rare birds, but the forests to the north secrete some paradisaical excursions. These include the Bosque Estatal de Guajataca, a forest known for some of the best hiking trails on the island. Some brilliant and serendipitous accommodation possibilities lie in store in this region too.

◉ Sights & Activities

The region is primarily known for its beguiling natural attractions, lying north and northeast of the town of San Sebastián.

Forests crisscrossed by the island's best trail system and Puerto Rico's most idyllic swimming holes are the headliners.

San Sebastián Market MARKET
(Hwy 111, Plaza Agropecuaria; ⊗dawn-8pm Fri) One of Puerto Rico's strangest markets takes place on Fridays amidst a labyrinth of stalls at San Sebastián's Plaza Agropecuaria. Whether you're in need of a rifle, a rare bird or just some good old-fashioned *pinchos* (Puerto Rico's take on a kebab), you should find it here.

Museo de História MUSEUM
(⊗10am-4pm Thu-Sun) FREE This ornate mint-green turn-of-the-century edifice has been impressively refurbished to grace San Sebastián's central plaza with its crowning sight. Inside, rooms are preserved with late 19th- and early 20th-century furniture and furnishings.

★Gozalandia WATERFALL
(La Cascada del Guama; off Rte 446; Parking $5; ⊗9am-6pm daily) Sometimes a little piece of paradise lies in store even in the least obvious of locales, and Gozalandia is San Sebastián's: a flurry of dramatic cascades 5km north of town that tumbles into some inviting plunge pools. The crashing river here is backed by steep forest and is a truly beautiful spot to spend some hours soaking up the quietude.

There are two key cascades. At the lower it is possible, with care, to climb behind the waterfall, whilst at the upper, there is a rope swing. Near the parking area, the Sha's (p226) restaurant rustles up great cocktails using fresh fruits, and it is rarely crowded.

Note that the owner of the land on which the cascades are found still advertises the place as La Cascada del Guama even though most know it as Gozalandia.

Bosque Estatal de Guajataca FOREST
(Hwy 446; ᴘ) Despite its diminutive size (2430 acres), the Bosque Estatal de Guajataca contains more trails (27 miles) than any other forest in Puerto Rico – including El Yunque. Set in dramatic karst country, the distinctive terrain oscillates between 500ft and 1000ft above sea level and is characterized by bulbous mogotes (sheer limestone pinnacles) and rounded *sumideros* (funneled depressions). Covered by a moist subtropical forest, there are 45 species of bird to be found here along with 186 different types of tree.

Most of the main hikes depart from, or near, the **ranger station** (☎787-872-1045; Rte

446; ⊙8am-5pm) on Rte 446. True to form, this office, 5 miles into the forest, is not always open, and when rangers do emerge they don't always have much in the way of printed information. The moral: come prepared. The best bet is to call the DRNA (p262) in San Juan before you arrive at the forest, find things closed and feel a little lost. 'Official' maps of the area are usually hand-drawn, photocopied and not to scale.

The most popular hike is the 1.5-mile **Interpretative Trail** (Rte 446): this passes an **observation tower** (Rte 446; ⊙24hr; P) and several other points of interest (be sure to hike to the observation tower to get the best views of the surrounding countryside). It's a moderate walk that takes about two hours.

Trail Number One breaks off from the Interpretative Trail and heads toward **Cueva del Viento** arguably the highlight of the entire forest. There, wooden stairs will take you down into the depths of a dark cave rich with stalactites and stalagmites (bring a flashlight). Let rangers know if you are going into the caves.

There are also a scattering of picnic tables where locals gather around grills, and plantations of blue mahoe trees. The area is a favorite habitat of the endangered Puerto Rican boa.

The nearest eating facilities are a bakery and a supermarket at the intersection of Hwys 446 and 457.

Lago Guajataca   LAKE
(Rte 119; ⊙6am-6pm Tue-Sun) Lago Guajataca is a serene man-made lake with some of Puerto Rico's best fishing – evidenced by two private clubs for anglers hoping to hook some of the bountiful stock of tucunaré and barbudo fish. The easiest approach to the lake is along Hwy 2 to Rte 119 and then into the forest to the DRNA office (☑787-896-7640; Rte 119 Km 22.1; ⊙6am-6pm Tue-Sun). If you want to fish, you'll need to get a permit here: you can pick up a loaner bamboo fishing pole (no bait) too.

🛏 Sleeping & Eating

Nino's Camping & Guesthouse CAMPGROUND $
(☑787-896-9016; www.facebook.com/Ninos-Camping-and-Guest-House-174026676099314; Rte 119 Km 22.1; campsites from $25, cabins up

to 8 people $199; P ☀) Near Lago Guajataca, this is a nice lakeside option, operated by a friendly family. The little cabins have everything except sheets and utensils. Discounts are given for longer stays and there's a swimming pool and an activities room on-site. It can also rent kayaks and operates fishing ventures for groups.

★**San Sebastián Bed & Breakfast** B&B $$
(☑787-942-2867; http://sansebastianbb.com; Andres Méndez 21; r $120; ❋ 🛜) Exquisite breakfasts with feisty local coffee are prepared at this centrally located residence in San Sebastián, one of Puerto Rico's few bed-and-breakfasts. The five rooms are simple but the host is charismatic and extremely informative about the local area.

Hacienda El Jibarito HOTEL $$
(☑787-280-4040; www.haciendaeljibarito.com; Rte 445 Km 6.5; s/d from $149/195; P ❋ ☀) 🅿
This innovative and idyllic ecolodge bills itself as an 'agro-tourist complex,' that is, a hotel doubling up as a hacienda (agricultural estate). Although it retains suitably rustic touches such as hammocks, rocking chairs and antique farming implements, it's a bit softer than the back-to-nature experience you usually get up in the hills.

Sha's PUERTO RICAN $
(Gozalandia, off Rte 446; mains $7-15; ⊙11:30am-7pm) This open-sided restaurant above the waterfalls at Gozalandia serves decent *mofongo* (mashed plantains with meat). They also concoct tasty cocktails using fresh fruit and copious amounts of – you guessed it – rum.

ℹ Getting There & Away

San Sebastián is best approached via Hwy 111, 20km east from where the road branches off from Hwy 2 by Aguada. Rte 119 branches off northeast from San Sebastián to Lago Guajataca (12km). From San Sebastián it's 5km north on Rte 446 to Gozalandia or 11km to the Bosque Estatal de Guajataca. Driving any of these minor roads to get to the region's attractions requires extreme care: expect narrow potholed lanes with extreme rainfall a regular occurrence.

Understand
Puerto Rico

PUERTO RICO TODAY 228

Puerto Rico struggles with dire economic conditions even as it tries to sort out its status with the United States.

HISTORY 230

Puerto Rico's dramatic history has unfolded at the Caribbean crossroads of Africa, Europe and the Americas.

LIFE IN PUERTO RICO 240

Puerto Rican culture is a blend of modern American hustle with breezy Caribbean traditions.

SOUNDS OF PUERTO RICO 245

Ready to dance? Puerto Rico is the legendary birthplace of salsa and reggaetón.

ARTS.......................................250

Puerto Rico has a rich artistic tradition, from vibrant folk art to breathtaking contemporary art.

PUERTO RICO LANDSCAPES.................254

Lush rainforests, dreamy beaches and arid hills make up this amazingly diverse, compact island.

WILDLIFE OF PUERTO RICO..................258

Brightly colored birds flit above, while below a riot of tropical fish dart through Puerto Rico's sparkling waters.

Puerto Rico Today

Drive any distance on Puerto Rico's deplorable roads and your teeth will rattle to the perfect metaphor for the Commonwealth: it's on a very bumpy path. Its finances have gone from bad to worse and it is at risk of following Detroit into bankruptcy. Meanwhile, its best-educated workers see greater opportunity in the United States. And the very relationship with the giant to the north shows no signs of being resolved any time soon.

Best on Film

Maldeamores (2007) Luis Guzmán stars in this film about love's little ironies.

Lo que le pasó a Santiago (1989) Nominated for an Oscar, this is a mysterious, lyrical tale of unexpected love.

Rum Diary (2011) Johnny Depp as Hunter S Thompson in his booze-filled days in San Juan as depicted in his book of the same name.

La guagua aérea (1993) A rueful comedy about Puerto Ricans who moved to the US in the '60s.

Best in Print

When I Was Puerto Rican (Esmeralda Santiago; 1993) This memoir tackles immigration and cultural assimilation.

Parrots Over Puerto Rico (Susan L Roth & Cindy Trumbore; 2013) A beautiful and lyrical look at the island's people, nature and parrots.

Simone (Eduardo Lalo; 2012 (Spanish), 2015 (English) A moody meditation set amid the neighborhoods of San Juan.

Spiks (Pedro Juan Soto; 1973) These short stories concern the struggle of Puerto Rican emigrants to the US in the '50s.

A Question of Status

A commonwealth of the United States of America, Puerto Rico is a semi-autonomous territory whose constitutional status has long been a political oxymoron. Puerto Ricans enjoy many protections and benefits that US citizens have, but they are not allowed to participate in federal elections and have only a nonvoting 'Resident Commissioner' in the US House of Representatives.

A non-binding resolution in 2012 showed that the majority of the island's voters favor US statehood. President Obama committed to funding an 'official' referendum that would decide Puerto Rico's political fate, and set aside $2.5 million for this purpose (although no date was specified).

The question remains, particularly under Donald Trump's presidency, whether any Puerto Rican vote favoring statehood could be linked to a mandated admission process to the US as the 51st state. President Trump's views on this, and relationship with the island, have so far seemed nuanced to say the least. But on becoming Puerto Rico's 12th Governor in 2017, pro-statehood Ricky Rosselló succeeded in getting Senate to pass a bill paving the way for the first 'statehood or independence' vote in Puerto Rico's history, set for June 11, 2017.

Environmentalism & Energy

Energy issues have long sparked debate among Puerto Ricans, whose energy costs outweigh those of their US neighbors (electricity costs are virtually double the US average) despite them having, on average, half the salaries to pay for them with. The island's ailing electricity grid was responsible for an island-wide three-night blackout in September 2016.

As the island has no petroleum, gas or coal reserves, and these three currently account for 98% of its electricity generation, it's easy to see where the problem lies. Solar energy is being slowly increased, and the Santa Isabel wind-turbine farm near Salinas on the south coast is the Caribbean's largest, but many further measures are needed to increase the paltry percentage of Puerto Rican power coming from renewable sources. On a small island, however, securing new energy sources is not always easy.

The Economic Downturn

Like so many other places in the world, Puerto Rico's economy was precipitated on a downwards spiral with the global financial crisis that hit hard beginning in 2007. The effect on the Commonwealth was immediate and stark: unemployment soared to 16%, a level unthinkable just a few years earlier when the island was touted as an economic miracle.

Meanwhile, government spending rose as efforts were made to prop up the economy. By 2012, the island's budget deficit was a whopping $2.2 billion. Efforts to raise taxes and limit spending have met with mixed results. And Puerto Rico has taken a far more blasé approach than other countries facing economic ruin. Why? Well you only need to look north to the US to see salvation.

Bailing out Puerto Rico, however, carries no political gain for the US. Plus, with US spending down, there's little money for a bailout. Instead, Puerto Rico's finances may survive because it is too big to be allowed to fail. For years the Commonwealth's municipal bonds have been beloved by mutual funds and other investors, lured by their high interest yields and supposed security. Were Puerto Rico to collapse, it would have disastrous consequences for some of the world's largest financial institutions.

Collapse, at the beginning of new Governor Ricky Rosselló's tenure in 2017, is still a very prevalent threat. Public debt stands at over $70 billion, so concerning to the US that it appointed a board to oversee all measures undertaken to tackle the deficit, which in turn will hamper Rosselló's power to resolve anything.

Several other factors have been hindrances to economic resuscitation. Puerto Ricans are leaving for the mainland US in greater numbers than ever before. If the island's bright young things only envisage their future beyond its shores, it becomes that much harder for Puerto Rico's economy to bounce back. In addition, the tourism sector, which accounts for an estimated 7% of GNP, has been hard-hit by 2015's Zika outbreak. And President Donald Trump has thus far appeared a lot less sympathetic to the Puerto Rican pecuniary plight than his predecessor.

Many see statehood as the best road to recovery and there is a glimmer of hope in this respect. One of the pro-statehood Rosselló's first acts was to call the island's first ever referendum on its status with the options of 'statehood' and 'independence', to take place in June 2017.

POPULATION: **3.5 MILLION**

POPULATION GROWTH RATE: **-1.73%**

GDP (PER CAPITA): **$28,300**

LIFE EXPECTANCY: **79 YEARS**

UNEMPLOYMENT: **11.9%**

belief systems
(% of population)

70 Roman Catholic

25 Protestant

3 other

2 none

if Puerto Rico were 100 people

80 would be white
12 would be mixed-race (including Taíno)
8 would be black

population per sq km

PUERTO RICO   USA   DOMINICAN REPUBLIC

≈ 35 people

History

Puerto Rico occupies a crucial juncture in the geographical and political history of the Americas. The most defining event in its annals was the nearly 400-year rule of the Spanish, whose checkered history of colonization, genocide, military triumph and defeat are seen everywhere, especially at El Morro fort in Old San Juan. Then there's the dramatic arc of the Commonwealth's struggle to define itself after the US occupation in the late 1800s. Protests, terrorism and passion have fueled the debate.

Taíno Roots

It's unfortunate that, similar to so many other indigenous peoples of the Americas, the best record of Taíno culture is written by those who would annihilate it. Through the journals of Ramón Pané, a Catalonian friar who was traveling with the second Columbus expedition, we are given a vivid firsthand account of the Taíno lifestyle, customs and religious beliefs. Although told with an unintentionally comic cultural and religious bias, it's precious information and often more accurate than other similar histories in the Americas. In his 1505 *Account of the Antiquities – or Customs – of the Indians,* Pané gives a breathless report of Puerto Rico's native residents, describing cities with wide, straight roads, elaborate religious rituals and small communities of 'artfully made' homes behind walls of woven cane. Their diet was derived from tropical fruit grown in orchards that grew oranges and citron that reminded Pané of the ones in Valencia or Barcelona. The beauty of the Taíno culture only exists as an echo today, but it made an indelible influence on contemporary Puerto Rico.

Some historians claim that a small group of Taíno escaped the 16th-century Spanish genocide and hid in Puerto Rico's Central Mountains where they survived until the early 19th century, but there's no proof of this claim.

Taíno Life on Puerto Rico

We know now that the Taíno were an Arawakan group with societies that were well established on Puerto Rico and the other Greater Antilles (Cuba, Hispaniola and Jamaica) when Columbus first turned up in the area in 1493. Arawaks first settled the island around AD 700, following a migration north from the Orinoco River delta in present-day Venezuela.

TIMELINE	2000 BC	430–250 BC	AD 1000
	Puerto Ferro Man, a native from the Ortoiroid culture that had migrated north from the Orinoco basin in present-day Venezuela, lives on the island of Vieques	The Ortoiroids are displaced by the Saladoids, a horticultural people skilled at pottery. Saladoids laid the early building blocks for a singular Caribbean culture.	The Taíno – who also come from the Orinoco basin – emerge as a dominant culture; they name the island Borinquen, meaning 'the Great Land of the Valiant and Noble Lord.'

By AD 1000 a distinctive Taíno culture had emerged based on agriculture, fishing, hunting and the production of cassava bread.

Pané speaks in depth about the complex religious cosmology of the Taíno, a system that had creation stories that often surprised Pané with their Christian parallels. They believed in a single, eternal god who was omnipresent and invisible, and often also worshiped the mother of this god, who was known by a number of names. Each home held a stone or wood idol, usually about 3ft tall, called a *cemí,* which would receive their prayers. The practice of making these statues translated seamlessly into Christianity. Today *santos* (carved figurines representing saints), of the same height, are available across the island.

The native Taíno belief in the afterlife was quite different from the Christian dogma though, and in it there are some basic elements that would survive in other hybrid religions in the islands. Take for instance the Taíno belief in the walking dead, which bears a certain resemblance to famous tenants of Haitian Vodou. According to Taíno, the dead can return from the afterlife, a place called Coaybay, and walk among the living. In Taíno belief the dead walked through the villages and forests at night so they could eat tropical *guanábana* fruit. They also believed that women from Coaybay could have sexual communions with living men. The only way to tell the living from the dead was to touch someone on the belly, as they believed that the dead had no navel.

The small, round wooden huts of the Taíno people were called *bohíos,* where they smoked *cohibas* (cigars) and slept in *hamacas* (hammocks). They called their newly adopted island Borinquen (Land of the Noble Lord) and made pottery, wove baskets and carved wood. The native society was relatively democratic and organized around a system of *caciques* (Taíno chiefs) who oversaw a rank of medicine men, subchiefs and, below them, workers.

For leisure, the Taíno built ceremonial ball parks where they played a soccer-like game with a rubber ball between teams of 10 to 30 people. At Tibes near Ponce in the south, and at Caguana near Utuadu in the north, archaeologists discovered impressive courts, marked by rows of massive stone blocks. Drums, maracas and güiros provided the game's percussive accompaniment – instruments that resound in Puerto Rican traditional and popular music today.

One recent genetic study of 800 Puerto Ricans found 61% had mitochondrial DNA from a female Amerindian ancestor, 27% inherited mitochondrial DNA from a female African ancestor and 12% had mitochondrial DNA from a female European ancestor.

Colonization of the Taíno

Columbus first saw Puerto Rico on November 19, 1493 – a date simultaneously celebrated and mourned today. Columbus' 17 ships landed on the island's west coast for water, somewhere in the area near Rincón. But the visit was extremely brief, as Columbus' main base in the region was on Hispaniola (known today as Haiti and the Dominican Republic). There

1493	1508	1509	1511
On November 19, during his second voyage to the New World, Christopher Columbus lands on Puerto Rico's west coast. He christens the island *San Juan Bautista.*	Juan Ponce de León leads Spanish colonists to Puerto Rico in search of gold. He establishes the island's first colony – Caparra – in the north on swampy land close to San Juan harbor.	Ponce de León becomes first governor of San Juan Bautista (Puerto Rico) after Spain refuses to grant Columbus' son, Diego, rights to the lands discovered by his (recently deceased) father.	Subjected to brutal exploitation, the Taíno stage their first unsuccessful revolt against their Spanish overlords. Ponce de León is subsequently replaced as governor in favor of Diego Columbus.

was a period of relative quiet between his 'discovery' of Puerto Rico and the arrival of Ponce de León, who landed on the island in the August of 1508. León was here for good; he was sent by the Spanish crown to set up a colonial base for the Caribbean in Puerto Rico and look for gold. At first, León's expedition was amicably received by the chief of all chiefs, a *cacique* called Agüeybana.

But the good relationship didn't last long. Approximately 100 years before the Spanish arrived, Taíno culture was challenged by the Caribs, a warlike tribe from South America who raided Taíno villages for slaves and fodder for cannibalistic rites. When Ponce de León took possession of the island, the simmering tensions between the Taíno and Caribs were still evident and sometimes misinterpreted by the Spanish as Taíno aggression. In reality the Taíno were a friendly, sedentary people who put up little resistance to the new colonizers. Although León's letters to the crown describe this as a period of relative peace, he had difficulty making the Taíno understand that he was now in charge, and indigenous people were understandably resistant to their newfound roles as subservient laborers.

> The first black person to arrive in Puerto Rico was Juan Garrido, a conquistador allied to Juan Ponce de León. He first set foot on the island in 1509.

When León was unable to get the Taíno to fall in line with the arduous tasks of mining and farming for the Spanish, Queen Isabella issued an edict in simple terms: 'You will force the said Indians to associate with the Christians of the island.' Though the Spanish crown issued paltry monetary payments for the labor, it was tantamount to slavery.

By 1511 the forced labor and religious conversion of the Taíno had destroyed any shred of initial goodwill that may have existed between tribal leaders and the Spanish. When Agüeybana died, his nephew, called Agüeybana II, took over and tensions came to a head. Though accounts differ about the lead-up to the first Taíno uprising, the most colorful version goes like this: in an effort to test the Spaniards' suggestion of religious

AGÜEYBANA

Agüeybana (meaning 'Big Sun') was the most powerful *cacique* (Taíno chief) in Puerto Rico when Europeans first discovered the island. A trusting character who was curious about the European travelers, Agüeybana's close relationship with Juan Ponce de León was instrumental in Spanish colonization of the Caribbean. Told in a prophecy about the coming of a 'clothed people,' Agüeybana warmly received the Spanish explorer in 1508; some historical accounts, notably written by the Spanish, claim that he believed the Europeans were deities. He hosted a ceremony of friendship and led León and a delegation of his men on a scouting expedition of the island, from which Puerto Rico's first maps were drawn. But León struggled to convince Agüeybana to assist him with his two main priorities: mining Puerto Rico for gold and converting indigenous people to Christianity.

1513	1521	1595	1598
Following the decimation of the local Indian population through disease and outright slaughter, the first West African slaves arrive on the island to work in the new economy.	The city of San Juan is founded on its present site and the island changes its name from San Juan Bautista to Puerto Rico.	With permission from the Queen of England, British privateer Sir Francis Drake attempts to attack and loot San Juan with 26 ships but is repelled by the city's formidable defenses.	Spain's Phillip III forbids growing ginger, which is more lucrative for farmers, commonly smuggled and traded for slaves. The king demands they grow sugar to benefit the crown.

protection and life beyond death, Agüeybana II lured a Spanish soldier to a lake where he was promised a number of women would be bathing. Instead, a Taíno warrior drowned him while tribal leaders watched. Soon greater aggression was planned.

A few small raids on new Spanish settlements in the south went in favor of the Taíno, but as soon as León learned of the incidents, he unleashed his technologically advanced soldiers on the Taíno warriors. The battle that quelled the uprising was shocking in its brutality. An estimated 11,000 Taíno were killed in military campaigns by a Spanish force numbering only 100.

Testimonies vary as to how many Taíno inhabited Borinquen at the time of the Spanish invasion, though most anthropologists place the number between 20,000 and 60,000. In 1515 – after nearly a decade of maltreatment, a failed rebellion, disease and virtual slavery – only 4000 remained. Thirty years later a Spanish bishop put the number at 60.

While Taíno blood may have all but disappeared in modern Puerto Rico, native traditions live on. Puerto Rican Spanish is dotted with native words like yucca (a root vegetable), iguana, *manatí* (manatee – a sea mammal), maracas and ceiba (Puerto Rico's national tree); and some terms have even found their way into modern English: think *huracán* for hurricane and *hamaca* for hammock.

The Invaders

It's easy to imagine Puerto Rico's disparate invaders scheming in the shadowy ports of the Caribbean and the gilded halls of Europe. To evade the guns of El Morro and sack the San Juan harbor would write history – for pirates and princes alike. Not long after the fort was commissioned by Spanish King Charles V in 1539, it came under siege from those seeking strategic power in the Caribbean. Everyone from daring British dandy Francis Drake to storied cutthroats like Blackbeard tried their luck against San Juan's formidable defenses.

One of the colony's earliest invaders, Francis Drake first arrived in Puerto Rico in 1595 pursuing a stricken Spanish galleon – holding two million gold ducats – that took shelter in San Juan harbor. While the plucky Brit may have singed the king of Spain's beard in Cádiz a decade earlier, the Spaniards quickly got revenge in Puerto Rico when they fired a cannonball into Drake's cabin, killing two of his men, and – allegedly – shooting the stool from underneath him. Drake left the island empty-handed and died the following year of dysentery in Panama.

San Juan was attacked by the British navy again three years later under the command of the third earl of Cumberland. Learning from Drake's mistakes, Cumberland's 1700-strong army landed in what is now Condado and advanced on the city via land from the east. After

In 2016, the city of Arecibo erected North America's largest statue, the Birth of the New World, accepting it after a clutch of American cities rejected the monument. The statue, showing Christopher Columbus at the helm of a vessel bound for the Americas, stands near a site of extreme importance for the island's indigenous Taíno people.

1625	1786	1797	1850–67
The Dutch navy besieges San Juan and burns it to the ground, but they are prevented from taking total control by Spanish forces manning the fortifications in El Morro.	The early signs of Puerto Rican identity blossom with the publication of the first book dedicated to specifically Puerto Rican history, *Historia Geográfica, Civil y Política de Puerto Rico* by Fray Íñigo Abbad y Lasierra..	A third and final attempt by the British to take San Juan is led by General Abercromby during the Seven Years' War, but the Spanish once again stand firm.	The Puerto Rican liberation movement gathers strength under the inspirational leadership of Ramón Emeterio Betances, a poet, politician, diplomat and eminent surgeon.

a short battle, the city surrendered and the British occupied it for the next 10 weeks, before a dysentery epidemic hit and forced an ignominious withdrawal.

In response to frequent British incursions, San Juan's defensive walls were repeatedly strengthened, a measure that helped repel an ambitious attack by the Netherlands in 1625. The Dutch fired over 4000 cannonballs into the city walls before landing 2000 men at La Puntilla. Although the invaders managed to occupy the city temporarily and take the Fortaleza palace, the Spanish held El Morro fort and, after less than a month, the Dutch retreated, razing the city as they went.

San Juan's second great fort, San Cristóbal, was inaugurated in the 1630s and the city saw no more major attacks for almost two centuries. It wasn't until 1797 that the British, at war again with Spain, tried one last time. Still, even though they had over 60 ships and 10,000 men they eventually withdrew in bloodied and breathless exasperation.

Smuggling, Sugar & Spain

The total number of American soldiers killed in Puerto Rico during the Spanish–American War of 1898 was four.

Just look at a map and Puerto Rico's strategic position – between the shores of North, Central and South America – is immediately evident. During Spain's early settlement in the 16th century, the empire knew that Puerto Rican harbors were key to transporting the limitless wealth of the Americas. But the crown's insistence on a centralized government was an arrogant political position that would cost Spain dearly and shape the development of Puerto Rico.

In the mid-1500s Spain insisted that all imports and exports from its growing empire be trafficked through ports in Spain. But Seville was some 2½ months away by sail and the policy was immediately inadequate for controlling the island's many ports. A number of forces – including new Spanish colonies in gold-rich Peru and Mexico – led to the rise of an enormous, well-organized black market in Puerto Rico.

This unchecked flow of goods and money hastened the development of Puerto Rico's *other* ports – Ponce and Arroyo among them – where sugarcane and goods from the Americas were moved out of sight of Spanish authorities.

The power vacuum was quickly filled by merchants operating with their own agenda. Through the 16th and 17th centuries, cities of the south grew rich from trade with Caribbean neighbors – certainly illegal, but completely unknown to the distant king.

Even after Spain gave more power to local authorities in San Juan in the 18th century, the brisk black-market exchange of sugar, ginger and slaves between Puerto Rico and its neighbors (including the young United States) continued in the south, funding many of the majestic homes and fountains tourists visit today.

1858	1868	1873	1898
Samuel Morse introduces wired communication to Latin America for the first time with the installation of a line in Arroyo.	Revolutionaries inspired by Betances take the town of Lares and declare a Puerto Rican republic, in the event known afterward as the Grito de Lares, but the uprising is repelled by Spanish forces sent from San Sebastián.	In the wake of the Grito de Lares, the Spanish authorities institute various political and social reforms in Puerto Rico, including the abolition of slavery, freeing 30,000 slaves.	US forces blockade San Juan and land a 16,000-strong force unopposed at Guánica on the south coast, ending the Spanish–American War; Spain cedes Puerto Rico to the USA.

JUAN PONCE DE LEÓN

Soldier, sailor, governor, dreamer and politician, the life story of Juan Ponce de León reads like a *Who's Who* of late-15th- and early-16th-century maritime exploration. Aside from founding the Spanish colony of Puerto Rico in 1508, this daring, yet often short-sighted, Spanish adventurer partook in Columbus' second trans-Atlantic voyage, charted large tracts of the Bahamas, discovered the existence of the Gulf Stream and was the first recorded European to set foot in what is now known as Florida.

Born in Valladolid, Spain, in 1460, de León served his military apprenticeship fighting against the Moors during the Christian reconquest of Granada in 1492. The following year he arrived in the New World on Columbus' second expedition and settled on the island of Hispaniola, where he was proclaimed deputy governor of the province of Higüey. Following Columbus' death in 1506, the Spanish crown asked de León to lead the colonization of Borinquen, an island first explored by Columbus in 1493.

Despite initially currying favor with the native Taíno Indians, the Spaniard's relationship with his new neighbors quickly deteriorated. In 1512, he was replaced and given a new task: explore the region. After circumnavigating the Bahamas, de León elected to divert northwest and, in the process, inadvertently 'discovered' Florida.

After several forays along Florida's coast (which de León thought was an island), the explorer returned to Puerto Rico via Cuba and Guadalupe in 1515 and stayed there for the next six years. In 1521, de León organized another trip to Florida. This time they landed on the west coast of Florida but were quickly beaten back by Calusa Native Americans. Wounded in the thigh by a poisoned arrow, de León was shipped back to Havana where he died in July 1521. His remains were returned to Puerto Rico where they are interred in the Catedral de San Juan.

African Roots

As throughout the Caribbean, slavery was the engine of the Puerto Rican economy through the late 18th and early 19th centuries, and has left an indelible mark on Puerto Rican culture. The two types of slaves that were brought to the island – *ladinos,* born and acculturated in Spain, and *bozales* and Yoruba people, brought from Africa – first mined meager gold and silver deposits. Once these deposits were depleted, slaves propped up the sugarcane industry and agriculture on the coastal areas of the island. While the rest of the island's population experienced normal growth, the slave population skyrocketed throughout the late 18th century. A census figure in 1765 shows 5400 slaves in Puerto Rico; by 1830 it had increased to more than 31,000, mainly due to the introduction of new slaves directly from Africa and other parts of the Caribbean. However, despite these increases, by 1795 the majority (more than 60%) of black and mulatto people living in Puerto Rico were free. This trend,

1900	1917	1937	1942
US Congress passes the Foraker Act, granting a US–run government in Puerto Rico; American Charles Allen is installed as governor, aided by an 11-man executive council that includes five Puerto Ricans.	The Jones Act makes Puerto Rico a territory of the US and unilaterally grants islanders US citizenship and a bill of rights; English becomes the official language.	Student *independentistas* (independence advocates) clash with police on Palm Sunday; 20 people die and over 100 are injured in what becomes known as the 'Masacre de Ponce.'	A German submarine fires on Isla de la Mona, a largely uninhabited island off Puerto Rico's west coast. It was one of the few incidents of WWII in the Caribbean.

unusual for the Caribbean, is often attributed to an asylum policy that granted freedom to fugitive slaves from throughout the region.

By the late 1830s, after years of racial violence in the Caribbean and abolitionist movements, it became clear that slavery was increasingly less justifiable. Sugar barons combined their slave holdings with low-wage workers called *jornaleros* and continued to accrue immense wealth.

Many slave uprisings occurred and began to intertwine with a political movement for emancipation led by Julio Vizcarrondo, a Puerto Rican abolitionist living in Spain, as well as island-based political leaders such as Segundo Ruiz Belvis, Román Baldorioty de Castro and Ramón Emeterio Betances. After years of struggle the Spanish National Assembly abolished slavery on March 22, 1873.

Described by the late cultural and social writer Jose Luis González as *el primer piso,* or 'the first floor' of Puerto Rican culture, influences from the Commonwealth's history of slavery continue to shape the country today. In Puerto Rico's music, art and religious icons, African traditions are powerfully felt.

Former leader of the Puerto Rican Nationalist party, Pedro Albizu Campos was of African, Taíno and Basque descent. He graduated from Harvard University with a law degree in 1921 and was fluent in eight languages.

From Spanish Colony to American Commonwealth

As two Greater Antilles islands ruled by Spain for nearly four centuries, Cuba and Puerto Rico share a remarkably similar history. Both were colonized in the early 1500s, both retain vestiges of their indigenous Taíno culture, both were heavily influenced by the African slave trade and both remained Spanish colonies a good 80 years after the rest of Latin America had declared independence. The irony, of course, lies in their different paths after 1898 and the fact that today Puerto Rico is intertwined with the US. Cuba's relationship with the US has stayed chilly since it was considered a former Soviet satellite and 'public enemy number one.'

Two Wings of the Same Dove

While the bulk of Spain's South American colonies rose up under the leadership of revolutionary emancipator Simón Bolívar in the 1820s, Puerto Rico and Cuba's conservative Creole landowners elected to stay on the sidelines. But, as economic conditions worsened and slavery came to be regarded as an ailing colonial anachronism, the mood started to change.

During the 1860s links were formed between nationalists and revolutionaries on both islands, united by language and inspired by a common foe. The cultural interchange worked both ways. Great thinkers like Cuban national hero José Martí drew early inspiration from Puerto Rican surgeon and nationalist Ramón Emeterio Betances, while Mayagüez-born General

1948	1952	1953	1967
With US Congressional approval, Puerto Ricans craft their own constitution and elect their first governor, Luis Muñoz Marín, former president of the Senate, who holds the post for 16 years.	The constitution of Puerto Rico is approved by referendum, making the island an Estado Libre Asociado (a US commonwealth); the Puerto Rican flag is flown – legally – for the first time.	Immigration from Puerto Rico to the US peaks as an estimated 75,000 Puerto Ricans move to New York City. Almost one in 10 New Yorker residents are from Puerto Rico.	Puerto Rico holds first plebiscite on the issue of Puerto Rican statehood, but votes overwhelmingly to remain a commonwealth; the independence parties gain only 1% of the votes.

Juan Rius Rivera later went on to command the Cuban Liberation Army in the 1895–98 war against the Spanish.

It was Puerto Rican nationalists who fired the first shot, proclaiming the abortive Grito de Lares in 1868. Following Puerto Rico's lead two weeks later, Cuba's machete-wielding *mambises* (19th-century Cuban independence fighters) unleashed their own independence cry. Both ultimately failed.

Cuba and Puerto Rico's political divergence began in 1900 when the US Congress passed the Foraker Act, making Puerto Rico the first unincorporated territory of the US. Cuba, meanwhile, thanks to the so-called Teller Amendment (passed through Congress before the Spanish–American War had started), gained nominal independence with some strings attached in 1902.

Resistance to the new arrangement in Puerto Rico was spearheaded by the Partido Unión de Puerto Rico (Union Party), which for years had been demanding greater democratic rights. The Union Party was led by Luis Muñoz Rivera, one of the most important political figures in the history of Puerto Rico and a diplomat who was willing to compromise with the US on key issues. Under pressure from President Woodrow Wilson he ultimately ceded on his demand for outright independence in favor of greater autonomy via an amendment to the Foraker Act.

GRITO DE LARES

As well as boasting the world's largest radio telescope and its youngest-ever boxing champion, Puerto Rico also holds the dubious distinction of having created history's shortest-lived republic. The independent republic of Puerto Rico, proclaimed during the abortive Grito de Lares (Cry of Lares) in 1868, lasted slightly less than 24 hours.

Worn down by slavery, high taxes and the asphyxiating grip of Spain's militaristic rulers, independence advocates in the Caribbean colonies of Puerto Rico and Cuba were in the ascendancy throughout the 1850s and '60s.

The main Puerto Rican attempt at armed insurrection came on September 23, 1868. Over 600 men and women marched defiantly on the small town of Lares near Mayagüez, where they were met with minimal Spanish resistance. Declaring a Puerto Rican republic from the main square, the rebels named Francisco Ramírez Medina head of a new provisional government. But the glory didn't last. Marching next on the nearby town of San Sebastián, the poorly armed liberation army walked into a Spanish military trap and were quickly defeated by superior firepower.

This failed revolution did lead to some long-term political concessions. In the years that followed, the colonial authorities passed liberal electoral reforms, granted Puerto Rico provincial status and offered Spanish citizenship to all *criollos* (island-born people of European descent).

1970	1978	1985	1999
Marisol Maralet becomes the first Puerto Rican to win the title of Miss Universe. Over the next 40 years, four more Puerto Ricans win the title, the most of any country in the contest's history.	Two independence supporters are shot by police posing as revolutionary sympathizers in the Central Mountains; the incident exposes deep political fissures and government corruption.	A mudslide following Tropical Storm Isabel kills 129 people in the hills near Ponce, making it the island's worst natural disaster in a century.	Major protests break out on the island of Vieques against the US Navy, following the killing of islander David Sanes Rodríguez during military target practice.

In 1917, just months after Muñoz Rivera's death, President Woodrow Wilson signed the Jones Act. It granted US citizenship to all Puerto Ricans and established a bicameral legislature whose decisions could be vetoed by the US president. No Puerto Ricans were involved in the debate over citizenship.

Searching for Status

A special cask of high-grade rum was set aside by a brewer in 1942 with orders that it be opened only when Puerto Rico becomes an independent nation. When (or if) that happens, free drinks for everyone!

Questioned by many before the ink had even dried, the Jones Act failed to provide any long-term solutions. On the contrary, the debate over Puerto Rico's relationship with the US continued to intensify, defining the political careers of two major figures who would emerge on the island in the late 1920s and early '30s: Pedro Albizu Campos, leader of the pro-independence Partido Nacionalista (Nationalist Party); and Luis Muñoz Marín, who established the Partido Popular Democrático (PPD; Popular Democratic Party) in 1938.

As the son of the widely respected Muñoz Rivera, Luis Muñoz Marín took a conciliatory approach to challenging the colonial situation. While the US Congress sidestepped the status question, Muñoz Marín's PPD pressed for a plebiscite to allow Puerto Ricans to choose between statehood and independence. In the late 1930s and early 1940s, the majority of the PPD favored independence. However, neither President Franklin D Roosevelt nor the Congress seriously considered it as an option, and laws were enacted to criminalize independence activities.

Blanca Canales, leader of the abortive Jayuya Uprising in 1950, is popularly considered to have been the first woman to have led an armed revolt against the US government.

Rather than take to the mountains to fight – as Fidel Castro in Cuba later did – Muñoz Marín adopted a strategy that incorporated the status question with other issues affecting the Puerto Rican people, such as the dire economic and social effects of the Great Depression. His deciding moment came in 1946 when he rejected independence and threw his political weight behind an effort to grant the island a new status. In 1948, with Marín's support, Congress granted Puerto Rico the status it has today as an Estado Libre Asociado, or ELA, the Free Associated State. This intended to give the island more political autonomy, despite close ties with the US.

In 1952, this status description was approved by a referendum held on the island. Voters also approved Puerto Rico's first constitution that was written by islanders. Muñoz Marín became the first governor of Puerto Rico to be elected by Puerto Ricans. The new status and newly granted US citizenship for Puerto Ricans led to what is commonly known as the 'Great Migration.' Attracted to better economic opportunities in the US, Puerto Ricans left the island by the tens of thousands. In 1953 alone an estimated 75,000 Puerto Ricans arrived in New York City. Miami and Chicago also hosted large Puerto Rican populations and the period would forever transform the face of urban communities of the United States.

2000	2003	2005	2006
Puerto Ricans elect former San Juan mayor Sila Maria Calderón of the Popular Democratic Party as the first woman governor of the Commonwealth.	After four years of protests and 60 years of occupation, the US Navy pulls out of Vieques; the former military land is promptly designated a US Fish & Wildlife Refuge.	Guerrilla pro-independence leader Filiberto Ojeda Ríos is killed in a shootout with US federal agents. The incident causes widespread anger and demonstrations on the island.	An acute budgetary crisis forces the shutdown of schools and government offices across the island for two weeks as legislative officials try to address a $740-million deficit in public funds.

Nevertheless, despite claims by the new governor and his supporters that the status question was finally resolved with ELA, for all intents and purposes, nothing changed: the US Congress still had plenary powers over Puerto Rico. Although islanders became exempt from paying federal income taxes, they still had no representation in Congress (apart from a nonvoting delegate), could not vote in US national elections, and were still being drafted into the US Armed Forces to fight alongside young Americans in foreign wars.

Over the years a number of referenda and plebiscites have been held, ostensibly to allow the Puerto Rican people to decide the future of the island's status. Two official plebiscites, in 1967 and 1993, resulted in victories for 'commonwealth' status or the ELA. Other votes have been held, with the status options and the approach to self-determination defined in different ways. All of these popular votes have been shaped by the ruling party at the time of the vote: either the pro-ELA PPD, or the pro-statehood Partido Nuevo Progresista (PNP; New Progressive Party). None have been binding for the US Congress.

In 1998, as the island was getting ready to mark the 100th anniversary of US control, Congress acknowledged that the current status was no longer viable. A bill called for a plebiscite in which Puerto Ricans would vote on only two status options: either statehood or independence. It did not provide ELA or any other form of 'enhanced commonwealth' as an option, which angered members of the PPD. Ultimately, the legislation went nowhere.

In 2012, a non-binding vote on the island's political status was held on Puerto Rico and drew an impressive turnout of 78% of eligible voters. A majority favored statehood, which sends the issue squarely back to the US government for resolution. Current US President Donald Trump's relationship with Puerto Rico is nuanced. The new Governor of Puerto Rico, Ricky Rosselló, is pro-statehood.

A popular vote in 1990 making Spanish the official language in Puerto Rico was revoked just two years later to reinstate both Spanish and English as joint Commonwealth languages.

2009	2012	2016	2017
Sonia Sotomayor becomes the 111th Justice of the US Supreme Court. Of Puerto Rican descent, Sotomayor is the first Hispanic justice in the history of the court.	In a non-binding referendum, 54% of voters favored rejecting Puerto Rico's status as a territory of the US. In a separate question about preferred status, 61% favored statehood.	As Donald Trump becomes the next US President, Puerto Rico elects a pro-statehood Governor, Ricky Rosselló: the latest twist in the island's journey towards (or away from) settling on a status that satisfies everyone.	One of Ricky Rosselló's first acts as Governor is to schedule the island's first 'statehood or independence' referendum, to take place on June 11, 2017.

Life in Puerto Rico

Puerto Rican culture is a kaleidoscope with four constantly overlapping elements – Taíno, Spanish, African and American. As such, the dynamic culture is incredibly hard to pin down in words. One side of the street looks like the Bronx, while the other is all Latin America, with bananas sold out of the back of a truck. The commonwealth exports well over half of its population to the United States, yet expatriates exhibit fierce loyalty to the island they call home.

Lifestyle

Modern practicalities of the island's political and cultural position have meant that, for three or four generations now, many Puerto Ricans have grown up bouncing between mainland US cities and their native soil. Even those who stay put assimilate by proxy: young people in a wealthy San Juan suburb may wander the mall past American chain stores and chat about Hollywood blockbusters; obversely, their counterparts living in the uniformly Puerto Rican neighborhoods of New York or Chicago may have a day-to-day existence that more closely resembles Latin America. This makes the full scope of their bilingual and multicultural existence difficult to comprehend for outsiders. Many Puerto Ricans are just as comfortable striding down New York's Fifth Ave for a little shopping during the week as they are visiting the *friquitines* (roadside kiosks) with their families at Playa Luquillo on the weekend.

In 2015, the statisticians produced one of their most damning stats about Puerto Rico yet: for the first time in history, more Puerto Ricans were living in the continental US (4.9 million) than there were in Puerto Rico (3.5 million).

Where Puerto Rico and the US most diverge in a practical sense may be in economics. A glance beyond the shiny buildings of San Juan shows the toll taken by worldwide recession coupled with the island's own woes. A large number of manufacturing jobs left the island over the last decade, taking skilled managers with them and leaving factories to rust. With an unemployment rate of 11.9% and average salaries around $28,000 (roughly half the US average), the local aphorism is that if you need a job, fly to Orlando – a journey made easy by their US citizenship.

From Rincón to Vieques, visitors will find Puerto Ricans to be incredibly friendly and open; they like nothing better than to show off their beloved Borikén (the island's Taíno name). You'll also note that, despite their obsession with big American cars and big shopping complexes, Puerto Ricans also have their lives defined by some of life's simpler pleasures. A favorite island pastime is to wade into warm ocean waters just before sunset – beer in hand and a few more in the cooler – to shoot the breeze with whoever else is out enjoying the glorious spectacle of changing skies.

Multiculturalism

Like most Caribbean cultures, Puerto Ricans are genetically an ethnic mix of Native American, European and African. About 80% of the island classifies itself as white (meaning of Spanish origin, primarily), 8% as black, and 12% as other, or mixed, which includes Taíno. Along the coast of Loíza, where African heritage is most prominent, distinct features from the Yoruba people abound, while in the mountains, a handful of people still claim distant Taíno bloodlines. Many of them are right; advanced ethnographic study of Puerto Ricans in recent years uncovered a strong connection to the island's first settlers.

Puerto Ricans might tell you that ethnic discrimination doesn't exist on their island, but politically correct Spanish speakers may be aghast at some of the names Puerto Ricans use to refer to each other – words like *trigueño* (wheat-colored) and *jabao* (not quite white). It may sound derogatory (and sometimes it is), but it can also simply be a less-than-thoughtful way of identifying someone by a visible physical characteristic, a habit found in much of Latin America. You'll also hear terms like *la blanquita*, for a lighter-skinned woman, or *el gordo* to describe a robust man. Identifying which terms are racial slurs, rather than descriptive facts, will be a hard distinction for non-islanders to make, and it's wisest to steer clear of all such vernacular. Compared with much of the Caribbean, Puerto Rico is remarkably integrated and even-keeled about ethnicity. This may result from a long history of being a somewhat heterogeneous island with the powers-that-be changing wildly and frequently: even in the island's first census back in 1899, around 62% defined themselves as white, 32% as 'mixed' and 6% as black.

The island's most important challenge is to correct the historical fact that the poorest islanders – those descended from the slaves and laborers who were kept from owning land until the early 20th century – have been short-changed when it comes to higher education. As in the United States, the issue of racial and economic inequality in Puerto Rico – while still visible – has improved immeasurably in the last 50 years. While urban deprivation and a lack of provision of housing are ongoing issues, the relative economic conditions in modern Puerto Rico are significantly better than in most other countries in the Caribbean.

LIFE IN PUERTO RICO MULTICULTURALISM

Practice your Spanish by reading *El Nuevo Día*, Puerto Rico's biggest-selling daily newspaper, online at www.elnuevodia.com (it's got an English section, too).

READING UP ON PUERTO RICAN CULTURE

From sexual revolution to struggles for the commonwealth's independence to island-saving eco-activism, start your cultural journey to Puerto Rico in the pages of a book.

Down These Mean Streets (Piri Thomas) Peppered with the street slang of Spanish Harlem, this gritty classic takes a cold and sober look at the challenges of violence, drugs and racism during the first wave of Puerto Rican immigration to New York City.

Boricuas: Influential Puerto Rican Writings – An Anthology (edited by Roberto Santiago) This collection of essays and stories presents an incredibly diverse and wide-ranging insight into Puerto Rican authors, many of whom are scarcely translated into English. If you read one book to sample Puerto Rican writing, this is it.

The Disenchanted Island – Puerto Rico and the United States in the Twentieth Century (Ronaldo Fernández) Required reading for Latin American studies students, this chronicle of the island's struggle for independence is passionately told, putting the relationship between Puerto Rico and the United States under a microscope.

Imposing Decency: The Politics of Sexuality and Race in Puerto Rico, 1870–1920 (Eileen J Suárez Findlay) This brassy, bold historical reading of Puerto Rico feminism is rooted in Puerto Rico's working-class sexual revolution during the turbulent years of the American colony.

Islands Under Fire: The Improbable Quest to Save the Corals of Puerto Rico (Kevin McCarey) The US Navy was bombing much of Culebra in the 1970s and damage to the coral reefs was becoming extreme. McCarey joined up with an oddball band of activists to bring the destruction to a halt. It's a romp of a book you'll be unable to put down.

Religion

Like many former Spanish colonies, Roman Catholicism is practiced widely, with an estimated 70% of Puerto Ricans identifying as Catholic. But both Catholics and Protestants – the second-largest religious group – have been widely influenced by centuries of indigenous and African folkloric traditions. Slaves brought from West Africa between the 16th and 19th centuries carried with them a system of animistic beliefs that they passed on through generations of their descendants.

The *santos* (small carved figurines representing saints) that have been staple products of Puerto Rican artists for centuries descend to some degree from Santería beliefs in the powers of the saints (although many Puerto Ricans may not be aware of the sources of this worship). Many Puerto Ricans keep a collection of their favorite *santos* enshrined in a place of honor in their homes, similar to shrines that West Africa's Yoruba people keep for their *orishas* (spirits), like Yemanjá, the goddess of the sea.

Belief in the magical properties of small carved gods also recalls the island's early inhabitants, the Taíno, who worshipped little stone *cemíes* (figurines) and believed in *jupías,* spirits of the dead who roam the island at night to cause mischief.

Tens of thousands of islanders consult with *curanderos* (healers) when it comes to problems of love, health, employment, finance and revenge. Islanders also spend significant amounts of money in *botánicas:* shops that sell herbs, plants, charms, holy water and books on performing spirit rituals.

Puerto Rico's intangible folk culture, the esotericism of its myths and cultural peculiarities dating back to Taíno times, were always passed down generation to generation in the island's remoter locales. The first writer to commit those to prose was Cayetano Coll y Toste in his *Leyendas y Tradiciones Puertorriqueñas* (1925).

Women in Puerto Rico

Puerto Rican culture, like much of Latin American, is too often stigmatized as a 'macho' world where women play traditional roles, bearing children, cooking meals and caring for the home. Stereotypes paint Puerto Rican men in a similarly simplistic light – possessive, jealous and prone to wild acts of desperation when in love. Although many women generally perform all those duties (and more) in the most traditional Puerto Rican family structures, recent history has seen the island break significantly with the punitive gender discrimination that can be common in other Latin American countries and throughout the Caribbean. But a more substantive look at Puerto Rican culture reveals a much greater complexity to the role of women in contemporary Puerto Rico.

Puerto Rican women have excelled at business, trade, sport and, most importantly, politics – often with more measurable achievement than their counterparts in the United States. San Juan elected a female mayor decades before a woman won a comparable office in the US, and, in 2000, Sila María Calderón was elected governor of Puerto Rico. She ran on a campaign that promised to end government corruption, and clean house she did. In the US, Supreme Court Justice Sonia Sotomayor is of Puerto Rican descent and has strong ties to the island.

Other women's issues that tend to be loaded with political and social baggage in the United States have a relatively progressive position in

PUERTO RICO'S BEAUTIES

On most progressive issues of gender equality, Puerto Rico can shame other Latin American countries...at least until it's time to dust off the rhinestone tiara and satin sash and crown a beauty queen. Puerto Rico simply adores the beauty pageant. The island's near obsession with pageants has paid off, too. In the big enchilada, the annual Miss Universe, Puerto Ricans are something of a cinch. The island has brought home a stunning five wins in the pageant's history, the most recent in 2006.

San Germán (p192)

Puerto Rican culture. For instance, abortion is legal in Puerto Rico (although the rest of the Caribbean, outside of Cuba, is uniformly opposed to it). In Puerto Rico, even socially conservative politicians remain acutely aware of the effects of a high birthrate on family living and quality of life.

The effect that the relatively progressive place women have in Puerto Rican society has on travelers is very noticeable for women traveling alone. Although typical safety precautions should be followed, solo women travelers attract much less attention than in other corners of Latin America.

Sports

Though the silent, stone-lined Taíno ball courts of Tibes and Caguana pay homage to Puerto Rico's long dedication to sports, they speak nothing of the ferocious energy that fires the competitive spirit of islanders today. For such a geographically small place, Puerto Rico plays a disproportionately large role in modern sport, especially in boxing and baseball.

Baseball

Puerto Rico's official pastime is *béisbol* (baseball), a modern game that bears a vague resemblance to the ceremonial *batú* of Taíno ancestors and draws telling parallels with the island's contemporary economic and cultural relationship with the US. As much as Puerto Rico's beleaguered economy is reliant on support from the US federal government, the *Liga de Béisbol Profesional Roberto Clemente* (Professional Baseball League Roberto Clemente; www.ligapr.com) – named after the legendary player of the early 1970s – is bankrolled by America's own Major League Baseball (MLB).

Players with island roots often make their most significant contributions to the Puerto Rican diaspora while working in New York and Chicago. The

El Boricua is an online monthly bilingual cultural magazine for Puerto Ricans worldwide. It can be found at www.elboricua.com. The word *boriuca* derives from the Taíno *boriken*, meaning 'land of the great and valiant Lord.'

pros that rise from the island's stadiums are often celebrated as icons when they make it to the big time in the US.

While the official pastime gets plenty of lip service and Puerto Ricans follow the US Major Leagues avidly, the great passion for baseball is found in school and amateur leagues, although the Puerto Rican pros play a full season, November to January. These winter league games, as they are called, attract diehard fans, and – importantly – scouts from the major league teams in the US. Currently there are six teams in the league. Catching a winter league game can be a terrific cultural experience and it's dirt cheap by American standards. Tickets are usually around $10 or less and a cold beer will only set you back $3. San Juan's Hiram Bithorn Stadium is a great place to watch a game.

US Major League teams also hold spring training camps in Puerto Rico and regularly use the island's league as a farm team. Early-season exhibition games are held in spring, including the televised San Juan Series, at the Hiram Bithorn Stadium.

Boxing

Puerto Rico has spawned enough fighters to fill its own boxing Hall of Fame, including the youngest world champion in boxing history and one of the sport's greatest-ever knockout specialists.

The standard was set in the 1930s when wily bantamweight Sixto Escobar became the first Puerto Rican to win a world-championship belt, knocking out Mexican Baby Casanova in Montreal in 1936. In his homeland, Escobar became an overnight hero.

The 1970s introduced the two Wilfredos – Benitez and Gómez. Benitez, nicknamed 'The Radar,' was a childhood boxing sensation. Raised in New York City, he became the youngest-ever world champion when he defeated Colombian Antonio Cervantes in a World Junior Welterweight Championship bout in 1976. Just 17 at the time, The Radar defended his title three times before losing to Sugar Ray Leonard in 1979. Gómez, known as Bazooka, was a punching phenomenon from San Juan who retains one of the highest knockout ratios, with 42 knockouts in 46 fights. Rated number 13 in Ring magazine's list of all-time best punchers, Gómez is the subject of the 2003 documentary Bazooka: The Battles of Wilfredo Gómez.

As much a showman as a fighter, Hector 'Macho' Camacho was Puerto Rico's most flamboyant star. Born in Bayamón but raised in New York, Camacho aped the style of Muhammad Ali by leaping into the ring dressed as Captain America before a fight. During a 20-year career he fought everyone from Roberto Duran to Julio César Chávez. He tested local loyalties in an all–Puerto Rican world-title fight against Felix Trinidad.

Trinidad, from Cupey Alto, is another modern boxing legend who won world titles at three different weights, including a 1999 victory over Oscar de la Hoya.

Puerto Ricans continue to score well in boxing. One of the greatest recent stars is Danny García; he's been on a roll since he won the world welterweight title in 2010. José Pedraza also achieved fame after winning the super featherweight title in 2011.

Tennis

Monica Puig, Puerto Rico's most successful modern-era tennis player, created history in 2016 by becoming the first Latin American woman to win gold at the Olympic Games, and the first to win Olympic gold whilst representing Puerto Rico.

Sounds of Puerto Rico

The music of Puerto Rico is a sonic reflection of the destination itself, a sound shaped by a dynamic history of revolution, colonialism and the cultural crosscurrents that blow between the island, New York City, Spain and Africa. The sound synonymous with Puerto Rico is certainly salsa, but that which pounds from the open doorways of most of the island's nightspots these days is usually reggaetón, a blazing blend of hip-hop and thudding Caribbean syncopations.

Popular Music & its Roots

To cram for your history lesson on Puerto Rican music in under four minutes, cue up 'Tradicional A Lo Bravo,' a hugely popular single from Puerto Rican reggaetón hitmaker Tego Calderon. Calderon's rapid-fire lyrical delivery and the pounding syncopated bass line is emblematic of the reggaetón movement, but the song also borrows a little something from the important musical traditions of the island. The brassy horns pay homage to salsa bands from the 1960s. The nylon string guitar nods to colonial traditions and *jíbaro* (rural troubador) music. The loping syncopation of the hand drums reference African-rooted Puerto Rican *bomba*. Somewhere, hidden among Calderon's potent swagger, you'll even hear the grinding scrape of a güiro, a percussion instrument made from a notched, hollowed gourd, which was a part of the musical battery of indigenous Taíno tribes.

From the lilt of precolonial folk music to the macho assault of reggaetón, Puerto Rican music has been an evolving part of, not a departure from, past traditions. Puerto Rico has also always been a musical melting pot and remains so today. The island's musical genres can shift as quickly as they are defined, shaped by strong influences from the US, Europe and across Latin America. These dynamic hybrids, whether present in reggaetón or contemporary rock, are a fundamental quality of the music. Then and now, these traditions often place as much importance on dancefloor expressions as on the sound itself.

Bomba y Plena

The bewildering conflux of traditions that collide in Puerto Rican music can be seen in the earliest popular music on the island, *bomba y plena*, two distinct yet often associated types of folk music. With origins in European, African and native Caribbean cultures, this is the basis for many of the sounds still associated with Puerto Rico and, like salsa, a musical form inexorably tied with dance.

The most directly African in origin is the *bomba*, a music developed by West- and Central-African slaves who worked on sugar plantations. A typical *bomba* ensemble included drums made from rum barrels and goatskin, *palitos* or *cuás* (wooden sticks that are hit together or on other wooden surfaces), maracas and sometimes a güiro. In the oldest forms (documented as early as the 1680s), dancers led the band, furiously competing with each other and the percussionists in an increasingly frenzied physical and rhythmic display. The tunes ended when either dancer or drummer became too exhausted to continue. Loíza Aldea, on the northeast coast, claims

The Puerto Rican Cuatro Project (www.cuatro-pr. org) is a nonprofit organization that has adopted the island's national instrument as a means of keeping its cultural memories alive. Its website is a must for those seeking to learn about Puerto Rican musical traditions.

bomba as its invention, and the streets rumble with it throughout summer, particularly during the Fiesta de Santiago, which begins at the end of July.

Plena, which originated in the more urban region around Ponce, is also drum-based but with lighter textures and a less forceful beat. Introduced by *cocolocos,* slaves who migrated north from islands south of Puerto Rico, *plena* uses an assortment of handheld percussion instruments. Locals once referred to the form as *el periodico cantado* (the sung newspaper), because the songs typically recounted, and often satirized, current events. The *plena* beat has strongly syncopated African roots and is a close cousin to calypso, *soca* and dancehall music from Trinidad and Jamaica.

Bomba y plena developed side by side on the coastal lowlands, and inventive musicians eventually realized the call-and-response of *bomba* would work well with *plena's* satirical lyrical nature, which is why the forms are often played back-to-back by ensembles. If you catch *bomba y plena* today, a historically accurate performance will be rare; in the 1950s a modernization of the sound paved the way for salsa by often adding horns and other European instruments, pan-Caribbean rhythmic elements and the clatter of Cuban percussion.

The most comprehensive online resource about Puerto Rican music is Music of Puerto Rico (www.musicofpuertorico.com).

Salsa

For most gringos, salsa's definition as a catch-all term for the interconnected jumble of Latin and Afro-Caribbean dances and sounds isn't easy to get

PUERTO RICO PLAYLIST

It's nearly a crime to distil three generations of Puerto Rico's vibrant club music into an iPod playlist, but the following romp includes singles spanning half a century, from classic salsa to contemporary reggaetón. If nothing else, use this as a starter to discover the diverse and unexpected charms of Puerto Rican music.

Tito Puente 'Ran Kan Kan,' *Babarabatiri* (1951)

Cortijo Y Su Combo 'El Bombon De Elena,' *...Invites You to Dance* (1957)

Celia Cruz 'Chango Ta Vani,' *La Incomparable* (1958)

Willie Colón 'Te Conozco,' *Cosa Nuestra* (1969)

El Gran Combo De Puerto Rico 'No Hay Cama Pa' Tanta Gente,' *Nuestra Musica* (1971)

Ismael Marinda 'Se Casa La Rumba,' *Abran Paso!* (1972)

Eddie Palmieri 'Nunca Contigo,' *The Sun of Latin Music* (1973)

Fania All-Stars 'Ella Fue (She Was the One),' *Rhythm Machine* (1977)

Frankie Ruiz 'Me Dejó,' *Mas Grande Que Nunca* (1989)

Marvin Santiago 'Fuego A La Jicotea,' *Fuego A La Jicotea* (1991)

Vico C 'Calla,' *Aquel Que Había Muerto* (1998)

Yuri Buenaventura 'Salsa,' *Yo Soy* (2000)

Tego Calderon 'Guasa, Guasa' from *Abayarde* (2003)

Daddy Yankee 'Plane to PR,' *El Cartel: The Big Boss* (2007)

Tito el Bambino 'El Tra,' *It's My Time* (2007)

Don Chezina 'Songorocosongo,' *Tributo Urbano A Hector Lavoe* (2008)

Calle 13 'No Hay Nadie Como Tú,' *Los de Atrás Vienen Conmigo* (2009)

Kany Garcia 'Feliz,' *Boleto De Entrada* (2009)

Cultura Profética 'Baja La Tension,' *La Dulzura* (2010)

Marlow Rosado y La Riqueña 'No Me Digan Que Es Muy Tarde Ya,' *Retro* (2012)

Los Wálters 'Porsche,' *Verano Panorámico* (2014)

Maracas decorated with the flag of Puerto Rico

a handle on, but for those who live in its areas of origin – Puerto Rico, Cuba and New York City – it's as much a lifestyle as a genre, with cultural complexities that go well beyond the 'spicy' jargon that's often bandied about.

Salsa tunes might sound vastly different from one another. They can be slow or brisk, flippant or heartrending. Salsa was born in the nightclubs of New York City in the 1960s and remains an iconic sound today.

The Source of the Sauce

In addition to the mishmash of African traditions that spread through the islands via the slave trade, Cuba's *son* – a traditional style that was widely reintroduced to global audiences in the '90s through *Buena Vista Social Club* – is a crucial ingredient in salsa. Originating in eastern Cuba, *son* first became popular in the 1850s, mixing guitar-based Spanish *cancións* and Afro-Cuban percussion, a fundamental formula that still makes the foundation of many salsa songs. Variations include the rumba, mambo and cha-cha.

Another element of salsa is merengue, which took root in Puerto Rico's neighboring island, the Dominican Republic, where it is the national dance. With its even-paced steps and a signature roll of the hips, it's probably the easiest Latin dance for beginners. Compared with salsa, the rhythmic underpinning has a more rigid structure, and though the music can gallop along at a wild pace, dancers keep their upper body in a graceful, poised stance.

Of all the variations that helped bring salsa into being, none is more important than the mambo – a flamboyant style of music and dance that marries elements of swinging American jazz with *son*. Again, the musical dialogue of the Caribbean islands is evident right down to the style's name; mambo is a Haitian word for a vodou priestess. It started in Cuba in the 1930s and soon spread to Puerto Rico and the US, where mambo became a cross-over fad.

The Birth & Near-Death of Salsa

It's wonderfully appropriate that salsa is called just that, given the number of sound styles that melded in Puerto Rico to produce the sound that was then exported to the world.

> Puerto Rico's national anthem, 'La Borinqueña,' is actually a *danza* that was later subtly altered in order to make it sound more grandiose and anthem-like.

In 1964, Johnny Pacheco, a visionary producer, created Fania Records, a label that helped make salsa a wildly popular commercial success. Scores of Puerto Rican, Cuban and Nuyorican singers became household names in the '60s, and when Carlos Santana's now-ubiquitous rock song 'Oye Como Va' hit stores in 1969, it may have marked the crest of the Latin wave.

Though the craze left a mark on American pop and jazz traditions, the crowds dwindled in subsequent decades as musical tastes shifted radically in the late 1970s. While Puerto Rican youth turned to rock-and-roll imports from the US through the '80s, traditionalists celebrated the sappy *salsa romantica* typified by crooners such as José Alberto.

Puerto Rican music started garnering big attention outside the Spanish-speaking world with the success of San Juan–born Enrique Martín Morales (better known to the planet as Ricky Martin). Martin's 1999 single 'Livin' La Vida Loca' plonked Puerto Rican pop on the planet's music map.

Salsa Today

Though salsa's faithful took plenty of solace in Fania records from the '80s, it wasn't until the 1990s that a modern Nuyorican – salsa crooner Marc Anthony, aka ex-Mr JLo – brought salsa back from the brink of obscurity and into a blinding popular spotlight, braiding its traditional elements with those of sleek and shiny modern Latino pop.

Although Anthony and Lopez remain salsa's premier couple, American audiences have also had fleeting infatuations with another Puerto Rican, Ricky Martin (Mr La Vida Loca). More recent Puerto Rican pop stars, such as the smart, jazz-fused group Cultura Profética, pick and choose the elements of the island's traditional sound to weave into contemporary records.

But the neo-traditionalist salsa from Bronx-born Puerto Rican singer India and heartthrob crooner Manny Manuel carry the torch from the graying generation who invented it. There are a number of new ensembles who keep turning out the salsa hits in rotation on Puerto Rican radio, though most of them hail from New York City. Watch for the superb El Gran Combo de Puerto Rico, a large group of masters who've packed festivals in the US and on the island for over 50 years. Also pretty cutting edge is Grammy winner Marlow Rosado y La Riqueña, fronted by the namesake composer/producer who mixes salsa, reggaetón, rock and more. And Marc Anthony continues to release chart-topping albums, most recently *3.0,* a salsa album featuring 'Vivir Mi Vida.'

Reggaetón

The raucous bastard-child of reggae, salsa and hip-hop is reggaetón, a rough-and-tumble urban sound that took over the unpaved streets of Loíza

---

THE 'BRIDGE' OF TITO PUENTE

Puerto Ricans and Cubans jovially argue over who invented salsa, but the truth is neither island can claim to be the commercial center of salsa success. That honor belongs to the offshore colony known as El Barrio: the Latin Quarter, Spanish Harlem, New York City. In the euphoria following the end of WWII, New York's nightclub scene boomed as dancers came in droves to bump and grind to the sound of mambo bands. At the time, the music carried a basic Latin syncopated beat, punctuated by horn sections that were typical of the great swing bands of Stan Kenton and Count Basie.

Then young Puerto Rican drummer Tito Puente came into the picture. After serving three years in the US Navy during the war and attending New York's Juilliard School of Music, Puente began playing and composing for Cuban bands in New York City. He gained notoriety for spicing up the music with a host of rhythms with roots in Puerto Rican *bomba*.

Puente became a star and the face of the salsa boom, bridging cultural divides with his music decades before multiculturalism was even considered a real word. Shortly after the legendary five-time Grammy winner's death in 2000, at the age of 77, a stretch of road in Harlem – East 112th St at Lexington Ave – was renamed Tito Puente Way.

PUERTO RICAN MUSIC: ALIVE & KICKING

Through slush and snow, you've been daydreaming all winter about that idyllic Puerto Rican night on the town, when rum flows like water, the band is hot as a tin roof and the likelihood of dislocating something on the dancefloor is high. Catching live traditional music isn't as easy as you might hope, but the following San Juan nightspots are known for salsa.

Nuyorican Café (☏787-977-1276; www.nuyoricancafepr.com; 312 San Francisco, Old San Juan; cover $5; ⊗8pm-late) San Juan's coziest dancefloor hosts live combos playing traditional favorites.

Club Brava (☏787-791-2781; www.bravapr.com; El San Juan Hotel, 6063 Av Isla Verde, Isla Verde; cover $20; ⊗10pm-late Thu-Sat) In a resort but known for its mix of house, reggaetón and salsa.

La Placita de Santurce (Calle Dos Hermanos, Santurce; ⊗5pm-late Thu-Sat; ☐T3, T5) The infamous Friday-night street party that attracts salsa bands.

El San Juan Hotel Lobby (☏787-791-1000; www.elsanjuanhotel.com; 6063 Av Isla Verde, Isla Verde; ⊗8pm-2am) Live salsa and meringue bands belie the seemingly staid surrounds.

Aldea, the Caribbean's answer to the ethos of American thug life. On a trip to a Puerto Rican nightclub, reggaetón dominates the turntables, and you'll likely wake up the next morning with your ears ringing.

As the name suggests, it draws heavily on reggae, though the simplest reduction of its sound is a Spanish-language hip-hop driven by the crushing bass of Jamaican raga, a bossy, electro-infused spin on reggae. An aggressive strain of reggaetón developed in urban areas of Puerto Rico in the 1980s, circulated underground on self-released mix tapes. In the 1990s it incorporated thunderous elements of Jamaican raga and came unto its own. Toss in the thud of a drum machine and some X-rated lyrics and you have yourself a bona fide musical revolution.

Unlike most traditionally postured Puerto Rican music/dance combos, reggaetón dancefloors feature a deliriously oversexed free-for-all, with its most popular move known as *perreo,* or dog dance – which leaves little to the imagination. Reggaetón stars such as Tego Calderon, Daddy Yankee, Don Omar and Ivy Queen have hit the mainstream.

Puerto Rican Folk

The earliest folk music on the island started with the percussion and wind instruments of the Taíno, and grew to incorporate elements as disparate as the island's ethnic composition: Spanish guitars, European parlor music and drums, and rhythms from West Africa. Indigenous instruments include at least half a dozen guitar-like string instruments that are native to the island, such as the aptly named four-string guitar-like *cuatro.*

In the mountains, sentimental and twangy folk music was played on *cuatros* by rural troubadours, called *jíbaros,* whose costume often includes a ragged straw hat. A number of traditional *jíbaro* songs – mostly rooted in some kind of Western European parlor music – are still popular at island weddings and family gatherings. An *aguinaldo* is sung by groups of wandering carolers at Christmastime, with lyrics that often explain the traditions of the holiday (perhaps unsurprisingly, many of the most famous ones include singing about pork).

Perhaps the most structurally complex of the island's folk music, *danza* is considered Puerto Rico's classical music. *Danza's* exact lineage is unknown, but it's generally considered to be modeled after *contradanza,* a social music and dance from Europe. *Danza* popularity blossomed in 1840 when it incorporated new music and dance steps called *habaneras* (another export of Cuba).

José Feliciano, a six-time Grammy award winner, taught himself to play guitar despite being born blind. He remains one of Puerto Rico's most successful crossover pop stars.

Arts

Although no match for the island's iconic music, Puerto Rico's other arts nevertheless vividly reflect the vibrant culture. Fittingly, Puerto Rico's writers use both Spanish and English to describe local life and issues around poverty, freedom, colonialism and the country's netherworld status within the US. Movies invariably reflect the screen-friendly local colors, as do the energetic visual arts, with galleries illustrating this tiny island's gargantuan artistic output constantly opening. With dance, Puerto Ricans enjoy physically expressing their nuanced musical rhythms.

Literature

Puerto Rico was without a printing press until 1807, and Spain's restrictive rule kept literacy rates low for almost 400 years. But indigenous literature developed nonetheless; the 19th and 20th centuries gave rise to writers who penned the island's identity: Alejandro Tapia y Rivera, Manuel Alonso, Dr Enrique Laguerre and Julia de Burgos.

As more islanders migrated to the US in the 1950s, Puerto Rican 'exiles,' known as Nuyoricans, produced powerful fiction. One of the most successful writers was Pedro Juan Soto, whose 1956 collection *Spiks* (a racial slur aimed at Nuyoricans) depicts life in the New York *barrios* with biting realism. Miguel Algarín, Miguel Piñero and Pedro Pietri started a

ICONS OF PUERTO RICAN LITERATURE

Alejandro Tapia y Rivera (1826–82) The 'Father of Puerto Rican literature' wrote poems, stories, essays, novels and plays. Long, allegorical poems include *Sataniada,* 'A Grandiose Epic Dedicated to the Prince of Darkness.'

Manuel Alonso (1822–89) Alonso wrote *El gíbaro* (1849), a collection of vignettes about cockfights, dancing, weddings, politics, race and the *espiritismo* (spiritualism) that characterize the island *jíbaro* (an archetypal witty peasant).

Dr Enrique Laguerre (1906–2005) Puerto Rico's first important international novelist. Published in 1935, *La llamarada* (Blaze of Fire) is set on a sugarcane plantation, based on Laguerre's time spent at Palacete Los Moreau near Isabela, where a young intellectual struggles with US corporate exploitation.

Julia de Burgos (1914–53) A major female poet, she responded in outrage when the island became US territory. Her work embodies two fundamental elements of Boricua identity: intense, lyrical connection to nature and fiery politics.

Giannina Braschi (1953–) One of the biggest names among the many Puerto Rican writers living in New York, Braschi writes about the state of freedom in her homeland – or lack thereof. Her three novels, *Empire of Dreams* (1994), *Yo-Yo Boing!* (1998) and *United States of Banana* (2011), have won international acclaim.

René Marqués (1919–79) An Arecibo-born playwright whose most important work is *La Carreta*, which follows a Puerto Rican family's journey from the sticks to San Juan and then New York in search of a better life.

PUERTO RICO ON FILM

For movies set in Puerto Rico or about Puerto Rican life in the *barrios* of New York, seek out:

Carlito's Way Starring Al Pacino and Sean Penn, this popular 1993 drama follows the exploits of Carlito Brigante, a Puerto Rican drug dealer in New York who struggles to go straight after his release from prison.

Rum Diary (Rum Punch) Shot entirely on location in 2011, Johnny Depp plays Hunter S Thompson in his early yet still-dissolute days when he worked as a journalist in San Juan during the early 1960s.

Angel Written and directed by Jacobo Morales (who also stars), this drama follows the story of a corrupt police captain and the man he wrongly imprisoned. It narrowly missed out on a 2008 Academy Award nomination.

GoldenEye The iconic Arecibo radio-telescope provided the backdrop for the famous climactic scenes of 007's 17th screen outing.

Pirates of the Caribbean: On Stranger Tides San Juan's dramatic forts made for atmospheric shots during the fourth installment of the film series in 2011 (Johnny Depp presumably spent a lot of time on set in Puerto Rico around this point).

Latino beatnik movement on Manhattan's Lower East Side at the first Nuyorican Poets Café.

Esmeralda Santiago's 1986 memoir, *Cuando era puertorriqueña* (When I Was Puerto Rican), became a standard in US schools for its eloquent portrayal of her childhood on the island and how the lessons learned there have shaped her success.

Eduardo Lalo is best known for his Romulo Gallegos Prize–winning novel *Simone* (2012), which, through an unusual narrative style, sets an almost hypnotic tone for its ramble through the city of San Juan. His first book, *En el Burger King de la calle San Francisco* (In the San Francisco Street Burger King), is a lyrical exploration of Old San Juan.

Another San Juan writer, Zoé Jiménez Corretjer, has won many awards for her contemporary poetry. Two other poets, Luz María Umpierre-Herrera and Sandra María Esteves, are particularly known for their poetic dialogue in which they each wrote two works to the other debating the roles of women in Puerto Rican society.

Cinema

Puerto Rico's balmy weather, historic architecture and modern infra-structure attract Hollywood productions. The first truly Puerto Rican movie (ie, with a Puerto Rican cast and crew), *Los Peloteros,* was made in 1953, and a homegrown industry only started to flourish in the late 1980s, thanks largely to one director: Jacobo Morales. He wrote, directed and starred in *Dios los cría* (God Created Them). The movie offered a critical look at Puerto Rican society and was lauded by critics and fans. His next offering, *Lo que le pasó a Santiago* (What Happened to Santiago), won an Academy Award nomination in 1990 for Best Foreign Film (the irony!). *Linda Sara* (Pretty Sara), his 1994 follow-up, earned him another.

Director Marcos Zurinaga also made a name for himself in the 1980s, first with *La gran fiesta* (The Big Party) in 1986, which focuses on the last days of San Juan's biggest casino, and then with the acclaimed *Disappearance of Garcia Lorca* (1997).

The most widely distributed and successful Puerto Rican film is probably Luis Molina Casanova's 1993 tragicomedy, *La guagua aérea* (A Flight of Hope), which explores the reasons behind Puerto Ricans' emigration in the

Rita Moreno (born in Humacao, 1931) managed the rare feat of winning an Academy Award *(West Side Story)*, a Grammy *(The Electric Company Album)*, a Tony *(The Ritz)* and two Emmys *(The Muppet Show* and *The Rockford Files)*. Only 11 others have won all four.

1960s. On the artistic front, *Mi santa mirada,* a 2012 short drama by Alvaro Aponte, follows a Puerto Rican drug dealer who decides to change his life. It was recognized at the Cannes Film Festival.

Visual Arts

San Juan's Museo de San Juan is a symbol of Puerto Rico's dedication to the visual arts, which can be traced back to the early days of Spanish colonization. The first great local artist to emerge was self-taught painter José Campeche (1751–1809). Masterpieces such as *Dama a caballo* (Lady on Horseback) and *Gobernador Ustariz* (Governor Ustariz) demonstrate Campeche's mastery of landscape and portrait painting, often inspired by the story of Jesus.

Another master, Francisco Oller (1833–1917) did not gain recognition until the second half of the 19th century. Oller was very different from Campeche; he studied in France under Gustave Courbet and was influenced by acquaintances including Cézanne. Like his mentor Courbet, Oller dedicated a large body of his work to scenes from humble, everyday island life. Bayamón, Oller's birthplace, maintains a museum to its native son, and many of his works are in San Juan's Museo de Arte de Puerto Rico. Both Oller and Campeche are honored for starting an art movement inspired by Puerto Rican nature and life, and they gave a distinct cultural and artistic identity to the island.

After a storm of poster art that covered the island in visual and verbal images during the 1950s and '60s, serious painters such as Julio Rosado del Valle (1922–2008), Francisco Rodón (b 1934) and Myrna Báez (b 1931) evolved a new aesthetic in Puerto Rican art, in which images rebel against the tyranny of political and jingoistic slogans. Báez is one of a new generation of female artists building on Puerto Rico's traditions to create exciting installation art. Her work is exhibited in many San Juan galleries.

One of the island's most famous contemporary artists was actually a Nuyorican – Rafael Tufiño (1922–2008), who was born in Brooklyn to Puerto Rican parents. Using vivid colors and big canvases, Tufiño was considered the 'painter of the people' because of his unflinching depiction of poverty on the island. His work has joined the permanent collection of the Museum of Modern Art, the Metropolitan Museum of Art and the Library of Congress.

The Museo de Arte de Ponce is one of the Caribbean's greatest art galleries, but a riveting new contemporary art space seemingly opens in Puerto Rico every year: the latest is the fantastic Museo de Arte in Mayagüez.

TRIO OF PUERTO RICAN FOLK ART

Search out examples of these folk-art treasures in some of the better shops on the quieter streets of Old San Juan.

Santos Drawing on the artistic traditions of carved Taíno idols called *cemíes,* these small statues represent religious figures and are enshrined in homes to bring spiritual blessings to their keepers.

Mundillo Made only in Spain and Puerto Rico, this fine lace was imported with early nuns, who made and sold it in order to finance schools and orphanages. Renewed interest in island folk arts, generated by the Instituto de Cultura Puertorriqueña, has revived the process.

Máscaras These frightening and beautiful headpieces are worn at island fiestas, and are popular pieces of folk art. The tradition of masked processions goes back to the Spanish Inquisition, when masqueraders known as *vejigantes* brandished balloon-like objects (called *vejigas;* literally, 'bladders'), terrifying sinners into returning to the church. In Puerto Rico, it merged with masking traditions of African slaves.

A mosaic in Loíza (p94) town square

Dance

The rolling gait of salsa is inexorably linked with the Puerto Rican identity, and the island's attitude toward dance often has a refreshing lack of North American reserve.

Over time, many classifiable musical forms – *bomba,* salsa, *plena* and *danza* – have evolved complementary dances based on syncopated rhythms and melodies. An early example was the formal *danza,* an elegant ballroom dance imported from Cuba. *Bomba* is another colorful import, with influences brought via African slaves. Boisterously energetic, *bomba* has spawned a plethora of subgenres such as *sica, yuba* and *holandes,* and is both spontaneous and exciting to watch.

Puerto Rico's signature dance is certainly salsa. With its sensuous moves and strong African rhythmic base, it seems like the perfect expression of Puerto Rico's cultural DNA – loose-limbed locals make it look as simple as walking.

To see the best free-form Puerto Rican dance, head to San Juan's steamy nightclubs, where being seen with the best moves is a matter of searing personal pride.

For eye-popping examples of Puerto Rico's vivid visual art, head to San Juan's Santurce district. Museums, galleries, outdoor art and impromptu graffiti combine for a visual riot as vibrant as the best salsa.

Puerto Rico Landscapes

It is the astonishing beaches that captivate most minds planning a first visit to Puerto Rico. But as seasoned aficionados know, the sand and surf intimate only a part of the full, rich picture of the topography. Shores also yield internationally crucial swathes of mangrove reserve, and behind the beachside hotels the mythical, densely forested contours of the Central Mountains cascade invitingly upwards. The island rears a number of crops: bananas, coffee, yams and citrons are of great importance.

Geology

Like almost all of the islands that sprang from the Caribbean Basin, Puerto Rico owes its existence to a series of volcanic events. These eruptions built up layers of lava and igneous rock and created an island with four distinct geographical zones: the central mountains, karst country, the coastal plain and the coastal dry forest. At the heart of the island, running east to west, stands a spine of steep, wooded mountains called the Central Mountains. The lower slopes of the cordillera give way to foothills, comprising a region on the island's north coast known as 'karst country.' In this part of the island, erosion has worn away the limestone, leaving a karstic terrain of dramatic sinkholes, hillocks and caves.

Forty-five non-navigable rivers and streams rush from the mountains and through the foothills to carve the coastal valleys, particularly on the east and west ends of Puerto Rico, where sugarcane, coconuts and a variety of fruits are cultivated. The island's longest river is the Río Grande de Loíza (64km), which flows north to the coast.

Puerto Rico – mainland and islands – claims almost 8900 sq km of land, making the Commonwealth about twice the size of the Mediterranean island of Corsica and a little over half the size of the US state of Connecticut.

Territorial Parks & Reserves

Puerto Rico has more than a dozen well-developed and protected wilderness areas, which offer an array of exploration and a few camping opportunities. Most of these protected areas are considered *reservas forestales* (forest reserves) or *bosques estatales* (state forests), although these identifiers are often treated interchangeably in government-issued literature and maps. Commonwealth or US federal agencies administer most of the natural reserves on the island, and admission to these areas is generally free.

Private conservation groups own and operate a few of the nature preserves, including Las Cabezas de San Juan and Humacao Nature Reserve in the east. The best time to visit nearly all of the parks is from November to March; however, Bosque Estatal de Guánica is an inviting destination year-round.

Major Parks & Reserves

El Yunque National Forest The emerald 28,000-acre highlight of the island's parks is this misty, magnificent rainforest. Dotted with idyllic waterfalls and covered in dense flora, it's home to some of Puerto Rico's most wild and

Salinas (p158)

endangered animals. With the island's best trails, El Yunque's lush forests and sun-splashed peaks are ideal for hiking and mountain biking.

Bosque Estatal de Guánica An immense patch of 10,000 acres on the southwest coast, this huge park is home to a tropical dry-forest ecosystem and a Unesco biosphere forest. Its arid scenery and beautiful birds make it good for hiking, swimming, biking and birdwatching.

Reserva Forestal Toro Negro This ruggedly beautiful and central mountainous park has landscapes that are as spectacular as El Yunque's, but with none of the infrastructure. If you want to get off the map (literally), this is the place.

Las Cabezas de San Juan This notable 316-acre coastal preserve is at the northeast corner of Puerto Rico. El Faro (the lighthouse) stands guard over the offshore cays. Its paved trails and interpretive centers make this a fine place for families, and it's a great spot to view the Laguna Grande bioluminescent bay.

Bosque Estatal de Río Abajo Densely forested and dotted with development, this state forest covers 5000 acres in karst country near the Observatorio de Arecibo. It has hiking trails and an aviary, where the Department of Natural Resources is working to reintroduce the Puerto Rican parrot and other endangered species.

Isla Mona The most isolated of Puerto Rico's nature sanctuaries lies about 50 miles west of Mayagüez, across the often-turbulent waters of Pasaje de la Mona. This tabletop island is sometimes called Puerto Rico's Galápagos or Jurassic Park because of its isolation. It's a tag made all the more eerie by the island's 200ft limestone cliffs, honeycomb caves and giant iguanas. Come here for solitude, hiking and caving.

Vieques National Wildlife Refuge Glimmering to the east are the 'Spanish Virgin Islands,' Culebra and Vieques, both of which have large tracts of land designated as National Wildlife Refuges under the control of the US Fish & Wildlife Service. At 18,000 acres, the Vieques refuge is the largest protected natural reserve in Puerto Rico and home to wild turtles and iguanas. It has

The San Fermin earthquake that hit western Puerto Rico in October 1918 measured 7.6 on the Richter scale and triggered a 20ft tsunami. The event caused more than $4 million worth of damage to the cities of Mayagüez and Aguadilla. It killed 116 people.

some of the Caribbean's best beaches; activities include snorkeling, swimming, hiking and cycling.

Environmental Issues

Puerto Rico has long suffered from a number of serious environmental problems, including population growth and rapid urbanization, deforestation, erosion of soil, water pollution and mangrove destruction. While Puerto Ricans still have a long way to go toward undoing generations of damage and preserving their natural resources, the past few decades have seen an increase in the level of awareness, resources and action dedicated to conservation efforts.

Tourism

Unchecked development has long been Puerto Rico's biggest environmental threat. Big developers and hotel companies regularly eye the country's lush coastline and pristine beaches in search of their next site. As economically beneficial as tourism might be, its continued expansion could lead to a law of diminishing returns. In their quest to make a livelihood from tourism, some have ended up causing extensive damage, as in the case of the bioluminescent bay at La Parguera, where oil pollution from tourist boats has significantly dimmed the luminescent glow.

The National Astronomy & Ionosphere Center (www.naic.edu) website has information about the Observatorio de Arecibo and about the heavens for the general public as well as for academic types.

Population Growth & Urbanization

Population growth and rapid urbanization have long posed the greatest threats to the island's environment, although this has moderated somewhat, simply because the population is falling as people head to the US mainland looking for work. Still, Puerto Rico currently has a higher population density than any of the 50 US states, with an average of 408 people per sq km. It also supports one of the highest concentrations of roads in the world (certainly the bumpiest).

Deforestation & Soil Erosion

Clear-cut logging operations ended in the 20th century, leaving untold acres of rich mountain topsoil plugging the mouths of rivers and streams. In the 1920s and '30s, conservationists and the US colonial government set aside and reforested an extensive network of wilderness reserves, mostly in karst country and the Central Mountains. Today these reserves are mature forests and cover nearly the entire central part of the island – about one-third of Puerto Rico's landmass. Meanwhile, the demands of development continue to threaten unprotected natural areas.

ENVIRONMENTAL GROUPS

Many organizations working to protect Puerto Rico's environment also offer excellent tours or activities that visitors can join.

Surfrider Foundation (www.surfrider.org) Puerto Rico's beaches get a lot of use, and often they get littered: this organization arranges beach cleanups, and you can get involved, or ask them about their other environmental projects.

Corporación Piñones Se Integra (p93) A non-profit that strives to preserve and restore San Juan's urban waterways; you can support them by renting a kayak or bicycle to explore the waterways and other unsung areas of the metro area.

Para la Naturaleza (p73) Operates a number of private nature reserves and has many volunteer projects available to participate in on its website.

Water Issues

Many streams, rivers and estuaries on the coastal plain have been polluted by agricultural runoff, industry and inadequate sewer systems. Environmental groups lobbying for the cleanup of these cesspools have made little headway. Visitors should not be tempted to swim in rivers, streams or estuaries near the coast. On a positive note, efforts are being made to clean up San Juan's urban estuaries.

Mangrove Protection

Widespread economic development after WWII devastated vast mangrove swamps, particularly along the island's north shore. In the 1990s, progress was made in reversing this damage, including the creation of a 2883-acre nature reserve at Bahía de Jobos on the south coast.

Environmentalists had more reason to celebrate in 2013 with the creation of the Corredor Ecológico del Noreste (Northeast Ecological Corridor), which will protect some 3000 acres of mangroves, beaches and sea-turtle nesting sites on the north coast east of Luquillo.

Heavy-Metal Pollution

Both the land and sea life around Vieques were literally under siege from the US government during the years of naval bombardment. The US Navy left Vieques in 2003 and the island was deemed a Superfund site shortly after the pullout. Though progress has been made, much of the Vieques National Wildlife Refuge is closed to the public until heavy metals, unexploded ordnance and leftover fuels and chemicals can be taken care of.

Puerto Rico's highest point is Cerro de Punta (4389 ft/1338m) in the Central Mountains but, offshore to the north, its lows are of greater significance. The Puerto Rico Trench is the deepest point in the Atlantic Ocean, reaching a murky extent of 28,374 ft/8648m.

Wildlife of Puerto Rico

Seeking out the wildlife of Puerto Rico can be very rewarding. The island's jungle-clad mountains and surreal variety of terrain – including some of the wettest and driest forests in the subtropical climate – have a bit of everything (albeit no huge beasts or flocks of colorful birds). The island's most famous creature is the humble common coqui. The nocturnal serenade of this small endemic frog is the poignant soundtrack of the island, an ever-present reminder of Puerto Rico's precious natural environment.

Amphibians & Reptiles

Puerto Rico's long coastline is one of its most inviting environments to both human and animal visitors. Despite heavy development, a handful of the island's beaches are still nesting sites for two of the world's most critically endangered turtles, the hawksbill and leatherback sea turtles. An excellent place to view the nesting process is on the isolated northern beaches of the island of Culebra.

The hawksbill and leatherback sea turtles are among the 61 species of reptiles and 25 species of amphibians on the island – one of the most diverse collections of such animals in the world. Certainly the most famous amphibian is the tiny but highly vocal coqui frog (its distinctive nighttime croak has been measured at 10 decibels), which has been adopted as a national symbol. But it's not the only frog on the show. The sapo *concho*, the Commonwealth's only endemic toad, has done something the coqui never could: close roads. Parts of Hwy 333 along the south coast of Bosque Estatal de Guánica have been fenced off to help protect this endangered creature's breeding grounds, and results have paid off: toad numbers are jumping up again.

Iguanas are often kept as semiwild pets and pose unlikely obstacles on numerous Puerto Rican golf courses. The most notable wild species is the Mona ground iguana, which still survives in large numbers on the western island of Mona – often dubbed the Galápagos of the Caribbean because of its unique biological diversity.

Puerto Rico boasts 11 varieties of snake, none of which are poisonous. The most impressive is the Puerto Rican boa, which averages 7ft in length; it is also endangered, but hikers may spot one in the karst region of the northwestern state forests and in El Yunque.

Learn all about the coqui frog and other animals that inhabit Puerto Rico in *Natural Puerto Rico* by Alfonso Silva Lee, an exhaustive but entertaining book on island wildlife.

Marine Life

Spending time in the water off Puerto Rico's shores at the right time of year can reveal excellent marine life. Pods of humpback whales breed in the island's warm waters in winter. In the late winter of 2010, southern shores off the island also saw more orca (killer whales) than ever before recorded. Local fishermen attribute this to the relatively warm waters of the Caribbean bringing more dolphins for the orca to eat. Most whale-watching tour operators leave from Rincón, with the tour season usually beginning in early December and ending in March.

Though looking for whales may be a hit with tourists, the Antillean manatee (the town of Manatí, on the north coast, is named after the mammal) is more dear to Puerto Ricans. These so-called sea cows inhabit shallow coastal areas to forage on sea grasses and plants. Manatee numbers have dropped in recent decades due to habitat loss, poaching and entanglement with fishing nets, but they are generally thought to be coming back. To see a manatee, rent a kayak and float along the mangrove-lined shores in the southeast of the island, around the Bahía de Jobos.

Of course, the majority of travelers are captivated by seeing the tropical fish and coral off the island's shores. The continental shelf surrounds Puerto Rico on three sides and blesses the island with warm water and excellent coral reefs, seawalls and underwater features for diving and snorkeling. Especially off the west coast, the water is clear and filled with fish, including parrot fish, eels and sea horses. An abundant supply of sea grass is home to crabs, octopus, starfish and more.

Mammals

Very few of the land mammals that make their home in Puerto Rico are native to the island; most mammal species – from rats to cows – have been accidentally or intentionally introduced to the island over the centuries.

Bats are the only native terrestrial mammal in Puerto Rico. They exist in large numbers in the caves of karst country, but most travelers will only catch glimpses at dusk while visiting Bosque Estatal de Cambalache or the Cavernas del Río Camuy.

Puerto Rico is also home to the distinctive Paso Fino horse, a small-boned, easy-gaited variety. The Paso Finos have been raised in Puerto Rico since the time of the Spanish conquest, when they were introduced to the New World to supply the conquistadores on their expeditions throughout Mexico and the rest of the Americas. The horses are most dramatic on the island of Vieques, where they roam in semiwild herds across the landscape, although the animals are also celebrated in a festival in the south coast town of Guayama.

Other mammals of interest to travelers are two small colonies of monkeys, both introduced by scientists. The first lives on the 39-acre Cayo Santiago where a group of rhesus monkeys arrived for scientific study in 1938. Today they've burgeoned into a community of more than 900 primates and can be spotted from snorkeling tour boats. The second scientific monkey colony that grew out of control is on Isla de Monos off La Parguera, which is a standard part of the tour of the mangrove canals.

Birds & Bugs

With more than 250 species spread over 3500 sq miles, Puerto Rico is an excellent place to dust off your binoculars and engage in a bit of tropical birdwatching. The Commonwealth's most famous bird is also one of its rarest: the elusive Puerto Rican parrot (aka the Puerto Rican Amazon). Numbers of the bright-green bird were down in the mid teens during the 1970s, but thanks to concerted conservation efforts the wild population has recovered to a still-precarious 60 to 80. The parrots exist in the wild in the El Yunque and Río Abajo forest reserves, although seeing one is akin to winning a lottery ticket.

Among the 17 endemic birds is the Puerto Rican tody, a small green, yellow and red creature that frequents the moist mountains of the Central Mountains and the dense thickets of the south coast where it feeds on insects.

The coastal dry forest of Guánica might be the biggest draw for serious birdwatchers looking to whittle down their life list. It features more than 130 bird species, comprising largely of songbirds. Some of these are migratory birds, such as the prairie warbler and the northern

There are seven known regions worldwide that are phosphorescent – meaning they glow in the dark thanks to micro-organisms called dinoflagellates living in the water – but Puerto Rico's are considered among the brightest and the best. Head to Bioluminescent Bay (Bahía Mosquito) in Vieques, Bahía de Fosforescente at La Parguera and Laguna Grande north of Fajardo.

Puerto Rico's biggest snake, the Puerto Rican boa, can reach 7ft in length. Found mainly in the remote northern karst forests, it's not a threat to humans.

WILDLIFE OF PUERTO RICO MAMMALS

HIKING FOR THE BIRDS

Exotic birdlife is the wildlife of choice to spot on nature hikes. The most obvious destination for budding ornithologists is El Yunque National Forest, situated close to the capital. The El Portal Visitors Center on Hwy 191 has good, basic information on the local birdlife. Another choice is Bosque Estatal de Guánica, where the solitude of the trails may help facilitate spying some of the 130-odd bird species found there.

The island's richest species diversity can be spied in the Cabo Rojo area, particularly around Las Salinas salt flats, where migratory birds from as far away as Canada populate a unique and highly varied ecosystem. Call in at the Centro Interpretativos Las Salinas de Cabo Rojo (p191) to speak with informed local experts.

parula. Many are nonmigratory species, including the lizard cuckoo and the critically endangered Puerto Rican nightjar.

Along the coast, one of the joys of winter beachcombing is watching the aerial acrobatics of brown pelicans as they hunt for fish. Stray out along the salt flats and far-flung headlands of Cabo Rojo, a migratory ground for 25 bird species, and you may glimpse another of the island's endemic feathered friends, the yellow-shouldered blackbird.

The island also has a supply of unusual flying and crawling insects, including a large tropical relative of the firefly called the *cucubano,* and a centipede measuring more than 6in in length with a sting that can kill. Much to the chagrin of generations of foreign visitors there are also zillions of blood-hungry mosquitoes.

Flora

Puerto Rico's tropical climate and unique rain patterns create a veritable greenhouse for a huge variety of plant life, which thrives on tropical heat, tons of rain and lots of moisture in the air. As soon as you leave San Juan's urban zone, you'll see green everywhere.

Mangrove swamps and coconut groves dominate the north coast, while the El Yunque rainforest, in the east, supports mahogany trees and more than 50 varieties of wild orchid. Giant ferns thrive in the rainforest as well as in the foothills of karst country, while cacti, mesquite forest and bunch-grass reign on the dry southwest tip of the island. The dry forests near Guánica grow a variety of cacti, thorny scrub brush and plants equipped for harsh, dry conditions.

The hills of the Central Mountains are densely forested and flowering trees punctuate the landscape. Look for the butterfly tree, with its light-pink flower resembling an orchid, the bright orange exclamation of the African tulip and the deep red of the royal poinciana, which are cultivated near the Christmas season.

Exotic shade trees have long been valued in this sunny climate, and most of the island's municipal plazas sit beneath canopies of magnificent ceibas or kapoks (silk-cotton trees), the flamboyán (poinciana), with its flame-red blossoms, and the African tulip tree.

Islanders often adorn their homes with flowers, and tend lovingly to fruit trees that bear bananas, papaya, *uva caleta* (sea grape), *carambola* (star fruit), *panapen* (breadfruit) and *plátano* (plantain). Never do the floral hues of Puerto Rico come together on song more than at Aibonito's Festival de Flores (p218) in June.

Of course, sugarcane dominates the plantations of the coastal lowlands, while farmers raise coffee on the steep slopes of the Central Mountains.

For birdwatchers heading to Puerto Rico or the Caribbean, *A Guide to the Birds of Puerto Rico and the Virgin Islands* by Herbert Raffaele is a must-have. If you don't luck out and spot a wild Puerto Rican parrot, one of the 10 most endangered species in the world, there are over 300 in captivity in various zoos and sanctuaries.

Survival Guide

DIRECTORY A–Z 262

Accommodations 262

Climate 263

Customs Regulations . . .263

Electricity 264

Embassies &
Consulates. 264

Food 264

Gambling 264

GLBTI Travelers. 264

Health. 264

Insurance. 265

Internet Access. 265

Legal Matters 265

Maps. 265

Money. 265

Public Holidays. 266

Safe Travel. 266

Telephone 266

Tourist
Information 266

Travelers with
Disabilities. 266

Visas. 267

Volunteering 267

Women Travelers 267

TRANSPORTATION. . 268

GETTING THERE &
AWAY 268

Entering the Country. . .268

Air. 268

Sea 268

GETTING AROUND 269

Air. 269

Bicycle 269

Boat 269

Car 269

Hitchhiking 271

Local
Transportation 271

LANGUAGE 272

Glossary. 277

Directory A–Z

Accommodations

Puerto Rico has a wide range of accommodations. Book ahead in high season.

Hotels Available island-wide in price ranges from $60 to $400+ nightly, with a good selection under $200.

Bed-and-Breakfasts A relatively new mid-range accommodation option; owners always live on or near the premises and breakfast is included.

Guesthouses These range from family-run places with a few rooms to larger motel-like stays; many can also be apartments under another name.

Resorts World-class properties line San Juan's beachfront and other coastal areas. There are, however, few all-inclusive resorts.

Camping Possible on Culebra and in a handful of nature parks.

B&Bs

An accommodation category still in its early days in Puerto Rico, bed-and-breakfasts have been growing in numbers on the island of recent years. Comparable in quality with many of the better hotels and often indistinguishable from boutique hotels, the hallmarks of Puerto Rican bed-and-breakfasts is that they are family-owned places where the owners live on the premises to attend to your needs and always rustle up a good breakfast included in the room price, which varies between $100 and $300.

There is now a **Puerto Rico Bed and Breakfast Association** (www.puertoricobedandbreakfasts.com) where you can find out more.

Camping

Camping is a difficult proposition in Puerto Rico, as reservations must usually be made at least 15 days in advance (perhaps not coincidentally at least a day longer than most tourists' vacations). Reservation offic-

es and ranger stations have maddeningly erratic hours and the quality of facilities varies greatly.

Beach camping You can find campsites on or near the sand on Vieques and Culebra. It's also possible at some of the beaches along the northeast coast, moving from Luquillo east.

National Forests and Forest Reserves Contact the **Departamento de Recursos Naturales y Ambientales** (DRNA, Department of Natural Resources; ☏787-999-2200; www.drna.gobierno.pr; Km 6.3, Rte 8838, Río Piedras; ⊙8am-noon & 1-4pm Mon-Fri; ⓂCupey) at least 15 days in advance for reservations and a permit. Commonwealth-run forest-reserve campgrounds are likely to have showers and RV hookups available; national forest campgrounds tend to be less developed.

Guesthouses

Places calling themselves 'guesthouses' can differ vastly from one to the next. While some guesthouses may have as few as two rooms, others may have dozens. One guesthouse may look like a roadside motel, another may be a beach house with a pool. The phenomenon of Airbnb has hit Puerto Rico in earnest and 'guesthouses' now are, in the majority of cases, rental apartments with few further amenities. Most guesthouses are mid-range in price.

Hotels

Puerto Rico has many top-end resort hotels and a growing number of boutique options. Most major chains have properties in San Juan and all other sizeable cities. Despite a difficult economic climate, there are still new resorts opening and others being lavishly restored.

At all hotels and resorts, watch out for mandatory 'resort fees' that can add charges of $50 a day or more to room prices. Service charges are also common at top-end places.

Paradores

The Puerto Rico Tourism Company (PRTC; www. seepuertorico.com) endorses about 20 *paradores* (inns) scattered across the island and they are a mixed bag. Some are modern and generic hotels, others are quaint, oozing with charm. Some are beautifully housed in old coffee plantations.

Rental Accommodation

Consult Airbnb.com and vrbo.com for scores of rental listings in a variety of locations and price ranges around the island.

Climate

Barranquitas

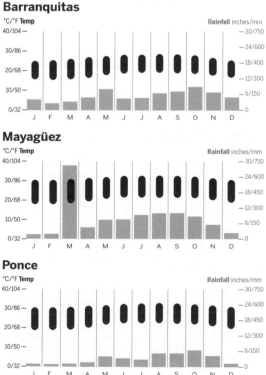

Mayagüez

Ponce

Customs Regulations

Goods brought into the US in greater quantity than the duty-free customs allowances are subject to taxes and tariffs and must be declared at customs.

Cigarettes/Cigars Each person over 18 can bring 200 cigarettes or 100 cigars duty free into Puerto Rico or the US.

Currency US law permits you to bring in or take out as much as $10,000 in US or foreign currency, traveler's checks or letters of credit without formality.

Gifts US citizens are allowed to import, duty free, $400 worth of gifts from abroad, while non-US citizens are allowed to bring in $100 worth.

Liquor Each person over the age of 21 can bring 1L of liquor, duty free, into Puerto Rico or the US. From Puerto Rico, you can take out as much purchased alcohol and tobacco as you wish without paying any duty on it.

Plants Declare any plants, fruits or vegetables at the airport. The US department of agriculture restricts many island plants.

Electricity

Type A
120V/60Hz

Type B
120V/60Hz

Embassies & Consulates

Most nations' principal diplomatic representation is in Washington DC, which means many countries do not maintain consulates in Puerto Rico. Consulates in here tend to be the honorary kind that have very limited services – if any – for travelers. The following may be of use:

French Consulate (787-767-2428; www.consulfrance-miami.org; 270 Av Muñoz Rivera, Suite 301, Hato Rey; phone inquiries 9am-noon Mon, Wed & Fri, in-person by appointment only; Roosevelt)

Spanish Consulate (787-758-6090; www.exteriores.gob.es; Mercantil Plaza, 2 Av Ponce de León; 8:30am-1:30pm Mon-Fri)

Netherlands Consulate (787-399-0830; www.the-netherlands.org; Mercantil Plaza, 2 Av Ponce de León; by appointment only)

Dominican Republic Consulate (787-725-9550; www.domrep.org; 1607 Av Ponce de León, Suite 101, Santurce; 9am-2pm Mon-Fri)

Food

Food is an intrinsic part of Puerto Rican culture and the Commonwealth offers a flavorsome array of dining options, from side-of-a-dusty-road food trucks to trendy farm-to-table bistros. For more on Puerto Rico's cuisine, see p34.

Gambling

Gambling is legal in Puerto Rico, takes a variety of forms and is quite prevalent. Though mostly confined to the large-resort casinos of San Juan, other hotels with smaller casinos exist elsewhere. All casinos will offer a variety of slot machines and some table games. There is a horse track and cockfighting arena in San Juan. Other places to watch cockfights (galleras) elsewhere on the island are largely seedy affairs. You'll likely see vendors selling lottery tickets around the island, and a mechanical horse-racing game, with rules similar to roulette, at small town fiestas and along the side of the road.

GLBTI Travelers

Puerto Rico is probably the most gay-friendly island in the Caribbean. San Juan has a well-developed gay scene, especially in the Condado district (and also in Santurce) for Puerto Ricans and visitors. Vieques and Culebra have become popular destinations for an international mix of gay and lesbian expatriates and travelers. Rincón, whilst some way behind other destinations in specifically gay venues, is a gay-friendly destination too. Ponce and Mayagüez, as sizeable university cities, are also liberal places.

In the cities and in major resort areas, it's easier for gay men and women to live their lives with a certain amount of openness. As you travel into the middle of the island, it's more difficult to be out, as people are not used to seeing same-sex couples displaying affection publicly.

As of 2015, same-sex couples can legally marry and apply to adopt.

Health

For medical emergencies, dial 911.

Availability & Cost of Health Care

Cities and larger towns have at least one high-standard hospital. Elsewhere there is usually at least one good clinic. The service is of a standard comparable to elsewhere in the mainland US.

Environmental Hazards

Animals Do not pet or feed any animal, except domestic animals known to be free of infectious diseases. Spiny sea urchins and coelenterates (coral and jellyfish) are a hazard in some areas.

Mosquitoes Except for infrequent outbreaks of dengue fever, mosquito-borne illnesses are usually not a concern in Puerto Rico. A bug spray containing DEET is best to ward off insects, but use sparingly as it kills natural organisms in island bays and inlets.

Sandflies The notorious 'no-see-ums.' These invisible bugs come out mostly in the early evening. Culebra and Vieques can be particularly thick with them, so lay on the DEET.

Sun Yes, it's subtropical, so apply high-protection sunscreen.

Water Tap water does not taste great but is safe to drink.

Viral Infections

DENGUE FEVER

Dengue fever is a viral infection found throughout the Caribbean. In Puerto Rico the incidence usually peaks between September and November. Dengue is transmitted by Aedes mosquitoes, which often bite during the daytime and are usually found close to human habitations. They breed primarily in artificial water containers such as jars, barrels, plastic containers and discarded tires. It's common in urban environments.

Dengue causes flu-like symptoms, including fever, muscle aches, headaches, nausea and vomiting, often followed by a rash. The aches may be quite uncomfortable, but most cases resolve in a few days. Severe cases usually occur in children under age 15 who are experiencing their second dengue infection.

There is no vaccine and no treatment for dengue fever except taking acetaminophen/paracetamol (Tylenol) and drinking fluids. Severe cases may require hospitalization. The cornerstone of prevention is protection, so use DEET-based mosquito repellent.

ZIKA VIRUS

Zika is a viral infection transmitted primarily, as with Dengue fever, through Aedes mosquitoes. It was first identified in Uganda in the 1940s, but a severe outbreak across the Americas in 2015 and 2016 also affected Puerto Rico with particular seriousness. As of early 2017,

the tally of Zika cases was over 30,000.

The relatively mild symptoms include slight fever, skin rash, conjunctivitis, muscle and joint pain, and normally last for two to seven days, after which sufferers normally make a complete recovery. The main risk with Zika is in how it affects pregnant women. There have been studies showing a link between infected pregnant women and babies born with microcephaly (particularly small heads).

Infection can be transmitted through the bite of the mosquito, most likely during the day in early morning and evening, but the infection can be sexually transmitted too. Cases were declining as of early 2017, but the risk of catching the infection has deterred many visitors.

Insurance

Check your health and/or your homeowners insurance to see what is and is not covered in terms of problems that may arise on the road. You may want to consider travel insurance for lost luggage, trip cancellations and delays, health coverage and more.

Worldwide travel insurance is available at www.lonelyplanet.com/bookings. You can buy, extend and claim online anytime – even if you're already on the road.

Internet Access

Wi-fi is common in places to stay, cafes and public places and squares. In this book, the wi-fi symbol means that wi-fi is available throughout the property unless otherwise noted, while the internet symbol means there are public internet terminals available.

Legal Matters

The thing to remember is that in the majority of legal matters, things follow exactly

the same pattern as they do in the mainland US.

➡ Puerto Rico follows US laws in all criminal and most legislative matters. If you are arrested, you have the same rights as you would elsewhere in the US.

➡ If you're stopped by the police, remember there's no system of paying fines on the spot. Don't attempt to pay the officer.

➡ Although English is widely spoken, many police in rural areas do not speak English.

Drinking Laws

Alcohol is deeply ingrained in the island's social scene – more so than in parts of the US and Europe. Puerto Rico has few 'blue laws' prohibiting the times and places where alcohol can be consumed.

➡ Minors are not permitted in bars and pubs, even to order nonalcoholic beverages.

➡ Old San Juan has laws to prevent drinking in the streets, and violators are subject to heavy fines.

➡ Driving under the influence of alcohol will result in stiff fines, jail time and penalties.

➡ Drinking on the beach is legal.

Maps

Apps from Apple and Google have Puerto Rico well covered. There are also many free maps available that will do in most cases. When you hire a vehicle from a rental agency they give out complimentary maps that suffice for getting around most places. You'll find more detailed maps at drug and convenience stores. The best maps for Puerto Rico can be purchased from the US Geological Survey.

Money

➡ Major bank offices in San Juan and Ponce will exchange foreign currencies. There are also exchange desks at San Juan's Luis Muñoz Marín International Airport and major resorts.

➡ ATMs are easily found in all but the smallest towns.

➡ Tipping in restaurants averages 15% to 20% but is not as expected as it is in mainland US.

Public Holidays

US public holidays are celebrated along with local holidays in Puerto Rico. Banks, schools and government offices (including post offices) are closed, and transportation, museums and other services are on a Sunday schedule. Holidays falling on a weekend are usually observed the following Monday.

New Year's Day January 1

Three Kings Day (Feast of the Epiphany) January 6

Eugenio María de Hostos' Birthday January 10

Martin Luther King Jr Day Third Monday in January

Presidents' Day Third Monday in February

Emancipation Day March 22

Palm Sunday Sunday before Easter

Good Friday Friday before Easter

Easter A Sunday in late March/ April

José de Diego Day April 18

Memorial Day Last Monday in May

Independence Day/Fourth of July July 4

Luis Muñoz Rivera's Birthday July 18

Constitution Day July 25

José Celso Barbosa's Birthday July 27

Labor Day First Monday in September

Columbus Day Second Monday in October

Veterans' Day November 11

Thanksgiving Fourth Thursday in November

Christmas Day December 25

Safe Travel

Hazards in the Water

The currents of Puerto Rico's beaches can be deadly, with the biggest hazards being riptides and dangerous ocean currents. Obey all posted signs on beaches. If you get caught in a riptide that carries you away from shore, never panic or swim against it, you'll only get worn out. Instead, swim parallel to the shoreline and when the current lessens make your way back to shore.

Hazards on the Road

Puerto Rican drivers are more aggressive than drivers on the mainland US, and rules of the road are taken as more of a suggestion. Keep your cool and proceed with caution. Mountain roads can be very narrow and have sudden drop-offs and rough surfaces. Beep before driving into blind curves. If you come to a point in the road too narrow for both cars to pass, the car on the uphill side should reverse and let the other driver pass. GPS can easily malfunction here, too, and direct you up what might officially be a road but is actually a 4×4-only track.

If you're driving and see a police car with its blue lights on, don't worry, police in Puerto Rico are required to have their lights lit whenever driving. Police will sound a siren during emergencies.

Hiking & Camping

➡ Never head into the forest without leaving someone your planned itinerary.

➡ Minor cuts and scrapes can get infected easily in this climate; carry disinfectant.

➡ Getting lost is easy; invest in a good topographical map for serious hikes.

Weather & Natural Disasters

Although somewhat predictable, Puerto Rico can get pounded with tropical storms and hurricanes, which can result in a number of serious disruptions for visitors, including washed-out roads and trails, and shuttered attractions. Hurricane season is usually between the beginning of June and the end of November. If you're visiting during this time there's still likely nothing to worry about.

Telephone

The good news for US cellphone users is that Puerto Rico is treated as just another state in terms of coverage and roaming fees.

International Calls

To call home from Puerto Rico:

➡ First dial 🖉011, the international dialing prefix in the US.

➡ Dial the country code of the country you want to call. For Australia, dial 🖉61; the UK, 🖉44; Ireland, 🖉353; New Zealand, 🖉64.

➡ Dial the rest of the number.

Tourist Information

Puerto Rico Tourism Company is the Commonwealth's official tourist bureau. It has a fair range of general-interest materials and a decent website, See Puerto Rico (www.seepuertorico.com). Privately produced tourist magazines and brochures are abundant.

Travelers with Disabilities

Travel in Puerto Rico is becoming easier for people with disabilities as the country is subject to the Americans with Disabilities Act (ADA). Public buildings (including hotels, restaurants, theaters and museums) are now required by law to be wheelchair-accessible and to have appropriate restroom facilities.

PRACTICALITIES

Weights & Measures Puerto Rico follows the American imperial system with two major exceptions: all distances on road signs are in kilometers and gas is pumped in liters.

TV & Radio American TV is broadcast across the island. Radio is mostly in Spanish. Places to stay will have the full compliment of US cable/satellite channels.

Newspapers Some main newspapers have good websites. *El Nuevo Dia* (www.elnuevo-dia.com) is Puerto Rico's leading news publication and it also has one of the island's most popular websites. It has an English section, too.

Smoking Banned in most public places, including hotel rooms and restaurants.

Public transportation services (buses, trains and taxis) must be made accessible to all, including those in wheelchairs, and telephone companies are required to provide relay operators for the hearing impaired.

Many banks now provide ATM instructions in Braille. ADA-compliant curb ramps are common, and some of the busier roadway intersections have audible crossing signals. Playa Luquillo has a beach especially for the mobility-impaired, and ferries to Culebra and Vieques are accessible.

Resources

Download Lonely Planet's free Accessible Travel guide from http://lptravel.to/AccessibleTravel.

Visas

➔ You only need a visa to enter Puerto Rico if you need a visa to enter the US, since the Commonwealth follows the United States' immigration laws. For many countries, an ESTA (Electronic System for Transport authorization, https://esta.cbp.dhs.gov/esta) must nevertheless be applied for.

➔ As a commonwealth, Puerto Rico subscribes to all the laws that apply to traveling and border crossing in the United States.

➔ US citizens can enter with proper proof of citizenship, such as a driver's license

with photo ID, a passport or a birth certificate.

➔ Visitors from other countries must have a valid, scannable passport. Countries participating in the Visa Waiver Program – the EU, Australia, New Zealand and much of Latin America – don't need visas to get in.

➔ International travelers will most likely transit through an East Coast hub such as New York City or Miami, or arrive from Europe on one of several new, cheap, direct flights.

➔ US Department of State (www.state.gov) has up-to-date information about visas, immigration etc.

Volunteering

As a relatively rich country in close geographic and economic proximity to the United States, Puerto Rico offers limited opportunities for volunteering.

Rainforest management The Earthwatch Institute (www.eyeontherainforest.org) partners with Las Casas de la Selva to run one- to three-week research missions to the Bosque Estatal de Carite, where participants learn forest management skills and aid in the rejuvenation of the tropical rainforest. Volunteers stay in tents in the Casas de la Selva complex inside the park and spend their time planting seedlings, studying trees and monitoring local frog populations.

Beach cleanup The Surfrider Foundation (www.surfrider.org)

has chapters in San Juan and Rincón. They organize plastics and beach cleanups, and run public education programs.

Turtle watching The US Fish and Wildlife Refuge runs a volunteer turtle watch on Culebra's Playa Brava during nesting season. You can access this project through CORALations (www.coralations.org), a nonprofit organization that is involved in coral reef protection.

Wildlife protection The **Vieques Conservation and Historical Trust** (Map p134; ☎787-741-8850; www.vcht.org; 138 Flamboyán, Esperanza; tours from $20; ☺9am-5pm) accepts volunteers for a wide variety of projects, including assisting with animals and reefs, maintaining a tank of rescued marine animals, and feeding animals.

Women Travelers

Puerto Rico's status as a US commonwealth means that women have a position in society not dissimilar to that in the United States.

Puerto Rican women crisscross the island all the time by themselves, so you won't be the only solo woman on the ferry or public bus, but as a foreigner you will attract a bit more attention. Most of it will be simple curiosity, but a few may assume you'd much rather be with a man if you could. If you don't want the company, most men will respect a firm but polite, 'no thank you.'

Transportation

GETTING THERE & AWAY

For a Caribbean castaway destination, Puerto Rico is well-connected, mainly thanks to an important airport and cruise-ship port in San Juan.

Flights, cars and tours can be booked online at lonely planet.com/bookings.

Entering the Country

Luis Muñoz Marín International Airport (San Juan) San Juan's LMM airport (SJU) receives the vast majority of flights to Puerto Rico, especially international ones. It has all services (except wi-fi), including major car-rental companies and fairly cheap, flat-rate taxis to the nearby tourist centers.

Old San Juan and Ponce Piers Cruise ships dock at the busy ports at the base of Old San Juan, and at Port of the Americas near Ponce's La Guancha

Paseo Tablado. Fabulous food and drink are all nearby, although from Ponce's port you'll need a taxi to get to the center.

Air

There are a few airports on the island that service international flights.

Luis Muñoz Marín International Airport (San Juan Airport; www.aeropuertosju. com) is San Juan's main airport and where almost all flights arrive or depart.

Rafael Hernández Airport (Aguadilla Airport; http://aguadilla.airport-authority.com) receives a few international flights, with several airlines flying to New York, Newark and Orlando from here. Other mainland US destinations are served too, with specific routes changing frequently. A few other Caribbean destinations such as Santo Domingo, St Lucia and Aruba are also served.

Small planes fly to the British Virgin Islands from **Isla Grande Airport** (Fernando Luis Ribas Dominicci Airport), Benjamín Rivera Noriega Airport (Culebra Airport) and Antonio Rivera Rodríguez Airport (Vieques Airport).

Most major destinations in mainland US are served by airlines including American Airlines, United, Delta, Spirit, LATAM, Air Canada, Emirates, Air France, KLM and British Airways. Other direct international routes of interest include London and Oslo (Norwegian), Frankfurt (Condor) plus St Thomas in the US Virgin Islands and Santo Domingo in the Dominican Republic (Seabourne Airlines).

Sea

Cruise Ship

San Juan is the second-largest port for cruise ships in the western hemisphere

---

CLIMATE CHANGE & TRAVEL

Every form of transport that relies on carbon-based fuel generates CO_2, the main cause of human-induced climate change. Modern travel is dependent on airplanes, which might use less fuel per kilometer per person than most cars but travel much greater distances. The altitude at which aircraft emit gases (including CO_2) and particles also contributes to their climate change impact. Many websites offer 'carbon calculators' that allow people to estimate the carbon emissions generated by their journey and, for those who wish to do so, to offset the impact of the greenhouse gases emitted with contributions to portfolios of climate-friendly initiatives throughout the world. Lonely Planet offsets the carbon footprint of all staff and author travel.

(after Miami). Over one million cruise-ship passengers pass through the ports in Old San Juan annually, and all the major cruise-ship lines operate cruises from here.

Following substantial investment, Ponce's **Port of the Americas** (Muelle de Ponce) also now has cruises calling.

Ferry

A ferry service supposedly connects Puerto Rico with the Dominican Republic. **America Cruise Ferries** (Map p52; ☑Mayaguez 787-832-4800, San Juan 787-622-4800; www.acferries.com; return adults from $189, cars from $250) was running the large *Caribbean Fantasy* from Old San Juan to the Don Diego port near Santo Domingo in the Dominican Republic, but at the time of research this 13-hour route had problems and was not operating.

Yacht

➡ Hopping aboard a yacht destined for the West Indies from North America or Europe is a highly popular way of getting to Puerto Rico.

➡ Marinas are located at most major resorts and at principal ports around the Puerto Rican coast. The biggest marinas are at San Juan, Fajardo (east coast), Salinas and Ponce (south coast).

➡ Upon reaching the island you *must* clear immigration and customs unless you are coming directly from a US port or the US Virgin Islands.

➡ There are numerous online clearinghouses for those seeking yacht-crew positions (both experienced and inexperienced). Examples include **Crewfinders** (www.crewfinders.com) and **Yacht Crew Register** (www.yachtcrewregister.com).

GETTING AROUND

Air

Because Puerto Rico is such a small island, its domestic air transportation system is basic. Daily flights connect San Juan with Mayagüez on the mainland, and with the offshore islands of Culebra and Vieques.

Cape Air (☑1-800-227-3247; www.capeair.com) and **Jet-Blue** (☑1-800-538-2583; www.jetblue.com; Luis Muñoz Marín INternational Airport) fly to Mayagüez on the west coast; these airlines also fly to Vieques from here.

Isla Grande Airport (Fernando Luis Ribas Dominicci Airport) Culebra and Vieques are served from San Juan's secondary airport, both by **Vieques Air Link** (☑888-901-9247, 787-741-0508; www.viequesairlink. corn; Antonio Rivera Rodríguez Airport) and **Air Flamenco** (☑787-741-8811, 877-535-2636; www.airflamenco.net; Antonio Rivera Rodríguez Airport).

Benjamín Rivera Noriega Airport (Culebra Airport) **Vieques Air Link** (☑787-742-0254, 888-901-9247; www.viequesairlink.com; Aeropuerto Benjamín Rivera Noriega, Hwy 251) and **Air Flamenco** (☑877-535-2636, 787-742-1040; www.airflamenco.net; Benjamín Rivera Noriega Airport, Hwy 251) connect Culebra with Vieques and either Isla Grande or Luis Muñoz Marín airports in San Juan.

Antonio Rivera Rodríguez Airport (Vieques Airport) Vieques Air Link and Air Flamenco connect Vieques with Culebra and either Isla Grande or Luis Muñoz Marín airports in San Juan.

Eugenia María de Hostos Airport (Mayagüez Airport) **Cape Air** (☑1-800-227-3247; www.capeair.com) Fly several times daily between here and San Juan's Luis Muñoz Marín airport.

Bicycle

Bicycles should be considered a recreational, rather than practical, form of transportation for all but the most ambitious of travelers. Cycling hasn't traditionally been a popular means of getting around the island and the bad road conditions make this unlikely to change soon.

The hazards of cycling in Puerto Rico include nightmare traffic, dangerous drivers and a general lack of awareness about cyclists' needs. Most natives simply aren't used to seeing touring bikes on the road. Never cycle after dark. For further advice contact the Puerto Rican Cycling Federation.

You can usually rent a bike in tourist areas.

Boat

Charter Yacht

All of the island's major resorts have marinas where you can charter yachts or powerboats, either with a crew or 'bareboat.' Crewed boats come with a skipper and crew, and you don't need any prior sailing experience. With bareboat charters, you can rent the boat and be your own skipper.

Some charter companies:

Sail Caribe (Map p108; ☑787-889-1978; www.sailcaribe.com; Marina Puerto del Rey, Fajardo; yacht rental per week from $2500)

Erin Go Bragh (☑787-860-4401; www.egbc.net)

Ferry

Public ferries link Fajardo with Culebra and Vieques.

Car

Despite the occasional hazards of operating a car in Puerto Rico, driving is currently the most convenient way to get around the countryside, see small towns, cross sprawling suburbs and explore wide, open spaces. In fact, most Puerto Ricans like to travel by car wherever possible, and only get out to use their own two feet when wheels really won't get them any further. Like it or not, if you want to see anything of the island you'll pretty much have to drive: public transport is about as poor as it gets, and cycling on certain roads, the Ruta Panorámica included, is deemed too dangerous.

Driver's License

Any valid driver's license can be used to rent and operate a car or scooter in Puerto Rico. If you stay longer than 90 days, residency laws require you to get a Puerto Rican license.

Fuel

Major oil companies maintain gas stations across the island, which generally stay open until about 7pm (later around major highways). Don't let your tank go dry, though, because the next station could be a long way up the road. In rural areas, stations may close on Sunday.

Insurance

Liability insurance is required in Puerto Rico, as in most US states. Insurance against damage to the car, called Collision Damage Waiver (CDW) or Loss Damage

Waiver (LDW), is usually optional, but will often require you to pay for the first $100 or $500. Some credit-card companies cover car rentals, so extra coverage may not be needed. Always take some insurance – accidents happen far too easily. Most rental agencies prohibit taking a car to Culebra or Vieques.

Parking

Finding parking can be a real problem in San Juan and central Ponce. Do not park at curbs painted red or yellow. Parking fees at the hotels average about $20 per day.

Rental

Car-rental rates in San Juan are very competitive; elsewhere, not so much. A car costing $30 or less a day in San Juan will cost $60 or more in smaller cities and on the islands. Some companies prohibit taking rentals from the mainland to Culebra and Vieques.

All of the major international car-rental companies operate on the island, especially at the airport in San Juan. There are also local firms, especially in smaller cities and on the islands.

Road Conditions & Hazards

➡ Puerto Rico's roads are in an abysmal state. Expect bumps, potholes, broken guard rails and worse.

➡ Puerto Rico has more cars per square mile than any other place on earth – twice as many as Los Angeles County – expect traffic jams.

➡ Puerto Rican's driving habits are casual in the extreme; a sure sign of a tourist driver is the use of turn signals. Sudden stops, turns in front of oncoming traffic and other unsafe moves are common. Drivers often ignore stop lights and signs.

➡ Watch out for island animals – dogs, chickens, horses, pigs – that wander across the roads, particularly in the mountains and on Culebra and Vieques.

➡ Secondary roads through the mountains are in generally poor condition, with lots of rough surfaces and very narrow passes.

➡ Police always keep warning lights on. Emergencies are signaled by a siren.

➡ Puerto Rico's best roads are its Expressway toll roads, which include numbers 22 (San Juan–Arecibo), 66 (San Juan–Canóvanas), 52 (San Juan–Ponce) and 53 (Fajardo–Yabucoa). Have correct change, usually 50¢ to $2, ready at toll booths.

➡ Confusingly, whilst speed is measured here in mph (miles per hour) the road signs measure distance in kilometers.

CAR RENTAL TIPS & TRICKS

➡ Booking online in advance can save a lot of money. Try www.kayak.com for a comparative overview of rental rates.

➡ Some major rental car companies are located several miles from the LMM air terminal. Though most have shuttles, be sure they provide transportation to and from the airport.

➡ Unlike in the US, many airport-based car-rental agencies are not open 24 hours. If you have a late flight home, you'll have to arrange to drop off your car early, or pay an expensive 'airport drop-off fee', which is only waived in cases where the original office you hired from is closed at the time you return the vehicle.

➡ Larger companies will accept debit cards, but expect them to put at least a $500 hold on your funds until the car is safely returned.

➡ If you rent a car from a major airport, it is possible to drop the car off at another location for a small additional fee.

ROAD DISTANCES (MILES)

	Aguadilla	Aibonito	Arecibo	Cabo Rojo Point	Fajardo	Mayagüez	Ponce	Rincón
Aibonito	95							
Arecibo	33	61						
Cabo Rojo Point	70	122	70					
Fajardo	115	69	83	145				
Mayagüez	17	80	49	22	142			
Ponce	63	34	45	50	95	46		
Rincón	11	94	43	35	125	14	60	
San Juan	83	46	52	122	38	100	74	93

Road Rules

➜ Driving rules here are basically the same as they are in the US; traffic proceeds along the right side of the road and moves counterclockwise around traffic circles.

➜ It is legal to turn right at a red light, except where signs state otherwise.

➜ It is legal to ignore red lights (if safe to do so) between midnight and 5am.

➜ Watch for school zones, where the speed limit is 15mph (strictly enforced during school hours).

➜ Most highway signs employ international symbols, but distances are measured in kilometers, while speed limits are posted in miles per hour.

➜ Seat belts and motorcycle helmets must be worn; children younger than four years must travel in child safety seats.

Hitchhiking

Hitchhiking is rare in Puerto Rico and not recommended. Most of the time, you're gawped at in disbelief even for walking a short distance along a road.

Local Transportation

Public Transportation

San Juan has an efficient bus system and a metro (Tren Urbano), which will eventually expand to cover places like Caguas. Elsewhere services are more casual.

Públicos

Públicos are essentially public minibuses that run prescribed routes during daylight hours. Traveling via público offers a great local experience, but it requires a lot of patience and time. Some públicos make relatively long hauls between places such as San Juan and Ponce or Mayagüez, but most make much shorter journeys, providing a link within and between local communities.

Comfort Van rides are not especially comfortable, as drivers will try to put as many passengers in one van as possible. Vans can be old, stinky and extremely hot and crowded. Travel can be slow as the driver stops frequently to let people on and off.

Cost Público is by far the most inexpensive way to travel long distances in Puerto Rico. The longest run on the island (about three hours) will not cost more than $15. It depends on the number of passengers, the vehicle and, quite often, the driver.

Destinations The destination will be clearly written in the front window of the van. If you go to an unusual destination, you will likely be stranded for a return trip.

Frequency Públicos will leave when the van is full. In the early morning and evening, when people are going to and from work, the terminals will be most busy. Some públicos, such as the ones that run to popular beaches, may only operate on the weekend.

Schedules For fares and schedules, inquire with locals any place públicos stop. There is no central source of info.

Terminals There will be major público terminals near the center of every midsized or large city. Elsewhere, públicos make their pickups and drop-offs at a van stand on or near a town's central plaza.

Taxi

Taxis are available in most of the mid-sized to large cities on the island. Often, flagging a taxi in a public plaza is faster than calling for one. Drivers almost never use meters, so make sure to establish the cost before beginning your journey. San Juan is the exception to this: its government-regulated 'tourist taxis' have fixed rates.

Language

Spanish spelling is phonetically consistent, meaning that there's a clear and consistent relationship between what you see in writing and how it's pronounced. Most Latin American Spanish sounds are pronounced the same as their English counterparts – if you read our red pronunciation guides as if they were English, you'll be understood just fine. Note that the kh in our pronunciation guides is a throaty sound (like the 'ch' in the Scottish loch), v and b are similar to the English 'b' (but softer, between a 'v' and a 'b'), and r is strongly rolled. Some Spanish words are written with an acute accent (eg días) – this indicates a stressed syllable. In our pronunciation guides, the stressed syllables are in italics. Spanish nouns are marked for gender (masculine or feminine). Endings for adjectives also change to agree with the gender of the noun they modify. Where necessary, both forms are given for the phrases in this chapter, separated by a slash and with the masculine form first, eg perdido/a (m/f).

When talking to people familiar to you or younger than you, use the informal form of 'you', tú, rather than the polite form Usted. In all other cases use the polite form. The polite form is used in the phrases provided in this chapter; where both options are given, they are indicated by the abbreviations 'pol' and 'inf'.

BASICS

Hello.	Hola.	o·la
Goodbye.	Adiós.	a·dyos

WANT MORE?

For in-depth language information and handy phrases, check out Lonely Planet's *Latin American Spanish Phrasebook*. You'll find it at **shop.lonelyplanet.com**, or you can buy Lonely Planet's iPhone phrasebooks at the Apple App Store.

How are you?	¿Qué tal?	ke tal
Fine, thanks.	Bien, gracias.	byen gra·syas
Excuse me.	Perdón.	per·don
Sorry.	Lo siento.	lo syen·to
Yes./No.	Sí./No.	see/no
Please.	Por favor.	por fa·vor
Thank you.	Gracias.	gra·syas
You're welcome.	De nada.	de na·da

My name is ...
Me llamo ...   me ya·mo ...

What's your name?
¿Cómo se llama Usted? ko·mo se ya·ma oo·ste (pol)
¿Cómo te llamas?   ko·mo te ya·mas (inf)

Do you speak English?
¿Habla inglés?   a·bla een·gles (pol)
¿Hablas inglés?   a·blas een·gles (inf)

I (don't) understand.
Yo (no) entiendo.   yo (no) en·tyen·do

ACCOMMODATIONS

I'd like to book a room.
Quisiera reservar una   kee·sye·ra re·ser·var oo·na
habitación.   a·bee·ta·syon

How much is it per night/person?
¿Cuánto cuesta por   kwan·to kwes·ta por
noche/persona?   no·che/per·so·na

Does it include breakfast?
¿Incluye el desayuno?   een·kloo·ye el de·sa·yoo·no

campsite	terreno de cámping	te·re·no de kam·peeng
hotel	hotel	o·tel
guesthouse	pensión	pen·syon
youth hostel	albergue juvenil	al·ber·ge khoo·ve·neel
I'd like a ... room.	Quisiera una habitación ...	kee·sye·ra oo·na a·bee·ta·syon ...

single	*individual*	een·dee·vee·*dwal*
double	*doble*	*do*·ble
air-con	*aire acondicionado*	*ai*·re a·kon·dee·syo·*na*·do
bathroom	*baño*	*ba*·nyo
bed	*cama*	*ka*·ma
window	*ventana*	ven·*ta*·na

DIRECTIONS

Where's ...?
¿Dónde está ...? don·de es·*ta* ...

What's the address?
¿Cuál es la dirección? kwal es la dee·rek·*syon*

Could you please write it down?
¿Puede escribirlo, por favor? *pwe*·de es·kree·*beer*·lo por fa·*vor*

Can you show me (on the map)?
¿Me lo puede indicar (en el mapa)? me lo *pwe*·de een·dee·*kar* (en el *ma*·pa)

at the corner	*en la esquina*	en la es·*kee*·na
at the traffic lights	*en el semáforo*	en el se·*ma*·fo·ro
behind ...	*detrás de ...*	de·*tras* de ...
far	*lejos*	*le*·khos
in front of ...	*enfrente de ...*	en·*fren*·te de ...
left	*izquierda*	ees·*kyer*·da
near	*cerca*	*ser*·ka
next to ...	*al lado de ...*	al *la*·do de ...
opposite ...	*frente a ...*	*fren*·te a ...
right	*derecha*	de·*re*·cha
straight ahead	*todo recto*	*to*·do *rek*·to

EATING & DRINKING

What would you recommend?
¿Qué recomienda? ke re·ko·*myen*·da

What's in that dish?
¿Que lleva ese plato? ke *ye*·va e·se *pla*·to

I don't eat ...
No como ... no *ko*·mo ...

That was delicious!
¡Estaba buenísimo! es·*ta*·ba bwe·*nee*·see·mo

Please bring the bill.
Por favor nos trae la cuenta. por fa·*vor* nos *tra*·e la *kwen*·ta

Cheers!
¡Salud! sa·*loo*

I'd like to book a table for ...
Quisiera reservar una mesa para ... kee·*sye*·ra re·ser·*var* oo·na *me*·sa pa·ra ...

When's (the next flight)?
¿Cuándo sale (el próximo vuelo)? *kwan*·do sa·le (el *prok*·see·mo *vwe*·lo)

Where's (the station)?
¿Dónde está (la estación)? don·de es·*ta* (la es·ta·*syon*)

Where can I (buy a ticket)?
¿Dónde puedo (comprar un billete)? don·de *pwe*·do (kom·*prar* oon bee·*ye*·te)

Do you have (a map)?
¿Tiene (un mapa)? *tye*·ne (oon *ma*·pa)

Is there (a toilet)?
¿Hay (servicios)? ai (ser·*vee*·syos)

I'd like (a coffee).
Quisiera (un café). kee·*sye*·ra (oon ka·*fe*)

I'd like (to hire a car).
Quisiera (alquilar un coche). kee·*sye*·ra (al·kee·*lar* oon *ko*·che)

Can I (enter)?
¿Se puede (entrar)? se *pwe*·de (en·*trar*)

Could you please (help me)?
¿Puede (ayudarme), por favor? *pwe*·de (a·yoo·*dar*·me) por fa·*vor*

Do I have to (get a visa)?
¿Necesito (obtener un visado)? ne·se·*see*·to (ob·te·*ner* oon vee·*sa*·do)

(eight) o'clock	*(las ocho)*	las (o cho)
(two) people	*(dos) personas*	(dos) per·*so*·nas

Key Words

appetizers	*aperitivos*	a·pe·ree·*tee*·vos
bar	*bar*	bar
bottle	*botella*	bo·*te*·ya
bowl	*bol*	bol
breakfast	*desayuno*	de·sa·*yoo*·no
cafe	*café*	ka·*fe*
children's menu	*menú infantil*	me·*noo* een·fan·*teel*
cold	*frío*	*free*·o
dinner	*cena*	*se*·na
food	*comida*	ko·*mee*·da
fork	*tenedor*	te·ne·*dor*
glass	*vaso*	*va*·so
highchair	*trona*	*tro*·na

Signs

Abierto	Open
Cerrado	Closed
Entrada	Entrance
Hombres/Varones	Men
Mujeres/Damas	Women
Prohibido	Prohibited
Salida	Exit
Servicios/Baños	Toilets

hot (warm)	caliente	kal·yen·te
knife	cuchillo	koo·chee·yo
lunch	comida	ko·mee·da
main course	segundo plato	se·goon·do pla·to
market	mercado	mer·ka·do
menu (in English)	menú (en inglés)	me·noo (en een·gles)
plate	plato	pla·to
restaurant	restaurante	res·tow·ran·te
spoon	cuchara	koo·cha·ra
supermarket	supermercado	soo·per·mer·ka·do
vegetarian food	comida vegetariana	ko·mee·da ve·khe·ta·rya·na
with/without	con/sin	kon/seen

Meat & Fish

beef	carne de vaca	kar·ne de va·ka
chicken	pollo	po·yo
duck	pato	pa·to
fish	pescado	pes·ka·do
lamb	cordero	kor·de·ro
pork	cerdo	ser·do
turkey	pavo	pa·vo
veal	ternera	ter·ne·ra

Fruit & Vegetables

apple	manzana	man·sa·na
apricot	albaricoque	al·ba·ree·ko·ke
artichoke	alcachofa	al·ka·cho·fa
asparagus	espárragos	es·pa·ra·gos
banana	plátano	pla·ta·no
beans	judías	khoo·dee·as
beetroot	remolacha	re·mo·la·cha
cabbage	col	kol
carrot	zanahoria	sa·na·o·rya
celery	apio	a·pyo

cherry	cereza	se·re·sa
corn	maíz	ma·ees
cucumber	pepino	pe·pee·no
fruit	fruta	froo·ta
grape	uvas	oo·vas
lemon	limón	lee·mon
lentils	lentejas	len·te·khas
lettuce	lechuga	le·choo·ga
mushroom	champiñón	cham·pee·nyon
nuts	nueces	nwe·ses
onion	cebolla	se·bo·ya
orange	naranja	na·ran·kha
peach	melocotón	me·lo·ko·ton
peas	guisantes	gee·san·tes
(red/green) pepper	pimiento (rojo/verde)	pee·myen·to (ro·kho/ver·de)
pineapple	piña	pee·nya
plum	ciruela	seer·we·la
potato	patata	pa·ta·ta
pumpkin	calabaza	ka·la·ba·sa
spinach	espinacas	es·pee·na·kas
strawberry	fresa	fre·sa
tomato	tomate	to·ma·te
vegetable	verdura	ver·doo·ra
watermelon	sandía	san·dee·a

Other

bread	pan	pan
butter	mantequilla	man·te·kee·ya
cheese	queso	ke·so
egg	huevo	we·vo
honey	miel	myel
jam	mermelada	mer·me·la·da
oil	aceite	a·sey·te
pasta	pasta	pas·ta
pepper	pimienta	pee·myen·ta
rice	arroz	a·ros
salt	sal	sal
sugar	azúcar	a·soo·kar
vinegar	vinagre	vee·na·gre

Drinks

beer	cerveza	ser·ve·sa
coffee	café	ka·fe
(orange) juice	zumo (de naranja)	soo·mo (de na·ran·kha)
milk	leche	le·che

tea	té	te
(mineral) water	agua (mineral)	a·gwa (mee·ne·ral)
(red/white) wine	vino (tinto/ blanco)	vee·no (teen·to/ blan·ko)

EMERGENCIES

| **Help!** | ¡Socorro! | so·ko·ro |
| **Go away!** | ¡Vete! | ve·te |

Call ...!	¡Llame a ...!	ya·me a ...
a doctor	un médico	oon me·dee·ko
the police	la policía	la po·lee·see·a

I'm lost.
Estoy perdido/a.   es·toy per·dee·do/a (m/f)

I had an accident.
He tenido un   e te·nee·do oon
accidente.   ak·see·den·te

I'm ill.
Estoy enfermo/a.   es·toy en·fer·mo/a (m/f)

It hurts here.
Me duele aquí.   me dwe·le a·kee

I'm allergic to (antibiotics).
Soy alérgico/a a   soy a·ler·khee·ko/a a
(los antibióticos).   (los an·tee·byo·tee·kos) (m/f)

SHOPPING & SERVICES

I'd like to buy ...
Quisiera comprar ...   kee·sye·ra kom·prar ...

I'm just looking.
Sólo estoy mirando.   so·lo es·toy mee·ran·do

May I look at it?
¿Puedo verlo?   pwe·do ver·lo

I don't like it.
No me gusta.   no me goos·ta

How much is it?
¿Cuánto cuesta?   kwan·to kwes·ta

That's too expensive.
Es muy caro.   es mooy ka·ro

Can you lower the price?
¿Podría bajar un   po·dree·a ba·khar oon
poco el precio?   po·ko el pre·syo

There's a mistake in the bill.
Hay un error   ai oon e·ror
en la cuenta.   en la kwen·ta

ATM	cajero automático	ka·khe·ro ow·to·ma·tee·ko
credit card	tarjeta de crédito	tar·khe·ta de kre·dee·to
internet cafe	cibercafé	see·ber·ka·fe

| **post office** | correos | ko·re·os |
| **tourist office** | oficina de turismo | o·fee·see·na de too·rees·mo |

TIME & DATES

What time is it?	¿Qué hora es?	ke o·ra es
It's (10) o'clock.	Son (las diez).	son (las dyes)
It's half past (one).	Es (la una) y media.	es (la oo·na) ee me·dya

morning	mañana	ma·nya·na
afternoon	tarde	tar·de
evening	noche	no·che
yesterday	ayer	a·yer
today	hoy	oy
tomorrow	mañana	ma·nya·na

Monday	lunes	loo·nes
Tuesday	martes	mar·tes
Wednesday	miércoles	myer·ko·les
Thursday	jueves	khwe·ves
Friday	viernes	vyer·nes
Saturday	sábado	sa·ba·do
Sunday	domingo	do·meen·go

Numbers

1	uno	oo·no
2	dos	dos
3	tres	tres
4	cuatro	kwa·tro
5	cinco	seen·ko
6	seis	seys
7	siete	sye·te
8	ocho	o·cho
9	nueve	nwe·ve
10	diez	dyes
20	veinte	veyn·te
30	treinta	treyn·ta
40	cuarenta	kwa·ren·ta
50	cincuenta	seen·kwen·ta
60	sesenta	se·sen·ta
70	setenta	se·ten·ta
80	ochenta	o·chen·ta
90	noventa	no·ven·ta
100	cien	syen
1000	mil	meel

January	enero	e·ne·ro
February	febrero	fe·bre·ro
March	marzo	mar·so
April	abril	a·breel
May	mayo	ma·yo
June	junio	khoon·yo
July	julio	khool·yo
August	agosto	a·gos·to
September	septiembre	sep·tyem·bre
October	octubre	ok·too·bre
November	noviembre	no·vyem·bre
December	diciembre	dee·syem·bre

PUBLIC TRANSPORTATION

boat	barco	bar·ko
bus	autobús	ow·to·boos
plane	avión	a·vyon
train	tren	tren
first	primero	pree·me·ro
last	último	ool·tee·mo
next	próximo	prok·see·mo

I want to go to ...
Quisiera ir a ... kee·sye·ra eer a ...

Does it stop at ...?
¿Para en ...? pa·ra en ...

What stop is this?
¿Cuál es esta parada? kwal es es·ta pa·ra·da

What time does it arrive/leave?
¿A qué hora llega/ a ke o·ra ye·ga/
sale? sa·le

Please tell me when we get to ...
¿Puede avisarme pwe·de a·vee·sar·me
cuando lleguemos kwan·do ye·ge·mos
a ...? a ...

I want to get off here.
Quiero bajarme aquí. kye·ro ba·khar·me a·kee

a ... ticket	un billete de ...	oon bee·ye·te de ...
1st-class	primera clase	pree·me·ra kla·se
2nd-class	segunda clase	se·goon·da kla·se
one-way	ida	ee·da
return	ida y vuelta	ee·da ee vwel·ta
airport	aeropuerto	a·e·ro·pwer·to
aisle seat	asiento de pasillo	a·syen·to de pa·see·yo

bus stop	parada de autobuses	pa·ra·da de ow·to·boo·ses
cancelled	cancelado	kan·se·la·do
delayed	retrasado	re·tra·sa·do
platform	plataforma	pla·ta·for·ma
ticket office	taquilla	ta·kee·ya
timetable	horario	o·ra·ryo
train station	estación de trenes	es·ta·syon de tre·nes
window seat	asiento junto a la ventana	a·syen·to khoon·to a la ven·ta·na

DRIVING AND CYCLING

I'd like to hire a ...	Quisiera alquilar ...	kee·sye·ra al·kee·lar ...
4WD	un todo-terreno	oon to·do-te·re·no
bicycle	una bicicleta	oo·na bee·see·kle·ta
car	un coche	oon ko·che
motorcycle	una moto	oo·na mo·to
child seat	asiento de seguridad para niños	a·syen·to de se·goo·ree·da pa·ra nee·nyos
diesel	petróleo	pet·ro·le·o
helmet	casco	kas·ko
hitchhike	hacer botella	a·ser bo·te·ya
mechanic	mecánico	me·ka·nee·ko
petrol/gas	gasolina	ga·so·lee·na
service station	gasolinera	ga·so·lee·ne·ra
truck	camion	ka·myon

Is this the road to ...?
¿Se va a ... por se va a ... por
esta carretera? es·ta ka·re·te·ra

(How long) Can I park here?
¿(Por cuánto tiempo) (por kwan·to tyem·po)
Puedo aparcar aquí? pwe·do a·par·kar a·kee

The car has broken down (at ...).
El coche se ha averiado el ko·che se a a·ve·rya·do
(en ...). (en ...)

I have a flat tyre.
Tengo un pinchazo. ten·go oon peen·cha·so

I've run out of petrol.
Me he quedado sin me e ke·da·do seen
gasolina. ga·so·lee·na

GLOSSARY

aldea – village, hamlet
Arcaicos – Archaics; first known inhabitants of Puerto Rico

bahía – bay
balneario – public beach
barrio – neighborhood, city district
bateyes – Taíno ball courts
boca – mouth, entrance
boleros – ballads
bomba – musical form and dance inspired by African rhythms and characterized by call-and-response dialogues between musicians and interpreted by dancers; often considered as a unit with plena, as in *bomba y plena*
Boricua – Puerto Rican; a person of Puerto Rican descent
Borinquen – traditional Taíno name for the island of Puerto Rico
bosque estatal – state forest
botánica – shop specializing in herbs, icons and associated charms used in the practice of *Santería*

cacique – Taíno chief (male or female)
callejón – narrow side street, alleyway
capilla – chapel
Caribs – original colonizers of the Caribbean, for whom the region was named
casa – house
cayos – cays; refers to islets
cemíes – small figurines carved from stone, shell, wood or gold, representing deities worshiped by the Taínos
centros vacacionales – literally 'vacation centers'; form of rental accommodation popular with island families, with facilities ranging from basic wooden cabins on the beach to two-bedroom condos
cerro – hill, mountain
Changó – Yoruba god of fire and war believed to control thunder and lightning; one of several principal deities worshiped in Santería (see also orishas)

comida criolla – traditional Puerto Rican cuisine
Compañía de Parques Nacionales – CPN; National Park Company
coquí – a species of tiny tree frog found only in Puerto Rico; the island's mascot
cordillera – a system of mountain ranges
criollo – island-born person of Spanish parentage; in colonial times considered inferior by peninsular Spaniards (see also mestizo)
culebrenses – residents of Culebra
curandero – healer

danza – form of piano music and stylized figure-dance with Spanish origins, fused with elements of island folk music
Departamento de Recursos Naturales y Ambientales – DRNA; Department of Natural Resources & Environment

espiritismo – spiritualism
Estado Libre Asociado – associated free state; the term describes Puerto Rico's relationship with the USA

fiesta patronal – the annual celebrations staged in Puerto Rican cities and towns to honor each community's patron saint
fortaleza – fortress
friquitines – roadside kiosks
fuerte – fort

galería – gallery
garitas – turreted sentry towers constructed at intervals along the top of Old San Juan's fortifications
gringo – term used on the island to describe Americans

hacienda – agricultural estate, plantation

iglesia – church

Igneris – Indian group of the Arawakan linguistic group; early settlers of Puerto Rico
independentistas – advocates for Puerto Rican independence

jíbaro – country person, often cast as archetypal Puerto Rican

laguna – lake or lagoon
lechonera – eatery specializing in suckling pig
LMM – abbreviation for San Juan's Luis Muñoz Marín International Airport
malecón – pier, waterfront promenade
máscaras – masks (see also vejigantes)
mercado – market
Mesónes Gastronómicos – a Puerto Rico Tourism Company–sponsored program involving a collection of restaurants around the island that feature Puerto Rican cuisine
mestizo – person of mixed ancestry; usually Indian and Spanish (see also criollo)
mogotes – hillocks
mundillo – traditional form of intricately woven lace, made only in Puerto Rico and Spain

norte – north
Nuyoricans – Puerto Rican 'exiles' in the US

orishas – Yoruba deities worshiped in Santería, often associated with Catholic saints (see also Changó)

palacio – palace
parador – country inn
parque – park
pasaje – passage
playa – beach
plazuela – small plaza plena – form of traditional Puerto Rican dance and song that unfolds to distinctly African rhythms beat out with maracas, tambourines and other traditional percussion instruments; often associated with bomba

pleneros – *plena* singers
ponceños – residents of Ponce
PRTC – Puerto Rico Tourism Company
públicos – shared taxis, usually minivans equipped with bench seats, which pick up passengers along a prescribed route and provide low-cost local transport islandwide
puerta – gate, door
puerto – port
punta – tip, end

reserva forestal – forest reserve
ron – rum

sanjuaneros – residents of San Juan

Santería – Afro-Caribbean religion representing the syncretism of Catholic and African beliefs, based on the worship of Catholic saints and their associated *Yoruba* deities or *orishas*
santero – an artist who carves *santos;* one of many names for practitioners of the rites of *Santería*
santos – small carved figurines representing saints, enshrined and worshipped by practitioners of *Santería*
sonda – sound
supermercado – supermarket
sur – south

Taínos – indigenous Puerto Ricans

tienda – store
turismo – tourism
turista – tourist

universidad – university
urgente – urgent

valle – valley
vegetales – vegetables
vejigantes – traditional Puerto Rican masks (see also *máscaras*)
ventana – window
vereda – path, trail
vino – wine

Yoruba – West Africans brought to Puerto Rico as slaves
zoológico – zoo

Behind the Scenes

SEND US YOUR FEEDBACK

We love to hear from travelers – your comments keep us on our toes and help make our books better. Our well-traveled team reads every word on what you loved or loathed about this book. Although we cannot reply individually to your submissions, we always guarantee that your feedback goes straight to the appropriate authors, in time for the next edition. Each person who sends us information is thanked in the next edition – the most useful submissions are rewarded with a selection of digital PDF chapters.

Visit **lonelyplanet.com/contact** to submit your updates and suggestions or to ask for help. Our award-winning website also features inspirational travel stories, news and discussions.

Note: We may edit, reproduce and incorporate your comments in Lonely Planet products such as guidebooks, websites and digital products, so let us know if you don't want your comments reproduced or your name acknowledged. For a copy of our privacy policy visit lonelyplanet.com/privacy.

OUR READERS

Many thanks to the travelers who used the last edition and wrote to us with helpful hints, useful advice and interesting anecdotes:

Aaron Owens, Adrienne Nielsen, Charles Ferrer, Christine Hassel, Dean Johnson, Elisabet Barcelo, Ellen Tamburello, Keely Koenig, Luisa Marangoni, Lyn Stoesen, Matthew Valentine, Nancy Ault, Raquel Rodriguez, Sandra van Mulken, Stan Sonnega, Susan Myers.

WRITER THANKS
Liza Prado

Mil gracias to all the locals whose names I never learned but whose help was essential to me. Special thanks to my long lost *sanjuanero* friend Carlos Rivas, Kathy Gannett in Esperanza and Keishya Salko in Punta Santiago. Thank you to mom, dad, Joe, Elyse and Susan for all the kid help, and to Eva and Leo for waiting so patiently to play. And to Gary, my heart, thank you for your support and love; there's no way I could do what I do without you.

Luke Waterson

Thank you Aurelio, Juan Julio and his stalwart JCB for rescuing me when my car came off the road and was teetering on the edge of a rather deep ravine. And, welcome as a piña colada on a sultry afternoon, was the assistance of Tamaris, José and Eddie in San Juan, Trevor in Isabela, Lisa in Rincón and Kurt in Jayuya. At LP, gratitude streams across the oceans to co-writer Liza and editor Bailey for helping bring this book together.

ACKNOWLEDGEMENTS

Climate map data adapted from Peel MC, Finlayson BL & McMahon TA (2007) 'Updated World Map of the Köppen-Geiger Climate Classification', Hydrology and Earth System Sciences, 11, 163344.

Cover photograph: A man stands on a boat looking at a Puerto Rican beach, Artifan/Shutterstock ©

THIS BOOK

This 7th edition of Lonely Planet's *Puerto Rico* guidebook was researched and written by Liza Prado and Luke Waterson. The 6th edition was written by Ryan Ver Berkmoes and Luke Waterson; the 5th edition was written by Nate Cavalieri and Beth Kohn. This guidebook was produced by the following:

Destination Editor Bailey Freeman

Product Editor Sandie Kestell

Senior Cartographer Anthony Phelan

Book Designers Ania Bartoszek, Gwen Cotter

Assisting Editors Gabrielle Innes, Kate Morgan, Gabrielle Stefanos, Maja Vatrić

Cover Researcher Naomi Parker

Thanks to Ronan Abayawickrema, Angela Tinson

Index

A

accommodations 262-3, see also individual locations
activities 25-7, 39-44, see also individual activities
Adjuntas 223-4
Aguadilla 210-12, **160**
Agüeybana 232
Aguirre 157
Aibonito 217-18
air travel 268, 269
Alonso, Manuel 250
animals 258-60, see also individual species
Arawak people 230-1
architecture 11, 22, **11**, **86**
area codes 19
Area Recreativa Doña Juana 221
Arecibo 201-3
art galleries, see museums & galleries
arts 250-3, see also individual arts
ATMs 18, 266

B

Báez, Myrna 252
Bahía de Fosforescente 166
Bahía de Jobos 157-8
Bahía Mosquito 131
ballet 85
balnearios, see beaches
Baño de Oro 99
Baño Grande 99
Baños de Coamo 159
Bacardí rum 37, 93, 185
bargaining 21
Barranquitas 218-20
baseball 12, 88, 243-4, **12**
Bayamón 92-3

Map Pages **000**
Photo Pages **000**

beaches 22
Balneario Boquerón 188
Balneario Condado 69
Balneario de Carolina 69-70
Balneario el Ojo del Buey 200
Balneario Escambrón 69
Balneario Morrillos 202-3
Pata Prieta 135
Piñones 94
Playa Azul 105
Playa Ballena 164
Playa Brava 121
Playa Buyé 188
Playa Caña Gorda 164-5
Playa Caracas 132-3
Playa Carlos Rosario 120
Playa Combate 190
Playa Condado 69
Playa Crash Boat 211
Playa de Cerro Gordo 199-200
Playa El Convento 108
Playa El Gallito 135
Playa Escondida 135
Playa Flamenco 120, 121
Playa Grande 135
Playa Isla Verde 69
Playa Jobos 207
Playa La Chiva 134-5
Playa La Plata 133-4
Playa Larga 114
Playa Lucía 114
Playa Luquillo 105
Playa Mar Chiquita 202
Playa Media Luna 135
Playa Melones 122
Playa Naguabo 112
Playa Navío 135
Playa Negra 135
Playa Ocean Park 69
Playa Resaca 121
Playa Santa 192
Playa Sardinera (Isla Mona) 196

Playa Seven Seas 108
Playa Shacks 207
Playa Survival 207
Playa Tamarindo (Culebra) 120-1
Playa Tamarindo (Guánica) 164
Playa Wilderness 211
Playa Zoni 121
Punta Arenas 135
Punta Soldado 121-2
Starfish Beach 135
Sun Bay 135
beauty pageants 242
beer 37
béisbol 12, 88, 243-4, **12**
Betances, Ramón Emeterio 233, 236
bicycling 42-3, 269, see also mountain biking
Aguadilla 211
Culebra 123
Isabela 208
Piñones 93
Toro Verde Nature Adventure Park 219
Vieques 136
biohazards 132
bioluminescent waters 14, 46, **15**
Bahía de Fosforescente 166
Bahía Mosquito 131
Laguna Grande 110
Las Cabezas de San Juan 16, 107-8, **16**
Reserva Natural Laguna de Joyuda 187
birds 259-60
birdwatching 260
Bosque Estatal de Guánica 163-4
El Yunque National Forest 99
Refugio de Boquerón 188
Reserva Natural Laguna de Joyuda 187

Birth of the New World Statue 202
boas 258
boat tours 109, 123, 136, 168
boat travel 269
bomba 245-6
Bonus Nuclear Power Plant 175
books 228, 241, 250-1
Boquerón 188-90
bosques estatales, see territorial parks & reserves
boxing 244
Braschi, Giannina 250
budget 19
bus travel 271
business hours 19

C

Cabo Rojo area 186
Caguas 215-16
Calderón, Sila María 238, 242
Camacho, Hector 'Macho' 244
Campeche, José 252
camping 104, 189, 262
Campos, Pedro Albizu 236
Canales, Blanca 238
Cañón de San Cristóbal 217
canyoning 73, 206, **17**
Caparra 54
car rental 270
car routes
  karst country 205, **205**
  Ruta Panorámica 115, 222
  south coast 159
car travel 269-71
Carnaval 25, 151
Carrasquillo, Edwin Báez 215
Casa Acosta y Flores 194
Casa Bacardí Rum Factory 93
Casa Bavaria 220

Casa Blanca 62
Casa de la Masacre de Ponce 150
Casa de Lola Rodríguez de Tió 194
Casa del Libro 59
Casa Morales 194
Casa Museo Canales 223
Casa Museo de la Música 162
Casa Museo Luis Muñoz Rivera 218
Casa Perichi 194
Casa Wiechers-Villaronga 149-50
casinos 88
Cataño 92-3
cathedrals, *see* churches & cathedrals
caves
  Cueva del Viento 226
  Cueva del Indio 202
  Isla Mona 195
  Parque de las Cavernas del Río Camuy 204
caving 73, 206
Cayo Afuera 131
Cayo de Tierra 131
Cayo Luis Peña 120
Cayo Santiago 112
cell phones 18
Cementerio Santa María Magdalena de Pazzis 62
central mountains 48, 213-26, **214**
  accommodations 213
  climate 213
  food 213
  highlights 214
  history 215
  travel seasons 213
  travel to/from 215
Centro Ceremonial Indígena de Tibes 154
Cerro de Punta 221, 257
ceviche 35, **12**
children, travel with 45-6, 54
churches & cathedrals
  Capilla del Cristo 59
  Catedral de Nuestra Señora de la Candelaria 182-3
  Catedral de San Germán de Auxerre 193
  Catedral de San Juan 59

Catedral Nuestra Señora de Guadalupe 149
Iglesia de Porta Coeli 192
Iglesia de San José 59
Iglesia del Espíritu Santo y San Patricio 95
Iglesia San Blas 159
Parroquia de San Antonio de Padua 218
cinemas 85, 88
classical music 85
climate 18, 25-7, 263, *see also individual regions*
Coamo 159-62
coffee 14, 36-7
coffee plantations 36
  Hacienda Buena Vista 154
  Hacienda Pomarrosa 220-1
  Hacienda San Pedro 223, **14**
  Hacienda Tres Angeles 224
Columbus, Christopher 202, 231, 233
comida criolla 34-8
consulates 264
coquí frogs 17, 258, **17**
cooking courses 72
Corozo Salt Flats 191
costs 19
credit cards 18
cruise ships 90, 268-9
cruises 177, *see also* boat tours
Cuba 236-7
Culebra 47, 116-28, **117**, **119**, **161**
  accommodations 116, 124-5
  activities 122-4
  beaches 120-2
  climate 116
  drinking & nightlife 126
  entertainment 126
  food 116, 125-6
  highlights 117
  history 118
  shopping 126
  sights 118-20
  tourist information 127
  travel seasons 116
  travel to/within 127-8
Culebra National Wildlife Refuge 118
culture 228-9, 240-4
Cumberland, Earl of 233
currency 18
customs regulations 263

cycling, *see* bicycling

D

dance 73, 253
dangers, *see* safety
danza 253
de Burgos, Julia 250
de León, Juan Ponce 235
deforestation 256
dengue fever 265
Dewey 119, 124, 125, 126-8, **122**
Día de los Reyes 25
disabilities, travelers with 266-7
diving 12, 23, 40-1, *see also* snorkeling
  Aguadilla 211
  Culebra 122-3, **44**
  Fajardo 109
  Isla Caja de Muertos 153
  Isla Desecheo 209
  Isla Mona 196
  La Parguera 168, **13**
  Naguabo 112-13
  Rincón 176-7
  San Juan 71
  Vieques 136
Dorado 199-201
Drake, Sir Francis 232
drinking 265
drinks 34-8, *see also* coffee, rum
driver's licenses 270
driving, *see* car rental, car routes, car travel

E

east coast 47, 96-115, **97**
  accommodations 96
  climate 96
  food 96
  highlights 97
  history 97-8
  travel seasons 96
  travel to/within 98
economy 228-9
El Capitolio 64
El Combate 190
El Faro de las Cabezas de San Juan 108
El Faro de Punta Mulas 129-30
El Morro 54-5, **21**
El Hippie Petroglyphs 99
El Yunque 47, 96-105, **100-1**
  accommodations 103-4

activities 99-103
sights 98-9
tourist information 104-5
tours 103
travel to/from 105
El Yunque National Forest 10, 98-105, **10**, **160-1**
electricity 264
embassies 264
emergencies 19
Ensenda Honda 119-20
environmental groups 256
environmental hazards 132, 264-5
environmental issues 228-9, 256-7
Escobar, Sixto 244
Esperanza 130-2, 137-8, 139-40, **134**
Estación Experimental Agrícola Federal 184
etiquette 21
events 25-7
exchange rates 19

F

Fajardo 107-11, **108**
Faro de los Morrillos 202
Faro Punta Tuna 114
Faro y Parque Histórico de Arecibo 202
Feliciano, José 249
Feria Dulce Sueño 25
ferry travel 269
festivals & events 25-7, *see also individual festivals & locations*
Fiesta de San Juan Bautista 26
film 228, 251-2
first-time visitors 20-1
fishing
  Fajardo 109
  La Parguera 169
  Lago Guajataca 226
  Naguabo 112
  Rincón 177
  San Juan 71
  Vieques 137
folk art 252
food 12, 24, 34-8, 264, **17**, **38**, *see also individual locations*
  cooking courses 72
  friquitines (food trucks) 35, 140
  fruits 36
  lechón 17, 37, 219
  mofongo 37, **38**

piragüeros 35
pork 17, 37, 219
seafood 35-6
soups 36
Foraker Act 237
forests, see territorial
parks & reserves
forts
El Morro 54-5, **21**
Fortín Conde de Mirasol
129
Fuente de los Leones
149
Fuerte Caprón 169
Fuerte del Cañuelo 93
Fuerte San Cristóbal 55
Fuerte San Gerónimo 64
La Fortaleza 61-2
frogs 17, 258, **17**
friquitines 35, 140

G
galleries, see museums &
galleries
gambling 264
Garrido, Juan 232
gay travelers 84, 264
geography 254
geology 254
Gilligan's Island 165
golf 200
Aguadilla 211
Dorado 200
Isabela 208
Luquillo 106
Grito de Lares 237
Guánica 163-6, **164-5**, **2-3**
Guavate 219
Guayama 155-7
guesthouses 263

H
haciendas
Hacienda Buena Vista
154
Hacienda de Santa
Lucía 114
Hacienda Pomarrosa
220-1
Hacienda San Pedro
223, **14**
Hacienda Tres Angeles
224
hang gliding 112, 113
Hatillo Mask Festival 27,
203, **27**
health 264-5
Highway 110 210
Highway 181 115

hiking 24, 41-2, 46, 216, see
also hiking trails
Bosque Estatal de Carite
216
Bosque Estatal de
Guajataca 225-6
Bosque Estatal de
Guánica 163-4, 260
Bosque Estatal de Río
Abajo 206
Cañón de San Cristóbal
217
Culebra 123-4
El Yunque National
Forest 10, 41, 99, 101-3
Reserva Forestal Toro
Negro 221
Vieques 137
safely 266
hiking trails, see also
hiking
Big Tree Trail 102
Camino Ballena 164
Camino El Bolo 221
Charco Azul Trail 216
Cueva del Viento 39, 226
El Radar Trail 216
El Toro Trail 102-3
El Yunque Trail 39, 102
La Coca Trail 102
La Mina Trail 39, 102, **44**
Los Morrillos
Lighthouse 39, 192
Mt Britton Trail 103
Trade Winds National
Recreation Trail 102-3
Vereda La Torre 39
Vereda Meseta 164
Hiram Bithorn Stadium 88
history 230-9
colonization 231-4
incorporation into US
237-9
slavery 235-6
Spanish rule 234-7
statehood 238-9
Taíno people 230-3
hitchhiking 271
holidays 266
Hombre de Puerto Ferro
132
horseback riding
Isabela 208
Naguabo 113
Vieques 137
horses 142, 259
hotels 263

I
Igneris people 156

iguanas 167, 195, 258
immigration 268
indigenous peoples 156,
230-3
insurance 265
internet access 265
internet resources 19
Isabel Segunda 129-30,
138-9, 140-1, **133**
Isabela 207-10
Isla Caja de Muertos 153
Isla Caracoles 166
Isla Culebrita 118-19
Isla de Cabras 92-3
Isla de Magueyes 166-8
Isla de Monos 166-8
Isla de Ratones 187
Isla Desecheo 209
Isla Mata la Gata 166
Isla Mona 195-6
itineraries 28-33

J
Jardín Botánico de la
Universidad de Puerto
Rico 69
Jayuya 222-3
Jiménez Corretjer, Zoé 251

K
karst country 205, **205**
kayaking 43
Culebra 123
Fajardo 109
La Parguera 168
Luquillo 105
Piñones 93-4
Rincón 177
San Juan 70-1
Vieques 136
kitesurfing 43, 70, 200, **161**

L
La Fortaleza 61-2
La Guancha Paseo Tablado
150
La Parguera 166-70,
167, **12**
La Piedra Escrita 223
Lago Caonillas 204, 206
Lago Dos Bocas 204, 206
Lago Luchetti 162-3
lagoons, urban 70
Laguerre, Enrique Dr 250
Laguna Grande 110
Lalo, Eduardo 251
languages 18, 21, 272-8
Lares 237

Las Cabezas de San Juan
Reserva Natural 16,
107-8, **16**
Las Paylas 106
lechón 17, 37, 219
legal matters 265
lesbian travelers 84, 264
lighthouses
El Faro de las Cabezas
de San Juan 108
El Faro de Punta Mulas
129-30
El Morro 54-5
Faro de los Morrillos 202
Faro Punta Tuna 114
Faro y Parque Histórico
de Arecibo 202
Los Morrillos Lighthouse
192
Punta Higüero
Lighthouse 175
literature 228, 241, 250-1
live music 22
local transportation 271
Loíza 94-5
Luis Peña Channel Natural
Reserve 120-1
Luquillo 105-7

M
manatees 157, 259
mangroves 257, **2**
maps 265
Maricao 224-5
markets
Artisans Fair 89
Mercado de Río Piedras
69
Mercado Juan Ponce de
León 153
Nueva Plaza del Mercado
153
Old San Juan Farmers
Market 78
San Sebastián Market
225
Marqués, René 250
Masacre de Ponce 150
máscaras 252
Martin, Ricky 248
Mayagüez 182-6, **183**
measures 267
medical services 264
Mirador La Piedra Degetau
217-18
mobile phones 18
mofongo 37, **38**
money 18, 19, 265-6
monkeys 112, 167
Monte Resaca 121

Moreno, Rita 251
mosquitoes 264-5
mountain biking 14, 42-3, **15**, see also bicycling
  Barranquitas 219
  Bosque Estatal de Guánica 163-4
  Refugio Nacional Cabo Rojo 191
multiculturalism 240-1
mundillo 252
Muñoz Marín, Luis 218, 236
museums & galleries
  C787 Studios 67
  Casa Bacardí Rum Factory 93
  Casa de Lola Rodríguez de Tió 194
  Casa del Libro 59
  Casa Museo Canales 223
  Casa Museo Luis Muñoz Rivera 218
  Centro de Arte Alejandro Franceschi 162
  Centro de Bellas Artes (Guayama) 155-6
  Centro de Bellas Artes de Caguas 215
  Espacio 1414 67
  Espacio Emergente 92
  Faro y Parque Histórico de Arecibo 202
  Mausoleo Familia Muñoz Rivera 218
  Museo Castillo Serrallés 150-1
  Museo de Arte (Mayagüez) 182
  Museo de Arte Contemporáneo de Puerto Rico 67
  Museo de Arte de Ponce 147
  Museo de Arte de Puerto Rico 66-7
  Museo de Arte e Historia (Arecibo) 202
  Museo de Arte e Historia de Dorado 199
  Museo de Artes Populares de Caguas 215
  Museo de Entomología y Biodiversidad Tropical 69
  Museo de Historia (San Sebastián) 225

Map Pages **000**
Photo Pages **000**

  Museo de Historia, Antropología y Arte de Río Piedras 68
  Museo de la Historia de Ponce 150
  Museo de la Historia de San Germán 193
  Museo de la Música Puertorriqueña 149
  Museo de las Américas 55, 58
  Museo de Oller 92
  Museo de San Juan 59
  Museo del Cemí 223
  Museo del Tobacco 215
  Museo Felisa Rincón de Gautier 59
  Museo Histórico de Culebra 120
  Museo y Centro Cultural Casa del Rey 199
  Parque de las Ciencias Luis A Ferré 92
  Vieques Conservation & Historical Trust 132
  Volkylandia 162
music 22, 85, 245-9, **247**, see also live music

N
Naguabo 111-14
national parks, see territorial parks & reserves
newspapers 267
north coast 48, 197-212, **198**
  accommodations 197
  climate 197
  food 197
  highlights 198
  history 199
  travel to/from 199
  travel seasons 197
Nuyorican 251, 252
Nuyorican Café 85, **13**

O
Obama, Barack 228
Observatorio de Arecibo 203-4
Oller, Francisco 252
opening hours 19
outdoor activities 39-44, see also individual activities

P
paddleboarding
  San Juan 70-1
  Vieques 136

Palacete Los Moreau 207
Palmas del Mar 112-13, **9**
paradores 263
parks & plazas
  La Placita de Santurce 65
  Malecón 166
  Parque Ceremonial Indígena Caguana 204, **23**
  Parque de las Palomas 61
  Parque de los Próceres 184
  Parque del Tercer Milenio 64
  Parque la Ventana al Mar 64-5
  Parque Nacional Laguna del Condado Jaime Benítez 65-6
  Parques Luis Muñoz Rivera 64
  Plaza Colón 184
  Plaza de Armas 60
  Plaza de Colón 59-60
  Plaza de Recreo (Barranquitas) 218
  Plaza de Recreo (Rincón) 173
  Plaza de Recreo (Yauco) 162
  Plaza de San José 61
  Plaza del Quinto Centenario 60
  Plaza Las Delicias 147, 149, **23**
  Plazuela de la Rogativa 61
  Plazuela Las Monjas 60
Parque de Bombas 149, **10**
Parque de las Cavernas del Río Camuy 204
parrots 10, 259, 260
Paseo de la Princesa 58-9, **5**
Paso Fino horses 259
passports 268
phosphorescence, see bioluminescent waters
Piñones 93-4
piragüeros 35
planning, see also individual regions
  budgeting 19
  calendar of events 25-7
  children, travel with 45-6, 54
  first-time visitors 20-1
  food & drink 34-8
  internet resources 19
  itineraries 28-33
  outdoor activities 39-44

Puerto Rico basics 18-19
Puerto Rico's regions 47-8
  travel seasons 18, 25-7
plants 260
Playa de Joyuda (town) 186-8
Playa Húcares (village) 112
Playa Salinas (town) 158-9
playas, see beaches
plazas, see parks & plazas
plena 246
politics 228
pollution 257
Ponce 10, 48, 144-55, **145**
  accommodations 151-2
  climate 144
  drinking & nightlife 153
  festivals & events 151
  food 152-3
  highlights 145
  history 146-7, 150
  shopping 153-4
  sights 147-51
  tourist information 154
  travel seasons 144
  travel to/from 154-5
  travel within 155
Ponce massacre 150
population 229, 256
Pozuelo 155-7
pre-Taino peoples 156
public holidays 266
public transportation 271
públicos 271
Puente, Tito 248
Puerta de San Juan 59
Puerto del Rey 109
Puerto Rican parrots 10, 259, 260
Puerto Rico JazzFest 25, 74, **27**
Punta Higüero Lighthouse 175
Punta Santiago 112

R
racism 241
radio 267
Raíces Fountain 59
rainforests, see El Yunque National Forest
rappelling 43
Refugio de Boquerón 188
Refugio de Vida Silvestre Iris L. Alameda Martínez de Buquerón 188
Refugio Nacional Cabo Rojo 191-2

reggaetón 248
religion 229, 242
renewable energy 228-9
reptiles 258
reservas, see territorial
 parks & reserves
Rincón 171-82, **172**,
 174, **16**
 accommodations 177-9
 activities 176-7
 climate 171
 drinking & nightlife 180-1
 festivals & events 177
 food 179-80
 highlights 172
 shopping 181
 sights 173-5
 tourist information 181-2
 travel seasons 171
 travel to/within 182
road distance chart 271
road hazards 270
road rules 271
Roberto Clemente
 Coliseum 88
rock-climbing 217
Rosselló, Ricky 239
rum 37, 93, 185, 222
Ruta Panorámica 115, 222

S
safety 266
 camping 266
 diving & snorkeling 41
 health 264-5
 hiking 266
 hitchhiking 271
 road safety 270
 San Juan 89-90
 swimming 266
 Vieques 142
 weather 266
sailing, see boat tours
Salinas 158-9, **255**
salsa 13, 247-8, 253, **13**
salt flats 191
San Fermin earthquake
 255
San Germán 192-5, **193**, **11**
San Juan 47, 50-95, **51**,
 52-3, **86-7**
 accommodations 50,
 74-8
 activities 70-2
 beaches 69-70
 children, travel with
 65, 94
 climate 50

Condado 64-5, 75-6,
 80-1, 84, **66-7**
 courses 72-3
 drinking & nightlife 83-5
 entertainment 85-8
 festivals & events 74
 food 12, 50, 78-83, **12**
 Hato Rey 67-8
 highlights 51
 history 54
 Isla Verde 77-8, 82-3,
 84, **72**
 itineraries 60
 La Perla 62, 64
 Miramar, 65-7, **66-7**
 neighborhoods 61
 Ocean Park 65, 76-7,
 81-2, 84, **77**
 Old San Juan 9, 54-63,
 74-5, 78-80, 83-4,
 56-7, 8-9, 86-7
 Puerta de Tierra 64
 Río Piedras 68-9
 Santurce 65-7, 82, 84-5,
 66-7
 shopping 88-9
 sights 54-69
 tourist information
 89-90
 tours 73
 travel seasons 50
 travel to/from 90
 travel within 91-2
 walking tours 62-3, **63**
San Juan National Historic
 Site 55
San Sebastián 225-6
santos 252
seafood 35-6
smoking 267
snakes 258
snorkeling 12, 23, 40-1, **12**,
 see also diving
 Culebra 122-3
 Fajardo 109
 Isla Caja de Muertos 153
 La Parguera 168
 Naguabo 112
 Rincón 176-7
 San Juan 71
 Vieques 136
south coast 48, 144-70, **145**
 accommodations 144
 climate 144
 food 144
 highlights 145
 history 146
 travel seasons 144
 travel to/from 146

Spanish–American War
 234
spas 71-2
sports 24, 88, 243-4, see
 also individual sports
squares, see parks &
 plazas
street art 79
surfing 16, 39-40
 Aguadilla 211
 Culebra 122-3
 Isabela 207-8
 Luquillo 105
 Rincón 16, 176, **2**, **16**
 San Juan 71
 Yabucoa 114
swimming 12, 177, 266

T
Taíno people 230-3
Tapia y Rivera, Alejandro
 250
taxes 21
taxis 271
Teatro La Perla 150
telephone services 18, 266
tennis 244
territorial parks & reserves
 254-6
 Bosque Estatal de Carite
 216-17
 Bosque Estatal de
 Guajataca 225-6
 Bosque Estatal de
 Guánica 163-4
 Bosque Estatal de
 Guilarte 224
 Bosque Estatal de
 Maricao 224
 Bosque Estatal de Río
 Abajo 206
 Bosque Estatal de Susúa
 162
 Centro de Visitantes de
 Pesca y Vida Silvestre
 de Cabo Rojo 191
 Humacao Nature
 Reserve 112
 Las Cabezas de San
 Juan Reserva Natural
 16, 107-8, **16**
 Refugio de Boquerón
 188
 Refugio de Vida Silvestre
 Iris L. Alameda
 Martínez de Boquerón
 188
 Refugio Nacional Cabo
 Rojo 191-2
 Reserva Forestal Toro
 Negro 220-2

Reserva Nacional de
 Investigación
 Estuarina de Bahía de
 Jobos 157
 Reserva Natural
 Humedal Punta
 Tuna 114
 Reserva Natural Laguna
 de Joyuda 187
 Vieques National Wildlife
 Refuge 129
theater 85
thermal baths 159
time 18
tipping 21, 266
tollways 201
Toro Verde Nature
 Adventure Park 219
tourism 256
tourist information 266
tours 43
transportation 268-71
travel to/from Puerto Rico
 268-9
travel within Puerto Rico
 269-71
trekking, see hiking
Trinidad, Felix 244
turtles 124, 195, 258
TV 267

U
Universidad
 Interamericana 193-4
urbanization 256
US military presence
 121, 128
US statehood 228

V
vacations 266
Vieques 47, 116-17, 128-43,
 117, **130-1**
 accommodations 116,
 137-9
 activities 135-7
 beaches 132-5
 climate 116
 drinking & nightlife 141
 festivals & events 137
 food 116, 139-41
 highlights 117
 history 128
 shopping 142
 sights 128-32
 travel seasons 116
 travel to/from 143
 travel within 143
Vieques National Wildlife
 Refuge 129

viewpoints 99, 169
visas 18, 267
visual arts 252, **253**
volunteering 267

W
walking, *see* hiking
walking tours
  San Juan 62-3, **63**
water pollution 257
waterfalls
  Cañón de San Cristóbal
   217

Gozalandia 225
La Coca Falls 99
La Mina Falls 99
Las Paylas 106
weather 18, 25-7, 263, 266,
  see also individual
  regions
websites 19
weights 267
west coast 48, 171-96, **172**
  accommodations 171
  climate 171
  food 171

highlights 172
history 172-3
  travel seasons 171
  travel to/from 173
whales 258-9
whale-watching 43, 177
wildlife 17, 23, 258-60
Wilfredo, Benitez 244
Wilfredo, Gómez 244
women in Puerto Rico
  242-3
women travelers 267

Y
Yabucoa 114-15
yacht travel 269
Yauco 162-3
yoga 72-3

Z
Zika virus 265
ziplining 17, 43, 206, 221
Zoológico de Puerto
  Rico 184

Map Legend

Sights
- Beach
- Bird Sanctuary
- Buddhist
- Castle/Palace
- Christian
- Confucian
- Hindu
- Islamic
- Jain
- Jewish
- Monument
- Museum/Gallery/Historic Building
- Ruin
- Shinto
- Sikh
- Taoist
- Winery/Vineyard
- Zoo/Wildlife Sanctuary
- Other Sight

Activities, Courses & Tours
- Bodysurfing
- Diving
- Canoeing/Kayaking
- Course/Tour
- Sento Hot Baths/Onsen
- Skiing
- Snorkeling
- Surfing
- Swimming/Pool
- Walking
- Windsurfing
- Other Activity

Sleeping
- Sleeping
- Camping

Eating
- Eating

Drinking & Nightlife
- Drinking & Nightlife
- Cafe

Entertainment
- Entertainment

Shopping
- Shopping

Information
- Bank
- Embassy/Consulate
- Hospital/Medical
- Internet
- Police
- Post Office
- Telephone
- Toilet
- Tourist Information
- Other Information

Geographic
- Beach
- Gate
- Hut/Shelter
- Lighthouse
- Lookout
- Mountain/Volcano
- Oasis
- Park
- Pass
- Picnic Area
- Waterfall

Population
- Capital (National)
- Capital (State/Province)
- City/Large Town
- Town/Village

Transport
- Airport
- BART station
- Border crossing
- Boston T station
- Bus
- Cable car/Funicular
- Cycling
- Ferry
- Metro/Muni station
- Monorail
- Parking
- Petrol station
- Subway/SkyTrain station
- Taxi
- Train station/Railway
- Tram
- Underground station
- Other Transport

Note: Not all symbols displayed above appear on the maps in this book

Routes
- Tollway
- Freeway
- Primary
- Secondary
- Tertiary
- Lane
- Unsealed road
- Road under construction
- Plaza/Mall
- Steps
- Tunnel
- Pedestrian overpass
- Walking Tour
- Walking Tour detour
- Path/Walking Trail

Boundaries
- International
- State/Province
- Disputed
- Regional/Suburb
- Marine Park
- Cliff
- Wall

Hydrography
- River, Creek
- Intermittent River
- Canal
- Water
- Dry/Salt/Intermittent Lake
- Reef

Areas
- Airport/Runway
- Beach/Desert
- Cemetery (Christian)
- Cemetery (Other)
- Glacier
- Mudflat
- Park/Forest
- Sight (Building)
- Sportsground
- Swamp/Mangrove

OUR STORY

A beat-up old car, a few dollars in the pocket and a sense of adventure. In 1972 that's all Tony and Maureen Wheeler needed for the trip of a lifetime – across Europe and Asia overland to Australia. It took several months, and at the end – broke but inspired – they sat at their kitchen table writing and stapling together their first travel guide, *Across Asia on the Cheap*. Within a week they'd sold 1500 copies. Lonely Planet was born.

Today, Lonely Planet has offices in the US, Ireland and China, with a network of over 2000 contributors in every corner of the globe. We share Tony's belief that 'a great guidebook should do three things: inform, educate and amuse'.

OUR WRITERS

Liza Prado
Curator, San Juan, El Yunque & East Coast, Culebra & Vieques Liza Prado has been a travel writer since 2003, when she made a move from corporate lawyering to travel writing (and never looked back). She's written dozens of guidebooks and articles as well as apps and blogs to destinations throughout the Americas. She takes decent photos, too. Liza is a graduate of Brown University and Stanford Law School. She lives very happily in Denver, Colorado, with her husband and fellow LP writer, Gary Chandler, and their two kids.

Luke Waterson
Central Mountains, Rincón & West Coast, North Coast, Ponce & South Coast Raised in the remote Somerset countryside in Southwest England, Luke quickly became addicted to exploring out-of-the-way places. While completing a Creative Writing degree at the University of East Anglia, he shouldered his backpack and vowed to see as much of the world as possible. Fast-forward a few years and he has traveled the Americas from Alaska to Tierra del Fuego and developed an obsession for Soviet architecture and pre-Columbian ruins in equal measure. He divides his time between Wales and Slovakia, on which he keeps the world's leading English-language content site on Slovak travel and culture, www.englishmaninslovakia.co.uk. Luke also wrote the Plan, Understand and Survival Guide sections.

Published by Lonely Planet Global Limited
CRN 554153
7th edition – October 2017
ISBN 978 1 78657 142 7
© Lonely Planet 2017   Photographs © as indicated 2017
10 9 8 7 6 5 4
Printed in China